Encyclopedia of
Children,
Adolescents,
and the Media

Encyclopedia of
Children,
Adolescents,
and the Media

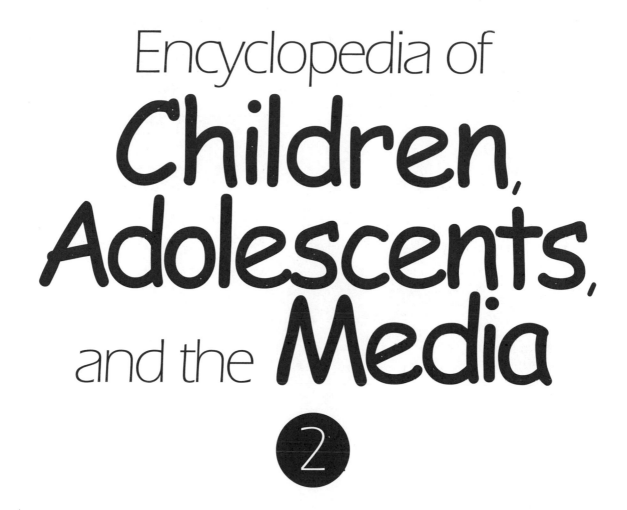

2

Edited by

Jeffrey Jensen Arnett
Clark University, Worcester, Massachusetts

A SAGE Reference Publication

SAGE Publications
Thousand Oaks ■ London ■ New Delhi

For information:

 SAGE Publications, Inc.
2455 Teller Road
Thousand Oaks, California 91320
E-mail: order@sagepub.com

SAGE Publications Ltd.
1 Oliver's Yard
55 City Road
London EC1Y 1SP
United Kingdom

SAGE Publications India Pvt. Ltd.
B-42, Panchsheel Enclave
Post Box 4109
New Delhi 110 017 India

Printed in the United States of America

Library of Congress Cataloging-in-Publication Data

Encyclopedia of children, adolescents, and the media/[edited by] Jeffrey Jensen Arnett.
    p. cm.
Includes bibliographical references and index.
ISBN 1–4129–0530–3 or 978-1-4129-0530-5 (cloth : alk. paper)
    1. Mass media and children—Encyclopedias. 2. Mass media and teenagers—Encyclopedias.
3. Internet and children—Encyclopedias. 4. Internet and teenagers—Encyclopedias. 5. Video games
and children—Encyclopedias. 6. Video games and teenagers—Encyclopedias. I. Arnett, Jeffrey
Jensen. II. Title.
HQ784.M3E53 2007
302.23083—dc22   2006016723

This book is printed on acid-free paper.

06   07   08   09   10   10   9   8   7   6   5   4   3   2   1

Publisher:	Rolf Jenke
Acquiring Editor:	Jim Brace-Thompson
Development Editors:	Diana E. Axelsen
	Eileen Gallaher
Editorial Assistant:	Karen Ehrmann
Production Editor:	Beth A. Bernstein
Copy Editors:	April Wells-Hayes
	Jacqueline Tasch
Typesetter:	C&M Digitals (P) Ltd.
Indexer:	David Luljak
Cover Designer:	Michelle Lee Kenny

Contents

Editorial Board

List of Entries

Reader's Guide

The Reader's Guide is provided to assist readers in locating articles on related topics. It classifies articles into 17 general topical categories: Advertising; Advocacy Groups; Books and Print Media; Computers and Electronic Media; Cross-Cultural Perspectives; Developmental Stages; Gender and Sexuality; Media Education; Media Effects; Media Use; Movies; Music; Public Policy; Research Methods; Television; Theories; and Violence and Aggression. Entries may be listed under more than one topic.

Advertising

Adult Mediation of Advertising Effects
Advertising, Host Selling and
Advertising, Purchase Requests and
Advertising, Sexuality in
Advertising, Viewer Age and
Aggression, Advertising and
Alcohol Advertising, Effects of
Alcohol Advertising, International
Branding
Cigarette Advertising, Effects of
Cigarette Advertising, History of
Consumer Development, Phases of
Consumerism
Contraceptive Advertising
Designated Driver Advertising Campaigns
Federal Communications Commission,
    Advertising and
Food Advertising, Content in
Food Advertising, Eating Disorders and
Food Advertising, Gender, Ethnicity, and Age
Food Advertising, Influence of
Food Advertising, International
Food Advertising, Regulation of
Food Advertising, Obesity and
Food Advertising to Children
Food and Beverage Advertising in Schools
Licensing, Merchandising and

Product Placements, Alcohol
Product Placements, Cigarettes
Product Placements, Food
Promotional Tie-Ins
Purchase Influence Attempts
Relationship Marketing
Schools, Advertising/Marketing in
Sponsored Educational Material (SEM)
Tobacco Advertising, International
Tweens, Advertising Targeting of
Viral Marketing

Advocacy Groups

Action for Children's Television (ACT)
Advertising Council, The
American Academy of Pediatrics
Center for Media Education (CME)
Children Now
Children's Advertising Review Unit (CARU)
Children's Television Charter
International Clearinghouse on Children,
    Youth, and Media
Internet Watch Foundation
Kaiser Family Foundation
Media Advocacy
Media Education Foundation
Media Matters Campaign
Motherhood Project

Cross-Cultural Perspectives

Developmental Stages

Gender and Sexuality

Movies

Music

Public Policy

Research Methods

Television

Theories

Violence and Aggression

About the Editor

Jeffrey Jensen Arnett is a research professor at Clark University in Worcester, Massachusetts. During fall 2005, he was a Fulbright Scholar at the University of Copenhagen. He has taught at Oglethorpe University in Atlanta, the University of Missouri, and the University of Maryland. He received his Ph.D. in developmental psychology from the University of Virginia and was a postdoctoral fellow for 3 years at the University of Chicago.

Dr. Arnett is the author of *Emerging Adulthood: The Winding Road from the Late Teens Through the Twenties,* along with numerous scholarly articles in this area. He is also the author of the textbook *Adolescence and Emerging Adulthood: A Cultural Approach.* In addition to editing the *Encyclopedia of Children, Adolescents, and the Media,* he is the editor of the *International Encyclopedia of Adolescence.* He is also editor of the *Journal of Adolescent Research.*

Within the area of psychology and media, Dr. Arnett's primary interests include adolescents' uses of music and their responses to cigarette advertising. For the past decade, he has served as an expert witness on adolescents' responses to cigarette advertising in litigation against the major tobacco companies.

About the Associate Editors

Jane D. Brown is the James L. Knight Professor in the School of Journalism and Mass Communication at the University of North Carolina–Chapel Hill (UNC–CH). She is an expert on how the media are used by and influence adolescents' health and has studied the influence of the media on adolescents' tobacco and alcohol use, aggression and sexual behavior.

Brown is the coeditor and coauthor of four books, including *Sexual Teens, Sexual Media* (2002). Her research has been published in adolescent as well as media/communication journals, including the *Journal of Adolescent Health, Pediatrics, Journal of Communication,* and *Mass Communication and Society.*

She has served on the CHHD-W Population Sciences Committee (PSC) study section and the national boards of Advocates for Youth, The National Campaign to Prevent Teen Pregnancy, and the Trojan Sexual Health Advisory Council, and the selection committee for the William T. Grant Foundation's Young Scholars Program. She received a PhD from the University of Wisconsin–Madison.

Keith Roe is Director of the PhD School of the Faculty of Social Sciences at Catholic University of Leuven, Belgium. In 1991, he was appointed Professor of Communication in the Department of Communication at the university, and he served as chair of the department from 1996 to 2000. In 2000, he was elected Dean of the Faculty of Social Sciences, a position he held until 2003. He previously served as a Visiting Professor at the University of North Carolina–Chapel Hill and the Annenberg School for Communication at the University of Pennsylvania. From 1985 to 1990, he was Research Fellow at the University of Gothenburg (Sweden), including periods as a Visiting Scholar in Budapest and Humboldt University (Berlin).

Dr. Roe has led a significant number of large-scale research projects and has published widely on the media use of children and adolescents. He is currently joint editor of *Communications: The European Journal of Communication* and an advisory editor of *Poetics: Journal of Empirical Research on Culture, Media and the Arts; Young: The Nordic Journal of Youth Research;* and the *Journal of Children of Media.*

He earned a BSc in social sciences from Loughborough University in Leicestershire, UK, in 1971, an MEd from the University of Nottingham (England) in 1978, and a PhD from the University of Lund (Sweden) in 1983. In 1984, he was awarded the International Communication Association prize for the best PhD thesis of the year in mass communication.

L. Monique Ward is Associate Professor in the Department of Psychology at the University of Michigan. Her research interests center on children's and adolescents' developing conceptions of both gender and sexuality, and on the contribution of these notions to their social and sexual decision making. She is particularly interested in studying how children interpret and use the messages they receive about male-female relations from their parents, peers, and the media. Her work also explores intersections between gender roles, body image, and sexuality. Her research has been published in a diverse set of scholarly journals, including *Developmental Psychology, Journal of Research on Adolescence, Psychology of Women Quarterly, Journal of Sex Research,* and *Journal of Adolescent Research.* She serves on an APA-sponsored task force investigating the sexualization of girls.

She received a PhD in developmental psychology from the University of California at Los Angeles.

Barbara J. Wilson is Professor and Chair of the Department of Speech Communication at the University of Illinois at Urbana–Champaign. Before joining the University of Illinois, she was on the faculty at the University of California, Santa Barbara, for 12 years. Her area of expertise is the social and psychological effects of the mass media, particularly on youth.

Dr. Wilson is coauthor of *Children, Adolescents, and the Media* (Sage, 2002) and three book volumes of the *National Television Violence Study* (Sage, 1997–1998). In addition, she has published more than 50 scholarly articles and chapters on media effects and their implications for media policy. Her recent projects focus on preschoolers' attachment to media characters, parents' and children's fright reactions to kidnapping stories in the news, and children's attraction to media violence.

Dr. Professor Wilson currently serves on the editorial boards of seven academic journals. She has served as a research consultant for Nickelodeon, the National Association of Television Program Executives, Discovery Channel Pictures, and the Centers for Disease Control and Prevention. She earned a PhD from the University of Wisconsin-Madison.

Contributors

Debashis 'Deb' Aikat
University of North Carolina at Chapel Hill

Michelle Arganbright
Washington State University

Jeffrey Jensen Arnett
Clark University

Erica Weintraub Austin
Washington State University

Stephen Balkam
Internet Content Rating Association

Elizabeth Bandy
Stanford University

Rachel Barr
Georgetown University

Angie Colette Beatty
Saint Louis University

Kimberly Bell
University of Dayton

Genelle Belmas
California State University, Fullerton

Andrea M. Bergstrom
University of Massachusetts–Amherst

Gordon L. Berry
University of California, Los Angeles

Kimberly L. Bissell
University of Alabama

Gail Masuchika Boldt
University of Iowa

Heinz Bonfadelli
University of Zurich

David Brake
London School of Economics

Daniel W. Brickman
University of Michigan

Jane D. Brown
University of North Carolina at Chapel Hill

J. Alison Bryant
Indiana University

Jennings Bryant
University of Alabama

Moniek Buijzen
University of Amsterdam

Andrew Burn
University of London

Brad J. Bushman
University of Michigan

Xiaomei Cai
George Mason University

Sandra L. Calvert
Georgetown University

Joanne Cantor
University of Wisconsin–Madison

Ulla Carlsson
Göteborg University

Nicholas L. Carnagey
Iowa State University

Courtney Carpenter
University of Alabama

Armin Castello
University of Freiburg, Germany

Lisa Cavanaugh
Duke University

Jesse J. Chandler
University of Michigan

Michael Charlton
University of Freiburg, Germany

Yi-Chun Yvonnes Chen
Washington State University

I-Huei Cheng
University of Alabama

Ariel R. Chernin
University of Pennsylvania

T. Makana Chock
Syracuse University

Dimitri A. Christakis
University of Washington

Glenda B. Claborne
University of Washington

Lynn Schofield Clark
University of Colorado

David Ian Cohen
Sesame Workshop

Sarah M. Coyne
University of Central Lancashire

Abe Crystal
University of North Carolina at Chapel Hill

R. Glenn Cummins
Kennesaw State University

Frank E. Dardis
Pennsylvania State University

Solomon Davidoff
New England Institute of Art

John Davies
University of North Florida

Esteban del Río
University of San Diego

Timothy Dewhirst
University of Saskatchewan

Stephanie Hemelryk Donald
University of Technology, Sydney

Nicola Döring
Ilmenau University of Technology

William Douglas
University of Houston

Hardy Dreier
University of Hamburg

Meenakshi Gigi Durham
University of Iowa

Patricia Edgar
World Summit on Media for Children Foundation

Heidi Hatfield Edwards
Pennsylvania State University

Steven Eggermont
Katholieke Universiteit Leuven

Rutger C. M. E. Engels
Radboud Universiteit Nijmegen

Keren Eyal
University of Arizona

Kirstie Farrar
University of Connecticut

Douglas A. Ferguson
College of Charleston

Mark Finney
University of Colorado at Boulder

Stacy Fitzpatrick
University of Minnesota, Twin Cities

Ulla G. Foehr
Stanford University

Jeanne Funk
University of Toledo

Debra Furr-Holden
Pacific Institute for Research and Evaluation

Christina Romano Glaubke
Children Now

J. Robyn Goodman
University of Florida

Donna Grace
University of Hawaii

Daren A. Graves
Harvard Graduate School of Education

Sherryl Browne Graves
Hunter College

Bradley S. Greenberg
Michigan State University

Patricia Greenfield
Los Angeles Children's Digital Media Center

Kimberly S. Gregson
Ithaca College

Mark D. Griffiths
Nottingham Trent University

Jo Groebel
Europäisches Medieninstitut e.V.

David Gudelunas
Fairfield University

Ingunn Hagen
Norwegian University of Science and Technology

Christine H. Hansen
Oakland University

Derek L. Hansen
University of Michigan

Katherine Hanson
Sesame Workshop

Sam A. Hardy
University of Virginia

Kristen Harrison
University of Illinois

Uwe Hasebrink
Hans-Bredow-Institut

Lisa Henriksen
Stanford University School of Medicine

Nokon Heo
University of Central Arkansas

Kymberly Higgs
University of Dayton

Renee Hobbs
Temple University

R. Michael Hoefges
University of North Carolina

Cynthia A. Hoffner
Georgia State University

Marjorie J. Hogan
Hennepin County Medical Center, Minnesota

Andrea Holt
University of Alabama

Yifeng Hu
Pennsylvania State University

Stacey J. T. Hust
Washington State University

Elizabeth Hutton
Pennsylvania State University

Jeroen Jansz
University of Amsterdam

Krishna Jayakar
Pennsylvania State University

Nancy Jennings
University of Cincinnati

Robert Jensen
University of Texas at Austin

Jeannette L. Johnson
Friends Research Institute, Inc.

Sriram Kalyanaraman
University of North Carolina at Chapel Hill

Nadia Kaneva
University of Colorado at Boulder

Mary Kearney
University of Texas at Austin

Sarah N. Keller
Montana State University–Billings

Janna L. Kim
San Francisco State University

Jinhee Kim
San Francisco State University

William Kinnally
Florida State University

Christoph Klimmt
Hannover University of Music and Drama, Germany

Myra Gregory Knight
University of North Carolina at Chapel Hill

Silvia Knobloch-Westerwick
Ohio State University

Jennifer A. Kotler
Sesame Workshop

K. Maja Krakowiak
Pennsylvania State University

Marina Krcmar
University of Connecticut

Friedrich Krotz
University of Erfurt

Robert Kubey
Rutgers University

Susanne Kubisch
University of Hamburg

Kenneth A. Lachlan
Boston College

Jennifer L. Lambe
University of Delaware

Anna Langhorne
University of Dayton

Elisabeth Lasch-Quinn
Syracuse University

Alice Y. L. Lee
Hong Kong Baptist University

Sang Lee
West Virginia University

Dafna Lemish
Tel Aviv University

Ron Leone
Stonehill College

Dana S. Levin
University of Michigan

Cynthia Lewis
University of Minnesota

Meredith Li-Vollmer
University of Washington

Deborah L. Linebarger
University of Pennsylvania

Rich Ling
Telenor R&D

Sonia Livingstone
London School of Economics and Political Science

Elizabeth P. Lorch
University of Kentucky

Amy Shirong Lu
University of North Carolina at Chapel Hill

Tannis M. MacBeth
University of British Columbia

Robert Magee
University of North Carolina at Chapel Hill

Sampada Sameer Marathe
Pennsylvania State University

Nicole Martins
University of Illinois at Urbana–Champaign

Sharon R. Mazzarella
Clemson University

Michael McDevitt
University of Colorado

Michael A. McGregor
Indiana University

Brenda A. Miller
Pacific Institute for Research and Evaluation

Kathryn C. Montgomery
American University

Roy L. Moore
University of Kentucky

Kristin C. Moran
University of San Diego

Michael Morgan
University of Massachusetts–Amherst

Robin Nabi
University of California, Santa Barbara

Jamie Campbell Naidoo
University of Alabama

Amy I. Nathanson
Ohio State University

Mary Beth Oliver
Pennsylvania State University

Shani Orgad
London School of Economics and Political Science

Bill Osgerby
London Metropolitan University

Laura M. Padilla-Walker
University of Nebraska–Lincoln

Edward L. Palmer
Davidson College

Angela Paradise
Universtity of Massachusetts–Amherst

Ingrid Paus-Hasebrink
University of Salzburg

Norma Pecora
Ohio University

Kate Peirce
Texas State University

Elizabeth Perse
University of Delaware

Bruce E. Pinkleton
Washington State University

Richard W. Pollay
University of British Columbia

Marjorie Rhodes
University of Michigan

Victoria Rideout
Kaiser Family Foundation

Rocío Rivadeneyra
Illinois State University

James D. Robinson
University of Dayton

Liliana Rodriguez
University of Massachusetts–Amherst

Keith Roe
Katholieke Universiteit Leuven

Sarah F. Rosaen
University of Michigan at Flint

David R. Roskos-Ewoldsen
University of Alabama

Ingegerd Rydin
Halmstad University

Avi Santo
University of Texas at Austin

Stephanie Lee Sargent
Virginia Tech

Ronda M. Scantlin
University of Dayton

Erica Scharrer
University of Massachusetts–Amherst

Cyndy Scheibe
Ithaca College

Deborah Schooler
San Francisco State University

Juliet B. Schor
Boston College

Marc C. Seamon
Marshall University

Sean S. Seepersad
California State University, Fresno

Timothy Shary
Clark University

John L. Sherry
Michigan State University

Yu Shi
New York University

L. J. Shrum
University of Texas at San Antonio

Razvan Sibii
University of Massachusetts–Amherst

Nancy Signorielli
University of Delaware

Charlene Simmons
University of Tennessee at Chattanooga

Arvind Singhal
Ohio University

Ulrika Sjöberg
Halmstad University

Paul Skalski
University of Minnesota, Duluth

Leslie Snyder
University of Connecticut

Stephen Soitos
University of Massachusetts

Denise Sommer
University of Jena, Germany

C. Lynn Sorsoli
San Francisco State University

Brian G. Southwell
University of Minnesota

Glenn Sparks
Purdue University

Renske Spijkerman
Addiction Research Institute (IVO), Rotterdam

Carmen Stavrositu
Pennyslvania State University

Jeanne Rogge Steele
University of Minnesota

Leila Katharina Steinhilper
University of Erfurt

Michael T. Stephenson
Texas A&M University

Susannah R. Stern
University of San Diego

Carmen Stitt
University of Arizona

Patricia A. Stout
University of Texas at Austin

Jeffrey J. Strange
Public Insight, Portland, Oregon

Victor C. Strasburger
University of New Mexico School of Medicine

Carolyn Stroman
Howard University

Kaveri Subrahmanyam
*California State University at Los Angeles and
    the UCLA Children's Digital Media Center*

S. Shyam Sundar
Pennsylvania State University

Daniel Süss
University of Applied Sciences, Zurich

Tamara Swenson
Osaka Jogakuin College

Ron Tamborini
Michigan State University

Mark Tarrant
Keele University

Jessica L. Taylor
University of Pennsylvania

Laramie D. Taylor
University of California, Davis

Tom ter Bogt
University of Amsterdam

Shayla Thiel
DePaul University

Khia A. Thomas
University of Michigan

Teresa L. Thompson
University of Dayton

Yan Tian
University of Missouri, St. Louis

Rosemarie T. Truglio
Sesame Workshop

Jeanine W. Turner
Georgetown University

Joseph Turow
University of Pennsylvania

Kathleen Tyner
University of Texas at Austin

Patti M. Valkenburg
Universiteit van Amsterdam

Jan Van den Bulck
Katholieke Universiteit Leuven

Regina J. J. M. van den Eijnden
Addiction Research Institute

Bas van den Putte
Universiteit van Amsterdam

Rebecca Van de Vord
Washington State University

Judith Van Evra
St. Jerome's University in the University of Waterloo

Veerle Van Rompaey
Katholieke Universiteit Leuven

Cecilia von Feilitzen
International Clearinghouse on Children, Youth

Peter Vorderer
University of Southern California

Carson B Wagner
Ohio University
University of Texas at Austin

Kim Walsh-Childers
University of Florida

Christa Ward
University of Georgia

L. Monique Ward
University of Michigan

Ron Warren
University of Arkansas

S. Craig Watkins
University of Texas at Austin

James B. Weaver, III
Virginia Tech

René Weber
Michigan State University

David K. Westerman
Michigan State University

Leslie R. Williams
University of Pennsylvania

Teena Willoughby
Brock University

Barbara J. Wilson
University of Illinois at Urbana–Champaign

Mallory Wober
Michigan State University

Richard T. A. Wood
Nottingham Trent University

Tracy Worrell
Michigan State University

Brian M. Young
University of Exeter

Byron L. Zamboanga
Smith College

Dolf Zillmann
University of Alabama

Lara Zwarun
University of Texas at Arlington

Introduction

It was 1904, and G. Stanley Hall, writing his magnum opus on adolescent development, was concerned about rising crime rates among American youth. He discerned a variety of causes, but one key source of the problem was the media. As Hall saw it, a young man may be induced to commit crimes in part because "his mind becomes inflamed with flash literature and 'penny dreadfuls'" that portray crime as glamorous and heroic (p. 361). This was not the only problem of youth that Hall attributed to media influences. Johann von Goethe's 1774 novel, *The Sorrows of Young Werther,* remained popular in Hall's time—with pernicious effects, according to Hall. "The reading of romance has great influence on the development of youthful passion. Werther has created a distinct psychosis known as Wertherism" (p. 387).

Hall and his contemporaries could hardly have imagined the media environment that today's children and adolescents experience. The "literature" Hall worried about is still there, but now print media take a back seat to the newer, electronic forms: television, radio, recorded music, movies, mobile phones, electronic games, and the Internet. American children and adolescents use media for an average total of 6.5 hours per day, according to the Kaiser Family Foundation's landmark 2005 study of 8-to-18-year-olds—more time than they spend in school, far more time than they spend with their families. Totals are similar in other industrialized countries.

The fact that media use has become such a central part of the daily experience of children and adolescents all over the world makes this a propitious time to compile the *Encyclopedia of Children, Adolescents, and the Media.* Because the media children and adolescents use are so diverse, and because media use pertains to so many different aspects of children and adolescents'

development, this was a monumental project, with the two volumes containing a total of 463 entries. There were 4 associate editors and 19 advisory board members, all of them outstanding scholars in media research. A total of 496 authors contributed entries.

Media are pervasive worldwide as part of children and adolescents' daily experience; accordingly, we sought to make the contents of the encyclopedia international. There are specific regional entries on Asia, Europe, and Latin America, as well as specific country entries for the two most populous countries in the world, China and India, and on Japan, which has been such an important contributor to children's media worldwide. Many of the other entries contain information drawn from a variety of countries.

Many people today, including many media researchers, share Hall's concern that the influences of media on children and adolescents are primarily negative, and this concern is reflected in the contents of the encyclopedia. Two of the largest topic categories are gender and sexuality (47 entries) and violence (31 entries). These entries show that the content of the media consumed by children and adolescents is dominated by sexuality and (especially) violence. Anyone who doubts Freud's theory that sex and aggression are the primary wellsprings of human nature need only spend a day perusing the media environment of the average child or adolescent. Toddlers and children enjoy cartoons wherein the main characters invent humorously creative ways of beating the snot out of each other; girls embrace the models of princess or tart (or princess-tart) offered by cartoon characters and pop stars; boys thrill to electronic games that involve pretending to kill bad guys and aliens; adolescents like best the movies and music that contain the most explicit sexual and violent content.

Although there is little doubt about the content of the media children and adolescents consume, the question of effects has been a challenging one in media research from its inception. Does sexual and violent content influence children and adolescents, or are the children and adolescents who are most attracted to sexual and violent content already different from other children, already more prone to sexual risks and aggression? Different scholars have different answers to this question, and the 37 entries on theories in this encyclopedia offer a variety of takes on it. Still, there is broad consensus among media researchers that media use is not merely correlated with children's development but also influences their development.

I admit that I originally came to this question as a skeptic, having learned in my training as a developmental psychologist to be wary of simple statements of cause and effect. However, eventually I was convinced of the effects of media by the accumulation of evidence—not just correlational or experimental studies but longitudinal studies, field studies, ethnographic studies, and natural experiments—and I believe that most thorough readers of this encyclopedia will be convinced as well, as they read through the entries describing the results of studies that used these different methods. Yes, children and adolescents make media choices based on their individual characteristics, and some more than others prefer sexual and violent content, but the effects of such content on their development are real, and we doubt them at our peril—and our children's peril.

Not only is sexual and violent content a source of concern. Also worrisome is the huge volume of advertising to which children and adolescents are exposed through the media. The 40 entries on advertising offer a wealth of compelling and unsettling details, and like the entries on sex and violence, taken together the entries on advertising leave little doubt about advertising's effects on children and adolescents (and here I can add that, as a parent of twin 6-year-olds who regularly clamor for whatever is relentlessly advertised on the Cartoon Network, I did not need to be convinced). Even schools, formerly places where the barrage of advertising in modern society was kept at bay, have now opened their doors to invite the barrage in, as shown here in entries on topics such as Sponsored Educational Materials and Commercial Television and Radio in Schools.

Given the many concerns about media use among children and adolescents, it is understandable that adults have organized in various ways to address those concerns. The encyclopedia contains entries on 22 advocacy groups, which comprise a wide range of national and international efforts to improve the quality (or at least minimize the damage) of the media content children and adolescents receive. There are also 39 entries in the area of public policy, showing the many approaches that have been taken nationally and internationally to control what media producers market to children and adolescents. In addition, 23 entries in the area of media education describe the methods that have been developed to teach children and adolescents to be discerning consumers of the media that surround them nearly all day every day, and to recognize and defuse media attempts to manipulate their desires, needs, and consumption habits.

Although the weight of opinion in the entries in the encyclopedia is decidedly in the direction of the concerns and potential negative effects of media, many entries show how children and adolescents benefit from their media use. Television may be mostly a vast wasteland saturated with sex and violence, but the best television provides children and adolescents with an entertaining educator and opens their minds and imaginations to new worlds. Music provides children and (especially) adolescents with materials for building personal and group identities and helps them to manage unruly moods. Movies can provide wonderful, inspiring stories. Mobile phones and email allow children and adolescents to connect to a broad network of friends and family much more often than was possible in the past. The Internet is a portal to an infinite store of information about every imaginable topic. Even print media have retained their power to inspire children and adolescents, as the recent *Harry Potter* craze has demonstrated. Who could have predicted that children and adolescents all over the world would become riveted to a series of 500+ page books about a boy who attends a school for wizards? This example helps remind us that media are, at their best, wonderful sources of enjoyment for children, adolescents, and the rest of us.

Although we sought to be as comprehensive as possible in putting together the two volumes of the encyclopedia, we decided early on not to include entries on specific media characters or performers. There were three reasons for this. First, if we had opened the door to this, it would have been difficult to stop (once we had an entry for Metallica, how could we have denied an entry to Megadeth?). Second, notwithstanding the enduring popularity of characters such as Tom and Jerry or performers such as Madonna, most media characters and performers popular among children and adolescents have a rather short time in the spotlight. (There was a popular singer a few years ago, Britney something—remember her?) They come and go, and entries on them would already seem dated by the time the encyclopedia was published. Third and most important, the focus of the encyclopedia is on children and adolescents' experiences with media rather than on the specific media products they use. If boys are avid players of the electronic game *Grand Theft Auto*, what is important about this, for our purposes, is their avid involvement in a highly violent electronic game, not the fact that the specific game is *Grand Theft Auto*. Next month or next year, another violent electronic game may come along and supersede *Grand Theft Auto* in popularity, but the important issues pertaining to boys' involvement in violent electronic games will endure.

In closing, I would like to thank the many people involved in producing the encyclopedia. First, my eminent associate editors, Jane D. Brown, Keith Roe, L. Monique Ward, and Barbara J. Wilson. They did a fabulous job of helping me assemble the hundreds of authors for the encyclopedia. Each of them edited many of the entries, and each also contributed at least one entry. Second, the 19 advisory board members, who suggested many of the entries we included in the encyclopedia and who were also key in assembling the authors for the project. It was a great honor to work with such a stellar group of media scholars. Third, at Sage Publications, the development editors Eileen Gallaher and Diana Axelsen, and Beth Bernstein, the production editor; all of them were extraordinarily capable in administering the project and getting all the entries into good shape, and they were delightful to work with.

Finally, I would like to dedicate my work on this encyclopedia to the memory of my mother, Marjorie Littlefield Arnett, who entertained us throughout my childhood with a wry running commentary on the stupidity and venality of most advertising, no doubt providing me with a "media education" that endures to this day. This is for you, Mom.

—Jeffrey Jensen Arnett
Clark University

FURTHER READINGS

Hall, G. S. (1904). *Adolescence: Its psychology and its relation to physiology, anthropology, sociology, sex, crime, religion, and education* (Vols. 1 & 2). Englewood Cliffs, NJ: Prentice Hall.

L

LANGUAGE, IMPACT OF THE INTERNET ON

The Internet is a visual medium that uses a mixture of text, images, and sound. Its communication applications, such as email, instant messaging, and chat rooms, are especially popular among youth. These younger users seem to be adapting to the unique demands of online communicative environments by creating a chat code of their own. Research has begun to document the features of this chat code and suggests that users are creating this code by adapting strategies from oral and written contexts. Concerns have been raised that the use of this chat code will transfer to conventional forms of oral and written discourse and, just as important, may enable youth to shut parents and other adults out of their world.

FEATURES OF ONLINE COMMUNICATION

First and foremost, online communication occurs in an environment that is devoid of face-to-face cues such as eye contact, gaze, body orientation, and gesture. Second, although it takes place in the written medium, online communication is like spoken language, particularly unplanned speech, in that it typically consists of shorter, incomplete, grammatically simple, and even incorrect sentences. Furthermore, research suggests that users omit copulas, subject pronouns, and articles. Thus, it appears that the language used on the Internet (also called *Netspeak*) may be an amalgam of written and spoken language—a register of written language with many of the stylistic features of spoken language. The spontaneous conversational contexts of most online communication present conditions that push this written medium in the direction of oral language characteristics.

FEATURES OF ONLINE CHAT CODES

Ethnographic investigation of online teen chat rooms suggests that users are creating this chat code by utilizing the resources of oral and written English in creative ways. Some codes specific to chat rooms include the distinctive visual appearance of nicknames created by combining letters and numerals in creative ways (e.g., MizRose7, MORN8SUN); the request for numerals to identify interested conversation partners (press 14 if ya wanna chat 2 a 14/f/cali); the use of a standard graphic format to reveal identity information (17/m/fl, which stands for "17-year-old male from Florida") and the ubiquitous a/s/l (age/sex/location) code.

Anecdotal reports suggest that the same process is occurring with regard to the language codes that are being created and used in instant messaging conversations. For instance, common utterances such as *r u there* (are you there?), *brb* (be right back), and *pos* (parent over shoulder) highlight the pressure toward brevity to approximate the timing of oral discourse but within a written context.

IMPLICATIONS OF THE CHAT CODE

Reports from researchers and media alike suggest that younger users are creating and using the code as they adapt to each new technology. This is not surprising, given that younger people are generally at the vanguard of cultural innovations, and this has certainly been the case with language changes in the computer medium. One implication of this is that children and teenagers are more adept at this code than their parents and can use it to mask the true nature of their online activities from their parents. A related concern is children and adolescents who are growing up using this code will think nothing of using it in written forms of discourse, where such language is inappropriate.

—*Kaveri Subrahmanyam and Patricia Greenfield*

See also Chat Rooms, Social and Linguistic Processes in; Email; Instant Messaging; Internet Relay Chat (IRC); Mobile Telephones

FURTHER READINGS

Baron, N. S. (1998). Letters by phone or speech by other means: The linguistics of email. *Language and Communication, 18,* 133–170.

Crystal, D. (2001). *Language and the Internet.* Cambridge, UK: Cambridge University Press.

Freiermuth, M. R. (2002). *Features of electronic synchronous communication: A comparative analysis of online chat, spoken and written texts.* Ph.D. dissertation, Oklahoma State University.

Greenfield, P. M. (1984). *Mind and media: The effects of television, video games, and computers.* Cambridge, MA: Harvard University Press.

Greenfield, P. M. (1999). Cultural change and human development. *New Directions in Child and Adolescent Development, 83,* 37–60. San Francisco, CA: Jossey-Bass.

Greenfield, P. M., & Subrahmanyam, K. (2003). Online discourse in a teen chatroom: New codes and new modes of coherence in a visual medium. *Journal of Applied Developmental Psychology, 24, 713–738.*

LANGUAGE, PROFANITY IN

See PROFANITY, TRENDS IN

LANGUAGE LEARNING, TELEVISION AND

To fully address the issue of television and language learning, we must consider at the very least what is meant by language development, as well as the age of the child who is attempting to learn from television. First, language learning might be divided into two broad categories, *grammatical development* and *lexical development*. Furthermore, we might also distinguish between *initial language learning* and *vocabulary extension*, the latter being a process that continues throughout life.

Overall, it appears that television can teach language in some real but limited ways. Children—and, indeed, adults—can learn new words and extend their vocabularies. However, the complexity of grammar is difficult to parse from speech—especially speech of the kind that one garners from television. After all, there is no interaction per se, and the speaker can not arrange his or her grammar to best suit the needs of the listener. Lastly, television does not appear to be able to teach initial words to toddlers.

Most research that examines preschoolers between the ages of 2 and 5 years has shown that young children can in fact acquire new words by watching television. For example, in a series of laboratory studies, Rice and colleagues showed preschoolers animated programs that contained infrequently used words (e.g., *gramophone*). After seeing the clip twice in the span of a week, children who saw it performed significantly better when matching the word with a picture than did control children who had not seen the clip. On average, 5-year-olds learned more than 3-year-olds.

In a similar study by Singer and Singer, children who attended a child-care program were randomly assigned either to watch 10 episodes of *Barney* or to engage in free play in another room at the facility, over a 2-week period. Prior to exposure, children were pretested on vocabulary words that would appear in *Barney.* After the exposure period, children were tested again. Children who had seen *Barney* performed significantly better than those in the control group on their knowledge of words used in the *Barney* episode.

There is also evidence from longitudinal studies, the designs of which offer greater external validity. Rice and colleagues examined the vocabulary growth of children over a 2 ½-year period. Children who watched *Sesame Street* more frequently experienced greater vocabulary growth even when parent education and initial vocabulary scores were controlled for. However, this finding was only true of children who were 3 years old at the beginning of the study; 5-year-olds did not make such extensive gains. Therefore, it appears from both experimental designs and longitudinal survey research that preschoolers can, in fact, learn new words from television.

However, it appears that children do not effectively learn grammar from television. Although the data here are not as robust, due to difficulties in data collection on this issue, correlational research studies that have examined grammatical development have found that exposure to television is negatively correlated with grammatical development. Language acquisition experts suggest that human interaction in which the learner is part of the dyad may be the only way to access the complexity of grammar.

Finally, most research using both experimental and survey design has focused only on the ability of television to teach *new* words to children—not to teach them *initial* words. That is, studies look at long-term vocabulary extension of children who are older (3 years of age or older) and who therefore have relatively extensive productive and receptive vocabularies. The process of learning new words is not identical to that of learning initial words. In the latter case, very young children must learn what words are; must understand that they can refer to objects, concepts, and ideas; and must learn to identify a word as belonging to the category of noun, adjective, or verb. In other words, initial language acquisition is a more complex process than later vocabulary extension. With the popularity of programs (e.g., *Teletubbies, Baby Einstein*) now targeting preverbal children, it may well be important to understand the impact of these programs on initial language acquisition. However, there is a dearth of studies examining this topic. However, in one study, Krcmar and colleagues examined the ability of toddlers (aged 12 to 24 months) to learn new words from *Teletubbies*. Using the fast mapping paradigm and a clip from *Teletubbies* with an edited voice-over, the authors found that, until children were approximately 20 months of age, they were able to learn novel words only from a live, adult speaker—and not from the adult speaker on videotape or from the dubbed *Teletubbies* clip. This suggests that very young children cannot learn initial words from television until they are almost 2 years old.

So, can television teach language to children? Perhaps the best answer is this: Television teaches words, not language, which is best learned through human interaction.

—*Marina Krcmar*

See also Infants and Toddlers, Developmental Needs of; Infants and Toddlers, Media Exposure of; Information Processing, Active vs. Passive Models of; Information Processing, Developmental Differences and; Media Literacy, Approaches to; Reading, Literacy and; Reading, Patterns of; Television, Attention and; Television, Viewer Age and

FURTHER READINGS

Fisch, S. M., Truglio, R. T., & Cole, C. F. (1999). The impact of *Sesame Street* on preschool children: A review and synthesis of 30 years' research. *Media Psychology, 1,* 165–190.

Krcmar, M., & Grela, B. G. (2004). Learning vocabulary from television: Toddlers, television, and attention. *Literacy Today, 39,* 19–20.

Lemish, D., & Rice, M. (1986). Television as a talking picture book: A prop for language acquisition. *Journal of Child Language, 13,* 251–274.

Naigles, L., Singer, D., Singer, J., Jean-Louis, B., Sells, D., & Rosen, C. (1995a). *Barney says, "Come, go, think, know": Television reveals a role for input in later language acquisition.* Hartford: Connecticut Public Broadcasting.

Naigles, L., Singer, D., Singer, J., Jean-Louis, B., Sells, D., & Rosen, C. (1995b, June). *Watching "Barney" affects preschoolers' use of mental state verbs.* Paper presented at the annual meeting of the American Psychological Society, New York.

Pingree, S., Hawkind, R. P., Rouner, D., Burns, J., Gikonyo, W., & Neuwirth, C. (1984). Another look at children's comprehension of television. *Communication Research, 11,* 477–496.

Rice, M. (1983). The role of television in language acquisition. *Developmental Review, 3,* 211–224.

Rice, M. (1984). The words of children's television. *Journal of Broadcasting, 28*(4), 445–461.

Rice, M., & Haight, P. (1986). "Motherese" of "Mr. Rogers": A description of the dialogue of educational television programs. *Journal of Speech and Hearing Disorders, 51,* 282–287.

Rice, M., Huston, A., Truglio, R., & Wright, J. (1990). Words from *Sesame Street*: Learning vocabulary while viewing. *Developmental Psychology, 26,* 421–428.

Rice, M., & Woodsmall, L. (1988). Lessons from television: Children's word learning when viewing. *Child Development, 59,* 420–429.

Sachs, J., Bard, B., & Johnson, M. (1981). Language learning with restricted input: Case studies of two hearing children of deaf parents. *Applied Psycholinguistics, 2,* 33–54.

Selnow, G. W., & Bettinghaus, E. (1982). Television exposure and language development. *Journal of Broadcasting, 26,* 469–479.

Singer, D. G., & Singer, J. L. (1998). Developing critical viewing skills and media literacy in children. *Annals of the American Academy of Political and Social Science, 557,* 164–179.

Tomasello, M. (1990). The social bases of language acquisition. *Social Development, 1,* 67–87.

Tower, R. B., Singer, D. G., Singer, J. L., & Biggs, A. (1979). Differential effects of television programming on preschoolers' cognition, imagination, and social play. *American Journal of Orthopsychiatry, 49,* 265–281.

Woodward, A., & Markman, E. (1998). Early word learning. In W. Damon, D. Kuhn, & R. Siegler (Eds.), *Handbook of child psychology: Vol. 2. Cognition, perception, and language.* New York: Wiley.

LATIN AMERICA, MEDIA USE IN

Latin America is a diverse region with varying degrees of media development. Although Latin American media systems are dedicated to producing content that is inherently "Latin," the development of the systems has followed a commercial North American model, with various levels of direct U.S. investment in particular systems (Sinclair, 2004). The major producers of Latin American programming are Mexico, Brazil, and Venezuela, with significant domestic production and distribution as well as extensive exportation around the globe.

Children in Latin America, like other children around the world, spend a considerable amount of time using mass media, especially television. The concerns about television and children in Latin America are the same concerns faced by North Americans. On average, children are watching television about 3 hours per day, and nearly 45% of children have television sets in their bedrooms. More than 40% of Latin American children watch television alone, especially as they age (Meirelles, 2005). According to the Pan Latin American Kids Survey, conducted in 1998, 45% of people agree that there is too much sex on TV, and 55% believe there is too much violence ("Sex & Violence," www.zonalatina.com).

According to a survey conducted in Latin America in 2002, television is the main source of entertainment for 34% of children ages 12 to 19. Radio usage varies between boys and girls, with 23% of boys naming radio as a main source of entertainment, whereas 35% of girls use the radio most ("Media as the Main Sources of Entertainment," www.zonalatina .com). Most households in Latin America have access to both radio and television; in some rural areas, access to television is more common than access to a telephone.

MASS MEDIA IN MEXICO, BRAZIL, AND VENEZUELA

Mexico

Grupo Televisa is the largest and most influential media conglomerate in Mexico, controlling television networks, magazines, newspapers, and other mass media. Televisa's popularity was unchallenged during the 1970s and 1980s, when on any given evening 90% of the television audience watched one of the four Televisa channels.

Televisa provides children's programming under the Televisa Niños brand, the line-up of which is filled by domestic productions. One of the most popular programs is *El Chavo del Ocho,* a live-action sitcom, which has been on the air for 35 years. It targets children 6 to11 years old and is shown throughout Latin America as well as on Spanish-language television in the United States. *Plaza Sésamo,* the Mexican version of *Sesame Street,* is a co-production of Televisa and Sesame Workshop and targets a preschool audience. Other programming for children on Televisa includes *telenovelas,* drama serials that use the soap opera form but are tailored to audience members aged 6 to 12. In addition, *Señal Tu* is a radio program in Mexico created by kids for kids and distributed through the Televisa radio network; it provides news, information, and gossip about favorite celebrities.

In 1993, TV Azteca entered the Mexican marketplace after acquiring two government-operated channels. Since that time, TV Azteca has increased its audience share to nearly 30% of the prime-time audience by providing alternative programming to that of Televisa (Sinclair, 2004). While TV Azteca does some of its own production for adult entertainment and news, it relies more heavily on imports for its children's programming, especially Disney. TV Azteca's Channel 7 includes the *Disney Club,* which showcases *Lilo y Stitch* and other programs highlighting the Disney brand.

Brazil

Rede Globo has had a near-monopoly of the Brazilian media since the 1960s, when Roberto Marinho established the network with investment from the U.S.-based Time-Life Corporation. Currently, the most popular genre of programming through the television arm of Rede Globo is the telenovela. TV Globo has extensive production facilities, in which nearly all of its programming is produced. Like Mexico's Televisa, Globo has become a major exporter of telenovelas to Portugal and, by dubbing their programs into Spanish, to other Latin American countries as well as to the United States.

Children's programs on TV Globo include *Disney en TV,* which features Disney programs dubbed into Portuguese. TV Globo dedicates about 10% of its programming to children, usually in the morning between 9:30 and 12:00. A popular program is *TV XuXa,* a live-action variety show in which the host, Keka, leads children on different adventures. TVE Brasil, a public station based in Rio de Janeiro, has programming for children in the morning from 10:00 until noon and later between 1 and 6 p.m., for a total of 5 hours of programming per day. Some programs are domestic productions and include *A Turma do Perere,* a program that teaches children about Brazilian folklore, and *Castelo Rá-tim-Bum,* an educational program targeted to 4-to-8-year-olds that features math and science lessons. The public channel also airs shows imported from PBS in the United States, such as *Caillou* and *Zoboomafoo* (Leite, 2005).

Venezuela

Although Venezuela is a smaller media market than either Mexico or Brazil, the system is also dominated by a single broadcaster, Venevisión, founded in 1960 by Diego Cisneros. Venevisión is not the only choice in Venezuela, but it does attract the widest audiences with its telenovelas and news programming. Children's programming on Venevisión includes *El Chavo de Ocho* from Mexico and Disney shows such as *Lizzie McGuire.* A Venezuelan production, *Atómico,* is a children's variety show broadcast from 4 p.m. to 6 p.m. Monday through Friday on the network.

In addition to national networks, both Televisa and Venevisión own part of Univisión, the largest Spanish-language network in the United States, which provides children's programming for Spanish-speaking audiences in the United States. Although Mexico, Brazil, and Venezuela provide some national children's television programming, there is a lack of diversity and few choices for children who do not have access to direct-to-home satellite networks.

CHILDREN'S PROGRAMMING ON CABLE AND SATELLITE CHANNELS

Access to cable and satellite channels has increased across Latin America, making more television programming available for adults as well as children. Of the 103.4 million people in Mexico, 96% of the population have access to television in the home, and about 14% have cable, whereas 4.5% subscribe to direct-to-home satellite systems. Of the 176 million Brazilians, 88% have access to television in the home, 9% subscribe to cable, and another 4.2% have direct-to-home satellite television. In Venezuela, of the population of 24.3 million, 96% have access to television in the home, 20% have access to cable, and close to 6% have access to satellite channels (www.worldscreen.com).

The international children's television landscape is mimicking adult network expansion as networks expand to make programming available in countries around the world. Not only is CNN international, Disney and Nickelodeon are as well. Of cable channels in Latin America, the most popular is the Disney Channel, followed by the Cartoon Network and Discovery Kids, with Nickelodeon coming in sixth, demonstrating that families with cable use it for access to children's programming. The Disney Channel has been successful in its international expansion by marketing the Disney brand and dubbing its programs and movies into Spanish and Portuguese for distribution throughout Latin America. In Brazil, however, the Disney Channel ranks 17th, and the Cartoon Network holds the number one spot. Mexican television households also rank the Cartoon Network first, with the Disney Channel coming in second, according to IBOPE cable household ratings. Although not yet as popular as other networks, Nickelodeon is quickly penetrating Latin American markets by launching networks in a variety of countries by dubbing their programs into Spanish and Portuguese. Some of the Nickelodeon programs that have been featured around the globe include *Rugrats, Blue's Clues,* and *SpongeBob SquarePants.*

MTV Latin America, owned by Viacom (the same corporation that owns Nickelodeon) appeals to young audiences by including North American and Latin American artists on the channel. The localization strategy of MTV is to appeal to the domestic audience by including local on-air personalities with whom the audience can identify. In Brazil, Viacom has established

Viacom Networks Brasil, which includes VH1 in Portuguese and is customized for Brazilian viewers. It also operates existing businesses in the market, such as MTV. In Brazil, MTV receives 38% of all advertising revenue aimed at teenagers (Leite, 2005).

AOL/Time Warner's Cartoon Network has been expanding globally as well, with specific channels in Europe, Latin America, and Japan. The Cartoon Network offers the same programming available on all of its international networks but dubs in the domestic language. Many of the programs originate in Japan and the United States and include *Teen Titans, Ed, Edd n Eddy,* and *Powerpuff Girls.* The cartoon genre is particularly popular with children and has proven to be a successful export. Changing the language of animated characters is easier and less expensive than with live action.

Disney has been an international brand almost since its inception. In the current marketplace, it is not slowing down in terms of international recognition and has also increased its viewer numbers through product marketing. The Disney Channel is available through 13 specialized international channels, including channels in Germany, Latin America, and the Middle East. It has 20 million international network subscribers. Disney children's programming, however, does not end with the Disney Channel. Fox Kids Europe has 33 million subscribers, and Fox Kids Latin America has 14.3 million subscribers; these are both Disney companies. Some current popular Disney programming includes *Lilo & Stitch, Lizzie McGuire,* and the *Digimon* series, which Disney acquired through its agreement with Saban Entertainment, a Japanese company.

The availability of international children's networks does not necessarily mean that this type of programming is what the audience prefers, but the ease of dubbing makes it possible to localize a program seamlessly in a way that eliminates its foreignness. In this way, most children's television programming becomes transparent text that appeals to an audience in any cultural context. Although local audiences prefer local programming, children do not necessarily view cartoons created in the United States or Japan as foreign.

THE IMPACT OF MASS MEDIA

Critics question the impact of foreign imports from the United States and Japan on the cultural values of children in Latin America, where access is not limited to international networks but through single and block program sales to domestic broadcasters. Children, in particular, may be more susceptible to the influence of television than teens or adults due to their cognitive development stages, during which children are constantly learning about themselves and others in their social and cultural environment. Local culture is intertwined with global culture; children from around the world share the same interests, watch the same programming, play the same games, and share in the media preferences available in their living rooms, which create spaces for the negotiation of identity based on exposure to both global and local influences.

In addition, there is growing concern about the impact of advertising on children's values, including increased materialism. A full 54% of children in Latin America aged 7 to 11 agreed with the statement, "I love to watch ads on television," and when separated by country, 58% of Mexican children, 48% of Brazilian children, and 71% of Venezuelan children love to watch ads. Commercialization is not new to the mass media in these countries, as many use a commercial model. The new concern, however, is advertisements for North American products and the perception that these products are better. Of children who agree that they "love to watch ads on television," 53% agree that "North American products are better" ("TV Advertising and Children in Latin America"). In addition, there has been recent attention to the relationship between television viewing and obesity, especially in urban areas of Latin America, where heavy television viewing is correlated to obesity because of the displacement of other activities ("Television = Obesity?").

EDUCATIONAL PROGRAMMING

It is widely accepted that television can be used as an educational tool throughout Latin America. Castro (2004) explains that educational or prosocial messages should be salient throughout the program and appropriate for the target audience. If used properly, such messages can be advantageous for marginalized groups, especially children who may not have access to public education.

An example of an educational program is the coproduction of Televisa in Mexico and Children's Television Workshop (now Sesame Workshop), resulting in *Plaza Sésamo* as an adaptation of *Sesame Street.* In the early 1970s, a production team from Mexico was the first to truly change the look and content of *Sesame Street* to promote specific values of the

Mexican culture. Since *Plaza Sésamo* is shown in other Spanish-speaking Latin American countries, special consideration was taken to ensure that it would appeal to a diverse audience of children. The aim of the *Plaza Sésamo* production team was to create 130 half-hour episodes entirely in Spanish under the guidance of the Latin American research and production team. Today, each program is created through the co-production process: approximately half the episode consists of original productions filmed in Mexico City, and the other half is composed of short scenes that are considered by the Workshop as culturally neutral, that is, not having any exclusively American values or symbols, such as coins, the flag, or historical figures. *Plaza Sésamo* can be seen throughout Latin America.

THE TELENOVELA

The *telenovela* (soap opera) is the most popular programming genre for Latin American audiences; telenovelas are created for all audience segments. They differ from the daytime soap operas popular in the United States because telenovelas have endings, usually after about 150 hour-long episodes. The most popular are broadcast Monday through Friday during prime time and appeal to a broad general audience. During the day, telenovelas are targeted toward children up to age 12. The early-evening telenovela is reserved for the teenage audience, with more adult-themed novelas broadcast between 8 p.m. and 11 p.m.

Telenovela viewing is indeed popular with children, with 29% of those under 12 watching telenovelas alone or with their mothers. In fact, 41% of Latin Americans think telenovela viewing is an activity for the whole family, whereas 40% agree that viewing can unite the family (Gonzalez, 1993).

Telenovelas aimed at children usually feature child actors as the primary characters and involve story lines that are appropriate for the audience, focusing on school and family issues. In Mexico, telenovelas for children have proven to be successful, enjoying high ratings during the afternoon broadcasts on Televisa. The primary audience for these programs are 6-to-12-year-olds, who enjoy, for example, *Amy la Niña de la Mochila Azul* (*Amy, the Girl with the Blue Backpack*) and *Sueños y Caramelos* (*Dreams and Candies*). Teen telenovelas revolve around topics relevant to that age group and include discussions of intimate relationships, drug use, and peer pressure. Often, telenovelas will incorporate prosocial messages to reach teenagers in ways that are less obtrusive than other educational sources. Miguel Sabido, who became a telenovela producer at Televisa during the 1970s, designed the entertainment-education approach in Mexico. Use of the telenovela genre has proven to be an effective method of incorporating messages for all age groups, but particularly teens.

When considering preferences in television viewing, 89% of children across Latin America choose cartoons as their favorite type of television programming, with movies coming in second at 52%. Telenovelas are listed as a favorite genre for 60% of girls and about 28% of boys ages 7 to 11. Gender differences can also be found for other popular genres; nearly 40% of boys choose action-adventure, and about 25% of girls cite it as a genre they like to watch. Some 50% of boys ages 7 to 11 like to watch sports on television, whereas fewer than 20% of girls say they watch sports programming ("Favorite Television Programs," www.zonalatina.com/ZIdata167).

MOVIES

In addition to watching television, Latin American children enjoy watching movies, which are often imported from the United States. The global film market is dominated by Hollywood productions. When Latin Americans were given a choice among Hollywood movies, movies from their own country, movies from other Latin American countries, and movies from Europe, 78% of teenage males said they preferred Hollywood films, as did 79% of females. When the survey respondents were separated by country, 85% of Brazilians, 71% of Venezuelans, and 66% of Mexicans preferred Hollywood films. The lower numbers in Mexico may be due to the recent popularity and international success of Mexican movies such as *Amores Perros* and *Y Tú Máma También*.

MUSIC

Music in Latin America, as in most regions of the world, inspires youth culture because musicians are able to use music as a vehicle of free expression by working outside the constraints of other mass media. Musical traditions in the region are a mix of sounds from the Caribbean, Central America, and South America, creating such genres as samba, tango, mambo, and salsa. During the 1970s, young people embraced salsa music as the musical sound of Latin

America (Berrios-Miranda, 2004). As Latin Americans migrated to other parts of the world, the sounds and music traveled with them. Popular salsa artists include Tito Puente and Celia Cruz, who have captured the attention of salsa fans worldwide.

Rock en español is the blending of various musical forms from Latin America with the harder rock sounds of the North. The genre began in the early 1960s, which coincided with the modernization of many Latin American cities as well as the commercial development of other media forms. Much of the rock en español produced during the 1970s was a subversive voice against oppressive governments throughout the region; teenagers have been attracted to this musical genre because of the freedom to express alternative political views. Contemporary rock en español has found audiences of Latina/os in the United States and has gained much attention, especially in the border regions (Kun, 2002).

Popular Latin American musicians have found success in the North American market by appealing to audiences eager to listen to what has been called the "Latin explosion." Youth in the United States embraced such Latin American singers as Gloria Estefan in the 1980s and Ricky Martin and Marc Anthony in the 1990s, each of whom records albums in Spanish and English to appeal to audiences throughout the Americas. Bilingual singers are not new, but the intense marketing of Latina/os is now seen as an effective way to sell more records.

MAGAZINES

The magazine industry in Latin America is characterized by audience segmentation, whereby many magazines appeal to specific audience interests. Pan-regional magazines appeal to broad general audiences throughout Latin America and focus on news and finance. Spanish-language versions of American magazines such as *Vogue* and *Cosmopolitan* attract young female readers, while *Maxim,* also an American magazine, attracts young men. These and other American magazines are available in many countries.

Mexico has a wide variety of magazines appealing to every interest, including magazines published for children and teenagers. Two examples from Mexico include *El Cienpiés,* which features trivia, activities, and other information for young children, and *Eres,* which targets teenage girls with celebrity gossip and advice columns. *Artrevida* is a Brazilian magazine targeted to teenage girls, with celebrity news, advice columns, and fashion tips. Another magazine for teens is *Capricho,* which has a more "alternative" feel and focuses on music, celebrity news, and fashion. Teenagers are also attracted to adult fashion, gossip, and sports magazines. Current information about the use of magazines by young people in Latin America is unavailable.

INTERNET

Internet use in Latin American countries varies according to technological availability and access to computers. Young people who do have access through home or school are embracing the Internet, making Latin America the fastest-growing Internet market in the world, with a 19% increase in users from 2004 to 2005. As of September 2005, 16.4% of the population in Mexico were regular Internet users; in Brazil, 12.3% of people use the technology. In fact, Brazil and Mexico account for 57% of all users in Latin America (Internet World Statistics, www.internet worldstats.com). Popular activities online include shopping, downloading music, and instant messaging. Of teenagers using the Internet, 47% of males and 36% of females download music on a regular basis ("Downloading Music," www.zonalatina.com/Z1data 241). Teenagers use the Internet for instant messaging ("Instant Messaging," www.zonalatina.com/Z1data 225.htm) and other forms of mediated interpersonal communication.

Websites are available for Spanish- and Portuguese-speaking children. Nearly all the domestic television programs have associated websites featuring games for children to play online. Nickelodeon, Disney, and the Cartoon Network also have Spanish and Portuguese web pages that allow Latin American children to form interactive relationships with the characters. As the availability and popularity of the Internet becomes more widespread, young people will undoubtedly spend more time online. As this happens, concern intensifies about access to inappropriate material and use of the technology by pedophiles to gain access to children.

Children in Latin America spend a significant amount of time using mass media to be entertained, educated, and informed. Although there are varying degrees of development throughout the region, one common denominator among children throughout

Latin America, and indeed the world, is that they watch television. Although international children's networks are expanding, domestic channels that provide local or foreign programs are still the most commonly watched by Latin American children. The behavioral and social effects of exposure to media sex, violence, and advertising are of concern to Latin Americans, as are the consequences of exposure to foreign cultural values originating in the United States.

—*Kristin C. Moran*

See also Electronic Games, International; Entertainment-Education, International; Globalization, Media and; International Clearinghouse on Children, Youth, and Media; Internet Use, International; Latina/os, Media Use by; Radio, International; Television, International Viewing Patterns and

FURTHER READINGS

Berrios-Miranda, M. (2004). Salsa music as expressive liberation. *Centro Journal, 16*(2), 159–173.

Blosser, B. (1990). Through the pantalla Uruguaya (Uruguayan screen): The television environment for children in Uruguay. *Studies in Latin American Popular Culture, 9*, 149–169.

Castro, A. C. (2004). *Televisión educativa o televisión para aprender.* La Iniciativa de Comunicacion. Retrieved November 23, 2005, from http://www.comminit.com/la

Cole, R. (Ed.). (1996). *Communication in Latin America: Journalism, mass media, and society.* Wilmington, DE: Scholarly Resources.

Downloading music in Latin America. Retrieved November 20, 2005, from http://www.zonalatina.com/Z1data241.htm

Elsmar, M. (Ed.). (2003). *The impact of international television: A paradigm shift.* Mahwah, NJ: Erlbaum.

Favorite television programs of Latin American children. Retrieved October 19, 2005, from http://www.zonalatina.com/ZIdata167.htm

Fox, E. (1997). *Latin American broadcasting: From tango to telenovela.* London: John Libbey Media.

Gonzalez, J. (1993). La Confradía de las emociones interminables. In N. Mazziotti (Ed.), *El Espectáculo de la pasión: Las telenovelas latinoamericanas.* Buenos Aires: ABRN Producciones Gráficas.

Hollywood Inc., Latin America. Retrieved November 20, 2005, from http://www.zonalatina.com/ZIdata155.htm

IBOPE cable household ratings, 2005. Retrieved November 12, 2005, from http://www.zonalatina.com/cable0509

Instant messaging users in Latin America. Retrieved November 20, 2005, from http://www.zonalatina.com/Z1data225.htm

Internet world statistics. Retrieved December 1, 2005, from http://www.internetworldstats.com

Kun, J. (2002). Rock's reconquista. In R. Beebe, D. Fulbrook, & B. Saunders (Eds.), *Rock over the edge: Transformations in popular music culture.* Durham, NC: Duke University Press.

Latin America. Retrieved November 18, 2005, from http://www.worldscreen.com/latinamerica.php

Latin American children's choice of TV programs. Retrieved October 19, 2005, from http://www.zonalatina.com/ZIdata162.htm

Leite, G. (2005). *Pauta y mercado de la televisión infantil.* La Iniciativa de Comunicacion. Retrieved November 22, 2005, from http://www.comminit.com/la

Media as the main sources of entertainment. Retrieved November 20, 2005, from http://www.zonalatina.com/ZIdata264.htm

Meirelles, A. H. (2005). *Niños y consumo televisivo en América Latina.* La Iniciativa de Comunicacion. Retrieved November 19, 2005, from http://www.comminit.com/la

Pan Latin American kids survey. Retrieved November 18, 2005, from http://www.zonalatina.com/ZIdata

Sex and violence on television. Retrieved October 19, 2005, from http://www.zonalatina.com/ZIdata16.htm

Sinclair, J. (2000). *Latin American television: A global view.* New York: Oxford University Press.

Sinclair, J. (2004). The globalization of Latin American media. *NACLA Report on the Americas, 37*(4), 15–19.

Sinclair, J., Jacka, E., and Cunningham, S. (Eds.). (1996). *New patterns in global television: Peripheral vision.* New York: Oxford University Press.

Television=Obesity? Retrieved November 20, 2005, from http://www.zonalatina.com/ZIdata285

Television program preferences in cable households. Retrieved October 19, 2005, from http://www.zonalatina.com/ZIdata103.htm

TV advertising and children in Latin America. Retrieved October 19, 2005, from http://www.zonalatina.com/ZIdata144.htm

LATINA/OS, MEDIA EFFECTS ON

The underrepresentation of Latinos and Latinas in the media and their overrepresentation among consumers of media have led to concern that Latina/o youth may be at particular risk for media influence. However, there are only a few empirical studies that examine the impact of media on Latina/o youth. The research studies that have been conducted explore the role of media on Latina/o viewers' self-perceptions, focusing on self-esteem, ethnic identity, and body image. Another set of studies has examined connections between Latino youth's media use and their attitudes and belief systems, including ideas about gender and academic achievement. Finally, there have been studies to determine the influence of media on the health concerns of Latina/o adolescents.

Concern has arisen that the absence of Latina/o media personalities and repeated exposure to stereotypical portrayals of Latina/os may lead viewers to believe that these attributes characterize Latina/os in the real world. It is believed that heavy media use will cause Latina/o viewers to believe that Latina/os are inferior and that being a Latina/o is bad, thereby diminishing self-esteem. However, empirical evidence has not substantiated this hypothesized connection. Subervi-Velez and Necochea found that Latina/o children's general viewing amounts were only mildly related to their self-esteem, and in a positive direction. Therefore, Latina/o children who watched more English-language television had a more elevated self-esteem. Surprisingly, watching Spanish-language television was not related to the children's self-esteem.

Others have raised concerns over the influence of these media images on the ethnic identity of Latina/o youth. Although no published study has directly linked media use with the ethnic identity of Latina/o children and adolescents, studies have examined other relevant issues, such as acculturation. Studies have found a consistent relationship between media use and acculturation. Research with Latina/o adolescents has shown that those who are less acculturated use Spanish-language media to a greater extent. In addition, watching English-language television increases the acculturation level among newer Latina/o immigrants. Another set of studies has examined the links between media use and perceptions of Latina/o media personalities. Findings indicate that, when Latina/os watch more television, they are less likely to rate the televised depictions of Latina/o characters as fair. This result is consistent with the finding of Children Now that Latina/o children perceived that minority characters were underrepresented and more likely to be cast in negative roles than European American characters. This set of studies establishes a connection between Latina/o youth's media use and their feelings about their ethnic group and identity.

Other analyses of how media use shapes the self-conceptions of Latina/o youth have focused on issues of body image and body satisfaction. Focus group studies have explored Latina college students' perceptions of magazines' images and found that participants preferred a body ideal that corresponded with the ultra-thin media ideal and pursued this ideal through diet, exercise, and some unhealthy practices. Although the late adolescents emphasized their own cultural ideals and were aware that physical differences due to their ethnicity excluded them from attaining the mainstream media ideal, some were still unable to resist the negative impact on their self-image. A number of participants identified magazines as the most influential sources for body image ideals. Although these focus group results are informative, these connections have yet to be supported by survey data. Jane, Hunter, and Lozzi's survey of 87 Cuban American women aged 18 to 25 years found that neither amount of television nor amount of magazine exposure was a significant predictor of beliefs and attitudes associated with eating disorders. Thus, from these findings a mixed picture emerges, one in which Latinas speak of mainstream media ideals influencing their body image attitudes and behavior, even though their media exposure levels have not been found to be associated with these outcomes in any published work.

In addition to examining the role of media on the self-perceptions of Latina/o youth, a small number of studies have investigated the effect of media on the attitudes of Latina/o children and adolescents. One set of studies has examined gender-role norms. Experimental studies with Latina/o children found that exposing children to stereotypical or nonstereotypical gender occupations on television influenced their own ideas about gendered occupational roles and their own career aspirations. Those who viewed men and women in gender-typed occupations had more stringent ideas about the occupational roles of men and women, indicating that televised portrayals could affect ideas about gender and career choices. A more current study conducted by Rivadeneyra and Ward with Latina/o high school students found that greater levels of exposure to English- and Spanish-language television programming and the perception of television content as realistic were associated with more traditional views about gender roles. These connections remained even when acculturation level and generational status were taken into account. However, these relationships were only found with the girls in the study and did not exist with the boys, indicating a gender difference in the link between media use and gender-role attitudes.

Two published studies have also looked at the role of media use on the academic outcomes of Latina/o adolescents. An early study by Tan and colleagues found connections between media use and the grade point average of Latina/o high school students. Those who read newspapers were more likely to have a higher grade point average. On the other hand, those who watched television for entertainment were more likely to have a lower grade point average. More current research by the same author found that watching American television was related to higher educational aspirations among ninth-grade Latina/os. The authors suggest that viewing English-language television may help Latina/o immigrants understand U.S. culture, and therefore they may become more savvy educational consumers.

Finally, the impact of media use on health-related behaviors has also been examined with Latina/o youth. As with other ethnic groups, connections have been found between receptivity to pro-tobacco media and tobacco use among Latino adolescents. However, Latina/os, along with other ethnic minority groups, are less receptive to these messages than are European American adolescents. Program evaluation studies of media literacy programs have found that these can deter the initiation of cigarette use, the experimental use of marijuana, and the initiation of alcohol drinking and binge drinking among Latino middle school students.

—*Rocío Rivadeneyra*

See also Advertising, Ethnicity/Race in; Body Image, Ethnicity/Race and; Children Now; Ethnicity, Race, and Media; Ethnicity/Race, Media Effects on Identity; Hip Hop, Ethnicity/Race in; Immigrants, Media Use by; Latin America, Media Use in; Latina/os, Media Images of; Latina/os, Media Use by

FURTHER READINGS

Children Now. (1998). *A different world: Children's perceptions of race and class in media.* Retrieved from http://www.childrenow.org

Goodman, J. R. (2002). Flabless is fabulous: How Latina and Anglo women read and incorporate the excessively thin body ideal into everyday experience. *Journalism and Mass Communication Quarterly, 79*(3), 712–727.

Hofstetter, C. R., Hovell, M. F., Myers, C. A., & Blumberg, E. (1995). Patterns of communication about AIDS among Hispanic and Anglo adolescents. *American Journal of Preventive Medicine, 11*, 231–237.

Jane, D. M., Hunter, G. C., & Lozzi, B. M. (1999). Do Cuban American women suffer from eating disorders? Effects of media exposure and acculturation. *Hispanic Journal of Behavioral Sciences, 21*(2), 212–218.

Rivadeneyra, R., & Ward, L. M. (2005). From *Ally McBeal* to *Sábado Gigante*: Contributions of television viewing to the gender role attitudes of Latino adolescents. *Journal of Adolescent Research, 20*, 453–475.

Stilling, E. A. (1997). The electronic melting pot hypothesis: The cultivation of acculturation among Hispanics through television viewing. *Howard Journal of Communication, 8*, 77–100.

Subervi-Velez, F. A., & Necochea, J. (1990). Television viewing and self-concept among Hispanic American children— A pilot study. *Howard Journal of Communication, 2*, 315–329.

Tan, A., Fukioka, Y., Bautista, D., Maldonado, R., Tan, G., & Wright, L. (2000). Influence of television usage and parental communication on educational aspirations of Hispanic children. *Howard Journal of Communication, 11*, 107–125.

Unger, J. B. (2003). Peers, family, media, and adolescent smoking: Ethnic variation in risk factors in a national sample. *Adolescent and Family Health, 3*, 65–70.

LATINA/OS, MEDIA IMAGES OF

In the United States context, the terms *Latino* and *Latina* describe people who trace their ancestry to nations and cultures in Latin America. Media images construct meaning about Latina/os through visual representation. While Latina/os make up a significant and historically situated population in the United States, entertainment and news media typically neglect to include them in stories and images. Historically, the relatively few images in general market media marginalize and stereotype Latina/os. Although negative and stereotypical images persist, more recent celebrations of Latina/o stars and styles provide positive imagery in popular culture as Latina/os become incorporated into the American mainstream, fueled in part by 2000 U.S. Census reports that Latina/os make up more than 13% of the total U.S. population, surpassing African Americans as the second-largest ethnic or racial group after whites. Spanish-language radio and television programs are common throughout the

United States, with many shows catering to children. Contemporary media texts in Spanish directed at children work within the representational strategies of multiculturalism and present more visible and positive images of Latina/os than might be found in general market media.

Because Latina/os constitute a large and linguistically, culturally, and racially diverse group, media images do much to create a coherent notion of Latina/o identity and solidarity, which is referred to as *Latinidad.* As media audiences, children learn about Latina/os and about the nature of Latinidad through media images, and these images become part of the negotiation and formation of identity for Latina/o children. Persistent negative stereotypes in entertainment and news media can influence how children construct meanings about themselves and others and encourage bias and racism. Positive images in children's media, such as the characters Dora and Diego in the popular Nickelodeon series *Dora the Explorer,* represent Latina/os as part of a multicultural society.

Considering general market media representations since World War II, entertainment and news images present audiences with consistent negative stereotypes of Latina/os. Negative stereotypes suture people to a few visually simple images that demean, belittle, and marginalize. For Latina/os, Hollywood films project images of villains or sexualized lovers, and television programs feature maids and shady characters. Television and advertising images aimed at children have historically used humiliating and demeaning stereotypes for entertainment and product promotion, such as Speedy Gonzales and the Frito Bandito. With pressure from Latina/o advocacy groups, scholars, and critics, such characters are less frequently seen although not absent from media images. In news discourses, Latina/os continue to be criminalized and underrepresented. Local television news features stories of Latina/o teenage gang members and creates moral panic by racializing public issues such as immigration and crime. Children involved in these issues are often brought into news stories and constructed as part of public problems. Together, entertainment and news media provide ample examples of negative stereotypes and marginalizing images.

Despite the history of Latina/os living within the United States prior to the nation's founding, only recently have Latina/os garnered close attention and accommodation by mainstream corporations, politicians, and general market media corporations. The 2000 U.S. Census data showed rapid growth of a young Latina/o population. Media images that celebrate Latinidad have become more common in recent years as media companies, advertisers, and marketing demographers attempt to construct messages for Latina/o audiences. Film and television feature more positive Latina/o characters than in decades past, and television and print journalism include photographic representations of Latina/os that celebrate Latinidad and the contributions of artists and performers to U.S. culture. Much of the so-called "Latin pop explosion" that occurred at the turn of the 21st century provided positive images of singers and dancers such as Ricky Martin and Jennifer Lopez, who stand as teen icons. The ascent of multiculturalism as a dominant ideology in U.S. culture also casts Latina/o media images in positive light. While celebratory images of Latinidad represent changes in representation welcomed by many Latina/os, critics and scholars also warn that positive imagery neglects to confront social inequity that shapes the lived experience of Latinidad.

In contemporary entertainment media images targeted to children, many positive Latino/a characters populate storybooks, television, and films in Spanish and English. At the same time, media images of Latina/os in children's media remain understudied.

—*Esteban del Río*

See also Advertising, Ethnicity/Race in; Body Image, Ethnicity/Race and; Food Advertising, Gender, Ethnicity, and Age; Hip Hop, Ethnicity/Race in; Latin America, Media Use in; Latina/os, Media Effects on; Latina/os, Media Use by

FURTHER READINGS

Martínez, K. Z. (2004). *Latina* magazine and the invocation of panethnic family: Latino identity as it is informed by celebrities and *papis chulos. Communication Review, 7*(2), 155–174.

Mastro, D. E., & Greenberg, B. S. (2000). The portrayal of racial minorities on prime-time television. *Journal of Broadcasting and Electronic Media 44*(4), 690–703.

Mayer, V. (2003). *Producing dreams, consuming youth: Mexican Americans and mass media.* New Brunswick, NJ: Rutgers University Press.

Ramírez Berg, C. (2002). *Latino images in film: Stereotypes, subversion, and resistance.* Austin: University of Texas Press.

Valdivia, A. N. (2000). *A Latina in the land of Hollywood and other essays in media culture.* Tucson: University of Arizona Press.

LATINA/OS, MEDIA USE BY

As Latina/os have become one of the largest ethnic minority groups in the United States, the group has begun to attract the attention of researchers. The media world of Latina/o children and adolescents seems to be unique in several important ways. First, Latina/o youth indicate greater exposure to certain types of media, most significantly television, indicating an average of one more hour of television viewing per day than Caucasian youth. Second, Latina/o youth are exposed to Spanish-language media, a media world that may include different images and messages from those found in English-language media. Finally, Latina/o children may have different audience involvement behaviors than children of other ethnic groups, and there is some indication that they are more likely to view to learn, to identify most closely with minority media personalities, and to perceive some aspects of the television world as more realistic.

TELEVISION VIEWING AMOUNTS

In 1999, a large survey (N = 3,155) conducted by the Kaiser Family Foundation with children ages 2 to 18 found that, on average, Latina/o children spent about one hour more per day (7:05 hours) with media than European American children (6:00 hours). Among younger children (2-to-7-year-olds), this difference was accounted for by differences in television viewing. Latina/o children (ages 2 to 18) watched an average of 3:31 hours of television per day, significantly more than European American children (2:22 hours), but significantly less than African American children (3:56 hours). Other studies have found similar television viewing amounts for Latina/o youth, ranging from 3.71 hours per day for high school students to 4.14 hours per day for younger children. In terms of cable access, Latina/o children (42%) are less likely to have premium cable television at home, compared to African American children (55%).

As with young people from other ethnic groups, the largest proportion of Latina/o youth indicated that they watched children's entertainment programming (59%) and children's educational programming (45%). However, a lower proportion of Latina/o children and adolescents (37%) indicated that they watched comedy programming compared to African American children and adolescents (49%). Additionally, a lower

proportion of older Latina/o children (ages 8 to 18: 16%) viewed television dramas compared to European Americans (25%).

SPANISH-LANGUAGE TELEVISION

Latina/o youth are often exposed to a second television world that is *not* part of the media diet of most non-Spanish speakers: Spanish-language television created both in the United States and in Latin America. Among Latina/os in the United States, Spanish-language television is both popular and accessible, with Univisión (the number one Spanish-language network in the United States) reaching close to 95% of the U.S. Latina/o audience, and Telemundo (the number two network) reaching approximately 84%. Evidence from advertising research suggests that Spanish-language TV may hold more credibility and possibly more influence among Latina/os than English-language TV.

This is not to say that Latina/os watch only Spanish-language television. In fact, research has found that much of the Latina/o television audience watches many of the same programs viewed by the general U.S. television audience. One study with Latina/o high school students found that 25% of their television viewing time was dedicated to watching Spanish-language programming. Although Latina/o youth are consistent viewers of Spanish-language television, it is not the only television viewing they are doing or even the majority of it. Both television worlds are important in studying this group. Findings indicate that language use, acculturation, and immigrant status are related to the language of television programming viewed, with Spanish speakers, new immigrants, and those who are less acculturated being more likely to watch Spanish-language television.

OTHER MEDIA CONSUMPTION

In terms of other media consumption, Latina/o children reported watching significantly more movies (21 minutes a day) than European American children (8 minutes a day) and similar amounts to black children (19 minutes a day). Similar trends were found for video games, with Latina/o children reporting 24 minutes of video game exposure, significantly more than what European American children reported but similar to what black children reported.

Latina/o children were found to be similar to children of other ethnicities in terms of their music media exposure. Younger Latina/o children (ages 2 to 7) reported listening to the radio about 25 minutes a day and to CDs and tapes for 23 minutes a day. Older Latina/o children and adolescents (ages 8 to 18) reported listening to radio about 56 minutes a day and to CDs and tapes for 1 hour and 8 minutes a day. These amounts were similar to amounts reported by other ethnic groups in the same age groups. One of the few differences found in exposure to audio media was that Latina/o children were less likely to report having a CD player at home (86%) compared to European American children (92%). In addition, there were differences in the musical genres that were listened to, with Latina/o youth most likely to report listening to "Latin/salsa" music than any other ethnic group and more likely than European American youth to listen to "rap/hip hop."

Significant differences were found in terms of exposure to print media and computer time among Latina/o children. Although Latina/o youth reported spending the same amount of time with print media as youth of other ethnicities (about 38 minutes with all print media), a greater percentage of Latina/o children (23%) than European American children (12%) reported not having read on the previous day. In terms of computer exposure, Latina/o youth were less likely to have computers in their homes (48%) than European American youth (78%). Surprisingly, there were no ethnic-group differences in the amount of computer time for the total sample. However, when taking into account computer users only, Latina/o youth reported spending significantly more time on the computer (2:12 hours per day) than European American youth (1:35 hours per day).

AUDIENCE INVOLVEMENT

In addition to sheer number of hours exposed to media, it is also important to assess audience involvement behaviors, including identification with media personalities, motivations for media use, and perceived reality of the media world. Research studies with Latina/o children and adolescents indicate that they prefer Latina/o characters and that, in the absence of Latina/o characters, Latina/o youth name African American television personalities as the celebrities they look up to the most. There is also some indication that Latina/o viewers may be more likely than Caucasian viewers to use TV intently to learn about the world. Survey data from more than 1,000 adults found that Latina/os were more likely than Caucasians to report using TV "to learn about myself" and "to learn new things." Work with younger participants has found that Latina/o youth were more likely to say that they learn interesting things from TV (23%) than European American youth (15%) and less likely to say they are "just killing time" when watching TV (48% versus 53% of European American youth). Additionally, Latina/o youth in one study believed more strongly than Caucasian youth that the portrayals of Mexican Americans on television were realistic.

—Rocío Rivadeneyra

See also Advertising, Ethnicity/Race in; Ethnicity, Race, and Media; Ethnicity/Race, Stereotyping; Ethnicity/Race, Media Effects on Identity; Hip Hop, Ethnicity/Race in; Immigrants, Media Use by; Latin America, Media Use in; Latina/os, Media Effects on; Latina/os, Media Images of; Music, Personal Identity and

FURTHER READINGS

Albarran, A., & Umphrey, D. (1993). An examination of television motivations and program preferences by Hispanics, Blacks, and Whites. *Journal of Broadcasting and Electronic Media, 37,* 95–103.

Rivadeneyra, R., & Ward, L. M. (2005). From *Ally McBeal* to *Sábado Gigante*: Contributions of television viewing to the gender role attitudes of Latino adolescents. *Journal of Adolescent Research, 20,* 453–475.

Roberts, D. F., Foehr, U. G., Rideout, V. J., & Brodie, M. (1999). *Kids and media at the new millennium.* Palo Alto, CA: Kaiser Family Foundation.

Supervi-Velez, F. A., & Colsant, S. (1993). The television worlds of Latino children. In G. L. Berry & J. K. Asamen (Eds.), *Children and television: Images in a changing sociocultural world* (pp. 215–228). Newbury Park, CA: Sage.

LICENSING, MERCHANDISING AND

Merchandising and licensing seem to be nearly the same thing; the main difference between these two processes is in their goals. Licensing is meant to increase the revenues of a product or service; merchandising is a marketing instrument used to bring more attention to a product in new or existing markets. Merchandising is used by the owner of a trademark or copyright in the marketing process to draw as much attention as possible to a product or service, whereas licensing is based on an agreement between partners. The owner of a trademark or copyright focuses on finding new markets with low risks. A licensee, on the other hand, tries to cut marketing costs by taking advantage of a well-known and accepted image that he or she hopes to transfer to his or her new product or service. Both licensing and merchandising play an important role in the handling of products and services targeted to children, adolescents, and their parents. A pioneer in the licensing of media products and characters is the Walt Disney Company, which licenses its characters and the Disney brand to partners all over the world.

TYPES OF LICENSING

Licensing of trademarks and service marks has become an important way to gain additional income from existing trademarks, but it has not always been a common practice. There are many different types of licensing, the most important being character licensing, personality licensing, event licensing, and brand licensing. Character licenses are the rights to use fictional characters for products and services. To use a character from a movie for books, posters, or video games, a company must have a license agreement with the owner of the character's copyright. In the case of personality licensing, the contract deals with a real person. Under such a license, a person's name and image cannot be used without permission. Event licensing involves popular events such as sports games and music concerts. The most popular kind of licensing, however, is brand licensing, in which a new company obtains the right to use a well-known brand to establish its business on the market.

NATIONAL REGULATORY DIFFERENCES

Many countries have traditionally forbidden the licensing of trademarks because the trademark that is licensed would no longer serve its perceived primary purpose: to indicate the source or origin of a product or service. As a result, some countries developed the concept of registered user agreements. This permits a person other than the original owner of the trademark to be an authorized user of this trademark in his or her own business. However, the problems with licensing have decreased significantly, and today most countries accept licensing as a way to enter new markets.

REASONS FOR LICENSING

One possible reason for a company to license a trademark is to extend the trademark's geographic range and the range of products with which it is associated with a minimum of risk for the owner of the original trademark. Still, the feasibility and advisability of licensing a trademark must be analyzed on a case-by-case basis. Many factors come into play, including the goods involved, the outlook and strategy of the owner of the trademark, and national market conditions. Possible license agreements include contracts with licensees in individual countries, contracts that cover bigger geographical regions (such as Western Europe), and contracts that deal with certain product lines, such as toys. In some licenses, the original licensee has the right to grant regional sublicenses to push products onto new markets.

A license agreement is usually a written document that is subject to the contractual laws of a particular jurisdiction. No matter what type of licensing arrangement is involved, the license must guarantee the trademark owner control over the quality of the licensed products. This means there must be consequences for the licensee who produces below-standard products using the license. Another part of a license agreement is a marketing schedule, which may enable the main owner of the trademark to push new products onto the market by licensing a trademark to several different licensees. This can generate a great deal of attention for the product through the marketing campaigns of the various licensees.

Another aspect of licensing agreements is the payment of royalties from the licensee to the licensor based on any number of factors. The risk for the licensee is in the amount of the royalty he or she must pay to the owner of the trademark. In the worst case, the cost will be too high for the licensee to profit from having the license. Such royalties often involve complex tax considerations and in some countries are subject to government agency approval. Many countries require licenses to be recorded with a local trademark office or other government agency. If such a requirement is not fulfilled for a given license, the license may be invalid in the region, and the trademark may be cancelled on the grounds of non-use.

On the whole, the main reason for licensing is to get additional profit from licensees in new markets. A common case involves the content owner of a popular book selling the license for a movie based upon the book; an additional possibility could be a license for a computer game as well. A recent example of a successful trademark and copyright licensor is Marvel Comics. Superheroes from the Marvel Universe have been very successful in movies, in games, and on TV. The many presentations of Spiderman and his popular colleagues have brought Marvel profits that would have been impossible without licensing.

—*Hardy Dreier*

See also Advertising, Market Size and; Advertising, Regulation of; Disney

FURTHER READINGS

Böll, K. (1999): *Merchandising und Licensing. Grundlagen–Beispiele–Management.* München, Germany: Vahlen.

Jeremiah, J. R. (1997). *Merchandising intellectual property rights.* Chichester, UK: Wiley.

Zu Salm, C. (2001): Character Licensing: Von der Lizenzierung eines Charakters zur Etablierung einer Kinder-Dachmarke. In K. Böll (Ed.), *Handbuch Licensing* (pp. 123–163). Frankfurt am Main: Deutscher Fachverlag.

LITERACY

Concern that media use might have negative effects on literacy and educational achievement among children can be dated back to the growth of popular literature in the mid-19th century and was greatly amplified by the rapid of diffusion of television in the 1950s. Recently, the hypothesis has received a fresh impulse from the rapid diffusion of new information and communication technologies.

THE CONCEPT OF LITERACY

Most commentators are agreed that literacy means something more than "functional literacy" (i.e., the basic ability to read and write), although there is little agreement as to just what constitutes that something. Traditionally, it involved being well educated or knowledgeable or, to use more recent terminology, possessing large amounts of academic and cultural capital. Consequently, it has long been generally assumed that universal education is a prerequisite for the attainment of high levels of literacy in a society.

However, some historians dispute this view, citing evidence that, in some countries, mass literacy was achieved before the introduction of universal schooling, implying that there is more than one route to literacy. Another view sees literacy as something composed not of neutral, technical, and universal elements but of competencies that are culturally and temporally specific to various social contexts (and their dominant groups), a view frequently adopted by ethnic and other minority groups. Recently, there has been a trend toward breaking down the concept into various "subliteracies"—such as print literacy, media literacy, visual literacy, computer (or e-)literacy, and information literacy—implying the acquisition of specific and not necessarily transferable competencies within each subdomain. In his comprehensive treatment of the interaction between media, cognition, and learning, Gavriel Salomon saw the neuropsychological evidence that different symbolic modes of information are processed in different parts of the brain as pointing to the conclusion that different kinds of content are processed by different cognitive systems, with varying amounts of mental translation involved. Thus, he argued, although watching TV may require less conscious effort than reading a book, TV viewing may facilitate learning for those who experience difficulty with print modes, albeit learning of a different kind. By extrapolation, this view has led some observers to suggest that electronic digital developments may be taking us toward entirely new forms of literacy that will be unlike any current forms of literary practice.

MEDIA AND LITERACY

There is a long-standing assumption that the invention of printing was primarily responsible for the development of literacy in the West and that other means of mass communication (such as TV and computers) must also, in one way or another, fundamentally affect it. However, some historians also question this assumption, arguing that levels of literacy were already rising in Europe before printing was invented and that the resulting demand for texts provided the impetus for printing rather than vice versa. Others see industrialization, rather than printing, as the primary motor driving the growth in literacy. If these (disputed) claims are correct, the whole traditionally assumed causal link between different forms of media and different forms of literacy is called into question.

PREVALENT THEORETICAL PERSPECTIVES

Nevertheless, an extensive body of research has explored the relationship between media and literacy. Building on the extensive overview of the subject by Susan Neuman, four major theoretical assumptions underlying research into the effects of media on literacy and educational achievement may be discerned. Three of them are negative: *displacement theory* (that media take time away from reading and schoolwork), *information processing theory* (that reading-based activities activate the mind, whereas activities such as TV viewing are mentally pacifying), and *short-term gratification theory* (that media have radically changed children's expectations with regard to learning by stimulating the demand for constant novelty, pace, and stimulation). The fourth theoretical assumption is positive: *interest stimulation theory* (that media can enhance learning by stimulating interests). The positive potential of TV was underlined by Patricia Greenberg, who argued that TV is an intrinsically democratic medium that can make learning available to groups of children who fare less well in traditional educational situations. Conversely, in a number of polemical attacks in the 1980s, Neil Postman accused the media in general, and television in particular, of destroying print literacy as well as other aspects of academic and cultural accomplishment.

RESEARCH EVIDENCE: A SUMMARY

The predominant model tested has been a simple negative effects model dominated by TV use. Various educational consequences of excessive TV use have been postulated, such as poor concentration, reading and writing difficulties, and poor examination results. However, this negative effects hypothesis has never received consistent, convincing support. Attempts to operationalize and test alternative models have been rare, although one perspective that has received significant empirical support is based on the insight that the educational system helps to structure society by allocating students to different status groups and, by extrapolation, thereby also structures general cultural dispositions and styles, including media uses and preferences. In other words, the causal relation between education and media use is here reversed. In general, research in the field has seldom been sustained or systematic. There is no common agreement on the definition of literacy; most studies have been cross-sectional and have been conducted within a wide variety of disciplines, using a wide array of methods of measurements and analysis, thereby making meaningful comparison of results impossible. Consequently, there is little consensus among researchers. Finally, the rapid diffusion of digital information and communication technologies has radically altered the whole research context and has imposed new theoretical and methodological parameters upon it.

—*Keith Roe*

See also Cognitive Development, Media and; Digital Literacy; Media Effects, Models of; Media Literacy, Aims and Purposes of; Media Literacy, Approaches to; Media Literacy, Key Concepts in; Media Literacy Programs; Reading, Impact of TV on

FURTHER READINGS

Adoni, H., & Nossek, H. (2001). The new media consumers: Media convergence and the displacement effect. *Communications: The European Journal of Communication, 26*(1), 59–83.

Greenfield, P. M. (1984). *Mind and media: The effects of television, video games, and computers.* Cambridge, MA: Harvard University Press.

Kress, G. (2003). *Literacy in the new media age.* London/New York: Routledge.

Martin, A., & Rader, H. (2003). *Information and IT literacy: Enabling learning in the 21st century.* London: Facet.

Neuman, S. (1991). *Literacy in the television age.* Norwood, NJ: Ablex.

Postman, N. (1986). *Amusing ourselves to death.* London: Heinemann.

Roe, K. (1995). Adolescent's use of socially disvalued media: Towards a theory of media delinquency. *Journal of Youth and Adolescence, 24*(5), 617–631.

Salomon, G. (1994). *Interaction of media, cognition and learning.* Mahwah, NJ: Erlbaum.

LONELINESS

Loneliness researchers Leticia Peplau and Daniel Perlman have identified at least three common elements that characterize loneliness. First, loneliness is a subjective feeling in which a person perceives a deficiency in his or her social relationships. Therefore, the person wants more social interaction than he or she currently has. Second, loneliness is an emotional experience usually described as a painful, negative, and aversive feeling. Third, it is also usually associated with feelings of isolation and rejection.

LONELINESS IN ADOLESCENCE

To understand loneliness in adolescence, one first needs to make the distinction between a temporary, mild degree of loneliness that is easily overcome (state loneliness) and a longer-lasting, severe degree of loneliness that is difficult to overcome (trait loneliness). All adolescents may experience some degree of the mild state of loneliness. For instance, adolescence is a time of identity building, and to some degree adolescents need to be alone to process their own thoughts and feelings and build their own identities. During these alone times, adolescents may make use of several different types of media, such as the Internet, music, and television. These media can help adolescents in their identity building; for example, adolescents may use the Internet to research a wide variety of topics they find interesting, or they may listen to music to reinforce their current identities. Research has shown that, although these alone times can produce loneliness, adolescents report greater positive affect after spending some time alone. In other cases, the longer-lasting trait loneliness may be an indication of an underlying problem that needs to be addressed. Trait loneliness suggests that these adolescents may have characteristics that keep them locked in a cycle of loneliness. Three main characteristics are (1) how they think about themselves and their expectations about others when forming relationships, (2) their level of social skills, and (3) how they cope with loneliness.

Several researchers have shown that lonely adolescents may think in ways that keep them from forming meaningful relationships and thus make them feel lonely. Lonely adolescents may think that they are not capable of forming relationships, that they are not worthy of anyone else's affections, or that they will be rejected in social situations. Many of these thoughts occur automatically, and adolescents may be unaware of how much their thinking influences their behavior in social situations. For example, they may not initiate conversations in social situations for fear of being rejected, or they may say little in conversations because they believe the other people in the conversation are not interested in what they have to say.

Researchers have also shown that lonely adolescents have poor social skills. Poor social skills include inability to initiate or sustain a conversation, not knowing how to appropriately disclose information about self, insensitivity to social cues that other people exhibit, and not knowing how to be responsive to other people in conversations. For example, adolescents may disclose too much or too little information in conversations, thus making other people in the conversation feel uncomfortable and perhaps unwilling to continue further communication.

Poor coping has also been pointed out by researchers as another contributing factor for loneliness. Positive ways of coping with loneliness allow an adolescent to deal with feelings of loneliness and move on. Such coping might include talking with others about how they feel, engaging in activities such as exercising, studying, engaging in a hobby, and so on. However, poor and negative ways of coping with loneliness keep adolescents locked in a cycle of loneliness. These poor coping activities include brooding about their loneliness, watching television, overeating, and using drugs. All these activities provide only a temporary reprieve from adolescents' feelings of loneliness and fail to address the underlying issues of why they feel lonely.

LONELINESS AND THE MEDIA

Some researchers have argued that media help adolescents feel less lonely, whereas others have argued that it may cause adolescents to feel lonelier. In some cases, researchers have argued that media use can have a cathartic effect; reading loneliness poetry or listening to music about loneliness, for example, may help adolescents relieve some of their feelings of loneliness. In other cases, researchers have argued that solitary media activities (such as watching television, playing computer games) displace the time that adolescents can spend on more social activities such as sports.

One type of media that has been investigated further to determine its effect on loneliness is the Internet. An interesting feature of the Internet is that it can be a solitary activity (such as Web surfing) or a social activity (for example, chat rooms and instant messaging). Research provides evidence that the Internet tends to "make the rich richer and the poor poorer." The Internet may help foster greater communication among adolescents who already have good social skills and a substantial group of friends, through such features as text messaging (via Internet and cell phones), email, and so on. However, lonely adolescents with negative thinking patterns and poor social skills often have trouble forming relationships online. They may form superficial, temporary relationships that are not effective in helping them overcome their loneliness. Though there is less evidence of it, the Internet may also help the "poor get richer." Internet websites that provide information about loneliness and online loneliness discussion groups may help to change the lonely adolescents' ways of thinking and behaving that keep them feeling lonely.

Whatever the type of media usage, if it does not help the adolescent resolve the underlying issues causing the loneliness, it will not provide effective relief from loneliness. In some cases, the loneliness that adolescents feel may be only temporary, like the feelings at the end of a romantic relationship. Adolescents may use media in these cases to provide a cathartic effect and help them cope with their feelings of loneliness. In other cases, adolescents may feel lonely all the time because of some underlying issue, such as negative thinking patterns, poor social skills, and poor coping patterns. In these cases, media use may be less effective in reducing their feelings of loneliness over a period of time.

—*Sean S. Seepersad*

See also Bedrooms, Media Use in; Catharsis Theory; Internet Use, Social; Media Effects, Models of; Online Relationships; Peer Groups, Joint Use of Media in

FURTHER READINGS

Hojat, M., & Crandall, R. (1989). *Loneliness: Theory, research and applications.* Newbury Park, CA: Sage.

Peplau, L. A., & Perlman, D. (Eds.). (1980). *Loneliness: A sourcebook of current theory, research and therapy.* New York: Wiley.

Rokach, A., & Brock, H. (1998). Coping with loneliness. *Journal of Psychology, 132,* 107–128.

Rotenberg, K. J., & Shelley, H. (1999). *Loneliness in childhood and adolescence.* Cambridge, UK: Cambridge University Press.

Seepersad, S. (2003). *Understanding loneliness using attachment and system theories and developing an applied intervention.* Unpublished manuscript. Retrieved from http://www.webofloneliness.com/publications/critical/loneliness.PDF

Seepersad, S. (2004). Coping with loneliness: Adolescent online and offline behavior. *CyberPsychology and Behavior, 7,* 35–39.

Tyler, T. R. (2002). Is the Internet changing social life? It seems the more things change, the more they stay the same. *Journal of Social Issues, 58,* 195–205.

M

MAGAZINES, ADOLESCENT BOYS'

Little academic research has explored either the content or effects of magazines targeted at adolescent boys. What little research is publicly available is market research; such work largely describes who reads what magazines and suggests that teenage boys in the United States gravitate toward hobby or special-interest magazines rather than male equivalents of the lifestyle magazines popular among adolescent girls. In fact, some researchers have suggested that teenage boys perceive the very idea of lifestyle magazines as essentially feminine, and they reject the idea of such a magazine designed for them.

Most research that asks what magazines teenage boys read has been conducted by Mediamark Research, Inc., for the Magazine Publishers of America (MPA), a trade group. Of magazines MPA describes as "teen interest," half of the highest circulation titles are primarily of interest to males. These include *Boy's Life,* the official magazine of the Boy Scouts of America or BSA (with a reported circulation of 1.28 million), three magazines focusing on video games and game play (e.g., *Game Informer* with a reported circulation of 1.32 million), and *Sports Illustrated for Kids* (with a reported circulation of 760,000). Of these, the only one clearly produced exclusively for boys, of course, is *Boy's Life,* and its circulation figures may not reflect the same degree of interest or readership as those of other titles. Many local units of the BSA purchase subscriptions for all boys enrolled in any of their programs, including boys as young as 7 years old.

An alternative indicator of what magazines teenage boys read is the percentage of a given title's readers who are teenage boys. Although this does not indicate in absolute terms how many boys read these magazines, it does suggest the importance of teen audiences to a specific magazine. In 2004, Mediamark Research, Inc., reported that the magazines reporting the highest percentage of teenage boys in their readership are primarily magazines designed for automotive and motor sport enthusiasts. Examples include *Dirt Rider* (30% of readers are teenage boys), *4 Wheel and Off Road* (20% of readers are teen boys), and *Popular Hot Rodding* (18% of readers are teenage boys). Readers of professional wrestling fan magazines are also disproportionately likely to be teenage boys (e.g., *WWE Magazine*, with 20% of its readers being teenage boys). It is helpful to compare these figures with those from magazines actually designed for teenage girls—the readership of *Seventeen* is only 36% teenage girls, and the readership of *YM* is only 47% teenage girls.

No formal analyses have explored the contents of magazines targeted at or read predominantly by teenage boys in the United States. One such study has been undertaken in the Netherlands, however. Whereas the United States has no prominent lifestyle magazines for teenage boys, in the Netherlands, a lifestyle magazine for teenage boys is published and enjoys a sizable readership. A comparison between its contents and those of a popular, comparable magazine for girls found that the boys' magazine focused more on hobbies (such as motor sports and technology) and celebrities, the girls' more on fashion and beauty. The study's author concludes that the boys' magazine reinforces masculine stereotypes in much the same way girls' magazines reinforce feminine stereotypes.

Some research on the effects of advertising in youth-oriented magazines has included men's lifestyle magazines such as *Maxim* and *FHM* (also called "lad magazines"). Although the typical readers of such magazines are significantly older than teens, it is likely that many teen boys also read them. Lad magazines contain content evocative of magazine genres popular among teen boys (e.g., sections on technology, cars, and celebrities) as well as content comparable to that found in girls' lifestyle magazines (e.g., sections on fashion and consumer products). The magazines are also frankly sexual and feature numerous images of provocatively dressed and posed women as well as articles about sex. Advertisements for alcohol are common, and alcohol is a common element in articles about sex. Reading lad magazines has been linked in at least one study to perceptions that alcohol use is commonplace and acceptable, to expectations that alcohol use brings positive effects, and to increased alcohol consumption among middle school students. No research on the effects of other elements of lad magazine content has been published as of this writing.

—*Laramie D. Taylor*

See also Advertising, Effects on Adolescents of; Magazines, Adolescent Girls'; Sexual Information, Teen Magazines and

FURTHER READINGS

Mediamark Research, Inc. (2004). *Teen market profile.* Retrieved May 24, 2006, from http://www.magazine.org/content/files/teenprofile04.pdf

Taylor, L. D. (2005). All for him: Articles about sex in American lad magazines. *Sex Roles, 52*(3/4), 153–163.

Thomsen, S. R., & Rekve, D. (2004). The differential effects of exposure to "youth-oriented" magazines on adolescent alcohol use. *Contemporary Drug Problems, 31*(1), 31–58.

Willemsen, T. M. (1998). Widening the gender gap: Teenage magazines for girls and boys. *Sex Roles, 38*(9/10), 851–861.

MAGAZINES, ADOLESCENT GIRLS'

With their subscription rates numbering in the millions, teen magazines are viewed as a ubiquitous socializing force among girls in the Western world. Early research on teen magazines began in the 1970s, with Angela McRobbie's groundbreaking content analysis of the popular British publication, *Jackie.* Since then, research evidence has slowly accumulated elsewhere to provide detailed descriptions of the content of teen magazines, to understand how adolescent girls interpret magazine messages, and to examine links between magazine reading and girls' beliefs and behaviors. Among researchers' most frequently cited concerns is the narrow range of topics discussed in teen magazines and their emphasis on girls' need to look good and attract boys.

TEEN MAGAZINES AS A UNIQUE MEDIUM IN GIRLS' LIVES

Currently, mainstream teen magazines (e.g., *Seventeen, YM, Teen*) represent one of the largest segments of a thriving consumer magazine industry. Researchers estimate that nearly all girls in the United States read teen magazines occasionally and that more than 70% of girls read them on a regular basis. By providing detailed instructions that promise to help girls improve their physical appearance and relationships, teen magazines communicate a level of intimacy with their readers that is rarely shared by other media. Indeed, some researchers have likened the "how to" nature of magazine messages to the type of advice that is provided by an older and more knowledgeable sister or girlfriend. Consistent with this view, research suggests that most readers find teen magazines to be a trustworthy and valuable source of information.

CONTENT OF TEEN MAGAZINES

The vast majority of studies investigating teen magazines are content analyses, which provide detailed descriptions of the quantity and quality of magazine messages. Content analyses reveal that the most common topics discussed in teen magazines focus on fashion, beauty, domestic life, and romantic relationships. In particular, teen magazines have been found to support traditional gender roles, placing high value on girls' physical appearance and their capacity to attract boys and maintain heterosexual romantic relationships. As notable as the presence of messages supporting traditional gender roles is the absence of other types of content. In particular, researchers have noted that girls' interest in education, careers, travel, sports, public service, or politics is rarely mentioned. Moreover, the topics covered in mainstream teen magazines appear to be relatively consistent regardless of the particular magazine in question, the era in which it was published, or its country of origin. Indeed, themes identified in teen magazines published in the United States, Canada, Great Britain, Australia, New Zealand, and the Netherlands are strikingly similar across several decades.

MESSAGES ABOUT FEMININITY AND GENDER ROLES

Through the topics covered and the advice given, teen magazines provide strong and often contradictory messages about what it means to be a girl and about how girls should act in relationships with others. Specifically, teen magazines adhere to traditional norms of femininity that portray girls as dependent, preoccupied with their physical appearance, and consumed by heterosexual desire. In a content analysis of *Seventeen* spanning more than 30 years (1961–1985), Kate Peirce found that in all three decades, about 60% of the editorial content was devoted to discussions about girls' appearance and their interest in keeping house (i.e., decorating, cooking), whereas little attention was devoted to topics of personal development and growth. In a follow-up analysis of fiction stories presented in *Seventeen* and *Teen*, she found that the female protagonists were almost always portrayed as weak and dependent on others to solve their problems. Moreover, analyses of *Seventeen*, *YM*, and *Teen* indicate that these magazines explicitly encouraged girls to be confident and "be themselves," but the implicit message was that they should do so in order to attract boys. Thus, in teen magazines, heterosexual romance is described as a significant and serious component of adolescent development, and one that will ultimately bring happiness and meaning to girls' lives.

Two studies have examined teen magazines' portrayals of the working world. One analysis of fiction articles in *Seventeen* and *Teen* showed that occupations were often gender stereotyped. Whereas women were usually depicted in service and caretaking occupations (e.g., nurses, social workers, and sales clerks), men were depicted in a wider variety of careers, many of which were prestigious or required high educational attainment (e.g., doctors, lawyers, and bankers). Over a decade later, a second study found that the most frequently mentioned occupations in *Seventeen* were based in the entertainment industry. Becoming an actress, musician, dancer, or model not only was depicted as a

realistic aspiration for girls and young women, but also was regarded with much admiration and prestige.

MESSAGES ABOUT BEAUTY AND BODIES

A recurring theme in teen magazines is that feminine success can be achieved by making oneself physically beautiful. Via advertisements, images, and editorial content, girls are encouraged to wear cosmetics and to keep up-to-date with the latest fashion trends. Guidelines are provided by expert advisers, such as supermodels and celebrities, and often require that readers purchase a variety of beauty products. Many researchers express concern over magazines' competing needs to serve adolescent girls and satisfy their advertisers. They argue that advertisers benefit when magazines exploit girls' insecurities about their physical appearance during a period characterized by rapid physical growth and change.

Teen magazines have also been charged with promoting an ideal of thinness. Analyses of magazine images show that they promote a homogeneous and often unattainable standard of beauty; models are almost always Caucasian, tall, long-legged, light-skinned, curve-free, and air brushed to physical perfection. In addition, girls' bodies are presented as objects that need to be carefully monitored through exercise, dieting, costuming, and comportment.

Teen magazines convey ambivalent messages about body functions. Content analyses of menstrual product advertisements indicate that in teen magazines, menstruation is described both as a natural process and as a source of considerable embarrassment and discomfort. Advertisements for menstrual medications emphasize the importance of "staying slim" during the menstrual period and describe how menstrual products offered girls the "protection" they needed to "feel safe" against staining and unwanted odors. Thus, in teen magazines, girls' bodies are portrayed as not only thin but also sanitary and odor-free.

MESSAGES ABOUT SEXUALITY AND SEXUAL HEALTH

A growing body of studies has focused on depictions of sexuality in teen magazines. Research indicates that the amount of sexual content in teen magazines has increased dramatically in recent years, even as the proportion of health-related sexual information has diminished. By the 1990s, the most frequently discussed sexual topics were general references to sexual activity, followed by messages about sexual decision making, virginity, and female sexual responsibility. Some other issues that were openly addressed by teen magazines, albeit less frequently, were one-night stands, sexual abuse, incest, oral sex, erotic dreams, masturbation, and emergency contraception. Although the range of sexual topics in teen magazines has broadened and become more explicit in recent years, several researchers point out that references to gay and lesbian issues are still conspicuously absent.

Teen magazines are replete with sexual scripts, which dictate how women and men are supposed to act in dating and sexual relationships. For the most part, these scripts support a sexual double standard, describing boys as active and aggressive sexual initiators and girls as sexual objects and limit-setters who are responsible for the negative sexual consequences of intercourse. Several researchers have examined magazines' contradictory portrayals of female sexuality, which encourage girls to dress and behave in sexually provocative ways but to abstain from sexual activity. Contradictory messages are also seen in teen magazine portrayals of losing one's virginity. Although one study found that *Seventeen* increasingly recognized girls' capacity to experience sexual desire, this nontraditional script was overshadowed by more frequent messages about girls' ambivalence toward sexuality, their potential to be sexual victims, and the morality of their sexual decisions.

GIRLS' INTERPRETATION OF MAGAZINE MESSAGES

Qualitative research has examined how adolescent girls approach and interpret the content of teen magazines. Although most girls report reading magazines for entertainment purposes or to fill time, many say that they turn to magazines for guidance and to learn about other girls' lives. Indeed, advice columns, quizzes, and nonfiction articles rank among girls' favorite sections, as they provide a look into what are presented as typical concerns of other adolescent girls. Research suggests that girls do not necessarily accept magazine messages at face value. Rather, readers engage with the text, comparing the content with their own lived experiences and mulling over the magazines' recommendations.

Girls' selection and interpretation of magazine content may be moderated by race/ethnicity and age. In particular, research suggests that compared to white girls, African American girls perceive the content of mainstream teen magazines to be less realistic and less relevant to their lives. In interviews, African American girls dismissed editors' suggestions for hair care and cosmetics as irrelevant and were critical of these magazines' restrictive standard of beauty. Older African American girls were especially astute at identifying the lack of diversity in teen magazines.

LINKING GIRLS' READING TO THEIR BELIEFS AND BEHAVIORS

Few studies have attempted to link girls' reading of teen magazines to their beliefs and behaviors. Research that has examined such connections has focused on girls' feelings about their bodies. Research suggests that sheer exposure to teen magazines (i.e., how often magazines are read) is unrelated to girls' attitudes about their bodies. However, the extent to which girls compare themselves to magazine images has been associated with a variety of negative body-related outcomes, including worse appearance self-esteem, higher body dissatisfaction, greater drive to be thin, and more pathogenic weight control behaviors. Thus, the relation between magazine reading and girls' body attitudes and weight-related behavior seems to be best explained by social comparison theory. Notably, most of these studies use correlational data and therefore cannot determine whether reading these magazines has an influence on beliefs and behaviors related to body image or whether girls with certain body image beliefs and behaviors are most drawn to the magazines.

In a noteworthy longitudinal and experimental study, girls were randomly selected to receive a 15-month subscription to *Seventeen* magazine. Results indicated that exposure to teen magazines was associated with lower body satisfaction, but not uniformly across all girls. Although there was no main effect for the experimental manipulation, girls in the experimental condition who reported higher body dissatisfaction at baseline had a significant growth in negative affect about their bodies several months later. The authors concluded that magazine exposure effects are likely to be short-lived except among girls who exhibit heightened vulnerability.

ALTERNATIVES TO MAINSTREAM TEEN MAGAZINES

Alternatives to mainstream teen magazines have become increasingly available to adolescent girls. The late 1990s witnessed the rise of a number of niche magazines targeting specific segments of the population, including preteen girls (e.g., *Cosmo Girl*), and girls of color (e.g., *Word Up!*). Zines (also, *grrrl zines*) are another alternative magazine form that has emerged in the past two decades. Zines are usually independently published magazines that are written by and for adolescent girls. A stated objective of many zine writers is to challenge dominant cultural standards of femininity and beauty and to offer messages about female empowerment and social justice. Formal research on zine writers and readers is still quite limited at this time.

—*Janna L. Kim*

See also Advertising, Effects on Adolescents of; Advertising in Girls' Magazines; Body Image in Girls and Young Women; Ethnicity, Race, and Media; Gender Roles in Magazines; Research Methods, Content Analyses; Schemas/Scripts, Sexual; Sexual Information, Teen Magazines and; Social Learning Theory/Social Cognitive Theory; Socialization and Media; Zines

FURTHER READINGS

Carpenter, L. M. (1998). From girls into women: Scripts for sexuality and romance in *Seventeen* magazine, 1974–1994. *The Journal of Sex Research, 35*, 158–168.

Currie, D. H. (1997). Decoding femininity: Advertisements and their teenage readers. *Gender and Society, 11*, 453–477.

Duke, L. (2000). Black in a blonde world: Race and girls' interpretations of the feminine ideal in teen magazines. *Journalism and Mass Communication Quarterly, 77*, 367–392.

Durham, M. G. (1998). Dilemmas of desire: Representations of adolescent sexuality in two teen magazines. *Youth and Society, 29*, 369–389.

Evans, E. D., Rutberg, J., Sather, C., & Turner, C. (1991). Content analysis of contemporary teen magazines for adolescent females. *Youth and Society, 23*, 99–120.

McRobbie, A. (2000). *Feminism and youth culture*. New York: Routledge.

Peirce, K. (1990). A feminist theoretical perspective on the socialization of teenage girls through *Seventeen*. *Sex Roles, 23*, 491.

Stice, E., Spangler, D., & Agras, W. S. (2001). Exposure to media-portrayed thin-ideal images adversely affects vulnerable girls: A longitudinal experiment. *Journal of Social and Clinical Psychology, 20*, 270–288.

MAGAZINES, CHILDREN'S

Children's magazines are those periodicals that target children ages 6 months to 13 years old, a diverse group of magazines that range from board books with rounded corners to high-gloss periodicals that mimic more mainstream magazines. Some children's magazines are widely circulated, such as *Boys' Life* (circulation 1.45 million) and *Highlights* (circulation 3 million). In recent years, the children's magazine market has grown. Since 1993, more than 150 new children's magazines have been launched.

Children's magazines target several age groups and cover diverse subject areas. For instance, *Babybug* (circulation 25,000) is a nontraditional magazine that targets the youngest of readers (6 months to 2 years). A board book with rounded corners and no staples, it features bright, simple pictures with rhymes and simple sentences. Despite its unusual format, *Babybug* and any serial publication that targets children are included in the children's magazine industry. Whereas adult magazines are categorized by gender, race, and subject area, the magazine industry does not segment children's magazines in this way. Children's magazines cover such topics as wildlife and natural history (e.g., *Ranger Rick* and *National Geographic for Kids*), international issues (e.g., *Short Story International*), and consumer reports (e.g., *Zillions*). Furthermore, some children's serial publications are versions of mainstream magazines targeted to adults, such as *Sports Illustrated for Kids* (circulation 600,000), which was launched in 1989.

One study of children's use of magazines have found that about 11% of children ages 5 to 7 and 15% of children ages 8 to 10 reported reading magazines the previous day. Overall, magazine reading remains constant as children age. Children's magazines have often been used to try to encourage young children to become lifetime readers and learners.

By most accounts, children's magazines date back to the 1700s. At the beginning, they were largely pedantic in nature and were created to help children learn about themselves and the world around them.

One of the oldest children's magazines still in publication is *Jack and Jill* (circulation 326,000), which was first published in 1938. It focuses on children's health and nutrition. *Highlights*, first published in 1946, has one of the largest circulations among children's magazines. It targets children from 2 to 12 years old and contains a wide array of content, with an emphasis on puzzles and games.

The magazine industry today hardly resembles the educational, nonglossy formats that were prevalent when *Jack and Jill* and *Highlights* were first published, having experienced fairly dramatic changes in both design and marketing content. With the inclusion of advertising, most children's magazines today have the look and feel of more mainstream magazines. These changes are due to increased competition from a larger number of magazines and from other media outlets, such as television.

Mass media scholars have largely ignored children's magazines, but a few scholars have focused on the potential messages that children may receive from this content. Although most research focuses on the potential lack of educational content in newer serials, some takes a media effects perspective. For example, Susan Lynn and her colleagues analyzed the gender portrayals in advertisements in *Sports Illustrated for Kids*. They found that male characters outnumbered female characters and were more often shown in dominant roles, whereas girls were shown in limited athletic and gender-stereotyped roles.

Other scholars have been concerned with children's magazines as marketing media. Overall, such investigations arise from concern about the potential effects of marketing on children (e.g., encouraging unhealthy eating or consumerism). Some children's magazines are linked to a specific children's toys (e.g., *Barbie*, which was published from 1984 to 1996) or corporation (e.g., *Nickelodeon Magazine*), and some scholars argue that they are little more than public relations material. For most magazines, however, the marketing is limited to advertisements. Earlier children's publications, such as *Jack and Jill* and *Highlights,* did not include advertising, but now many children's magazines do.

—*Stacey J. T. Hust*

See also Advertising, Effects on Children of; Gender Roles in Magazines; Infants and Toddlers, Developmental Needs of; Infants and Toddlers, Media Exposure of; Media Effects; Media Effects, History of Research on; Preschoolers, Media Impact on Developmental Needs of

FURTHER READINGS

Cline, L. (1998, March). Magazines for children. *Mothering,* p. 52.

Fishel, C. (1998, May-June). Pee-wee reads. *Print, 52*(3), 94–99.

List, S. K. (1992, February). The right place to find children. *American Demographics, 14*(2), 44–48.

Lynn, S., Walsdorf, K., Hardin, M., & Hardin, B. (2002). Selling girls short: Advertising and gender images in *Sports Illustrated for Kids. Women in Sport and Physical Activity Journal, 11*(2).

Roberts, D. F., Foehr, U. G., Rideout, V. J., & Brodie, M. (2004). *Kids and media in America.* Cambridge, UK: Cambridge University Press.

MANGA (JAPANESE COMIC BOOKS)

Manga, Japanese comic books or graphic novels (novels told using the comic form), are legitimate forms of popular art and literature in Japan, enjoyed by children, young people, and adults. The pen-and-ink drawings are printed on newsprint in magazines with dimensions similar to phonebooks. The magazines include series installments of 20- to 50-page manga from established artists and complete stories from newer artists. Magazines have from 200 to 800 pages. In addition to the manga, the magazines include comics in a four-panel format similar to those in American newspapers. Successful series are compiled and reprinted in paperback format on higher-quality paper. Popular manga are made into anime (animated films or television series).

The term *manga* literally means "rambling picture." It developed from a style of Japanese woodblock prints, *ukiyoe,* that commonly depicted actors, sumo wrestlers, and beautiful courtesans. Hokusai, a 19th-century artist, first applied the term for the woodblock prints in his 15-volume *Hokusai Manga,* a popular collection of caricatures of samurai and nobles. The art of manga has been traced to scrolls from the 12th century that depict animals engaged in human activities, including frogs depicted as priests.

Manga's current form combines Japanese and Western drawing techniques. After World War II, manga grew in popularity. Manga by Osamu Tezuka, who adapted several novels to the graphic form before creating *Astro Boy* (1952), proved particularly popular and established the modern artistic style. Although styles vary by artist, manga frequently portray wide-eyed characters, particularly adolescents, and androgynously beautiful women and men. Younger manga artists are encouraged to imitate established artists. Numerous volumes giving advice on drawing in the manga style are available in Japanese, English, and other languages.

Manga dispel a stereotype about Japan as a humorless nation. In addition to manga's depiction of a wide range of social phenomena, from the social order to sexism and racism, the stories and artwork include humor, satire, language puns, and exaggeration not typically associated with Japanese society. This is at odds with the general characterization of Japan as a culture that prefers the ambiguous and subtle to the explicit and straightforward. Manga are anything but subtle.

Manga have an international following, particularly among high school and college students, with popular titles translated into at least 30 languages. Most fans and artists insist that magazines be printed in Japanese format, reading from right to left. The first and longest running series in English, *Oh My Goddess,* began in 1994. Initially, manga in the United States were popular only with male comic collectors and were sold in specialty shops. The availability of manga in mainstream bookstores spurred sales of other styles of manga, particularly series favored by teenage girls. Manga represent the fastest-growing segment of the American publishing market, with 2004 sales reaching $204 million, 35% higher than 2003. Manga sales in Japan have declined recently, but the 2004 sales still surpassed $4 billion. More than 9 million websites provide information about manga in English.

Different types of manga have distinctive appearances and are considered age specific. The most popular manga are those for teenage boys (*shonen*) and teenage girls (*shojo*), although these also have adult fans. Teen manga may include futuristic elements, although series based on traditional stories are also produced.

One popular *shonen* manga title is *Dragon Ball* (Japan 1984–1995; United States 2000), by Akira Toriyama. This fantasy action series is based on the Chinese folktale *Journey to the West* and follows the hero's martial arts adventures from childhood through old age. Most manga for teenage boys have similar premises. They rely on action by male protagonists, include humor amid the action, and depict camaraderie between male characters in sports or battles.

Shojo manga, popular with teenage girls, have strong female protagonists and portray emotions along with the action. The stories often include magic, futuristic settings, and romantic interests. Popular *shojo* manga titles such as *Ceres, Celestial Legend* (Japan 1996–2000; United States 2004), by Yuu Watase, mix teenage angst with adventure and romance. The story

The manga series *Oh My Goddess, called "Aa Megami-Sama"* in Japanese, is frequently labeled as a *shojo manga* because of the romantic appeal of the goddess Belldandy, shown here. However, the manga's focus on the interactions of Keiichi (who could be any teenage boy) with the goddess and her sisters, Urd and Skuld, gives the series a crossover appeal with *shonen* fans. The original Japanese version of the romantic comedy, by manga artist Kosuke Fujishima, began in 1988, and the first anime movie in the series was released in 2000.

SOURCE: © Kosuke Fujishima.

line of *Ceres, Celestial Legend* is similar to any fairy tale of a mortal taking something from a celestial maiden that prevents her from returning to her world. One specific kind of *shojo* manga includes depictions of sexuality that may shock those unprepared for teenagers who magically switch genders, sibling romances, relationships between humans and aliens, and affairs between two androgynously beautiful male characters. That some titles have not been the subject of parental objections is generally attributed to Americans' unfamiliarity with manga. American publishers concerned about sexuality in manga seek series that do not include graphic depictions, as fans protest when series are altered from the originals.

Besides teens, some types of manga are targeted for children, young men (*seinen*), and young women (*josei*). Children's manga are cute and humorous. Unlike children's manga, adult manga do not include *furigana* (reading aids added over *kanji*, Japanese characters borrowed from Chinese). *Josei* manga have realistic portrayals of life, including romance and sex. *Seinen* manga have the widest range of artistic styles and content, from avant-garde postmodernism to therotic or even pornographic. The gritty and futuristic avant-garde manga are popular with most fans, and other manga deal with historic themes and literary adaptations.

—*Tamara Swenson*

See also Anime

FURTHER READINGS

Cornog, M., & Perper, T. (2005). Non-Western sexuality comes to the U.S.: A crash course in manga and anime for sexologists. *Contemporary Sexuality, 39*(3), 1–6.

Glazer, S. (2005, September 18). Manga for girls. *New York Times,* Section 7, pp. 16–17.

Gravett, P. (2004). *Manga: 60 years of Japanese comics.* London: Laurence King.

Hall, E. (1977). *Beyond culture.* Garden City, NY: Doubleday.

Ito, K. (2005). A history of manga in the context of Japanese culture and society. *Journal of Popular Culture, 38*(3), 456–475.

JETRO. (2005, July). Japanese publishing industry. *Japan Economic Monthly.* Retrieved from http://www.jetro.go.jp/en/market/trend/industrial

Krefta B. (2003). *The art of drawing manga.* New York: Barnes & Noble.

Reid, C. (2005, April 18). U.S. graphic novel market hits $200M. *Publishers Weekly, 252*(16), 15.

Schodt, F. L. (1996). *Dreamland Japan: Writings on modern manga.* Berkeley, CA: Stone Bridge Press.

MEAN WORLD SYNDROME

Mean world syndrome is the tendency for heavy TV viewers to believe that the world is a more hostile and unfriendly place than it actually is, to be more afraid of becoming a victim of violent crime, and to be more distrustful of others. The mean world effect is derived from cultivation theory as developed by George Gerbner in 1969. According to the theory, repeated exposure to media has small but cumulative effects on people's beliefs about what the real world is like.

There are first- and second-order components to mean world beliefs. First-order components are simple distortions in beliefs about the prevalence of crime. Second-order components are the ways these beliefs influence value judgments and attitudes toward th world.

Research has provided the strongest support for first-order components. Heavy TV viewers (defined as those who watch 4 hours per day or more) are more likely to believe in a mean world because television violence is more vivid than most day-to-day experiences and thus is remembered better. Vivid images have a disproportionate influence on decisions because people often base their decisions on the first thoughts that come to mind, rather than on accurate information. Thus, heavy TV viewers are more fearful about becoming victims of violence, more distrustful of others, and more likely to perceive the world as a dangerous, mean, and hostile place (Cantor provides a review of this research). Although the effects are cumulative over time, Peterson and Zill found evidence of mean world beliefs in children as young as 7 years old.

The degree to which people rely on television as a source of information depends on whether viewers think television provides an accurate depiction of the real world. News reports influence mean world beliefs more than other types of media, probably because they are perceived as more accurate. Also, Linda Heath and John Petraitis found that violent media makes people more afraid of crime in their own city than in their own neighborhood, probably because they have more firsthand experience with their own neighborhood. Television violence may also appear more accurate if people have experiences that confirm the mean world it portrays. Heavy television viewers who have experienced real-world violence are especially likely to endorse mean world beliefs.

There is also some evidence that biased estimates of violence change people's behavior. Heavy TV viewers are more likely to purchase a gun or a guard dog than are light TV viewers, and they show greater tolerance of police brutality and restrictions of civil liberties. Robert Putnam has even suggested that reduced trust in others causes the breakdown of *social capital* (civic participation), although further research is needed.

—*Jesse J. Chandler and Brad J. Bushman*

See also Cultivation Theory; Fantasy–Reality Distinction; News, Children's Exposure to; News, Children's Responses to

FURTHER READINGS

Cantor, J. (1998). *"Mommy, I'm scared": How TV and movies frighten children and what we can do to protect them.* San Diego, CA: Harvest/Harcourt.

Gerbner, G. (1969). Toward "cultural indicators": The analysis of mass mediated message systems. *AV Communication Review, 17,* 137–148.

Heath, L., & Petraitis, J. (1987). Television viewing and fear of crime: Where is the mean world? *Basic and Applied Social Psychology, 8,* 97–123.

Peterson, J. L., & Zill, N. (1981). Television viewing in the United States and children's intellectual, social, and emotional development. *Television and Children, 2,* 21–28.

Putnam, R. D. (1996). The strange disappearance of civic America. *The American Prospect, 1,* 34–48.

Shrum, L. J. (1997). The role of source confusion in cultivation effects may depend on processing strategy: A comment on Mares (1996). *Human Communication Research, 24,* 349–358.

MEDIA, FUTURE OF

This entry makes some informed guesses about the potential changes in media technologies and forms, especially those popular among children and young people. Although it mainly describes expected changes in Western countries, these media and formats are also increasingly available in other parts of the world.

GLOBALIZATION

The globalization in media channels and forms is likely to increase. Improved satellite technologies will decrease differences across boundaries, while the media technology divide may increase within nations. In many countries, children and young people will be able to watch a number of international channels, for example, Cartoon Network, Nickelodeon, Jetix, and the Disney channels. Adolescents will continue to enjoy global music channels such as MTV and Music First. Popular genres among children will be cartoons and situation comedies. Among young people, reality genres will remain popular, as will international competition program concepts like *Idol*. Feature films will remain popular, and so will programs about animals, nature, and different cultures, contemporary as well as ancient. Among young people, American entertainment about romance and dating (e.g., *Friends*) will stay popular. More interactive forms such as chat TV will increase in popularity.

CHANGES IN TELEVISION USE

Television will remain the main medium among children and young people in terms of number of people watching and time used for the medium. However, there will be two main developments in the way children and young people relate to TV, reinforcing tendencies that are visible today. First, children and young people's TV viewing will increasingly be part of their multitasking: Children will watch TV at the same time as they do something else: eating, playing, or performing school homework. TV will be used especially in interaction with the computer. Children will spend time in front of the computer instant messaging, chatting, or checking out websites about TV programs or TV personalities while they watch TV. Another important change in TV viewing habits will be the tendency to time shift. Young people will tape their favorite programs on DVD recorders and video or download on personal computers and burn them. They may watch the recorded programs when it is more convenient for them. Television game consoles will also remain popular among children and young people, especially among young boys.

COMPUTER USE

The main media of the future will be computers and mobile phones. These technologies will become increasingly important in the everyday lives of children and young people. Children will learn to use computers at preschool age, either in their homes or preschool institutions. A number of games and websites are already available for the youngest children, and more will be developed. Computers will increase in significance as the children grow older, with this multimedia machine functioning as a game player, a communication tool (email and chat), a means of personal expression (websites and personal profiles), a site for Internet access, and a tool for homework; the computer will often contain a CD-ROM and DVD player. In addition, the Internet will be used for consuming other media—for downloading music (e.g., to an iPod), skimming the main news or newspaper headlines, listening to the radio, and watching programs one missed on TV. The Internet may also be used for shopping or for keeping in contact with friends, for example, through instant messaging. More young people will also acquire Web cameras; especially for teenagers with a boy- or girlfriend, this will be a popular way to keep in touch across geographical distances.

MOBILE PHONES

The mobile phone will also remain popular among young people, and increasingly, it will be introduced to even younger children. Many parents will want their children to have a mobile phone so that parents can keep in touch with children and organize school and leisure transport. Children will continue to use the mobile phone, especially for SMS messages with their friends. Mobile phones will be used to coordinate their daily social lives and also for flirting. A negative side is that the mobile phone can also be used for bullying, when some youngsters send threatening or negative comments to others. In addition, advertisers will aim to reach young people and children through mobile advertising and sales campaigns. The mobile phone will also be used to convey more visuals, such as personal pictures or shots from situations and vacation spots and for music (MP3s).

NEW TECHNOLOGIES

Media tools will become smaller and more mobile. One example is iPods: Children and young people will be able to store their favorite music, downloaded from the Internet or copied from their own and their friends' CDs. Children will listen to music on CD players when they walk or use transportation. Another increasingly popular technology will be small DVD players designed for traveling, particularly by car. Families will purchase such DVDs for their children so children can watch films or play games in the back of the car.

PRIVATIZATION OF MEDIA USE

Another tendency will be a privatization of media use within the family. Due to cheaper and smaller technological tools and increasing living standards in the West, children will increasingly have their own media technologies in their bedroom. There will be an even stronger tendency toward a bedroom culture, where teenagers' rooms are furnished with PC/Internet, TV, console games, DVDs, CD players, and so on. In this sense, there will be greater opportunities for children and young people to use media the way they want. But parents will also increasingly feel a need to regulate media, to make websites and programs with pornographic, pedophile, or violent content unavailable for their children. Filter technologies will increasingly be available to assist parents in such regulation efforts. Some parents will also become concerned with the increasing commercial pressure on their children and thus try to limit their children's access to such messages.

—*Ingunn Hagen*

See also Computer Use (various entries); Media Genre Preferences; Multitasking; Regulation, Television

FURTHER READINGS

Haddon, L. (2004). *Information and communication technology in everyday life: A concise introduction and research guide.* Oxford, UK: Berg.

Hoover, S. M., Clark, L. S., & Alters, D. F. (2004). *Media, home, and family.* New York: Routledge.

Livingstone, S. (2002). *Young people, new media: Childhood and the changing media environment.* London: Sage.

Livingstone, S., & Bovill, M. (2001). *Children and their changing media environment: A European comparative study.* Mahwah, NJ: Erlbaum.

Rideout, V., Roberts, D. F., & Foehr, U. G. (2005, March). *Generation M: Media in the lives of 8–18 year olds* (A Kaiser Family Foundation Study). Retrieved January 25, 2006, from http://www.kaiserfamilyfoundation.org/entmedia/7250.cfm

MEDIA, MEANINGS OF

In the 19th century, natural scientists had to name many newly discovered objects and processes. Most of the new terms were precise and effective, and they have stood the test of time. During the past half century, what has come to be called *media studies* has expanded greatly and in many directions, creating a need for definitions in this field. The word *media* has been treated as a singular, although the dictionary insists it is plural. It may be used to refer to organizations, such as newspaper publishers or television stations; to the content that is transmitted (such as a program or a book); to hardware such as a data disc; or to the whole phenomenon of communication between sender and receiver.

Medium, the singular form of *media,* is derived from Latin and originally meant middle or between. It refers best to what some have called the channel or the pathway for information between the sender and receiver. Because psychologists believe that information carried by each of the modalities to each of the senses is processed in different ways and parts of the brain, Joseph Wober proposed a detailed system of words to deal with these communication actors and processes.

Under this system, the term *message systems* refers to complex entities such as television companies and advertisers; these encode and display information via what might well be termed *sign agents* (e.g., programs, billboards, electronic speakers). From these screens, surfaces, and electronic (and human and animal) speakers, information passes through the media, of which the air carries three: light produces sight, molecular pressure carries sound, and particular molecules convey scent, thus reaching the three distance senses. Three other sensory systems internal to each human being transmit thermal, pressure, and movement and positional information. There are thus (at least) six media consisting of the pathways along which information reaches a human brain. In this view, there are no "new media," although new message systems and new sign agents are continually being devised and marketed. When Marshall McLuhan coined his aphorism "The medium is the message," this is surely what he meant—that the route by which data reach the brain has substantial consequences for how the brain deals with messages and therefore what kinds of meanings we can make of them.

This proposed set of labels indicates that television and the movies each involve two media (sight and sound); print works one medium (sight); radio and the many forms of sound speakers, one medium each; and perfume, one medium. A riot engages three or possibly four media (sight, sound, bodily pressure, smell). Individuals have to learn how to interpret signals received via each (sensory) medium; the skills for encoding messages (e.g., making programs, writing texts) and for decoding them (e.g., understanding movies, reading print) are different, and each requires the mastery of specific skills. In technically advanced societies, most people learn these skills without noticing the process; however, in other cultures and among individuals with learning deficits, these may be specific to particular sense modalities.

These labels invite us to think of the differences between encoding and decoding skills (making and understanding messages); such skills may be more or less well developed by our experiences specific to each medium. These labels also invite attention to the scope with which each medium can transmit information with more or less sophisticated codes. Vision is currently uppermost in print-literate cultures although the balance may be altering, with sound gaining in its diversification.

—Joseph M. Wober

See also Media, Future of

FURTHER READINGS

Wober, J. M. (1988). *The use and abuse of television: A social psychological analysis of the changing screen.* Hillsdale, NJ: Erlbaum.

MEDIA ADVOCACY

Mass media are powerful in presenting issues and shaping opinions in the society, and media advocacy is an approach that attempts to influence media's coverage of an issue and to help a relevant policy achieve public awareness and support. According to Lawrence Wallack, Lori Dorfman, and their colleagues, the purpose of media advocacy is to contribute to the development of social and policy initiatives that promote health and well-being. In general, media advocacy efforts focus on issues related to health and human well-being, and the goal is usually to get more news coverage for a topic and to shape the relevant debates in a desired fashion.

Media advocacy efforts largely emphasize news coverage because news has a crucial impact on people at both the personal and public levels. At the personal level, news media may provide information and elicit changes in individuals' knowledge and attitudes about a topic, and it may even stimulate a person to take actions. At the public level, mass media can raise awareness of certain issues among the public and policymakers and can contribute to improving conditions in the society. For example, a news report on former president Ronald Reagan's colon cancer and publicity following the death of television journalist Katie Couric's husband, who had the same disease, motivated people to get tests to detect the same health problem. A series of newspaper articles on infant mortality led to legislative support for providing low-cost prenatal care.

HOW MEDIA ADVOCACY WORKS

Several theoretical notions are often mentioned to explain why and how advocacy efforts through news media may work. In particular, agenda setting and framing theory provide good perspectives to understand the important role of news media in the process of advocating an issue or a public policy.

Agenda Setting

Agenda setting proposes that media can influence the public agenda regarding what issues are considered important; framing theory suggests that the way media frame or present an issue can influence how people think about it. Specifically, the initial research on agenda setting proposed that the media coverage and placement of an issue could influence the public to consider the issue an important topic. That is, the media agenda sets the public agenda: The issues selected and covered by media become the issues on the top of public's mind. For example, Maxwell McCombs and Donald Shaw analyzed media coverage of the 1968 presidential election. They found that issues receiving the most media coverage were also the issues voters considered important. This study was followed by many others that found much the same thing, leading to a large body of literature on agenda setting. In short, early research on agenda setting described that media determine what issues audiences think about.

More recent research on agenda setting suggested that media could further influence how audiences think about an issue. Scholars suggested that the media could also influence whether people associated positive or negative attributes with a policy or person. For example, Guy Golan and Wayne Wanta found that a political candidate who was covered more favorably in media was more likely to be perceived in a positive light. Such influence is called second-level agenda setting.

Framing Theory

Relevant to second-level agenda setting, framing theory proposes that there are some consistent patterns in the way that media cover an issue and that these patterns influence how audiences conceive the issue. As Robert Entman argued, the ways in which media frame an issue determine what information people can select from and what will be left out, as well as what issues will be considered salient. Framing theory also suggests that what and how information is presented in media can impact people's recognition of problems, their diagnoses of what causes these problems, and their judgments and selection of solutions. Framing theory holds that because message framing influences how people's cognitive schema and attribution process are constructed, it can determine how media content is comprehended and incorporated with existing knowledge and can even shape the attitudes and behaviors people adopt. Thus, as advocates attempt to communicate with target audiences, message framing plays an important role in shaping an issue during the agenda setting process.

MEDIA ADVOCACY RELATED TO YOUTH

Some activist groups or organizations use media advocacy strategies to promote children's and adolescents' health and well-being. Some of their efforts have generated positive outcomes and have been documented as successful cases in health promotion through a media advocacy approach. For example, the Mothers Against Drunk Driving (MADD) organization has been successful in obtaining and sustaining media attention as well as public support for policies to reduce drunk driving. In one case reported in a 1991 issue of *Lobbying and Influence Alert*, MADD mobilized to generate media coverage and public responses to a drunk driving law in Hawaii; the law would have deleted a provision allowing for nearly automatic license revocation for drivers who refused to take a Breathalyzer™ test when stopped by the police. MADD staged actions in front of Hawaii's Eternal Flame war memorial on Memorial Day and pointed out the "flaw in the law" to the press and the public. The messages were framed to create the belief that we should remember not only those killed in war but also those killed on the highways and that enactment of the flawed law would enable drunk drivers to avoid punishment. The speech podium for the event carried phone numbers of the governor's and senate president's office, and within a week, thousands of phone calls had been received there. Accompanied with grassroots campaigns to collect signatures on petitions and promote phone calls to legislators, MADD ultimately made sure the provision was deleted. This case offers a good example of how media advocacy can be a successful approach to obtaining media coverage and public awareness and to achieving a goal of promoting an important issue or supporting a public policy.

—*I-Huei Cheng*

See also Advertising Campaigns, Prosocial; Agenda Setting; Anti-Drug Media Campaigns; Media Effects; Media Literacy (various entries); Public Health Campaigns; Schema Theory; Television, Prosocial Content of

FURTHER READINGS

Brown, J. D., & Walsh-Childers, K. (1994). Effects of media on personal and public health. In J. Bryant & D. Zillmann (Eds.), *Media effects: Advances in theory and research* (pp. 389–416). Mahwah NJ: Erlbaum.

Entman, R. M. (1993). Framing: Toward clarification of a fractured paradigm. *Journal of Communication, 43*(4), 51–58.

Golan, G., & Wanta, W. (2001). Second-level agenda setting in the New Hampshire primary: A comparison of coverage in three newspapers and public perceptions of candidates. *Journalism and Mass Communication Quarterly, 78*(2), 247–259.

Hallahan, K. (1999). Seven models of framing: Implications for public relations. *Journal of Public Relations Research, 11*(3), 205–242.

MADD gets mad. (1991). *Lobbying and Influence Alert, 1*(3), 1–2.

McCombs, M., & Shaw, D. L. (1972). The agenda setting function of mass media. *Public Opinion Quarterly, 26,* 176–187.

Stillman, F. A., Cronin, K. A., Evans, W. D., & Ulasevich, A. (2001). Can media advocacy influence newspaper coverage of tobacco: Measuring the effectiveness of the American stop smoking intervention study's (ASSIST) media advocacy strategies. *Tobacco Control, 10,* 137–144.

Treno, A. J., Breed, L., Holder, H. D., Roeper, P., Thomas, B. A., & Gruenewald, P. J. (1996). Evaluation of media advocacy efforts within a community trial to reduce alcohol-involved injury: Preliminary news results. *Evaluation Research, 20*(4), 404–423.

Wallack, L., & Dorfman, L. (2001). Putting policy into health communication: The role of media advocacy. In R. E. Rice & C. K. Atkin (Eds.), *Public communication campaigns* (3rd ed., pp. 389–401) Thousand Oaks, CA: Sage.

Wallack, L., Dorfman, L., Jernigan, D., & Themba, M. (1993). *Media advocacy and public health: Power for prevention.* Newbury Park, CA: Sage.

Walsh-Childers, K. (1994). Newspaper influence on health policy development. *Newspaper Research Journal, 15*(8), 89–104.

MEDIA CELEBRITIES

Much of young people's media consumption is driven by celebrities. Movie actresses, sports heroes, music performers, models, and television performers attract children and adolescents to the media. They are important agents of media socialization, frequent issues in peer communication, and objects of admiration. Celebrities provide orientation and social information to young audiences and shape their knowledge, attitudes, and behaviors significantly.

CONCEPTUAL APPROACHES

Various theories address the relation between young people and media celebrities. McCutcheon, Lange, and Houran recently introduced the concept of *celebrity worship* and distinguished intensities of commitment with a celebrity, which range from mild forms (such as keeping informed about a celebrity) to extreme and pathological forms (such as overidentification and obsession with a media star). Hoffner investigated *wishful identification,* which refers to young media users' imagining that they are like or actually are a media character. This notion thus includes elements of positive admiration and imitation of star behavior. Yet another body of theory is parasocial interaction and relationships (PSI/PSR). PSI/PSR research has demonstrated that young media users perceive and process media characters in ways similar to individuals from their real social environment. PSI/PSRs can display highly diverse qualities, including admiration and idolization, but also negative dispositions (e.g., toward singers performing a disliked style of music). The concept thus can encompass a range of attachments from weak ties between audience and celebrity to very intense relationships. Cohen, for instance, reports that teenagers suffer from breakups of PSRs with favorite TV performers (e.g., if the celebrity disappears from a TV series), which indicates the affective relevance of such relationships, especially for young people. Overall, a variety of similar theoretical models of the involvement of young audiences with media celebrities have been advanced, and they do not necessarily assume solely idolization as the major quality of such involvement.

IMPACT OF CELEBRITIES ON IDENTITY FORMATION

Young people's interest in media celebrities has raised the questions of whether and how such media relationships contribute to identity development. Boon and Lomore report that strong commitment to media celebrities (even for characters that are fictional or dead) is common among adolescents. Most important, a substantial portion of their sample of young people reported that the bond with their favorite celebrity had motivated them to change parts of their identity. For instance, 60% of the respondents said that their preferred celebrity had altered their personal attitudes and values, and almost 15% confirmed that they had changed their appearance to become more similar to their idol. Inspired by their favorite celebrity, many respondents also modified their lifestyle and engaged in activities their idol had framed in a desirable way. These findings suggest that social learning as described by Bandura is the most likely psychological mechanism behind the effects of celebrities on identity formation.

Brown, Basil, and Bocarnea studied audience responses to the death of Diana, Princess of Wales. They found that involvement with Diana not only increased use of media content related to her death, but also facilitated a worse image of the tabloid press, whose paparazzi were considered by some to be partly responsible for Diana's lethal accident. This study thus demonstrated the effect of involvement with an idol on specific attitudes. Overall, the literature suggests that stars are important agents of adolescent identity development and socialization. Direct effects are accompanied by indirect effects of celebrities on youth culture (e.g., the impact of hip-hop celebrities on American gang style), which add to the overall relevance of media idols on young audiences. The determinants of the quality and intensity of young people's parasocial relationships with celebrities (as well as the determinants of the actual celebrity preferred) remain to be investigated in more detail, however.

CONSEQUENCES

Because of the frequent and intense admirer-celebrity relationships found among young people, a variety of beneficial and problematic consequences can arise from those relationships. For instance, corporate and social agents use celebrities to influence young audiences for their purposes: Celebrity endorsement has emerged as a key technique in product marketing. Celebrity support for political parties and leaders has been found to evoke political attitude change in young audiences. And worship for slim celebrities can cause negative effects on young media users' body image. It is, therefore, reasonable to continue research on celebrity idolization (and other forms of parasocial relationships) and its consequences for young people and to advise parents and teachers to keep informed about the social (and potentially intimate) bonds with celebrities that children and adolescents create, maintain, and break up.

—*Christoph Klimmt*

See also Adolescents, Developmental Needs of, and Media Fan Cultures; Gender Identity Development; Loneliness; Music, Group Identity and; Music, Personal Identity and; Parasocial Interaction; Peer Groups, Impact of Media on; Peer Groups, Influences on Media Use of; Soap Operas, Effects of; Social Learning Theory/ Social Cognitive Theory; Socialization and Media; Television, Morality and Identification With Characters on; Youth Culture

FURTHER READINGS

Bandura, A. (2001). Social cognitive theory of mass communication. *Media Psychology, 3*(3), 265–299.
Boon, S. D., & Lomore, C. D. (2001). Admirer-celebrity relationships among young adults. Explaining perceptions of celebrity influence on identity. *Human Communication Research, 27*(3), 432–465.
Brown, W. J., Basil, M. D., & Bocarnea, M. C. (2003). Social influence of an international celebrity: Responses to the death of Princess Diana. *Journal of Communication, 53*(4), 587–605.
Caughey, J. L. (1984). *Imaginary social worlds.* Lincoln: University of Nebraska Press.
Cohen, J. (2004). Parasocial break-up from favorite television characters: The role of attachment styles and relationship intensity. *Journal of Social and Personal Relationships, 21*(2), 187–202.
Giles, D. (2002). Parasocial interaction: A review of the literature and a model for future research. *Media Psychology, 4,* 279–305.
Hoffner, C. (1996). Children's wishful identification and parasocial interaction with favorite television characters. *Journal of Broadcasting and Electronic Media, 40,* 389–402.
Jackson, D. J., & Darrow, T. I. A. (2005). The influence of celebrity endorsements on young adults' political opinions. *Harvard International Journal on Press/Politics, 10*(3), 80–89.
Klimmt, C., Hartmann, T., & Schramm, H. (in press). Parasocial interactions and relationships. In J. Bryant & P. Vorderer (Eds.), *Psychology of entertainment.* Mahwah, NJ: Erlbaum.
Maltby, J., Giles, D., Barber, L., & McCutcheon, L. E. (2005). Intense-personal celebrity worship and body image: Evidence for a link among female adolescents. *British Journal of Health Psychology, 10*(1), 17–32.
McCutcheon, L. E., Lange, R., & Houran, J. (2002). Conceptualization and measurement of celebrity worship. *British Journal of Psychology, 93,* 67–87.
Silvera, D. H., & Austad, B. (2004). Factors predicting the effectiveness of celebrity endorsement advertisements. *European Journal of Marketing, 38*(11–12), 1509–1526.

MEDIA EDUCATION, FAMILY INVOLVEMENT IN

Media education refers to intentional efforts of teachers at school or of parents in families to influence, teach, and help to train children and adolescents to become media literate. *Media socialization* in a broader sense refers to the whole of the mostly nonintentional and longitudinal processes of accessing, selecting, and using a variety of different media in the family, with peers, and at school, and to the effects of these processes on children and adolescents. Explicit media education, based on a curriculum and intended to realize media literacy as a positive outcome, is predominantly practiced in the context of school, whereas nonsystematic and unplanned processes of media socialization characterize most family settings. There seems to be a shift from explicit family media education in the form of negative and restrictive parental control of children's media use to more positive and participatory forms of media socialization based on mutual communication between parents and children. This shift from external control to internal self-regulation reflects a tendency to see media not only in a negative way as a potential threat but also as a productive resource for the development of children's identity.

MEDIA LITERACY

Resulting from media education and media socialization, *media literacy* is a complex and manifold competence that is conceptualized and defined in various ways by different scholars based on diverse theoretical approaches. In general, it is understood as the ability to access, select, understand, analyze, and evaluate as well as to create and to communicate media messages. But depending on the specific theoretical premises of media literacy, the focus may be on the critical and ideological evaluation of media messages or on the appreciation of its aesthetic and formal features. In addition to this message orientation, other more media-centered approaches accentuate that media literacy is about understanding the technological, economical, political, and cultural structures, processes, and constraints of the modern media system—that is, being able to understand how media function in society. More user-specific concepts emphasize media use as intentional, active, and need-oriented social behavior. The goal of media education consequently is the self-confident and determinate media user, who is not dependent on or addicted to media but who uses the media and their messages as positive resources in creative and social responsible ways.

THE CHANGING FAMILY MEDIA ENVIRONMENT

Children and young people access and use media primarily in the family context, especially during early childhood, and a plentitude of media is accessible in most families today. The modern home has become the site and focal point of a multimedia culture. In the 1970s, there was a significant shift from print media to audiovisual or screen culture; and in recent years, the modern household has been increasingly transformed by new computer-based interactive media such as the Internet. This ongoing transformation of the family media environment was accompanied by both anxieties and optimistic expectations. Pessimists such as Neil Postman lamented the end of childhood, the decay of print culture, and the loss of traditional values and the socializing role of the family as a consequence of the dominance of television entertainment. On the other hand, computer industry leaders such as Bill Gates or new media experts such as Nicholas Negroponte optimistically foresee and stress new educational possibilities and participatory opportunities for the so-called digital generation.

As a result of the contradictory public discourse, media educational goals and strategies of parents are often insecure and contradictory. Empirical research demonstrates that especially upper-class and privileged families have positive attitudes toward print media and stress books in their media education by buying books for children and reading aloud to them. Television education is an even more fundamental part of family education. The use and functions of television structure the daily routines of family life but also create considerable conflict between parents and children. One important cause is parental uncertainty about whether and how to regulate television use, together with negative attitudes toward television as an educational tool. But very often, parental guidance and control address only the time and amount of children's viewing. Furthermore, this is done in a more or less strict way only in early childhood, and most parents do not focus on understanding and interpreting television content. As a result, the main goal of family media education often is to protect vulnerable youth from negative media influences but not to teach them actively how to select and use media in a competent, creative, and responsible way. According to a 1999 Kaiser Family Foundation report, a surprising amount of children's media use in the United States is unsupervised; this is certainly influenced by the fact that a third of children between 2 and 7 years old and two thirds of older children have a TV in their bedroom.

Although the recent diffusion of modern interactive media has created new uncertainties, it was accompanied by mostly positive parental expectations. Therefore, diffusion and adoption of personal computers and the Internet took place more rapidly in affluent families, and as a result, gaps in access to new media increased. On the other hand, research shows that young people use the computer and the Internet mostly for entertainment purposes and to communicate with others, but rarely for educational reasons.

QUESTIONS AND RESULTS OF RESEARCH

Most research in the domain of media, children, and family is still descriptive. It focuses on the availability, uses, and functions of the different media in the family environment. In addition, newer studies are also theoretically oriented, for example, the Young People New Media project in more than a dozen European countries. The focus of this Livingstone study is the changing media environment of today's children and its consequences for uses and functions of old and new media. A special research question deals with the diffusion of information and communication technology. The leading research hypothesis is that higher socioeconomic segments generally are more motivated and able to acquire and use new media first because of financial resources, innovativeness, or educational expectations. As a result, the "haves" are better able to take advantage of these new media developments than the "have-nots," and existing inequalities in access and use will widen. Besides these social disparities, there are also gender gaps: Boys seem to be more fascinated by computers or the Internet than girls. But it is still unclear if these gaps will persist or if there will be a trickle-down effect as there was for the telephone and television in the past.

The study also analyzes differences between several types of households. *Media-rich homes* have greater than average access to a wide variety of old and new media: books, television, VCR, personal computers, Internet, or telephone. These households tend to be middle class, and parents in these homes claim to feel comfortable using computers themselves. In contrast, ownership of media in *traditional homes* is average for all media except the newest, such as computers or the Internet. But the main reason seems to be not financial but attitudes toward media and the family life cycle, for example, the absence of older children. Parents in traditional homes generally feel that television provides children with good programs and that children's viewing is appropriately controlled. Television and VCR are common in *media-poor homes*, but access to all other media is under average. These households are likely working class and poorer.

Other questions deal with different value orientations and styles of parental media education—for example, authoritative versus participatory—and their relations to regulation of children's media use or to interpersonal discussions with children about media topics. In a similar way, Chaffee and McLeod in the 1970s and Lull in the 1980s developed theoretical approaches dealing not so much with explicit media educational goals and practices of parents, but more with different family communication patterns such as laissez-faire, protective, pluralistic, or consensual. Empirical studies have indicated that the amount of television viewing by parents is correlated with the TV viewing of their children. But this parental modeling effect is mediated by family communication patterns. For example, it was hypothesized that children in socially oriented families would use television to fulfill integrative functions whereas concept-oriented families would use television more for educational purposes.

—*Heinz Bonfadelli*

See also Developmental Differences, Media and; Family Environment, Media Effects on; Media Education, Schools and; Peer Groups, Impact of Media on; Socialization and Media; Youth Culture

FURTHER READINGS

Bryant, J. (Ed.). (1990). *Television and the American family.* Hillsdale, NJ: Erlbaum.
Kubey, R., & Donovan, B. W. (2001). Media and the family. In D. G. Singer & J. Singer (Eds.), *Handbook of children and the media* (pp. 323–339). Thousand Oaks, CA: Sage.
Livingstone, S., & Bovill, M. (Eds.). (2001). *Children and their changing media environment: A European comparative study.* Mahwah, NJ: Erlbaum.
Süss, D. (2004). *Mediensozialisation von Heranwachsenden* [Media socialization of adolescents]. Wiesbaden: VS Verlag.

MEDIA EDUCATION, INTERNATIONAL

Media education is a term used to refer to the process involved in learning how to critically analyze and create media messages. The term originated in England, where it is generally synonymous with *media literacy.* The widespread use of the term *media education* arose, in part, as a result of the challenges associated with translating the term *literacy* into various world languages.

PROGRAMS IN GREAT BRITAIN

Most people would agree that Great Britain has the most well-established program of media literacy education in the world. Media education, which first appeared in the 1930s in England, grew out of a classical tradition of literary criticism that established a premise that modern society and its cultural manifestations were alienating and mechanistic. According to this view, young people needed to be protected from the deadening and distracting dimensions of mass media and popular culture. It was thought this could be accomplished by providing them with concepts and skills needed to discriminate between the elite culture of the literary tradition and newer media-based cultural forms. In the 1950s and 1960s, Richard Hoggart's book, *The Uses of Literacy,* and Stuart Hall and Paddy Whannel's book, *The Popular Arts,* signaled the beginning of a shift in thinking among scholars, who began moving away from making a "high culture/low culture" dichotomy toward analyzing the media through an examination of authorship, audience reception, meaning making, and cultural identity in a sociocultural context. With the rise of British cultural studies in the 1970s, a number of scholars and practitioners began to focus on the pedagogical dimensions of teaching about

media. Journals such as *Screen Education* provided educators with opportunities to share, reflect on, and formalize ideas from the experimental teaching that was widely under way as film and popular media began to be used more widely in the classroom with children, adolescents, and young adults. In 1985, Len Masterman's book, *Teaching the Media,* became widely influential, reaching an international audience of scholars and educators with interests in media literacy. By 1989, media education was a compulsory part of British education and located as a subject area within English. Many organizations have been important in supporting the work of teachers and students, including the British Film Institute, the English and Media Centre, the Institute on Education at London University, and many others.

Students in England can take courses and examinations in media studies at both the GCSE and A-levels. GCSE is the first academic program for adolescents, usually culminating at age 16. The A-level examination is the academic flagship of the education program for those between 16 and 18 years old in England, Wales, and Northern Ireland. A-levels enable those

Moving Images in the Classroom is a curriculum resource developed by the British Film Institute to help strengthen students' skills of critical analysis in responding to images in the secondary classroom. It includes eight instructional practices that can easily be used by teachers with most films, documentaries, and other audiovisual materials. The curriculum resource is available free from the website of the British Film Institute, Education Division, at http://www.bfi.org .uk/education/teaching/miic.

SOURCE: http://www.bfi.org.uk/education/teaching/miic.

who wish to remain in school or college after the age of compulsory schooling to continue their education for another 2 years. An A-level student in media studies could expect to cover topics such as the Hollywood studio system, the history of public service broadcasting in the United Kingdom, marketing in the music industry, and gender in teen magazines. Students would face the challenge of creating a media product as a member of a creative team and would learn to apply analytic concepts including media institutions, languages, audiences, and representation, referencing theories such as uses and gratifications or narrative structures. Even in Great Britain, media education leaders acknowledge that there is still little formal initial training for teachers and too little emphasis on media literacy at the elementary level.

ACTIVITIES OF NATIONAL AGENCIES AND THE EUROPEAN UNION

Some media education initiatives exist as part of the mission of a national agency, as in the case of CLEMI, the French national organization for media and education. It was created in 1983 with the mission of developing teacher training activities to encourage the use of news media and promoting young people's ability to better understand the world and develop critical thinking skills. CLEMI provides educational training to more than 15,000 teachers annually.

Some European nations have established grassroots organizations, like the MED, the Italian Media Education Association, which has an active organization of scholars and educators involved in creating and implementing curricula, providing teacher education, and conducting research. Recently, an online network for media educators, Media-Educ, was formed to foster the development of stronger and more coherent media education initiatives in Europe. At a 2004 conference held in Belfast, Northern Ireland, participants explored questions concerning the curricular location of media education in schools, approaches to teacher education, relationships between media educators and professional media organizations, and the value of practical media production work for students. A number of Scandinavian and Eastern European nations, including Sweden, Russia, and Hungary, have educators who are implementing media literacy education with the support of scholars and activists in those nations.

The European Union has also provided support for media education. In 1989, education ministers of the European Union recognized the principle of media education as a basic entitlement of every citizen from the earliest years of schooling. Since then, most European nations have included some kind of requirement for media education in their school curricula. Regulatory bodies have developed an interest in media education as a counterbalance to the increasingly complex problem of media regulation in a digital age, and there has been some corporate interest in sponsoring media education activity.

MEDIA EDUCATION IN CANADA

Media literacy has a long history in Canada, where the Ontario-based Association for Media Literacy has supported the work of educators there since 1978. This organization maintains a website, publishes a newsletter, and organizes conferences, summer institutes, and workshops for teachers, and its success has inspired the creation of similar associations in eight other provinces.

MEDIA EDUCATION IN AUSTRALIA

Australian Teachers of Media (ATOM) is an independent, nonprofit, professional association in Australia for media teachers and others who wish to use media effectively in their classrooms. ATOM aims to foster and encourage a generation of students who are both multiliterate and technologically savvy. The organization sponsors competitions for student-produced multimedia, provides opportunities for teacher education, and hosts statewide conferences.

MEDIA EDUCATION IN ASIA

In most of Asia, media literacy is still in an initial stage of development. Media educators in Japan, Korea, and other Asian nations work primarily in nonschool settings or promote media literacy as a component of parent education. In 2005, a 4-day conference was held in China to introduce the concept of media literacy and to explore how parents and teachers can help teach young people to critically evaluate the media.

INTERNATIONAL EFFORTS: UNESCO

International cooperation has helped to create a worldwide movement for media literacy education. In 1982, a group of educators from more than a dozen nations met under the auspices of UNESCO at the first international symposium on media education at Grunwald, Federal Republic of Germany. This group declared,

> Rather than condemn or endorse the undoubted power of the media, we need to accept their significant impact and penetration throughout the world as an established fact, and also appreciate their importance as an element of culture in today's world. The role of communication and media in the process of development should not be underestimated, nor the function of media as instruments for the citizen's active participation in society. Political and educational systems need to recognize their obligations to promote in their citizens a critical understanding of the phenomena of communication.

UNESCO has continued to sponsor international gatherings of media literacy educators worldwide and, partly as a result of these conferences, media literacy has begun to emerge in Latin America, Eastern Europe, Africa, and Asia. International conferences on media education have been effective in building a coalition of leaders in many nations. This has resulted in some experimental cross-national initiatives that bring teachers and students from several countries into contact using media production and media analysis activities. It is anticipated that such initiatives will continue to develop in the 21st century.

—*Renee Hobbs*

See also Media Education, Family Involvement in; Media Education, Schools and; Media Literacy, Key Concepts in; Media Literacy Programs

FURTHER READINGS

Bazelgette, C., Bevort, E., & Savino, J. (Eds.). (1992). *New directions: Media education worldwide.* London and Paris: British Film Institute & CLEMI.

Buckingham, D. (2004). *Media education: Literacy, learning, and contemporary culture.* London: Polity.

Hall, S., & Whannel, P. (1965). *The popular arts.* New York: Pantheon Books.

Hoggart, R. (1998). *The uses of literacy.* New Brunswick, NJ: Transaction. (Original work published 1957)

Masterman, L. (2001). *Teaching the media.* London: Routledge. (Original work published 1985)

UNESCO. (1982). *Grunwald declaration on media education.* Retrieved May 24, 2006, from http://www.unesco.org/education/pdf/MEDIA_E.PDF

MEDIA EDUCATION, POLITICAL SOCIALIZATION AND

Media contribute to political socialization by providing youth with perspectives that give them a foothold in the political system. Information obtained from news media allows adolescents to form opinions, to talk about politics, and to gain motivation for civic participation. However, children and teenagers must pay attention to news media if they are to benefit. Educators and activists lament an erosion of youth interest in public affairs and sinking rates of youth exposure to newspapers and television news. In recent years, a more optimistic picture has come into focus with successful innovations that incorporate media in community activism and in civic education.

RESEARCH ON MEDIA IN POLITICAL SOCIALIZATION

Political socialization is the process by which young people acquire knowledge, dispositions, and social

Students at Franklin Elementary School in Wausau, Wisconsin, voted on Election Day 2004 as part of an activity sponsored by Kids Voting USA. In this innovative curriculum, students monitor political advertisements and candidate statements in media during the final weeks before Election Day. Classroom discussion about news coverage allows students to refine opinions as they prepare for their first voting experience.

SOURCE: © KidsVotingUSA.org. Photographer: Bill Forbes.

skills that allow them to participate effectively in civic affairs. The origin of empirical research on civic development is often traced to Herbert Hyman's book *Political Socialization*, published in 1959. Through the 1960s and 1970s, researchers mostly ignored media as a contributing factor in political development, and families were viewed as the most important influence on this process. This assumption seemed reasonable given the many years in which parents could directly or indirectly communicate cues about politics. Scholars presumed that children would readily adopt the partisan identification of parents along with other orientations such as political tolerance, confidence in government, and support for voting. However, researchers found that the influence of families was quite minimal, beyond modest correlations for party preference. Scholarship during this era also explored the effects of schools. Once again, the results were meager. Beyond the direct transmission of textbook knowledge, the civics curriculum appeared mostly inconsequential in political development.

Researchers in communication began to investigate influences of mass media in the 1970s. In one study, investigators asked teenagers to rate parents, teachers, friends, and media according to their value in providing information and personal opinions on current affairs. Media stood out as the most important source for both information and opinions. Subsequent research confirmed that habitual media exposure is a robust predictor of adolescents' knowledge about issues, parties, and government.

PATTERNS OF MEDIA USE

Although television and newspapers often reinforce each other as socializing agents, they are used for distinct purposes in political learning. A child is typically introduced to public affairs through TV, beginning with attention to sports and weather. TV news is easier to comprehend than newspaper content, allowing viewers to pick up discrete bits of information such as the names of candidates. For children, broadcast news exposure is more strongly related to political knowledge than is print news.

TV consequently represents a bridge to politics, providing easy access. But for children to achieve higher levels of political sophistication, they must supplement or replace TV with newspaper reading as they enter adolescence. Print media offer greater depth in news coverage, allowing readers to comprehend political processes and to integrate disparate ideas. Newspaper reading for most children begins in elementary school with exposure

to the comics and sports pages. The biggest jump in newspaper reading occurs at ages 10 to 12, when reading skills are typically mastered. Higher stages of cognitive development increase the likelihood of newspaper reading as content becomes easier to comprehend.

REFINEMENTS IN THEORY

Contemporary theorists reject a transmission model in which children and teenagers simply absorb information from TV, newspapers, and the Internet. Instead, media are consequential in civic development by virtue of how they are incorporated in primary groups. Children and adolescents must actively *use* the news in interpersonal communication to fully benefit from media exposure. In this regard, families, schools, and peer groups represent overlapping spheres for civic development to the extent that adolescents share knowledge and exchange opinions obtained from media. Thus, the most optimal learning occurs when media exposure occurs in concert with the testing and validation of opinions in conversation. Both news attention and discussion are necessary for adolescents to shape raw impressions into refined perspectives.

INNOVATIONS AND REFORM

However, the potential for media to contribute to political development has scarcely been realized in the United States. With interest in news waning, young people increasingly rely on late-night comedy and other entertainment programs for political information. Not surprisingly, surveys show that the extent of adolescents' knowledge of public affairs is, at best, worrisome. Educators have responded by experimenting with ways to engage youth via media use and media production. In the Kids Voting USA curriculum, for example, students dissect campaign advertisements and monitor news coverage of candidates during election campaigns. Michael McDevitt and Steven Chaffee found that these activities prompt adolescents to initiate conversations with parents about election issues. These discussions, in turn, motivate parents to pay more attention to news as they anticipate future conversations. This "trickle-up influence" is particularly evident in families of low socioeconomic status, where parents were typically not socialized to politics in their own youth. Students' media use in the home thereby offers low-income parents a second chance at citizenship.

Media literacy—the ability to analyze, evaluate, and produce media of various types—represents another promising strategy for cultivating civic growth. Communication scholar Robert Kubey notes that the United States trails other English-speaking nations in media education, and recent research shows that civic curricula are particularly effective when rooted in media literacy. Examples of this approach include students producing documentaries on community issues, broadcasting their own news programs, and using websites to compare candidate positions. In an era in which citizenship is increasingly expressed through electronic and digital forums, media literacy is likely to become a higher priority for civic education.

—*Michael McDevitt*

See also Media Education, Schools and; Media Effects; Media Literacy Programs; News, Children's Exposure to; News, Children's Responses to

FURTHER READINGS

Atkin, C. (1981). Communication and political socialization. In D. Nimmo & K. Sanders (Eds.), *Handbook of political communication* (pp. 299–328). Beverly Hills, CA: Sage.

Center for Information & Research on Civic Learning & Engagement. (2003). *The civic mission of schools*. New York: CIRCLE and Carnegie Corporation of New York.

Kubey, R. (2004). Media literacy and the teaching of civics and social studies at the dawn of the 21st century. *American Behavioral Scientist*, *48*(1), 69–77.

McDevitt, M., & Chaffee, S. H. (2002). From top-down to trickle-up influence: Revisiting assumptions about the family in political socialization, *Political Communication*, *19*(3), 281–301.

MEDIA EDUCATION, SCHOOLS AND

With the media occupying such a large presence of the daily lives of children and teens, calls have been issued for schools to take up the study of media, beginning as early as kindergarten and continuing through 12th grade. Proponents of media education in the classroom argue that in the modern world, the subject of the media deserves a place alongside more traditional topics such as social studies, science, and math. The term *media education* is often used synonymously with *media literacy*, describing endeavors that entail learning to "read" the media in an informed manner and with a healthy dose of skepticism.

DEFINITION AND DEBATES

Despite the calls for media education in schools, researchers, teachers, parents, and others have had difficulty agreeing on how this should be accomplished. Should media education adopt a protectionist tone (e.g., "you shouldn't watch that"), or will that turn young people off and make them resistant to the curriculum? How political should media education be, especially if it is conducted in public schools? Should negative effects of media on children and teens be emphasized, or should positive roles and media appreciation take center stage? Does media education include learning how to make media (e.g., learning audio or video production or how to make a website), or is media analysis the primary concern (e.g., developing and applying critical thinking skills)?

While these and other debates continue, a basic definition of media literacy has been offered by Patricia Aufderheide. It states that media literacy is the ability to create, access, analyze, and evaluate the media in all its forms. Aufderheide also identified a small list of key aspects. Media education should help young people learn that media "construct reality," which basically means that media shape understandings and interpretations of the world. It should promote comprehension of the ways in which media portrayals are unrealistic (or are "constructions of reality"). Media education should advance knowledge of the potentially complex and varying ways that media affect audiences. It should help students to understand *how* media are made as well as *why* they are made (which introduces discussion of the commercial enterprise of making media). Finally, media education should foster awareness that media messages have inherent values associated with them. For instance, the relative absence of an ethnic group from prime-time television can serve to devalue the group, whereas the abundance of commercial messages in media can promote consumerism as a positive value.

EXAMPLES AND EFFECTIVENESS

A number of media education curricula have been implemented in schools with both children and teens, and the effects of these efforts have been studied using social scientific research methods. The curricula vary widely in terms of age group targeted, the topic that they take on, and the exercises and assignments that they entail. Yet, they share a common objective: to increase critical thinking about media, often with the desire to intervene in media effects.

Advertising

A small number of published studies exist on the role of school-based media education in bolstering students' resistance to advertising. In one study conducted by Renee Hobbs and Richard Frost, 11th graders participated in a lengthy curriculum with an emphasis on the critical analysis of advertisements (among other topics). Later, participants were more likely than control-group members to be able to identify the purpose of an ad, its target audience, and the techniques used to create it. In studies by Erica Weintraub Austin and colleagues, media literacy training among third graders led to enhanced understanding of tobacco advertising techniques, diminished perception that most young people use tobacco, and increased endorsement of anti-tobacco advocacy.

Violence

A handful of media education studies on media violence have been published. Lawrence and Sharon Rosenkoetter and colleagues gave first through third graders a lengthy curriculum on the topic, which included such exercises as learning about special effects and discussing lack of realism. Rowell Huesmann and colleagues had slightly older children complete a shorter curriculum that included writing an essay about why television violence can be harmful. In Erica Scharrer's study, sixth graders participated in a five-lesson curriculum that discussed ways of portraying violence that are likely to encourage negative effects (e.g., as accompanied by rewards, as occurring with few consequences) and applied these ideas to a series of clips. The research evidence from these and other studies shows increases in knowledge about and critical attitudes toward media violence among media education participants, as well as decreases in identification with aggressive characters or aggression.

Body Image

Feeling dissatisfied with one's weight or the way one looks is another negative media effect that media education interventions have attempted to remedy. In a study conducted by Heidi Fuller and colleagues, fourth graders participated in a curriculum in which they discussed how computers can digitally enhance models' appearance and how unrealistic female characters appear in Disney films. In focus groups, media literacy participants were more likely to give careful thought to media portrayals of beauty and bodies compared to those

in a control group. A 10-lesson media literacy and eating disorder prevention program with 9-to-11-year-olds, studied by Michael Levine and associates, included units on the analysis of nutrition and weight messages in commercials. After participating, students had gained knowledge on the topic, and the older participants displayed more positive attitudes toward overweight people compared to control-group members.

OBSTACLES

Despite these promising studies, the incorporation of media education into the day-to-day agenda of kindergarten through 12th-grade classrooms in the United States has been sporadic and slow going. Although every state now lists media literacy in its curricular framework (thereby showing a certain degree of "buy-in"), teachers often are not given the training or resources necessary to systematically integrate it into the classroom. Thus, in the adoption of media education in schools, the United States lags considerably behind other countries such as Australia, Canada, and the United Kingdom.

Overall, media education holds much promise for providing children and teenagers with the tools they need to deconstruct the media. Although a number of barriers and debates have marked its growth, there is mounting evidence that educating young people about the media in school can have a positive effect on their knowledge, attitudes, and behavior.

—*Erica Scharrer*

See also Center for Media Education (CME); Digital Literacy; Media Education, Family Involvement in; Media Education, International; Media Education Foundation; Media Literacy Programs

FURTHER READINGS

Aufderheide, P. (1997). Media literacy: From a report of the national leadership conference on media literacy. In R. Kubey (Ed.), *Media literacy in the information age: Current perspectives*. New Brunswick, NJ: Transaction.

Austin, E. W., & Johnson, K. K. (1997). Immediate and delayed effects of media literacy training on third-graders' decision making for alcohol. *Health Communication, 9,* 323–350.

Austin, E. W., Pinkleton, B. E., Hust, S. J. T., & Cohen, M. (2006). Evaluation of an American Legacy Foundation/ Washington State Department of Health media literacy pilot study. *Health Communication, 18,* 75–96.

Fuller, H. A., Damico, A. M., & Rodgers, S. (2004). Impact of a health and media literacy curriculum on 4th-grade girls: A qualitative study. *Journal of Research in Childhood Education, 19,* 66–79.

Hobbs, R., & Frost, R. (2003). Measuring the acquisition of media literacy skills. *Reading Research Quarterly, 38,* 330–355.

Huesmann, L. R., Eron, L. D., Klein, R., Brice, P., & Fischer, P. (1983). Mitigating the imitation of aggressive behavior by changing children's attitudes about media violence. *Journal of Personality and Social Psychology, 44,* 899–910.

Levine, M. P., Smolak, L., & Schermer, F. (1996). Media analysis and resistance in primary school children in the primary prevention of eating problems. *Eating Disorders: The Journal of Treatment & Prevention, 4,* 310–322.

Rosenkoetter, L. I., Rosenkoetter, S. E., Ozretich, R. A., & Acock, A. C. (2004). Mitigating the harmful effects of violent television. *Journal of Applied Developmental Psychology, 25,* 25–47.

Scharrer, E. (in press). "I noticed more violence": The effects of a media literacy program on knowledge and attitudes about media violence. *Journal of Mass Media Ethics.*

MEDIA EDUCATION FOUNDATION

The Media Education Foundation (MEF) is a non-profit organization that produces and distributes educational videos designed to promote critical thought, conversations, and activism about media and culture. Founded in 1991 by University of Massachusetts Amherst Professor Sut Jhally, the organization takes up issues of media consolidation, consumer culture, and media depictions. Its mission is "to answer the challenge posed by the radical and accelerating corporate threat to democracy," according to a recent catalog and brochure. The videos typically feature footage from the media content in question (e.g., music videos, news coverage, television programs, video games, etc.), deconstructed by experts, scholars, and activists who discuss research findings and make critical observations pertaining to the topic.

Professor Jhally's first video, *Dreamworlds*, was an incisive critique of the music video industry and its depiction of women and girls. A legal move to stop its distribution, which was later withdrawn, brought considerable media attention to his research and inspired the creation of the Media Education Foundation. Now, staff at MEF estimate that more than 2 million college students have seen the popular video; a third updated installment, titled *Dreamworlds 3: Desire, Sex, and Power in Music Videos*, was released in 2006. The MEF catalog currently includes dozens of videos, with new titles continually in the works.

Among the other bestsellers in the MEF catalog are the *Killing Us Softly* videos, featuring media critic Jean Kilbourne's critical assessment of gender in advertising. The third installment in the series, *Killing Us Softly 3: Advertising's Image of Women*, was released by MEF in 2000. Another top seller is *Tough Guise: Violence, Media, & the Crisis in Masculinity*, in which Jackson Katz, a leading anti-violence educator who has worked with professional sports teams and other groups of men, raises issues of school and dating violence and the portrayal of masculinity in the media. Other MEF videos have taken on a wide range of social and cultural issues including (but not limited to) media representations of alcohol and drinking (*Spin the Bottle*), of social class (*Class Dismissed: How TV Frames the Working Class*), of body and beauty (*Slim Hopes: Advertising & the Obsession With Thinness*), and of gays and lesbians (*Off the Straight and Narrow: Lesbians, Gays, Bisexuals & Television*).

Another MEF production *Hijacking Catastrophe: 9/11, Fear & the Selling of American Empire*, released in 2004, discussed U.S. foreign policy and media coverage of the events of September 11, 2001, and the war in Iraq. It met with widespread critical acclaim. The video also expanded the audience for MEF videos beyond the usual high school and college or university setting. *Hijacking Catastrophe* opened in select movie theaters across the country, was reviewed in a number of mainstream and alternative media outlets, and has sold an unprecedented number of copies.

MEF also offers free educational resources on its website for educators to use in the classroom as supplements to the videos. Discussion questions, media literacy activities, summaries of the topics covered in the videos, exercises for research and writing, and links to additional sources are available. In addition to those resources, the MEF website features interviews with media scholars and activists, news updates, and clips from each of the organization's videos.

—*Erica Scharrer*

See also Center for Media Education; Media Advocacy; Media Education, Schools and

WEBSITE

Media Education Foundation: www.mediaed.org

MEDIA EFFECTS

Research on how children respond to media and on the nature of media effects still is most extensive with regard to the effects of television viewing on children's development. There rarely is one universal effect of media use, but specific aspects of such use may predict positive or negative outcomes in at least some children and teenagers. Recent surveys of time spent with various media suggest that television remains the dominant medium, beginning very early in childhood and extending through adolescence. Total media consumption and total television viewing by children and youth have changed little over the last several years, suggesting a source of stability in effects on development.

At the same time, the pace of change in media availability, in the functions of media, and in the portability of media far outstrips that of research into media effects. Patterns of media consumption reflect increasing specialization, as children and teenagers show more frequent use of cable channels and selectively recorded programs. The increased presence of media in children's bedrooms, greater storage capability of media devices, and extensive use of wireless technology and cellular telephone functions have provided children and teenagers with greater access to media; this access has been accompanied by a sharp increase in media multitasking. Despite numerous studies of the effects of television on children's development, what we know about media effects in general and effects of television in particular must be viewed as subject to change as technologies and the power and functions of media in children's lives continue to evolve.

EFFECTS ON COGNITIVE DEVELOPMENT, EDUCATION, AND ACHIEVEMENT

Concerns about television's potential harm to children's thinking and school achievement and hopes for its potential educational benefits have existed virtually since the medium's introduction. There are several bases for worries about risks to cognitive development and education. One hypothesis is that extensive early exposure to electronic media may affect brain development in infants and toddlers, leading to adverse effects on cognitive development. Although some studies report negative associations between the total amount of very early exposure to television and measures of language and attentional abilities, effects of some content can be positive, and no specific evidence of effects on early brain development has been produced.

A second explanation for potential negative effects is founded on a distinction between foreground and background television. The former refers to programming produced for young children and often selected by them or their parents for intentional viewing, whereas the latter consists of programming produced for a general audience, which serves as a backdrop for children's other activities. Background television may constitute the bulk of television exposure among infants and toddlers, a situation even more the case before the advent of television programs (e.g., *Teletubbies*) and videos (e.g., *Baby Einstein*) designed specifically for this youngest age group. Whereas the question remains open as to whether foreground television can be used productively with a very young audience, there is growing evidence that background television is disruptive to toddlers' play behavior and social interaction and that an early rearing environment characterized by more background noise is associated with poorer cognitive development. Television as a major component of background noise is a common phenomenon for very young children who live in households where television is left on most of the time, and according to a Kaiser Foundation study, this situation may exist in nearly half of U.S. households.

A third basis for concerns about negative effects on cognitive development and achievement throughout childhood and adolescence is displacement theory, which proposes that time spent with television takes time away from more valuable activities, such as reading and imaginative play. Evidence supporting this proposal is mixed. In a number of studies, children who view TV most heavily seem to spend less time engaged in activities that encourage cognitive development and, in turn, show the lowest achievement. For light to moderate television viewers, program content, family interaction, and opportunities for other activities moderate television's effects on children's achievement and creativity. It also should be noted that some studies find positive associations among usage levels of various media, with children who report higher television use also reporting more time spent reading and using computers and with no association between television viewing and grades in school.

What of television's potential educational benefits? Limited evidence suggests that viewing of specific programs contributes positively to very young children's vocabulary development. For preschoolers, there is substantial evidence of language learning and increases in school readiness. A growing number of programs for preschool children (e.g., *Sesame Street, Blue's Clues,* and *Dora the Explorer*) have well-articulated curricula and are informed by research on young children's attention and comprehension. Such programs are associated with growth in problem solving, flexible thinking, literacy, and vocabulary development, with some of these effects translating to long-term positive effects on educational achievement. Programs designed for school-age children also have been successful in teaching skills and increasing familiarity with content areas but must contend with the additional challenge of maintaining older children's interest with a compelling narrative while blending educational content with the narrative structure. The growing Internet usage by children and teens (including time shared with television and responding to what they are watching on television) offers future avenues for engaging older children in beneficial activities.

EFFECTS ON SOCIAL BEHAVIORS

Concern regarding television's effects on children's social development has been most apparent in the long-standing debate over the link between televised violence and children's aggression, but it extends to other areas, such as development of gender and ethnic stereotypes and the comprehension and expression of emotions. Several overlapping theories suggest why television content may exert effects in these areas.

Arousal theory emphasizes physiological responses that can be produced by television programs. Programs causing emotions also produce bodily responses, such as increased heart rate from excitement during a violent or suspenseful show. Although there are individual and age differences, the excitement of shows that produce physical arousal will attract many children. However, arousal theory also predicts that with increased exposure, children need stronger stimulation to reach the same level of arousal and emotional reactions and so can become desensitized to violence and other themes that provoke emotions. In support of this perspective, children show reduced responses to real-life aggression after viewing televised violence.

Albert Bandura's social cognitive theory asserts that children learn many social behaviors by observing those modeled by others. Factors that increase children's likelihood of trying a behavior include whether they can identify with the person modeling the behavior and whether the model succeeds in achieving a goal or in obtaining a reward. Heavy exposure to television characters who achieve goals by behaving in aggressive, violent, or stereotypical ways may encourage children to use similar strategies in their own lives. Numerous studies provide evidence that heavy exposure to televised violence is linked to increased aggressive behavior in children and adolescents.

Script theories address ways in which television influences the development of children's knowledge and beliefs about the world. Based on experiences with real and media events, children construct generalized representations of what to expect in certain situations or of certain people. In turn, children's expectations may guide their behaviors. Children who observe frequent aggressive solutions to conflict situations are more likely to expect others to behave aggressively. One specific version of script theory, cultivation theory, proposes that heavy viewing leads people to see the world as it is portrayed on television. For example, television programs overrepresent the occurrence of violence and exaggerate the presence and the power of white males. Consistent with cultivation theory, heavy viewers are relatively likely to see the world as mean and threatening and to develop ethnic and gender stereotypes.

Some evidence supports each of these theories. However, results from any single study cannot establish a clear causal link *from* television *to* a particular behavior. The strongest argument is possible when multiple sources of evidence based on multiple methods converge, as has occurred for the conclusion that viewing televised violence contributes to aggressive behavior. Even in this case, heavy viewing of violent television is documented as only one contributor to the development of aggressive behavior, and it is most likely to affect children who are prone to aggressive behavior for other reasons (e.g., children growing up in contexts in which aggression is viewed as a relatively acceptable response to conflict).

An additional question concerning media effects on social development concerns potential associations of media use and developing social relationships. A recent Kaiser Foundation survey of media use among 8-to-18-year-olds revealed that children and adolescents who reported spending more time using media also reported spending more time with their parents and in pursuing other hobbies. This finding may reflect one more aspect of media multitasking: that children and teens find media use a comfortable context for spending time with parents. However, it does not reveal the quality of parent-child interactions or other aspects of social relationships. These investigators also reported that heavy media users are less likely to talk out problems with parents and that the children and teens who reported least contentment with their lives also spent more time playing video games and less time reading than their more contented peers. Another factor connecting media use to social relationships may relate to variations in how media are used in different households. Analogous to disruption by background television of play behavior and parent-child interactions among very young children, responses to the survey suggested potentially more disruption from media in households where media use is unregulated and television is left on most of the time.

EFFECTS ON HEALTH BEHAVIORS

As children develop and move through adolescence, they make a growing number of choices that influence health, choices that may become part of a long-term lifestyle. Early in development, children's health-related choices may include preferences for particular foods, participation in physical activities, and decisions to engage in risky activities. Later in childhood and in their teen years, choices expand to include the use of substances with health consequences such as tobacco, alcohol, and illicit drugs, as well as choices about sexual behaviors. Media use during childhood and adolescence, especially viewing of television and movies and music consumption, may contribute to the development of health-related knowledge, attitudes, and behaviors.

One potential mechanism for influence may stem from incidental effects of portrayals of health-related behaviors in entertainment media and in television product advertisements. Based on the three theoretical perspectives described earlier, portrayals of health-related behaviors might influence children's and adolescents' concepts of what is normal (in youth culture or in the adult world), what is acceptable, and what is associated with positive characteristics or responses from others.

Food preferences and physical activity. Advertising for food products targeted at children is likely to emphasize high-fat, high-sugar foods. The findings of some studies indicate that exposure to TV ads contributes to children's short-term and long-term food preferences, although parents' preferences exert stronger influence. There is some evidence that TV viewing as a *behavior* may relate to overweight and obesity during childhood and adolescence by contributing to decreases in physical activity and increases in calorie consumption, but other investigations report no relation or a positive relation between media use and physical activity.

Substance use and sexual behavior. Tobacco and drug use are portrayed infrequently on U.S. television programs, although somewhat more commonly in movies. Alcohol use is shown frequently in television programs and in movies and is promoted heavily in product ads, with both situations typically portraying alcohol use as a normative, problem-free adult behavior. The number of sexual scenes on television has nearly doubled since 1998, with many portrayals comic but others including references to commitment issues and safer sex. The effects of these portrayals are mixed; the most consistent finding is that the overall amount of viewing of entertainment television and advertising is related to positive alcohol expectancies and alcohol use among adolescents.

A second possible mechanism for influence is the use of mass media as a means to deliver intentional interventions to change or reinforce health-related attitudes, beliefs, and behaviors. Although a number of mass media efforts have failed to effect change, theoretically driven campaigns targeted at specific at-risk groups have reduced risky behaviors including tobacco use, drug use, and unprotected sex.

—Elizabeth P. Lorch

See also Media Effects, Family Interactions and; Media Effects, History of Research on; Media Effects, Models of; Media Exposure

FURTHER READINGS

Anderson, D. R., Bryant, J., Wilder, A., Crawley, A. M., Santomero, A., & Williams, M. E. (2000). Researching *Blue's Clues:* Viewing behavior and impact. *Media Psychology, 2,* 179–194.

Anderson, D. R., Huston, A. C., Schmitt, K. L., Linebarger, D. L., & Wright, J. C. (2001). Early childhood television viewing and adolescent behavior: The Recontact Study. *Monographs of the Society for Research in Child Development 68* (1, Serial No. 264).

Anderson, D. R., & Pempek, T. A. (2005). Television and very young children. *American Behavioral Scientist, 48,* 505–522.

Calvert, S. (1999). *Children's journeys through the information age.* Boston: McGraw-Hill.

Christakis, D., Zimmerman, F., DiGiuseppe, D., & McCarty, C. (2004). Early television exposure and subsequent attentional problems in children. *Pediatrics, 113,* 708–713.

Fisch, S. (2000). A capacity model of children's comprehension of educational content on television. *Media Psychology, 2,* 63–91.

Hornik, R. C. (2002). *Public health communication: Evidence for behavior change.* Mahwah, NJ: Erlbaum.

Kaiser Family Foundation. (2005). *Sex on TV.* Menlo Park, CA: Author.

Linebarger, D. L., & Walker, D. (2004). Infants' and toddlers' television viewing and language outcomes. *American Behavioral Scientist, 46,* 1–22.

Murray, J. P. (1998). Studying television violence: A research agenda for the 21st century. In J. K. Asamen & G. L. Berry (Eds.), *Research paradigms, television, and social behavior.* Thousand Oaks, CA: Sage.

Naigles, L. R., & Mayeux, L. (2001). Television as incidental language teacher. In D. G. Singer & J. L. Singer (Eds.), *Handbook of children and the media* (pp. 135–152). Thousand Oaks, CA: Sage.

Nelson, K. (1973). Structure and strategy in learning to talk. *Monographs of the Society for Research in Child Development, 38*(Serial No. 149).

Neuman, S. B. (1991). *Literacy in the television age.* Norwood, NJ: Ablex.

Rideout, V., Roberts, D. F., & Foehr, U. G. (2005). *Generation M: Media in the lives of 8–18-year-olds.* Menlo Park, CA: Kaiser Family Foundation.

Rideout, V., Vandewater, E., & Wartella, E. (2003). *Zero to six: Electronic media in the lives of infants, toddlers, and preschoolers.* Menlo Park, CA: Kaiser Family Foundation.

Wachs, T. D. (1986). Ambient background noise and early development. *Children's Environments Quarterly, 3,* 23–33.

Wright, J. C., Huston, A. C., Scantlin, R., & Kotler, J. (2001). The Early Window project: *Sesame Street* prepares children for school. In S. M. Fisch & R. T. Truglio (Eds.), *"G" is for "growing": Thirty years of research on children and* Sesame Street (pp. 97–114). Mahwah, NJ: Erlbaum.

MEDIA EFFECTS, FAMILY INTERACTIONS AND

Communication is an essential, indispensable element for the formation and maintenance of families. Indeed, social interaction is the vehicle through which family members establish, maintain, and dissolve their intimate relationships. Within this unique social system, the mass media have become an integral, if not routine part of family life. This entry examines some aspects of how the mass media impact interactions within families, focusing on parents, children, and adolescents.

The typical American family home is permeated with media technologies, including multiple television and radio sets, media players, and computers systems, and often, the children are the most avid media consumers. A 2005 study of children 8 to 18 conducted by the Kaiser Family Foundation found, for instance, that children spent almost 6½ hours daily using mass media. However, because many children used multiple media simultaneously (referred to as media multitasking), the average total exposure to all media exceeded 8½ hours each day. Media multitasking appears to be facilitated by an abundance of media technologies within the typical child's bedroom. A television (68%) with a VCR/DVD player and video game console (50%) are commonplace, and almost a third of the children in the Kaiser study reported having a computer in their bedroom, many with Internet access. Overall, 86% of the children indicated that there was at least one computer in their home, 75% with Internet access. At the same time, less than half (46%) of the children reported having any family rules about media use, with most of these children stating that such rules were rarely enforced.

The prominence of mass media in the lives of children and adolescents raises several questions: What effect do the media have on family communication? Do the mass media stimulate or impede family interactions? Do the mass media provide an electronic hearth around which family members can congregate or provide a barrier separating individuals? Interestingly, the body of research suggests the answer to all of these questions is yes, highlighting the fact that the relationship between mass media use and family communication is multifaceted and highly interdependent.

Although rapid changes in both the institution of the family and in mass media technologies are not well reflected in contemporary research, some conclusions can be advanced. First, how families define themselves and create a socially constructed set of roles, values, and norms exercises considerable influence over the media experiences of its members. Work explicating family communication patterns, for example, revealed that parents' values and norms regarding communication were predictive of family media habits. *Social-oriented* parents, for example, emphasize harmony, conformity, and getting along with others, and their families are most likely to use media for social purposes such as solidarity, companionship, and conversation. *Concept-oriented* parents, on the other hand, encourage expression of ideas, critical thinking, and open debate of opinions, and their families perceive the mass media as tools to instill values and facilitate constructive arguments.

During the 1950s, which are often referred to as the "Golden Age" of television, television was the mass media centerpiece around which the family often gathered. In many contemporary households, this traditional model of media effects on family interactions has been replaced by a rapidly escalating trend towards privatization of mass media use.

SOURCE: © CORBIS.

Second, mass media have the potential to enhance family communication in several ways. Television, for example, can bring families together into a common social environment, foster a feeling of togetherness, and enrich nonverbal interactions between family members. More generally, the mass media can provide texts (e.g., stories, music, and jokes) that can stimulate family conversations and provide a reference point for discussion of sensitive and complex issues. This notion is illustrated by recent research showing that "teen Internet mavens"—savvy young Internet users who can quickly access product information—are exerting considerable influence in family economic decision-making processes. Furthermore, it has become relatively common practice to use text messaging, email, bulletin boards, and blogs to substantially expand both the quantity and quality of communication within the family, the extended family, and the family's broader social network.

Third, traditional models of media effects on family interactions, those that attribute a unique centrality to television within households, are no longer viable. The era of television as the mass media centerpiece around which the family gathers has been replaced by a rapidly escalating trend toward privatization of mass media use. Several studies, for example, have demonstrated that children with TVs in their bedrooms are less likely to engage in coviewing with other family members. Building on this evidence, many commentators have voiced concerns that the emergence of computers in children's bedrooms might further inhibit interaction and involvement among family members. As yet, however, evidence of this "social time displacement" notion is mixed. This may be due, at least in part, to the fact that incorporation of the computer within the family system does not necessarily require the negotiation of new family media habits but instead may only require modification of ones previously developed to accommodate the individualized use of earlier technologies such as TV and video games.

Finally, there is reason to suspect that the utility of the mass media as a physical and psychological obstacle allowing family members to avoid interaction with one another has been substantially enhanced in our contemporary media environment. It has long been recognized that television is often used by children and other family members as a way of coping with stress and heading off family tension. Recent research suggests, however, that a transition may have begun, and the Internet is increasingly becoming the medium of choice for many who seek refuge during difficult times within the family. Children and adolescents exhibiting excessive Internet use, for example, consistently display stress-related characteristics such as loneliness, anxiety, and low self-esteem, and for many, the Internet provides both an entertaining distraction and a safe communal environment. Adults, of course, can also exhibit obsessive Internet use for essentially the same reasons. Taken together, these considerations raise the possibility that for some, the Internet could offer an alluring alternative to family interaction, involvement, and problem solving, thus further exacerbating problems within a stressful or dysfunctional household.

—James B. Weaver, III and Stephanie Lee Sargent

See also Family Environment, Media Effects on; Kaiser Family Foundation; Media Effects (various entries); Media Entertainment; Movie Viewing, Adolescents'; Movie Viewing, Children's; Television, Child Variables and Use of

FURTHER READINGS

Alexander, A. (2001). The meaning of television in the American family. In J. Bryant & J. A. Bryant (Eds.), *Television and the American family* (2nd ed., pp. 273–287). Mahwah, NJ: Erlbaum.

Belch, M. A., Krentler, K. A., & Willis-Flurry, L. A. (2005). Teen Internet mavens: Influence in family decision making. *Journal of Business Research, 58,* 569–575.

Gentile, D. A., & Walsh, D. A. (2002). A normative study of family media habits. *Applied Developmental Psychology, 23,* 157–178.

Hughes, R., Jr., & Hans, J. D. (2001). Computers, the Internet, and families: A review of the role new technology plays in family life. *Journal of Family Issues, 22,* 778–792.

Kestnbaum, M., Robinson, J. P., Neustadtl, A., & Alvarez, A. (2002). Information technology and social time displacement. *IT & Society, 1,* 21–37.

Leung, L. (2004). Net-generation attributes and seductive properties of the Internet as predictors of online activities and Internet addiction. *CyberPsychology & Behavior, 7,* 333–348.

Livingstone, S., & Bovill, M. (2001). *Children and their changing media environment: A European comparative study.* Mahwah, NJ: Lawrence Erlbaum.

Lull, J. (1990). *Inside family viewing: Ethnographic research on television's audiences.* London: Routledge.

Roberts, D. F., Foehr, U. G., & Rideout, V. (2005, March). *Generation M: Media in the lives of 8–18 year-olds* (Publication 7251). Menlo Park, CA: Kaiser Family Foundation.

Sang, F., Schmitz, B., & Tasche, K. (1993). Developmental trends in television coviewing of parent-child dyads. *Journal of Youth and Adolescence, 22,* 531–542.

Vangelisti, A. L. (2004). *Handbook of family communication.* Mahwah, NJ: Erlbaum.

MEDIA EFFECTS, HISTORY OF RESEARCH ON

Since the study of media effects began during World War I, several different theories have served as the conceptual framework for this research. In the early days of scientific effects studies, many social critics assumed powerful and uniform media effects. In part, this was because of the historical bias in the popular press toward chronicling instances of powerful media effects. But some aspects of these assumptions about powerful effects reflected the prominence of stimulus-response models in psychology, and others emerged because of widespread public uncertainty and concern about the social and psychological impact of the new mass media, especially on children and adolescents. After the Depression, a limited-effects model emerged, ascribing to media consumers the ability to select and evaluate media. Following the 1960s, new perspectives evolved on the mechanisms of media effects, and research began to address cognitive, affective, and physiological effects as well as behavioral effects of media. Recent advances in research tools, statistical modeling, and methodological approaches, along with increased sophistication in theories of child and adolescent development, have combined to give communication scholars more accurate and holistic models of media effects on young media users.

The study of media effects began during World War I, in large part in response to concerns about propaganda spread by the military at home and abroad. Later, critics expressed similar concerns about what were perceived to be incredibly potent advertising and public relations efforts being employed by rapidly expanding corporations that were seen as ruthless and inhumane.

Initially, many social scientists, as well as the public, believed that mass media produced rather uniformly powerful effects on their unsuspecting audiences. This immense and presumably subversive power of media messages on vulnerable audiences was described in various and sundry colorful ways: Mass media supposedly fired messages like dangerous bullets, or injected messages like strong drugs propelled through hypodermic needles. These metaphors gave rise to the bullet or hypodermic needle theories of powerful media effects. Other scholars have labeled these early theoretical models the theory of uniform media influences.

The standard history of media effects research typically attributes the rise of these powerful effects theories to the development of a mass society of fragmented individuals who received similar messages from the mass media of communication. Several early media theorists focused on the dramatic changes taking place in society during the late 19th and early 20th centuries and the resulting effects on the masses. They noted the importance of mass behavior, which typically was attributed to the urbanization and industrialization of the early 20th century. Urbanization, in turn, allegedly was due primarily to the social factors that detached people from their local cultures and local group settings.

Several early books on mass media were written with an underlying acceptance of the bullet or hypodermic needle theories; that is, they assumed an immense power of mass communication messages over their audiences. These included Walter Lippmann's *Public Opinion*, Harold Lasswell's *Propaganda Technique in the World War*, and George Bruntz's *Allied Propaganda and the Collapse of the German Empire in 1918*. The powerful-effects model also undergirded the creation of the influential Institute for Propaganda Analysis (1937–1942), which was devoted to informing the public about propaganda, because of the fear that without critical education about propaganda, democracy could not withstand the onslaught of subversive mass media messages.

Lippmann, a journalist and philosopher, provided an extremely important impetus to communication research in *Public Opinion,* which is often viewed as a foundational element of the intellectual history of agenda-setting research. In this classic work, Lippmann called on his experiences with propaganda during World War I and emphasized the role of the news media in influencing audiences' perceptions about important issues in very powerful ways. Moreover, Lippmann's colorful prose (e.g., "the world outside and the pictures in our head") helped frame public opinion research for future generations of communication scholars.

The powerful-effects model is sometimes said to have served as the conceptual basis for a series of early empirical investigations sponsored by the Payne Fund in the 1920s, but in fact, the investigators typically considered factors such as age and cognitive abilities that could mitigate potentially powerful media effects. Although these investigators sought to determine the influence of the motion picture on children—and they typically found that movies could be powerful instruments of education, attitude change, emotional impact, health, and behavior change—such effects were in no way found to be uniform for all children and youth.

With a few notable exceptions, the powerful-effects model (or theory of uniform media influences) seems to have remained the dominant paradigm of media effects until after the Depression, when empirical studies began to indicate that effects from mass media were not as powerful as originally thought. Rather than a society of fragmented individuals who received all-powerful messages from mass media, the view shifted

to one of a society of individuals who generally were not alienated, who interacted within groups, and who were active in selecting and discarding media messages. This active audience was perceived as limiting the effects of media messages and as having considerable potency of its own. Studies by Paul Lazarsfeld and associates at Columbia University's Bureau of Applied Social Research, such as the voting studies reported in *The People's Choice* in 1948, revealed that individual opinion leaders often served as well-informed or expert interpreters of media messages for their peers, a process that sometimes mitigated media impact. Other social scientists, such as Carl Hovland, who was then working for the U.S. War Department, confirmed that mass media had only limited effects on individuals. Hovland conducted controlled experiments that assessed attitude change among soldiers who viewed training or motivational films. He found that many of the films had little or no effect on the soldiers' attitudes or motivations.

The limited-effects model became better established in 1960 with the publication of Joseph Klapper's *The Effects of Mass Communication*. This classic work reviewed hundreds of media effects studies from the 1920s through the 1950s and attempted to make blanket generalizations on the subject of mass media effects. Klapper called for a new, *phenomenistic* approach to research in the field, which emphasized particular factors that limited the effects of mass media messages on individuals. In his work, audience members were typically perceived as using media messages that reinforce existing opinions, abilities, and beliefs.

In the decades following the 1960s, mass media research thrived as the field of mass communication became firmly established at research universities throughout the United States and began to gain credibility worldwide. As new approaches to studying media effects emerged, especially in domains other than public opinion, voting, and marketing, many new theories and research findings did not fit neatly into the limited-effects paradigm; therefore, the media effects portfolio was expanded to include new studies that indicated moderate to powerful media effects under certain conditions.

Those theories asserting more robust media effects included Marshall McLuhan's sense extension theory, presented in *Understanding Media*, which alleged that media effects do not result from exposure to media content per se but from the essential form of a medium that is routinely and almost universally consumed. In other words, medium effects are often cultural in scope. Such effects were thought to alter basic patterns of information processing, perception, and cognition among an entire population of users. Compelling empirical evidence to support or refute such claims about culturally universal media effects is largely lacking, but McLuhan's ideas captured the public's imagination and drew considerable attention to other types of media effects research.

The role of social constraints and audience interpretations (or media reception theory) began to receive widespread credence as mediating or mitigating factors in media effects. One critical change that often yielded more pronounced media effects was a shift toward examining dimensions of media effects other than their behavioral impact. In fact, studies assessing cognitive, affective, and physiological effects often made the point that changes in knowledge, attitude, and affect were important in their own right, even if they did not necessarily lead to immediate and overt changes in behaviors. Moreover, in the last two decades of the 20th century, many investigators began to focus on the *process* of effects, including precursors of effects (e.g., attention, comprehension, information acquisition) and reception processes perse (e.g., selective exposure, empathy).

In addition, more compelling support for robust media effects under certain conditions emerged, as research methodologies and statistical tools became more sophisticated, especially during the past quarter century. For example, an elaborate investigation by Sandra J. Ball-Rokeach, Milton Rokeach, and Joel W. Grube called the *Great American Values Test* revealed that the effects of viewing a 30-minute television program on values were robust when people were confronted with inconsistencies in their basic beliefs versus their behaviors.

The latter part of the 20th century saw the development of more powerful research tools (e.g., meta-analysis), advances in statistical modeling (e.g., structural equation modeling), and the emergence of new methodological approaches (e.g., epidemiological models). Moreover, the more widespread and sensitive usage of longitudinal designs and field experiments further clarified previous findings from media effects investigations and revealed that many of the most robust sorts of media effects accumulate over time and with continued media use (i.e., cumulative effects)

As a result of this burgeoning body of increasingly consensual evidence, a number of professional associations (e.g., the American Medical Association, American Academy of Pediatrics, American Psychological Association, and Parent-Teachers Association) have issued public policy statements regarding the role of media consumption in the psychological well-being and public health of young people. The vast majority of these statements have implicitly or explicitly adopted moderate (and occasionally powerful) media effects models, including statements that under certain social and ecological conditions (e.g., family structure, parenting style, media use style), regular and prolonged exposure to certain types of media fare (e.g., violence, pornography, commercials for fast foods) contributes to mental or physical health problems (e.g., increased aggression or hostility, ADHD, obesity), especially among children and adolescents. Such moderate (and even powerful) media effects claims and models have become a mantra of postmodern information societies.

—*Jennings Bryant*

See also Media, Future of; Media Effects; Media Effects, Models of

FURTHER READINGS

Bryant, J., & Thompson, S. (2002). *Fundamentals of media effects.* New York: McGraw-Hill.

Harris, R. J. (2004). *A cognitive psychology of mass communication* (4th ed.). Mahwah, NJ: Erlbaum.

Perse, E. M. (2001). *Media effects and society.* Mahwah, NJ: Erlbaum.

MEDIA EFFECTS, MALTREATED CHILDREN AND

Media research on maltreated children specifically focuses on television and defines maltreatment as physical, sexual, verbal, or emotional abuse or neglect of children by their parents. Emotionally disturbed children also fit into this category; these children tend to be from unstable homes, often have behavioral problems in school, and are sometimes institutionalized. Maltreated children have become a source of interest in media research because they watch television more than other children. Media theories, such as social learning and cultivation theory, suggest that individuals who are heavy viewers of television are more vulnerable to its effects. Typically, maltreated children watch television between 3.5 and 8 hours per day, compared to 3 hours for nonmaltreated children; institutionalized children typically watch the most television. In addition, a few studies have found that fewer rules are associated with television viewing in the homes of maltreated children. In the 1970s, William A. Donohue and Thomas R. Donohue started this line of research, and since then, Joyce Sprafkin and Kenneth D. Gadow have also conducted many investigations. This entry first discusses the negative effects revealed by this line of research and then examines a few positive outcomes that have also been identified.

A number of studies have examined the ability of maltreated children to recognize television images as fantasy rather than reality. Literature suggests that children, in general, are not able to distinguish between fantasy and reality until about the age of 8 years. This is an important ability because fright reactions, persuasion, the belief that the world is like television, and other outcomes can emerge from not being able to distinguish these differences. The results suggest that emotionally disturbed children are more likely than nondisturbed children to believe television content is real and that commercials are truthful. In general, this suggests that emotionally disturbed children can come to perceive the television world as the real world and be more likely to want, request, and buy advertised products. In one study, emotionally disturbed children received instruction on distinguishing between real and fantasy presentations on television and in commercials. In comparison to children who did not receive the instruction, those who did were more able to recognize the difference between fantasy and reality on television, but the instructions had no impact on perception of commercials.

Several investigations by Thomas R. Donohue have studied the effect of television on maltreated children's value judgments and choice of role models. Overall, maltreated children prefer violent to nonviolent programs and violent television characters to nonviolent ones. Another consistent finding is that when maltreated children are asked for their reaction to a fictitious situation, the behavior they predict for themselves is more aggressive than the behavior they predict for their friends, family, and favorite television characters. However, they usually do not describe their own behavior as antisocial in nature. In fact, maltreated children sometimes report television characters as acting more disruptive than they would

behave in different situations. In most of these fictitious situation comparisons, the child's best friend is rated as the most similar to the subject and thus the most aggressive, followed by their favorite television character. Children usually predict that behavior of parents and other important adult figures in their lives would be significantly less aggressive than their own. Some of these investigations have also noted that emotionally disturbed children see television children and television parents as happier than their own families. One study found that abused children are less likely than nonabused children to be able to identify a favorite character, a favorite adult character, and favorite television families.

This inability to name a favorite character could be explained by a set of unpublished studies by Sarah F. Rosaen, which compared maltreated and nonmaltreated children in terms of their relationships to television characters. The results suggest that the attachment children have formed with their parents is an important predictor of the likelihood that they will feel close to television characters. The findings revealed that children who want a relationship with their parent but do not have one are the most likely to feel close to television characters, whereas children who avoid relationships with their parents because of parents' unreliability seldom form relationships with television characters. Because maltreated children experience both of these types of attachment to parents more than nonmaltreated children do, the Donohue results concerning the ability to identify television favorites may have occurred because that sample of abused children displayed avoidant attachment.

Another set of studies has focused on differences in reactions to aggressive content. This research has been of particular interest because maltreated children tend to be more aggressive behaviorally than nonmaltreated peers. Social learning theory has been extensively tested, and a consistent causal link has been noted between viewing violent content and aggressive behavior. Building on this research, Sprafkin and Gadow have conducted three studies on the relationship in maltreated populations. Two studies suggest that maltreated children have higher levels of aggression after viewing violent cartoons. One investigation found that older emotionally disturbed children (about 10 years old) showed more aggressive responses after viewing violent cartoons. In another study, researchers had emotionally disturbed and learning disabled children watch a violent or nonviolent cartoon and then asked the children to decide whether to help or hurt another child. Children who viewed the aggressive cartoon pressed the "hurt" button for a longer time, with emotionally disturbed children pressing it longer than learning disabled children.

Finally, a few investigations have found positive outcomes from exposing emotionally disturbed and academically handicapped boys to television programs designed to promote better problem-solving skills. In general, the children exposed to the television programs exhibited slightly more socially acceptable behavior, slightly decreased social isolation, and small gains in emotional control and personality functioning in comparison to a group not exposed to the television program. Measures of teacher's perceptions in one study supported these findings.

—*Sarah F. Rosaen*

See also Advertising, Effects on Adolescents of; Advertising, Effects on Children of; Aggression, Television and; Cartoons, Violence in; Cultivation Theory; Family Environment, Media Effects on; Fantasy–Reality Distinction; Fear Reactions; Parasocial Interaction; Social Learning Theory/Social Cognitive Theory

FURTHER READINGS

Donohue, T. R., Henke, L. L., & Morgan, L. A. (1988). The impact of television's role models on physically abused children. *Child Study Journal, 18*(3), 233–247.

Elias, M. J. (1983). Improving coping skills of emotionally disturbed boys through television based social problem solving. *American Journal of Orthopsychiatry, 53*(1), 61–72.

Sprafkin, J., & Gadow, K. D. (1988). The immediate impact of aggressive cartoons on emotionally disturbed and learning disabled children. *The Journal of Genetic Psychology, 149*(1), 35–44.

MEDIA EFFECTS, MODELS OF

Media effects, a central focus of the study of mass communication, are driven by two main concerns. First, mass communication is surrounded by a legacy of fear. Parents and educators are worried about the potential negative impact of the media, and such worries drive a good deal of research about children's use of movies, radio, television, and the Internet. A second reason for the study of media effects is the realization that mass communication can be an effective tool to promote educational outcomes and prosocial lifestyles. This awareness drives research on the educational, political, and health effects of media. Throughout history, thoughts about media effects have been framed by different models or ways of characterizing media effects. This entry presents two different ways to categorize approaches to the study of media effects: an historical approach that focuses on the degree of power of the mass media and an approach that focuses on the dimensions of different media effects.

HISTORICAL MODELS OF MEDIA EFFECTS

Models are simplified representations of some aspect of reality. Models of media effects focus on explanations of the impact of mass communication. Different models provide different explanations and emphases for how the mass media affect the audience. The history of the study of media effects is typically viewed as a series of models that differ in the relative power they ascribe, respectively, to the media and to the audience. Each phase of research presented a model that dominated thinking and research to explain how media effects occurred.

The first phase relied heavily on sociological and psychological paradigms of the early 20th century through the late 1930s. Early research on media effects was based on sociological views of the mass society that saw the audience as normless and socially isolated and on psychological research that focused on stimulus-response. According to the "magic bullet" or "hypodermic needle" models of media effects, mass media messages were seen as powerful stimuli that could directly and quickly evoke predictable responses from passive and socially isolated audience members. Harold Lasswell's 1927 research on the properties of propaganda falls squarely within this model, as does Robert Merton's research on the overwhelming audience response to American singer Kate Smith's appeals in a World War II war bond drive. This model, characterized as a direct effects model of media effects, viewed the audience as helpless to resist the well-crafted messages of powerful sources.

The second phase of media effects research emerged from evidence that media's power was often limited. Although news reports characterized the audience response to the radio broadcast of *The War of the Worlds* as widespread and profound, researchers found that only a portion of the audience was really frightened by the fictional tale of invaders from outer space. Studies showed that a variety of audience characteristics either magnified or diminished the likelihood of fear. Other notable research programs provided other evidence that media effects were not as direct as originally thought. The Erie County (Ohio) voting study found that in a presidential election, personal contact could be more influential than media messages. World War II studies found that soldiers' resistance to filmed persuasion was limited by personal factors and experiences. Research of the era supported a limited-effects model of media effects. This model held that people were powerful and able to resist media messages. Instead of studying the effects of powerful sources, this model focused on the power of the audience. Important concepts in this model are selective exposure, selective attention, and selective recall. In general, people were seen as selecting media messages according to their own interests and attitudes. If they encountered messages contrary to their preexisting attitudes, selective perception and recall would limit the impact of those messages. According to the limited-effects model, reinforcement was the most common outcome of media effects. In 1960, Joseph Klapper summarized the limited-effects model as asserting that mass communication affects media consumers through interconnected mediating factors and influences rather than serving as a necessary and sufficient direct cause of specific effects.

This model dominated until the mid-1960s. With the arrival of television, it quickly became clear that the rapid adoption of this new medium overcame the power of selective exposure. Early studies, for example, showed that television viewers learned about political candidates from campaign ads, even if they were not particularly interested in the election. New theories of media effects emerged based on the impact of consistent messages carried across media channels. These theories, however, focus on cognitive and affective media effects (i.e., what people think and feel). Maxwell McCombs and Donald Shaw, for example, found a strong agenda-setting media effect in the 1968 presidential election: Because the news media, for the most part, highlight the same issues, events, and people, the audience believes that these issues, events, and people are important. Thus, the media have the power to set the agenda for the audience. George Gerbner and Larry Gross found that the consistent patterns of television content—violence, overrepresentation of white

males, and underrepresentation of women, racial-ethnic minorities, children, and older adults—affect audiences' perceptions about their world. Cultivation research holds that exposure to television content affects people's beliefs about society and instills fear. This model of powerful but limited effects focused on television's impact on social reality—how society is configured and what is important. Although these effects reflect powerful mass media, the effects are limited. The agenda-setting model, for example, holds that the media do not tell people what to think but rather what to think about. Cultivation theory holds not that television makes people act violently, but that it makes them think that society is violent. Effects are perceptual, not behavioral.

This historical view of media effects serves an organizing function for mass communication research. These models might very well reflect their historical eras. For example, the uncertainty of a society between two world wars might have given the media more power. There are, however, critics of this historical approach. The limited-effects phase, for example, was useful to the broadcast industry, which was resisting substantial government regulation at the time. Most important, research on the children's audience certainly did not follow this progression. Some of the earliest studies about the impact of movies on children (the Payne Fund studies) considered how many factors in children's lives (e.g., parental influence, family and social environment) intervened in the effects of movie content.

This historical view illustrates that different models of media effects place different emphasis on either the media or audience as the prime explanation for media effects. The study of media effects is now driven by a range of theories or specific explanations that assert direct connections between various aspects of media content and specific outcomes of media use. Now, scholars find it useful to organize their thinking about media effects along specific dimensions. Some of these dimensions delineate the type of effects; others elaborate the conditions of media impact.

DIMENSIONS OF MEDIA EFFECTS

Cognitive-Affective-Behavioral Effects

This dimension focuses on the types of effects: cognition (belief and knowledge acquisition), affect (attitudes and emotional responses), and behavior (action).

These distinctions are important because it is clear that media content can have separate effects along those separate dimensions. Cultivation research, for example, focuses on how exposure to violent images on television leads viewers to believe that the world is a violent place (a cognitive effect) and to become more fearful (an affective effect). Communication campaign research is built on the awareness that researchers need to direct audiences through stages of media effects, moving from attention, comprehension, and memory (cognitive effects) to decision and action (behavioral effects). This dimension reminds us that cognition and affect are important effects, but they do not always translate directly into behavior.

Micro- Versus Macrolevel Effects

This dimension is another that focuses on the type of media effect—that is, the level of media influence. Microlevel effects focus on the impact of the mass media on specific individual audience members. Research on microlevel effects examines what individual children learn from educational programming, which types of adolescents might be more likely to initiate smoking, or what kind of messages would be persuasive to different types of audiences. Microlevel research generally grows from a psychological perspective and focuses on short-term effects.

Macrolevel effects occur at the societal or cultural level. Some scholars argue that a focus on microlevel effects obscures macrolevel effects. Focusing on how media affects individuals can limit our observations of the larger changes occurring around us. For example, research on the effectiveness of *Sesame Street* showed that all children—regardless of socioeconomic background—learned from the program. This research concealed a macrolevel effect, however. *Sesame Street* was contributing to a growing gap in school preparedness because children from higher socioeconomic status (SES) families learned from the program at a faster rate than children of lower SES groups. Some scholars believe that media's strongest impacts are the most subtle, involving shifts in society and culture.

Intentional Versus Unintentional

Some effects are purposive and planned whereas others are accidental. Intentional media effects include learning from educational media, brand awareness as a result of commercial messages, adoption of healthy

practices as a result of public service announcements, and changes in public opinion as a result of political campaign messages. Unintended media effects include aggressive behavior as a result of media violence, the adoption of unhealthy behaviors (e.g., underage drinking) as a consequence of advertisements, and political apathy as a result of negative political advertising.

Content Dependent Versus Content Irrelevant

Much research on media effects focuses on the impact of specific media content. That is, we are concerned about how the deluge of holiday toy commercials leads children to be materialistic. Or, we are concerned about how smoking in movies glamorizes and normalizes smoking. Or, we are concerned that children might model the aggressive behavior they see on television. Although there is a good deal of evidence that media content can cause effects, there is awareness that other media effects can be content irrelevant and grow out of media use.

The most commonly researched content-irrelevant effect is displacement. Parents and educators have been concerned about entertainment media's displacement of educational media. A body of research has examined how children's television use is linked to lower levels of academic achievement. This research is based on the assumption that television use (or, today, computer games and Internet use) displaces reading and schoolwork. Other displacement effects focus on how entertainment media use keeps people from becoming politically involved. In 1948, Paul Lazarsfeld and Robert Merton proposed that the media led to a "narcotizing dysfunction," in which political action is displaced by public affairs media use.

In another area of content-irrelevant media effects research, scholars speculate on how the forms of different media lead to different learning styles. Many writers have argued that television's pacing and commercial interruptions lead to shortened attention spans.

Short-Term Versus Long-Term

It is important to understand whether different media effects are enduring. Not all effects are long term. Some theories of media effects argue that media content teaches children unrealistic and stereotypical views society, but research does not always specify how long these effects persist. Is it possible that exposure to different media messages—or real-world experiences—can alter unrealistic perceptions? Understanding the persistence of media effects suggests how to mitigate negative effects and how to enhance positive effects.

Reinforcement Versus Change

The most visible media effects studies highlight how the mass media change the audience—for example, how violent media content makes children more aggressive. Or how political advertising leads people to change their voting intentions. Or, how alcohol advertising leads adolescents to drink. These are certainly important aspects of the study of the mass media, but there is evidence that media's strongest impact is reinforcement and stabilization. Because it is easier to observe change than reinforcement, we often forget the media's power to stabilize—to keep people from changing. The power of the mass media to reinforce might be stronger than their power to change. Violent media content, for example, might have a greater impact on some youngsters because it provides justification for their aggressive tendencies. In a media environment where audiences are exposed to countless persuasive messages, media advocates need to create messages that keep people committed to prosocial behavior.

—*Elizabeth M. Perse*

See also Desensitization Effects; Displacement Effect; Uses and Gratifications Theory; Violence, Effects of

FURTHER READINGS

DeFleur, M. L., & Ball-Rokeach, S. (1989). *Theories of mass communication* (5th ed.). New York: Longman.
Perse, E. M. (2001). *Media effects and society*. Mahwah, NJ: Erlbaum.

MEDIA ENTERTAINMENT

The media are an integral part of children's and adolescents' everyday life. According to the Kaiser Family Foundation, on a randomly selected day, U.S. children from 8 to 18 years old use media for more than 6 hours a day, and they primarily prefer entertainment media. Children's experience of media entertainment is an everyday phenomenon that is complex and that differs from the adult experience in many ways. Research has addressed a number of these differences, although the focus has been primarily on television use.

Entertainment is becoming increasingly important in everyday life, as the growing proportion of entertainment among all media offerings demonstrates. Some researchers already refer to "the age of entertainment" instead the information age. One possible explanation for the growing popularity of entertainment media is the decrease in the number of hours worked and the corresponding increase in leisure time. On the other hand, the economic situation has improved in industrialized countries, and more people can afford media hardware such as cellular phones.

Entertainment experiences depend on different factors: the supporting medium, the special format of the product, and its preparation, as well as subject-centered (expectancies, attitudes, knowledge, desires, moods, etc.) and situational aspects. Although entertainment is a mostly positive experience, one can undergo very different cognitive and emotional states during entertainment reception (e.g., suspense, sadness, frustration, or self-reflection).

ENTERTAINMENT PREFERENCES

Even very young children have a clear idea about what media content they want to experience. Movies with a mixture of humor, action, suspense, and romance are most appealing. But the content also has to be original, comprehensible, and interesting, and it has to offer a relationship to the media character. Age, sex, and socioeconomic status are moderating variables for these preferences. Whereas girls seem to prefer media content in which no one is hurt, boys like to see violence on the screen. Researchers find large differences between girls and boys, particularly in the choice of media role models. Preschool boys are interested in masculine heroic actors, such as sport stars, soldiers, and cops; girls like feminine figures such as fairies, princesses, or ballerinas, but they also accept male role models. Perhaps male actors normally have more attractive roles than women do and are therefore much more interesting as role models. When children grow up, these entertainment preferences become more characteristic. One reason might be the stronger affiliation to peers who exert pressure on children and adolescents to behave according to their gender.

DEVELOPMENTAL CHARACTERISTICS OF ENTERTAINMENT RECEPTION

Children's prerequisites for entertainment experiences are quite different from those of adults, as children are undergoing significant mental and physical changes and continuously experience volatile emotional and cognitive reactions, interests, and preferences. An important developmental feature concerning children's media usage is their capacity for information processing. Young children often have comprehension problems when using media, mostly because they are unable to distinguish between primary and secondary messages. As a consequence, they may consider secondary action more important than the central information of a narrative. Furthermore, children may perceive several connected scenes as independent of each other, complicating their understanding of the plot. Also, children's attention to media differs from the attention of adults: Children watching TV might display attentional inertia—the longer they face the screen, the longer they continue to face it. And vice versa: The longer spectators direct their attention to something other than the screen, the more difficult it will be to call their attention back to it. This phenomenon affects children's entertainment experience.

Another characteristic concerns the distinction between real and fictional media content. Very young children think that all media content is real. When children get older, however, they distinguish between reality and fiction, with the help of perceptual clues; for example, they understand that cartoons are not real. Later, they may know that Big Bird from *Sesame Street* is a person in a costume but believe the Cosby family really exists. Children's perception of media characters also differs from that of adults. Young children attach more importance to the appearance of characters than to their behavior. Children might evaluate an attractive person as good and an unattractive person as a bad character. Although children demonstrate an early ability to take the perspective of other people, a complex empathy with the actors on the screen is not yet fully developed in infants and young children. Finally, adults and children have different emotional experiences while using entertainment media. Research examining emotional reactions toward scary films has shown that young children are more afraid of concrete visual threats, whereas older children are more scared of humans with negative motives.

PROSPECTS

Although media psychology and communication researchers have been working in this area for years, some deficits remain: All too often studies focus exclusively on television and neglect the young users of other entertainment media. Future research has to fill this gap, as the usage of entertainment media starts earlier in life.

—*Peter Vorderer and Leila Katharina Steinhilper*

See also Developmental Differences, Media and; Gender, Media Use and; Media Genre Preferences; School-Age Children, Impact of the Media on

FURTHER READINGS

Anderson, D. R., Lorch, E. P., Field, D. E., Collins, P. A., & Nathan, J. G. (1986). Television viewing at home: Age trends in visual attention and time with TV. *Child development, 57,* 1024–1033.

Bryant, J. A., & Bryant, J. (2003). Effects of entertainment televisual media on children. In E. L. Palmer & B. M. Young (Eds.). *The faces of televisual media: Teaching, violence, selling to children* (pp. 195–217). Mahwah, NJ: Erlbaum.

Cantor, J., & Sparks, G. G. (1984). Children's fear responses to mass media: Testing some Piagetian predictions. *Journal of Communication, 34,* 90–103.

Duck, J. M. (1990). Children's ideals: The role of real-life versus media figures. *Australian Journal of Psychology, 42,* 19–29.

Hoffner, C., & Cantor, J. (1991). Perceiving and responding to mass media characters. In J. Bryant & D. Zillmann (Eds.), *Responding to the screen: Reception and reaction processes* (pp. 63–101). Hillsdale, NJ: Erlbaum.

Huston, A. C., & Wright, J. C. (1998). Mass media and children's development. In I. E. Sigel & K. A. Renninger (Eds.), *Handbook of child psychology: Vol. 4. Child psychology in practice* (pp. 999–1058). London: Wiley.

Kaiser Family Foundation. (2005). *Generation M: Media in the lives of 8–18 year-olds.* Retrieved June 29, 2005, from http://www.kff.org/entmedia/loader.cfm?url=/commonspot/security/getfile.cfm&PageID=51809

Livesley, W. J., & Bromley, D. B. (1973). *Person perception in childhood and adolescence.* London: Wiley.

Ritterfeld, U., Klimmt, C., Vorderer, P., & Steinhilper, L. (2005). The effects of a narrative audio tape on preschoolers' entertainment experience and attention. *Media Psychology, 7*(1), 47–72.

Valkenburg, P. M., & Janssen, S. C. (1999). What do children value in entertainment programs? A cross-cultural investigation. *Journal of Communication, 49*(2), 3–21.

Vorderer, P., & Ritterfeld, U. (2003). Children's future programming and media use between entertainment and education. In E. L. Palmer & B. M. Young (Eds.), *The faces of televisual media: Teaching, violence, selling to children* (pp. 241–262). Mahwah, NJ: Erlbaum.

Zillmann, D., & Vorderer, P. (Eds.). (2000). *Media entertainment: The psychology of its appeal.* Mahwah, NJ: Erlbaum.

MEDIA EXPOSURE

A recent study published by the Kaiser Family Foundation reported that American youth between the ages of 8 and 18 spend about 6½ hours with media daily, nearly 4 hours of which is television use. Is this too much exposure? Thousands of studies have established that excessive media use, particularly when filled with depictions of sex, violence, and other deviant behaviors can skew certain youth's worldviews and increase the likelihood of risky behaviors. Certainly, other factors such as parenting, environment, and biology greatly influence children's attitudes and behaviors. Yet, in our highly mediated world, the media's presentation of social reality almost certainly impacts youth's perceptions of society and acceptable behavior. Therefore, a conscious reduction of the amount of media exposure, ideally combined with parental mediation and discussion, would likely prove beneficial to youth of all ages. This entry examines two sources of concern among parents and educators regarding youth and media exposure: violence and sex. Efforts to curb excessive media consumption are then discussed.

YOUTH VIOLENCE AND AGGRESSION: LINKS TO MEDIA EXPOSURE

More than 1,000 scientific studies of various populations over three decades conclude that viewing violence on television increases the probability that viewers will be more fearful, will become more desensitized to real-world violence, or will become violent themselves. Longitudinal, cross-cultural studies have shown that children who watched more violence on television were more likely than those who watched less television violence to be aggressive as teenagers and young adults, even after controlling for various demographic factors. Violent or deviant behavior has also been linked with certain musical preferences, such as rap and heavy metal. It has been estimated that up to 15% of violent behavior in the United States can be attributed to television viewing.

SEX AND SEXUAL ATTITUDES: THE ROLE OF MEDIA

The pervasiveness of sexual content in today's media is undeniable, with American media being considered the most sexually suggestive and irresponsible. In addition to television shows, particular emphasis has also been placed on the sexual content of music videos.

About 36 studies published since the early 1980s have examined links between media exposure and the sexual attitudes, assumptions, and behaviors of youth, with the overall trend indicating that media exposure is in fact linked to sexual outcomes. The degree of association between media and sexual attitudes or behavior in these studies varied depending on certain demographic factors and the type of media examined. These findings yielded conditional yet consistent evidence that media exposure of youth relates to their sexual attitudes, behaviors, and expectancies toward sex.

Research demonstrates that youth learn about sexuality from the media. Television creates the sense that sex is normal for teenagers, and teenagers have reported normalized media depictions of teen sex as a reason for engaging in sexual activity. Youth have named media as a source of information about sex, sexuality, how to act, and the perceived prevalence of contraceptive use. According to studies by the Kaiser Family Foundation, although teenagers name parents and teachers as important purveyors of sexual information, between 40% and 60% of teens reported learning about pregnancy, birth control, sexuality, sexual health, or how to address sexual issues from television, movies, music, or magazines. We are left to question what sorts of information teens hone from media, considering that the teen pregnancy rate in the United States is the highest among developed countries worldwide.

EXPERIMENTAL EVIDENCE

One experiment, using a randomized controlled trial, assessed the effectiveness of an 18-lesson curriculum designed to reduce television, videotape, and video game use among third and fourth graders in San Jose, California. After a 10-day "TV turnoff" portion of the curriculum, the participants agreed to a media budget of 7 hours per week, and they handed in weekly parent signature slips to affirm compliance to the budget.

Using pre- and posttest peer ratings of aggression, children's aggression ratings for the experimental groups increased significantly less over the course of the school year than ratings of children in the control groups. Observed incidents of verbal and physical aggression were reduced 47% and 37%, respectively, for those children in the experimental group. Because of a small sample size, however, only the verbal aggression finding was statistically significant. There were no significant results to indicate that children in the experimental group felt the world was any less "mean and scary" than control group children did. Finally, children in the experimental group exhibited significantly less consumer behavior, as measured by the number of purchase requests directed toward their parents, than children in the control group.

Music videos have also received much attention in their potential to shape youth attitudes and behavior. One study showed a significant reduction in weekly violent incidents in a forensic hospital over a 55-week period, from 44 incidents per week to 27 incidents per week, after removing MTV (Music Television) from the available television channels, results that were further supported by time series analysis. While the experiment was performed with a specific population, it is unique in that it was able to actually measure effects directly attributable to decreased music video exposure. Longitudinal experiments such as this are normally difficult to conduct in the field with teenagers, many of whom attend to music videos on a regular basis at home or in the homes of their peers.

A CALL FOR ACTION: TURN OFF THE TV

In April of each year, Kaiser Permanente and the TV Turnoff Network sponsor TV-Turnoff Week, which encourages parents and children to discontinue use of their televisions for a full week and instead pursue other activities such as exercise, arts, crafts, and other endeavors. In 2004, an estimated 7.6 million people participated in TV-Turnoff Week. Other organizations calling for less media exposure and more media reform include Adbusters, KidsHealth for Parents, and the American Academy of Pediatrics.

—*Michelle Arganbright*

See also Computer Use, Rates of; Internet Use, Rates and Purposes of; Media Effects; Sexual Content, Age and Comprehension of; Violence, Effects of; Violence, Experimental Studies of; Violence, Natural Experiments and

FURTHER READINGS

Arnett, J. (1991). Heavy metal music and reckless behavior among adolescents. *Journal of Youth and Adolescence, 20*(6), 573–593.

Brown, J. D., Steele, J. R., & Walsh-Childers, K. (Eds.). (2002). *Sexual teens, sexual media.* Mahwah, NJ: Erlbaum.

Brown, J. D., & Witherspoon, E. M. (2002). The mass media and American adolescents' health. *Journal of Adolescent Health, 31,* 153–170.

Huesmann, L. R., Moise-Titus, J., Podolski, C., & Eron, L. (2003). Longitudinal relations between children's exposure to TV violence and their aggressive and violent behavior in young adulthood: 1977–1992. *Developmental Psychology, 39*(2), 201–221.

Kalof, L. (1999). The effects of gender and music video imagery on sexual attitudes. *The Journal of Social Psychology, 139*(3), 378–385.

Reddick, B. H., & Beresin, E. V. (2002). Rebellious rhapsody: Metal, rap, community, and individuation. *Academic Psychiatry, 26*(1), 51–59.

Robinson, T. N. (2003). The effects of cutting back on media exposure. In D. Ravitch & J. P. Viteritti (Eds.), *Kid stuff: Marketing sex and violence to America's children* (pp. 193–213). Baltimore: Johns Hopkins University Press.

Rössler, P., & Brosius, H. (2001). Do talk shows cultivate adolescents' views of the world? A prolonged-exposure experiment. *Journal of Communication, 51*(1), 141–163.

Strasburger, V. C. (1995). *Adolescents and the media: Medical and psychological impact.* Thousand Oaks, CA: Sage.

Villani, S. (2001). Impact of media on children and adolescents: A 10-year review of the research. *Journal of the American Academy of Child and Adolescent Psychiatry, 40*(4), 392–401.

Ward, L. M. (2003). Understanding the role of entertainment media in the sexual socialization of American youth: A review of empirical research. *Developmental Review, 23*(3), 347–388.

Weiman, G. (2000). *Communicating unreality: Modern media and the reconstruction of reality.* Thousand Oaks, CA: Sage.

WEBSITES

Adbusters: www.adbusters.org

American Academy of Pediatrics: http://www.aap.org/healthtopics/mediause.cfm.

KidsHealth for Parents: kidshealth.org

TV Turnoff Network: www.tvturnoff.org

MEDIA GENRE PREFERENCES

The study of media genre preferences pertains to individuals' selections of certain types of content within each medium (e.g., horror or documentary films, news or talk shows, rap or rock music, etc.). Media effects researchers attempt to determine how and why individuals choose certain types of media content. Individuals vary greatly in their selections and preferences of media genres. For example, some children are drawn to cartoons and others to sitcoms. Adolescents use their musical selections, whether rock, country, rap, or other, to differentiate themselves from others. The process of developing preferences for a particular genre is complex. Needs and motivations, individual differences, and moods are just some of the many factors that affect individuals' disposition toward various genres.

MOTIVATIONS

According to the uses and gratifications theory, individuals actively select media to fulfill specific needs and desires. Arnett specified five uses of media by adolescents, including entertainment, identity formation, high sensation, coping, and youth culture identification. Like adults, children and adolescents use the media for enjoyment; they get pleasure from watching a particular type of show or listening to a piece of music. Of course, what is enjoyable for one person is not necessarily enjoyable for another, so even when individuals have a common reason for using media, their selections may vary.

Adolescents also use the media to shape their ideas of who they are and where they fit in regard to others. A preference for a particular type of music, such as punk rock, may indicate an adolescent's identification with others who likewise enjoy this type of music. This choice of music may also reveal an adolescent's appreciation for a certain type of lifestyle, fashion, hairstyle, worldview, behavior, and so forth, that are associated with this genre.

Researchers have identified many motivations for using media in general and television in particular. Rubin identified six television viewing motivations of children and adolescents, including to learn, to pass time (or habit), for companionship, to escape or forget, for arousal, and for relaxation. He found that most children and adolescents watch television out of habit or when they have nothing better to do. Moreover, children and adolescents who used television for different purposes often selected dissimilar programs. For example, those who watched television because it was arousing, thrilling, or exciting preferred adventure or dramatic programs, whereas those who watched out of habit, to escape, or for companionship preferred situation comedies. Furthermore, those who watched out of habit were most likely to shun news or public affairs programming. Differences in individual goals thus influence genre choice.

INDIVIDUAL DIFFERENCES

The strengths of certain needs also affect media selection. For example, some individuals have a strong need for cognition or desire to think and understand whereas others do not. The strength of this need may determine not only the decision to use a particular medium, but also the type of programming that is selected. It is plausible that those who have a higher need for cognition would choose programming that is educational or informative. In support of this idea, Hawkins et al. found that individuals with a high need for cognition were less likely to pay attention to dramas and comedy shows than were those with a low need for cognition, but this difference was not found for news or informational programs.

Another trait that affects genre preferences is level of sensation seeking. High sensation seekers generally prefer novel and intense stimuli and often take more risks than do low sensation seekers. This difference may be due to divergent levels of arousal for high and low sensation seekers, such that high sensation seekers are less aroused by the same content or activities than are low sensation seekers. As a result, high sensation seekers prefer programming that elicits higher levels of arousal. Potts, Dedmon, and Halford found that high sensation seekers viewed more music videos, daytime talk shows, stand-up comedy programs, documentaries, and animated cartoons but fewer newscasts and drama programs than did low sensation seekers.

AGE, GENDER, AND ETHNICITY

The level of sensation seeking varies by age and gender. Arnett found that adolescents rate higher in sensation seeking than do adults and that males rate higher than females. This may explain why action-adventure films are most liked by adolescent males. Other genres associated with high sensation seeking include heavy metal and rap music, horror films, and violent programming, all of which are more commonly favored by males rather than females. Differences in media genre preferences for males and females may also be explained by gender role socialization. For example, boys may enjoy violent content because they learn that aggressive behavior is masculine. Gender role socialization may also explain why females favor romantic films (e.g., chick flicks) and musicals, whereas males tend to avoid these types of films.

Another variable that has been found to influence genre selections is ethnicity and race. Although during adolescence some feel the need to separate themselves from their ethnic or racial heritage, many embrace genres such as rap or country music, which is associated with their ethnic-racial background. In terms of television programs and films, viewers often select content that features characters of their race or ethnicity because they may be better able to relate to or identify with these characters.

Age also affects the types of media that children and adolescents favor. As children and adolescents develop and change, their preferences for certain media genres may change as well. For example, young children watch many cartoons, but as they get older, their interests shift to other types of programs, such as dramas and situation comedies. The same progression can be seen for other media, such as radio and film. Children often prefer Top 40 radio formats; however, teenagers often find a specific musical genre and pick radio stations accordingly. Although many factors, such as changing needs, may contribute to these types of shifts in favored genres, parental controls and media targeting also play a role.

ATTITUDES, DISPOSITIONS, AND PERSONALITY TRAITS

Personality, dispositional, and attitudinal differences also contribute to media selection. According to selective exposure theories, individuals choose media content that is consistent with their preexisting attitudes. Individuals who are racist, for example, may select content that confirms their supremacy over other races rather than content that refutes this belief. Selective exposure theories are supported by the findings of Rubin, West, and Mitchell, which reveal that fans of heavy metal and rap music have higher levels of aggressiveness and more negative attitudes toward

women than do fans of other musical genres. It is possible that the lyric content of many heavy metal and rap songs attracts adolescents who hold negative images of women or who are predisposed to aggressive behavior. Rap lyrics, which often focus on societal discontent, also attract adolescents who are generally more distrustful of others. However, it is not clear whether previously held attitudes always determine preferences for particular media genres, as selective exposure theories suggest, or whether the consumption of media content causes certain attitudes and behaviors.

Other variables that have, at times, been found to influence children's and adolescent's preferences for media genres include educational achievement, school commitment, acceptance of authority, and parental preferences. Roe found that school commitment and achievement were related to music and video choices. Specifically, adolescents who preferred harder types of rock music, such as heavy metal, lacked a commitment to school. Also, males who preferred violent videos had negative attitudes about school. One possible explanation for these findings is that those who perform poorly in school or who dislike it may desire to rebel against the mainstream and thus choose oppositional media such as heavy metal music and violent videos.

Traits such as being neurotic, psychotic, and extroverted also influence music and film preferences. Weaver found that people who were neurotic (i.e., emotional, socially isolated, and anxious) favored news and informational programming and dramas but avoided comedy and adventure programs; people who were psychotic (i.e., impulsive and nonconforming) liked more violent programming, dramas, and tragedies.

MOODS

According to mood management theories, moods influence people's preferences for certain media. The theory is based on the assumption that people seek to maximize pleasure and minimize pain. A person who is in a negative mood will want to change this mood and will select programming accordingly. Similarly, people who are bored seek exciting programming whereas those who are overly anxious choose relaxing content. Genre preferences may thus shift based on mood. Weaver and Laird found that women's genre preferences changed throughout their menstrual cycles because of changes in their affective states. When experiencing negative moods, women showed a preference for comedy shows; in positive moods, they favored drama or suspense programs. However, they were unaware of why their preferences had shifted.

Adolescents often report being attracted to media content that is congruent with their moods. For example, Gibson, Aust, and Zillmann found that adolescents reported that if they had recently been scorned by a love interest, they would choose to listen to love-lamenting songs, whereas if they had recently encountered a satisfying love situation, they would prefer love-celebrating songs. Therefore, it is possible that adolescents sometimes choose to listen to sad songs because these types of songs help them cope with depressing situations. Other genres of music may be chosen for similar reasons. Arnett found that adolescent males reported listening to heavy metal music most often when they were angry. Even though this type of music is characteristically bleak and is often criticized for promoting negative feelings and behavior, it can have a purgative effect. Some adolescents choose to listen to this type of music to release negative emotions and to improve their moods.

Media genre preferences—whether consciously or unconsciously determined, as suggested by the uses and gratifications theory and mood management theories, respectively—determine what media content people consume. Although many studies have examined the factors that affect these preferences, more research is needed to determine how these factors interact with each other.

—K. Maja Krakowiak

See also Adolescents, Developmental Needs of, and Media; African Americans, Media Use by; Depression, Media Use and; Gender, Media Use and; Latina/os, Media Use by; Mood Management Theory; Movie Viewing, Adolescents'; Movie Viewing, Children's; Music Listening, Uses of; Native Americans, Media Use by; Peer Groups, Influences on Media Use of; Radio, Listeners' Age and Use of; Selective Exposure; Sensation Seeking; Television, Motivations for Viewing of; Uses and Gratifications Theory

FURTHER READINGS

Arnett, J. J. (1991). Adolescents and heavy metal music: From the mouths of metalheads. *Youth and Society, 23,* 76–98.

Arnett, J. J. (1994). Sensation seeking: A new conceptualization and a new scale. *Personality and Individual Differences, 16,* 289–296.

Arnett, J. J. (1995). Adolescents' use of media for self-socialization. *Journal of Youth and Adolescence, 24,* 519–533.

Gibson, R., Aust, C. F., & Zillmann, D. (2000). Loneliness of adolescents and their choice and enjoyment of love-celebrating versus love-lamenting popular music. *Empirical Studies of the Arts, 18,* 43–48.

Hawkins, R. P., Pingree, S., Hitchon, J., Gorham, B. W., Kannaovakun, P., & Gilligan, E. (2001). Predicting selection and activity in television genre viewing. *Media Psychology, 3,* 237–263.

Potts, R., Dedmon, A., & Halford, J. (1996). Sensation seeking, television viewing motives, and home television viewing patterns. *Personality and Individual Difference, 21,* 1081–1084.

Roe, K. (1995). Adolescents' use of socially disvalued media: Towards a theory of media delinquency. *Journal of Youth and Adolescence, 24,* 617–631.

Rubin, A. M. (1979). Television use by children and adolescents. *Human Communication Research, 5,* 109–120.

Rubin, A. M., West, D. V., & Mitchell, W. S. (2001). Differences in aggression, attitudes toward women, and distrust as reflected in popular music preferences. *Media Psychology, 3,* 25–42.

Weaver, J. B., III. (1991). Exploring the links between personality and media preferences. *Personality and Individual Differences, 12,* 1293–1299.

Weaver, J. B., III, & Laird, E. A. (1995). Mood management during the menstrual cycle through selective exposure to television. *Journalism and Mass Communication Quarterly, 72,* 139–146.

MEDIA JOURNALS

Much of the research on children, adolescents, and the media is published in academic journals. Indeed, some have argued that research is not really knowledge until it has been published so that it can be shared with other scientists and practitioners.

Several distinctions are important for understanding journals. First, some journals are refereed, and other journals are not (the latter are often called vanity journals). When someone submits a potential article to a refereed journal, the editor asks a set of scholars (usually three or four) who are experts on the topic to review the manuscript. These experts critique the manuscript and make recommendations to the editor: to accept the manuscript for publication, to ask the author(s) to revise the manuscript (and make suggestions on how to improve the manuscript), or not to publish the manuscript. Ultimately, the editor makes the decision on whether to publish a manuscript or not, but the reviewers greatly aid in this process. For vanity or nonrefereed journals, either the editor asks authors to submit a manuscript, or the authors submit the manuscript and pay the journal to publish it. In either case, manuscripts are not sent to experts to review in nonrefereed journals. Refereed journals are generally considered better because having experts review the manuscript before publication generally improves the quality of the published manuscript.

A second distinction among journals is whether they are associated with some organization, such as the International Communication Association (ICA) or they are independent. Whether the journal is associated with a professional organization or not generally does not influence the quality of what is published in the journal, but generally, independent journals have more freedom because the organization that controls a journal *may* place limits on the types of articles the editor can accept for publication. Of course, independent journals also have limitations placed on them because the publisher wants to make a profit. There are three major academic organizations in the United States that study children, adolescents, and the media: the ICA, the Association for Education in Journalism and Mass Communication (AEJMC), and the National Communication Association (NCA).

The ICA publishes several journals, two of which include some research on children, adolescents, and the media. *Human Communication Research* tends to publish empirical research, some of which deals with children and the media. The *Journal of Communication* publishes a wider variety of articles, including a range of topics and research methodologies.

AEJMC also publishes a variety of journals, two of which include research on children, adolescents, and the media: The *Journal of Broadcasting & Electronic Media* and *Mass Communication and Society*. The *Journal of Broadcasting & Electronic Media* tends to publish empirical research (like HCR). *Mass Communication and Society* publishes articles from a number of different perspectives that deal with the media and larger social issues, many of which deal with children and adolescents.

The NCA also publishes a number of journals, including *Communication Monographs* and *Critical Studies in Mass Communication*. However, despite a large membership in the NCA's Mass Communication Division, the NCA journals do not publish a lot of research dealing with children, adolescents, and the media.

Independent journals that publish research on adolescents, children, and the media include *Communication*

Research and *Media Psychology*. As the title suggests, all of the research published in *Media Psychology* focuses on psychological approaches to understanding the media. *Media Psychology* publishes both empirical research and theoretical essays dealing with the media. *Communication Research* tends to publish empirical research on a number of topics related to communication including media, children, and adolescence.

These are the main media journals that publish research on children, adolescents, and the media. However, many other journals occasionally publish research on this topic; in psychology, for example, *Journal of Adolescence* (including a special issue on video games in 2004), *Journal of Adolescent Research*, *Journal of Applied Developmental Psychology* (including a special issue on children's educational TV in 2003), *Child Development*, *Journal of Personality and Social Psychology*, and *Journal of Applied Social Psychology*. In addition, there are many other specialized journals that publish research relevant to their topic area. For example, the journal *Aggressive Behavior* has published research on the effects of TV violence and video games. Likewise, *Addiction* and *Lancet*–both medical journals–have published research on health-related topics and children's television.

—*David R. Roskos-Ewoldsen*

See also Research Methods, Experimental Studies; Research Methods, Qualitative.

MEDIA LITERACY, AIMS AND PURPOSES OF

Media literacy refers to an expansion of alphabetic literacy and orality concepts to include the social uses of print, electronic, and digital media tools and records. The Aspen Institute Leadership Forum on Media Education defines media literacy as "the ability to access, analyze, evaluate and produce communication in a variety of forms." These forms include print, still images, moving images, interactive media, digital media, and audio.

In North America, the term *media literacy* was advanced in the 1980s by the Association for Media Literacy in Canada and institutionalized as a curriculum requirement in the province of Ontario. The Ontario Ministry of Education (1989) defines media literacy as

Having computers with Internet access is a key element in building media literacy among students. According to the National Center for Education Statistics, the ratio of students to computers with Internet access in U.S. public schools was 4.8 to 1 in 2002, compared to 12.1 to 1 in 1998, when it was first measured. The percentage of U.S. public schools with Internet access grew from 80% in 2000 to 99% in 2002. Efforts to implement media literacy programs in U.S. schools began in the 1970s, and today media literacy skills are directly or indirectly referenced in the learning standards for all 50 states, including standards for English and language arts, social studies, science, math, technology, art, and health. Advocates ranging from pediatricians to politicians support the work of elementary and secondary teachers in developing media literacy among children and adolescents.

SOURCE: © Nancy Louie/istockphoto.com; used with permission.

concerned with helping students develop an informed and critical understanding of the nature of the mass media, the techniques used by them, and the impact of these techniques. More specifically, it is education that aims to increase students' understanding and enjoyment of how media work, how they produce meaning, how they are organized, and how they construct reality. Media literacy also aims to provide students with the ability to create media products. (pp. 6–7)

The term *media literacy* is also one of a constellation of multiliteracies and, as such, is often used interchangeably with other literacy qualifiers such as information literacy, digital literacy, visual literacy, and 21st-century literacy, all seeking to convey a contemporary and expanded concept of literacy.

Media literacy is proposed as an outcome of the process of media education whereby practitioners teach *about* media as well as *through* the uses of a variety of media forms and content. Media education is characterized by two distinct and overlapping domains of media analysis and production, roughly analogous to the study of reading and writing in alphabetic literacy. Because of the complexity of literacy theory and practice, the term *media education* is often favored over *media literacy* by international media educators.

Media education encompasses the critical analysis and hands-on production of a wide range of texts and tools across diverse genres, including literacy artifacts found in popular culture, primary and secondary source materials, mass media, educational media, advertising, as well as blogs, podcasts, vodcasts, wikis, and the social uses of consumer media tools and discourses, such as text messaging. Practitioners also analyze media content within economic, historical, social, and cultural contexts, including the role of media institutions in society and the way that media aesthetics contribute to meaning. Media analysis activities are reinforced by hands-on, experiential production of print, electronic, and digital media in a variety of forms.

The aims and purposes of media literacy are diverse, reflecting dichotomies in the emerging field, akin to historical debates about the purposes and outcomes of alphabetic literacy for individuals, institutions, and societies. Practitioners hope to instill critical literacy skills, as well as media production skills that individuals can use to strategically communicate in a wide range of social contexts. Media literacy competency includes knowledge and skill indicators related to media construction, design of media content, narrative structures, commercialism, consumerism, political and social implications of media, the relationship between media form and content, the nature of media industries, media ethics, characteristics of media genre, representation and stereotyping, distribution strategies, media audiences, social uses of media content, and immersion in virtual environments. In short, media literate individuals are seen as active, as opposed to passive users of media.

Differences in the articulation of media literacy outcomes are rooted in the degree to which practitioners adhere to aims and purposes derived from at least two media education models. These models differ in that the first focuses on negative outcomes of media use whereas the second emphasizes its creative potential.

In the United States, awareness of the need for media literacy advanced as a by-product of media effects studies and the creation of television critical-viewing materials for children in the 1970s. From the perspective of the first model, media literacy is viewed as a prophylactic for presumed negative media effects, especially with young children. Sometimes referred to as a *protectionist* or *inoculation model* of media education, these approaches to media education seek to inhibit access to media content and tools thought to be harmful, particularly to children. Protectionist models for media literacy education promote strategies for critical viewing and parental control of media with children.

In contrast, *open-access models* of media education recognize personal pleasure in media use and promote self-expression in media production by individuals and groups in the belief that audiences, including children, purposefully negotiate meaning and are aware that media are constructed. Open-access models aim to advance media literacy education from strong freedom of expression foundations, stressing widespread media access as a cornerstone of democratic societies. This model favors relatively unrestricted access to tools, content, and distribution, with implications for related legal and policy issues such as copyright, media rating systems, media ownership, and community media standards.

Media education is integrated across both formal and informal learning environments, although data about the practitioners, approaches, and best practices in the field is still largely anecdotal and emerging. Media educators tend to emphasize the role of media analysis and production as literacy tools for learning, youth development, social justice, civic activism, artistic expression, and community building.

Formal media education programs are integrated across a range of disciplines, including language arts, the arts, math and science, and health, and indicators for media analysis and practice can be found explicitly in state and national standards documents across the United States, as well as internationally. For example, the state of Texas explicitly includes "viewing/representing" standards in the English, language arts, and reading strand of the Texas Essential Knowledge and Skills standards, which are intended for media education across grade levels. Other states also include standards language that encourages media analysis in the classroom across the disciplines. These standards serve as a rationale for increased teacher preparation in the integration, analysis, and production of new media across the curriculum in formal classroom settings.

Although hands-on media production can be found in public and private elementary and secondary schools across the United States, the term *youth media* is most often associated with production programs conducted in informal learning spaces by nonprofit or community-based organizations. Internationally, media production programs in both formal and informal educational settings are also referred to as *media studies.*

Youth media efforts place an emphasis on media production and grew out of technology access programs that were created to support a broader, more equitable and more diverse public access to information communication technologies and resources for all citizens. Youth media programs have overlapping missions related to the uses of the media arts for media appreciation, social activism, vocational readiness, academic preparation, and general youth development issues, such as preventative health practices and youth self-efficacy.

—*Kathleen Tyner*

See also Digital Literacy; Media Education (various entries)

FURTHER READINGS

Aufderheide, P. (Ed.). (1993). *Media literacy: A report of the national leadership conference on media literacy.* Aspen, CO: Aspen Institute.

Kubey, R., & Baker, F. (1997, October 27). Has media literacy found a curricular foothold? *Education Week,* p. 56.

Ontario Ministry of Education. (1989). *Media literacy resource guide: Intermediate and senior divisions 1989.* Toronto: Ontario Ministry of Education.

Texas Essential Knowledge and Skills for English Language Arts and Reading: Texas Administrative Code (TAC), Title 19, Part II, Chapter 110. Retrieved November 25, 2005, from http://www.tea.state.tx.us/rules/tac/chapter110/index.html

MEDIA LITERACY, APPROACHES TO

Media literacy is most commonly defined as the ability to access, analyze, evaluate, and produce communication in a variety of forms. In the United States, the concept of media literacy largely began with an emphasis on TV literacy; parents and educators were urged to protect children from misleading commercial messages and other harmful effects of television through discussion and analysis of what they saw on television. Since the early 1990s, media literacy theory and application have broadened considerably, going beyond this early emphasis on protectionism to focus on inquiry, empowerment, and education. Today, media literacy is considered to be a logical extension of traditional literacy applied to a wide range of media formats, including those that are print based (e.g., newspapers, magazines, books), audiovisual (e.g., radio, television, film, recorded music, video games), and digital (e.g., computer games, the Internet, podcasting).

The essence of media literacy involves critical thinking and communication skills that are developed through increased awareness of how media messages are constructed, practice in deconstructing or decoding those messages, understanding the economics and power structure of media industries, and training in digital technologies and media production. Specific media literacy skills include learning how to use media wisely and effectively, both in and outside of the classroom; knowing the basic language used in each media form; being able to judge the credibility and accuracy of information presented in different formats; evaluating the author's intent and meaning; appreciating the techniques used to persuade and convey emotion; being able to recognize bias and stereotypes in media messages; and being able to communicate effectively through different mediated formats.

MEDIA LITERACY IN EDUCATIONAL SETTINGS

Media literacy, then, overlaps with many other types of literacy that are central to K–12 and higher education, including information literacy, digital literacy, scientific literacy, visual literacy, and cultural literacy, and it has been identified as an essential skill for children and adolescents in the 21st century. In educational settings, media literacy training builds critical thinking, communication, and technology skills and has been shown to be an effective way for teachers to address different learning styles and show an appreciation for multiple perspectives. In the United States, media literacy skills are now directly or indirectly referenced in the learning standards for all 50 states, including those for English/language arts, social

studies, science, math, technology, art, and health. In social studies, the growing emphasis on document-based questions has led to wide acceptance of media literacy education as an effective pedagogical approach, especially for at-risk students and visual learners. Media literacy is also frequently used in the public health arena to address issues such as alcohol and tobacco use, nutrition, body image and eating disorders, and violence.

QUESTIONS FOR ANALYSIS

Five key concepts are widely recognized as fundamental to media literacy, whether applied to film, news, advertising, photographs, or textbooks: (1) All media messages are constructed; (2) each medium has different characteristics, strengths, and a unique language of construction; (3) audiences negotiate meaning, thus different people may interpret the same media message in different ways; (4) media messages are produced for particular purposes, including profit, persuasion, education, and artistic expression; and (5) media messages have embedded values and points of view.

Although there are many different approaches to the application of media literacy, most involve asking a key set of questions about any media message, such as Who produced it and who sponsored it, and what is their purpose? Who is the target audience, and how is the message specifically tailored to its members? What techniques are used to inform, persuade, entertain, and attract attention? How current, accurate, and credible is the information in this message, and how can we tell? Whose perspectives are included, and whose voices or perspectives are left out? What else is left out of this message that might be important to know?

MEDIA LITERACY, PARENTING, AND EARLY CHILDHOOD EDUCATION

Media literacy for parents and early childhood educators often focuses on setting limits for the amount and type of media used (especially with respect to television, video games, and computers), with initiatives like "Turn Off the TV Week" that are aimed at decreasing children's reliance on television as their major leisure activity. Recommendations for parents also include coviewing television with their children, discussing not only the commercial messages but also the stereotyped portrayals, assumptions about the appropriateness of violence, and other value messages. In early childhood education, media literacy typically includes teaching children to distinguish between program and commercial content, to identify tricks that advertisers use to make toys and foods appear better than they actually may be, and to be aware of misleading nutritional information presented in TV commercials for cereals, snacks, and heavily sugared beverages.

MEDIA PRODUCTION

Besides developing critical viewing and analysis skills, media literacy also involves teaching children and adolescents the technology and media production skills necessary to communicate effectively in today's world. Media production programs for youth have grown dramatically as video and digital technologies have become more affordable and accessible, and they have been especially effective in urban communities as a way of reaching disenfranchised teens. Often funded through afterschool programs or community

organizations, youth-based media productions now include news, documentaries, video poems, public service advertisements, and social action pieces.

MEDIA LITERACY RESOURCES AND RESEARCH

Information about applications of media literacy in different educational contexts is available through a huge number of published materials and online resources (see Table 1). Because the field of media literacy is quite new in the United States, there is still little empirical evidence documenting how well media literacy works, especially in educational contexts. Published research on the effectiveness of media literacy is scattered across a range of fields, including communications, education, and public health. Some studies have shown media literacy training to be effective in helping children and adolescents become more critical viewers of media, more skeptical about advertising and the

Table 1   Media Literacy Organizations and Web Resources

Action Coalition for Media Education http://www.acmecoalition.org
Grassroots organization promoting media literacy, independent media-making, and media reform.

Alliance for a Media Literate America http://www.amlainfo.org
National grassroots membership organization; sponsors biennial National Media Education Conference.

Center for Media Literacy http://www.medialit.org
Professional development; main source for purchase of media literacy resource materials in the United States

Just Think Foundation http://www.justthink.org
Works directly with youth and educators to build critical thinking skills and creative media production.

Media Awareness Network http://www.media-awareness.ca/english/index.cfm
Canadian web resource for media and information literacy with special sections for teachers and parents.

Media Education Foundation http://www.mediaed.org
Produces and distributes video documentaries on a range of media issues to increase citizen participation.

Media Literacy Clearinghouse http://medialit.med.sc.edu/
Award-winning website designed for K–12 educators with hundreds of links to curriculum resources.

Media Literacy Online Project http://interact.uoregon.edu/MediaLit/mlr/home/index.html
Online archive of articles, bibliographies, and other resources regarding media, children, and adolescents.

November Learning/Building Learning Communities http://www.anovember.com
Well-respected source for effective use of information/communication technologies to enhance learning.

Project Look Sharp http://www.projectlooksharp.org
Professional development; produces curriculum-driven media literacy materials for K–12 and college use.

Internet, and more resistant to persuasive messages and portrayals about unhealthy behaviors. Initial studies of media literacy integrated into classroom instruction and practice have found that it engages students and may strengthen critical thinking and listening skills, improve reading comprehension and analysis, and develop both writing and general communication skills.

—*Cyndy Scheibe*

See also Adult Mediation of Advertising Effects; Adult Mediation Strategies; Cognitive Development, Media and; Digital Literacy; Media Education, Family Involvement in; Media Education, International; Media Education, Schools and; Media Education Foundation; Media Literacy Programs; TV-Turnoff Week

FURTHER READINGS

Brown, J. A. (2001). Media literacy and critical television viewing in education. In D. G. Singer & J. L. Singer (Eds.), *Handbook of children and the media* (pp. 681–697). Thousand Oaks, CA: Sage.

Galician, M. (Ed.). (2004). High time for "*dis*-illusioning" ourselves and our media: Media literacy in the 21st century. Part I: Strategies for schools (K–12 and higher education). Part II: Strategies for the general public. *American Behavioral Scientist, 48*(1/2).

Goodman, S. (2003). *Teaching youth media: A critical guide to literacy, video production, and social change.* New York: Teachers College Press.

Hobbs, R., & Frost, R. (2003). Measuring the acquisition of media-literacy skills. *Reading Research Quarterly, 38,* 330–355.

Kubey, R. (Ed.). (1997). *Media literacy in the information age: Current perspectives* (Information and Behavior Series, Vol. 6). New Brunswick, NJ: Transaction.

Semali, L. M. (2000). *Literacy in multimedia America: Integrating media education across the curriculum.* New York: Falmer Press.

Silverblatt, A. (2001). *Media literacy: Keys to interpreting media messages* (2nd ed.). Westport, CT: Praeger.

Tyner, K. (1998). *Literacy in a digital age: Teaching and learning in the age of information.* Mahwah, NJ: Erlbaum.

MEDIA LITERACY, KEY CONCEPTS IN

Media literacy is often understood as the process of critically analyzing media messages, but it includes the ability to compose messages using media tools and technologies as well. In recent years, media literacy has been defined as an extended conceptualization of literacy, a view many educators embrace; in this perspective, media literacy includes the ability to access, analyze, evaluate, and communicate messages in a wide variety of forms. This definition arose in the early 1990s as media literacy educators from across the United States gathered at the Aspen Institute for a leadership conference on media literacy. The term *access* generally means the ability to locate information or find messages and to be able to comprehend and interpret a message's meaning. *Analysis* refers to the process of recognizing and examining the author's purpose, target audience, construction techniques, symbol systems, and technologies used to construct the message. The concept of analysis also includes the ability to appreciate the political, economic, social, and historical context in which media messages are produced and circulated as part of a cultural system. *Evaluation* refers to the process of assessing the veracity, authenticity, creativity, or other qualities of a media message, making judgments about a message's worth or value. Finally, the definition of media literacy includes the ability to *communicate* messages in a wide variety of forms (using language, photography, video, online media, etc.). Media literacy emphasizes the ability to use production processes to compose and create messages using various symbol systems and technology tools.

Media literacy is primarily conceptualized as a learning outcome within an educational framework that aims to give children and young people opportunities to learn about mass media, popular culture, and communication technologies. *Media literacy education* (or *media education*) are terms used to refer to the pedagogical processes used to develop media literacy. Because media literacy has developed from the work of educators from many disciplinary perspectives (including communication, education, the fine arts, and public health) in a number of different countries (including England, Canada, Australia, the United States, and others), questions of terminology, focus, and emphasis are debated. In the United States, two national membership organizations support the work of media literacy educators: the Alliance for a Media Literate America (AMLA) and the Action Coalition for Media Education (ACME).

There are many different types of genres and formats within specific media and communication technologies, and media literacy programs may address these specific forms directly. For example, media literacy programs have included a focus on critical analysis of newspapers and television news, print and TV advertising, magazines, popular music, and contemporary film. Many media literacy advocates and educators make use of a unifying framework: *key concepts* or questions that identify the central ideas associated with media literacy learning. The key concepts can be explored with children of different ages and with different types of media messages. These include the following:

Messages are constructions. The media do not present simple reflections of external reality. Rather, media messages are carefully crafted constructions that are the result of many decisions and determining factors.

Media messages are constructed using a creative language with its own rules. Individual media messages can be recognized within specific genres (e.g., cartoons, news, advertising, romance, horror, biography). Media messages make use of symbol systems, codes, and conventions that can be verbal, visual, auditory, musical, narrative, or digital. For example, in narrative films for children, the bumbling or evil adult is a character stereotype that is commonly used in creating conflict.

Audiences actively interpret messages. People construct meaning as they consume media messages. Message interpretation varies according to individual factors such as developmental level, personal needs and anxieties, situational factors, racial and sexual attitudes, and family and cultural backgrounds.

Media have embedded values and points of view. Explicitly or implicitly, media express ideological messages about issues such as human nature, social roles, authority and power, and the distribution of resources. Media messages provide the majority of the observations and experiences that people use to develop personal understandings of the world and how it works. Much of people's sense of reality is based on media messages containing representations that have been specifically constructed to embody points of view, attitudes, and values.

Media have commercial implications and exist within an economic context. Media literacy aims to encourage an awareness of how the media are influenced by commercial considerations and how economics and power affect message content, production techniques, and distribution. Many media products that children and young people consume are created as part of global business interests. Questions of ownership and control are important because a relatively small number of individuals decide what we watch, read, and hear in the media.

Media literacy can be developed within the family through informal communication between parents and children. Media literacy education has been implemented in elementary and secondary schools and in after-school programs. Over the past 20 years, there has been widespread growth in the resources and materials needed to teach media literacy to children and adolescents. A wide variety of instructional methodologies are used to teach media literacy, but most educators employ close analysis of media texts through questioning, role-playing or simulations, and media production exercises or activities. In the United States, most state education standards include media literacy outcomes as part of English language arts, fine arts, social studies, or health education, but implementation of media literacy is scattered and generally not widespread. Research on media literacy education has begun to demonstrate evidence about how children and young people can benefit from educational experiences that involve critically analyzing and composing messages using media tools and technologies.

—*Renee Hobbs*

See also Media Education, International; Media Literacy Programs

FURTHER READINGS

Center for Media Literacy. (2005). *Literacy for the 21st century: An overview and orientation guide to media literacy education. Part I: Theory.* Santa Monica, CA: Author. Retrieved from http://www.medialit.org/pdf/lit 2105.pdf

Schwarz, G., & Brown, P. (Eds.). (2005). Media literacy: Transforming curriculum and teaching. *National Society for the Study of Education Yearbook, 104*(1).

MEDIA LITERACY PROGRAMS

Media literacy education is the process used to develop media literacy, defined as the ability to access, analyze, evaluate, and communicate messages in a wide variety of forms. Children and young people can benefit from opportunities to learn about mass media, popular culture, and communication technologies. Media literacy programs may emphasize the critical examination of news, advertising, film, television, magazines, music, the Internet, and popular culture. Programs may also emphasize media production and creative expression.

Since the 1970s, media literacy has developed through the work of educators, artists, media professionals, and scholars who have implemented programs in schools and nonschool settings to explore mass media, popular culture, and communication technologies with children and young people. Many factors may lead educators to begin integrating media analysis and media production activities into the curriculum. Motivations may include a focus on increasing student motivation for learning; responding to ubiquitous elements of media culture, including sexism, violence, and materialism; expanding appreciation for alternative or noncommercial media; reducing the power of U.S. media corporations to control culture; enhancing technology skills; responding to student learning styles; strengthening students' recognition of how print and visual media work as forms of expression and communication; or enabling students to explore the constructed nature of cultural identity, social power, and values. Generally, most media literacy initiatives occur as the result of the initiative of a single individual or small team, working at a local level within the contexts of their school or nonprofit youth-serving organization.

Methods of instruction emphasize the process of critical analysis of a variety of print, visual, electronic, and digital texts through questioning and active discussion, as well as opportunities for children and young people to represent their own ideas through creating media in a wide variety of forms. Using critical questions to stimulate students' active cognitive response is increasingly a common classroom practice, and this instructional strategy has been extended to include the texts of popular culture, including television, movies, magazines, and popular music. Other instructional methods include role-playing, simulation, and media comparison-contrast activities. Media literacy has been integrated into all the K–12 subject areas, and numerous resource materials are available to support the work of elementary and secondary teachers in integrating media literacy into existing instruction. However, most media literacy programs, curriculum materials, and resources have been developed to align with the subject areas of English language arts and health education.

MEDIA LITERACY IN ENGLISH LANGUAGE ARTS

Media literacy has long been part of English language arts education in many K–12 schools in a number of English-speaking nations. In the United States, the National Council of Teachers of English first adopted policy language supporting media literacy education in 1975, stating that the organization should continue

> to encourage teacher education programs which will enable teachers to promote media literacy in students; and cooperate with organizations and individuals representing teachers of journalism, the social sciences, and speech communication to promote the understanding and develop the insights students need to evaluate critically the messages disseminated by the mass media. (National Council of Teachers of English, 1975, p. 1)

In 2003, the organization adopted a policy encouraging preservice, in-service, and staff development programs to focus on new literacies, multimedia composition, and a broadened concept of literacy. Educators with interests in media literacy generally adopt perspectives from the disciplines of the humanities, semiotics, and cultural studies to guide their work, although some make use of media effects or psychological research on learning theory. Literacy educators are now routinely using the word *text* to refer to all the expressive forms that people use to create and share meaning, including traditional literary genres as well as media and popular culture. In the United States, media literacy has also been used in large high schools as a theme to create small learning communities, enabling teachers from several subject areas to make use of media literacy concepts in their classrooms with a smaller group of learners.

One example of a media literacy program in English language arts is the Pacesetter English curriculum. This course was designed by the College Board as an integrated program on instruction, professional development, and assessment designed to support a rigorous fourth-year high school course. It includes substantial units on authorship, voice, film, language, and the mediation of culture through representation. In an evaluation study conducted by the College Board, teachers using Pacesetter English reported more use of film and video, and participating students demonstrated higher levels of both reading and writing compared to a demographically matched control group. Research has also provided evidence to show that media literacy can improve critical thinking and communication skills, including reading and writing skills.

A school-based media literacy program in a particular school might take many forms. At the middle school or high school levels, some teachers will include popular culture texts and media studies topics in their existing English or social studies classes. Other teachers may implement special instructional units on specific media genres, such as journalism and the role of news in society, advertising and cultural identity, or stereotyping in film or television. Others will examine similarities and differences between literature and film. Although plentiful teaching materials support teachers' work in this area, there is some resistance to media literacy education among educators. Because most teachers do not learn anything about media literacy in their undergraduate education programs at colleges and universities, many teachers are unfamiliar with the concept. In the United States, the No Child Left Behind Act has reduced the time available to teachers for enrichment activities like media literacy.

MEDIA LITERACY IN HEALTH EDUCATION

As a component of health education, media literacy curriculum materials have been created to address media violence and aggression, nutrition, body image, substance abuse prevention, and other topics. Most health educators in the United States now include some focus on analyzing advertising in the context of understanding substance abuse, including alcohol and tobacco. Hundreds of regional health conferences between 1995 and 2000 featured presentations and workshops demonstrating media literacy as part of health education, and health professionals are a major subgroup of the membership of the Alliance for a Media Literate America (AMLA), one of the two national membership organizations for media literacy. Major federal organizations including the Centers for Substance Abuse and Prevention, the White House Office of National Drug Control Policy, and the National Institute for Child Health and Human Development have supported media literacy as a means to promote child and adolescent health by developing curriculum materials, hosting teacher education conferences, or providing funding for programs. Research has shown that media literacy education can reduce susceptibility to tobacco use among children and increase skepticism about perceptions of the thin ideal in beauty

and fashion magazines among adolescent girls. In one study, parents of preschoolers who received media literacy education emphasizing nutrition and food advertising learned how to critically analyze television commercials about food products, which resulted in increased awareness of the need to communicate to their children about what is truthful in media messages.

YOUTH MEDIA PROGRAMS

An increasing number of nonschool programs are using media literacy concepts in their work with children and young people in after-school programs, summer camps, and other nonschool settings. The term *youth media* is emerging to describe the work of a broad range of nonschool organizations that use a variety of media and technologies to serve youth. Such programs typically involve older children and adolescents in some forms of critical analysis and media production activities. Youth media practitioners may emphasize media production as a form of social activism in local communities, and most youth media programs reflect the particular values of the social justice advocates, youth development specialists, media artists, and technology access providers who conduct these programs. Authentic representation and voice are emphasized in programs designed to give adolescents opportunities to strengthen leadership skills and advocate for issues of concern to them.

—*Renee Hobbs*

See also Media Education, International

FURTHER READINGS

Krueger, E., & Christel, M. (2001). *Seeing and believing: How to teach media literacy in the English classroom.* Portsmouth, NH: Boynton/Cook.

Kubey, R., & Hobbs, R. (2000). *Setting the research agenda for media literacy and health education* (Report of a conference held April 15–17 at Rutgers University, New Brunswick, NJ). Retrieved from http://www.mediastudies.rutgers.edu/mh_conference/index.html

National Alliance for Media Arts and Culture. (2003). *A closer look: Case studies from NAMAC's youth media initiative.* San Francisco: Author.

National Council of Teachers of English. (1975). *Position statement on promoting media literacy.* Retrieved March 1, 2006, from http://www.ncte.org/about/over/positions/category/media/107519.htm

Schwarz, G., & Brown, P. (Eds.). (2005). Media literacy: Transforming curriculum and teaching. *National Society for the Study of Education Yearbook, 104*(1).

MEDIA MATTERS CAMPAIGN

The American Academy of Pediatrics (AAP), the national organization for education and support of more than 60,000 pediatricians and pediatric specialists, has been involved in the research and policy on effects of the media on children and youth for decades. In 1983, the Task Force on Children and Television studied the impact of TV and suggested ways to emphasize and improve the educational content. Subsequently, the AAP Committee on Communications, later called the Committee on Public Education, created (and revised as needed) several policy statements concerned with the impact of media exposure.

In 1997, the AAP launched Media Matters, a national public education campaign to raise awareness and teach pediatricians, parents, children, and youth about mass media influence on health, including television, movies, popular music, the Internet, computer and video games, and advertising. Media Matters used a "train the trainer" approach, giving pediatricians knowledge and specific tools for educating children, youth, and families about media. In addition, pediatricians received information about the various health risks posed by media exposure, and they were encouraged to identify the possible role of media exposure in conditions such as obesity, aggressive behavior, substance use, or academic difficulties. A cornerstone of Media Matters is encouraging media education and promoting media literacy within families and communities, specifically learning and incorporating the ability to analyze media through critical viewing and thinking.

Pediatricians involve themselves in Media Matters through regional or national workshops and helpful resource kits. "Media Education in the Practice Setting" provides a written overview of the pediatrician's role in media and guidelines integrating media education into patient encounters. The material provides suggestions for healthy media use habits, echoing existing recommendations found in the AAP policy statements. "Media History," a checkoff form for parents about children's media use, allows pediatricians to focus on problem media habits and provide recommendations when necessary. Pediatricians often speak at schools, community events, and professional conferences or to the news media or government representatives, important venues for the dissemination of information about media education.

Media Matters includes other features supporting the public education goal of helping pediatricians, parents, children, and adolescents gain awareness about the influence of media on health:

- Campaign materials ("Media Education in the Practice Setting" and the "Media History" form)
- Public education brochures ("Understanding the Impact of Media on Children and Teens," as well as brochures for parents on media ratings, the Internet, and television) and fact sheets
- Scholarly articles on children, adolescents, and media
- Testimony on children, adolescents, and media
- The Holroyd-Sherry Award recognizing a physician's contribution to media as a public health issue
- A network of "Media Matters Team" pediatricians available for educating others in the field
- Support for the Los Angeles-based Media Resource Team (since 1994), providing consultation with the media industry regarding accurate portrayal of pediatric health issues
- Support for national initiatives, including National TV-Turnoff Week
- Media Matters website
- Links to other media education websites
- Letter-writing templates
- Leadership education conferences and workshops (funding dependent)
- Current AAP policy statements on a variety of topics, including
    Children, adolescents, and the Internet
    Children, adolescents, and television
    Gender stereotypes and body image in the media
    Media education
    Media influence and substance abuse
    Media violence
    Sexuality, contraception, and the media

—Marjorie J. Hogan

See also American Academy of Pediatrics; Media Effects, History of Research on; Media Effects, Models of; Public Health Campaigns

FURTHER READINGS

American Academy of Pediatrics. (1998). *Media education in the practice setting.* Elk Grove Village, IL: Media Matters.

Hogan, M. J. (2001). Parents and other adults: Models and monitors of healthy media habits. In D. G. Singer & J. L. Singer (Eds.), *Handbook of children and the media* (pp. 663–680). Thousand Oaks, CA: Sage.

WEBSITE

Media Matters: mediamatters@aap.org

MEDIA PRACTICE MODEL

The Media Practice Model is a graphic representation that illustrates how adolescents use media in their everyday lives. First presented in 1995, it grew out of a collaborative student/faculty project that explored how teenagers used the mass media (television, radio, magazines, movies, and newspapers) when forging their sexual identities. Since then, it has proved to be a robust way to describe the role of media in the lives of teens not only within the context of teenage sexuality but also in general. Breaking with a tradition of studying media primarily from a quantitative research perspective, the model was based on a series of qualitative studies that focused on adolescents' room culture. In their rooms (most often their bedrooms), teenagers of the 1990s listened to music, watched television, read magazines, talked on the phone, and did homework. A privileged few had access to the Internet. Millennial teens engage in these same activities in the privacy of their rooms, but they also spend time playing video games and connecting with friends through instant messenger, email, blogs, and online diaries and photo albums. Much of the time, teens' engagement with media involves identity work, the process of creating a sense of self in the context of their immediate and larger social worlds. Unconsciously or purposefully, they draw on the media to help make sense of their lives.

The media constitute a cultural tool kit from which teens can extract social capital, cultural models, mood enhancers, and (imagined) companions. Often, teens bring their finds from that tool kit into their bedrooms or dorm rooms, where they create a material culture of posters, collages, and media hardware. What shows up on the walls, floors, beds, and shelves in their rooms points to a below-the-surface media role that is complex, linked to developmental factors, and intertwined in everyday life. Room culture research confirming these realities led to the core ingredients of the media practice model.

Graphically simple but conceptually complex, the model draws on four important research streams—British cultural studies, practice theory in the tradition of Bourdieu and Willis, the sociocultural-historical school of Russian psychology, and mainstream communications and socialization theories—to explain the relationship between teens and media.

Adapted from Johnson's conceptualization of the production, circulation, and consumption of cultural texts, the model is drawn as a circuit to highlight the interrelatedness among its core components: identity and media selection, interaction, and application (see Fig. 1). The arrows in the model point to a chronological, not a causal relationship among these elements; their purpose is to suggest that teens' interactions with media are part of the dialectical, seamless process of becoming, of existing in the world. Media (meant to include media channels, content, and forms) are understood to be important cultural *mediating devices*, whose influence is amplified or restrained by active individuals engaged in the everyday activities and routines, called *practice*, that constitute daily life. It is significant that the influence of teens' everyday media activities is, in turn, influenced by their lived experience. Consequently, the term is placed above the circuit to signify that teens' differentiated, dynamic media practices will vary in accordance with their lived experience.

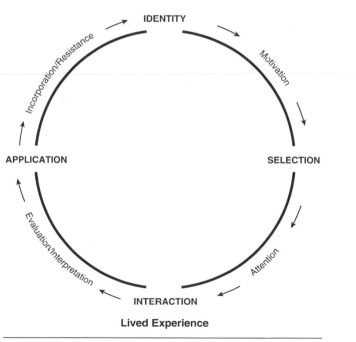

Figure 1   The Media Practice Model

SOURCE: J. R. Steele (1991).

Far more nuanced than the demographic variables of gender, age, and race, lived experience should be thought of as an individual's experience of *living through* a particular place and time with a unique body, intelligence quotient, sense of humor, threshold for anger, sensitivity about race, and so forth. It is a theme that Russian psychologist Lev Vygotsky took up from a developmental perspective in the 1920s. He emphasized the integral role of mediated action in development and insisted on the situated character of the cultural tools that mediate such action. In keeping with Vygotsky's perspective, the inclusion of lived experience positions media practice in the concrete sociocultural-historical reality that is unique for every individual.

Identity. We know from psychology and sociology that constructing a coherent sense of self is one of the key tasks of adolescence. Because teens draw heavily from media as they explore who they are and the "possible selves" they might become, identity is featured at the top of the circuit to underscore its central role in media practice. Research suggests that teens' sense of who they are (personal identity) and where they fit in the world (social identity) drives their choices about what media they will attend to under what circumstances (selection) and influences what they take away (application) from those encounters (interaction).

Selection. Technological advances provide 21st-century adolescents with a huge array of media options from which to draw. Possibly as a result of all these choices, today's teens and young adults are remarkably adept at multitasking. It is not unusual for a 16- or 20-year-old to talk on the phone, check email on the computer and keep an eye on the television, all at the same time. If the TV is muted, they also can enjoy their favorite music, possibly filtered through a surround-sound speaker system connected to a carousel CD changer that provides up to 6 hours of uninterrupted listening. Clearly, the amount of attention focused on such media activities will vary, depending on the immediate circumstances. Hence, motivation and attention appear on the perimeter of the circuit to emphasize that such intervening variables affect not only what media teens choose to attend to but also how attentive they actually are.

Interaction. Conceptualized in terms of practice, interaction is seen as active engagement with media. As such, it must be understood within the context of the whole person—the thinking, feeling, moving person who cannot separate the mind from the emotions, nor the emotions from the body's physiological reactions to affective stimuli. As such, interaction is defined as the cognitive, affective, and behavioral engagement with media that produces change. Evaluation and interpretation of media content are cognitive activities, whereas letting a song put one in the mood for love is a form of affective interaction. Like motivation and attention, these terms appear on the perimeter of the circuit to suggest their role as intervening variables. They are meant to be illustrative, not restrictive. Involvement, meaning-making, or decoding could readily replace them, depending on what was being explicated.

Application. This component of the model comes closest to what researchers traditionally have referred to as media effects. From the perspective of practice, it means the concrete and symbolic ways in which adolescents use media in their everyday lives as they work to become adults. The element of variability in media practice, albeit limited by content and the situated contexts in which media fare is produced and consumed, suggests that application is anything but fixed. Rather, teens can use media to reproduce in the self the attitudes, values, beliefs, and ways of being (incorporation) that they find in the media, or conversely, they can use media to move away from mainstream norms (resistance). What teens take from media, in the form of incorporation or resistance, is fed back into their evolving identities, affecting in turn the next or ongoing interaction with media. The Media Practice Model represents this seamless, dialogic flow.

—*Jeanne Rogge Steele*

See also Adolescents, Developmental Needs of, and Media; Cultural Identity; Developmental Differences, Media and; Media Effects, History of Research on; Media Effects, Models of

FURTHER READINGS

Johnson, R. (1987). What is cultural studies anyway? *Social Text: Theory/Culture/Ideology, 16*, 38–80.

Markus, H., & Nurius, P. (1986). Possible selves. *American Psychology, 41*, 954–969.

Steele, J. R. (1999). Teenage sexuality and media practice: Factoring in the influences of family, friends, and school. *Journal of Sex Research, 36*, 331–341.

Steele, J. R., & Brown, J. D. (1995). Adolescent room culture: Studying media in the context of everyday life. *Journal of Youth and Adolescence, 24*(5), 551–576.

Vygotsky, L. S. (1978). *Mind in society: The development of higher psychological processes*. In M. Cole,

V. John-Steiner, S. Scribner, & E. Souberman (Eds.), *Mind in society*. Cambridge, MA: Harvard University Press.

Willis, P. (1977). *Learning to labor: How working class kids get working class jobs*. New York: Columbia University Press.

MESSAGE INTERPRETATION PROCESS MODEL

The message interpretation process (MIP) model tracks media effects from an information processing perspective. The model (Figure 2) has evolved largely out of social cognitive theory, expectancy theory, and dual-process theories of attitude change. It proposes that logical comparisons and affective responses create routes to decision making that interact and feed into later-stage beliefs as messages progressively become internalized or rejected.

According to the MIP model, individuals apply heuristics to a message based on logic (such as credibility) or on affect (such as liking). They also can reflect on a message in considerable depth through logical analysis or wishful thinking. Furthermore, affect can append biases to otherwise logical analyses. College students, for example, incorporate media messages into their perceptions of social norms for other students' use of alcohol based on both media messages portraying the apparent desirability of alcohol use and the perceived realism of such messages.

According to the MIP model, individuals employ partly logical and partly affective interpretation strategies. These strategies require teachable skills. Accordingly, the model has been used successfully to evaluate media literacy interventions.

The model posits that individuals of all ages take an active role in their socialization through decision making that makes use of media messages. Because individuals process information through a series of decision-making filters, sometimes called benchmarks, a message can encounter rejection at any step. Consideration of these filters can prevent overly optimistic predictions of media effects. Conversely, evaluations that neglect the filters may underestimate the effects of media use because direct-effects models do not account for indirect effects that cumulatively have a considerable impact.

Perceived realism commonly represents the entry-level variable to the logic-oriented route in the decision-making model. Perceived realism refers to the extent to which a portrayal seems accurate and representative—that is, "like most people" in the real world. Realistic messages have a better chance of surviving a tougher filter, called perceived similarity, the assessment of how closely the portrayal reflects normative personal experiences. High similarity or congruence with perceived norms of relevant reference groups can lead to the next filter of identification, characterized by the desire to emulate a portrayal. Identification reliably predicts the expectation that doing something consistent with what has been seen in the media will bring positive results, known as expectancies, which reliably predict behavior. The entry-level filter representing the affect-oriented route to decision, which can bypass or bias the logic-oriented route, is how desirable or undesirable a message seems.

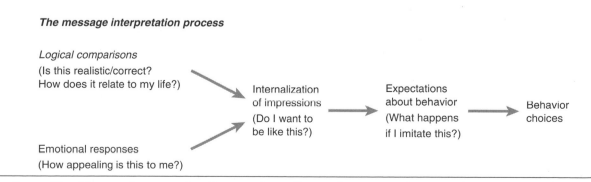

The message interpretation process

Logical comparisons
(Is this realistic/correct?
How does it relate to my life?)

Internalization
of impressions
(Do I want to
be like this?)

Expectations
about behavior
(What happens
if I imitate this?)

Behavior
choices

Emotional responses
(How appealing is this to me?)

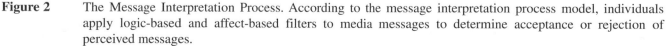

Figure 2   The Message Interpretation Process. According to the message interpretation process model, individuals apply logic-based and affect-based filters to media messages to determine acceptance or rejection of perceived messages.

SOURCE: Used by permission of Erica Weintraub Austin.

The MIP model has been tested on samples ranging from third graders to college-age students, with similar patterns emerging from the data, suggesting that it applies well across developmentally diverse populations. By identifying key interpretation-based filters that individuals use to evaluate messages, it can help explain why messages succeed or fail and can identify weaknesses in the interpretation process that media literacy interventions can strengthen.

—Erica Weintraub Austin

See also Adult Mediation Strategies; Information Processing, Active vs. Passive Models of; Information Processing, Developmental Differences and; Media Effects; Social Learning Theory/Social Cognitive Theory

FURTHER READINGS

Austin, E. W., Chen, M., & Grube, J. W. (in press). How does alcohol advertising influence underage drinking? The role of desirability, identification and skepticism. *Journal of Adolescent Health, 38*(4), 376–384.

Austin, E. W., & Knaus, C. S. (2000). Predicting the potential for risky behavior among those "too young" to drink, as the result of appealing advertising. *Journal of Health Communication, 5,* 13–27.

Austin, E. W., & Meili, H. K. (1994). Effects of interpretations of televised alcohol portrayals on children's alcohol beliefs. *Journal of Broadcasting & Electronic Media, 38,* 417–435.

Austin, E. W., Miller, A. R., Silva, S., Guerra, P., Geisler, N., Gamboa, L., et al. (2002). The effects of increased awareness on college students' interpretations of magazine advertisements for alcohol. *Communication Research, 29,* 155–179.

Austin, E. W, Pinkleton, B. E., Cohen, M., & Hust, S. T. J. (2005). Evaluation of an American Legacy Foundation/ Washington State Department of Health media literacy pilot study. *Health Communication, 18,* 75–95.

Austin, E. W., Pinkleton, B. P., & Fujioka, Y. (1999). Assessing pro-social message effectiveness: Effects of message quality, production quality, and persuasiveness. *Journal of Health Communication, 4,* 195–210.

Austin, E. W., Pinkleton, B. E., & Fujioka, Y. (2000). The role of interpretation processes and parental discussion in the media's effects on adolescents' use of alcohol. *Pediatrics, 105,* 343–349.

Austin, E. W., Roberts, D. F., & Nass, C. I. (1990). Influences of family communication on children's television interpretation processes. *Communication Research, 17,* 545–564.

Knaus, C., & Austin, E. W. (1999). The AIDS Memorial Quilt as preventative education: A developmental analysis of the Quilt. *AIDS Education and Prevention, 11,* 525–540.

Pinkleton, B. P., Austin, E. W., Cohen, M., & Miller, A. (in press). State-wide evaluation of the effectiveness of media literacy to prevent tobacco use among adolescents. *Health Communication.*

MOBILE TELEPHONES

During the past decade, adolescents and even preadolescents have begun using mobile (or cellular) telephones in unexpected numbers. In the early stages of its development and commercialization, the technology was often framed around its use in business and professional settings. However, the range of use and the groups who adopted the device far exceeded these early expectations. In the case of mobile telephony, adoption by adolescents—reported in Asia, Scandinavia and the broader European context, and Israel, and to a lesser degree in the United States—was truly one of the surprising dimensions.

Adolescent adoption has changed the dynamics of the industry and has exposed some of the taken-for-granted assumptions about the role of teens in society. Adolescent use was made possible through the drive by teens to interact with their peers and to cautiously emancipate themselves from their parents. It has also led to the reformulation of the mobile telephone market in the form of prepaid subscriptions, the rise of texting, and the establishment of secondary industries such as ring tones, icons, and mobile phone covers. The adolescent market also has contributed to the convergence of mobile music devices, camera phones, networked gaming, and a wide variety of other functions into a single portable device.

Adolescence is the context in which the adoption of mobile communication took place. Adolescence— a social institution that is particular to industrialization—is a phase of life where individuals can emancipate themselves from parents. Emancipation is necessary because in a rapidly changing world, the experience of the child will necessarily be different from that of his or her parents.

The peer group can be seen as the midwife of emancipation and provides a setting in which adolescents can participate in decision making, explore the boundaries of acceptable behavior, and test themselves in a social area outside of the protective—and perhaps stifling—familial sphere. The mobile telephone is an exceptional tool for this task.

Several specific social impacts of the mobile telephone on the situation of adolescents are worthy of mention. They include (1) microcoordination, (2) facilitation of identity development and emancipation, (3) safety and control, (4) the culture of texting, (5) gendering of the technology, (6) the role of the device in dating and in the exploration of sexuality, and finally (7) the role of the device in the area of bullying and deviance.

Microcoordination. Perhaps the most profound effect of the mobile telephone—for adolescents as well as other groups—is its contribution to the coordination of people in modern society. In an era when daily life often includes movement between a wide variety of locations (home, school, a job, free-time activities, entertainment locales, etc.) the traditional system of geographically fixed telephone locations is not as functional as mobile telephones. The latter enable users to call directly, regardless of the location of the caller and the person called, which allows for far more nuanced real-time microcoordination.

Facilitation of identity development and emancipation. The peer group is an important influence as adolescents become emancipated from their home of orientation and develop an independent identity. In the context of the peer group, individuals can participate in decision making, the establishment of peer style, and so on.

The mobile phone is important here on two counts. First, it provides a personalized communications channel that allows adolescents unprecedented access to each other. The peer group can engage in functional, expressive, and merely sociable interaction at the drop of a hat. Second, the mobile telephone—that is, the telephone handset—is an object of consumption on a par with other personal artifacts, such as glasses, watches, jewelry, and clothes. In its role as a fashion item, it lets adolescents test out their ability to consume appropriate artifacts. The decision to use one or another device is a decision regarding not only the functional aspects of the device but also the individual's sense of style. In both cases, the mobile telephone has a role in adolescents' development as independent actors separate from parents.

Safety and control. While adolescence is a period characterized by the individual seeking out wider horizons, issues of safety and parental control also get played out. Research has shown that the original motivation for having a mobile phone—at least the one that is used in discussions with parents—is that it provides a safety link. When adolescents begin to move into the broader world, parents are often motivated to provide their children with a way to get in touch "just in case something happens." The device also allows parents to gather information on their children's activities and to exercise some control over where they are and what they are up to, although teens can use strategies to manage this accessibility such as claiming that their battery was dead or that they had turned the sound off. The mobile phone also allows for expressive interaction when the child is away from home, for example, at summer camp, or in situations where parents are divorced.

The culture of texting. Texting is one of the quintessential teen media applications. This is particularly true in East Asia and in Europe. Adolescents were the first to use text messages, and they have developed the practice in terms of its linguistic dimensions and its role in the broader use of mobile communication. They have integrated texting into their daily lives, and the way that they stay in touch with peers and parents through texting has found a role even in the negotiation of romantic relationships. Adolescents have learned to use texting as an unobtrusive form of interaction, which can be used as a covert way to stay in touch while in more staid settings such as school. Adolescents have developed forms of interaction such as specialized abbreviations and slang, although this aspect of use is often overplayed in the press. Although current technologies are likely to be replaced by others that are more advanced, adolescents have pioneered the use of asynchronous, mobile text-based interaction.

Gendering of the technology. The mobile telephone has been adopted by male and female adolescents at different rates and for somewhat different purposes. Analysis has shown that males often adopt mobile communication devices and techniques earlier than females. However, the analysis also shows that females tailor the technology to social interaction. Whereas males may experience a stronger fascination with the technology in itself, females use the technology for social ends. Clearly, some females are quick to adopt technically sophisticated uses, and males also use the devices for social interaction. Nonetheless, males are often the first to investigate the potentials of the technology, whereas the females adopt the uses that facilitate social interaction.

Dating and exploring sexuality. Just as the mobile telephone gives the peer group an open channel for interaction, it also plays into the contact between adolescents as they establish, maintain, and end romantic relationships. During the preliminary stage of romantic interaction and after the nascent couple has met face-to-face, there may be a period when they exchange text messages. This is an easy way to work slowly through the process of determining the suitability of the other person. Messages can be carefully edited, in some cases, with the aid of friends. Texting may also turn into flirtatious or erotic interaction that is calculated to entice the prospective partner. Indeed, there is a correspondence between mobile telephone use and sexual experience. After the establishment of a relationship, the mobile telephone provides the couple with the ability to exchange endearments that might not otherwise be possible. It is reported that some couples have a nearly obligatory responsibility to send a last goodnight text message and a similar good-morning message. The mobile telephone has also found its role for couples in the process of breaking up. Reluctance to respond to text messages, inaccessibility via the mobile phone, and even "Dear John" or "Dear Johanna" text messages are used as a gentle—or perhaps cowardly—way to indicate that the romantic flame is burning out.

Bullying, deviance, and dangerous behavior. Finally, the mobile telephone has been used in various forms of deviance and bullying. In the United Kingdom, the phenomenon of "happy slapping," an assault on an innocent bystander, is videoed by a peer using a mobile phone camera. Bullying of student colleagues either by sending anonymous text messages or by taking illicit photographs of them in unguarded moments such as in the school shower is another common issue. Finally, research shows that teens who engage in a variety of deviant behaviors—theft, fighting, and narcotic use—also use the mobile telephone to coordinate among themselves. In the case of happy slapping and the text/camera phone bullying, there is clearly a link between the technology and the behavior. In the case of other types of deviance, the mobile phone has not caused the conduct but rather is used to implement an already existing behavior.

A final issue here is the use of the mobile telephone while driving. Although this is dangerous for all demographic groups, it has been found to be particularly dangerous for teen drivers.

Thus at several levels, the mobile telephone fits into the adolescent lifestyle, and because of this, it has become a symbol of youth par excellence.

—Rich Ling

See also Computer-Mediated Communication (CMC); Email; Instant Messaging; Internet Use, Social

FURTHER READINGS

Castells, M., Fernandez-Ardevol, M, Qiu, J. L., & Sey, A. (2004). *The mobile communication society: A cross-cultural analysis of available evidence on the social uses of wireless communication technology.* Los Angeles: Annenberg Research Network on International Communication.

Grinter, R., & Eldridge, M. (2001). y do tngrs luv 2 txt msg? In W. Prinz, M. Jarke, Y. Rogers, K. Schmidt, & V. Wulf (Eds.), *Proceedings of the Seventh European conference on computer supported cooperative work* (pp. 219–238). Dordrecht, the Netherlands: Kluwer.

Ito, M. (2005). Mobile phones, Japanese youth and the replacement of social contact. In R. Ling & P. Pedersen (Eds.), *Mobile communications: Renegotiation of the social sphere* (pp. 131–148). London: Springer.

Kasesniemi, E., & Rautianen, P. (2002). Mobile culture of children and teenagers in Finland. In J. Katz & M. Aakhus (Eds.), *Perpetual contact: mobile communication, private talk, public performance* (pp. 170–192). Cambridge, UK: Cambridge University Press.

Ling, R. (2005). Mobile communications vis-à-vis teen emancipation, peer group integration, and deviance. In R. Harper, A. Taylor, & L. Palen (Eds.), *The inside text: Social perspectives on SMS in the mobile age.* London: Kluwer.

Ling, R., & Helmersen, P. (2000). "It must be necessary, it has to cover a need": The adoption of mobile telephony among pre-adolescents and adolescents. In R. Ling & K. Thrane (Eds.), *The social consequences of mobile telephony.* Oslo, Norway: Telenor R&D.

Ling, R., & Yttri, B. (2002). Hyper-coordination via mobile phones in Norway. In J. E. Katz & M. Aakhus (Eds.), *Perpetual contact: Mobile communication, private talk, public performance* (pp. 139–169). Cambridge, UK: Cambridge University Press.

Nafus, D., & Tracey, K. (2002). Mobile phone consumption and concepts of personhood. In J. E. Katz & M. Aakhus (Eds.), *Perpetual contact: Mobile communication, private talk, public performance* (pp. 206–221). Cambridge, UK: Cambridge University Press.

Rakow, L. F., & Navarro, V. (1993). Remote mothering and the parallel shift: Women meet the cellular telephone. *Critical Studies in Mass Communication, 10,* 144–157.

Taylor, A., & Harper, R. (2001). *The gift of the gab? A design oriented sociology of young people's use of "MobilZe!"* (Working Paper). Guildford, UK: Author.

Townsend, A. M. (2000). Life in the real—mobile telephones and urban metabolism. *Journal of Urban Technology, 7,* 85–104.

MOOD MANAGEMENT THEORY

Mood management theory focuses on the ways in which individuals select media as a means of affecting or "managing" their moods. This theory generally predicts that individuals' media selections reflect, at least in part, motivations to intensify or prolong positive moods and to alleviate or diminish negative moods. Unlike uses and gratifications approaches, mood management theory does not assume that viewers are necessarily aware of their motivations for viewing or willing to articulate them. As a result, research from a mood management perspective typically employs experimental methods in which viewers' moods or affective states are manipulated, and resulting media selections are then observed or measured. The vast majority of research on mood management has employed adult samples; however, some research suggests that younger viewers may show patterns similar to those of adults in their use of media selections for mood management. A small number of studies have studied very young children, and some research suggests ways in which adolescents may use media for mood management.

Mood management theory offers numerous predictions concerning the ways in which individuals will use media to manage their mood states. For example, individuals who are overstimulated or stressed are predicted to select media content that is soothing or relaxing, whereas individuals who are understimulated or bored are predicted to select content that is lively and exciting. Likewise, individuals who are in bad moods are predicted to avoid media content that is negative or sad and to show preferences for media content that depicts uplifting and happy situations and characters.

Over the years, numerous studies have offered support for the basic assumptions and hypotheses of mood management theory across a wide variety of media content and genres. For example, research has shown that individuals in bad moods are inclined to select comedic entertainment (provided that the humor is not hostile), whereas they are disinclined to select newspaper stories featuring bad news. Similarly, individuals who are bored show an increased preference for exciting programming such as sporting events and game shows, whereas individuals who are stressed show an increased preference for more calming content such as nature programming and soothing musical performances.

There are several reasons why media consumption for purposes of mood management may become most pronounced during the adolescent years. First, adolescence is more strongly associated with intense mood swings, higher levels of stress, and greater self-reflection. Second, adolescents likely have greater control of their media selections than do young children. The idea that mood management may be particularly salient during the teen years and young adulthood is supported by research reporting that adolescents' consumption of media use is often related to exploring the "private self" and that their extensive use of music often reflects motivations related to emotional expression and stress reduction.

Whereas mood management theory has received abundant support in a variety of empirical studies, selection and enjoyment of some types of media content appear at odds with mood management predictions. For example, the enjoyment of tear-jerkers and the frequency with which mournful love songs are enjoyed by listeners (and particularly teen listeners) seem inconsistent with the idea that people use media to maintain positive moods. Similarly, a large number of children's programs feature decidedly sad or traumatic portrayals, including *Bambi, Charlotte's Web,* and *Old Yeller,* among others.

Under what circumstances might people find negative or sad media portrayals appealing? Perhaps surprisingly, some research suggests that individuals may be particularly likely to select such fare when they are in sad or bad moods—a finding that appears to be opposite to what mood management predicts. For example, Louise Mares and Joanne Cantor found that lonely older viewers were more interested in viewing entertainment featuring sad stories about older characters rather than stories featuring happy or successful characters. Furthermore, after viewing sad portrayals, lonely viewers reported more positive mood states than did lonely viewers who had seen uplifting portrayals. The idea that people in bad moods may be attracted to sad or negative media entertainment has also been demonstrated in terms of musical preferences. For example, Rhonda Gibson, Charles Aust, and Dolf Zillmann found that adolescents reported that they would have greater interest in listening to love-lamenting than love-celebrating music if they had been spurned by a romantic partner, whereas the opposite musical tastes were evident if they had learned that a romantic interest was reciprocated.

Although attraction to sad or negative media portrayals presents challenges to the assumptions of mood management theory, a variety of possible explanations for such preferences are consistent with mood management predictions. For example, some researchers have suggested that individuals may be able to make themselves feel better about their own situations by comparing themselves to others who are worse off. Alternatively, viewers who are sad or blue may choose to view sad entertainment as a way of reassuring themselves that they are not alone in their problems. Similarly, viewing the suffering of beloved characters may be informative to viewers in bad moods, as these types of portrayals may provide possible courses of action that could ultimately lead to mood repair.

Clearly, this list of possible reasons why viewers may select and enjoy media content that is designed to elicit bad or negative states is far from complete. However, these explanations share a common theme: the ultimate restoration of positive moods. Consequently, although choosing to view sad films or listen to mournful love songs may appear contradictory to mood management assumptions, such behaviors may well represent evidence for the validity and scope of this theory.

—Mary Beth Oliver and Jinhee Kim

See also Media Entertainment; Media Genre Preferences; Selective Exposure; Uses and Gratifications Theory

FURTHER READINGS

Bryant, J., & Miron, D. (2002). Entertainment as media effect. In J. Bryant & D. Zillmann (Eds.), *Media effects: Advances in theory and research* (2nd ed., pp. 549–582). Mahwah, NJ: Erlbaum.

Gibson, R., Aust, C. F., & Zillmann, D. (2000). Loneliness of adolescents and their choice and enjoyment of love-celebrating versus love-lamenting popular music. *Empirical Studies of the Arts, 18*, 43–48.

Larson, R. (1995). Secrets in the bedroom: Adolescents' private use of media. *Journal of Youth and Adolescence, 24*, 535–550.

Mares, M. L., & Cantor, J. (1992). Elderly viewers' responses to televised portrayals of old age: Empathy and mood management versus social comparison. *Communication Research, 19*, 459–478.

Masters, J. C., Ford, M. E., & Arend, R. A. (1983). Children's strategies for controlling affective responses to aversive social experience. *Motivation and Emotion, 7*, 103–116.

North, A. C., Hargreaves, D. J., & O'Neill, S. A. (2000). The importance of music to adolescents. *British Journal of Educational Psychology, 70*, 255–272.

Oliver, M. B. (2003). Mood management and selective exposure. In J. Bryant, D. Roskos-Ewoldsen, & J. Cantor (Eds.), *Communication and emotion: Essays in honor of Dolf Zillmann* (pp. 85–106). Mahwah, NJ: Erlbaum.

Zillmann, D. (1988). Mood management through communication choices. *American Behavioral Scientist, 31*, 327–340.

Zillmann, D. (2000). Mood management in the context of selective exposure theory. In M. E. Roloff (Ed.), *Communication yearbook* (Vol. 23, pp. 103–123). Thousand Oaks, CA: Sage.

MOTHERHOOD PROJECT

As a subdivision of the nonprofit organization, the Institute for American Values, the Motherhood Project strives to educate and promote the renewed concept of motherhood and help mothers meet the challenges of mothering in modern society.

Enola Aird founded the Motherhood Project in 1999. In the past few years, the Motherhood Project has been actively holding group meetings of mothers, organizing symposiums discussing issues directly dealing with the welfare of mothers and children, advocating children's and mothers' rights before Congress, and conducting original research examining the relationships between motherhood and society. The Motherhood Project has become one of the most influential advocacy groups for mothers and children. The Motherhood Project is advised by the Mothers' Council, which consists of mothers of diverse backgrounds.

The relationship between advertising and children's well-being is one of the major concerns of the Motherhood Project. In 2001, it published the report, *Watch Out for Children: A Mother's Statement to Advertisers*, in which it accuses the advertisers of harming children by instilling values that are at odds with the values mothers try to teach their children.

Self-control and caring for others are two examples. The report argues that all adults should watch out for children. Based on the values that mothers cherish to nurture their children, the Motherhood Project put forward a "Mother's Code for Advertisers," which takes account of all types of advertising. The code calls for advertisers to refrain from advertising to children at schools, targeting children under the age of 8, engaging in product placement in media programs, conducting research to develop advertising and marketing aimed at children and adolescents, advertising the concepts of selfishness and instant gratification, and sponsoring programs featuring gratuitous sex or violence.

Following up on *Watch Out for Children: A Mother's Statement to Advertisers*, in 2004, the Motherhood Project issued *A Mother's Day Report*, an open letter to the advertisers and marketers. The Mothers' Council sent out 66 letters to various industry leaders to urge them to take immediate actions to improve their self-regulatory practices. In addition, the Council also calls for the Children's Advertising Review Unit (CARU) of the National Advertising Review Committee to develop new guidelines to keep up with the new trends in advertising practices, create a seal of approval for those who adhere to the guidelines, and diversify its advisory board. Many companies responded to the open letter of the Motherhood Project. Moreover, both CARU and the Entertainment Software Rating Board have agreed to consider the suggestions.

The Motherhood Project also published its *Motherhood Study* in May 2005, in which it surveyed more than 2,000 mothers about the attitudes, values, and concerns that they have about motherhood in contemporary society. Among other findings, the mothers in the survey expressed concern about the influence of media, in particular advertisements, on their children. In the report, the Motherhood Project encouraged all mothers to voice their views and concerns to the organization and urged the public to listen to what mothers are saying.

—*Xiaomei Cai*

See also Advertising, Regulation of; Children's Advertising Review Unit (CARU)

WEBSITE

The Motherhood Project: http://www.motherhoodproject.org

MOTHERS, MEDIA PORTRAYALS OF

The word *mother* packs an emotional wallop, so it is not surprising that motherhood traditionally attracts attention in the media. Mothers nab headlines for juggling families and careers—and for killing their children. Depictions of mothers elicit laughter and tears on television and in movies. Their presence or absence in the workplace has shaped magazine content for decades. Since the 1980s, however, motherhood has sparked an unusual degree of interest and controversy. In 2000, *Ms. Magazine* declared it a media fixation.

MOTHERS IN THE NEWS

Journalistic portrayals of mothers tend to focus on the extremes—the exemplary and the horrific. Exemplary mothers include celebrities, who typically manage to maintain their looks, homes, and careers while still making time for their families. One example is Catherine Zeta-Jones, who appeared glamorous and triumphant at the Academy Awards in 2003 a few weeks before giving birth to her second child. At the other extreme are "killer moms." Examples include Susan Smith and Andrea Yates, mothers who drowned their children.

Less sensational mothers often appear in news stories about single motherhood, minority issues, and family health. Single mothers often have been described as single by choice, dependent on the government, or less than ideal parents, as was television's Murphy Brown. Minority mothers are disproportionately depicted in the news as "welfare queens" and linked with abusive use of alcohol and crack (a form of cocaine). Mothers in general are depicted as responsible for their children's health and welfare.

MOTHERS IN MAGAZINES

Magazines depict mothers in terms of contradictions. Some portrayals affirm a particular role; others condemn it. In mainstream magazines, four types of maternal contradictions are prominent: (1) mothers who are selfless/selfish, (2) mothers who foster independence/dependence in children, (3) mothers who succeed/fail in the domestic sphere or fail/succeed in the public sphere, and (4) mothers who are natural and instinctive/need expert help. Such depictions have fostered what some observers describe as "mother wars," pitting at-home and employed mothers against each other.

Contradictory portrayals have evolved over several decades. In the 1950s, popular women's magazines such as *Parents, Ladies Home Journal,* and *Good Housekeeping* reflected the type of families that sociologists had pronounced "normal," those with the father as breadwinner and the mother as homemaker. Mothers were depicted as nurturing, loving, and moral. The 1960s brought two portraits of mothers—career mothers/serious community volunteers and good wife/mother. Working mothers rose to prominence in the 1970s. Magazines depicted them as "wonder women." *Working Mother,* a magazine tailored to the needs of working women, championed federally funded day care. Magazines restyled housewives as *homemakers* engaged in the "most noble profession." In the 1980s, the image of working mothers lost much of its glamour. Magazines portrayed working mothers as neurotic and stressed out. Neotraditional mothers, who abandoned or put on hold their careers for the sake of their children, also were featured. In the 1990s, "new momism," which was characterized by mothers' dedication to their children, began to resemble the "feminine mystique" of the 1950s. Working mothers were portrayed as "absentee moms."

Maternal contradictions also characterize portrayals of lesbian mothers. In the straight press, lesbian mothers have alternately been labeled *nonprocreative*—a position inherently opposed to family values—or recruiters for an abnormal lifestyle, with normal families assumed to be heterosexual. Lesbian mothers have been depicted in the lesbian press as both traitors to their sexuality and leaders among feminists.

MOTHERS IN VISUAL MEDIA

Mothers have been portrayed on television since its inception, figuring prominently in situation comedies and soap operas. In the late 1940s and early 1950s, sitcom mothers played by Lucille Ball, Gertrude Berg, and others often refused to stay in their place, resisting the notion that women's roles should be confined to the domestic arena. By the late 1950s and early 1960s, these characters had been succeeded by more submissive mothers in shows such as *Father Knows Best* and *Leave It to Beaver.* The feminist movement brought more working mothers to television, primarily in blue-collar and service sector jobs. The majority, however, were full-time homemakers, as portrayed in shows such as *The Waltons.* In the 1980s, most TV women began going to work, and many TV mothers held glamorous jobs, as did Clare, the lawyer-mom on *The Cosby Show.* By the 1990s, the work status of television women more closely matched that of real women, with clerical work the most common job in both cases.

Motherhood has played an increasingly prominent role in soap operas. In soaps of the 1970s, pregnancies occurred only rarely and often had negative results. In the 1980s and 1990s, however, an increasing number of characters were portrayed as pregnant women or mothers. Themes often focused on marriage, shaky relationships, speculation about who fathered the child, and numerous health complications.

Television advertisements of the 1970s typically portrayed women as mothers or housewives and often depicted them as being of low intelligence. By 2000, women were more likely to be shown as nurturers. TV shows about black families typically portray mothers as single parents, good humored and dominant, efficient, and effective decision makers. Jewish and Italian mothers, in contrast, often are depicted as selfish, pushy, domineering, or whiny.

Film portrayals of mothers often parallel those of other media. Hitchcock's films portrayed both good and bad mothers, but three of his most famous—*Psycho, Marnie,* and *The Birds*—depicted terrible mothers who created life and then drew it in again. Imagery of false or destructive mothers is a staple of science fiction films. Disney films typically have marginalized mothers and elevated fathers. Several films of the 1980s and early 1990s employed portrayals of both career and traditional mothers, with career mothers portrayed less sympathetically.

MOTHERS IN OTHER MEDIA

Few studies have examined portrayals of mothers in auditory media, although one survey found that working mothers prefer radio to other types of mass media. Topics offered by radio shows that target mothers appear to parallel those of women's magazines. Similarly, few studies have focused on depictions of mothers on the Internet. Author Lisa Nakamura, however, dismisses as myth the notion that cyberspace is raceless, genderless, and sexuality free.

—*Myra Gregory Knight*

See also Family, Television Portrayals of; Family Relationships, Television and; Parenting Styles

FURTHER READINGS

Barnett, B. (2005). Perfect mother or artist of obscenity? Narrative and myth in a qualitative analysis of press coverage of the Andrea Yates murders. *Journal of Communication Inquiry, 29*(1), 9–30.

Crain, R. (2001, March 26). Husbands are boys and wives their mothers in the land of ads. *Advertising Age, 72*(13), 22.

Douglas, S. J., & Michaels, M. W. (2004). *The mommy myth: The idealization of motherhood and how it has undermined women.* New York: Free Press.

Gilliam, F. D. (1999). The "welfare queen" experiment. *Nieman Reports, 53*(2), 49–52.

Johnston, D. D., & Swanson, D. H. (2003). Invisible mothers: A content analysis of motherhood ideologies and myths in magazines. *Sex Roles, 49*(1/2), 21–33.

Nakamura, L. (2002). *Cybertypes: Race, ethnicity, and identity on the Internet.* New York: Routledge.

Steenland, S. (1995). Content analysis of the image of women on television. In C. M. Lont (Ed.), *Women and media: Content/careers/criticism* (pp. 179–189). Belmont, CA: Wadsworth.

Thompson, J. M. (2002). *Mommy queerest.* Amherst: University of Massachusetts.

MOTION PICTURE ASSOCIATION OF AMERICA (MPAA)

The Motion Picture Association of America (MPAA) is a trade association for the movie industry in the United States. The MPAA is best known for administering the voluntary film rating system. It is also active in lobbying on behalf of its members, including a campaign to preserve copyright interests in the digital age. MPAA membership consists of seven major studios: Disney, Sony, MGM, Paramount, Twentieth Century Fox, Universal, and Warner Brothers.

The MPAA was formed in 1922 in an effort to quell criticism of provocative movie content and deal with the public image of the industry in the wake of several high-profile scandals involving movie stars. Members of the movie industry accepted this self-regulatory system as preferable to the threat of government censorship.

One of the primary tasks of the MPAA is to assign ratings to forthcoming films. The purpose of the ratings is to provide parents guidance in making judgments about what movies they allow their children to see. The current rating system is largely age-based and includes:

G—General Audiences: All ages admitted

PG—Parental Guidance Suggested: Some material may not be suitable for children

PG-13—Parents Strongly Cautioned: Some material may be in appropriate for children under 13

R—Restricted: Under 17 requires accompanying parent or adult guardian

NC-17: No one 17 and younger admitted

In addition to rating movies themselves, advertisements and preshow trailers for films must also be screened by the MPAA.

The ratings system is criticized on several different levels. One argument is that the system as administered constrains depictions of sex far more than it does violence. Also, there is concern that the system encourages ratings based on relatively inconsequential elements of the movie (like the number of times sexually suggestive language is used) rather than looking at the film as a whole (e.g., does it responsibly portray the consequences of sexual activity). Furthermore, recent studies have demonstrated "ratings creep," whereby the MPAA tolerates content in a movie that a few years ago would have received a more restrictive rating.

In recent years, the MPAA has also become active in lobbying for changes in copyright laws to protect against unauthorized distribution of movies. The organization has pursued lawsuits against file-sharing sites on the World Wide Web, under the auspices of the Digital Millennium Copyright Act. Along with the Recording Industry Association of America, the MPAA has also filed lawsuits against specific individuals (mostly adolescents and college students) who have illegally downloaded copyrighted material.

Jack Valenti was president of the MPAA from 1966 to 2004. He had a high profile as an active lobbyist for the movie industry. Since Valenti's retirement, Dan Glickman, who was a Cabinet member under President Clinton, is serving as the organization's president.

—*Jennifer L. Lambe*

See also Aggression, Movies and; Movies (various entries); Peer Groups, File Sharing Among; Ratings Systems, Parental Use of; Regulation, Industry Self-Regulation; Regulation, Movies

WEBSITE

The Motion Picture Association of America: http://www.mpaa.org

MOVIES, HISTORY OF

Children and adolescents have been an important segment of the movie audience since the earliest years of the motion pictures. Until the advent of television, the movies were a regular feature of children's leisure hours, and they continue to be today in their modern incarnation on video and DVD. Young people have also been instrumental in determining what audiences saw (or did not see) at the movies. The public's concerns about the effects of movies on children and Hollywood's desire to appeal to the lucrative youth market have profoundly shaped American cinema.

THE SILENT FILM ERA

The earliest motion pictures were exhibited in the 1890s, first as a curiosity, then gaining popularity as an inexpensive entertainment shown in nickelodeons. By the 1910s, there were more than 10,000 nickelodeons in the United States, and motion pictures had become

Cast members of the *Our Gang* series go for a walk. Harold ("Hal") Roach produced this series of short comedies starting in 1922 and continuing until 1938, when he sold the series to MGM. Production of the comedies continued until 1944. The films, later syndicated for television as *The Little Rascals*, broke new ground with their naturalistic portrayals of children and integrated cast of white and African American characters. However, many critics charge that the films perpetuated the "pickaninny" stereotype of black children by depicting them as simple-minded, raggedy buffoons who spoke in exaggerated dialect.

SOURCE: © John Springer Collection/CORBIS; used with permission.

a mass media. Some of the earliest motion pictures were based on children's literature, such as George Méliès's *Cinderella* (1899), or featured children, such as Louis Lumiére's *Watering the Gardener* (1895).

In the silent film era of the 1920s, children largely watched the same films viewed by adults. Movie stars popular with young people at that time included Buster Keaton, Mary Pickford, Douglas Fairbanks, and the Keystone Cops. Charlie Chaplin was one of the most beloved entertainers of that period, and his 1921 film *The Kid* drew particularly from a young audience due to the performance of his child co-star, Jackie Coogan. Young audiences also reveled in the cartoon antics of Felix the Cat, the heroics of a German shepherd named Rin Tin Tin, and the adventures of Tom Mix, a movie cowboy notorious for his amazing stunts astride a horse. Youngsters in Great Britain enjoyed many of the same films as their American counterparts, as well as British-made silent films, such as those featuring a patriotic hero named Lieutenant Rose.

Although children mainly saw the same movies as their parents, they often saw them at separate afternoon matinee screenings. By showing movies for children at times when most adult moviegoers were working, theaters could fill otherwise empty seats. Moreover, because children were smaller, more ticket-buying children could be squeezed onto the movable benches found at the time in many nickelodeons. The conditions for children at these early matinees led to several tragic incidents, most notably in the United Kingdom, when overcrowding resulted in injuries and even fatalities due to suffocation.

The motion pictures' popularity with young people drew the attention of social reformers and religious leaders in the United States and Great Britain. They feared that the movies glorified immoral behavior—such as criminal activity and illicit love affairs—and influenced children to forgo more wholesome recreational activities. Concerns about children spurred calls for censorship in the early 1900s, resulting in the formation of city and state movie censorship boards. By the late 1920s, civic groups, women's associations, and religious groups increasingly called for federal censorship of the motion pictures. In response, the American motion picture industry agreed to regulate the content of the movies on its own with a voluntary production code (commonly known as the Hays Code).

Concerns about the influence of the movies on children also prompted social science research, most notably a 12-volume series entitled *Motion Pictures and Youth* (commonly known as the Payne Fund Studies), published in 1933. Among the findings of these studies were that school-age children attended the movies more frequently than adults—on average once a week—and that the movies significantly influenced play activities, grooming and dress styles, and courting behaviors of young people.

Flash Gordon, played by Buster Crabbe, fighting off the enemy in a scene from the 1938 science fiction serial *Flash Gordon's Trip to Mars*. This fifteen-episode film serial was one of three that were based on the comic strip *Flash Gordon*.

SOURCE: © Underwood & Underwood/CORBIS.

MATINEES AND FAMILY FILMS

Children's matinees continued to be a mainstay for movie theaters in the 1930s and 1940s. Standard matinee fare included cheaply made Westerns that garnered a loyal child audience. Some of children's favorite cowboy stars from this era included Hopalong Cassidy, Gene Autry, and Roy Rogers. Serial movies were also important to theater managers because their uncomplicated plots and cliff-hanger endings drew children week after week in anticipation of the next installment. One of the most memorable serials of the 1930s was *Flash Gordon* (1936), detailing the fantastic adventures of a space hero. The *Our Gang* series was a long-lasting matinee regular that featured a ragtag group of lovable urchins. Cartoons by the animator Walt Disney became regular additions to the matinee lineup after his *Steamboat Willie* (1928) launched an international craze its star, Mickey Mouse. The popularity of Disney cartoon shorts peaked in the 1930s, when Mickey Mouse Clubs (sponsored by the Disney company) sprouted at theaters across the United States and Great Britain. By the late 1930s, Disney found a rival in the Warner Brothers studio. Over the next two decades, Warner Brothers' *Looney Tunes* introduced a cast of memorable characters that included Porky Pig, Bugs Bunny, and Daffy Duck. Although the Warner Brothers cartoons were written with adults in mind, they found an appreciative audience at the children's matinees.

During the Great Depression of the 1930s, the decline in movie attendance prompted the development of a new genre known as "the family film." American movie studios, in their attempt to lure larger audiences to full-price showings, created more films designed to appeal to both children and their parents. (In addition, family-oriented content also fell easily within the dictates of the Hayes Code). The success of the family films, especially those starring child stars Shirley Temple and Deanna Durbin, have been credited for saving several studios from financial ruin. Many popular family films of the era were based on children's literature, such as *David Copperfield* (1935) and *The Wizard of Oz* (1939). In 1937, *Snow*

White premiered as Disney's first full-length animated feature and became one of the top-grossing films of the decade, establishing Disney as the preeminent family film studio.

In other countries, particularly in Europe, a different genre of children's films developed. Countries such as the Soviet Union set up studios specifically to produce films conceived solely for children's viewing. These movies were told from the perspective of the child and were cast with ordinary-looking child actors who reflected the lives of the children who watched them. Frequently subsidized by the government, studios generally had much lower revenue expectations for these films and had budgets that were a fraction of what Hollywood movies spent (as reflected in the generally low production quality). Although a few of these films reached the attention of the American movie audience, such as French director Albert Lamorisse's *The Red Balloon* (1956), most were intended for children's viewing only within their country of origin. The tradition of this genre of children's cinema continues in many countries around the world, including the Netherlands, Iran, and Denmark.

THE RISE OF THE YOUTH MARKET

During the 1950s, the leisure habits of American families shifted, as much of the middle class moved into the suburbs, and television found a place in many homes. With new forms of recreation and greater distances between households and movie theaters, fewer Americans were going to the movies. Hollywood began to court teenagers who had the leisure, disposable income, and inclination to seek entertainment outside of the home. The emergence of teenagers as the primary target market for motion pictures is evident in the proliferation of "teenpics" during this decade, including movies about adolescent rebellion such as *Rebel Without a Cause* (1955), rock and roll musicals such as *Jailhouse Rock* (1957), horror flicks and sci-fi thrillers such as *I Was a Teenage Werewolf* (1957) and *The Blob* (1958), and the "beach films" of the early 1960s, for example, *Beach Blanket Bingo* (1963).

Studios also continued to make family films in an effort to reverse a decline in movie attendance. Successful family films included expensive musical productions, such as *Doctor Doolittle* (1967) and *Mary Poppins* (1964). Disney continued its successful run of animated features in the 1950s and 1960s, including *Cinderella* (1950), *Alice in Wonderland* (1951), *Lady and the Tramp* (1955), and also produced a series of live-action features showcasing child-star Hayley Mills, including *The Parent Trap* (1964) and *That Darn Cat* (1965).

BOX OFFICE POWER

Escapist, nostalgic films such as *Star Wars* (1977), *Superman* (1978), and *Grease* (1978) were among the largest box office draws in the 1970s, and young people were among their most enthusiastic fans. The child audience was particularly crucial to the success of *Star Wars;* the film had been financed in part through the licensing of *Star Wars* toys and merchandise (a practice that is now commonplace). Movies for families and children continued to be successful revenue generators for Hollywood in the 1980s, with such blockbusters as *E.T.: The Extraterrestrial* (1982), which grossed $228 million in the year it was released. Disney, after a slump in the 1970s and early 1980s, returned to economic prosperity in 1989 with *Honey, I Shrunk the Kids* and *The Little Mermaid*. Teenpics also flourished in the 1980s with hits such as *The Karate Kid* (1983), *Risky Business* (1986), and a number of films by director John Hughes, including *Sixteen Candles* (1984) and *The Breakfast Club* (1985).

Although the overall number of moviegoers continues to decline, movie studios have found stable sources of revenue in child and teen audiences. In Japan, family films by the acclaimed animator Hayao Miyazaki consistently break box office records, including *Princess Mononoke* (1997), *Spirited Away* (2001), and *Howl's Moving Castle* (2004). Hollywood has also banked on a resurgence of the family film with the success of movies such as *Home Alone* (1990), *The Lion King* (1994), *Shrek* (2001), and *Finding Nemo* (2003)—all of which rank in the top 30 highest-grossing U.S. films. Teenage boys have long been a driving factor in the development of movies, and evidence of their primacy as an audience can be seen in the steady stream of action, horror, and sex comedy films. However, the enormous box office take from the 1997 film *Titanic* (the highest-grossing film ever) demonstrated to studio executives the power of adolescent girls, who went to see the movie in droves. As a result, the early 2000s have seen an increase in the number of films marketed for girls, such as *Bring It On* (2000) and *The Princess Diaries* (2001). Another recent trend has been studios making movies based on existing children's television programs or video games (generally ones owned by a parent media company), such as The *Rugrats Movie*

(1998), *The Lizzie McGuire Movie* (2003), and a string of movies based on the *Pokémon* games and television series.

—*Meredith Li-Vollmer*

See also Cartoons, History of; Disney; Motion Picture Association of America (MPAA); Movie Viewing, Adolescents'; Movie Viewing, Children's; Regulation, Movies

FURTHER READINGS

Bazalgette, C., & Staples, T. (1995). Unshrinking the kids: Children's cinema and family film. In C. Bazalgette & D. Buckingham (Eds.), *In front of the children: Screen entertainment and young audiences* (pp. 92–108). London: British Film Institute.

Doherty, T. (2002). *Teenagers and teenpics: The juvenilization of American movies in the 1950s.* Philadelphia: Temple University Press.

Jowett, G. S., Jarvie, I. C., & Fuller, K. H. (1996). *Children and the movies: Media influence and the Payne Fund controversy.* Cambridge, UK: Cambridge University Press.

Staples, T. (1997). *All pals together: The story of children's cinema.* Edinburgh, UK: Edinburgh University Press.

Wojcik-Andrews, I. (2000). *Children's films: History, ideology, pedagogy, theory.* New York: Garland.

MOVIES, PERCEIVED REALISM OF

Perceived realism refers to the extent to which audiences perceive mediated content to be realistic. Certain components of movies, such as the situations, characters, and settings, as well as children's expectations of reality can all affect assessments of realism. Researchers measure perceptions of realism by asking participants various questions about the level of general realism, the realism of emotions portrayed, the realism of actions, and the realism of demographics in mediated content.

During their development, children and adolescents use different strategies to evaluate the level of realism in movies. It is generally understood that children consider mediated content to be more realistic than do adults. Differences in perceptions of realism are important because content that is thought to be more realistic has been found to have greater effects on viewers, both negative and positive.

DEVELOPMENT OF CHILDREN'S REALISM PERCEPTIONS

Due to lack of experience and developmental factors, children's perceptions of reality differ from those of adults. Both the type of content that is being assessed and children's ages can influence their impressions of the realism in movies and television programs.

When questioned by researchers, children discuss the realism of mediated content in terms of characters and actions, and they think that characters' feelings are more realistic than their actions. Moreover, children's ideas about realism are multidimensional. Hawkins found that children's evaluations of media realism depend on the degree to which they think that content directly reflects reality (i.e., is a "magic window" to the world) and on how well mediated content matches their social expectations. Furthermore, although children's tendency to believe that what is portrayed is actually happening decreases with age, their assumption that portrayed situations resemble life situations does not necessarily decrease with age.

Some content is thought to be equally realistic by children of various ages. However, Morison, Kelly, and Gardner found that even though children of different ages may not differ in their overall assessments of realism, they use different processes to make these judgments. The criteria for realness evolve during different stages in children's development. Young children use content-specific cues (e.g., the presence of flying people) to explain why certain content is not possible and thus not realistic. As they get older, children recognize formal features (e.g., the use of puppets, music, animation, etc.) and use these features to assess realness; that is, children develop an awareness of movie and television production, which makes it possible for them to identify content that was produced using special effects, makeup, and other devices. For example, Morison and colleagues found that by the age of 7 or 8, children understand that certain formats, such as cartoons, are not real and that some of the situations portrayed in the media are not possible. Also, by the age of 5 or 6, children begin to be able to compare mediated content with their own experiences and perceptions of reality. However, according to Dorr, they usually do not use these comparisons to make judgments about realism until they get older.

By adolescence, children begin using different strategies to determine realism. They often contemplate the probability that what is presented will occur in real life. Nevertheless, even content that children can identify as unrealistic may affect their emotive reactions. For example, although scary portrayals that feature monsters or other supernatural beings are often perceived to be unrealistic, they still elicit fear.

THE EFFECTS OF PERCEIVING MEDIATED CONTENT AS REALISTIC

Perceived realism is important to the study of media effects because it has been found to influence the relationship between media exposure and media effects. In one study, those who thought that mediated content was realistic were generally more susceptible to influence, or at least more likely to use content to make judgments. In other words, content that is regarded as being realistic is more likely to affect attitudes, beliefs, and behaviors than is content that is thought to be unrealistic.

Perceived realism may be particularly influential in the creation of cultivation effects. When making judgments about the world, people are generally more likely to use situations and characters that are considered to be real to make those decisions. For example, people who watch a lot of television and who think that the content they watch accurately portrays reality are more likely to think that crime is very prevalent in society because they can easily think of televised examples of crime. Perceptions of realism may thus make media examples more accessible. As a result, those who believe that content is realistic may be more likely to make false assumptions about their social world based on media depictions.

Furthermore, Hawkins found that content that is thought to be realistic produces greater antisocial effects than content that is thought to be unrealistic or based in fantasy. Various studies showed that people who perceive certain content to be realistic have been found to make harsher judgments about the mentally handicapped, to believe that more peers are sexually active, and to act aggressively. Furthermore, realistic depictions of violence tend to cause more fear than stylistic or animated portrayals. Of course, the mediating effects of perceived realism are not always negative. For instance, Reeves found that children who judged television content to be realistic increased their pro-social behavior and decreased antisocial behavior. Consequently, although research suggests that perceived realism can be associated with harmful outcomes, the ways in which it can be used for positive influence is deserving of greater research attention.

—*K. Maja Krakowiak*

See also Cognitive Development, Media and; Cultivation Theory; Fantasy–Reality Distinction; Fear Reactions; Formal Features; Sex in Television, Perceived Realism of

FURTHER READINGS

Busselle R. W., & Greenberg, B. S. (2000). The nature of television realism judgments: A reevaluation of their conceptualization and measurement. *Mass Communication and Society, 3,* 249–286.

Cantor, J. (2002). Fright reactions to mass media. In J. Bryant & D. Zillmann (Eds.), *Media effects: Advances in theory and research* (pp. 287–306). Mahwah, NJ: Erlbaum.

Dorr, A. (1983). No shortcuts to judging reality. In J. Bryant & D. R. Anderson (Eds.), *Children's understanding of television: Research on attention and comprehension* (pp. 199–220). New York: Academic Press.

Dorr, A., Kovaric, P., & Doubleday, C. (1990). Age and content influences on children's perceptions of the realism of television families. *Journal of Broadcasting & Educational Media, 34,* 377–397.

Hawkins, R. P. (1977). The dimensional structure of children's perception. *Communication Research 4,* 299–320.

Minnebo, J., & Van Acker, A. (2004). Does television influence adolescents' perceptions of and attitudes toward people with mental illness. *Journal of Community Psychology, 32,* 257–275.

Morison, P., Kelly, H., & Gardner, H. (1981). Reasoning about the realities on television: A developmental study. *Journal of Broadcasting & Electronic Media, 25,* 229–241.

Noble, G. (1973). Effects of different forms of filmed aggression on children's constructive and destructive play. *Journal of Personality and Social Psychology, 26,* 54–59.

Reeves, B. (1978). Perceived reality as a predictor of children's social behavior. *Journalism Quarterly, 55,* 682–689, 695.

Taylor, L. D. (2005). Effects of visual and verbal sexual television content and perceived realism on attitudes and beliefs. *The Journal of Sex Research, 42,* 130–137.

MOVIES, RATING SYSTEMS AND

Ratings systems refer to symbols that indicate the age appropriateness of media content. Ratings have been used as systems of self-regulation, intended to respond to viewers' concerns and forestall threats of government regulation. The U.S. movie industry has had content advisory codes since the 1920s; however, the ratings system we know today was developed in

1968 by the Motion Picture Association of America (MPAA) and the National Association of Theater Owners (NATO). This system's significance lies in its influence over other media ratings.

Movie studios are not legally required to submit their films for a rating, so the system's success depends on voluntary participation. Finding theaters for unrated films, however, is difficult when theater owners enforce the age restrictions of the MPAA ratings. A Federal Trade Commission investigation of movie marketing indicated increasing enforcement rates by a majority of U.S. movie theaters. A similar situation exists in the home video industry, where a majority of members of the Video Software Dealers Association (including video store chains such as Blockbuster) have policies that restrict children's access to videos based on MPAA ratings. Those codes are also printed on the video and its case. The presumption of both theater owners and video retailers is that unrated movies are to be treated as age inappropriate. Historically, moviegoing audiences have been reluctant to attend unrated movies, although no data are available to indicate that the same is true in the home video market.

The process of rating movies is supervised by the MPAA, which begins by assembling a panel of 8 to 13 people who will screen and rate films. Panel members must be experienced parents, "possessed of an intelligent maturity," and capable of putting themselves in the role of most American parents. They are full-time employees of the Classification and Rating Administration, an independent agency set up to insulate them from industry pressure. Panel members serve terms of varying lengths, requiring the recruitment of new members on a regular basis. Panel members screen the movie using a variety of criteria, including the film's depiction of violence, language, nudity, sensuality, and drug abuse. Panel members are directed to consider the mix of such elements within the context of the film. After screening, panel members consider which rating most parents would consider appropriate and then discuss their initial judgments. In the end, a majority vote determines the film's rating. Each member completes a written form with his or her vote and the reasons for assigning that rating. The MPAA then notifies the studio and announces the film's rating.

In most cases, movie studios can accurately predict a film's rating. It is the studio's intent to maximize box office revenues, which means achieving a rating that will guarantee as wide an audience as possible. Hence, the lowest rating (appropriate for young children) and the highest ratings (where children under 17 are restricted) are viewed as compromising a film's profit potential. If a film receives a rating that compromises its marketing plans, there are two options. First, the studio may request to see the reasons the film received its rating and then re-edit the film to achieve a different rating. The second option is to appeal the rating to the Rating Appeals Board, a 14-member panel of MPAA and NATO representatives that serves as the final authority. After screening the film and hearing from both the studio and the chair of the rating board, the appeals board votes. A two-thirds vote is required to overturn the original rating.

MEANINGS OF THE RATINGS

The MPAA uses five ratings, each of which indicates the age level for which the film is appropriate. The lowest rating is G (General Audiences—All Ages Admitted). According to the MPAA, this rating indicates that the film contains nothing that parents would object to their young children seeing. This does not mean the movie is a children's film, however, nor does it mean that it is free of violence or disrespectful language.

The second rating level is PG (Parental Guidance Suggested; Some Material May Not Be Suitable For Children). This indicates that the film may contain some profanity, violence, or nudity, but not at levels that the Ratings Board feels should merit a strong caution. This separates a PG movie from PG-13 (Parents Strongly Cautioned; Some Material May Be Inappropriate for Children Under 13). This rating was created in 1984 to indicate more severe levels of violent content, profanity, or nudity, which parents might not feel appropriate for young children. Any film depicting drug use or including even a single use of sexually derived profanity requires at least a PG-13 rating.

The two highest rating levels indicate attendance restrictions for minors. The R rating (Restricted, Under 17 Requires Accompanying Parent or Adult Guardian) indicates the film contains adult material (including hard profanity, rough violence, sexual-oriented nudity, or drug abuse). Theaters are intended to enforce the adult-accompaniment restriction for R-rated films. They are also expected to bar all minors from seeing an NC-17 film (No One 17 and Under Admitted). Although it may not legally be termed obscene or pornographic, such a film would have strong sexual, violent, or aberrant behavior.

The ratings symbol displayed in movie advertisements includes wording indicating the type of objectionable content present (e.g., crude humor, mild violence, nudity, or sexual content). These content descriptors are intended to give parents more information in advance of seeing the movie; however, some have criticized them for not providing enough information about the offending content. A second criticism of movie ratings comes from research with parents conducted by the National Institute on Media and the Family. Those researchers assembled their own panels of parent raters, who disagreed with the MPAA ratings on a number of films. An additional criticism, most recently leveled in the Federal Trade Commission's 2001 report *Marketing Violent Entertainment to Children*, is that movie theaters do not consistently enforce age restrictions. Hence, a significant portion of teens and children report viewing R-rated movies in theaters, as well as on premium cable television networks (e.g., HBO).

—*Ron Warren*

See also Motion Picture Association of America (MPAA); Parental Advisory Labels and Rating Systems; Regulation, Industry Self-Regulation; Regulation, Movies; Television Rating Systems, Parental Uses of

FURTHER READINGS

Federal Trade Commission. (2004, July). *Marketing violent entertainment to children*. Retrieved May 10, 2006, from http://www.ftc.gov/bcp/conline/edcams/ratings/reports.htm

Valenti, J. (2005, September). How it all began. *Movie ratings: How it works*. Retrieved March 16, 2006, from http://www.filmratings.com/about/content.htm

MOVIES, ROMANTIC LOVE IN

The concept of romance has been defined in different ways. It applies to such notions as a brief love affair, an intense and enduring bond based on mutual feelings of love, a sudden flare-up of romantic passion, and a strong amorous fascination of one person for another. Many of these and other dimensions of romantic love have occurred as a dominant or central idea of legends and tales in most cultures. Telling and retelling stories on the subject of romance is regarded as part of the socialization process of family values and sex roles. Through romantic tales, diverse moral propositions on love and relationships are propagated. The perils of romantic relationships that do not comply with customary norms or may disrupt established social ties, for instance, are illustrated by stories in which the lovers are left damaged or disappointed.

Media portrayals of romance can affect viewers' attitude toward romantic relationships, and some research has described the responses of children and adolescents in this regard.

In their storytelling practices, 20th-century media industries have always been keen to take up the theme of romantic love. Romantic movie couples—Ilsa and Rick in *Casablanca*, Rose and Jack in *Titanic*, Scarlett O'Hara and Rhett Butler in *Gone With the Wind*, and Vivian and Edward in *Pretty Woman*—are evidence of the legendary and sometimes iconic position of romance in popular culture. A number of analyses into the status of romantic portrayals in mass media cultures have described the romantic theme as dominant and ubiquitous. Bachen and Illouz speak of an obsession in our culture for stories about romantic love and call film and advertising the privileged discourse of sexual and romantic desire. Romantic portrayals in movies are described as a textbook example of how the figural dominates in a postmodern culture. Bachen and Illouz point out that compared to the verbal narratives of the past, the present-day visually vivid and lifelike imagery of romance is more likely to evoke mechanisms of identification and to elicit sexual affect, fantasy, and daydreaming.

Romantic representations are rarely discussed from an academic viewpoint, however. Certain studies have examined the nature of romantic portrayals in movies, describing, for instance, how the principal theme of romantic movies has changed over time. Whereas characters in movies from the 1930s typically were torn between a marriage for money or a marriage out of love, in the 1950s and 1960s, the principal theme of romantic movies had become sexual attraction and an idealized vision of bachelorhood, termed "the playboy fantasy." Movies from the 1970s and 1980s were characterized by an ambiguous visualization of a desire for authentic romance, on the one hand, and a cynical attitude toward romantic love, on the other.

Some of the contemporary movie stereotypes about romantic relationships have been identified as love at first sight, lovers are predestined for each other, and perfect partners understand each other's needs, also occurred in an analysis of Disney feature-length films. Tanner and her colleagues found that romantic relationships in Disney films often are created by love at first sight and tend to be idealized as easy to maintain. Pardun explored the romantic content of movies that attracted a considerable proportion of the teenage audience in 1995, reaching somewhat different conclusions. In general, her analysis revealed that direct references to sexual content are rare in romantic scenes. The bifurcation between love and sex in teenage movies, already described by film analysts, appears to be confirmed empirically in this study. Furthermore, Pardun made a distinction between various themes in romantic imagery, leading to different conclusions about romantic content in movies. The detection of categories as "romantic friction" and "negative romance," for example, leads to the conclusion that a rather negative image of romance is depicted. While movies often emphasize the difficulties of interpersonal communication, love declarations appear to be relatively uncommon. Second, Pardun documented that most romantic scenes involving married characters could be described as "monotonous monogamy," suggesting an unexciting picture of married life. Finally, almost half of the romantic scenes in the study featured what was termed *nonprogressive romance*; this category classified behaviors such as kissing, dancing, and flirtation, when no signs are displayed that these actions would continue on a physical or sexual level. The magnitude of this category, and Pardun's additional finding that these nonprogressive scenes more or less exclusively feature young characters, indicate that preintercourse behaviors are depicted as quite normal for teenagers in movies.

Some of these analyses have inspired a critical attitude toward the idealized description of romance in popular media. For that reason, a handful of studies have explored whether portrayals of romance may produce unrealistic expectations and illusions. Segrin and Nabi, for example, have shown that adults who watch television programs that contain many references to romantic relationships hold more idealized beliefs about marriage. According to Haferkamp, heavy viewers expect that romantic partners must empathize perfectly with each other and read each other's thoughts if their relationship is to stand and succeed. Based on interviews with 8-to-17-year-olds, Bachen and Illouz described a gradual conversion from children's imagined vision of romance shaped by the media, to a tension between the romantic ideals as imposed by the media and adolescents' emergent awareness of how the dating arena is organized.

—*Steven Eggermont*

See also Adolescents, Movie Portrayals of; Contraceptive Information, Television and; Disney; Movies, Sexuality in; Movie Viewing, Adolescents'; Movie Viewing, Children's

WHERE DOES A WOMAN'S SYMPATHY LEAVE OFF ...AND HER INDISCRETION BEGIN?

"Years from now," Laura was saying softly, "when you talk about this— and you will—be kind..."

From the sensational stage success that ran 91 weeks...and starring the players who created the original Broadway roles

The love story of a teen-age boy and an understanding woman.

M-G-M presents in CinemaScope and Metrocolor

Tea and Sympathy

starring

Deborah Kerr · John Kerr

with Leif Erickson · Edward Andrews

screen play by Robert Anderson · based on the play by Robert Anderson · directed by Vincente Minnelli · produced by Pandro S. Berman

An M-G-M picture

Romantic love has occurred as a central idea of legends and tales in most cultures, and portrayals of romantic relationships that do not comply with customary norms can be a source of moral propositions about love and relationships. Adolescents' romantic development often creates great tension in adults as well as in teens themselves. In the movie *Tea and Sympathy* (1956), a 17-year-old boy who does not emulate his peers' desire for girls is suspected of being homosexual, until an older woman gently seduces him in an effort to confirm his heterosexuality. Her indiscretion destroys her marriage, but the film suggests that her sacrifice saved him from a life of torment, thus preserving patriarchal priorities and alleviating adolescent anguish. Teenage romance has offered diverse fodder for movie drama, from the playful promiscuity of *Love Finds Andy Hardy* (1938) to the fatal angst of *Ode to Billy Joe* (1976) and the maudlin tribulation of *A Walk to Remember* (2002).

FURTHER READINGS

Bachen, C. M., & Illouz, E. (1996). Imagining romance: Young people's cultural models of romance and love. *Critical Studies in Mass Communication, 13*, 279–308.

Gallician, M. (2004). *Sex, love, and romance in the mass media: Analysis and criticism of unrealistic portrayals and their influence.* Mahwah, NJ: Erlbaum.

Haferkamp, C. J. (1999). Beliefs about relationships in relation to television viewing, soap opera viewing, and self-monitoring. *Current Psychology, 18*, 193–205.

MacKinnon, K. (2003). Male spectatorship and the Hollywood love story. *Journal of Gender Studies, 12*(2), 126–136.

Pardun, C. J. (2002). Romancing the script: Identifying the romantic agenda in top-grossing movies. In J. D. Brown, J. R. Steele, & K. Walsh-Childers (Eds.), *Sexual teens, sexual media: Investigating media's influence on adolescent sexuality* (pp. 211-225). Mahwah, NJ: Erlbaum.

Segrin, C., & Nabi, R. L. (2002). Does television viewing cultivate unrealistic expectations about marriage? *Journal of Communication, 52*, 247–263.

Shary, T. (2002). *Generation multiplex. The image of youth in contemporary American cinema.* Austin: University of Texas Press.

Tanner, L., Haddock, S. A., Zimmerman, T. S., & Lund, L. (2003). Images of couples and families in animated Disney movies. *American Journal of Family Therapy, 31*, 355–374.

MOVIES, SEXUALITY IN

Sexual allusions, depictions, and story lines are an everyday ingredient of popular movies in the United States and in Europe. Teenagers are very likely to be a exposed to these messages for several reasons. Adolescents have been identified as a key segment of the movie audience. Asked about their recent visits to a movie theater, one teenager in five reported going to the movies two or three times a month. Roberts indicated that teenagers prefer to go to the movies in the company of peers and unaccompanied by an adult. Furthermore, the Motion Picture Association of America found that 58% of all movies made from 1968 to 2003 fell in the category R (Restricted). In 2003, 20% of the top-grossing films were R-rated. Most young viewers in Greenberg et al.'s study reported that they had viewed at least one R-rated movie before they reached the required age. A survey into the industry's practices revealed that 81% of the mystery shoppers who were younger than 17 were able to buy an R-rated movie on DVD.

The few studies that have analyzed how sexual messages are presented in movies demonstrated a high rate of recurrence of sexually oriented content. In 1993, Greenberg and his colleagues examined 16 R-rated movies known for their appeal to young viewers; these movies were rated restricted by reason of their sexual content. Overall, these movies contained 10.8 sexual acts per hour, or 17.5 coded sexual behaviors per movie. Bufkin and Eschholz found that 60% of the top movies in 1996 included at least one sex scene. About half of these movies were rated PG or PG-13. Kunkel and his colleagues showed that televised movies are the TV genre with the greatest likelihood of presenting overt sexual behavior. Compared to other types of television programs, movies show a much higher frequency of sexual content in prime time.

These and other analyses also revealed trends in the explicitness with which sexual activity is presented and the typical context in which it is portrayed. Studies have documented a rising level of explicitness. Abramson and Mechanic concluded that the most popular movies of 1959, 1969, and 1979 dealt with comparable sexual themes, emphasizing physical gratification rather than affection; the authors also found, however, that more and more explicit dialogues and imagery were used.

A number of studies observed no or few allusions to contraception in movies and highlighted the predominance of extramarital sexual acts. Greenberg and colleagues categorized 46% of the sexually oriented scenes in a sample of R-rated movies as "sexual intercourse between unmarried partners." With a ratio of 32:1, unmarried intercourse occurred much more frequently than intercourse between married partners. Dempsey and Reychert's analysis of popular videotape rentals showed that 85% of the sex-related scenes occurred among unmarried couples. Unmarried characters' sexual behaviors also tend to be depicted more explicitly: Where passionate kissing was the most common sexual activity among married couples, a considerable proportion of the sexual scenes with unmarried partners contained what was labeled as "implied intercourse."

As a general rule, conclusions about the sexual content of movies appear to correspond to conclusions about most other types of media content: With the characters involved in sexual scenes being typically young, unmarried, and favorable toward sexual behaviors, an alluring, glamorous, uncomplicated, and thoughtless image of sexual activity is presented. There is one difference, however; movies are more likely to display this image in an unashamed and explicit manner.

—Steven Eggermont

See also Contraceptive Information, Television and; Motion Picture Association of America (MPAA); Movie Viewing, Adolescents'; Movie Viewing, Children's; Movies, Rating Systems and; Sex, Media Impact on; Sex in Television, Content Analysis of

FURTHER READINGS

Abramson, P. R., & Mechanic, M. B. (1983). Sex and the media: Three decades of best-selling books and major motion pictures. *Archives of Sexual Behaviour, 12,* 185–206.

Bufkin, J., & Eschholz, S. (2000). Images of sex and rape: A content analysis of popular film. *Violence Against Women, 6*(2), 1317–1344.

Dempsey, J. M., & Reichert, T. (2000). Portrayal of married sex in the movies. *Sexuality & Culture, 4,* 21–36.

Federal Trade Commission. (2004). *Marketing violent entertainment to children: A fourth follow-up review of industry practices in the motion picture, music recording & electronic game industries* (Report to Congress). Retrieved May 10, 2006, from http://www.ftc.gov/bcp/conline/edcams/ratings/reports.htm

Greenberg, B. S., Siemicki, M., Dorfman, S., Heeter, C., Stanley, C., Soderman, A., & Linsangan, R. (1993). Sex content in R-rated films viewed by adolescents. In B. S. Greenberg, J. D. Brown, & N. L. Buerkel-Rothfuss (Eds.), *Media, sex and the adolescent* (pp. 29–44). Cresskill, NJ: Hampton Press.

Kunkel, D., Eyal, K., Finnerty, K., Biely, E., & Donerstein, E. (2005). *Sex on TV.* Washington, DC: Kaiser Family Foundation.

Motion Picture Association of America. (2004). *U.S. entertainment industry: 2003 MPA market statistics.* Los Angeles: Author.

Roberts, D. F. (2000). Media and youth: Access, exposure, and privatization. *Journal of Adolescent Health, 27*(2), 8–14.

MOVIES, SUBSTANCE USE IN

An assortment of social factors, such as peers, families, and living situations, have been identified as influential in adolescents' decision making about and attitudes toward substance use. In addition, among other media, movies have been recognized as significant sources of information about substance use that can influence young people's beliefs and expectations. Attending the movies remains one of the most popular pastimes for American teenagers, and watching movies at home on DVD, video, or by other means is becoming ever more commonplace. Especially because media portrayals of substance use seldom include negative consequences of tobacco, alcohol, and drug use, the effect of these portrayals on young people is both a concern for parents and a public health issue.

SMOKING IN THE MOVIES

Studies focusing exclusively on tobacco use have found that most films, both currently and historically, contain at least one instance of cigarette smoking, with R-rated films most likely to include instances of smoking. Generally speaking, smokers in films are male adults who are motivated to smoke when they are agitated, sad, happy, or relaxed. Whereas some scholars have found that characters shown smoking are depicted as having higher socioeconomic status and increased romantic and sexual activity (thus potentially serving as attractive models), others have not found such associations. Evident consequences for tobacco use are exceptionally rare in movies.

In terms of depictions of youth smoking, a study examining 200 of the most popular movie rentals from 1996 to 1997 found that 17% of youth characters (18 and under) smoked and that girls were slightly more likely to do so. More recently, research investigating the top-selling films featuring teenagers from 1999, 2000, and 2001 found that one sixth of the major teen characters were shown smoking cigarettes.

ALCOHOL CONSUMPTION IN THE MOVIES

Depictions of alcohol use in films have received less attention than tobacco representations, although studies analyzing drinking on television are more frequent. In one late 1990s analysis of films, researchers found four out of five films showed at least one major character drinking. Movie drinkers tended to be adults and to have a higher socioeconomic status, to be more attractive and romantic/sexual, and to be more aggressive than nondrinkers. The negative consequences of alcohol consumption are not commonly shown, although one tenth of the most popular movie rentals from 1996 to 1997 did contain an anti-alcohol message. This study also found that 22% of characters who appeared to be under the age of 18 drank, with 40% of them experiencing consequences as a result of their alcohol consumption. Two fifths of the teen characters in the most successful teen-centered films from 1999 to 2001 were shown drinking, although they were unlikely to suffer any negative consequences in either the short or long term.

DRUG USE IN MOVIES

Portrayals of illicit drug use, although frequently commented on in the popular press, have received little systematic scrutiny from the social science community. In one of the only studies to attend to drug use, in 1999, Don Roberts and his colleagues found that about one fifth of the 200 popular movies they analyzed portrayed illicit drug use, and only half of these portrayed any consequences. Eight percent of characters under the age of 18 in Roberts's study were shown using illicit drugs. Susannah Stern's analysis of teen characters in 1999–2001 films documented that one seventh of teen characters used drugs. Notably, this study also found that teen characters were rarely shown refusing an offer to do drugs or regretting any of their substance use behaviors. In 2001, Thompson and Yokota found no illicit drug usage in their study of animated, G-rated films, although they noted that three films showed characters consuming a substance that transfigured them, and two films showed characters injected with a drug.

CONSEQUENCES OF SUBSTANCE USE IMAGERY

Altogether, research indicates that movies commonly provide images of substance use, both by adults and teenagers. Such imagery can be a concern, especially given the dearth of depictions demonstrating the negative consequences that often follow substance use. Equally notable is the apparent message in many films, especially those targeting young people, that substance use is a normal and fun teen behavior. This trend may play some role in findings that many teens view drinking and smoking (and, to a lesser extent, drug use) as acceptable youth behaviors. Moreover, despite their awareness of the risks involved, many young people regard substance use as "cool" and fashionable. A study by the Institute for Adolescent Risk Communication in 2002, for instance, found that young people (ages 14 to 22) are more likely to associate smoking cigarettes or pot and drinking alcohol with "popular" peers, rather than "unpopular" peers. A quarter of high school students believe that people who smoke pot are more interesting and

more independent people. Such associations between substance use and being popular, autonomous, or unique may help to explain the enduring appeal of substance use among American youth.

Indeed, despite myriad public health campaigns and school- and community-based education programs, substance use among American young people continues to be widespread. Recent studies reveal, for example, that most teens have tried smoking, drinking, and using marijuana, and a smaller yet sizable group of young people partake of these substances on a fairly regular basis. Although some young people use substances with relatively little consequence, many others are less fortunate. Indeed, statistics detailing the number of young people who suffer the costs of substance abuse (such as fatalities from automobile accidents, drug overdose, and chronic illnesses such as lung cancer) are distressing.

The role the movies ultimately play in actual substance use among children and teenagers continues to be studied. In the meantime, many activist and children's rights groups continue to appeal to the film industry to present more socially responsible images of substance use in their narratives, and many have begun to pressure the Motion Picture Association of America to use the rating system to limit young people's access to substance use imagery in the movies (i.e., by giving any films that show cigarette smoking an automatic rating of R or higher). In additionally, more cross-sectional and longitudinal studies are being undertaken to better understand how movies may be affecting young people's attitudes and behaviors; initial work suggests that the media do play a role.

—*Susannah R. Stern*

See also Cigarette Use in Television and Movies; Drug Use, Depictions of; Public Health Campaigns

FURTHER READINGS

Dalton, M. A., Tickle, J. J., Sargent, J. D., Beach, M. L., Ahrens, M. B. & Heatherton, T. F. (2002). The incidence and context of tobacco use in popular movies from 1988 to 1997. *Preventive Medicine, 34*(5), 516–523.

Pechmann, C., & Shih, C. (1999). Smoking scenes in movies and antismoking advertisements before movies: Effects on youth. *Journal of Marketing, 63*(3), 1–13.

Roberts, D. F., Henriksen, L., & Christenson, P. G. (1999). *Substance use in popular movies and music.* Washington, DC: Office of National Drug Control Policy.

Sargent, J. D., Dalton, M. A., Beach, M. L., Mott, L. A., Tickle, J. J., Ahrens, M. B., & Heatherton, T. F. (2002). Viewing tobacco use in movies: Does it shape attitudes that mediate adolescent smoking? *American Journal of Preventive Medicine, 22*(3), 137–145.

Stern, S. (2005). Messages from teens on the big screen: Smoking, drinking, and drug use in teen-centered films. *Journal of Health Communication, 10*(5), 331–346.

Thompson, K. M., & Yokota, F. (2001). Depiction of alcohol, tobacco, and other substances in G-rated animated feature films. *Pediatrics, 107,* 1369–1374.

MOVIES, VIOLENCE IN

Children and adolescents' exposure to movie violence has long been an area of concern for parents, researchers, and health professionals. Indeed, violence appears to be a common theme in movies (and movie promos) frequently viewed by children and adolescents. Research findings in this area are cause for concern, especially in light of the vast research suggesting that children and adolescents' exposure to violent images can lead to fear, aggression, and desensitization.

In fact, these concerns, dating back to film's introduction to society, prompted the Payne Fund Studies, a series of research studies conducted in the late 1920s and early 1930s in which movies and their harmful effects on children were examined. Although this study provided early evidence of violent films' negative impact on children's behavior and attitudes, its findings should be interpreted with caution due to methodological flaws of the research design (e.g., problems in sampling, measurement shortcomings). Regardless, this milestone study has helped set the stage for more recent studies of violent movies and their effects.

DEFINITIONS AND DEBATES

Like the existing research on television violence, most investigations of movie violence draw on either George Gerbner's definition of violence (i.e., physical force, with or without weapon, against self or other) or the National Television Violence Study's definition of violence (i.e., a threat or use of physical force intended to harm one or more animate beings). More inclusive definitions of violence have been advanced; for example, Bradley Greenberg's definition includes verbal aggression.

At the core of the debate over definitions of violence is the fact that not all acts of violence are equal.

For example, the brutality of the Holocaust depicted in *Schindler's List* (a film frequently screened in high school classrooms for its educational merit) is quite distinct from the blood and gore found in the *Scream* trilogy (a series of films popular among teenagers for their entertainment and shock value). What about violence found in films viewed by young children? An example can be seen in *The Lion King,* when Mufasa is murdered by Uncle Scar while Mufasa's son Simba watches. Clearly, not all violence is equal in its severity, graphicness, and realism; yet, what the research shows is that there is a high level of violence in movies viewed by young people.

VIOLENT CONTENT

Several content analyses have been conducted to investigate the presence of violence in film. These studies vary in terms of the film genre, the film's target audience, and the contextual features coded (e.g., weapons, gender of perpetrator and victim, etc.). Yet, these studies share a common objective of documenting the quantity and type of violence in movies.

Violence in G- and PG-Rated Films

G-rated films, popular among children, are not as violence free as their rating would suggest. Fumie Yokota and Kimberly Thompson conducted a content analysis of 74 G-rated animated films (released between 1937 and 1999) to quantify portrayals of violence. They found that all 74 films contained at least one act of violence, with the average film containing 9.5 minutes of violence. In most incidents of violence, only the body was used as a weapon; however, swords, knives, and guns were also featured. Moreover, a majority of violence occurred when good or neutral characters were feuding with bad characters to resolve conflicts. Indeed, this message to children—that violence is an appropriate means to solve problems—is cause for concern.

Like G-rated films, PG-rated films are popular among children and young people. Andrew Pelletier and colleagues conducted a content analysis of the 50 top-grossing G- or PG-rated live action films released between 1995 and 1997 to examine firearm use (an indicator of violence, no doubt). The authors found that 40% of the films showed at least one major character carrying a firearm. Of those characters handling a gun, 50% made a threatening gesture, and 19% fired a gun. The authors conclude that firearms are frequently shown in films likely to be seen by children.

Violence in "Slasher" Films

Research on "slasher" films is also noteworthy, given the popularity of this film genre among teens and preteens. Commonly rated PG-13, these films feature suspense-evoking scenes in which an antagonist (usually a male) attacks one or more victims. Recent slasher films known for their graphic portrayal of violence include *I Know What You Did Last Summer* and *Scream.*

A small number of published studies exist on the presence of violence in slasher films. For instance, Fred Molitor and Barry Sapolsky analyzed 30 slasher films released in 1980, 1985, and 1989, finding that heavier amounts of violence appeared in films released in 1989 than those in the earlier years. A follow-up study by Barry Sapolsky, Fred Molitor, and Sarah Luque found that popular slasher films of the 1990s feature more violence than slasher films of the 1980s. Such a finding begs the question of whether rates of violence in today's slasher films have continued to rise.

Violence and Aggression in Movie Previews

The study of violence in movie previews has been an important extension of the research on movie violence. Movie previews are important determinants of viewers' film selections and are perceived to be precursors to the full-length film. A study by Mary Beth Oliver and Sriram Kalyanaraman examined violence in 107 movie previews featured on video rentals; findings indicated that 75% of the previews contained at least one act of aggression and nearly 46% contained at least one gun scene. It is important to note that more than two thirds of the previews for G-, PG-, and PG-13-rated films featured at least one violent scene. Such evidence suggests that movie previews consistently feature materials that may be inappropriate for younger audiences.

CONCLUSION

Several noteworthy conclusions can be drawn from research on this body of literature. Parents and caregivers should preview films or use online resources to judge appropriateness of films for their children. Co-viewing may be particularly important with G-rated animated films because parents cannot necessarily rely on the Motion Picture Association of America's (MPAA) rating system for information on violent content. Furthermore, given the research indicating portrayals of violence in G- and PG-rated movies, it is perhaps due time that the MPAA give serious consideration to replacing or supplementing the current age-based rating system with one based on content descriptors.

—*Angela Paradise*

See also Aggression, Movies and; Motion Picture Association of America (MPAA); Movie Viewing, Adolescents'; Movie Viewing, Children's; V-Chip (Violence Chip); Violence, Desensitization Toward; Violence, Effects of; Violence, Experimental Studies of; Violence, Extent of and Responses to; Violence, Historical Trends and

FURTHER READINGS

Molitor, F., & Sapolsky, B. S. (1993). Sex, violence, and victimization in slasher films. *Journal of Broadcasting & Electronic Media, 37*(2), 233–242.

Oliver, M., & Kalyanaraman, S. (2002). Appropriate for all viewing audiences? An examination of violent and sexual portrayals in movie previews featured on video rentals. *Journal of Broadcasting & Electronic Media, 46*(2), 283–299.

Pelletier A. R., Quinlan K. P., Sacks J. J., Van Gilder, T. J., Gilchrist, J., & Ahluwalia, H. K. (1999). Firearm use in G- and PG-rated movies. *Journal of the American Medical Association, 282*(5), 428.

Sapolsky, B. S., Molitor, F., & Luque, S. (2003). Sex and violence in slasher films: Re-examining the assumptions. *Journalism & Mass Communication Quarterly, 80*(1), 28–38.

Yokota, F., & Thompson, K. M. (2000). Violence in G-rated animated films. *Journal of the American Medical Association, 283*(20), 2716–2720.

MOVIE VIEWING, ADOLESCENTS'

From John Travolta's *Saturday Night Fever* and Molly Ringwald's *Breakfast Club* to Lindsey Lohan's *Mean Girls,* movies—despite their differences in genre—continuously receive accolades from adolescents. The reasons movies are so popular among adolescents have to do with the imagination and new sensations that movies bring to teens. Whereas adolescents make up only 16% of the U.S. population, they accounted for 28% of all movie admissions in 2004, according to annual movie admission records. Adolescents have consistently demonstrated high interest in movies. Among those teen moviegoers, 88% saw between 2 and 12 movies a year, and 54% of them were frequent moviegoers who watched movies at least once per month. For example, more than half of 15-to-16-year-olds had seen the majority of popular R-rated movies.

Research has found that media play a significant role in adolescent development, particularly in terms of identity development. Media portrayals of substance use also influence young viewers, and both parents and policymakers have urged that movie content be continuously and carefully scrutinized and adolescents' viewing habits be actively and closely monitored.

Movie watching seems to be considered a group activity among adolescents. According to the Kaiser Family Foundation, only 15% of 7th to 12th graders said they were alone when watching movies, whereas 74% of them said that they were with someone else, most often with friends, followed by siblings and parents. Among families with teenagers ages 12 to 17, 35% of the families reported going to the movies at least once per month, and only 17% of them never went to the movies. Adolescents have different preferences as to favorite types of movies. Of the 7th to 12th graders surveyed, 42% listed action movies as among their favorite choices, followed by comedy (38%), horror (25%), family films (22%), and romance (16%).

Movie watching is no longer confined to movie theaters owing to a higher access to movie rentals, movie channels on TV, and movie downloads and DVD rentals from the Internet. High concentrations of video rentals and retail outlets in many communities influence households' movie-watching and -buying habits. Of youths ages 9 to 17, 62% said that they watched at least one video a week. Video rentals boost audiences' active viewing experience in that individuals pay more attention to movie rentals than to television viewing. In addition, when adolescents are at home, they most often spend time watching TV or movies alone in their bedrooms. Because 97% of families own a VCR and consume more than eight new videos a year, adolescents' exposure to movies has dramatically increased.

Adolescents actively use media for entertainment, identity formation, high sensation, coping, and youth culture identification. Youth generally regard parents and peers as the most important sources of information, followed by movies and other mass media outlets. An increasing number of studies have investigated the effects of movies on adolescents' development. Especially because mass media are popular and easily accessible, they play an important role in adolescent socialization and identity exploration. Movies are a source of information about gender identity, relationships, and romantic experience. The need for identity formation is particularly crucial because adolescents gradually distance themselves from parents during this developmental stage. Mass media also provide adolescents with ideal images of physical and behavioral characteristics.

MEDIA PORTRAYALS OF SUBSTANCE USE

Adolescents' interpretation of mass media messages and their perception of media figures such as movie actors and actresses can affect them in other ways as well. For example, negative portrayals of health-related issues, such as tobacco and alcohol use in movies, particularly catch researchers' attention. Content analyses investigating the portrayals of tobacco and alcohol use in top-grossing films have found an increasing likelihood that adolescents will internalize the behaviors portrayed on the big screen. The presence of alcohol and tobacco use in movies is far more noticeable to adolescents than to adults because adolescents are intrigued by adultlike behaviors and are eager to emulate them.

One content analysis of the 25 top-grossing movies between 1988 and 1997 showed that 87% of the movies portrayed tobacco use. R-rated movies contained significantly more tobacco occurrences than did G, PG, and PG-13 movies, although even G-rated movies depicted tobacco usage to some degree. An analysis of films geared toward teens found rare portrayals of the negative consequences of smoking and drinking. In movies rated R and PG-13, two fifths of teen characters drank alcohol, and one sixth smoked cigarettes. Adult tobacco users portrayed in movies were likely to smoke when socializing, celebrating, and partying. Teens, however, were more likely to use tobacco when they were sad, rebellious, disobedient, or feeling the need to relax, look cool, or fit in with their peers.

Another content analysis, this of the top 10 films from 1985 to 1996, further showed that the majority of films supported both tobacco and alcohol use, while the hazards of smoking and drinking were rarely mentioned. Only one third of the films referred to negative consequences of substance use. In addition, comedies were more likely to portray positive alcohol consumption than were drama or action movies. Overall, the prevalence of tobacco and alcohol use was often portrayed by lead characters.

Depictions of teens' substance use in film could further strengthen adolescents' belief that such behaviors are common among peers in the real world. According to social learning theory and social cognitive theory, individuals acquire behaviors through a series of vicarious observations and imitations. Social learning theory emphasizes the process by which individuals primarily learn from modeling the behaviors of others. In addition, social cognitive theory posits that individuals learn things from which rewarding consequences and experiences can be drawn. Positive expectancies of substance use can be primed through the influential figures portrayed by characters whom adolescents respect. For example, when other known factors such as family's and peers' smoking behaviors are controlled, research indicates that adolescents are more likely to take up smoking and have favorable attitudes toward smoking if their favorite stars do so. The depiction of tobacco usage in movies has also been positively associated with predicted favorable attitudes and susceptibility toward smoking among fifth to eighth graders.

The message interpretation process (MIP) model further postulates the importance of perceived desirability, similarity, identification, and expectancies of mass media messages that predict adolescents' behavior. Positive portrayals and appeals in movies can stimulate the desire to emulate the portrayed behavior, such as drinking or smoking. The influence of movie stars on adolescents' desire to smoke has been partially attributed to the actors' physical and emotional characteristics. For example, positive expectancies of smoking can be evoked if smokers are played by young attractive actors. Once adolescents perceive that teen characters in movies are similar to them, positive expectancies of substance use can be strengthened, and the chances of adolescents emulating the portrayed behavior will increase.

Health practitioners, parents, and professional movie associations, among others, have called for restrictions on adolescents' access and overexposure to movie portrayals of substance use. Protective factors can reduce adolescents' exposure to smoking in movies. Parents, for example, can actively monitor adolescents and restrict them from viewing R-rated movies having positive portrayals of tobacco and alcohol use. Some even propose radical changes—for example, that movies portraying tobacco use in a positive light without mentioning its negative consequences should be rated NC-17 rather than PG-13 or R. Others suggest media literacy programs as an alternative approach to helping young people develop critical thinking abilities that may limit the influence of smoking and drinking representations in movies.

—Yi-Chun Yvonnes Chen

See also Adolescents, Developmental Needs of, and Media; Adolescents, Movie Portrayals of; Alcohol Advertising, Effects of; Cigarette Advertising, Effects of; Movies, Romantic Love in; Movies, Sexuality in; Movie Viewing, Children's

FURTHER READINGS

Arnett, J. J. (1995). Adolescents' uses of media for self-socialization. *Journal of Youth and Adolescence, 24*(5), 519–533.

Atkin, C. K. (1990). Effects of televised alcohol messages on teenage drinking patterns. *Journal of Adolescent Health Care, 11,* 10–24.

Austin, E. W., & Knaus, C. S. (2000). Predicting the potential for risky behavior among those "too young" to drink, as the result of appealing advertising. *Journal of Health Communication, 5,* 13–27.

Austin, E. W., & Meili, H. K. (1994). Effects of interpretations of televised alcohol portrayals on children's alcohol beliefs. *Journal of Broadcasting and Electronic Media, 38,* 417–435.

Bandura, A. (1986). *Social foundations of thought and action: A social cognitive theory.* Englewood Cliffs, NJ: Prentice Hall.

Brown, J. D., Steele, J. R., & Walsh-Childers, K. (Eds.). (2002). *Sexual teens, sexual media: Investigating media's influence on adolescent sexuality.* Mahwah, NJ: Erlbaum.

Dalton, M. A., Tickle, J. J., Sargent, J. D., Beach, M. L., Ahrens, M. B., & Heatherton, T. F. (2002). The incidence and context of tobacco use in popular movies from 1988 to 1997. *Preventive Medicine, 34,* 516–523.

Everett, S. A., Schnuth, R. L., & Tribble, J. L. (1998). Tobacco and alcohol use in top-grossing American films. *Journal of Community Health, 23*(4), 317–324.

Goldstein, A. O., Sobel, R. A., & Newman, G. R. (1999). Tobacco and alcohol use in G-rated children's animated films. *Journal of the American Medical Association, 281,* 1131–1136.

Greenberg, B. S., Linsangan, R. L., Soderman, A., Heeter, C., Lin, C., & Stanley, C. (1987). *Adolescents and their exposure to television and movie sex* (Project CAST, Report No. 4). East Lansing: Michigan State University, Department of Telecommunications.

Kaiser Family Foundation. (1999). *Kids and media at the new millennium: A comprehensive national analysis of children's media use.* Retrieved November 1, 2005, from http://www.kff.org/entmedia/1535-index.cfm

Sargent, J. D., Dalton, M. A., Heatherton, T., & Beach, M. (2003). Modifying exposure to smoking depicted in movies: A novel approach to preventing adolescent smoking. *Archive of Pediatric & Adolescent Medicine, 157,* 643–648.

MOVIE VIEWING, CHILDREN'S

Movies—the first mass media—have been a widely accepted form of family entertainment since the time of World War I. Almost half of all families with children under 12 attend the theater occasionally, while 26% attend frequently and 16% infrequently. Only 17% of families never attend movies in the theater. In general 9-to-11-year-olds go to the movies more frequently than either 6-to-8-year-olds or 12-to-14-year-olds. Current technology is significantly increasing children's access to a wide variety of movies, often in unsupervised settings, and marketers are expanding the target audience by producing videos for infants as young as 3 months.

Children's movies are often conceptualized as family movies and considered to be nonoffensive, wholesome, and entertaining. However, current research, including content analysis of television and movies, indicates that children are routinely exposed to a variety of poor role models, which then may influence decision making and behavior. Nevertheless, some movies for children are wholesome and nonoffensive, and they remain an important and profitable source of family entertainment.

Technological advances have brought movies into the home, ending theater control and significantly increasing availability of movies to children. Research indicates that children today spend more time sitting at home using media than playing outside, including viewing about 40 minutes of videos daily. With the introduction of the video recorder (VCR), followed by DVD players, and with the ability to download movies onto a computer, children's access to all types of movies is possible. In addition, beginning in the late 1990s, companies such as Baby Einstein and SoSmart began to produce developmental baby videos targeting infants as young as 3 months. To date, there seems to be little research on usage or potential effects of movie watching beginning at such a young age.

Based on the Motion Picture Association of America (MPAA) movie rating system currently in place, G-rated films are considered appropriate for children under the age of 8. They contain no sexual content, scenes involving drug use, offensive language, and minimal violence. G-rated movies are the most profitable for the industry, although far fewer are produced than R-rated films. Also included in the category of children's movies are those with a rating of PG, indicating that although these movies are considered appropriate for those children ages 8 to 13, parental guidance is suggested. PG movies may contain some profanity or violence, but no drug use or explicit sex.

Various studies indicate that the MPAA rating system is used and considered helpful by almost 70% of parents. It is important to note, however, that almost half of all parents set no rules for their children regarding what they watch on television. Of 2-to-7-year-olds, 32% have a television in their bedroom, and 16% have a VCR; for 8-to-18-year-olds, the numbers are 65% and 36%, respectively. It seems likely, therefore, that children's exposure to movies, often unsupervised, is increasing, thereby heightening concerns regarding the influence of movies in the lives of children.

Some scholars suggest that although the current movie rating system is helpful, it is not complete and is not informed by an understanding of child development. For example, younger children do not distinguish between fantasy and reality, do not understand beyond concrete information to abstract, and cannot put themselves in someone else's place to understand how they are feeling. Younger children are also less able to put together pieces of a story or to draw inferences from the narration than older children. These developmental issues are not considered within the current rating system.

Furthermore, studies suggest that children of all ages experience fright reactions to media and that these feelings have the potential to remain with the individual and influence behavior. Potential fright response is not addressed within the current rating system. Also of concern is the positive correlation indicated by research between movie watching and risky behavior, suggesting that behavior such as tobacco and alcohol use in movies should also be assessed in addition to drug use, which is currently considered when assigning a rating category.

In a recent study, Goldstein and colleagues investigated 50 G-rated animated Disney films and found that two thirds, including all seven films released in 1996–1997, depicted tobacco use by at least one character; one half depicted alcohol use. According to these authors, 13 of the animated movies released by Disney since 1992 portrayed tobacco use, with almost twice as many characters using tobacco classified as good.

—*Rebecca Van de Vord*

See also Movies, Perceived Realism of; Movies, Rating Systems and; Movies, Violence in; Movie Viewing, Adolescents'

FURTHER READINGS

Associated Press. (2005). *Study: G-rated movies most profitable: Film industry produces many more R-rated flicks.* Retrieved November 10, 2005, from http://www.msnbc.msn.com/id/8123387

Goldstein, A., Sobel, R., & Newman, G. (1999). Tobacco and alcohol use in G-rated children's animated films. *Journal of the American Medical Association, 281*(12), 1131–1136.

Kaiser Family Foundation. (1999). *Kids and media at the new millennium: A comprehensive national analysis of children's media use.* Data retrieved November 1, 2005, from http://www.kff.org/entmedia/1535-index.cfm

Motion Picture Association of America. (2004). *2004 US movie attendance study.* Encino, CA: Author.

Paik, H. (2001). The history of children's use of electronic media. In D. G. Singer & J. L. Singer (Eds.), *Handbook of children and the media.* Thousand Oaks, CA: Sage.

Strasburger, V., & Donnerstein, E. (1999). Children, adolescents, and the media: Issues and solutions. *Pediatrics, 103*(1), 129–139.

Villani, S. (2001). Impact of media on children and adolescents: A 10-year review of the research. *Journal of the American Academy of Child and Adolescent. Psychiatry, 40*(4), 392–401.

Walsh, D., & Gentile, D. (2001). A validity test of movie, television, and video-game ratings. *Pediatrics, 107*(6), 1302–1308.

Wilson, B., Linz, D., & Randall, B. (1990). Applying social science research to film ratings: A shift from offensiveness to harmful effects. *Journal of Broadcasting & Electronic Media, 34*(4), 443–468.

WEBSITES

Baby Einstein: http://www.babyeinstein.com
So Smart: http://www.sosmart.com/

MULTIMEDIA TOYS

In a general sense, *multimedia toy* is a name for digitally based interactive media that are marketed as toys for children. All types of "smart" toys—*smart* meaning that such a toy can react to what a child is doing or saying—can be considered multimedia toys, including such media as Sony's PlayStation and Nintendo's Game Boy. However, virtual pets are the best developed example of such toys.

A virtual pet is a more or less complex software program that can interact with a person (and so is able to control input and to produce output). This software

Introduced in 1999, Sony's AIBO is a robot similar to a dog that was created primarily for entertainment. The word *aibou* means "friend" or "buddy" in Japanese, and *AIBO* is an acronym for Artificial Intelligence Robot. Combining robotic and media technology, the Sony AIBO could play music and take pictures as well as recognize spoken commands. Although Sony discontinued this product in early 2006, it continues to offer software support, and there are a number of websites for owners of the multimedia toy.

SOURCE: © Julien Guertault. Reprinted with permission.

program can be online or installed on a computer, or it may have its own physical form, for example, as an entertainment robot. The first type, pets that exist only on a personal computer or on the Internet, most often appears as little animals—a cool camel, a happy hamster, or a virtual dog that the user can adopt and care for. An example of the second type, a virtual pet with its own physical body, is the *tamagotchi*. This toy, first released in 1996, is a rather simple plastic egg with a little screen and some buttons. The story included with the product describes the egg as the living place of an alien for whom the owner must care. It needs symbolic food, sometimes medicine, companionship, and other kinds of attention. If the owner takes good care of the tamagotchi, it will communicate happiness and love; if not, it will become a very unpleasant being or even die.

Empirical studies in Germany showed that several months after the tamagotchi was launched, it could be found in 16% of German households that included boys between 6 and 17 and even in 28% of households with girls of the same age group. But the audience for the toy was not limited to children; as reported by the media, even businessmen interrupted their work to care for their tamagotchis. After 2 years, the tamagotchi wave ended for most people, and today one can find huge cemeteries of tamagotchis on the Internet. But tamagotchis are still sold, and from time to time, the Japanese enterprise, Bandai, offers a new tamagotchi type; the last one was able to marry another tamagotchi and even have children. This type of computer game is also used for serious purposes, such as teaching young people what is involved in caring for a child.

There arc a variety of other multimedia toys similar to a pet, especially in Japan: thc AIBO (a robot similar to a dog), the Furby, cats and little bears, e-versions of a red snapper, and so on. These toys are no longer produced only for children. More than 100,000 AIBOs have been sold. The AIBO has a wireless connection to the Internet and is able to serve as a diary, play MP3 music, and watch your home, but it is mainly constructed as an entertainment robot. It is able to learn and to develop, and in its autonomous mode, it functions as a complex stimulus-response machine that follows its instincts, especially its "love instinct," to come into contact with human people. Of course, this $2,000 pet is mostly used by children, and in industrialized countries, most children have already been in contact with one or another virtual pet. But there are further target groups, including technically sophisticated people who can write further software for it and elderly or chronically ill people who are not able to or do not want to own a real animal.

Seen from the perspective of media and communication research, multimedia toys are media for interactive communication between a human and an intelligent machine or a software program. An early form of interactive communication was the ELIZA program developed by Joseph Weizenbaum, a computer science professor at MIT. ELIZA was simple but high-functioning software that analyzed people's input and responded to them. Another example of interactive media is the use of global positioning systems in cars to get directions to specific locations.

The marketing of virtual pets has shown that the industry may learn how robots must function to be marketed successfully. The success of future robots for home use will probably depend not only on the work such a robot is able to do but also on its interactive competence. For people and society, of course, other questions come up: What are the effects on children of growing up with virtual pets rather than real pets? Are devices such as AIBOs valuable for elderly or ill people or for those who need emotional support? What are the consequences for the self-consciousness of humankind of virtual pets and other multimedia toys that simulate human and animal cognitive intelligence and also emotions?

—*Friedrich Krotz*

See also Electronic Games (various entries); Interactive Media; Interactivity; Virtual Reality

FURTHER READINGS

Krotz, F., Hasebrink, U., Lindemann, T., Reimann, F., & Rischkau, E. (1999). *Kinder und Jugendliche und neue und alte Medien in Deutschland* [Children and young people and new and old media in Germany]. Hamburg: Hans-Bredow-Institut.

Turkle, S. (1998). *Leben im Netz* [Life on the screen]. Hamburg: Rowohl.

Weizenbaum, J. (1982): *Die Macht der Computer und die Ohnmacht der Vernunft* [Computer power and human reason] (3rd ed.). Frankfurt am Main: Surhkamp.

WEBSITES

AIBO: www.aibo.com
Information about online virtual pets: www.virtualpets.com

MULTITASKING

Multitasking is the practice of doing of more than one activity at the same time, for example, talking on the cell phone when driving. Multitasking in the context of computer use refers to the simultaneous access to or use of multiple computer applications, such as word processing, instant messaging, Web surfing, and email; it can also refer to simultaneous access to and use of multiple screens within one application. In contrast, media multitasking refers to the practice of using multiple media at the same time—such as the television and the computer, or television, telephone, and the computer, and so on. Multitasking in the context of computer use is an extension of dividing visual attention among multiple locations on a screen, a visual skill that is extensively used in action video game play.

Research suggests that a significant characteristic of Internet use among youth, and in particular adolescents, is extensive multitasking. It is not uncommon for an adolescent to be working on a report for school, carrying on multiple instant message conversations, and downloading music—all at the same time. Multitasking typically occurs in the context of instant message use, and adolescents have reported that they like instant messaging because it allows them to have multiple conversations while at the same time carrying out other tasks on the computer, such as homework and downloading music. Although adolescents have been found to have four to five simultaneous conversations, on average they appear to have one or two conversations going on at the same time. The most common activities that teens report carrying out while instant messaging include homework, listening to music, and email.

Carrying on multiple conversations simultaneously requires users to keep track of the conversation thread in each window and even more important, to place a reply in the correct window. Not only is this cognitively challenging, mistakes can have social ramifications. In one study of 16 teenagers, two participants reported that they had on one occasion accidentally placed a response not intended for the recipient in the IM window. Because of these challenges, some adolescents report that they limit the number of active windows that they may have open at a given time. At this point, there has been no research examining the strategies that are used to carry on simultaneous conversations within an instant messaging environment. However casual observation of teen instant message use suggests that teens use many of the same strategies that have been identified in the context of chat rooms, such as brevity, chat codes, skipping punctuation, and emoticons or smileys.

How is multitasking accomplished? Adult research on task switching involving tasks such as pattern classification and arithmetic problems suggests that task switching is made possible by executive control processes that supervise the selection, initiation, execution, and termination of each task. Research is needed to determine whether switching between different applications and different windows of the same application is controlled by such executive processes. Other questions include the cognitive consequences of multitasking; for instance, is the quality of work produced (e.g., research report for school) impacted when the user is engaging in other activities at the same time (e.g., instant messaging conversations)? Finally, metacognitive knowledge about multitasking may play an important role among youth in the future; for instance, youth who multitask should know when not to multitask (e.g., when doing difficult math homework) and should know that they have to be careful when talking to multiple conversation partners at the same time.

—Kaveri Subrahmanyam

See also Computer Use, Rates of; Instant Messaging; Internet Relay Chat (IRC); Mobile Telephones

FURTHER READINGS

Boneva, B. S., Quinn, A., Kraut, R. E., Kiesler, S., & Shklovski, I. (in press). Teenage communication in the instant messaging era. In R. Kraut, M. Brynin, & S. Kiesler (Eds.), *Information technology at home.* Oxford, UK: Oxford University Press.

Green, C. S., & Bavelier, D. (2003). Action video game modifies visual selective attention. *Nature, 423,* 534–537.

Greenfield, P. M., deWinstanley, P., Kilpatrick, H., & Kaye, D. (1994). Action video games and informal education: Effects on strategies for dividing visual attention. *Journal of Applied Developmental Psychology, 15,* 105–123.

Greenfield, P. M., & Subrahmanyam, K. (2003). Online discourse in a teen chatroom: New codes and new modes of coherence in a visual medium. *Journal of Applied Developmental Psychology, 24,* 713–738.

Grinter, R. E., & Palen, L. (2002). Instant messaging in teenage life. *Proceedings of the 2002 ACM Conference on Computer Supported Cooperative Work.* Retrieved September 13, 2005, from http://delivery.acm.org/10.1145/590000/587082/p21-grinter.pdf?key1=587082 & key2=7993366211&coll=GUIDE&dl=ACM&CFID=5 4574470&CFTOKEN=36221788

Gross, E. F. (2004). Adolescent Internet use: What we expect, what teens report. *Journal of Applied Developmental Psychology, 24,* 633–649.

Rubinstein, J. S., Meyer, D. E., & Evans, J. E. (2001). Executive control of cognitive processes in task switching. *Journal of Experimental Psychology: Human Perception and Performance, 27,* 763–797.

Schiano, D., Chen, C., Isaacs, E., Ginsberg, J., Gretarsdottir, U., & Huddleston, M., (2002, April 20–25). *Teen use of messaging media.* Paper presented at the Conference on Computing Factors in Human Systems, Minneapolis, MN.

MULTI-USER DUNGEONS/ DOMAINS (MUDs)

Multi-user dungeons/dimensions/domains (MUDs) are a text-based form of multiplayer online computer game. MUDs combine elements of *Dungeons and Dragons*-style role-playing games with Internet-based chat. Although somewhat overshadowed in recent years by the profusion of graphical video games, MUDs still maintain a following among children and adolescents and are notable for emphasizing social interaction and imagination in computer game play.

OVERVIEW AND HISTORY OF MUDS

MUD originally stood for multi-user dungeon, and most early MUDs were essentially computer versions of the popular high school dice-based role-playing game *Dungeons and Dragons* from the 1970s. Both types of games immersed players in a Tolkien-esque fantasy world of the imagination. The first Multi-User Dungeon was programmed by Essex University students Roy Trubshaw and Richard Bartle in the late 1970s. Building on the foundation of earlier single-player text-based computer games, they created a virtual space in which a user logs on, creates or opens a character, and then reads descriptions of places, objects, and others in the fantasy world. To interact, the player types words or commands. As a typical fantasy MUD game progresses, players work together to fight monsters and find treasure, thereby advancing their characters and gaining more experience and power. After its creation, the fantasy adventure-style MUD dominated for the next 10 years.

Following fantasy MUDs, other types began to appear, such as science fiction adventure-themed MUDs and MUDs with the adventure component completely removed. This latter type of MUD, called *TinyMUD* by creator James Aspnes in 1989, stressed social interaction over combat and gave users the power to extend the virtual world of the MUD using a simple programming language.

Numerous MUDs currently exist, with a wide variety of themes popular with children and teens. As of September 2005, the portal website, MUD Connector .com, lists more than 1,800 different MUDs, including ones based on specific fictional universes (e.g., *Harry Potter*, *Star Wars*), MUDs based on general fictional themes (e.g., horror, superheroes), religious MUDs, historical MUDs, educational MUDs, and purely social MUDs.

CHILDREN, ADOLESCENTS, AND MUDS

Pioneering MUD scholar Sherry Turkle suggests that it is not uncommon for children as young as 8 and 9 to play MUDs, featuring grade school favorites such as *Barbie*. Indeed, an examination of the MUDs listed on MUD Connector.com reveals a number of MUDs focused on fictional universes popular with children and especially adolescents. In addition, related forms of adolescent computer games are now taking place on Web message boards (e.g., "play-by-post gaming"). Few studies have focused specifically on this young segment of the user population, but a notable exception is the work of Amy Bruckman, who began a social MUD for children called MOOSE Crossing in the mid-1990s.

MOOSE Crossing was created to allow children age 13 and under to construct virtual worlds in a supportive community environment. Kids who enter this MUD can create virtual objects such as magic carpets and imaginary pets and build virtual rooms and cities, using a basic programming language. Visitors to MOOSE Crossing may also interact with other users from around the world. Bruckman's work on the effects of MOOSE Crossing suggests that this type of MUD teaches children creative writing, computer programming skills, and a constructionist approach to community building, in addition to being more intellectually engaging than graphical media.

MUDS AND IDENTITY EXPLORATION

Several authors have looked at the use of MUDs for identity exploration. Because they are faceless, anonymous realities, MUDs provide many users with a stage on which to construct and role-play different personas, including the opposite sex. Bruckman suggests this type of MUD play causes users to notice and reflect on gender issues in basic human interaction. MUD identity exploration can also have therapeutic effects, such as when introverts play extroverted characters or teens with family difficulties attempt to play from the perspective of a troublesome family member. Work by Turkle suggests that MUD role-playing often has the positive outcome of helping users work through issues of personal identity.

RELATIONSHIP DEVELOPMENT THROUGH MUDS

The use of MUDs for building interpersonal relationships has also received some scholarly attention. Sonja Utz examined friendship development in MUDs and found that 77% of a sample of 103 MUD users reported having relationships with others online. In addition, participants who were low in skepticism toward computer-mediated communication (CMC) and who used paralanguage features of MUDs to express feelings and emotions were more likely to develop friendships.

ADDICTION TO MUDS

There are also potential negative consequences of MUD play, the most prevalent of which may be addiction. Psychological addiction to the Internet and electronic games has been documented, and this phenomenon may be strongest among adolescents involved with social virtual worlds such as MUDs. Some MUD users interviewed by Turkle reported playing 10 to 12 hours per day and even in excess of 80 hours per week. Playing this frequently could negatively impact school achievement and more.

THE FUTURE OF MUDS

What will MUDs look like in the future? Most likely, the same as now, even though the mainstream of the computer industry continues to emphasize technological advancements. Some MUDs have incorporated basic graphics, but the essence of these experiences lies in text-based interaction. Popular new graphical social games such as the Massively Multiplayer Online Role-Playing Game (MMORPG), which have roots in the MUD, exist now to bring player-rich visual experiences, but MUDs still have advantages over these more advanced games. MUDs remain free, at a time when many multiplayer gaming worlds have a monthly fee. MUDs also enjoy many of the benefits that print media have over graphical and moving image media. As a result, they should continue to provide children and adolescents with rich sustenance for the mind and imagination for many years to come.

—*Paul Skalski*

See also Electronic Games, Addiction to; Internet Use, Addiction to; Internet Use, Social; Online Relationships

FURTHER READINGS

Bruckman, A. S. (1993). Gender swapping on the Internet. *Proceedings of INET '93*. Reston, VA: The Internet Society.

Bruckman, A. S. (1997). *MOOSE Crossing: Construction, community, and learning in a networked virtual world for kids*. Doctoral dissertation, Massachusetts Institute of Technology.

King, B., & Borland, J. (2003). *Dungeons and dreamers: The rise of computer game culture from geek to chic*. Emeryville, CA: McGraw-Hill.

Turkle, S. (1995). *Life on the screen: Identity in the age of the Internet*. New York: Simon & Schuster.

Utz, S. (2000). Social information processing in MUDs: The development of friendships in virtual worlds. *Journal of Online Behavior*, *1*(1). Retrieved August 4, 2005, from: http://www.behavior.net/JOB/v1n1/utz.html

MUSIC, GROUP IDENTITY AND

Around the age of 8, children begin developing an increasing sense of independence and enter a period of transition from parental guidance to self-determination. The transition involves a shift away from a family-centered existence toward one that favors peer affiliations. This move toward independence is evident in adolescents' increasing control of their media choices and changes in their media exposure. For example, by the age of 15, adolescents appear to decrease their exposure to television while increasing their exposure to music through radio, CDs, and MP3s. Music, particularly popular music, has the potential to be a defining characteristic for the formation of interactive peer groups. In fact, the amount of music listening has been directly associated with the amount of time a youth spends among friends as opposed to family. Furthermore, one of the remarkable aspects of the role of music preference in adolescents' selective association with peers is that it can inspire connections that are independent from notable social barriers such as class.

Adolescents' music-related expression has been likened to a badge of distinction or conformity. Those who display associations with music such as hard rock or rap may do so to set themselves apart from the norm, whereas those expressing connections to mainstream pop music may be displaying signs of conformity to the norm. Either way, the displays of music preference can be relevant sources of information for adolescents to use in the process of selective association because they provide a variety of cues for identifying and attracting peers with similar interests and attitudes. Once peer groups are formed, music can also serve as a vehicle for social interaction.

SELECTIVE ASSOCIATION

Adolescents, like other people, prefer to associate with peers who share their interests and attitudes. Factor analysis of reasons for listening to popular music indicates that one of the primary reasons is to create an external impression. In addition, many adolescents consider music taste to be a central attribute to consider when forming impressions of others and may use the expression of musical taste to imply an association with certain social groups. Knowledge of music taste can be valuable for forming impressions because music has connections to emotions and emotional values that are often not expressed publicly. The way such connections are perceived and interpreted can trigger attractive or aversive reactions. Perceptions of a shared music taste have been significantly associated with positive character appraisals and evaluations of friendship potential. For example, knowledge of rap music or heavy metal can serve as the foundation for new friendships as the fans seek out others who display some conformity to the style of dress, mannerisms, and symbols associated with the genre's popular groups. Such evaluations have also been linked to stereotypical perceptions associated with different music genres (e.g., rock music is associated with toughness, and heavy metal is associated with rebellion). Ultimately, perceptions of shared music taste appear to increase positive character appraisals and enhance the desire for friendship.

Knowledge of music taste can also influence perceptions of potential girlfriends or boyfriends. The notion of musical taste as social information has been explored in several contexts, including video dating. Researchers have found that expressions of musical tastes by college students are frequently used to determine dating potential. Bias toward different music genres had different effects based on gender. For example, an expressed bias toward classical music generally diminished the dating potential of males but enhanced the dating potential of females. Conversely, a bias toward heavy metal generally had a negative effect on the dating potential of males but positive effect on the potential of females. However, researchers observed a gender bias in the use of music taste as a factor for appraising potential dates. Males appear to place a greater social value on expressions of shared music taste than females.

SOCIAL INTERACTION

Interaction among peers is an information-sharing activity, and music is an important subject for discussion among adolescents. They talk about and critique artists, songs, CDs, and videos. Music knowledge has also been identified as having social capital. Research has identified positive associations between familiarity with popular music and popularity. Adolescents who believe they are knowledgeable about a style of music frequently assume the role of opinion leader among friends or peers. Furthermore, the desire to interact with peers can foster the active pursuit of music information in the media, and the information learned from the media or a social interaction can lead to interactions with others in an effort to share the knowledge gained. Finally, music CDs and MP3s are among the most widely exchanged media among adolescent peers, and the acts of exchange reinforce group bonds and identity.

—*William Kinnally*

See also Music Genres (various entries); Music Genres, History of; Music Listening, Gender Effects on

FURTHER READINGS

Arnett, J. (1996). *Metalheads*. Boulder, CO: Westview Press.

Christenson, P. G., & Roberts, D. F. (1998). *It's not only rock & roll: Popular music in the lives of adolescents.* Cresskill, NJ: Hampton Press.

Knobloch, S., & Mundorf, N. (2003). Communication and emotion in the context of music and music television. In J. Bryant, D. Roskos-Ewoldsen, & J. Cantor (Eds.), *Communication and emotion: Essays in honor of Dolf Zillmann* (pp. 491–509). Mahwah, NJ: Erlbaum.

Konecni, V. J. (1982). Social interaction and musical preference. In D. Deutsch (Ed.), *The psychology of music*. New York: Academic Press.

North, A. C., Hargreaves, D. J., & O'Neill, S. A. (2000). The importance of music to adolescents. *British Journal of Educational Psychology, 70,* 255–272.

Roberts, D. F., & Foehr, U. G. (2004). *Kids and media in America*. New York: Cambridge University Press.

Zillmann, D., & Gan, S. (1997). Musical taste in adolescence. In D. J. Hargreaves & A. C. North (Eds.), *The social psychology of music* (pp. 161–187). Oxford, UK: Oxford University Press.

MUSIC, IMPACT OF VIOLENCE IN

Children under 6 years of age spend an average of an hour a day listening to some type of music. This exposure almost doubles between the preteen and teen years, so that by age 15, the average adolescent spends 2½ hours a day listening to music, with girls listening more than boys. Possession of music equipment such as iPODs and MP3 players is high among preteens and teens, and it does not vary with household income or parental education. Scholars have argued that such findings support the notion that music is the most important medium for adolescents and that favorite songs may be a socializing force for young people as they work toward understanding themselves and others. For this reason, the popularity of gangsta rap and hip hop among teens today has come under public scrutiny, in part because of the violent lyrics in such music. This entry describes the amount of violence in music today and the types of effects that violent songs can have on aggressive behaviors and attitudes in adolescents.

VIOLENCE IN MUSIC TODAY

Surprisingly few studies have systematically analyzed the content of music that teens listen to. In the only published study to look specifically at lyrics, Armstrong analyzed the content of 490 gangsta rap songs between 1987 and 1993. He found that 22% of the songs contained violent and misogynist lyrics. Of the songs with violence, assault was the most frequently occurring criminal offense (50%), followed by murder (31%), rape (11%), and rape and murder combined (8%). Armstrong argued that this sample represented an early period in gangsta rap's development and that current rap songs have become more explicitly violent in nature. To support this claim, Armstrong analyzed Eminem's top-selling album, *Marshall Mathers LP,* and found that 11 of the album's 14 songs (78%) contained violent lyrics. Thus, Armstrong's findings for the late 1980s and early 1990s presumably underrepresent how much violence is in rap and hip hop today. Other studies have analyzed music videos rather than just the lyrics, and they find that rap music is the genre that contains the most violence.

IMPACT OF VIOLENT MUSIC ON HOSTILITY

Several studies show a relationship between listening to violent music and being aggressive. In one study, Rubin, West, and Mitchell surveyed 243 college students about their listening habits, emotions, aggressive attitudes, and attitudes toward women. Rap and heavy metal listeners exhibited significantly more aggressive attitudes than did fans of classic rock, rhythm and blues, country, and alternative rock. Studies have also shown that adolescents who report liking rap and heavy metal music are more likely to be suspended or expelled from school for behavior problems, to engage in delinquent behaviors, and to have arrest records. Such findings suggest a relationship between listening to violent music and acting aggressively, but the causal order of these variables is difficult to untangle. In other words, is it the rap and heavy metal music that causes aggressive behavior in adolescents? Or is it that troubled and aggressive teens are drawn to violent music genres? To sort this out, experiments are needed. In one of the most ambitious experimental tests, Anderson and colleagues exposed college students to violent or nonviolent songs in a series of five studies. The researchers found that songs with violent lyrics increased feelings of hostility in four of the five experiments, and this effect occurred across a range of humorous and nonhumorous songs.

Two theories can be used to explain the impact of violent music on aggression. Social learning theory posits that children and teens can learn attitudes and behaviors from role models, particularly those who are attractive in nature and who are rewarded for their behaviors. Therefore, highly popular bands and singers who encourage violence in their songs can teach aggression to young listeners. Once such attitudes and behaviors are acquired, cognitive priming theory explains how the media can activate aggressive thoughts, feelings, and even behaviors stored in a person's memory. For a short time after exposure then, a person is in a primed state, which may temporarily reduce an individual's inhibitions against behaving in an antisocial way.

IMPACT OF VIOLENT MUSIC ON AGGRESSION AGAINST WOMEN

Researchers have also assessed whether violent songs can enhance aggression against women in particular. St. Lawrence and Joyner exposed 75 male undergraduates to 17 minutes of sexually violent heavy metal rock, Christian heavy metal rock, or classical music and then measured attitudes toward women, acceptance of violence against women, and self-reported arousal. Males in both heavy metal conditions were significantly more likely to support sex-role stereotypes than were males in the classical music condition. Furthermore, both the sexually violent and the Christian heavy metal music increased acceptance of interpersonal violence against women and of rape myths (e.g., women who get raped hitchhiking get what they deserve), although this was only statistically significant for the Christian heavy metal listeners. Similar research has examined the impact of gangsta rap on attitudes toward women. Studies show that male participants with little previous exposure to the genre who are then exposed to gangsta rap lyrics express more adversarial views toward women than do men who are not exposed to such lyrics.

POLICY IMPLICATIONS AND CONCLUSIONS

The increasing popularity of violent music genres like gangsta rap has created a heated debate among members of the music industry, parents, and policymakers. In 1985, several wives of U.S. congressmen formed the Parents Music Resource Center (PMRC) because of their concern about violent and sexual music. The PMRC asked the Recording Industry Association of America (RIAA) to provide parental advisory labels on recordings that contained explicit content. After congressional pressure, the RIAA agreed to label explicit audio recordings. Today, the labels are applied by individual record companies and artists in the form of a black and white logo with the words "parental advisory, explicit content." Unfortunately, the labels have not been very effective because many parents do not seem to use them. Moreover, it appears that the labels can attract older children and adolescents to the very music that their parents want to restrict.

Compared to the vast amount of research on violent television programming, the literature available on violent music is very limited. The studies that exist do seem to indicate that exposure to violent songs can have harmful effects, at least in the short run. Future research needs to explore age differences more systematically, with a particular focus on preteens and teens. Research also needs to be more precise about

what types of lyrics and genres are most likely to encourage aggressive attitudes and behaviors and among which types of teens. Finally, longitudinal research is needed to assess the long-term impact of exposure to violent music.

—*Nicole Martins*

See also Depression, Media Use and; Hip Hop, Violence in; Music Genres, Heavy Metal; Music Listening, Uses of; Music Lyrics, Effects of

FURTHER READINGS

Anderson, C. A., Carnagey, N. L., & Eubanks, J. (2003). Exposure to violent media: The effects of songs with violent lyrics on aggressive thoughts and feelings. *Journal of Personality and Social Psychology, 84,* 960–971.

Armstrong, E. G. (2001). Gangsta misogyny: A content analysis of the portrayals of violence against women in rap music, 1987–1993. *Journal of Criminal Justice and Popular Culture, 82*(2), 96–126.

Rideout, V. J., Vandewater, E. A., & Wartella, E. A. (2003). *Zero to six: Electronic media in the lives of infants, toddlers, and preschoolers* (A Kaiser Family Foundation Report). Menlo Park, CA: The Kaiser Family Foundation.

Roberts, D. F., & Foehr, U. G. (2004). *Kids and media in America.* New York: Cambridge University Press.

Rubin, A. M., West, D. V., & Mitchell, W. S. (2001). Differences in aggression, attitudes toward women, and distrust as reflected in popular music preferences. *Psychology of Women Quarterly, 3,* 25–42.

St. Lawrence, J. S., & Joyner, D. J. (1991). The effects of sexually violent rock music on male's acceptance of violence against women. *Psychology of Women Quarterly, 15,* 49–63.

MUSIC, PERSONAL IDENTITY AND

During adolescence, defining a personal identity is an important developmental task. Many young people use music and musicians they adore to distinguish themselves from their peers. Thus, music choice often gives an important impression of an adolescent character under construction. Music is meant to be fun, to brighten life, but the development and expression of musical taste can also be a serious statement about one's values and attitudes, about the person one is or wants to be. Many adolescents see music and musicians as particularly relevant to gender identity, daily behavior, fashion expression, social manner, and worldview. The influence of the medium and its artists on overall identity development is pervasive, complex, and far-reaching in its cultural significance.

THEORIES ON IDENTITY

The concept of identity has become fundamental for the way people in industrialized societies experience and talk about themselves. We tend to think about ourselves as having a hard core of a self, character, or personality—a core that is developed in our youth and remains relatively stable and consistent over time; and we assume that through our individuality, we differ from other people in essential ways. It is hard to imagine, but the concept of personal identity dates back only to William James's social philosophy, which he developed a little more than a century ago. In addition, Erik Erikson's psychological identity theory first appeared in the 1960s. Talking about one's identity is so common that the social science roots of the concept are lost in the past. Identity as a psychological concept has passed into everyday language and experience, and it has become a mainstay of popular speech and self-description.

In his seminal work, *The Principles of Psychology*, William James (1842–1910) distinguished between the *I* and the *me*. The I refers to a deep-seated feeling that I exist as a subject; the me is that part of my subjectivity that the I reflects on, that is, the characteristics of myself that I can know and describe. Thus, the I is the real self of a person, and the me is the attitudes, values, and skills that I think of as characteristic for the individual that I am.

Psychoanalyst Erik Erikson (1902–1994) extended James's notions in his influential *Identity: Youth and Crisis*. Erikson posited the psychoanalytic theory that the ego (self) held an uneasy position between the two towering forces of the id (urgings of a broadly sexual and aggressive nature) and the superego (internalized morality). Erikson sought to further define and delineate the ego's territory, and in doing so, he coined the psychological term *identity*. He noticed that a popular concept of identity first appeared in the media in the 1940s, linked to the experience of many World War II veterans who seemed to have the feeling that they were not "the same person" as before they fought in

the war. Erikson argued that this loss of self and the severe psychological suffering attached to it proved how fundamental a basic sense of identity is.

The development of identity is a social process that starts in childhood and spurts during adolescence, when youngsters are expected to develop a more detailed personality. Identity development is a process of self-definition and differentiation in a social context. Erikson specifies identity development as the mutual blending of personality and culture until an identity with more or less unique features is established. Identity is achieved when somebody knows who he or she "is." He or she has a delineated self-concept, has an idea about relationships to salient others, has acquired a position in the work field and the community, and has made an ideological commitment. Although adolescence is a crucial period for the carving out of individuality, Erikson emphasizes that identity development is a lifelong, enduring process.

Other theorists have posited the notion that identity is of a changeable nature. Authors in the social constructivist tradition have questioned the concept of a central core of identity and stress that identity construction is an ongoing process in the face of interactions we have with other people and cultural forces. Depending on whom we meet, we can have different identities, implying that a single person may have multiple, sometimes even contradictory, identities. However, Jerome Bruner, one of the most influential psychologists of the 20th century, has stressed that identity construction does not always bifurcate. We construct our identities through the stories or narratives we tell about ourselves to other people (and to ourselves), and these stories do have a historical continuity and focus; therefore, we experience ourselves as the same kind of person over time.

MUSIC AS A SOURCE OF IDENTITY

Adolescence is a psychologically sensitive period for identity formation. Identity becomes progressively more differentiated with age. Adolescents develop their own identity through continuous comparisons with peers, leading to strong evaluations of what one should or shouldn't be, what is fit for one's identity and what is definitely not. During this period, music and musicians provide roles and role models, and sometimes conversely anti-role models, for the delineation of identity. Music taste may be more important among adolescents than among grownups, who have already achieved a more or less stable identity and can tolerate and even value music that is not directly in their taste spectrum. Music may be of the utmost importance for young people who are part of peer crowds or youth cultures that revolve around a musical center: punks, heavy metal fans, hip hop fans, or ravers, and so on.

Pop music's dominant themes relate to romance and sexuality, and as such, they are highly attractive for young people. The lyrics and visual language inform adolescents about the mechanisms of falling in love, loving someone, and dealing with love sickness, desperation, and loneliness. Songs may intimately relate to one's own circumstances. With the musical artist as someone inspiring or comforting, one may identify with this bigger than life special friend and tend to see him or her as a life example. In general, many adolescents hold artists in high regard because of their attitudes toward life and the ideas and values they promote through their work. Consequently, they take these artists as role models for what they want to be themselves. This may range from picking up clues about proper gender roles and sexuality, to imitating what to wear and how to express oneself socially, to internalizing sophisticated notions on social and political relations.

Music may contribute to gender identity. Girls tend to listen more to pop songs, dance music, and romantic ballads, whereas boys generally prefer louder, brasher music. These preferences are not the expression of natural, fixed differences. During the 1990s, for instance, boys became more interested in dance music, and girls acquired a stronger taste for rock. However, music may be framed as more masculine or more feminine, and even musical instruments are often perceived as more male or female. Music tastes vary to some degree, and so, too, the way in which boys and girls relate to their idols often differs. Whereas girls fantasize about closely relating to their favorite artists and being their special friend or lover, boys more often aggrandize themselves as potential stars on huge stages, that is, becoming idols themselves. Thus, both genders use music preference and their fantasies relating to idols or pop fame itself to amplify their gender identity. Pop music offers a range of examples with whom to identify; artists and lyrics encompass a wide variety of gender and sexual identities, ranging from extremely traditional to wildly liberal, from 100% heterosexual to radically gay or intriguingly ambivalent and diffuse.

Furthermore, artists have always been style icons, and although their music is diverse, they have had a decisive influence on dress, manner, and expression, molded and fitted into an individualized form by their fans. Artists have displayed a kaleidoscope of styles to emulate. These include the male "ducktail" hairstyle and the female bobby sox and poodle skirts of the rock and roll 1950s; the extremely long hair and the tie-died India cotton dresses of the hippies in the 1960s and 1970s; the ripped jeans and jackets and the sneakers of heavy metal in the 1980s; the baggy trousers and hoods of hip hop in the 1990s; and on into the future.

Last but not least, pop music has influenced the ideas and values of young people. The advent of rock and roll in the mid-1950s has linked to a rejection of the conservative mainstream ethic of modesty and hard work in favor of a more fun and leisure-oriented mentality. During the sixties, pop musicians were the forerunners of a cultural revolution that posited hedonistic principles of less strict sexual morals coupled with an anti-materialist, environmentally conscious, and pacifist set of ideas. Seventies punk has been framed as nihilist resistance to the capitalist system, and eighties and nineties hip hop has addressed issues of racism and poverty among minority groups in the United States. Music offers a wide spectrum of ideas to use in identity formation—from traditional Christian values and redneck conservatism, to over-the-top hedonism and leftwing politics. Stars such as Hilary Duff sang at the festivities around U.S. President Bush's inaugural in 2005. Other immensely popular artists such as Eminem and Kanye West accused Bush of dictatorial tendencies and not caring about black people. Thus, music covers a range of ideologies.

—Tom ter Bogt and Stephen Soitos

See also Adolescents: Developmental Needs of, and Media; Cultural Identity; Gender Identity Development; Music, Group Identity and

FURTHER READINGS

Hargreaves, D. J., Miell, D., & MacDonald, R. A. R. (2002). *What are musical identities, and why are they important?* In R. A. R. MacDonald, D. J. Hargreaves, & D. Miell (Eds.), *Musical identities* (pp. 1–20). Oxford, UK: Oxford University Press.

Tarrant, M., North, A. C., & Hargreaves, D. J. (2002). Youth identity and music. In R. A. R. MacDonald, D. J. Hargreaves, & D. Miell (Eds.), *Musical identities* (pp. 134–150). Oxford, UK: Oxford University Press.

MUSIC, REBELLIOUSNESS AND

Rebellion is a key topic in popular music lyrics, comparable to romance/sexuality. Many artists have sung lines similar to those of Pink Floyd in *Another Brick in the Wall*—"We don't need no education [. . .] Teachers, leave those kids alone." In the 1960s, while the importance of love as topic in music lyrics decreased, songs questioning societal conventions emerged in chart-topping music. Listening to music with rebellious lyrics is common today, and so is public criticism of such content. For instance, in testimony before a U.S. Senate committee, the American Academy of Pediatrics expressed great concern about possible impacts on teens of music lyrics containing references to drugs, sex, and violence.

REBELLION IN THE LYRICS OF POPULAR MUSIC

The two music genres that are primarily associated with rebellion and defiant messages are rock and, more recently, rap/hip hop. Interestingly, they are also the two most popular music genres in the United States. A content analysis by Knobloch-Westerwick et al. of rock and rap songs at the top of the charts in 1993 and 2003 revealed that the majority of these songs contain rebellious lines. Furthermore, compared to rock, rap/hip hop lyrics tend to allude more often to anti-normative but nonaggressive behavior, more specifically to drug use, partying/clubbing, and casual cursing, and they more often contain references to sexual acts.

But lyrics about antisocial, aggressive behavior, including violence or death, and lyrics about violent sexual acts, containing vulgar or offensive language and expressing hostility, are also commonplace in the charts. For instance, Yo-Yo referred to violence in the hit song from 1993, "Ibwin' Wit MY Crewin": "See, I'll hang yo ass by a tree, getting chopped while your neck snap at 3." This reactive music content occurs more often in rock music than in rap/hip hop. In both genres, rebellion has become more mundane in the last decade. Today, more than 80% of the most popular rock and rap/hip hop charts contain rebellion.

EFFECTS OF REBELLIOUS MUSIC

Rebellion in music comes in a variety of forms, and the various possible impacts have not been examined. Several studies investigated effects of aggressive music lyrics, which are to be considered a kind of rebellious music, but produced mixed findings. However, it was repeatedly demonstrated that such lyrics instigate aggressive thoughts and feelings. In turn, these aggressive inclinations may influence interpretations of ongoing social interactions. As an example, a teenager who listens to violent lyrics in a song while driving is likely to hold more aggressive thoughts, which can cause him or her to drive more aggressively. Hence, such content could create aggressive behavior.

APPEAL OF REBELLIOUS MUSIC

Many surveys have found that people with a need for distinction and sensation seeking report enjoying rebellious music such as heavy metal or punk. But as rebellion in music has become so widespread, the differentiation in listeners is more visible in rebellious adolescents' rejection of nonrebellious tunes, as found by Bleich, Zillmann, and Weaver. It has been suggested that rebelliousness, as it relates to preferences for nonconformist music, could be more closely connected to sensation seeking than to hostility and anger. Rebellion, as related to defiant music consumption, might not be motivated by latent hostility and aggression but by seeking of fun and arousal. Dillman Carpentier, Knobloch, and Zillmann identified fun-seeking rebelliousness and disinhibition as better predictors than hostility and frustration-motivated rebelliousness for actually observed selective exposure to rock and rap music. It appears as if defiant messages have become more mainstream, so that fun-seeking music listeners now gain excitement from rebellious song lyrics and these are no longer so much outside the norms, at least in the context of popular music. Conceivably, young adults may gravitate toward this type of music, not so much to celebrate aggression and violence, but to somehow define themselves socially.

Studies that examined how adolescents and young adults perceive same-age others based on expressed music preferences underline the importance of music for social perception. For example, a teenage boy who enjoys easy-listening music might be considered wimpy by his peers. It is fairly obvious that teenagers often employ music to alienate their parents, which can achieved by sheer volume, favored artists' looks and demeanor, lyrics, or provocative musical styles. For instance, The Beatles' hairstyle was irritating to many established adults at the time, and Elvis Presley's suggestive dancing violated general norms in the early days of rock. Apparently, rebellious music has to reinvent itself continuously to remain provocative. This seems more difficult today, given the saturation of the charts and the media with aggression or sexuality, which used to be outside the norms but is becoming commonplace.

—*Silvia Knobloch-Westerwick*

See also Aggression, Music and; Aggression, Music Videos and; Drug Use, Depictions of; Hip Hop, Youth Culture and; Hip Hop, Violence in; Music, Impact of Violence in; Music Genres, Heavy Metal; Priming Theory; Sensation Seeking; Violence (various entries)

FURTHER READINGS

Anderson, C. A., Carnagey, N. L., & Eubanks, J. (2003). Exposure to violent media: The effects of songs with violent lyrics on aggressive thoughts and feelings. *Journal of Personality and Social Psychology, 84*(5), 960–971.

Arnett, J. (1992). The soundtrack of recklessness: Musical preference and reckless behavior among adolescents. *Journal of Adolescent Research, 7*(3), 313–331.

Bleich, S., Zillmann, D., & Weaver, J. (1991). Enjoyment and consumption of de.ant rock music as a function of adolescent rebelliousness. *Journal of Broadcasting & Electronic Media, 35*(3), 351–366.

Dillman Carpentier, F., Knobloch, S., & Zillmann, D. (2003). The rebellion in rock and rap: A comparison of traits predicting selective exposure to rebellious music. *Personality & Individual Differences, 35*(7), 1643–1655.

Hansen, C. H., & Hansen, R. D. (2000). Music and music videos. In D. Zillmann & P. Vorderer (Eds.), *Media entertainment: The psychology of its appeal* (pp. 175–196). Mahwah, NJ: Erlbaum.

Knobloch, S., & Mundorf, N. (2003). Enjoyment of music and music television. In J. Bryant, D. Roskos-Ewoldsen, & J. Cantor (Eds.), *Communication and emotion* (pp. 491–509). Mahwah, NJ: Erlbaum.

Knobloch-Westerwick, S., Musto, P., & Shaw, K. (2006, June). *Rebellion in the top music charts: Defiant messages in rap/hip hop and rock music 1993 and 2003.* Paper presented at the International Communication Association conference, Dresden, Germany.

MUSIC, TRANSGRESSIVE HISTORY OF

Popular music has often been *transgressive,* meaning that it violates cultural norms and expectations. Although popular music has changed dramatically over the past century, it has been consistently portrayed as offending the moral standards of the mainstream and provoking the young into deviant behavior. This quality in popular music goes back at least to the rise of jazz in the early 20th century and has continued through rock, heavy metal, and rap/hip hop.

Jazz was the music of the youth culture from the early years of the 20th century through the 1940s, although its dominant form changed from New Orleans jazz to swing to bop. Jazz was seen from the beginning, by both its fans and its critics, as highly sensual music, music that would stimulate sexual desire. This characteristic of jazz was due to the musical qualities of the songs, not the lyrics. Many of the most popular jazz songs had no lyrics at all, and when there were lyrics, they were usually innocuous. The sexual quality of jazz derived from the music—its beat, its energy, its intensity.

The other quality that made jazz sexually charged was that it was dance music. In dancing to jazz, the young demonstrated its sexually transgressive power. Jazz dancing was spontaneous, energetic, and intense like the music, and partners grasped each other tightly and moved rapidly. Both adults and young people recognized the transgressive quality of jazz, especially with regard to sexuality, but adults feared it while the young embraced it with enthusiasm.

By the mid-1950s, jazz had been supplanted by rock and roll. Like jazz, the transgressive quality of rock and roll was in the music, not the lyrics. The lyrics of rock and roll classics like "Hound Dog," "Johnny B. Goode," and "Tutti Frutti" contain nothing offensive. But like jazz, the music of rock and roll was perceived by both its fans and its critics to be sexually arousing. The pounding beat of rock and roll, the loud raw sound of the electric guitars (amplified to unprecedented levels with new technology), and the passionate vocal styles of the singers seemed like an invitation to be sexually transgressive.

Also like jazz, rock and roll was dance music, and the dancing styles that accompanied rock and roll added to the transgressive appeal of it. Rock and roll dance styles were largely borrowed from jazz and shared with jazz dancing high energy, frequent close contact between partners, and a reliance on spontaneous, unscripted dance movements. This style of dancing reinforced and extended the transgressive sexual power of rock and roll.

Scholars who write on popular music usually make a distinction between the rock and roll music of the 1950s and the rock music that began in the 1960s and continues today. The beginning of rock is usually marked with the rise to prominence of the Beatles in 1964. Rock in the 1960s and early 1970s possessed a strong transgressive appeal. Sex was a transgressive area for rock, as it had been for jazz and rock and roll. For both rock and roll and rock, the transgressiveness was not so much in the lyrics as in the music and the style of the performers, but with rock, the styles of the performers became more extreme. The sexual exhibitionism of performers such as Jim Morrison of The Doors soon made Elvis's hip-shaking seem relatively tame.

In addition to sex, rock extended the transgressive into three other areas: drugs, politics, and Satan. Many 1960s performers were rumored to use drugs, and two well-known performers, Jimi Hendrix and Janis Joplin, died of drug overdoses. A type of rock known as acid rock developed (*acid* being slang for the drug LSD), in which the music suggested the psychological state experienced under a hallucinogenic drug. Although rock was transgressive with regard to sex, the link to drugs was perhaps even more transgressive because of the illegality of drug use and the potential for a deadly overdose.

Rock was also transgressive in the political views it expressed. Some rock songs openly advocated political revolution, some protested American involvement in the Vietnam War, and some expressed cynicism about the integrity of political leaders, for example, The Who's "Won't Get Fooled Again." Rock songs such as these were transgressive in rejecting the authority of political leaders and political institutions.

The other form in which rock was transgressive in the 1960s and early 1970s was in its use of Satan. The first rock performers to make use of Satan as a transgressive figure were the Rolling Stones. Through songs such as "Sympathy for the Devil" and album titles such as *Their Satanic Majesty's Request,* the Stones promoted an image of themselves as transgressors by associating themselves with the ultimate transgressor.

By the mid-1970s, rock had become mainstream and had lost a considerable part of its transgressive power. Along came punk, whose aim was to be outrageous, to break deliberately every taboo. Unlike jazz, rock and roll, and rock, styles in which the music was more important to fans than the lyrics, in punk, the music counted for little. The lyrics of punk songs were its most transgressive element. Topics of the songs varied widely and included unemployment, racism, the British monarchy, and sex, but the undercurrent of all the songs was anger, aggressiveness, hatred, and nihilism.

The style of punk was also blatantly and deliberately transgressive. Performers adopted names such as Johnny Rotten and Sid Vicious; they spit and even vomited on stage. Performers and fans alike sought to be shockingly transgressive in their appearance. Parts of the head were shaved and the remaining hair dyed in loud colors and spiked into plumes of various designs. "Jewelry" included safety pins through the nose or ears. Stage props included articles of sexual fetishism and bondage, as well as Nazi swastikas. Punk performers were not sympathetic to neo-Nazis—on the contrary, punk performers were active in the "Rock Against Racism" movement—but the swastika was useful as a transgressive device, another way to provoke outrage. Punk may have shown the limits of the appeal of the transgressive. The appeal of punk was brief and limited to a relatively small core of fans, perhaps because the music itself had little appeal, and transgressiveness alone was not enough to carry it for very long.

Heavy metal music originated in the 1960s with groups such as Led Zeppelin, Iron Maiden, and Black Sabbath, but it reached the peak of its popularity in the 1980s when heavy metal bands such as Metallica topped the charts. Heavy metal is transgressive musically in its loudness and its abrasiveness. The fact that most nonfans abhor the music only makes it more appealing to its fans, the "headbangers" or "metalheads," because it places them in an exclusive, daringly transgressive minority. Lyrically, heavy metal is transgressive in multiple ways. Many songs contain political content, and as in punk, this content is transgressive in attacking the legitimacy of a variety of social institutions. Songs attack corruption in politics, religion, and the legal system and deplore the destruction of the environment by multinational corporations. Some heavy metal songs use Satan as a transgressive symbol.

Violence is the most common theme in heavy metal songs, and the violence of the songs marked a new level of transgressiveness in popular music. The music of heavy metal is well-suited to expressions of violence. The rough distorted guitar sound, the pounding bass and drums, and the towering volume of it all is exceptionally effective in portraying lyrical themes of death, war, destruction, and murder. No prior popular songs had depicted scenes of such violence and brutality. Heavy metal was popular for a variety of reasons, including the creativity and musical talent of the performers and the political content of the songs, but the violent quality of the music and lyrics was certainly part of its transgressive appeal.

Rap (also called *hip hop*) began in the late 1970s as street music in New York City and achieved widespread popularity by the late 1980s. Today, it is far and away the most popular genre across American ethnic groups. Music does not carry a great deal of importance in most rap songs. What matters most in rap, and what gives it transgressive power, is the lyrics. Although not all rap songs have transgressive themes, the themes that have given rap its greatest popularity and notoriety as *gangsta rap* are transgressive themes of sexual exploitation and violence.

Sexual exploitation of women was an occasional theme in rock, punk, and heavy metal songs, but rap songs carried this theme to a new transgressive extreme by adding a deeper edge of contempt and routinely blending sex with violence. Women in rap songs are often referred to as *hos* (whores) and *bitches*. Rap lyrics rage and rant against women for deception, dishonesty, sexual temptation, and sexual resistance. Sexuality is frequently portrayed as the man's successful assertion of power over a woman. Women are depicted being raped, beaten, knifed, and shot, and they are often dehumanized, portrayed as deserving whatever contempt and violence they get.

In addition to sexual violence against women, violence is a theme of rap songs in other ways. Most of the prominent rap performers are African Americans, and rap often depicts violent confrontations among young men in poor, urban, largely black areas. Performers describe murders they have committed, brag about evading others' murder attempts, and warn adversaries not to cross them or face potential violence. Certain groups, such as gay men and Asian Americans, are singled out for contempt and threats.

Although some rock, punk, and heavy metal songs also contain lyrics with violent themes, rap is more transgressive by making violence the heart of the genre. Rap performers have generally sought to portray the violence in the songs as a statement of the economic and political realities of urban America, and therefore virtuous, rather than as simply transgressive for the sake of gaining attention and selling recordings. However, critics of rap have argued that rap performers contribute to the stereotype of young black men as potentially violent.

—*Jeffrey Jensen Arnett*

See also Hip Hop, Portrayals of Women in; Hip Hop, Violence in; Music, Impact of Violence in; Music, Rebelliousness and; Music Genres, Heavy Metal; Music Genres, Hip Hop; Music Genres, History of

FURTHER READINGS

Allen, F. L. (1964). *Only yesterday: An informal history of the 1920s.* New York: Harper & Row.

Arnett, J. (1996). *Metalheads: Heavy metal music and adolescent alienation.* Boulder, CO: Westview Press.

Arnett, J. J. (2003). Music at the edge: Popular music and adolescents' pursuit of the transgressive. In D. Ravich & J. Viteritti (Eds.), *Kids' stuff: Marketing sex and violence to America's youth* (pp. 125–142). Baltimore: Johns Hopkins University Press.

Berry, V. (1995). Redeeming the rap music experience. In J. S. Epstein (Ed.), *Adolescents and their music: If it's too loud, you're too old.* New York: Garland.

Brake, M. (1985). *Comparative youth culture: The sociology of youth cultures and youth subcultures in America, Britain, and Canada.* London: Routledge & Kegan.

Decker, J. L. (1994). The state of rap: Time and place in hip hop nationalism. In A. Ross & T. Rose (Eds.), *Microphone fiends: Youth music & youth culture.* New York: Routledge.

Frith, S. (1981). *Sound effects: Youth, leisure, and the politics of rock 'n' roll.* New York: Pantheon.

Lichter, P. (1978). *The boy who dared to rock: The definitive Elvis.* New York: Dolphin.

McDonald, J. R. (1988). Censoring rock lyrics: A historical analysis of the debate. *Youth & Society, 19,* 24–36.

Pattison, R. (1987). *The triumph of vulgarity: Rock music in the mirror of romanticism.* New York: Oxford University Press.

Rieff, P. (1973). *Fellow teachers.* New York: Harper & Row.

Sabin, R. (Ed.). (1999). *Punk rock: So what?* New York: Routledge.

Ward, G. C. (2000). *Jazz: A history of America's music.* New York: Knopf.

MUSIC GENRES, DANCE/HOUSE/TECHNO

The terms *dance, house,* and *techno music* are often confused and interchanged among the mainstream public. Each genre, however, actually has its own definition and unique history. Although details regarding the history and credit for the origin of each style vary, certain generalities can be made regarding the characteristics of each style and key influencers in the development of each particular sound. This entry defines and clarifies the definition of each genre, addresses some key elements in the creation of each genre's unique sound, and discusses the general historical background and some key innovators of each style.

DANCE/ELECTRONICA

Dance music, in the context of this particular grouping, does not simply mean "any music we can dance to." While individual interpretations abound, the term *dance* is generally used as an umbrella term that is virtually synonymous with *electronica,* which encompasses a number of musical subgenres.

Electronica is a broad term used to describe various forms of 1990s/21st-century electronic music; the style is mostly a hybrid of Chicago House, Detroit Techno, and New York Garage. The musical form emerged in the 1990s with the advent of sophisticated electronic turntables, drum machines, and computer software capable of producing myriad synthetic beats, melodies, and "loops" or "samples" (a portion of a song "cut" from the original track and played over and over again within a new track). Particularly in the late 1990s, the ever-evolving electronica style split into multiple subgenres, two of which included *house* and *techno.* This niche-ing and specialization of the subgenres of electronica is ongoing, as the mainstream pop music industry frequently attempts to co-opt and commodify each style.

HOUSE/CHICAGO HOUSE

House music—a term that originally referred to the kind of music heard at the Warehouse, a gay Chicago nightclub—originated mostly in Chicago and is attributed to Frankie Knuckes, who DJ-ed at the Warehouse between 1979 and 1983. House music evolved from the disco era in the early 1980s, drawing from various musical forms such as jazz, synth pop (which relies heavily on synthesizers), reggae, and R&B (rhythm and blues).

The formal characteristics of house music include a steady, rhythmic, up-tempo beat of 120–140 beats per minute (bpm), and it is composed mainly through the use of sequencers (electronic composition tools, including drum machines), synthesizers (electronic sound generators), and samplers (electronic devices used to record, manipulate, and play back existing sounds, usually pre-recorded music). The count is

usually 4/4, or four beats per measure of music, with heavy reliance on kickdrums (bass drum) and hihats (cymbal-like sounds) to produce a "low beat/high clap" effect. In addition to DJ Frankie Knuckles, DJs Farley "Jackmaster" Funk, Jesse Saunders, Steve "Silk" Hurley, and Ron Hardy are some of the pioneers of the house sound. The characteristic that most distinguishes house music from techno music is house music's heavy use of vocals and lyrics, often sampled and used separately from their original recordings.

Current house artists include D.H.T. and Daft Punk. The house genre can be further subdivided into categories such as hard house, deep house, and acid house, among others, each with its own stylistic peculiarities.

TECHNO/DETROIT TECHNO

The term *techno* is most commonly—and mistakenly—used to describe all forms of electronic music in general. In reality, techno music originated in Detroit, more precisely in the suburb of Belleville, and was first considered a subset of the Chicago house sound. The term *techno* was subsequently attached to create the term *Detroit techno* by the techno group The Belleville Three and dance music entrepreneur Neil Rushton in order to distinguish the techno style from Chicago house. The techno sound emerged from the styles of German musical innovators Kraftwerk and the Electro-Funk DJ Afrika Bambaataa. Detroit DJs most credited with honing the techno style include Kevin Saunderson, Juan Atkins, and Derrick May.

The techno style is known for its rhythmically repetitive and mechanically textured nature. Melodic content is usually minor, and lyrical content is sparse if used at all. Compositionally, techno follows a 4/4 pattern as house does. Unlike house music, however, techno has a faster beat—usually between 130 and 140 bpm, although further subgenres of techno are faster, harsher, and more intense, such as hardcore and Grabber, which reach up to 200 and 220 bpm, respectively. Furthermore, the techno style incorporates a 16-step pattern, where breaks, emphases, or changes in the musical pattern take place on every 16th or 32nd beat. The pattern-like nature of techno makes it ideal for mixing and overlapping to facilitate hours of continuous play by DJs. Techno music is highly sequencer driven, with overlapping drum patterns intermixed with electronic effects. The overall effect is a syncopated layering of sounds. The final product of a piece of techno music is called a *track* as opposed to a *song*.

As the techno sound grew in popularity, popular artists began to incorporate its style—one notable example is Madonna's "Ray of Light." Techno artists such as Moby and The Prodigy keep the techno sound within the mainstream. Subgenres of techno include trance, hardcore, ambient, Grabber, and speedcore, among others.

RAVES AND ECSTASY

One can hardly discuss techno without touching on the dance phenomenon known as the *rave*. Detroit techno made its way across the Atlantic to the United Kingdom and Germany, where it morphed into further subgenres and spawned the *rave culture,* which then migrated its way back to the United States along with new, European-inspired subgenres of the techno sound. Summarily, raves are dance gatherings where various forms of techno (and house) are played for hours, and sometimes days, at a time. The typical rave is usually accompanied by lighting effects such as strobe lights and laser beams of various colors, and many ravegoers carry or wear various types of glow sticks to create attractive lighted patterns while dancing. Large raves can attract tens of thousands. Raves are commonly associated with youth, who sometimes travel impressive distances to attend underground raves advertised via the Internet, word of mouth, or flyers distributed by hand.

Although many ravegoers do not use drugs, raves are commonly associated with the drug Ecstasy (MDMA, or methylenedioxymethamphetamine, also commonly known as E, X, or XTC), which creates feelings of euphoria and a sense of well-being and stimulates locomotor activity, thus enabling ravegoers who use the substance to dance for hours.

—Michelle Arganbright

See also Music Listening, Uses of; Raves

FURTHER READINGS

Blake, A. (Ed.). (1999). *Living through pop.* New York: Routledge.

Electronica/dance. (2004). Retrieved Oct. 14, 2005, from http://musicstore.real.com/music_store/genre?genreid=109&tab=info

Monroe, A. (1999). Thinking about mutation: Genres in 1990s electronica. In A. Blake (Ed.), *Living through pop* (pp. 146–158). New York: Routledge.

Redhead, S. (Ed.). (1997). *The clubcultures reader: Readings in popular culture studies.* Malden, MA: Blackwell.

Reynolds, S. (1999). *Generation ecstasy: Into the world of techno and rave culture.* New York: Routledge.

Rietvald, H. (1997). The house sound of Chicago. In S. Redhead (Ed.), *The clubcultures reader: Readings in popular culture studies* (pp. 124–136). Malden, MA: Blackwell.

Sounds like techno. (2003). Retrieved Oct. 17, 2004, from http://www2.abc.net.au/arts/soundsliketechno/swf/default.asp#Scene_1

Techno. (2004). Retrieved Oct. 14, 2005, from http://musicstore.real.com/music_store/genre?genreid=109&tab=info

U.S. Food and Drug Administration. (2000). *Guidance for industry: Street drug alternatives.* Retrieved October 17, 2005, from U.S. Department of Health and Human Services, Food and Drug Administration website, http://www.fda.gov/cder/guidance/3602fnl.pdf

MUSIC GENRES, HEAVY METAL

Heavy metal is a type of popular music that is characterized by a rough, distorted guitar sound, pounding bass and drums, and vocals that are yelled and screamed as much as sung, all of it typically played at a thunderous volume. There are many subgenres of heavy metal, including thrash metal, speed metal, power metal, and death metal, but they all share these musical characteristics. Across subgenres, violence is the most common lyrical theme, but many songs contain political content, attacking the legitimacy of a variety of social institutions such as politics, religion, and the legal system. Currently popular metal groups include Morbid Angel, Corrosion of Conformity, Cannibal Corpse, Atheist, Kreator, Overkill, and Rottweiler.

Heavy metal fans tend to be young (12 to 25 years old), white, and male, although there are exceptions. The popularity of the music spans social classes and nationalities—heavy metal is popular all over the world. For many fans, heavy metal is not just a musical preference but a central part of their identity. They call themselves "metalheads" or "headbangers" and frequently wear black concert T-shirts with the logo of a heavy metal band to display to others their allegiance to heavy metal. For them, the songs are not merely a form of entertainment but an ideology, a worldview, a way of explaining the world and their place in it.

The history of heavy metal goes back to the late 1960s and early 1970s and groups such as Led

Zeppelin, Iron Maiden, and Black Sabbath. The peak of heavy metal's popularity—and controversy—came during the 1980s, with performers such as Metallica, Ozzy Osbourne, Megadeth, Judas Priest, and Slayer selling millions of albums and performing in large arenas all over the world. Although heavy metal has declined slightly in popularity since then, the most popular metal groups still sell millions of albums and play in arenas around the world filled with fervently devoted fans. According to a recent Kaiser Foundation study by Donald Roberts, Ulla Foehr, and Victoria Rideout, hard rock/heavy metal is the third most popular music genre among American adolescents, after rap/hip hop, and alternative rock.

Although heavy metal has been the topic of considerable public concern and criticism, not all heavy metal is controversial. Metal is quite diverse, from "lite metal" groups such as Mötley Crüe and Kiss, which sing mostly about partying and sex, to groups such as Metallica, which address serious social issues such as war and environmental destruction, to groups such as Slayer whose themes are relentlessly violent. Controversy and criticism has focused not on the lite metal groups but on the other heavy metal groups, especially concerning issues of suicide and violence.

Is there any credible evidence that heavy metal promotes suicide or violence? Jeffrey Arnett (1996) addressed this question directly in research on heavy metal fans by asking them if they listen to the music when they are in any particular mood and if the music *puts* them in any particular mood. Consistently, they said they listen to the music especially when they are angry—not surprising, in view of the violent, angry quality of the music and lyrics. However, they also said consistently that the music has the effect of calming them down. Heavy metal songs have a cathartic effect on their anger; in other words, they use the music as a way of purging their anger harmlessly. The songs express their alienated view of the world and help them cope with the anger and frustration of living in a world they see as hopelessly corrupt. Because it has this cathartic effect on their anger and frustration, if anything, the music makes them *less* likely to commit suicide or violence than they would be if they did not have the music available to use for this purpose. This cathartic effect of heavy metal has also been demonstrated experimentally.

Of course, it remains possible that the despair and violence of the songs could act as an inspiration to suicide or violence in some extreme cases.

Adolescents can respond to the same media stimulus in widely different ways. However, for the great majority of the millions of adolescent metalheads, heavy metal appears to act as a useful outlet for difficult youthful emotions.

In addition to concerns about suicide and violence, there have been concerns that heavy metal promotes alienation among adolescents and makes them more likely to engage in risky behavior. It is true that metalheads tend to have a dark view of the world. They are alienated from mainstream society; cynical about teachers, politicians, and religious leaders; and highly pessimistic about the future of the human race. Many (although certainly not all) have troubled relationships with their parents. Arnett (1992) also found higher rates of risk behavior among metalheads than among other adolescents, in areas such as high-speed driving, drug use, and vandalism.

However, there is no evidence that adolescents' alienation or risk behavior can accurately be blamed on the music. On the contrary, adolescents who are already alienated are attracted to heavy metal because it articulates their alienation. Adolescents who have high rates of risk behavior are attracted to heavy metal for the same reason they are attracted to risk behavior: Both heavy metal and risk behavior appeal to adolescents who enjoy especially novel and intense experiences—who are high in sensation seeking, in other words.

Although love for heavy metal does not appear to cause alienation or risk behavior, one more definite effect of the music is that many metalheads take up electric guitar or another musical instrument in the hope of becoming a heavy metal star. More than one third of the metalheads Arnett interviewed in his study intended to be involved in heavy metal music as a career, usually as a heavy metal star performing before large, worshipful audiences. However, this aspiration was more fantasy than reality. Although many of the metalheads Arnett interviewed had begun to play an instrument, not one of them was a member of a working metal band.

Heavy metal is an ideology, and as with most ideologies, its adherents devote considerable attention to distinguishing who is a true believer and who is not. Although lite metal bands are often grouped under the heavy metal banner by outsiders, most metalheads regard such groups with contempt, as "posers" who are falsely presenting themselves as heavy metal performers. Metalheads use words like *true* and *real* to describe the metal bands they regard as legitimate. They regard themselves as part of a vanguard distinguished by an uncompromising focus on speaking the truth about the way the world really is, ugly as this truth may be. Nonbelievers may regard heavy metal as immoral and even abhorrent, but to metalheads, heavy metal is a statement of the highest morality, a beacon of courage and honesty in an otherwise corrupt and hopeless world.

—Jeffrey Jensen Arnett

See also Music, Impact of Violence in; Music, Transgressive History of; Music Listening, Problem Behavior and

FURTHER READINGS

Arnett, J. (1992). The soundtrack of recklessness: Musical preferences and reckless behavior among adolescents. *Journal of Adolescent Research, 7,* 313–331.
Arnett, J. J. (1996). *Metalheads: Heavy metal music and adolescent alienation.* Boulder, CO: Westview Press.
Roberts, D. F., Foehr, U. G., & Rideout, V. (2005). *Generation M: Media in the lives of 8–18 year-olds.* Washington, DC: Kaiser Family Foundation.
Walser, R. (1993). *Running with the devil: Power, gender, and madness in heavy metal music.* New York: Wesleyan.
Wooten, M. A. (1992). The effects of heavy metal music on affect shifts of adolescents in an inpatient psychiatric setting. *Music Therapy Perspectives, 10,* 93–98.

MUSIC GENRES, HIP HOP

Hip hop and rap emerged as African American music styles in the late 1970s. Since then, they have influenced not only an increasing spectrum of music, but also fashion, visual arts, television and film, literature, attitudes, and lifestyles as a whole. The hip hop lifestyle has its own media representations, magazines, and commercials, and it is an example of how music that was originally a part of alternative local protest movements has become a broader music and lifestyle trend in global culture.

The roots of rap as a musical form that concentrates on rhythmic text and intense beats are to be found among early 20th-century talking blues, spoken passages in gospel later, and electric rhythm and blues by Bo Diddley and especially by the famous singer James Brown, often called the grandfather of rap. Other influences are critical poems by African American writers and singers such as Gil Scott-Heron and by Jamaican reggae DJs who mixed sounds with

their turntables. In New York, house parties with similar music styles became a fashion in the 1970s, and the first rap record was published in 1979 by the Sugarhill Gang, "Rapper's Delight."

Mass success started with the old school Kurtis Blow and especially Grandmaster Flash with his hit single, "The Message." Rap by then had become a genre that would soon affect youth culture not only in the United States but across the globe. The movie, *Wild Style,* promoted music and life in the neighborhood (the 'hood) of big cities and gangland, as well as the new street art forms, graffiti and break dancing, and the technique of "scratching," whereby the DJ becomes the master of ceremonies when he mixes several records to create a new sound. A new fashion, with baseball caps, cargo jeans, and sneakers, was adopted by the young and later by the adult mainstream. From New York, rap moved to Los Angeles and other major cities. Soon, rap and hip hop (named after the electronic beats of rhythm machines used in this music) were big trends in both the music and lifestyle of the young generation, with super stars such as Run-DMC, L.L. Cool J, and, as the first white band, the Beastie Boys. In its further differentiation, major subtrends were gangsta rap with controversial artists, Public Enemy, later 2Pac, Dr. Dre, Ice Cube, and Snoop Dogg, and fusions with other music styles, such as jazz, pop, and even folk, with artists like Vanilla Ice, De La Soul, and Arrested Development. Women rappers also emerged on the scene, with stars such as Salt-N-Pepa and Queen Latifah. Rap and hip hop also made it into other regions of the world with performers such as the Streets in Great Britain, MC Solaar in France, and Fanta 4, Bushido, and Naidoo in Germany.

In particular, the gangsta rap culture promoted an alternative attitude and behavior for the young. Being a member of a gang, having a criminal record, and being involved in shootings were regarded as romantic heroism. But the hip hop lifestyle also soon became associated with symbols of an ultra-rich trash culture that prized gold chains, tuned luxury cars, and explicit sexual behavior, often promoting male dominance. Thus, the values of hip hop culture were seen to have moved from criticism of the establishment to superficial nouveau-riche macho lifestyles. But this is only one facet of hip hop and rap.

Musically, the big stars of the early 21st century developed texts, sounds, and melodies that rank among the most popular genres of the past hundred years. 50 Cent has become a superstar who not only rules the music polls but also is a major role model whose life is reported in youth, adult, and society magazines. Along with other African American stars like P. Diddy, he influences fashion and design, is featured in movies, such as *Get Rich or Die Tryin',* and is among the biggest celebrities around the world. Equally, white rappers have become part of the hip hop culture. Most prominently, music superstar Eminem tops the hit polls, appeared in the autobiographical movie, *8 Mile,* and is regarded as an international pop icon. Because some of these artists are reported to have been involved in crime and drug use, outsiders have challenged their value as role models for the young. However, rap and hip hop musicians obviously fulfill adolescents' desire for controversial heroes who follow an anti-establishment lifestyle. Thus, these latter-day stars are in the same tradition as Elvis Presley, the Rolling Stones, Iggy Pop, the Ramones, the Sex Pistols, and Nirvana.

In the early 21st century, elements of hip hop culture can also be found in television, the movies, literature, and visual arts. Again, an originally youth-based music form has had an impact on a whole culture. Apart from the numerous music video clips featured on TV channels such as MTV, hip hop elements appear in programs like "Pimp my Ride" and "Sweet Sixteen." Hip hop and a critical treatment of drug abuse are features of movies such as *New Jack City.* Rap clothes have been a global fashion trend since the early 1980s, now even challenging high fashion in terms of popularity and promoting a relaxed look in street wear with jeans, sweatshirts, and sneakers. For more than 20 years, rap fashion has been the accepted uniform of the young generation, and the look is also adapted by adults and worn even in business environments. Rap culture graffiti have become an art form, with top works of artists such as the late Keith Haring or Jean-Michel Basquiat fetching prices in the millions of dollars. The rhythm and structure of rap and hip hop texts have found their way into modern novels and the poems of both African Americans and other writers.

—*Jo Groebel*

See also Hip Hop, Youth Culture and; Music, Rebelliousness and; Youth Culture

FURTHER READINGS

Shapiro, P. (2005). *The rough guide to hiphop.* New York: The Rough Guide.

MUSIC GENRES, HISTORY OF

The concept of *music genre* (or *musical genre*) relies on the assumption that pieces of music can be grouped together into categories according to distinctive stylistic traits that enable audiences to tell them apart. This presupposes that various elements of music—such as melody, rhythm, harmony, form, and texture—can be both aggregated and distinguished by members of society for whom such typologies are meaningful.

CAVEATS

Some caveats need to be established when considering the history of music genres, especially as applied to children and adolescents. The first cautionary note is that different media (e.g., radio, recordings, film) commonly use different typologies of music genres. For example, radio uses terminology such as *urban contemporary, top 40,* and *contemporary hits,* which is not commonly employed in the music recording industry, despite the fact that radio is playing these recordings. For the most part, this entry focuses on music genre as used by the recording industry.

A second caveat is that genres that might be useful in describing the music of young children (e.g., bubble gum, television themes, musical nursery rhymes) have little utility when applied to adolescents and do not have widespread usage in the music industries. We focus on the more typical genre classifications that are employed across age levels.

A third limiting condition is that in postmodern society, in which the focus in media is on fragmentation of audiences, music is increasingly categorized into smaller subgenres. For example, reggae is frequently subdivided into ska, dub, reggaeton, ragga, and dancehall reggae. Such minute compartmentalization is useful primarily for marketing purposes (e.g., for so-called record clubs), but this entry does not take this microanalytical approach.

One final caveat: Much of the historical development of today's popular music forms has taken place from the mid-20th century onward. Prior to the development of rock music, popular music was largely limited to children's songs, such as "Rudolph, The Red-Nosed Reindeer," and a relatively anemic Top 20 composed of slow ballads, string orchestras, sing-along novelty songs, and sentimental music, typified by Dinah Shore's (1950) "Dear Hearts and Gentle

People." The emergence of rock and its many progeny created an explosion in popular music genres, skewing any discussion of the history of musical genres toward the modern era.

CLASSICAL MUSIC

The term *classical music* is somewhat problematic because it has at least three meanings. First, in restrictive usage, it refers to Western, especially European music of the classical music era, typically identified as the period from the mid-1700s through the first third of the 19th century. The musicians of this era contributed many enduring symphonies, string quartets, and sonatas. Haydn and Mozart are the prototypical composers of this period, and Beethoven served as the link between the classical and romantic periods. Second and in less restrictive usage, classical music includes Western music of the medieval, Renaissance, baroque, classical, romantic, 20th century, and contemporary periods that is composed by professionally trained artists using music notation and usually performed faithfully to the score—again, by professionally trained artists. Because formal training and education typically are required to perform such music, it is often referred to as "serious" music. A third, less common, usage of the term *classical music* refers to the serious music of non-Western cultures, such as Chinese classical music (court music) or Indian classical music (marga).

For our purposes, the second, less restrictive meaning of classical music is most relevant. This music had its origins in the monophonic chant music of the early Christian era, which retained its essential form through the Middle Ages. During the Renaissance, this music expanded to include motets and madrigals from England and the Netherlands, as well as the French chanson. During the late 16th century, Italian opera by composers such as Monteverdi became an important part of this tradition and was to dominate the early baroque period.

During the 17th century, classical music expanded to include keyboard suites, sonatas, organ music, and music for orchestras, including symphonies and concertos. Handel and Bach composed works for almost all of the musical genres of the high baroque period, and Bach contributed a corpus of liturgical music that remains a fixture in church music today.

In the rococo tradition of the early 18th century, a move toward simpler harmonies and a preponderance of instrumental music prevailed. Later in this century,

the elegant, complex, classic style of Haydn and Mozart dominated. Along with Beethoven, their works helped define the mainstream tradition of Western classical music, featuring piano sonatas, string quartets, and symphonies.

The romantic era dominated the 19th century, with the symphony taking center stage. In addition, program music, grand opera, and character pieces for piano were prominently featured. Important romantic composers include Schubert, Mendelssohn, Chopin, Liszt, Wagner, Brahms, and Verdi. Wagner, in particular, influenced the musical establishment through his powerful operas. During the latter portion of this century, Mahler and Richard Strauss represented a continuation of prior traditions, whereas Schönberg exemplified the New Viennese School, Debussy and Ravel the French impressionist composers, and innovators like Bartók introduced folk elements into classical traditions.

Twentieth-century classical music evolved into many different foci, including expressionism (e.g., Berg), serialism (e.g., Boulez), neoclassicism (e.g., Stravinsky), electronic music (e.g., Stockhausen), minimalism (e.g., Glass), and aleatoric music (e.g., Cage). The eclecticism of 20th-century composers has been balanced somewhat by accelerated interest in composing fresh exemplars of earlier classic traditions (e.g., baroque, romantic), yielding great complexity to the portfolio of contemporary classical music.

GOSPEL

The gospel genre includes songs whose lyrics have strong religious, especially Christian emphases. Two major traditions exist in the American gospel tradition. In the Anglo-American Protestant tradition, gospel songs were spawned from revival meetings of the 1800s, especially those featuring singer Ira Sankey, who wrote, sang, and popularized such hymns as "Trusting Jesus" and "Under His Wings" in association with the evangelistic crusades of Dwight L. Moody. Others contributing to this stream of gospel included Fanny Crosby, whose sentimental poem songs expressed fervent, first-person joy over the anticipated blessings of heaven, and the mournful staples of George Bernard, such as "The Old Rugged Cross."

African American Protestants also contributed a major stream to American gospel music, often providing simple melodies sung in full voice, accompanied by shouts, moans, whispers, clapping, and stomping.

The first recorded song in this tradition was Thomas A. Dorsey's "If You See My Savior" (1926), but the rich sounds of Mahalia Jackson and the Soul Stirrers (including Sam Cooke) popularized this tradition in the 1940s and 1950s. Quartets and choirs provided energetic religious stimulation in this "black gospel music" tradition, which also provided considerable influence to the later popular sounds of Elvis Presley, Ray Charles, and Little Richard, among many others.

By the early 1980s, contemporary Christian music had replaced black gospel music as the most popular gospel style, and artists such as Amy Grant, Michael W. Smith, and Sandi Patti thrived in this tradition and often crossed over into mainstream popular music. By the turn of the 21st century, praise and worship music was becoming an increasingly popular hybrid of gospel and was entering the Sunday services of many Protestant congregations.

JAZZ

Perhaps the most interdisciplinary genre of music with a uniquely American stamp is jazz, which developed from a cross-fertilization of ragtime, folk blues, American marching band music, the harmonic piano music of European composers such as Ravel and Debussy, Latin American dance music, and various African folk traditions, among other sources. Often called the first grassroots art form to develop in the United States, jazz is principally instrumental in nature and is a largely African American creation. Jazz has developed many subgenres, including Dixieland, swing/big band, bebop, free jazz, jazz-fusion, and smooth jazz.

The instruments most closely associated with jazz are the saxophone and trumpet, but also popular among jazz musicians are the trombone, piano, double bass, guitar, drums, clarinet, and banjo. The most distinctive feature of jazz is improvisation, and many jazz clubs continue to feature "improv" sessions, in which musicians spontaneously feed off of each other to develop original music and foster musical innovation.

Although most major U.S. cities have a jazz presence today, the roots of jazz are typically traced to the 1890s in New Orleans, where Dixieland was born. The Original Dixieland Jazz Band, a group of white street musicians, cut the earliest jazz record in New Orleans in 1917. Soon black artists such as Freddie Keppard, King Oliver, Jelly Roll Morton, and others co-opted this tradition.

The 1920s witnessed major changes in the jazz scene. Louis Armstrong's soulful trumpet solos accompanied by his innovative scatting were joined by the swing pianists of the James P. Johnson school (e.g., Count Basie, Duke Ellington), who were joined in turn by the complex ensemble performances of Jelly Roll Morton's Red Hot Peppers.

The 1930s saw major contributions to jazz from other locales, including Chicago, New York, Kansas City, and Memphis, with each city adding its own sound to the rapidly expanding and increasingly popular jazz genre. That decade also witnessed Benny Goodman's remarkable success with the big band sound, which opened the door for other dance bands (e.g., Tommy Dorsey, Glenn Miller), including bands with phenomenal vocalists (e.g., Artie Shaw with Billie Holiday, Chick Webb with Ella Fitzgerald).

During the 1940s, a reaction against the commercialization of big band jazz yielded way to the sound of bebop. Led by virtuosos such as Charlie "Bird" Parker on saxophone and Dizzy Gillespie on trumpet, jazz in this era become known for its fast tempos, innovative solo riffs, and wild chord progressions.

The 1950s saw the introduction of the cool style of West Coast jazz, with Gerry Mulligan (baritone sax), Chet Baker (trumpet), and Dave Brubeck (piano), among others. Meanwhile in the East, Cannonball Adderley, Max Roach, Sonny Rollins, and John Coltrane were taking funk to a new level with soul jazz. Simultaneously, the Modern Jazz Quartet and Thelonious Monk extended the life of bebop.

Free jazz was an important strain of the 1960s, with its attempt to replace jazz stereotypes with new inflections and procedures. Don Cherry, Cecil Taylor, and Miles Davis provided some of the important innovations in this tradition.

The latest trend in jazz is often called the fusion movement, or jazz fusion, as jazz discovered Latin, hard rock, bossa nova, and many other forms of modern music, to which it lent its own traditions and innovations. As always, the beauty of jazz is that as new traditions are formed, other artists take pride in maintaining all of the many heritage styles of jazz.

RHYTHM AND BLUES

Also known as R&B and rhythm 'n' blues, historically rhythm and blues has referred to forms of music that were neither jazz nor blues but rather were a more lightweight form of popular black music. Nowadays, R&B is often used as a synonym for any contemporary black popular music.

Perhaps the most important thing about R&B is that it was vital in spawning other forms of music, such as rock and roll, doo-wop, funk, hip hop, and rap music. The combination of funk and soul music then fused into contemporary R&B, which has remained a popular urban music form into the 21st century.

ROCK AND ROLL

Like rock, rock and roll has become an umbrella term used to describe all popular music recorded since the early 1950s. However, in its early iteration, rock and roll was a type of American popular music that fused rhythm and blues with other sources. Pioneered by Chuck Berry, rock and roll rose in popularity through the captivating performances of Bill Haley, Buddy Holly, and Elvis Presley in the 1950s. Performed by black and white artists, rock and roll became the most successful form of American popular music for several years, plus it attracted a loyal following in Europe and throughout the world.

Essentially a form of rhythmicized blues, rock and roll typically featured amplified guitars, saxophones, and a prominent rhythm section of drums, piano, and bass, with the rhythm section typically giving intense emphasis to the first beat of each 4/4 bar. The tempo of this musical form was fast, and the texts were often concerned with sex, drugs, and rock and roll itself.

Rock and roll saw a rebirth in the 1960s with the popularity of the Twist, enhanced by the dynamic performances of Chuck Berry. The Beach Boys also contributed significantly to this renaissance, which influenced British groups, such as the Beatles and the Rolling Stones. For the most part, however, the main music scene moved from rock and roll to rock music.

ROCK

Whereas the roots of rock and roll are in the South, rock music was the child of California and was born during the turbulent 1960s. The Byrds in Los Angeles and the Charlatans, the Great Society, Quicksilver Message Service, and others from San Francisco popularized this music, although the Jefferson Airplane was the first of the Northern California rock bands to strike it big with the public and obtain a major recording contract.

Rock was electric, and so was its featured instrument, the electric guitar. The use of amplified and often distorted sounds from electric guitars characterized this form, which spawned numerous legendary guitarists. Live performances were a mainstay of rock, which appealed largely to white audiences whose members often were at odds with mainstream America, especially where drugs, sex, and work were concerned.

The Beatles borrowed heavily from this tradition and added to it, making rock an Anglo-American musical form. Leading performers included the Rolling Stones, Eric Clapton, the Who, the Doors, Jimi Hendrix, the Grateful Dead, and Janis Joplin. Typically, rock held little appeal for black audiences or for rural white audiences in America.

The mainstream media (recording, broadcast, and film especially) adopted rock and fed off of it, popularizing it, including rock's notorious counterculture festivals (e.g., Woodstock). This media affinity continued throughout the 1970s, with Bruce Springsteen, Kiss, the Eagles, ZZ Top, and many others becoming media darlings. During the 1980s, Music Television (MTV) offered rock videos around the clock, further popularizing the genre worldwide.

Rock spun off numerous other forms or subgenres, including jazz rock, art rock, folk rock, heavy metal, punk, and new wave. At the same time, the term *rock* became diluted and stood for almost all media-disseminated popular music during the 1970s and 1980s. However, in recent years, the term is once again reclaiming its more narrowly defined focus.

PUNK

Few music genres are more controversial than punk, and that is the way its early adherents would have liked it. The first wave of punk bands, such as the Sex Pistols, the Clash, and the Ramones, thrived on being perceived as underground musicians, yet they helped mold mainstream rock from the outside. Punk also fostered a homegrown philosophy, foreshadowing the grunge and garage band movements of later years, and they encouraged their audience members to learn to play instruments and create their own music. The simplicity of the music form also contributed to this grassroots music, which created many independent record labels and fan zines, because the mainstream media seemingly chose not to foster the genre.

Punk also generated several subgenres. These include new wave, hardcore punk, post punk, and alternative rock. Alternative rock became increasingly mainstream during the latter portion of the 20th century.

HIP HOP

Hip hop music is largely the child of rhythm and blues. The hip hop culture began among Puerto Rican and African American youth in the inner city of New York City (especially the Bronx) in the early 1970s, and several rap or hip hop groups began recording in the late 1970s and early 1980s. By the turn of the century, hip hop was a staple of American popular music and was regularly performed around the world.

Hip hop has two primary elements—rapping and so-called DJing (mixing, scratching)—along with two secondary elements—tagging (graffiti, as known as writing) and break dancing. Typically, hip hop involves a rapper (or a group of rappers) chanting their stories in an intensely rhythmic, lyrical form that relies heavily on rhyming, alliteration, and sounds effects (synthesized, sampled, or produced by mouth). The beat is an instrumental track provided by a DJ or instrumentalists.

Early successful hip hop artists were Afrika Bambaataa, Coke La Rock, Clark Kent, and Kool Herc & the Herculoids. Commercially successful artists include LL Cool J, DJ Jazzy Jeff and the Fresh Prince, MC Hammer, N.W.A., Dr. Dre, Ice-T, Run-D.M.C., Snoop Dogg, and Mary J. Blige.

Hip hop is much more than music. It represents the soul of American ghetto youth and their struggle for self-expression. Its manifestations in language, art, dress, and other areas played a major part in mainstream American culture in the late 20th century. Some of its components, such as gangsta rap, have also been lightning rods for public criticism.

REGGAE

With its roots in urban Jamaican popular music, reggae appeared in the mid-1960s as a synthesis of American R&B, traditional African and Jamaican folk music, and ska. In texture, reggae is characterized by its emphasis on offbeat rhythmic patterns and changed chorals. It is popular as dance music and is often seen as the voice of the Rastafarian movement.

Retaining its popularity rather consistently in Jamaica over the years, reggae has achieved some intermittent popularity in the United States and in England. It also played an important role in influencing other musical forms, including punk rock and hip hop. Major reggae artists include Toots and the Maytals, Bob Marley and the Wailers, and Black Uhuru.

COUNTRY MUSIC

Also called country and western or honky-tonk music, country music was derived largely from traditional oral music brought from the British Isles to colonial America, especially to the South. As early as the 1920s, "fiddling" music was being promoted by recording companies, and Victor recorded fiddlers Henry Gilliland and Eck Robertson in 1922. Often called hillbilly music, this early form of country music relied on old narrative British ballads as well as newer American ballads, which were accompanied by banjo, harmonica, and guitar—as well as fiddles, of course. Dancing, including square dancing and clogging, often accompanied this music.

Derivations of this early music were popularized by Jimmie Rodgers and the Carter family, whose less indigenous approaches made the music more accessible to those outside the Scots-Irish tradition. In addition, fusion with the Western swing movement, as well as additions from the largely underground bluegrass movement, further broadened the appeal of country music. By the mid-1930s, a mainstream style had emerged, adding more features of urban music. Roy Acuff was a key practitioner of this hybrid style, which developed many of the future texts of country music—the harsh realities of death, desertion, crime, thwarted love, alcoholism, crime, and the like.

Commercial radio stimulated the diffusion of this music when clear-channel stations like WSB in Atlanta and WSN in Nashville began to play country music for their large audiences. The popularity of these stations inspired WBAP in Forth Worth and WLS in Chicago to begin to play country music, which expanded its scope well beyond the South.

In the 1950s, country became even more popular by adding elements of rock and roll, with some parts of the genre transitioning into rockabilly music. Even more critically, the Nashville sound—a polished form of country music—with its backbone in the Grand Ole Opry, began churning out country songs for more mainstream audiences. The formation of the Country Music Association in Nashville in 1958 further expanded the scope and reach of this style of country music, which was to reach prominence with artists like Kitty Wells, Hank Williams, Ray Price, George Jones, Johnny Cash, Merle Haggard, Jim Reeves, Loretta Lynn, Dolly Parton, Barbara Mandrell, and many, many others.

By the turn of the century, country music had become a huge commercial phenomenon, with many country artists (e.g., Faith Hill, Shania Twain, Garth Brooks) routinely crossing over to mainstream popular musical forms. Other forms of country, such as bluegrass, remained more loyal to their roots and also became increasingly popular.

ELECTRO-ACOUSTIC MUSIC

Music that makes creative use of electronic equipment—including producing, changing, or revising its basic properties—is often discussed under the generic rubric of *electro-acoustic music*. This includes many subgenres, including electronic music (which consists wholly or in part of sounds produced by synthesizers of other oscillators), computer music (music composed or generated digitally by computer), and *musique contrète* (the historical source of the electro-acoustic form in which sonic material is derived from recorded sound), and the like. Other popular categories of this genre include electronic dance music, space, new age, ambient, and electronica, which typically refers to electronic music without lyrics but is also a generic term for all electronic music.

Pioneers of this genre include Pierre Schaeffer, Herbert Eimert, Karlheinz Stockhausen, Robert Moog, Milton Babbitt, Mordon Mumma, John Cage, Lars Gunnar Bodin, Wendy Carlos, Tangerine Dream, Brian Eno, and Moby. Electronic music ranges in style from "elevator music" to *gabba* (Dutch hyper-techno).

OTHER MUSIC GENRES

It should be noted that numerous other forms of music, including some that are very popular, have not been discussed. Prominent among them are soul, salsa, disco, funk, world music, contemporary African music, and Latin music. All of these have major fan bases and contribute significantly to the cultural arts.

—*Jennings Bryant*

See also Hip Hop, Youth Culture and; Music Genres (various entries)

FURTHER READINGS

Grout, D. J., & Palisca, C. V. (2005). *A history of Western music* (7th ed.). New York: Norton.

Randel, D. (1986). *The new Harvard dictionary of music.* Cambridge, MA: Belknap.

Stambler, I. (1989). *The encyclopedia of pop, rock, and soul* (Rev. ed.). New York: St. Martin's Press.

MUSIC GENRES, POP/ROCK

Children have long mimicked their favorite rock and pop stars using hair brushes as microphones as they dance around to the radio, CDs, and MTV. As they reach adolescence, popular music becomes far more serious business, however. Ever since the mid-1950s when Elvis Presley gyrated on national television, and a few years later during the 1960s "British invasion," when the Beatles rocked Shea Stadium, adolescents have considered pop and rock music their own—a sign of adulthood, sexuality, rebellion, fun, and solidarity. Whereas pop music is often viewed by teens as a softer, more commercially available (and parentally accepted) genre of music, rock music is seen as a harder, more rebellious style. The genres are different stylistically, but they are often lumped together under the heading of pop/rock. Usually played with electric guitar, bass, and drums and often sung by a vocalist, rock is known for its strong backbeats and rebellious attitude, even though it is made up of countless subgenres that may or may not adhere to this general formula. The genre of rock is rooted in blues, jazz, rhythm and blues, and boogie-woogie styles but also is influenced by traditional folk, gospel, and country music. While Elvis is considered by some to be the mainstreaming influence of rock and roll, others argue that Chuck Berry's "Maybellene" and Bill Haley and the Comets' "Rock Around the Clock" actually represent the first major commercial success of rock music on the radio and through vinyl records. The origin of the name of rock and roll is generally attributed to the rocking motion taken up by Southern gospel singers, which refers to the motion they used when caught up in spiritual rapture of their religious music.

Rock music has evolved and branched into numerous different subgenres over the years, including surf rock (which relies on fast-tempo electric guitars and is mostly instrumental), hard rock (which features more intricate guitar solos and soaring vocals), heavy metal (which is generally a faster, guitar-and-bass heavier, louder form of hard rock), folk rock (which is often played with acoustic and electric instruments and is exemplified in the music of Bob Dylan), progressive rock (which is a complicated form of rock that often includes multiple keyboard instruments and musicians rooted in the classical tradition of playing), psychedelic rock (which is often inspired by psychedelic drugs of the 1960s and sometimes featured extensive solos based somewhat on jazz forms), garage rock (a very basic, pared-down rock that hearkens to the rock bands of the 1960s, such as The Animals), grunge (which almost always refers to the loud, grungy sounding guitar-based bands of the early 1990s, such as Nirvana and Pearl Jam), punk rock (which was stripped-down, three-chord rock without any slick production and which included an even more rebellious ethic than previous rock genres), alternative and indie rock (an enormous genre that first encompassed bands that simply would not receive play on mainstream radio but evolved into music that simply sounded different from and positioned itself as an alternative to classic rock), goth (which is music with dark themes that sounds somewhat like punk but is affiliated with a subculture in which its listeners dress in gothic-style clothing), emo (a combination of pop, punk, and rock that refers to *emotional* and means its musicians tend to sing more about love than violence), and many others. The subgenres of rock—which are too numerous to mention in this entry—continue to multiply as rock musicians create new sounds with different instruments and technologies.

Conversely, pop music is often perceived as more commercially successful and radio friendly (even though this is not necessarily the case), and soft rock music—and even mainstream rock music—is often categorized as pop music. In addition to being viewed as commercial music that relies primarily on vocal melodies and simple lyrics, pop music also uses many of the same conventions as rock, including electric guitars and bass, drums and vocals, and often keyboards and synthesizers and crosses over into the rock genre in many ways. Subgenres of pop may include rock, hip hop and rap (although these are generally a genre of their own), funk, disco, new wave (a more musically sophisticated offshoot of punk) techno, dance, and the more derogatory "bubblegum pop," which refers to throw-away kinds of pop songs with strong hooks and little musical proficiency or lyrical meaning that are largely enjoyed by the bubblegum

set, or young teens and children. In general, *pop* is sometimes considered a disparaging term because some critics believe that it stands for a betrayal of the defiant spirit of rock music and tends to rely on less skill and follows simpler musical conventions that are more marketable than rock. However, pop music does draw from the same roots and influences as rock, and the term pop has been used to describe the music of the most famous rock bands, including The Beatles, simply because the music is popular and melodious.

Today, popular pop and rock music is recognized for its economic power, particularly in relation to youth's desire for it. Multinational entertainment conglomerates depend on children and adolescents to purchase music not only as a means of personal entertainment but as a matter of personal identity. MTV, a network launched in 1981, has built an empire on playing videos and programming related to music and youth culture. Much of this programming could be considered advertising. From the show, *TRL* (which stands for "total request live" but actually bases its top 10 videos of the day not on the largest number of requests but rather on how much MTV is playing the videos), to its reality programming, MTV sells viewers not only music but a particular lifestyle. This lifestyle still embodies the idea of rebellion and freedom found in rock music, but it also depends a certain amount on adolescents being positioned as powerful consumers of both popular culture and consumer goods.

—*Shayla Thiel*

See also Music, Rebelliousness and; Music Genres, Dance/ House/Techno; Music Genres, Heavy Metal; Music Genres, Hip Hop; Music Genres, History of; Music Lyrics (various entries); Music Videos (various entries)

FURTHER READINGS

Christenson, P., & Roberts, D. F. (1998). *It's not only rock and roll: Popular music in the lives of adolescents.* Cresskill, NJ: Hampton Press.

George-Warren, H., Romanowski, P., & Pareles, J. (2001). The Rolling Stone *encyclopedia of rock and roll* (revised and updated for the 21st century). New York: Fireside Press.

Grossberg, L. (1987). Rock and roll in search of an audience. In J. Lull (Ed.), *Popular music and communication* (pp. 175–197). Beverly Hills, CA: Sage.

Marcus, G. (1999). *In the fascist bathroom: Punk in pop music, 1977–1992.* Cambridge, MA: Harvard University Press.

Shirley, D. (1997). *The history of rock and roll.* New York: Franklin Watts.

MUSIC LISTENING, AGE EFFECTS ON

Age is an important consideration when discussing music listening because it is one of only two demographic characteristics that consistently predict audio exposure. Researchers who examine overall media use by children and adolescents have identified a distinct change in behavior at approximately 8 years old. This entry thus focuses on two developmental periods—children (ages 1 to 7) and older children and adolescents (ages 8 to 18).

YOUNG CHILDREN (AGES 1 TO 7)

The developmental stage of the young child dictates much of the music listening experience. Infants as young as 5 months show signs of recognizing and learning rhythmic patterns and sequential relationships between sounds. Recognition of pitch develops later. However, those reactions are most likely responses to changes in the aural environment as the infants differentiate the music from other nonmusical sounds like speech. Such discriminating listening is further refined to the point where preschoolers increasingly connect musical sounds with emotions, such as associating major mode to happiness and minor mode to sadness.

Research suggests that children begin to develop musical taste around the age of 5. That is, they exhibit greater reactions to the rhythmic and tonal characteristics of music. By the age of 5, children favor harmonious over dissonant, tonal over atonal, and metrical over nonmetrical music. However, as they grow, the disparity in their reactions to the extremes (e.g., tonal versus atonal) increases such that 10-year-olds are much more accepting of music that is harmonious, tonal, and metrical. The changes in taste observed in children between ages 4 and 10 are commonly attributed to the combination of acculturation and psychological development during this period. Of course, parental involvement is a prime source of acculturation. More than half of parents of young children report singing or playing music for them each day. However, the frequency of music play decreases for toddlers and for second children as compared to first children.

Children between the ages of 2 and 7 listen to music about 45 minutes per day. At this age, the research suggests they spend a little more time with radio than other sources. Children are four times more likely to listen to

children's music and programming than Christian, classical, Top 40, or country and western music genres, each of which is heard by about 10% of children. By the age of 6, children are focusing more attention on popular music and start recognizing and forming opinions about the hit songs of the day. The interest in popular music grows steadily, and their openness to music decreases as they reach adolescence.

OLDER CHILDREN AND ADOLESCENTS (AGES 8 TO 18)

Development and Exposure

Music is frequently cited as the most important media for adolescents due in part to their physiological and psychological development. Around the age of 8, children begin developing a greater sense of independence, and they enter a period of transition away from parental guidance toward self-determination. This transition is accompanied by changes in adolescents' media exposure. Researchers have observed an increase in audio use between the ages of 8 and 18 while other media use (e.g., television) declines, particularly during the mid-teen years. Between the ages of 13 and 18, the typical adolescent spends more than 10,000 hours listening to music. On any given day, 85% of U.S. children between 8 and 18 years old listen to at least a few minutes of audio media (primarily music), and more than 40% of those children spend more than an hour and a half listening each day. Most adolescents are spending that time with popular music.

Popular music is widely recognized as being made by young people for young people. The combination of youthful performers and salient subjects and messages is accepted as one explanation for adolescents' tremendous pop music interest. There are many genres of popular music today, and adolescents frequently report listening to more than one genre. However, a couple of genres are clearly favored. Rap/hip hop and alternative rock are the most popular, although listening patterns differ based on ethnicity and gender. More than half the adolescents between the ages of 12 and 18 listen to some rap/hip hop music on a typical day. About half listen to alternative rock.

Context

The social context in which music is heard has been shown to interact with the genre of the music to yield different listening experiences. For example, listening to hard rock or heavy metal among friends has a positive effect while listening to those genres among family members leads to a negative effect.

The majority of adolescent music listening occurs in solitary or personal situations to supplement activities such as reading, studying, and talking on the phone. Preteens (10 to 12 years old) spend less than half of their active listening time alone. That amount increases substantially in the teen years when they are likely to spend nearly three quarters of their active listening time alone. Much of the solitary listening occurs in the bedroom because it is seen as a refuge for self-exploration and dealing with stress and negative emotions. Music plays a role in mood management by eliciting desired affective states. Music can be a source of inspiration and arousal during times of low self-esteem or can provide an environment for exploring feelings of sadness. Music also can provide companionship or a sense of connectedness in moments of loneliness. In social contexts like dances and parties, music stimulates or excites positive moods. This use is obvious when one imagines dances, but it holds true when listening to sad music with close friends because the listening creates a shared experience and connectedness between friends.

—*William Kinnally*

See also Music, Group Identity and; Music Genres (various entries); Music Listening, Gender Effects on

FURTHER READINGS

Christenson, P. G., & Roberts, D. F. (1998). *It's not only rock & roll: Popular music in the lives of adolescents.* Cresskill, NJ: Hampton Press.

Larson, R. (1995). Secrets in the bedroom: Adolescents' private use of media. *Journal of Youth and Adolescence, 24*(5), 535–550.

Roberts, D. F., & Foehr, U. G. (2004). *Kids and media in America.* New York: Cambridge University Press.

Schwartz, K. D., & Fouts, G. T. (2003). Music preferences, personality style, and developmental issues in adolescents. *Journal of Youth and Adolescence, 32*(3), 205–213.

Thompson, K. P. (1993). Media, music, and adolescents. In R. M. Lerner (Ed.), *Early adolescence: Perspectives on research, policy, and intervention* (pp. 407–418). Hillsdale, NJ: Erlbaum.

Zenatti, A. (1993). Children's musical cognition and taste. In T. J. Tighe & W. J. Dowling (Eds.), *The psychology of music: The understanding of melody and rhythm* (pp. 177–196). Hillsdale, NJ: Erlbaum.

MUSIC LISTENING, GENDER EFFECTS ON

Adolescence is a time of identity development, specifically with regard to sexuality and gender, and adolescents spend an enormous amount of time listening to popular music and music videos. Music is also of high importance for "tweens" (roughly ages 9-to-12-years-old), who are at an age when many are in their first more serious romantic relationship. Because popular music contains many portrayals of gender roles and gender-typed behavior, often related to sexuality and romantic relationships, music exposure during these life phases most likely affects gender roles and related behavior. This connection may actually be the reason why music is preoccupied with romance and sexuality and thus with gender roles, and why teens and tweens listen to music so frequently. Concerns about the reinforcement of gender stereotypes and about too much emphasis on sexuality have often been voiced. This entry examines gender-related music content, music preferences, and the effects of music listening.

GENDER PORTRAYALS IN MUSIC LYRICS AND VIDEOS

Portrayals of gender roles have always been common in popular music. The first systematic analyses of lyrics focused on the then-dominant portrayals of love and courtship. Although, in the 1960s, a shift occurred in popular music to less emphasis on love and romance, the physical aspects of love gained more importance over time (Knobloch-Westerwick, Musto, and Shaw provide an up-to-date overview of these developments). Content analyses of popular music lyrics are fairly rare, but some have examined depictions of gender roles. For female role stereotypes specifically, Cooper found that 96% of the sampled songs from the 1940s to 1970s contained such stereotyping. The importance of stereotyping aspects changed; for example, females' physical characteristics were mentioned significantly more often in each successive decade of the four that were examined.

Several studies investigated gender stereotyping in music videos and found gender-typed portrayals across the board. Findings showed that males and females are victims of aggression with equivalent frequency, but black males are more than three times as likely to be aggressors, and white females are most frequently victims. The authors have suggested that music videos may reinforce false stereotypes of aggressive black males and victimized white females. Other work showed that men appear nearly twice as often as women, and men engage in significantly more aggressive and dominant behavior; women, on the other hand, engage in significantly more implicitly sexual and subservient behavior and are more frequently the object of explicit, implicit, and aggressive sexual advances. An analysis of characters' behaviors in music videos concluded that males are depicted as more adventuresome and aggressive than females, whereas females appear more affectionate and fearful than males. It was also found that many female characters wear revealing clothing and that they initiate and receive sexual advances more often than males.

GENDER-TYPED MUSIC USES AND PREFERENCES

Listeners' gender has been found to be of critical importance for individual reactions to popular music. For example, in a study by Toney and Weaver, males showed the strongest positive reactions toward hard-rock videos whereas females liked soft-rock music videos the most. Christenson and Peterson found that young females expressed a higher preference for mainstream pop, disco, R&B, soul, and gospel than males, whereas males favored various kinds of rock and blues. Boys and girls also differ in the ways they use music to regulate mood. Research suggests that girls more often use music to control and improve mood, to overcome loneliness, to pass time, and to set a tone with others.

Gender is also important in how teens and tweens perceive peers in connection with music preferences. Research indicates that expressing gender-typed musical tastes may create a favorable impression on adolescent and young adult age peers. For example, Zillmann and Bhatia reported that young men found a young woman more attractive as a potential date if she was said to like classical music whereas young women found a depicted man more attractive if he appeared to like heavy metal music.

MUSIC EFFECTS ON THE GENDERS

Music listening has been shown to have both short- and long-term effects on gender-related perceptions.

The former can be explained with priming, the latter with cultivation theory.

For the short-term priming effects, exposure to stereotypical music videos can alter viewers' impressions of people observed in similar contexts, often making neutral behavior appear more sexualized and making actions that fit stereotypical gender schemas seem more favorable. For example, music with sexually explicit lyrics has been shown to prime sexual appeal as an evaluative criterion in peers of the opposite sex. In other words, when young people get together and meet others of the same age, while being exposed to sexually laden lyrics of popular music, they are more likely to judge a potential partner merely based on physical appearance and sexual desirability.

Cultivation effects of music exposure emerged in survey findings showing that higher amounts of music video viewing was associated with more traditional gender role attitudes and with assignment of greater importance to specific stereotypical attributes. It has also been reported that frequent music video use was linked to stronger acceptance of women as sexual objects.

CONCLUSION AND OUTLOOK

The evidence that listening to popular music reinforces gender stereotypes and primes sexuality as important is fairly clear and unequivocal. Yet, any possible actions based on these findings face the challenge of how to maintain free speech interests and still curtail potentially harmful music content. The Parents Music Resource Center's opposition to the use of violence, drugs, and sex in music has resulted in warning labels on CDs. The identification and classification of content related to gender stereotypes, however, may be more difficult to justify. Nonetheless, this debate will certainly continue, given recent trends such as extreme gender stereotypes in hip hop music portraying women as sexual objects.

—*Silvia Knobloch-Westerwick*

See also Gender, Media Use and; Gender Identity Development; Gender Roles in Music; Hip Hop, Portrayals of Women in; Music, Personal Identity and; Music Listening, Uses of; Music Lyrics, Music Television and

FURTHER READINGS

Christenson, P. G., & Peterson, J. B. (1988). Genre and gender in the structure of music preference. *Communication Research, 15*, 282–301.

Cooper, V. W. (1985). Women in popular music: A quantitative analysis of feminine images over time. *Sex Roles, 13*(9–10), 499–506.

Dillman Carpentier, F., Knobloch-Westerwick, S., & Blumhoff, A. (in press). Naughty versus nice: Suggestive pop music influences on perceptions of potential romantic partners. *Media Psychology.*

Gan, S.-L., Zillmann, D., & Mitrook, M. (1997). Stereotyping effect of black women's sexual rap on white audiences. *Basic and Applied Social Psychology, 19*(3), 381–399.

Gantz, W., Gartenberg, H., Pearson, M., & Schiller, S. (1978). Gratifications and expectations associated with pop music among adolescents. *Popular Music and Society, 6*(1), 81–89.

Hansen, C. H., & Krygowski, W. (1994). Arousal-augmented priming effects. Rock music videos and sex object schemas. *Communication Research, 21*, 24–47.

Knobloch, S., & Mundorf, N. (2003). Enjoyment of music and music television. In J. Bryant, D. Roskos-Ewoldsen, & J. Cantor (Eds.), *Communication and emotion* (pp. 491–509). Mahwah, NJ: Erlbaum.

Knobloch-Westerwick, S., Musto, P., & Shaw, K. (2006, June). *Rebellion in the top music charts: Defiant messages in rap/hip hop and rock music 1993 and 2003.* Paper presented at the International Communication Association conference, Dresden, Germany.

Toney, G. T., & Weaver, J. B. (1994). Effects of gender and gender-role self-perception on affective reactions to rock-music videos. *Sex Roles, 30*, 567–583.

Zillmann, D., & Bhatia, A. (1989). Effects of associating with musical genres on heterosexual attraction. *Communication Research, 16*(2), 263–288.

MUSIC LISTENING, IMPACT OF

Since the early 20th century, various sectors of society have expressed concerns about the effects of exposure to popular music on children and young adults. More recently, research has addressed the effects on young people of listening to a variety of music genres, especially heavy metal and hip hop. Such research has examined the effects of music listening on attitudes toward women and girls, attitudes toward racial stereotyping, general aggression, and other personality traits. Models using priming theory and information processing theory are among the explanations offered for such effects.

Beginning with jazz and blues in the 1920s, and then moving to rock and roll in the 1950s, commentary about the effects of secular music on attitudes, thoughts, and behavior have appeared in both major and local newspapers, as well as periodicals. In particular, some parents, politicians, school officials, and clergy have charged that such music fosters negative attitudes about women and girls, incites violence, and promotes drug use and reckless sexual behavior. For example, in a *Washington Post* article on January 29, 1922, the Chicago school superintendent describes jazz music as an evil force that corrupts dancing and decreases respect for womanhood.

Beginning in the 1980s, however, the genres of metal and hip hop music, particularly the subgenres of death metal and gangsta/pimp rap, have drawn even greater ire from these groups. In addition to the aforementioned concerns, some people have criticized both genres for being nihilistic and homophobic. In addition, some citizens have assailed metal music for celebrating what they perceive as Satanism and occultism, while condemning some types of political rap music for promoting militancy or racial separatism. An extreme example of public disapproval for these genres is exemplified by former U.S. Senator Robert Dole's attack on the film and music industries in 1995 for marketing what he described as "nightmares of depravity" to American citizens. Dole singled out rap music and media giant Time Warner, which had previously distributed the song "Cop Killer," which was recorded by rapper Ice-T's speed metal band, Body Count. Thus, concerns about the deleterious effects of rap, rock, and metal music provide the impetus for most of the research on the effects of listening to popular music.

Ethical concerns about exposing children and adolescents to sexual, violent, and other controversial content in popular music genres, such as rap, rock, and metal, have limited research on effects of popular music primarily to college students and other young adults. Thus, only two published studies have investigated the effects of popular music on adolescents, and both of them involve research by Johnson and various colleagues on the effects of exposure to rap music videos. One study concerned violent themes, whereas the other entailed the depiction of young women in sexually subordinate roles.

Most of the research on popular music deals with the effects of viewing music videos, rather than listening to music without visual accompaniment. However, although such studies greatly contribute to the literature, they do not reveal information about the effects of exposure to violent lyrics without video. In fact, such studies actually confound or make it difficult to tease apart the roles that visual and aural content play in any observed effects. Thus, research on the effects of music listening would be quite valuable.

Although there is a dearth of experimental research on popular music, particularly regarding effects on adolescents, some survey research lends support to the findings of these studies. Collectively, they provide evidence that both refute and confirm some commonly held beliefs about the effects of listening to various types of popular music. In addition, these studies offer insight into factors that mitigate the negative effects of aural music exposure.

LINKS BETWEEN MUSIC PREFERENCES, PERSONALITY STYLE, AND ATTITUDES

Recent survey research has explored associations between preferences for various music genres, dispositions, and attitudes. In particular, these researchers were interested in associations between music that some people consider rebellious or aggressive and personal attitudes and behavior. Because these researchers took different approaches to defining various music genres, the findings are mixed. Nevertheless, there is some overlap. In a 2003 study, Schwartz and Fouts found that adolescents who preferred "heavy" music (such as the metal, rock, and rap genres) tended to be independent, anticonformist, and aggressive and more likely to question other people's rules, motives, and abilities, compared to teenagers who prefer "lighter" music, such as pop, teen pop, and dance music. In addition, they found that those who preferred heavy music demonstrated lower self-esteem and higher self-doubt than did those who preferred lighter music.

These findings are consistent with earlier research, which suggests that adolescents use music as both a learning tool and a way of constructing their identity. According to Berry, children whose academic performance is poor tend not to identify with school, and they seek alternative ways to "fit in" and increase their

self-esteem, such as immersing themselves in alternative music cultures. Such cultures supply an identity replete with fashion, hairstyles, language, and ideology. Nonspecific to academic performance, however, Larson and Kubey found that music, more than other media, elicits more motivation and excitement from adolescents in general and more emotional involvement from girls in particular, as it addresses their concerns about sexuality, individualization, and autonomy.

With respect to light music, Schwartz and Fouts found that adolescents who preferred such music experienced greater difficulty with their developing sexuality and with reconciling childhood beliefs with new sexual impulses than both heavy and eclectic music listeners. Furthermore, light-music listeners were more preoccupied with fitting in and being accepted by their peers, as well as with following rules and being responsible people than these other types of listeners. Teenagers who had eclectic music tastes, on the other hand, experienced less difficulty negotiating their adolescence than either light or heavy music listeners. This suggests that they flexibly use music to alter, reflect, or validate their moods. However, it is unknown whether musical eclecticism facilitates adolescent adjustment or whether well-adjusted adolescents simply have eclectic tastes.

In other research on college students, one study grouped heavy metal music with rock and alternative, which the authors labeled "intense and rebellious." They found an association between preference for heavy metal and self-perceived intelligence and verbal ability, openness to new experiences, athleticism, physical attractiveness, and risk taking, whereas another study found that heavy metal listeners were more aggressive and expressed less regard for women. With respect to rap music, the former study grouped this style of music with soul and electronica (labeled "energetic and rhythmic"). They found that people who listen to such music tend to be extroverted, agreeable, liberal, and athletic and to perceive themselves as attractive. Similar to the findings of the other study, rap music listeners were more aggressive and distrusting than people who did not listen to rap music; however, rap listeners also exhibited greater self-esteem.

Survey research is quite useful in terms of linking attitudes and personality types with music preferences, but this method does not allow one to determine whether the music preferences influence attitudes and personality or vice versa. A recent quasi-experimental study, however, sheds some light on these mixed findings. In addition to the problems that arise when researchers take different approaches to defining or classifying music genres, Carpentier, Knobloch, and Zillmann argued that self-report measures of music preference are problematic because youths often use music to establish or maintain a self-image or peer-group membership.

Thus, they assessed various personality traits of a group of college students and then allowed them to selectively expose themselves to defiant rock and rap songs, nondefiant rock and rap songs, or no music at all. Defining proactive rebellion as the active pursuit of activities solely to elicit excitement, they found that respondents who expressed higher levels of this trait listened to more defiant music than their counterparts. Similarly, when they combined proactive and reactive (unpremeditated retaliation or aggression to a situation such as arguing with an authority figure who yells at you) measures of rebellion to create a single assessment of "negative dominance," they found that participants who scored lower on this trait listened to defiant music for a much shorter period than their counterparts. Furthermore, they found that a higher level of disinhibition (such as preferring wild parties) was associated with liking defiant music, whereas hostility was not. Consequently, Carpentier, Knobloch, and Zillmann concluded that the rebellion associated with a preference for defiant music, which induces impulsive and sometimes antisocial feelings and behaviors, is inspired by a quest for freedom rather than being induced by anger.

EXPERIMENTAL RESEARCH ON THE EFFECTS OF MUSIC EXPOSURE

Attitudes Toward Women and Girls

Only a handful of true experiments have been conducted on the effects of popular music listening, and they have primarily addressed concerns about sexual aggression and other negative attitudes and behaviors toward women and girls. In one such study, St. Lawrence and Joyner explored the effects on male college students of sexually violent heavy metal rock, Christian heavy metal rock, and classical music. They found that regardless of the lyrical content, young men who were exposed to either type of metal/rock music held more stereotypic and negative attitudes toward women than young men who listened to

classical music. Unexpectedly, they also found that men who were exposed to classical music reported greater levels of sexual arousal than men who listened to either type of metal/rock music.

Two other studies investigated the effects of exposure to misogynous or sexually violent rap music on relatively small samples of predominantly white male college students. In one study, Barongan and Hall examined whether—following exposure to either misogynous or nonviolent rap music—participants would choose to expose a young woman to a sexually violent movie clip (containing a rape scene), a clip depicting nonsexual aggression toward a woman, or one showing a pleasant conversation between a man and woman. They found that few participants in either music condition showed the sexually violent clip. However, men who listened to music that demeaned women were more likely to show the clip that depicted aggression against women than men who listened to nonviolent rap music.

In the other study, Wester, Crown, Quatman, and Heesacker explored the effects of gangsta rap music on participants who were unfamiliar with the gangsta rap subculture. They found that exposure to such lyrics led men to view their relationships with women as more adversarial or as a competitive sport in which they must prevail, compared with men who did not listen to gangsta rap lyrics. In addition, people who hold adversarial beliefs about relationships generally perceive members of the opposite sex as untrustworthy. When the music itself was presented without lyrics, there were no effects on participants' attitudes toward women.

Attitudes Toward Racial Stereotyping

Regarding the effects of popular music on attitudes about racial stereotyping, Johnson, Trawalter, and Dovidio investigated the effects of exposure to violent rap songs by male artists. They concluded that exposure to such music can have negative implications for African Americans and that these effects occur for both black and white evaluators. Regarding judgments about aggression, respondents reacted to a story about a young black or white man who drank beer and then behaved aggressively after discovering that his fiancée broke off their engagement to date his best friend. Both blacks and whites attributed the black man's behavior to an enduring negative disposition or personality, rather than to situational factors such as feelings of hurt and betrayal, more often than they did with the white man's behavior. However, white participants were more likely than blacks to attribute the black man's behavior to disposition.

With respect to perceptions of intelligence, when asked to evaluate an applicant for a managerial position at a microchip manufacturing company, researchers found that exposure to violent rap music caused whites to perceive the black job applicant as less qualified than the white applicant. The final step in this overall study involved evaluations of a male applicant for an aircraft pilot position, which required strong "spatial skills." Unlike intelligence and aggression, this characteristic has been absent from cultural racial stereotypes. Thus, as expected, researchers found that exposure to violent rap music did not interact with race of the applicant and respondent to influence judgments. Interestingly, however, black participants perceived the black applicant to be more qualified than the white applicant, whereas white participants perceived the applicants to be equally qualified. Supporting these findings, Rudman and Lee found that after listening to violent and misogynist rap music, people evaluated a black target less favorably than a white target.

General Aggression

In terms of general aggression, Anderson, Carnagay, and Eubanks conducted five experiments to demonstrate that exposure to violent rock songs affects aggressive thoughts in three different ways. Such songs caused young adult listeners to interpret ambiguously aggressive words (such as *rock* or *stick*) as aggressive and increased the speed with which they pronounced aggressive (compared to nonaggressive) words. In addition, men pronounced aggressive words faster than women. Last, violent songs increased the proportion of aggressive words that listeners completed.

COGNITION AND MUSIC EFFECTS

The Priming Process

Studies of effects of popular music most often use priming theory to explain the process by which exposure to various types of music exerts its effect. Priming refers to the increased accessibility or reactivation of cognitive pictures and thoughts (known as schemas) immediately following exposure to a stimulus. Of course, in order for a stimulus to reactivate thoughts, those thoughts must have been previously stored in

memory following exposure to some event. Thus, researchers have proposed network models that involve memory nodes in the brain to explain how various stimuli (such as music) are capable of influencing our thoughts and feelings. Nodes refer to clusters of associated concepts that are located in memory. However, unlike parts of the brain that are concrete or visible, either through visual examination or technology, such as the cerebrum or pituitary gland, one cannot physically locate these nodes in the brain. Thus, memory nodes represent an abstract yet descriptive concept.

According to Berkowitz, activated thoughts radiate outward from a particular node along the associative pathways of other nodes and remain activated at the node for a brief period, enabling activation of other related thoughts and feelings. Bargh found that priming may chronically or temporarily increase accessibility of information that pertains to a particular target, either consciously or automatically (beneath the threshold of awareness); this information is then capable of affecting subsequent judgments and behaviors. A useful way of thinking of this may be to envision the music or other stimulus as a flame and the brain as a large branch containing smaller limbs, which represent different types of emotions, thoughts, or memories. If the main branch is set afire, then the flame will travel to the smaller limbs and spark a variety of pictures, thoughts, and feelings. The initial fire will die out, but if the branch is exposed to flame repeatedly, the fire may travel to other parts of the tree or surrounding forest and create lasting changes to the landscape.

Regarding stereotype activation, Johnson et al. used stereotype priming, as distinguished from category priming, to explain how exposure to stereotypes about black people affects both interracial (between members of different races) and intraracial (between members of the same race) perceptions. According to Lepore and Brown, category priming occurs only when a particular category is cued in the absence of any stereotypic characteristics. For example, the category *rapper*, which may be primed by a visual image of a young African American wearing trendy urban attire (i.e., extremely baggy or "sagging" pants), might be sufficient to adversely affect judgments about black people. Stereotype priming, on the other hand, involves the direct cueing of stereotypic characteristics, such as a rapper whose discourse is hypersexual, violent, and materialistic, with or without the category label. Moreover, Lepore and Brown have found that the activation of stereotypes does not vary as a function of level of prejudice because priming one aspect of a cultural stereotype activates other stereotypic associations.

These findings support Devine's early research demonstrating the role of culture in the maintenance of stereotypes. She found that although participants with lower levels of prejudice expressed fewer racially pejorative thoughts about blacks, they were equally knowledgeable about existing stereotypes about that group by virtue of their participation in the larger culture. Thus, with respect to effects of exposure to violent and sexist music, although whites and men may express more stereotypical beliefs about blacks and women, respectively, these latter groups are likely to be aware of such stereotypes within American culture.

Information Processing Theory

Another useful tool for explaining the effects of listening to popular music is Huesmann's information processing model, which extends Berkowitz's neoassociationist model as well as Bandura's model of observational learning. Berkowitz emphasized the importance of situational cues or primers, whereas Bandura underscored the governing of social behavior by internal self-regulating processes and the role of direct reinforcements (i.e., rewards and punishments). Huesmann's model focuses first on cognitive scripts and then on their acquisition and retrieval from memory.

According to the Huesmann model, people employ a heuristic search process to retrieve a script from memory that is appropriate for the situation. In addition, this model highlights the role of normative beliefs or internalized prescriptions regarding the appropriateness of behavior, beliefs that serve to regulate or justify behavior. Huesmann argues that both scripts and normative beliefs are learned via a combination of observational learning, cognitive rehearsal of the observed material, and physically enacting behaviors (instrumental learning).

Common examples of scripts are the "boy meets girl" or "schoolyard bully picks on unpopular kid" scenarios, which are ubiquitous in media. In addition, many children and adults may draw from personal experiences. These experiences involve tactics that either worked or failed to achieve results in a situation, as well as rewards or punishments. For example, if a boy successfully gets a date by lying or presenting himself in an otherwise false manner, then he may continue such behavior. Thus, listening to violent or

sexual music, particularly over an extended period, may influence attitudes toward particular groups (e.g., girls or African Americans), and these attitudes serve as scripts for future behavior.

—*Angie Colette Beatty*

See also Cognitive Script Theory; Media Effects, Models of; Music Genres, Heavy Metal; Music Genres, Hip Hop; Music Listening, Problem Behavior and; Priming Theory

FURTHER READINGS

Anderson, C. A., Carnagey, N. L., & Eubanks, J. (2003). Exposure to violent media: The effects of songs with violent lyrics on aggressive thoughts and feelings. *Journal of Personality and Social Psychology, 84,* 960–971.

Bargh, J. A. (1997). The automaticity of everyday life. In R. S. Wyer, Jr. (Ed.), *The automaticity of everyday life: Advances in social cognition* (Vol. 10, pp. 1–61). Mahwah, NJ: Erlbaum.

Barongan, C., & Hall, G. C. N. (1995). The influence of misogynous rap music on sexual aggression against women. *Psychology of Women Quarterly, 19,* 195–207.

Berkowitz, L. (1984). Some effects of thoughts on anti- and prosocial influences of media events: A cognitive-neoassociation analysis. *Psychological Bulletin, 95,* 410–427.

Berry, V. T. (1990). Rap music, self-concept, and low-income adolescents. *Popular Music and Society, 14,* 89–107.

Binder, A. (1993). Constructing racial rhetoric: Media depictions of harm in heavy metal and rap music. *American Sociological Review, 58,* 753–767.

Bryson, B. (1996). "Anything but heavy metal": Symbolic exclusion and musical dislikes. *American Sociological Review, 61,* 884–899.

Carpentier, F. D., Knobloch, S., & Zillmann, D. (2002). Rock, rap, and rebellion: Comparisons of traits predicting selective exposure to defiant music. *Personality and Individual Differences, 35,* 1643–1655.

Devine, P. G. (1989). Stereotypes and prejudice: Their automatic and controlled components. *Journal of Personality and Social Psychology, 56,* 5–18.

Huesmann, L. R. (1998). The role of social information processing and cognitive schema in the acquisition and maintenance of habitual aggressive behavior. In R. G. Geen & E. Donnerstein (Eds.), *Human aggression: Theories, research, and implications for social policy* (pp. 73–109). San Diego, CA: Academic Press.

Huesmann, L. R., & Guerra, N. G. (1997). Children's normative beliefs about aggression and aggressive behavior. *Journal of Personality and Social Psychology, 72,* 408.

Huesmann, L. R., Moise, J. F., & Podolski, C. (1997). The effects of media violence on the development of antisocial behavior. In D. M. Stoff, J. Breiling, & J. D. Maser (Eds.), *Handbook of antisocial behavior* (pp. 181–193). New York: John Wiley.

Jo, E., & Berkowitz, L. (1994). A priming effect analysis of media influence: An update. In *Media effects: Advances in theory and research* (pp. 43–60). Mahwah, NJ: Erlbaum.

Johnson, J. D., Trawalter, S., & Dovidio, J. F. (2000). Converging interracial consequences of exposure to violent rap music on stereotypical attributions of blacks. *Journal of Experimental Social Psychology, 36,* 233–251.

Lacayo, R. (1995, June 12). America's cultural revulsion. *Time,* pp. 24–30.

Larson, R. W., & Kubey, R. (1983). Television and music: Contrasting media in adolescent life. *Youth and Society, 15,* 13–31.

Lepore, L., & Brown, R. (1997). Category and stereotype activation: Is prejudice inevitable? *Journal of Personality and Social Psychology, 72,* 275–287.

Rentfrow, P. J., & Gosling, S. D. (2003). The do re mi's of everyday life: The structure and personality correlates of music preferences. *Journal of Personality and Social Psychology, 84,* 1236–1256.

Rubin, A. M., West, D. V., & Mitchell, W. S. (2001). Differences in aggression, attitudes toward women, and distrust as reflected in popular music preferences. *Media Psychology, 3,* 25–42.

Rudman, L. A., & Lee, M. R. (2002). Implicit and explicit consequences of exposure to violent and misogynous rap music. *Group Processes and Intergroup Relations, 5,* 133–150.

Rusting, C. L. (1998). Personality, mood, and cognitive processing of emotional information: Three conceptual frameworks. *Psychological Bulletin, 124,* 165–196.

Schwartz, K. D., & Fouts, G. T. (2003). Music preferences, personality style, and developmental issues of adolescents. *Journal of Youth and Adolescence, 32,* 205–213.

St. Lawrence, J. S., & Joyner, D. J. (1991). The effects of sexually violent rock music on males' acceptance of violence against women. *Psychology of Women Quarterly, 15,* 49–63.

Wester, S. R., Crown, C. L., Quatman, G. L., & Heesacker, M. (1997). The influence of sexually violent rap music on attitudes of men with little prior exposure. *Psychology of Women Quarterly, 21,* 497–508.

MUSIC LISTENING, PROBLEM BEHAVIOR AND

Throughout history and across cultures, music has been part of celebratory and religious gatherings and ceremonies. Due to music's power to provide an appropriate auditory context for festive and solemn events, as well as its ability to enhance moods and to comfort, great potency is attributed to this medium. In weighing music's power, some philosophers, religious leaders, and educators have stressed that music listening not only may have positive consequences but also is also a potentially dangerous medium. For instance, Greek philosopher Plato (428–ca. 347 BC) argued that music teaching was an essential part of education but that music in the soft and sorrowful Lydian mode—one of four major modes established by the Greeks—would feminize men and was even unfit to be listened to by women. The complaint that music consumption may induce or aggravate problems has survived into the present day and was most prominently heard when popular music found a mass audience in the second quarter of the 20th century. In the 1920s, jazz music, and more specifically the Charleston dance craze, was seen as an incentive to immoral behavior, leading to all kinds of social illnesses from female smoking to premarital sex and alcohol and drug abuse. The development of modern pop music since the mid-1950s has led to claims that some artists and some genres are a real threat to youth. Pop music listening has been associated with the development of a wide array of problem behaviors ranging from devil worship, suicide, and depression to substance misuse, aggression, and delinquency. In public debates throughout the 20th century, certain critics have described some types of music as possessing the power to induce violence, drug abuse, and self-harm and to undermine sexual morals and accepted religious notions. However, although correlations have been found between music preferences and problem behavior among adolescents, the issue of causality remains problematic.

CLAIMS ABOUT THE NEGATIVE INFLUENCES OF POP MUSIC

Young people use pop music to choose their fashion styles, to sharpen their worldview, and to define their identity. For most young people, pop music is an important medium, and many model themselves to some extent on examples provided by pop stars and their ideas. Consequently, it has been suggested that pop and rock music may have negative effects on behavior as well. For instance, in the 1950s, rock and roll's meteoric ascent led conservative white critics to conclude that racial boundaries would be blurred by this "Negro" music reaching a mass white audience.

Even though its greatest star of the period, Elvis Presley, was white (and had to be, perhaps, in order to achieve his level of fame during that period), an old fear of the sensual and explicit nature of black music's rock and roll roots surfaced, and Elvis's suggestive pelvic movements were interpreted as provoking a decline in sexual morals. In his third appearance on the nationally broadcast *The Ed Sullivan Show* on January 6, 1957, Elvis was shown only from the waist up, so as not to offend conservative viewers.

In the 1960s, many pop musicians were the most prominent heralds of a new ideology implying fundamental changes in the ethics of work, leisure, sexuality, substance use, and religion. They were often accused of being a threat to society. To illustrate how fast the times were changing, John Lennon casually mentioned that in 1966, the name *Beatles* had meaning for more people on this planet than the name *Jesus*. This led to severe criticism by U.S. religious organizations and to the public burning of Beatles' records in some American cities. Music seemed to be at the heart of a cultural war. Pop stars and other advocates of a liberal youth culture propagating anti-bourgeois, anti-materialist and pro-drug and pro-sex attitudes battled conservative standard bearers who feared the corruption of the young and the end of civilization.

In the eighties and nineties, two genres in particular have been criticized for their potential danger to young people. Organizations such as the Parents Music Resource Center (PMRC) believe that heavy metal and rap (hip hop) corrode sexual morals and encourage violence and drug use with their obscene and brutal lyrics. Some religiously inspired critics have even asserted that some rock records contain secret satanic messages only clearly discernable when they are played backward. Although never supported by scientific research, these claims of *backward masking* made it to U.S. courts, where heavy metal bands such as Judas Priest and Ozzy Osbourne had to defend themselves against claims that their music and its supposedly hidden messages drove fans to violent and suicidal acts.

As recently as 1999, the music of self-proclaimed anti-Christ superstar Marilyn Manson has been pinpointed as contributing to the mind-set of two young people who shot 12 students and a teacher at their high school in Columbine, Colorado, on April 20, 1999. Rapper Ice-T ("Cop Killer," 1992), and fellow rappers of Niggers With Attitude (N.W.A.; "Fuck Tha Police," 1992) were accused of provoking violence against the police in their compositions. Generally, the genre of gangsta rap has been criticized for its sensationalized portrayal of romance and sex and its glamorizing of drug use, violence, and delinquency.

EFFECTS OF MUSIC ON PROBLEM BEHAVIOR

Research on the links between adolescent cultural-style preferences and their adjustment suggests that preferences for heavy metal and hip hop may indeed be associated with a range of problem behaviors. Studies in English-speaking countries such as the United States, Canada, and Australia have disclosed a set of attitudes and externalizing problem behaviors that have been labeled "the heavy metal syndrome." Heavy metal fans tend to have a more problematic relation to school: They receive lower grades, and they have higher truancy and dropout rates. They experiment with alcohol and drugs at an earlier age and may continue to use and abuse these substances more frequently than their peers who disdain their musical choice. Heavy metal fans are more often involved in reckless, rule-violating, and risky sexual behavior. They report high-speed driving, driving while intoxicated, and having unsafe sex more frequently. Male heavy metal fans may hold relatively hostile attitudes toward other people more often and show more violence and delinquency in general. Several other studies performed in these same countries found that rap fans, compared to nonfans, also often exhibit more externalizing problem behaviors, such as drug use, engagement in unsafe sex, aggression, and delinquency. A fascination for the louder and brasher forms of rap music may increase the tolerance for violence, boost sexist attitudes, and divert educational drive. Dwelling in a symbolic universe glorifying pimplike hustlers may have the effect of a decrease in academic aspirations.

Other empirical studies have found that a preference for heavy metal is also associated with more internalizing problems. For instance, Canadian females who like heavy metal music are characterized by more depression, deliberate self-harm, and suicidal thoughts than mainstream-oriented girls. Both female and male U.S. heavy metal fans show higher levels of suicide ideation. While metal fans seem prone to more externalizing and internalizing distress, rap fans do not seem to display these types of problems as much. In a Dutch study, no elevated levels of depression, anxiety, or self-harm were found among fans of urban music (rap or R&B).

THE ISSUE OF CAUSALITY

Although associations have been found between metal or rap preference and problem behavior, most researchers stress that the results of these studies must be interpreted cautiously. If associations are found, they are weak, indicating that for most fans, even music that is labeled deviant is simply fun to listen to, contributes to a good mood, and may decrease problems.

Furthermore, although research provides evidence for some associations between music listening and problem behavior, music may not be a factor that independently contributes to problem behavior. For instance, heavy metal fans in the United States are more likely to report nonsupportive families and a marginal social position. They are more frequently on poor terms with their parents and dislike or oppose basic social institutions such as school and church or society in general. Heavy metal fans' social positioning may at least partially explain the link between their music preference and their emotional distress and problem behavior. In most studies, the link between a preference for heavy metal and problem behavior risk disappears or substantially decreases with controls for other risk factors, such as a strained relationship with parents, feelings of alienation in terms of self-estrangement or powerlessness, and an inclination to sensation seeking and drug use. This may imply that adolescents who already experience problems or have a certain psychological makeup seek music that, to a certain extent, reflects these problems or their personality. Thus, preferences for certain genres of music have been linked to problem behavior, but research has failed to settle the issue of causality; that is, it is still unclear whether music listening causes problems or people who are in some way troubled listen to certain kinds of music.

Several processes have been proposed in discussions about mechanisms behind the associations between music and problem behavior. One line of reasoning is that adolescents' music preferences influence their behaviors: Depressive or antisocial content in music activates antisocial or depressing cognitive schemas, which may in turn lead to actual antisocial behavior or depression. Second, youngsters may imitate the perceived lifestyle characteristics attributed to the music or artists with which they identify. Third, if adolescents are actual members of a clique (i.e., friendship group) holding certain music preferences, they may conform to acceptable group norms, and if these are deviant, they may engage in substance use and risky or rule-violating behavior themselves. Fourth, the desire to become affiliated with a certain musical/youth cultural style may guide adolescents toward deviant behaviors.

Other authors have downplayed music's effects and conceptualized music preferences as a mediator between personality characteristics and adolescent externalizing behavior. Children with prominent traits such as sensation seeking or rebelliousness may, at the start of adolescence, seek music styles and youth cultural affiliations that reflect their activity level, curiosity, and need for arousal. High-energy music and associated youth cultures geared to adventurousness and excitement can attract these young people disproportionably. Basic personal characteristics, later cultural preferences, and membership in peer groups that occasionally break social rules to seek stimulation may result in (collective) externalizing behavior in the future path of adolescent development. In this model of a developmental sequence, music and youth cultures function as a bridge between personality and relatively prevalent risky and rule-violating behaviors that are specific to middle and late adolescence.

SELECTIVE PUBLIC OUTCRIES

Certain exuberant genres that are popular among young audiences, such as Charleston-style jazz, rock and roll, metal, and rap, have attracted a disproportionate amount of public attention because of their supposed danger in spoiling the young. Other music genres, more popular among adults, are also potentially linked to problem behavior but have attracted far less attention. For instance, studies have shown that a preference for country music is correlated with an increased risk for alcohol abuse and depression, and opera aficionados more often think of suicide as a definite cure for problems. Public indignation over music's negative influences is a selective process, particularly when referring to teenage music, and it is heavily subject to stereotyping. Over the past two decades, the public debate in the United States has framed heavy metal as harmful to children, and rap music has been marked as a threat to the community, but never a cry was heard for a ban of genres such as country and opera.

—Tom ter Vogt and Stephen Soitos

See also Aggression Music and; Depression, Media Use and; Hip Hop, Violence in; Media Effects, Models of; Music Genres, Heavy Metal

FURTHER READINGS

Arnett, J. (1992). The soundtrack to recklessness: Musical preferences and reckless behavior among adolescents. *Journal of Adolescent Research, 7,* 313–331.

Binder, A. (1993). Constructing racial rhetoric: Media depiction of harm in heavy metal and rap music. *American Sociological Review, 58,* 753–768.

Mulder, J., Ter Bogt, T., Raaijmakers, Q., & Vollebergh, W. (in press). Adolescent music preferences and problem behavior. *Journal of Youth and Adolescence.*

Roe, K. (1995). Adolescents' use of the socially disvalued media: Towards a theory of media delinquency. *Journal of Youth and Adolescence, 24,* 617–631.

MUSIC LISTENING, USES OF

Researchers who examine adolescents' use of music generally focus their attention on audio sources such as CDs, tapes, MP3 files, and radio. Although these sources can be used for nonmusic content such as books and news, adolescents overwhelmingly favor them for listening to music. Most discussions of adolescents' music use address five basic areas of interest: household availability of playback devices, time spent listening to audio media, the contexts in which adolescents listen, preferred music styles, and the motives for listening.

HOUSEHOLD AVAILABILITY

Music sources are extremely common in the houses of adolescents throughout the United States. The typical child between the ages of 8 and 18 is likely to live in a house with three CD/tape players and three radios. About 97% of children in that age range live in a home with at least one radio, and 98% have at least one CD/tape player in their home. Furthermore, more than 80% of U.S. adolescents report having one radio and/or CD/tape player in their bedroom. Adolescents also value the portability of music players. As of 2004, 61% owned a portable CD player, and 18% owned an MP3 player. Interestingly, adolescents' access to audio media differs from other media in that there are no significant differences in access related to

age, ethnicity, race, or parent education and income. However, the amount of time children spend with music is not uniform across age, gender, or racial characteristics. As children age, the amount of time spent listening to music increases.

TIME SPENT LISTENING

On any given day, 85% of U.S. children between 8 and 18 years old listen to at least a few minutes of audio media (primarily music), and more than 40% of those children spend more than an hour and a half listening each day. A child between the ages of 8 and 10 listens to nearly an hour of music each day. Children in late adolescence (15 to 18 years old) listen to music for more than 2.5 hours per day. Younger girls (8 to 14 years old) spend more time listening to music than boys that age. However, by late adolescence, there is virtually no difference by gender. Younger African American children (2 to 10 years old) listen to more radio than their white counterparts.

The amount of time spent with music has been a source of consternation for media researchers because of music's role as a backdrop for other activities including other media (e.g., TV, Internet). Adolescents are becoming increasingly adept at multiple media use. About 25% of adolescents' total media time is spent simultaneously using more than one type of media. Of course, the aural nature of music makes it a prime choice for multiple media activity.

CONTEXTS FOR MUSIC LISTENING

Music is not only suitable for multiple media use but also has an important role during nonmedia group or individual activities. As children age, they increasingly use music with their peers or siblings. From the age of 12, children are exposed to popular music in the company of friends at parties and dances. In addition, by early adolescence, radio and recordings are increasingly used in solitary or personal situations to supplement activities such as reading, studying, and talking on the phone. Of course, late adolescents rarely spend a minute in a car (either alone or with others) without music playing.

MUSIC GENRES

Whether listening with friends at a party or alone in their bedrooms, adolescents prefer popular music.

The number of music genres increased greatly during the late 20th century, but adolescents clearly favor two basic genres: rap/hip hop and rock. About 65% of adolescents between the ages of 12 and 18 listen to rap/hip hop music on a typical day. More than 30% of children in that age range report listening to alternative rock on any given day. Although rap/hip hop is popular among adolescents regardless of their race, race has been identified as a good predictor of musical taste. African American adolescents are more likely to listen to rap/hip hop (about 80%) as well as R&B/soul, reggae, and gospel/Christian. White adolescents also listen to rap/hip hop but report listening to a wide array of rock-oriented genres, including alternative rock, hard rock, ska/punk, classic rock, and rave/techno. Regarding gender, differences are evident in only a few areas. Girls are more likely to report listening to soft rock and country and western, and boys are more likely to report listening to heavy metal.

MOTIVATIONS FOR MUSIC LISTENING

Researchers have identified several motives for music listening, regardless of genre preference; these fall into two basic categories: psychological benefits and psychosocial benefits. The psychological benefits are often described in terms of mood management, social stimulation, relaxation, relief of boredom, filling in silence. The psychosocial benefits include self-expression/identity and social utility.

As with other entertainment media, adolescents (and adults) often use music to manage their mood states. The mood management motive is evident in social and solitary listening contexts. In social contexts such as parties and dances, music stimulates or excites positive moods. Conversely, music is used by stressed or annoyed adolescents in solitary environments such as their bedrooms to soothe nerves or relieve anxiety. Adolescents who feel understimulated are likely to use music to relieve boredom or for filling silence. In addition, some adolescents report that listening to music can provide a sense of companionship, especially when they are feeling alienated.

Besides manipulating moods and providing comfort, music is also used for self-identification and self-expression. Music listening plays an important role in the shift toward independence from parents. Music listening can be the impetus for social interaction and the development of interpersonal relationships as well as self and group identities. Similarly, some adolescents approach pop music knowledge as social capital that can be used to improve their social status among their peers.

—*William Kinnally*

See also Mood Management Theory; Music Genres (various entries); Music Listening, Impact of

FURTHER READINGS

Arnett, J. J., Larson, R., & Offer, D. (1995). Beyond effects: Adolescents as active media users. *Journal of Youth and Adolescence, 24*(5), 511–518.

Avery, R. K. (1979). Adolescents' use of the mass media. *American Behavioral Scientist, 23*(1), 53–70.

Christenson, P. G. (1994). Childhood patterns of music uses and preferences. *Communication Reports, 7*(2), 136–144.

Christenson, P. G., & Roberts, D. F. (1998). *It's not only rock & roll: Popular music in the lives of adolescents.* Cresskill, NJ: Hampton Press.

Roberts, D. F., & Foehr, U. G. (2004). *Kids and media in America.* New York: Cambridge University Press.

Schwartz, K. D., & Fouts, G. T. (2003). Music preferences, personality style, and developmental issues in adolescents. *Journal of Youth and Adolescence, 32*(3), 205–213.

Van den Bulck, J., & Van den Bulck, B. (2000). The influence of perceived parental guidance on children's media use: Gender differences and media displacement. *Journal of Broadcasting and Electronic Media, 44*(3), 329–348.

MUSIC LYRICS, EFFECTS OF

Music lyrics encompass a variety of themes such as love, death, work, fun, substance use, politics, and so on. Song lyrics can also be abstract or explicit. In fact, much of the criticism that some songs receive focuses on the content of the lyrics, particularly those that contain sex- or violence-oriented material. Concerned critics contend that negative music lyrics can influence youth attitudes, values, and behaviors. However, the extent to which song lyrics are influential depends, first and foremost, on the individual's ability to comprehend the lyrics they hear.

Researchers have examined comprehension of lyrics by asking adolescents to report their interpretation of certain lyrics and then comparing their interpretations with the true meaning as defined by experts. A summary of this research suggests that most adolescents do not fully comprehend the definitive or true meaning of song lyrics. Given these findings, the role of memory is an important consideration. The ability to accurately recall specific lyrics will impact one's ability to reflect on and comprehend the meaning of a song. Studies have addressed this by having adolescents listen to a song and then report on its meaning or read a transcript of the lyrics before interpreting the music. These studies suggest that when lyrics are heard, they are not as easily or accurately remembered or interpreted as when the lyrics are read. Because information can be reviewed if necessary, reading lyrics can help facilitate memory acquisition and increase the information available for interpretation and more accurate comprehension. Unless a song is heard repeatedly, it is unlikely that an adolescent will fully retain the content of the lyrics.

Background characteristics of youth help explain why differences in comprehension of song lyrics have emerged. Compared to adolescents and college students, young children are likely to interpret song lyrics more literally. Cognitive developmental research has consistently found that young children tend to think concretely and to develop abstract thinking abilities only as they grow older. The interpretation and meaning of song lyrics also differ as a function of social class, race, and gender; that is, adolescents who come from similar backgrounds and have similar experiences are likely to interpret lyrics in roughly the same manner. Altogether, the current research suggests that children differ from adolescents in music comprehension based on their cognitive abilities. Moreover, lyric comprehension differs, depending on adolescent demographics.

The comprehension of song lyrics is complex and dynamic. Based on schema theory, adolescents are not blank slates; rather, they comprehend lyrics using their own unique set of experiences. These experiences help form the basis of an individual's schemas (simple mental representations of complex events), which play a relevant role in interpreting new information. Life's daily distractions make it difficult for us to partake in deep processing of song lyrics. Such distractions can elevate cognitive load, thus increasing the likelihood that people will rely on existing schemas or any available cues to interpret lyrics. In essence, when conditions make it difficult for adolescents to deeply process music lyrics (e.g., at parties, listening to iPOD while doing other activities), their preexisting schemas or any available cues in the song will influence their interpretation of the lyrics. For

example, a preadolescent boy who is dancing with someone he is attracted to might hear the lyrics, "say you'll be there" (by the Spice Girls) and easily misinterpret the song to mean that boys should always be there for their girlfriends, when in fact, the song lyrics imply casual, no-strings-attached sex.

As evident in prior research, the understanding of adolescents' comprehension of music lyrics requires a multifaceted approach. The developmental importance of cognitive ability is highlighted in the fact that younger children are less likely to comprehend the true meaning of song lyrics compared to adolescents and emerging adults. One must also consider the impact of memory and its effect on adolescents' ability to accurately interpret song lyrics. Furthermore, background characteristics also play an important role because they help color how one understands music lyrics. Similarly, prior knowledge and experience can shape the meaning imposed on song lyrics, especially under highly distracting situations. Also, the impact of music lyrics on adolescents' and emerging adults' lives will depend on the degree to which the lyrics are actually understood. Teenagers are experiencing considerable psychological and physical changes associated with puberty; thus, adolescents can sometimes live tumultuous lives that can make it difficult to pay close attention to the things happening around them, such as the lyrics of the songs to which they are listening.

—*Byron L. Zamboanga and Liliana Rodriguez*

See also Cognitive Development, Media and; Music Listening, Impact of; Music Listening, Uses of; Music Lyrics, Music Television and; Schema Theory; Schemas/ Scripts, Gender

FURTHER READINGS

Christianson, P. G., & Roberts, D. F. (1998). *It's not only rock & roll: Popular music in the lives of adolescents.* Cresskill, NJ: Hampton Press.

Epstein, J. S. (1994). *Adolescents and their music.* New York: Garland.

MUSIC LYRICS, MUSIC TELEVISION AND

Over the past 50 years, there have been dramatic changes in the styles of contemporary popular music, but despite dynamic changes in the types of musical genres favored by adolescents and young adults (the major consumers of popular music), the lyrical theme of being in love remains the most common. The manner in which the experience of being in love is described in song lyrics, however, has changed during the past five decades. Lyrics expressing romantic love dominated the 1940s and 1950s. With the advent of folk and folk rock music in the 1960s, song lyrics began to express the physical side of love. Songs with themes of drug use (marijuana and LSD) and protest against war also emerged as a reflection of the times. The rise of disco dance music in the 1970s brought a resurgence of songs about romantic love and having fun. In the 1980s, the lyrics of popular rock music included themes of infatuation and a greater emphasis on sexual attraction. Along with the acceptance of greater sexual permissiveness in Western society, sexual lyrics have become increasingly common. Songs with violent lyrics also emerged in the 1980s, particularly in punk rock and heavy metal music. Songs with occult themes were not uncommon. The increase in themes of sex, violence, satanism, and drugs and alcohol became a controversial topic during the decade of the 1980s, as groups such as the Parents Music Resource Center came out strongly against popular music lyrics, resulting in voluntary labeling of song lyrics by the recording industry. The growth of rap music and its subgenre, gangsta rap, during the 1990s brought an ever-increasing level of sexual, violent, and misogynistic lyrics. Controversial lyrical themes of sexual violence against women, including rape, torture, and degradation, are not uncommon in some forms of recorded rap music.

Since the 1980s, when song lyrics became a topic of national controversy, a number of research studies have been conducted to explore the effects of antisocial song lyrics on listeners. The majority of studies have investigated the effects of violent or sexually violent lyrics on hostile and aggressive attitudes. Most studies show that violent and sexually violent lyrics do impact listeners' attitudes, at least in the short term. A set of experiments by Anderson, Carnagey, and Eubanks, for example, demonstrated that violent lyrics increased aggressive thoughts and hostility, at least in the short term. In another study, Wester, Crown, Quatman, and Heesacker found that young men exposed to sexually violent lyrics reported more adversarial attitudes toward the women in their relationships. Contemporary psychological theories predict that exposure will have long-term as well as short-term effects on listeners, but longitudinal studies are needed to determine long-term effects of listening to antisocial music lyrics.

In 1981, the world of contemporary popular music was dramatically altered by the advent of Music Television (the MTV Networks). For the first time, music and film were combined in a new medium, the music video. Music videos are extremely popular among adolescent and young adult viewers, and listeners generally like music videos more than recorded music alone. As a result of the strong appeal of music videos, MTV has grown from a single broadcasting station in New York to become a global phenomenon. Recently, MTV announced its 100th non-U.S. cable station. In the United States, several other cable networks offer music videos to selected audiences (e.g., Country Music Television and Black Entertainment Television). Music videos allow viewers to watch and listen to their favorite performers simultaneously, and the visuals add meaning to the songs.

Since its inception, the music video has added to the music lyric controversy because of the nature of the visual content. Images containing sex and violence have engendered the most criticism. Music videos typically include visuals that dramatize the song's lyrics; therefore, the kinds of visual content shown tend to be consistent with the content of lyrical themes. Many content analyses have been conducted to investigate the nature of music video visuals, and they generally document high levels of sexual and violent images, antisocial behavior, and sexist portrayals of women. In recent years, sexual imagery has received more study than violent imagery has. Several studies during the late 1980s investigated violent visual content. In these studies, the percentages of videos containing violence ranged from a low of 15% to more than 50%. When videos contained violence, they averaged about 2.7 violent acts per video. Violent and sexual imagery are often combined in the same video. Sherman and Dominick reported that about 45% of the videos samples contained both types of imagery.

In various content analyses of the visual images in music videos, sexual imagery has been reported in about 40% to 75% of music videos. The depictions, however, tend to be mild and nongraphic, typically consisting of touching, kissing, and suggestive body movements. Images of sexual intercourse or other actual sex acts are almost never shown. Sexual imagery is most frequently depicted in the form of scantily or provocatively clad women posed or dancing suggestively. When nudity is shown, sexual areas of the body (female nipples, male and female genitalia) are generally blocked from view; although minimally covered breasts and bikini- or thong-clad female buttocks are prevalent images. Sexual images of women are much more common than those of men, and they vary somewhat across musical genres and across networks. In a recent content analysis of videos across four music television channels by Hansen and Hansen, BET surpassed CMT, VH1, and MTV in the percentage of videos containing visual images of scantily or provocatively clad women (about 77%), but MTV's sister station, VH1, was close behind (about 71%). However, both men (about 45%) and women (about 35%) were much more likely to be portrayed as sexually aggressive in videos shown on BET (showing predominantly rap and R&B videos) than on any of the other networks studied (the others ranged from 8% to 21%). Across all networks, women were two to three times more likely to be presented as sex objects than men were, and female sex objects were most prevalent on BET (they appeared in about 67% of the rap and R&B videos). The degree of sexuality also appears to differ across genres. Durant and colleagues found that sexuality was much more likely to be a significant component of rap or R&B videos than of other kinds of music videos, such as adult contemporary, rock, or country.

—*Christine H. Hansen*

See also Music Videos, Effects of

FURTHER READINGS

Anderson, C. A., Carnagey, N. L., & Eubanks, J. (2003). Exposure to violent media: The effects of songs with violent lyrics on aggressive thoughts and feelings. *Journal of Personality and Social Psychology, 84*(5), 960–971.

Baxter, L., DeRiemer, C., Landini, A., Leslie, L., & Singletary, M. (1985). A content analysis of music videos. *Journal of Broadcasting and Electronic Media, 29,* 333–340.

Durant, R. H., Rome, E. S., Rich, M., Allred, E., Emans, S. J., & Woods, E. R. (1997). Tobacco and alcohol use behaviors portrayed in music videos: A content analysis. *American Journal of Public Health, 87*(7), 1131–1135.

Gore, T. (1987). *Raising PG kids in an X-rated society.* Nashville, TN: Abingdon.

Gow, J. (1990). The relationship between violent and sexual images and the popularity of music videos. *Popular Music and Society, 14*(4), 1–10.

Greeson, L. E., & Williams, R. A. (1986). Social implications of music videos for youth. *Youth and Society, 18,* 177–189.

Hansen, C. H., & Hansen, R. D. (2000). Music and music videos. In D. Zillmann & P. Vorderer (Eds.), *Media entertainment: The psychology of its appeal.* Mahwah, NJ: Erlbaum.

Sherman, B. L., & Dominick, J. R. (1986). Violence and sex in music: TV and rock 'n' roll. *Journal of Communication, 36,* 79–93.

Sun, S.-W., & Lull, J. (1986). The adolescent audience for music videos and why they watch. *Journal of Communication, 36,* 115–125.

Wester, S. R., Crown, C. L., Quatman, G. L., & Heesacker, M. (1997). The influence of sexually violent rap music on attitudes of men with little prior exposure. *Psychology of Women Quarterly, 21,* 497–508.

MUSIC VIDEOS, AMOUNT OF VIEWING AND

The Kaiser Family Foundation's 2005 study, *Generation M: Media in the Lives of 8-18 Year Olds* revealed that children and adolescents spend an average of 1.44 hours a day listening to music. Boys spend about an hour and a half a day listening to music; girls spend about 2 hours. About a third of those listening to music were often using other media at the same time. Music videos make up a significant part of music listening among youth in the United States. The Parents Television Council reported in March 2004 that the MTV network was watched by 73% of boys and 78% of girls between 12 and 19 years old. Boys watched an average of 6.6 hours per week, and girls watched for an average of 6.2 hours per week. Although music listening can play positive roles in the lives of teens and adolescents, parents and policymakers have expressed concerns about their exposure to music videos with violent or sexual content, as well as content that portrays substance use. Amount of viewing is a key variable, however. Moderate exposure to the negative content in music videos appears unlikely to adversely affect healthy individuals who have many other interests and activities, good family relationships, and strong academic and social skills. For those with fewer strengths or options in their lives, the potential for negative influence appears to be much greater.

MTV, now almost 25 years old, was a cornerstone of the movement to make the music video the accessible medium it is today. In 2001, PBS On-line reported that MTV reached more than 350 million households globally, and in 2004, the Parents Television Council reported that MTV was watched by 73% of boys and 78% of girls ages 12 to 19. In addition to music videos, however, MP3s are now everywhere, and music lyrics and video clips, some of which contain more sex and violence than those available in stores, can be downloaded and shared, increasing the presence and potential impact of music in children's lives. A Yahoo press release in 2003 indicated that its music section, LAUNCH, streamed more than a billion music videos to consumers that year. That quadrupled the number streamed in the first 10 months of the previous year, underscoring the increasing popularity of using the Internet to watch music videos. According to the Kaiser Foundation study, nearly two thirds of 8-to-18-year-olds have downloaded music from the Internet, and almost half have streamed a ratio station through the Internet. Nearly one in five has an MP3 player.

Children and adolescents sometimes use music to relax, to fill time, to avoid doing other things, to provide a background as they do homework, or to escape into a more fanciful world. At other times, they may use music in more social ways such as listening with friends. As one of their strongest media influences, music helps children and adolescents express, think about, and deal with the complex social, family, identity, and school/work challenges they face. The potential for significant impact on their use of other media and on their developing beliefs and attitudes is huge, and they can learn both positive and negative lessons about how to live their lives.

Even a modest amount of viewing of music videos results in significant exposure to glamorized depictions of alcohol and tobacco use, sexuality, aggression, violence, and weapons. In 2004, a Parents Television Council publication reported that in 171 hours of MTV programming, young viewers were seeing an average of nine sexual scenes per hour, with about 18 sexual depictions, and 17 examples of sexual innuendo or sexual dialogue, compared with just under six instances of sexual content in later hours when only adults would be watching. Similarly, there were many more instances of foul language and profanities on MTV than during the later broadcasts aimed at adults. There is a good deal of violent content as well, including violence against women. Almost half of the children said they watch something different when they are alone than when they watch TV with their parents, and 25% of them chose MTV.

Parents, teachers, pediatricians, and researchers have raised concerns about the effects of heavy viewing of such content. The American Academy of Pediatrics, for example, voiced concern about the popular music video formats available to the 70% of American households that have cable. It suggested that when music lyrics are illustrated in the videos, their potential influence may be greater because viewers who may not have understood or listened closely to some of the lyrics cannot avoid the many, often disturbing visual images. A good deal of research also indicates that the frequent depictions of violence, negative and demeaning portrayals of women, stereotypic images, and portrayals of alcohol use and tobacco use can affect children negatively and influence their beliefs, attitudes, and behavior. There are some findings, for example, of an association between frequent depictions of alcohol and smoking and the greater likelihood that heavy viewers of that content will drink or smoke.

In large numbers of music videos, violence and sexual behavior are presented in dramatic ways, compared with few if any depictions of less dramatic or glamorous behavior, such as cooperation or academic achievement. Viewing such content can affect children's and adolescents' attitudes about those behaviors as well. Exposure to massive amounts of aggressive and violent behavior has been shown to be negatively associated with prosocial behavior in some studies. Stars of music videos also have an influence as models or icons with whom children and adolescents identify. If identification with media stars occurs, their behavior can influence children's behavior and attitudes directly, or the viewers can experience some of those behaviors vicariously.

—*Judith Van Evra*

See also Developmental Differences, Media and; Media Genre Preferences; Music Genres (various entries); Music Listening, Impact of; School-Age Children, Impact of the Media on; Violence (various entries)

FURTHER READINGS

National Institute on Media and the Family. (2002). *MTV*. Retrieved March 22, 2006, from http://www.media familyorg/facts/facts_mtv.shtml

Roberts, D. F., Foehr, U., & Rideout, V. (2005). *Generation M: Media in the Lives of 8-18 Year Olds* (Kaiser Family Foundation report). Retrieved March 22, 2006, from http://www.kff.org/entmedia/7251.cfm

The Social Impact of Music Violence. (1997, November 6). Testimony of the American Academy of Pediatrics before the Senate Subcommittee on Oversight of Government Management, Restructuring, and the District of Columbia. Retrieved from http://www.aap.org/advocacy/Washing/t1106.htm

Van Evra, J. (2004). *Television and child development* (3rd ed.). Mahwah, NJ: Erlbaum.

Williams, C. (2004, March). *MTV smut peddlers: Targeting kids with sex, drugs, alcohol* (Parents Television Council report). Retrieved March 22, 2006, from http://www.parentstv.org/PTCpublications/reports/mtv2005/main.asp

MUSIC VIDEOS, EFFECTS OF

Music videos appeared on the Music Television Network (MTV) in New York for the first time in 1981, and almost since their inception, they have been controversial. Music videos combine popular music with video, allowing viewers to listen to the music and see the performers at the same time. Music videos also frequently include images or a video story to enhance the song lyrics. Following the advent of MTV, several other music channels emerged in the United States (e.g., VH1, MTV's sister station; Black Entertainment Television [BET], and Country Music Television [CMT]), each targeting different segments of the viewing population. Over the past two decades, music videos have become a global phenomenon, and MTV recently announced its 100th non-U.S. music station.

Most of the controversy over music videos has involved the presence of sexual, violent, misogynistic, and antisocial images. Sexual and violent content has received the most scrutiny. For example, in 1988, the National Academy of Pediatrics came out strongly against the presence of sexual and violent content in music videos, arguing that these images make music videos unwholesome viewing for children. High levels of sexual and violent imagery in music videos have been documented by numerous content analyses. High levels of antisocial behavior (i.e., rebellious and socially unacceptable behaviors) also have been documented, along with sexist and sex-role stereotypic treatment of women. A great deal of evidence has now accumulated that the themes common in music videos, such as violence and sexism, can prime listeners' own schemas for social behavior, resulting in greater affinity for and acceptance of socially negative attitudes and behavior.

A number of nonexperimental studies have been conducted to look at the relationship between exposure to music videos and attitudes and personality of viewers. Several studies have found links between exposure and sexual attitudes. For example, Tiggeman and Pickering found that among college-age women, time spent viewing MTV predicts sexual permissiveness as well as more tolerant attitudes toward sexual harassment and a "drive-for-thinness," a potential precursor of anorexia and bulimia. Affinity for sexual content in music videos has been related to how much time young women spend viewing music videos, and for both young men and young women, heavy viewers reported a greater number of sexual behaviors in the real world than light viewers did.

The kinds of popular music aired most frequently differ greatly across music video networks, and although young people's preferences for music can cross music genres, fans tend to spend most of their time with their favorite type of music. Most research studies have explored personality and behavior attributes associated with a preference for particular kinds of popular music and music videos rather than exposure to music videos in general, and in many studies, music preferences appear to be linked to clusters of traits and attitudes.

Pop music (also called adult contemporary music), largely the domain of VH1, is considered the mainstream music for adolescents and young adults. Because pop music generally revolves around nonviolent themes of love, courtship, friendship, and having fun, it has received only cursory mentions in the research literature. For similar reasons, other less controversial genres, such as country music, soul music, classic rock, and alternative rock have not been studied. Most research has focused on the kinds of music that have created the most public controversy: punk rock, hard rock and heavy metal, and rap music. Fans of these three genres show a number of reliable differences in personality characteristics and attitudes. Studies have shown that fans of punk music, for example, appear to be less accepting of authority than fans of other music genres, and the strength of their anti-authority attitudes are directly related to the amount of time they report listening to punk music. In contrast, Hansen and Hansen found that fans of hard rock and heavy metal have been found to be higher in antisocial personality traits such as Machiavellianism and machismo and lower in the need for cognition. A study by Arnett showed that fans of hard rock and heavy metal are also higher in attributes related to risk taking, such as sensation seeking and recklessness. Less is known about the attributes associated with fans of rap music, but they may be more impulsive and more likely to seek external stimulation through motor activity and extroverted behavior. In studies comparing fans of heavy metal and rap music with fans of other kinds of music, heavy metal and rap music fans reported more hostile attitudes toward others and more negative attitudes toward women than fans of other kinds of music. A preference for rap and heavy metal has also been found to correlate positively with drug use, arrests, sexual activity, and school behavior problems and to correlate negatively with academic performance. Unfortunately, because studies of this type are correlational in nature, causal direction cannot be established with certainty.

Experimental research conducted to test the effects of music videos on viewers, however, has produced a number of highly consistent results indicating that exposure to music videos has predictable effects on cognition and behavior, and effects tend to parallel video content. Most researchers have investigated the impact of short exposures to videos containing sexual, violent, sexist, and antisocial lyrics and images compared to exposure to videos without these themes. In a study by Greenson and Williams, those who experienced even a short exposure to videos with high levels of violent and sexually permissive content were more likely to endorse these values than subjects who watched neutral music videos. In similar studies, young men exposed to violent rock music videos have reported an increase in aggressive attitudes toward women, and exposing young black men to violent rap music videos resulted in greater endorsement of violent behavior in a hypothetical situation involving conflict. In addition, exposure to rock music videos containing antisocial behavior has been shown to result in greater acceptance of antisocial behavior by subjects of both genders.

Studies of the effects of videos with sex-role stereotypic and misogynistic themes have reported the same kinds of content-related effects. For example, when compared to subjects who watched rock music videos with neutral themes, male and female subjects exposed to videos that portrayed women in sex-role stereotypic (i.e., male dominant, female submissive) roles reported

much greater liking for women who behaved in a sex-role stereotypic manner than for women who behaved counterstereotypically; those who watched the neutral videos preferred women who behaved nontraditionally. In a study by Johnson, Adams, Ashburn, and Reed comparing the effects of nonviolent rap music videos that contained images of sexually subordinate women with a no-video control condition, adolescent black females exposed to the sexist videos reported much greater acceptance of teen dating violence.

—*Christine H. Hansen*

See also see Hip Hop, Violence in; Music Listening, Effects of; Music Listening, Problem Behavior and; Music Lyrics, Music Television and; Violence, Effects of

FURTHER READINGS

Arnett, P. (1991). Heavy metal music and reckless behavior among adolescents. *Journal of Youth and Adolescence, 20*(6), 573–593.

Greenson, L. E., & Williams, R. A. (1986). Social implications of music videos for youth. *Youth and Society, 18,* 177–189.

Hansen, C. H. (1989). Priming sex-role stereotypic event schemas with rock music videos: Effects on impression favorability, trait inferences, and recall of a subsequent male-female interaction. *Basic and Applied Social Psychology, 10*(4), 371–391.

Hansen, C. H., & Hansen, R. D. (1990). Rock music videos and antisocial behavior. *Basic and Applied Social Psychology, 11*(4), 357–369.

Hansen, C. H., & Hansen, R. D. (2000). Music and music videos. In D. Zillmann & P. Vorderer (Eds.), *Media entertainment: The psychology of its appeal.* Mahwah, NJ: Erlbaum.

Johnson, J. J., Adams, M. S., Ashburn, L., & Reed, W. (1995). Differential gender effects of exposure to rap music on African-American adolescents' acceptance of teen dating violence. *Sex Roles, 33,* 597–605.

Rubin, A. M., West, D. V., & Mitchell, W. S. (2001). Differences in aggression, attitudes toward women, and distrust as reflected in popular music preferences. *Media Psychology, 3,* 25–42.

Tiggeman, M., & Pickering, A. S. (1996). Role of television in adolescent women's body dissatisfaction and drive for thinness. *International Journal of Eating Disorders, 20*(2), 199–203.

Took, K. J., & Weiss, D. S. (1994). The relationship between heavy metal and rap music and adolescent turmoil: Real or artifact? *Adolescence, 29,* 613–621.

N

NARRATIVE STORIES

While everyone loves a good story, the value of narrative stories goes far beyond enjoyment. Cultures transmit much of what is important through narrative stories, including moral messages. Through stories, the complexities of human interactions are portrayed. Children's ability to comprehend narratives is an important activity that allows them access to the cultural stories that pervade their daily lives across a variety of media. Although children are in middle childhood before they have the cognitive skills to understand these programs well, even infants and young children can understand stories if production features are used to highlight important content and if parents and teachers help children by repeating and summarizing important program messages and play with children in the process.

DEVELOPMENTAL DIFFERENCES IN NARRATIVE COMPREHENSION

In 1970, Andrew Collins divided the typical television story into central content, which is essential for understanding the story plot, and incidental content, which is irrelevant to the plot. He and his colleagues later divided the central material into (a) content explicitly or implicitly presented in the story and (b) content that is implicitly presented. Whereas explicit content is concretely presented and easily accessible, children have to figure out the meaning of implicit content, which is much more difficult for them. At a young age, children remember more incidental than central content, a pattern that changes when children are about age 9 or 10.

Understanding televised narratives involves several relatively complex cognitive activities. First, children must separate the central, plot-relevant material from the incidental, irrelevant material. Then, children must order and link the key central events over changes in time and space. Finally, children must understand the implicitly presented content by going beyond the information given and inferring character feelings and motives.

HOME AND SCHOOL INTERVENTIONS

Although infants and young children do not have the cognitive skills that older children have, their comprehension can be improved in various ways. These include interventions that take place in the home or school, such as repeating and rehearsing the important story content, as well as interventions that are put into the story, such as visual and verbal summaries to emphasize story messages.

Repeating the content is one way to enhance story comprehension. For instance, Catherine Snow (2005) demonstrated that stories presented in books are better remembered after parents read them several times to their child. Similarly, Rachel Barr and her colleagues (2003) demonstrated that repeatedly seeing the same story also helps infants remember television depictions. Snow found that repetition allows children to keep the content constant while consolidating what they know.

In a classic television study, Lynette Friedrich and Aletha Stein (1975) examined how verbally rehearsing and acting out (i.e., role-playing) the important program messages in an episode of *Mister Rogers' Neighborhood* affected children's learning of the socially desirable program content. In the verbal rehearsal condition, an adult summarized the important central story content for children, a practice that helped girls remember the socially desirable program content. In the role-play condition, puppets were used to help children rehearse the key program content, a practice that helped boys behave in socially desirable ways.

PROGRAM INTERVENTIONS

Some of the same interventions that help children in the real world can also help children learn when they are built into the actual production. For instance, Daniel Anderson and his colleagues (2000) demonstrated that repeatedly showing vignettes and building summaries into the production can help young children understand the important program messages.

The production features used to present television content, such as action, sound effects, and dialogue, can also help children understand televised narratives. For example, Sandra Calvert and Tracey Gersh (1987) demonstrated that sound effects can help children understand the important television story content by getting children to look at just the right moment. Rachel Barr and her colleagues (2003) have demonstrated similar beneficial outcomes when using sound effects in programs made for infants. These studies suggest that using production features carefully can help very young children get program messages that they might otherwise miss.

Production features can also help children understand television content because they are similar to how young children think. For example, Sandra Calvert and her colleagues (1982) discovered that visual character actions and verbal character dialogue can help children understand the important program content because children can see pictures in their mind's eye and can also use the language they hear characters say as a way to think about the story content.

—*Sandra L. Calvert*

See also Coviewing; Media Effects; Schema Theory; Television, Attention and; Television, Prosocial Behavior and; Television, Viewer Age and

FURTHER READINGS

Anderson, D. R., Bryant, J., Wilder, A., Crawley, A., Santomero, A., & Williams, M. E. (2000). Researching *Blue's Clues*: Viewing behavior and impact. *Media Psychology, 2*, 179–194.

Barr, R., Chavez, V., Fujimoto, M., Muentener, P., & Strait, C. (2003, April). *Repeated exposure and cartoon sound effects enhance on infant imitation from television.* Poster presented at the Society of Research on Child Development, Tampa, FL.

Calvert, S. L., & Gersh, T. L. (1987). The selective use of sound effects and visual inserts for children's television story comprehension. *Journal of Applied Developmental Psychology, 8*, 363–375.

Calvert, S. L., Huston, A. C., Watkins, B. A., & Wright, J. C. (1982). The relation between selective attention to television forms and children's comprehension of content. *Child Development, 53*, 601–610.

Collins, W. A. (1970). Learning of media content: A developmental study. *Child Development, 41*, 1133–1142.

Collins, W. A., Wellman, H., Kenison, A., & Westby, S. (1978). Age-related aspects of comprehension and inference from a televised dramatic narrative. *Child Development, 49*, 389–399.

Friedrich, L. K., & Stein, A. H. (1975). Prosocial television and young children: The effects of verbal labeling and role playing on learning and behavior. *Child Development, 46*, 27–38.

Snow, C. (2005). *What are the best practices in reading to children?* Retrieved August 20, 2005, from http:// gseweb.harvard.edu/~snow/Q%26As.htm

NATIONAL CAMPAIGN TO PREVENT TEEN PREGNANCY

The National Campaign to Prevent Teen Pregnancy is a nonprofit organization launched in 1996 at then-President Bill Clinton's urging. The campaign's mission was to reduce the teen pregnancy rate in the United States by one third over the following 10 years. By 2000, the pregnancy rate had dropped 28% from a high in 1990 of 117 pregnancies per 1,000 females ages 15 to 19 years old to 84 per 1,000. The latter teen pregnancy rate is still one of the highest in the industrialized world.

The National Campaign is led by a board of directors chaired by former New Jersey Governor Thomas H. Kean, four task forces (on the entertainment media; religion, public values, and public policy; effective programs and research; and state and local action), a national youth advisory group, and bipartisan advisory panels in both the U.S. Senate and the House of Representatives. Through these groups and a staff of about 20, the National Campaign takes a multipronged approach to reducing teen pregnancy. By the end of the 1990s, the campaign had become one of the primary resources available for preventing teen pregnancy and claimed to have almost reached its goal.

One of the most notable elements of the National Campaign is use of entertainment education as a strategy for getting sexually responsible messages to teens and parents. The National Campaign has partnered with more than 70 media companies, including *Teen People* magazine, the WB Network, and Fox Broadcasting; the media agree to include pregnancy prevention articles and scenarios in their entertainment programs. The campaign has worked closely with the producers of the hit teen show, *Dawson's Creek*, for example, to develop story lines that include portrayals of teens pledging abstinence, condom negotiation and use, and the risks of multiple partners and unprotected sex. The articles and shows often direct adolescents to the campaign's website, where they and their parents can learn more about pregnancy prevention.

In partnership with national advertising agencies, the National Campaign also produces a widely distributed series of print and television public service announcements, including a controversial "Sex Has Consequences" campaign that some critics claim does more to stigmatize youth than it does to prevent teen pregnancy. They also initiated the National Day to Prevent Teen Pregnancy, which encourages teens to take an online quiz reflecting on the best course of action in tough sexual situations. In 2005, more than a half million youth completed the quiz.

The National Campaign treads a careful nonideological line in a time when teen sexuality is hotly debated. Rather than engage in the ongoing debates over abstinence education or condom availability, the campaign steadfastly argues that reducing teen pregnancy is a good investment because a number of social problems including school failure, crime, and child abuse and neglect might be reduced if more children were born to parents who were ready and able to care for them.

The campaign has published more than 25 research-based reports and fact sheets on a range of topics, from the influence of parents on their teens' sexual behavior to best practices for teen pregnancy prevention programs. Campaign leaders have also

testified before key congressional committees and hosted briefings for congressional staff.

—*Jane D. Brown*

See also Sex, Media Impact on

FURTHER READINGS

Constantine, N., & Benard, B. (2000, July). Dirty campaign? *Youth Today.* Retrieved from http://crahd.phi .org/dirtycampaign.html

National Campaign to Prevent Teen Pregnancy. (1997). *Whatever happened to childhood? The problem of teen pregnancy in the United States.* Washington, DC: Author.

Singh, S., & Darroch, J. E. (2000). Adolescent pregnancy and childbearing: Levels and trends in developed countries. *Family Planning Perspectives, 32*(1), 14–23.

NATIONAL COMMISSION ON ADOLESCENT SEXUAL HEALTH

The National Commission on Adolescent Sexual Health was convened in 1994 by the Sexuality Information and Education Council of the United States (SIECUS), a nonprofit organization that advocates for comprehensive education about sexuality. SIECUS brought together 21 experts, chaired by Robert Johnson, director of adolescent medicine at the New Jersey Medical School. The commission reviewed existing literature about adolescents' sexual health and held a series of meetings over the course of a year to establish guidelines for educating adolescents about sexuality.

Their findings and recommendations were published in a report, *Facing Facts: Sexual Health for America's Adolescents.* The report was endorsed by 48 organizations, including the American Medical Association, the National Council of the Churches of Christ, Planned Parenthood Federation of America, Girls Inc., and the YWCA of the U.S.A.

The commission concluded that "responsible adolescent intimate relationships should be based on shared personal values and be consensual, nonexploitative, honest, pleasurable, and protected against unintended pregnancies and sexually transmitted diseases, if any type of intercourse occurs" (p. 4). The report includes guidelines for parents, adolescent health-care providers, sexual health curricula, and the media.

The commission, recognizing that "the mass media have become a major source of young people's information about sexuality" (p. 26), encouraged the media to provide accurate information and model responsible behavior. Specifically, the commission called for writers, producers, programming executives, reporters, and others to provide diverse and positive views of a range of body images because thin, beautiful people are not the only people who have sex; to include portrayals and discussion of protection against unwanted pregnancy and sexually transmitted diseases; and to outline the possible negative consequences if protection is not used. The guidelines also encourage the portrayal of typical sexual interactions as respectful and nonexploitative and an increased depiction of effective parent-child communication about sexuality and relationships.

The commission also called on the media to lift barriers to contraceptive and condom product advertising and to provide ways for young people to obtain additional information about sexuality and sexual health, for example, by listing addresses of public health organizations and support groups.

The commission's guidelines have been used by many organizations as a benchmark for sexuality education curriculum development and for interaction with the media about portrayals of sexual behavior.

—*Jane D. Brown*

See also Contraceptive Advertising; Sex, Media Impact on

FURTHER READINGS

Sexuality Information and Education Council of the United States (SIECUS). (1994). *Facing facts: Sexual health for America's adolescents.* Retrieved from http://www.siecus.org/pubs/Facing_Facts.pdf

NATIONAL TELEVISION VIOLENCE STUDY

The National Television Violence Study (NTVS) constitutes the largest and most systematic content analysis of television programming ever conducted and reported in a single investigation. Published in two volumes and a third executive summary volume, the work represents more than 10,000 hours of TV content gathered over a 3-year period (1994–1997). The programs were recorded and coded in an effort to document the amount and types of violence that appear on television. The sampling frame included programs aired between the hours of 6 a.m. and 11 p.m. on any of 23 television channels. Unlike many published samples, the shows were selected randomly and included ABC, CBS, NBC, and Fox as well as independent stations, public broadcasting stations, basic cable stations, and premium cable channels—HBO, Showtime, and Cinemax. Sports networks such as ESPN and news channels such as CNN were not included in the sample. On the basis of study findings, a number of recommendations were made for the television industry, policymakers, and parents.

The study was funded by the National Cable Television Association and conducted by researchers from four universities (University of California at Santa Barbara, University of Texas at Austin, University of Wisconsin at Madison, and the University of North Carolina at Chapel Hill). The group from Santa Barbara examined portrayals of violence in entertainment programming. The group from Austin focused on portrayals of violence on reality programming. The group from Wisconsin studied the impact of TV violence ratings and advisories on the viewing behavior of parents and children. The group from Chapel Hill explored the impact of anti-violence public service announcements (PSAs).

The NTVS researchers also benefited from an advisory council consisting of representatives from a total of 18 national organizations. These organizations included professional associations from the television industry, academic and scholarly organizations, and health organizations as well as legal, parental, and educational organizations. This panel was charged with ensuring the academic integrity of the studies and with providing the researchers feedback about the studies. The feedback was intended to represent a wide variety of perspectives and voices to supplement and not override the researchers' decisions and conclusions.

Three forms of violence were coded in this investigation: credible threats of physical force, actual acts of physical force, and harmful consequences of unseen violence. The inclusion of manifest and underlying codes for violence is significant because, all too often, researchers ignore underlying events that actually happen off-screen. These omissions result in the underestimation of the occurrences of violence on TV.

A founding principle of the NTVS is that not all violence poses the same degree of risk. Rather, the context of the violence partially determines whether the portrayal will be harmful to viewers. Based on an extensive review of the literature on the effects of media violence, the NTVS researchers identified a range of contextual features that may increase or decrease the risk of harmful effects:

Attractive perpetrator

Attractive victim

Justified violence

Unjustified violence

Conventional weapons

Extensive/graphic violence

Realistic violence

Rewards and punishments

Pain/harm cues

Humor

As described in the subsequent NTVS findings, consideration of these contextual features indicates that most TV violence is portrayed in ways that pose risks to viewers.

OVERALL TV PROGRAMMING

Television portrayals of violence were relatively stable over the 3-year period. About 61% of all programs on television contained some violence. Nearly 40% of that violence was enacted by "good" characters—characters likely to be employed as models by viewers. Similarly, more than 33% of the "bad" characters engaging in violent behavior were not punished within the program. In fact, in more than 70% of the violent scenes, characters behaving in a violent manner were not criticized by other characters, did not appear to feel any remorse for their actions, and were not punished at the time. During the 1996–1997 TV season, 67% of the programs in prime time contained violence. Findings indicated that children watching 2 hours of cartoons a day would see somewhere in the area of 10,000 violent incidents in a calendar year.

Generally, acts of violence are sanitized or trivialized. Depictions typically do not contain information about the long-term consequences of the violence, and half of the time, the programs do not contain portrayals of the harm or pain caused to the victim by the

violent agent. During the 3-year period, the amount of violence found on the broadcast networks and basic cable increased, and the highest percentage of programs containing violence could be found on the premium cable channels. Over that same 3-year period, less than 5% of the programs contained an anti-violence message. The typical violent program contained at least six acts of violence per hour, and more than 40% of the violent scenes were either couched in a humorous context or contained an element of humor.

REALITY PROGRAMMING

Reality programs are less likely to contain violence than television programming overall. More than 39% of the reality programs contained violence, compared to 61% of the overall programming. However, violence portrayals vary greatly among the genres of reality programming. All of the police reality shows contained violence, whereas only 15% of the talk shows contained acts of violence. Other genres of reality programs (tabloid news and documentaries) also contained high levels of violence, while entertainment and public affairs programs were much closer to the 39% average for reality programs. It is interesting to note that the number of reality programs increased from 384 to 526 over the 3-year period, and the percentage of programs containing violence was stable at about 39% each year; thus, the overall amount of violence did not decline over that same period.

RATINGS, ADVISORIES, AND VIOLENCE

TV parental guidelines are the codes or ratings applied to television programming in an effort by the industry to provide parents with information about the age-appropriateness and content of a particular program. The system, which is analogous to the Motion Picture Association of America (MPAA) ratings, was introduced in January 1997. The two ratings for children's programming are TVY (i.e., program is appropriate for all children) and TVY7 (i.e., program is appropriate for children 7 years and older). About 42% of the children's shows rated TVY—and 69% of the programs rated TVY7—contained violence. Some effort to employ the ratings as a way to help parents help children avoid violence is evident. General audience program ratings—those programs not identified as children's programs—are a different story. Nearly half of the programs rated TVG, TVPG, and TV14 contained violence. In short, violence is just as common in programs rated appropriate for all viewers (TVG) as it is in programs that suggest parental guidance (TVPG) and programs that are not appropriate for children under the age of 14 (TV14).

Other findings suggest that only 7% of the programs containing violence were rated, and only about 5% of all the programs aired during the 1996–1997 season were rated. The premium channels typically air movies and employ the MPAA coding system. It is interesting to note that fewer than 1% of those movies were rated G or general interest and suitable for all audiences. The vast majority of the movies (68%) were rated either PG or PG-13. When a rating is displayed, there is seldom an accompanying voice-over or audio warning for viewers. Obviously, parents in another room or multitasking will be unlikely to see the ratings that appear for a program. Furthermore, only one program in the composite week was rated TVMA, or a program most appropriate for mature audiences. Although the number of TVMA programs undoubtedly varies from channel to channel, it is clear that very few programs received the TVMA rating during the three seasons analyzed. Finally, programs aired during prime time were more likely to be rated than programs appearing during other time slots during the day. This appears to be an effort at ensuring the most watched programs contain ratings.

ANTI-VIOLENCE MESSAGES

In addition to the massive content analysis efforts described above, five separate experiments containing 1,600 subjects were also conducted to examine the impact of the content on audience members. In these studies, violence was defined as "overt depictions of a credible threat of physical force or the actual use of such force intended to physically harm an animate being or group of beings." These experiments investigated the impact of violence on interest level, arousal, and mood of the respondents, as well as the effect of conflict management training. The Chapel Hill group also examined message design considerations for PSAs and concluded that the depiction of negative consequences to violence increases the effectiveness of anti-violence PSAs. In fact, the more extreme the negative consequence, the more effective the PSA was at changing the attitudes of students between the ages of 11 and 15. Interestingly, the students reported believing that showing anti-violence PSAs with no

consequences would be a relatively ineffective strategy for changing attitudes about violence, a result that mirrors the findings of the Chapel Hill group.

RECOMMENDATIONS

The NTVS concludes with recommendations to the television industry, policymakers, and parents. Recommendations for the television industry include increasing efforts to show the negative consequences of programmatic violence, incorporating more anti-violence messages into story lines, and reducing the number of violent acts in general and specifically on children's programming. In addition, the rating system could be more effective if networks were encouraged to adopt it, used the system more systematically, included oral ratings along with the visual ratings that appear in programs, and avoided using age-based ratings.

Anti-violence PSAs or media campaigns need to rely less on celebrity endorsements and more on narrative strategies, including the negative consequences of violence. They should also avoid corporate logos and keep tags to a minimum; these distract the viewers and reduce the amount of time available for anti-violence messages to reach their audience.

Policymakers need to continue monitoring violence on television and recognize that context plays an important role in understanding violence on TV. More effort needs to be made to educate parents about the potential effects of violence and the ratings system. Policymakers need to ensure that the ratings system is not discontinued or used in a less than systematic fashion.

Finally, parents are encouraged to learn more about the content available on television, to be more involved with their children's TV viewing, and to talk with their children about violence and the new television rating system. All of these recommendations come from the findings presented in the NTVS and are generally consistent with the 3,500 or more studies on media violence that have been conducted in the United States alone.

—James D. Robinson,
Ronda M. Scantlin, and Yan Tian

See also Public Service Announcements (PSAs); Television Violence; Television Violence, Susceptibility to; Violence, Desensitization Toward; Violence, Effects of; Violence, Longitudinal Studies of

FURTHER READINGS

National Television Violence Study. Retrieved from www.ccsp.ucsb.edu/execsum.pdf

National Television Violence Study (Vol. 3). (1998). Thousand Oaks, CA: Sage.

Wartella, E., Olivarez, A., & Jennings, N. (1998). Children and television violence. In U. Carlsson & C. von Feilitzen (Eds.), *Children and media violence: UNESCO international clearinghouse on children and violence on the screen* (pp. 55–62). Göteborg, Sweden: Göteborg University, Nordicom.

NATIVE AMERICANS, MEDIA USE BY

The Native Americans of the 21st century are a diverse and complex group of people whose demographic patterns and cultural multiplicity result from five centuries of interaction between the indigenous population of North America and the Europeans who colonized the continent. From 1492 to about 1890, Native Americans endured a 400-year military struggle; it ended at Wounded Knee, South Dakota, on December 29, 1890. According to the 2000 U.S. Census, 4.1 million Americans (1.5% of the U.S. population) report their race as Native American or Alaska Native (U.S. Census Bureau, 2005). This number includes 2.5 million people, or 0.9% of the total U.S. population, who report only American Indian and Alaska Native background, in addition to the 1.6 million people, or 0.6% of the total, who report American Indian and Alaska Native in combination with another race. There are about equal numbers of Native American males and females, and they are a young people, with an average age of 28 years. Almost one third of Native Americans are children under the age of 18, whereas only 7% are age 65 and older. Far from a homogeneous population, with more than 500 tribes, the many Native American subpopulations are culturally distinctive, diverse, and complex. The Native American population is often thought of as being isolated on reservations, but the majority—by 2000, more than 60%—actually live in urban environments. More than 550 tribes are recognized by the U.S. government, including 223 village groups in Alaska. The Census 2000 identified Native American tribal groupings with 100,000 or more people as Cherokee, Navajo, Latin American Indian, Choctaw, Sioux, and Chippewa.

COMMUNICATION STYLES

In general, Native American communication styles are vastly different from the communication styles of other U.S. citizens. These communication styles affect media preferences, and they should be kept in mind by those developing new media specifically for Native Americans. Of course, communication styles vary among tribes and individuals, but there are several common elements among Native Americans

Patience. Concepts of time appear to be different for Native Americans; they often take more time to make decisions and consider possibilities and ways of being. Patience is a way of being, a way of seeing, a way of thinking, and a way of conducting oneself in the world. Silence is common among Native Americans, one manifestation of patience, which in turn is a respectful way of communicating. Often mistaken for shyness, silence is a form of communication in many Native American cultures. For Native Americans, silence often represents a period of reading body language and nonverbal communications. It is also a time in which American Indian clients may evaluate and test the specialists attempting to assist them.

Listening and observing. Most Native Americans may appear quiet and not as talkative as others, but this quietude is a skill that is taught, encouraged, and valued among them. Native Americans do a lot more listening than talking, and this behavior is seen as a sign of respect. Seeing, knowing, experiencing, and understanding involve listening intently and observing keenly the seen and unseen world, as well as understanding the relationship between these worlds. According to Fixico (2003), Indian thinking not only involves listening for sounds, but hearing while understanding the unseen.

Oral tradition. Storytelling is the foundation of the Native American oral tradition. The aforementioned patience, listening, and observing are essential skills for understanding the metaphors and relationships inherent in storytelling. Oral tradition typically passes stories down from generation to generation; these stories preserve the culture, transmit the history, tell personal biographies, entertain, educate, and inform. Stories serve different functions. For example, creation stories help explain the beginning of the physical and spiritual universe. Some stories are metaphors for explaining cultural values. Native Americans typically are a visual and oral culture and use stories as a means of conveying information or teaching morals and values.

Modesty value. Many Native American cultures have different behaviors around eye contact, and Coyhis (1999) estimates that close to half of Native American cultures do not maintain eye contact. To be modest is to be polite and respectful and to honor the other person. Modesty is manifested by not staring into the eyes of the other, but rather looking away.

Nonlinear thinking. To think like an Indian means that things, feelings, knowledge, and events are seen in their context to each other and that this contextual relationship is cyclical. Viewing life through a nonlinear lens lets people see their relationship to both their past and their future as a continuum that includes both ancestors and legacies. All things are related, and everything is involved. An approach to life that is circular provides context and relationship. Groups become more important than individuals, and individuals are not left in isolation but related to all things around them. Thus, thinking and communication become inclusive, not exclusive.

Humor. Humor is often a part of Native American cultures, and it may be used in many ways. Humor can be a way to increase comfort level or serve as part of the storytelling process. Finally, humor may serve as a defense mechanism against pain, trauma, distress, or an embarrassing situation.

NATIVE AMERICAN INVOLVEMENT IN THE MEDIA

Native Americans find their media images everywhere, and young children's conceptions often first develop out of media portrayals. Unfortunately, Native American children first see negative or outrageously unrealistic images of themselves. They see their faces on established brand names and trademarks that use Native American representations, such as Jeep Cherokee, Sue Bee Honey, or Crazy Horse Malt Liquor. Merskin (2001) found that these images are a result of assumptions about Native Americans and contribute to negative stereotyping and racism. Movies and television shows such as *Dances With Wolves, How the West Was Lost,* or *Northern Exposure* tend to rely on stereotypical images of Native Americans or show

them existing in the past. Merskin found that film presented more positive images of Native Americans than did television. Because children have television in their homes on a daily basis, this is of particular concern. Studies of the role of television in the development and maintenance of stereotypes are particularly troubling, given that Graves (1999) showed that television reinforces and maintains stereotypes in children that potentially contribute to prejudice and discrimination, a finding confirmed by others, including Rutland, Cameron, Milne, and McGeorge (2005). Sports teams that Native American youth may see on TV have Native American names, such as the Atlanta Braves, Cleveland Indians, Washington Redskins, and Florida State Seminoles. More disturbingly, several universities have mascots who are merely termed "chiefs" or "Indians," for example, Arkansas State University, Catawba College in North Carolina, and the University of Louisiana-Monroe. Most of these mascots dress up like make-believe Indians in exaggerated warfare outfits with red-painted faces.

Print Media

A Cherokee man named Sequoyah, who described the pages of books as "talking leaves," is credited with developing the Cherokee writing system in the 1820s. There is some debate over whether Sequoya actually invented the system or was simply the last of his tribe's scribe clan (the rest having been massacred). Since that time, Native Americans have written newspaper and magazine articles, fiction and nonfiction books, poetry, and lyrics. Trahant (1995) suggests that the media have created false images of the Native American and that until Native Americans project their own images, these false images will persist. Fortunately, many Native American authors have contributed to the ranks of successful mainstream books. Authors such as Louise Erdrich, Sherman Alexie, and Vine Deloria have contributed to an understanding of the complexities of Native American culture that is guided not by the dominant worldview but instead by depictions *of* Native Americans *by* Native Americans. Several bibliographies and guides on the Internet identify books portraying positive and accurate images of Native American youth and recommend the writings of contemporary and past Native Americans. Appropriate books that do not reinforce negative stereotypes can be found on the Internet, including the American Library Association's website.

Internet

Inaccurate perceptions of Native American culture are being used in the classroom, partially because much of the information used in classrooms is downloaded from well-meaning, but non-Native Internet sites. This information includes uninformed and stereotypical expressions of Native American culture. For this and other reasons, in 2001, the National Museum of the American Indian launched a website to introduce appropriate Native American media for youth and adults. The site provides information about new productions and media makers, as well as special projects that are related to Native American media. The mission of the Film and Video Center of the National Museum of the American Indian is to provide appropriate information about the work of Native Americans in media. The Native Networks website offers information on Native Americans in media. A comprehensive index of Native American media resources on the Internet delivers information on every available media format for Native Americans.

Radio

Radio, especially Internet-assisted radio, is one of the most far-reaching advances that help support Native American communication for youth. Typically produced by Native Americans, many of these stations broadcast specialty programs and documentaries for Native American adults and youths. Special stations, such as the Center for Native American Public Radio, help coordinate the work of the Native American Public Radio System, which comprises 32 Native-owned public radio stations located across 12 states, along with the American Indian Radio on Satellite (AIROS) in Lincoln, Nebraska, and the Koahnic Broadcasting in Anchorage, Alaska (see the Native Networks website on Internet and Radio). Since 1992, the Koahnic Broadcasting Corporation has conducted an Alaska Native Youth Media Institute in Anchorage. High school students receive individualized media instruction from Native American media professionals, who teach students about writing, recording, and producing audio for radio broadcast and Internet distribution. At the end of each institute, students produce a radio feature program that is broadcast by Native American radio stations across the country.

Video

To meet the need for media images that do not misrepresent Native Americans, the National Museum of the American Indian has actively sponsored the work of young Native American media makers for the past 5 years. In a special teen video program of the 2000 Native American Film and Video Festival, three works produced by youth from the United States and Canada were screened in a special program with a Native American teen and youth audience (see the Native Youth Media section of the Native Networks website). The National Museum of the American Indian also holds workshops on youth video production. Several other media projects foster the work of Native American youth. The Four Directions Project provides Native American youth with skills in computer-based technology and video. The Video Program at the Indian Island School of the Penobscot Nation offers video production training for youth in grades 3 through 8. The program has produced award-winning short animated videos that incorporate Penobscot traditions from youth perspectives. The Native Visions Program at the Center for American Indian Health of the Johns Hopkins University is a media training program that brings media professionals to reservation communities to conduct media training workshops with teens. There are many other media projects that are offered to Native American youth.

In 1999, a study of Native American children's perceptions of race and class in the media, which centered on news and entertainment, was conducted (Children Now, 1999). Children from many Native American communities, from the reservations of New Mexico to urban centers in Seattle, participated in focus groups that were organized around understanding Native American children's perceptions of how race and class were portrayed in the media. These children concluded that they rarely saw other Native American children on television. When they saw Native American adults on television, they were portrayed as poor, drunk, living on reservations, or dancing around fires. Youth rarely saw Native American representatives in the news. Coverage in the newspapers offered unfavorable stories about Native Americans that centered on such things as fighting over land or casinos. The youth who were interviewed felt passionately about their desire to see themselves in positive and realistic Native American roles on the screen and in the press. They would like to see smart

Native American kids who go to school on the reservation or in the city, or strong boys or girls who do well at sports, or mothers and fathers who don't drink.

—*Jeannette L. Johnson*

FURTHER READINGS

Children Now. (1999). *A different world: Native American children's perceptions of race and class in the media.* Retrieved October 10, 2005, from https://publications .childrennow.org

Coyhis, D. (1999). *Understanding Native American culture.* Colorado Springs, CO: Author.

Forquera, R. (2001). *Urban Indian health.* Seattle, WA: Kaiser Family Foundation.

Geiogamah, H., & Pavel, D. M. (1993). Developing television for American Indian and Alaska Native children in the late 20th century. In G. L. Berry & J. K. Asamen (Eds.), *Children and television: Images in a changing sociocultural world.* Newbury Park, CA: Sage.

Graves, S. B. (1999). Television and prejudice reduction: When does television as a vicarious experience make a difference? *Journal of Social Issues, 55*(4), 707–713.

Hirschfelder, A., & Montano, M. (1993). *The Native American almanac.* Englewood, NJ: Prentice Hall.

McHenry, T. (2002). Words as big as the screen: Native American languages and the internet. *Language Learning & Technology, 6*(2), 102–113.

Merskin, D. (2001). Winnebagos, Cherokees, Apaches, and Dakotas: The persistence of stereotyping of American Indians in American advertising brands. *Howard Journal of Communication, 12*(3), 159–169.

Native American Library Association. (n.d.). *Selective bibliography and guide, "I" is not for Indian: The portrayal of Native Americans in books for young people* (n.d.). Retrieved from www.nativeculturelinks.com/ ailabib.htm

Office of Technology Assessment. (1986). *Indian health care.* Washington, DC: U.S. Government Printing Office.

Rutland, A., Cameron, L., Milne, A., & McGeorge, P. (2005). Social norms and self-presentation: Children's implicit and explicit intergroup attitudes. *Child Development, 76*(2), 451–466.

Sanchez, J. (2003). How American public schools using down-linked news media shape American Indian identity. *Howard Journal of Communications, 14*(1), 39–48.

Snipp, C. M. (1996). The size and distribution of the American Indian population: Fertility, mortality, migration, and residence. In G. D. Sandefur, R. R. Rindfuss, & B. Cohen (Eds.), *Changing numbers, changing needs: American Indian demography and public health* (pp. 17–52). Washington, DC: National Academies Press.

Stiffarm, L. (1992). The demography of Native North American: A question of American Indian survival. In M. A. Jaimes (Ed.), *The state of Native America: Genocide, colonization, and resistance* (pp. 23–54). Boston: South End Press.

Thornton, R. (1987). *American Indian holocaust and survival: A population history since 1492.* Norman: University of Oklahoma Press.

Thornton, R. (1996). Tribal membership requirements and the demography of "old" and "new" Native Americans. In G. D. Sandefur, R. R. Rindfuss, & B. Cohen (Eds.), *Changing numbers, changing needs: American Indian demography and public health* (pp. 103–112). Washington, DC: National Academies Press.

Trahant, M. N. (1995). *Pictures of our nobler selves: A history of Native American contributions to news media* (Publication N. 95-F05). Nashville, TN: The Freedom Forum First Amendment Center.

U.S. Census Bureau. (1937). *Fifteenth census of the United States 1930: The Indian population of the United States and Alaska.* Washington, DC: U.S. Government Printing Office.

U.S. Census Bureau. (2002, February). *The Native American and Alaska Native population: 2000.* Retrieved October 26, 2004, from http:www.census.gov/ prod/2002pubs/c2kbr0–15.pdf

U.S. Census Bureau. (2005). *2000 Census of Population and Housing, Profiles of General Demographic Characteristics.* Retrieved March 29, 2005, from http:// factfinder.census.gov/home/aian/aianaff2000.html

Wilson, T. P. (1992). Blood quantum: Native American mixed bloods. In M. P. P. Root (Ed.), *Racially mixed people in America* (pp. 108–125). Newbury Park, CA: Sage.

WEBSITES

American Library Association: http://www.ala.org/ala/ alsc/alscresources/forlibrarians/servingnatamer/serving native.htm

Four Directions Project: http://www.4directions.org

Index of Native American Media Resources on the Internet: http://www.hanksville.org/NAresources/indices/NA media.html

Native American media: http://www.nativeculturelinks .com/media.html

Native Networks website: http://www.nativenetworks.si .edu/eng/green/index.htm

Native Networks, Internet and Radio: http://www.native networks.si.edu/eng/purple/radio.htm

Native Networks, Media Projects: www.nativenetworks .si.edu/eng/yellow/fymm.htm

Native Networks, Native Youth Media: http://www.native networks.si.edu/eng/rose/youth_media.htm

NATURAL EXPERIMENTS, IMPACT ON COMMUNITY ACTIVITIES

For many decades, most North Americans have habitually chosen watching television over other in-home leisure activities. TV viewing also displaces many leisure activities away from home, either in other dwellings or out of doors. A natural experiment in Canada provided the opportunity to compare the effects of television viewing in three towns assigned the pseudonyms of *Notel, Unitel,* and *Multitel.* Although their communications profiles were different, the three towns were similar in size, demographic variables such as socioeconomic status (SES), the cultural backgrounds of the residents, and the types of industry in the area. Each town had a population of about 700 but served an area four times as large through its schools and services. The purpose of the experiment was to compare Notel residents' participation in other leisure activities during the year before they first obtained television reception (Phase 1) with their participation 2 years later (Phase 2). The study also compared Notel's data with information from Unitel, with one Canadian public channel, and Multitel, with four (the same Canadian public channel and three American private channels).

This opportunity to conduct research on the effects of television was unusual and important because causal inferences can be made in natural experiments, provided that alternative possible explanations of the results (threats to internal validity) can be ruled out. This encyclopedia entry focuses primarily on the study conducted by Tannis MacBeth Williams and Gordon Handford (1986) with students in grades 7 through 12 in the three communities, with some results for adults included for comparative purposes.

The main goal of the study was to find out the extent to which residents of Notel, Unitel, and Multitel participated in their town's community activities. A method called ecological psychology, or behavior-settings analysis, was particularly well suited to this goal. In the 1950s, Barker and Wright (1955/1971) did a behavior-settings analysis of a town in the United States that they called *Midwest.* They theorized that each unit of the environment, or behavior setting, places limits on the range and type of behavior likely to occur there, sometimes for physical reasons but also because of social and other conventions. Their system

provides a method for specifying environmental units that can be applied to entire communities such as Notel, Unitel, and Multitel, towns about the same size as Midwest.

In an initial visit to each town during Phase 1 and then again 2 years later, several people in each of the following categories were interviewed: retailers, town clerks and elected officials, officers of community clubs/organizations, recreation-commission personnel, school teachers, newspaper editor, police, clergy, and children. The interview information was used to determine the public behavior settings. Researchers also obtained copies of the previous year's community newspaper to find items referring to community activities, organizations, meetings, special events, and so on.

The list of activities and events unique to each town was organized into the 12 categories Barker and Wright used to describe Midwest. These were sports; open areas, such as parks, playgrounds, and swimming holes; businesses, such as stores and offices; civic activities, such as the post office and town hall; out-of-school educational activities such as music lessons and adult classes; meetings of clubs and other nonsports organizations; medical activities, such as visits to the hospital or doctor's office; community dances, parties, and suppers; special days, such as weddings, funerals, and elections; religious activities; entertainment, such as special movies, parades, and bingo; and other activities, such as fund-raising events, town cleanup campaigns. Information on these 12 categories was obtained using a questionnaire with about 275 items for each town in each phase. Another questionnaire assessed participation in 58 private leisure activities such as bicycling, reading books, and exercising. Whereas separate community activity behavior-setting questionnaires were developed for each phase of the study in each town, the same private leisure activity questionnaire was given in all three towns in both phases.

When completing the questionnaires, each person indicated whether and how she or he was involved in each activity during the preceding year. All students in grades 7 through 12 completed the questionnaires at school. Summarizing across the three towns and two phases, community activity data were obtained from 337 students ages 12 and under, 629 13-to-15-year-olds, and 382 16-to-19-year-olds. Private leisure activity surveys were completed by a total of 1,203 youths 18 and under. Adults completed an additional

1,044 community activity surveys and 900 private leisure activity surveys, summarizing across the three towns and two phases.

Taken together, the findings indicated that television has little if any impact on the number of community activities *available,* but it has a noticeable impact on *participation* in those activities. Summing across all 12 activity categories and all ages, involvement in community activities was greatest in the absence of TV in Notel and fell significantly following its arrival. There also was evidence of greater participation in the towns with one public TV channel, CBC (Notel in Phase 2, Unitel in both phases), compared to a town with four channels—CBC and the three major U.S. private networks, ABC, CBS, and NBC (Multitel in both phases). Television affected central as well as peripheral involvement in community activities. Television use was related to participation for some kinds of activities but not for others.

TV's negative impact was greatest for sports, and the effect was stronger for youths than for adults. For example, mean participation in sports by all youths (18 and under) in Phase 1 was 16.0 in pre-TV Notel, which was statistically significantly greater than participation in Unitel (11.6) and Multitel (6.3). The town differences among youth in Phase 2 were not statistically significant (11.6, 11.5, and 8.3). The evidence implicating TV in decreased attendance at community dances, suppers, and parties also was reasonably clear, and again, the effect for youths was stronger than for adults. In Phase 1, the pre-TV Notel mean (4.24) was higher than those for Unitel (2.56) and Multitel (2.37). In Phase 2, youth participation means in all three towns did not differ significantly (3.30, 2.60, 2.62). There also was some evidence that availability of TV decreased attendance at meetings of clubs and other nonsports organizations, but this was mainly the case for adults in the longitudinal sample, not for youths. The results for participation in the category, special days, revealed that before TV was available in Notel, adults there attended more special day events than did adults in Unitel and Multitel; 2 years later, participation in special community events had fallen for youths as well as adults in Notel.

One of the major age-related findings was that when TV was not available, the oldest group of Notel residents (age 56 and older) participated in their community's activities as much as did younger adults ages 20 to 35, although not as much as the Notel youths age 19 and under. For Unitel and Multitel in both phases,

and for Notel in Phase 2, there was a significant drop in participation by adults age 56 and older by comparison with the preceding age group (36-to 55-year-olds). This was true for active participation in the sports category as well as overall participation in community activities. This suggests that the availability of television may affect the degree of age segregation characteristic of a community. If the older people attend fewer community activities, younger people who do attend have less opportunity to interact with older people. Greater age segregation may also have occurred for the category of community dances, parties, and suppers, except in this case, attendance decreased following the arrival of TV for Notel adolescents from Phase 1 to Phase 2. These age-related results suggest a qualitative component to the quantitative changes in community life associated with the impact of television.

It is clear from these results as well as those obtained by other researchers that TV's role in hindering or facilitating participation in other leisure activities is complex. Some activities—for example, active participation in sports—probably are displaced more or less directly, but others, especially those that can take place at the same time as TV viewing, probably are not. What are the processes involved in choosing to watch television versus playing a sport, reading, or attending a club meeting or community dance, party, or supper? In North America, watching TV is done more often out of habit or as a default activity than as a conscious decision to watch a particular program instead of doing one of many other possible activities. At least some of the time, for some people, watching television may displace other leisure activities because its ready availability makes the experience of finding something to do, something to make, or a game to play, alien. In other words, participation in leisure activities may operate in a self-perpetuating upward or downward spiral because the availability of TV attenuates the choice process.

It is important to acknowledge that some people have less choice than others because their access to other leisure activities is seriously limited by factors such as low socioeconomic status, illness, or other disability. For others, it may be safer to stay home, and alternatives to TV may or may not be available there.

These results regarding participation in community activities make it clear that television affects the leisure pursuits of children, adolescents, and adults. The results of other studies conducted in Notel,

Unitel, and Multitel, most notably those dealing with creativity, reading skills, problem-solving skills, and use of other media, indicate that some of the activities displaced by TV play an important role in fostering achievement, at least in certain areas and for certain people. By influencing how people play, TV may also influence how they think and work.

This study of participation in community activities in Notel, Unitel, and Multitel was cited by a prominent political scientist at Harvard University, Robert Putnam (2000), who analyzed the role of television in the decline in the United States at the end of the 20th century in social capital, including both civic participation and trust, particularly among young people.

—*Tannis M. MacBeth*

See also Notel, Unitel, Multitel Study; Research Methods, Natural Experiments

FURTHER READINGS

Barker, R. G., & Wright, H. R. (1971). *Midwest and its children*. Hamden, CT: Archon Books. (Original work published 1955)

Putnam, R. (2000). *Bowling alone: The collapse and revival of American community*. New York: Touchstone.

Williams, T. M., & Handford, A. G. (1986). Television and other leisure activities. In T. M. Williams (Ed.), *The impact of television: A natural experiment in three communities* (pp. 143–213). New York: Academic Press.

NATURAL EXPERIMENTS, IMPACT ON CREATIVITY AND SCHOOL ACHIEVEMENT

Because children and adolescents spend a significant amount of time watching television, the effects of watching TV on students' reading skills, vocabulary, creativity, spatial ability, and IQ scores are of concern to parents, educators, researchers, and policymakers. Tannis MacBeth and colleagues took advantage of a natural experiment in three Canadian towns to do a before-and-after study of the effects of television on a variety of cognitive skills. The study examined the effects of television viewing in three towns assigned the pseudonyms of *Notel, Unitel,* and *Multitel.* Although their communications profiles were different, the three towns were similar in size (about 700),

demographic variables such as socioeconomic status (SES), the cultural backgrounds of the residents, and the types of industry in the area.

In Phase 1, the researchers obtained data in Notel just before it obtained television reception for the first time, as well as in Unitel, which had had one Canadian (public) channel for about 7 years, and Multitel, which had had four channels (three from the United States as well as the same Canadian channel as Unitel) for about 15 years. They also obtained data in all three towns 2 years later in Phase 2 of the project. This encyclopedia entry focuses on the data that have particular relevance to education.

READING SKILLS

Many researchers have found that students who report watching more TV tend to be poorer readers and to do worse in school than students who watch less TV. On average, students who obtain lower scores on tests of general intelligence also tend to be poorer readers, to read less, to read different material, to do worse in school, and to watch more TV. The significant negative relationship between reading achievement and TV viewing, however, becomes smaller after the relationship of IQ to both TV and reading scores is removed. The difficulties in interpreting correlational data among the many variables related to TV and school achievement underscore the importance of the opportunity to study Notel students before and after TV reception became available because causal inferences can be made in natural experiments, provided that alternative possible explanations (threats to internal validity) of the results can be ruled out.

When first learning to read, children focus on decoding individual letters and words. Later, reading becomes more automatic and fluent, with a brief glance being sufficient to process an entire phrase. Raymond Corteen and Tannis MacBeth Williams (1986) examined this fluent/automatic phase of reading in all three towns in Phase 1, just before Notel obtained TV, gathering data on students in grades 2, 3, and 8, and 2 years later in Phase 2 on students in grades, 2, 3, 4, 5, 8, and 10. Two years after Phase 2, grade 2 students in all three towns were reassessed. Each student was tested individually. Children looked into a device that controls the amount of time the item is available to be seen; they had to read a series of items from a standardized reading test that were shown very briefly. Some were words, some were phrases, and some were nonsense words, that is, words that follow English spelling rules but are not true words, for example, *sked*. About 500 students in total were tested. In addition to this individual test of fluent reading skills, Phase 1 students completed a group reading test that assessed both comprehension and vocabulary. These group reading tests were given in all three towns to 813 students in grades 1 through 7 near the end of the school year, 6 months after the arrival of TV in Notel.

The results from the individual tests of fluent/ automatic reading skills varied according to both gender and grade level. The pattern was clearer when the relationship of IQ scores to the other variables was controlled. When all of these findings were considered, the weight of the evidence indicated that the availability of television slows down the acquisition of fluent reading in the early elementary grades, but, once acquired, good reading skills are not lost. The group test results corroborated these individual test results. In Phase 1, Notel students in grades 2 and 3 obtained higher vocabulary and comprehension scores on the group reading test than did Unitel and Multitel students, who did not differ.

It would be difficult, if not impossible, for researchers to directly observe the relationship between use of TV and acquisition of reading skills, but the pattern of results from this and other studies is consistent with the following hypotheses offered by MacBeth (1996). When no TV is available, many or even most children may practice reading enough to become fluent in the early elementary grades, but learning to read is difficult for almost all children. They have to "crack the code," and beginning readers do so slowly, with great difficulty. At the initial decoding stage, they are unable to read for pleasure and still enjoy having others read to them. At this stage, reading is hard work, and watching TV is more fun for most students; those who have the most difficulty reading probably find TV most attractive. The brighter children without learning disabilities may obtain sufficient practice in school or may read more at home than other children, either on their own or with the help of others.

The rewards of learning to read probably are greater for those who acquire the skills more quickly. Parents who consider reading to be an important skill may provide more encouragement, or parents with a greater orientation to print than to other media may more often encourage and provide help with reading. By the later

elementary grades, children who are poor readers have little opportunity to practice in school. The curriculum focuses on acquisition of reading skills only in the early grades, so beyond that point, poor readers are likely to read less outside school and to watch more TV. As other researchers have found and as noted earlier, in the later grades, use of TV, IQ scores, reading skills, and amount and type of reading are interrelated. In effect, the availability of TV and other media technologies may lead to an increase in the proportion of reading dropouts, especially among the less intelligent students in the early grades. However, this hypothesized influence of TV is indirect; the real cause is insufficient reading practice, so cutting down on time with TV might be necessary but would not be sufficient to produce good readers. The negative correlation between reading achievement and use of TV typically found in the later grades may be the outgrowth of a process that began in the early elementary grades, and not primarily due to the current influence of TV on reading skill. Older students who watch a lot of TV and read relatively little may do so because they are poor readers, rather than the other way round.

VOCABULARY

In addition to the vocabulary measure described above, which was part of the reading test given in a group (classroom) setting, the researchers obtained data for two other vocabulary tests. In Phase 1, 61 children in kindergarten and grade 1 in Notel and Unitel were individually given the Peabody Picture Vocabulary Test (PPVT), a measure of receptive vocabulary in which the examiner says a word and the child points to the one of four drawings that depicts it. Also in Phase 1, 160 children in all three towns who were in grades 4 and 7 were given the Wechsler Intelligence Scale for Children (WISC) vocabulary test. This task requires the child to provide definitions for a series of words the examiner says. Two years later, in Phase 2, the WISC vocabulary test was given to 284 students in grades 4, 6, 7, and 9. The results of the PPVT and WISC tests (as well as those for creativity discussed next) are described by Linda Harrison and Tannis MacBeth Williams (1986). There was no evidence to support the hypothesis that TV would have a positive effect on children's vocabulary, as no pattern in the results linked exposure to TV to the PPVT or WISC vocabulary scores, either positively or negatively.

CREATIVITY

The question of whether TV facilitates or inhibits various aspects of viewers' thinking, including creativity, has been much debated. Creativity is difficult to define and even more difficult to measure, especially in children, but there is substantial agreement that it includes both ideational fluency, that is, the ability to generate many ideas that fulfill certain requirements, and ideational originality, that is, the ability to generate unique or unusual ideas. The Notel, Unitel, and Multitel study examined both.

Children's creativity was assessed by Linda Harrison and Tannis MacBeth Williams (1986) with the alternate uses task, asking, for example, "Tell me all the different ways to use a newspaper." Scores were assigned for both the total number of appropriate responses (fluency) and the uniqueness/originality of each response. In Phase 1, a total of 160 children in grades 4 and 7 in the three towns were assessed. In Phase 2, 137 of the same students, now in grades 6 and 9 (the longitudinal sample), were reassessed, along with 147 students in grades 4 and 7 (the cross-sectional sample).

The results were clear, and the pattern was similar for the total number of ideas as well as their uniqueness and for both cross-sectional and longitudinal comparisons. Before their town had TV, Notel students had higher creativity scores on average than did students in both Unitel and Multitel. In Phase 2 when Notel had had TV for 2 years, however, the scores of Notel, Unitel, and Multitel students did not differ. From Phase 1 to Phase 2, only the scores of Notel students changed significantly, and they decreased.

These results indicate that TV viewing has a negative impact on children's creative thinking. This seems likely to be an indirect effect occurring because some other activities are displaced, for example, doing puzzles or playing games requiring multiple answers/ solutions that might have facilitated creativity. Having more varied experiences in the absence of TV may make a difference. Television also may displace "doing nothing," and the latter may encourage reflection and thinking about ideas.

TV may also displace some activities that require deeper information processing. Gavriel Salomon (1983) has reported evidence that the amount of invested mental effort (AIME) required to watch North American TV is low. Children and adults know this and, according to Salomon, tend to watch TV in a relatively mindless as opposed to a more mindful way. Salomon contends that young children learn that TV requires only lower levels of information processing, that is, encoding (taking in information directly) and chunking (parsing or grouping information), and no mental elaboration. In other words, TV does not require working over or transforming information. Children and adults accustomed to using these relatively mindless processing skills with TV also may use them to process information in other situations, even when the skills are inadequate to the task. The content of TV also may provide relatively few models of divergent thinking (coming up with many plausible answers or solutions) as opposed to convergent thinking (one correct answer). In short, this set of hypotheses revolves around the notion that North American TV tends to be oriented more toward entertainment than toward reflective thinking and persistence, so TV viewing does not facilitate performance on tasks that require these skills.

SPATIAL ABILITY

Although the researchers had hypothesized that television might affect children's spatial ability because it requires viewers to become TV literate by learning to decode two-dimensional spatial representations of three-dimensional space, they found no evidence for either a positive or a negative effect of TV on spatial ability.

IQ SCORES

During Phase 1, group test IQ scores were obtained from the permanent school records of 631 students across the three towns. These scores were used primarily as a control when assessing the role of TV in relation to other variables potentially related to IQ, such as reading, but the researchers also conducted some other analyses to assess the relationships among IQ scores, school achievement, and use of print and other media.

IQ scores from individual tests administered by professionals are considered to be more valid and reliable than scores from group tests, in part because the latter depend on reading ability. As mentioned earlier, the vocabulary and spatial ability tests given to students in grades 4 and 7 in Phase 1 and in grades 4, 6, 7, and 9 in Phase 2 were the WISC Vocabulary and Block Design IQ tests.

The study found evidence that children's use of television and other media varies with IQ, as measured both individually and in group tests. Higher IQ students watched less TV and used more print media than did lower IQ students. One of the most intriguing findings in the entire Notel, Unitel, Multitel natural experiment concerned the relations among IQ scores, reading ability, print use, and the availability of TV. When TV was available in their town, substantial intercorrelations were found among children's IQ scores, reading skills, amount of reading, and type of material read, as has been typical of other research conducted since TV became widely available. In this natural experiment, however, when TV was not available, IQ was more independent of reading skill and print use. In Phase 1, Notel students' IQ scores were not related to their performance on an individual measure of fluent reading skill. In addition, although Notel students' group IQ scores were significantly related to their Phase 1 group test reading scores, they were less strongly related to those scores than was the case for Unitel and Multitel students. These results are consistent with MacBeth's hypothesis, discussed earlier, that one effect of TV is more reading dropouts.

—*Tannis M. MacBeth*

See also Notel, Unitel, Multitel Study; Research Methods, Natural Experiments

FURTHER READINGS

Corteen, R. S., & Williams, T. M. (1986). Television and reading skills. In T. M. Williams (Ed.), *The impact of television: A natural experiment in three communities* (pp. 39–86). Orlando, FL: Academic Press.

Harrison, L. F., & Williams, T. M. (1986). Television and cognitive development. In T. M. Williams (Ed.), *The impact of television: A natural experiment in three communities* (pp. 87–142). Orlando, FL: Academic Press.

MacBeth, T. M. (1996). Indirect effects of television: Creativity, persistence, school achievement, and participation in other activities. In T. M. MacBeth (Ed.), *Tuning in to young viewers: Social science perspectives on television* (pp. 149–219). Thousand Oaks, CA: Sage.

Salomon, G. (1983). Television watching and mental effort: A social psychological view. In J. Bryant & D. R. Anderson (Eds.), *Children's understanding of television: Research on attention and comprehension* (pp. 181–198). New York: Academic Press.

NATURAL EXPERIMENTS, IMPACT ON GENDER ROLES

What are the effects of media portrayals on gender-related attitudes and beliefs? Content analyses of television and other media have consistently demonstrated since the 1950s that males are overrepresented, with two to three times as many male as female characters on TV. Both males and females are portrayed most often in traditional gender roles, that is, in stereotyped ways. Whereas it is relatively easy from a methodological point of view to document gender portrayals in various media, both quantitatively and qualitatively, it is substantially more difficult to document the effects of those portrayals. To the extent that viewers/readers/listeners are exposed to similar messages regarding gender through their real-life experiences and their exposure to various media, it may be impossible to isolate the influence of any particular medium on its users' attitudes and behavior. However, this entry describes two studies that do provide evidence of the impact of televised models and messages on children's perceptions of female and male gender roles and on female adolescents' dieting behaviors and their self-perceptions regarding their appearance.

EFFECTS OF TV ON GENDER-ROLE ATTITUDES

The Notel, Unitel, Multitel Study by Tannis MacBeth and colleagues allowed for the isolation of the effects of televised portrayals of gender from other sources of gender-related messages by studying gender-role attitudes in three Canadian towns (given the pseudonyms *Notel, Unitel,* and *Multitel*) before and 2 years after TV was introduced in Notel. Although their communications profiles were different, the three towns were similar in size (about 700), demographic variables such as socioeconomic status (SES), the cultural backgrounds of the residents, and the types of industry in the area. This natural experiment compared the gender-role attitudes of Notel children with those of children in Unitel and Multitel.

In one segment of a wide-ranging natural experiment, Meredith Kimball (1986) focused on children's gender-role attitudes. She used the Sex-Role Differentiation Scale (SRD) to assess students' beliefs about the appropriate and typical behaviors of girls and boys "your own age" (Peer Scale). The students also were asked to rate how frequently their own mother and father performed certain tasks (Parent Scale).

For the Peer scale, students rated each item on a scale from *1 (not true)* to *7 (very true)*. There were 61 items spread across five subscales: traits (e.g., tough, hardworking), behaviors (e.g., do dishes, swear), job suitability when grown up (e.g., bus driver, clerk in a store, a judge), authority relations (e.g., do what their parents say), and peer relations (e.g., keep secrets their friends tell them). For each item, the child rated how typical that behavior, characteristic, or future suitability of a job was both for boys their own age and for girls their own age. Their score was the sum of the differences between the two gender ratings for all 61 items. This scale measures degree of sex typing, that is, the extent to which the child differentiated between male and female peers by gender-typing them. The data were checked for the possibility that a child would differentiate or gender-type in a nontraditional way, for example, rating girls their age higher than boys their age on "tough," but this never occurred.

For the Parent Scale, the same procedure was used for rating and scoring the 41 items, except in this case students were asked about their own mother's (or stepmother's) behavior and their own father's (or stepfather's) behavior. The Parent Scale has four subscales: activities (e.g., does the family laundry), discipline (e.g., sees to it that the children do their homework), support (e.g., helps you with things when you're having trouble with it), and power (e.g., has the most to say about where to go on family outings). Each item is rated on a 7-point scale from *1 (never)* to *7 (often)* for each parent.

The participants were all students in grades 6 and 9 in each of the three towns in both Phase 1 (just before Notel obtained television) and Phase 2 (2 years later). The total sample included 130 students in Notel, 135 in Unitel, and 166 in Multitel. Longitudinal data were not obtained from the same children (e.g., those in grades 6 and 9 in Phase 1 who were in grades 8 and 11 in Phase 2). They were told not to put their names on the questionnaires so that they would be completely anonymous.

To ascertain the generalizability of their findings from these three small towns to larger urban populations, the researchers also analyzed data obtained 8 months prior to Phase 1 from 105 students in grades 5 and 8 in Vancouver, Canada's third-largest city.

Taken together, the bulk of the evidence from the analyses of the Peer Scale indicated that television made students' perceptions and attitudes with regard to gender roles more strongly gender-typed, that is, more traditionally stereotyped. Before their town had TV, Notel students' perceptions of their peers were more egalitarian than those of students in Unitel and Multitel. Two years after the arrival of TV, Notel students' gender-role perceptions had become more sex-typed, so that in Phase 2 there were no statistically significant differences among the three towns. Of the 12 data points for the Peer Scale results, only two were anomalous: Unitel boys had very high scores in Phase 1, reflecting more sex-typed perceptions than boys in Multitel as well as in Notel, and Unitel girls' perceptions in Phase 1 were less gender-typed than those of girls in Multitel as well as in Notel. But 10 of the 12 data points revealed a pattern indicating that TV viewing contributes significantly to stereotyped gender-role attitudes.

With regard to perceptions of their own parents' behavior, there was no evidence that exposure to TV had any effect. The Parent Scale scores did not vary according to town or phase of the study. On average, boys in grade 6 reported less sharing of various household and child-rearing tasks by their parents than did girls, but there was no gender difference in the parent reports of grade 9 students.

The finding that exposure to TV resulted in more stereotypical attitudes regarding gender roles of their peers but had no effect on the gender-typing of their own parents' behavior is noteworthy. It could be interpreted as indicating that the TV gender portrayals have a greater impact on gender-typing than observations of their own parents' behavior.

The results for the Peer and Parent Scales for children who grew up with TV in Unitel and Multitel were very similar to those for children who had grown up with TV in Canada's third-largest urban city, supporting the generalizability of the results regarding the effects of TV.

EFFECTS OF TV ON EATING DISORDERS

A natural experiment that showed a media effect on a gender-related issue, eating disorders, was conducted by Anne E. Becker, a medical anthropologist from the United States who studied eating habits in Fiji.

Traditionally, robust body shapes for both women and men have been preferred there, reflecting the importance in their culture of generous feeding and voracious eating. Television arrived in Fiji in 1995, with one channel that primarily carried programs from the United States, Australia, and the United Kingdom. In a prospective, cross-sectional, multi-wave study, Becker and her colleagues assessed two different sets of girls ages 15 to 19 years, the first 64 in 1995 within a few weeks of TV's arrival in Nadroga, and the other 65 in 1998. The proportion who reported ever having vomited to control weight increased from 0 to 11.3% over that period, and the proportion who scored high on a test of risk for disordered eating grew from 13% to 29%. In 1998, girls who lived in a house with a TV set were no more overweight than girls who lived in a house with no TV, but they were three times more likely to show symptoms of eating disorders. Three years after television arrived in Nadroga, 74% of the young women reported sometimes feeling "too big or fat," and 69% said they had dieted to lose weight. They also reported being interested in weight loss as a means of modeling themselves after the fictional TV characters they admired. The authors described their findings as reflecting an especially strong impact of television, given the long-standing cultural traditions that previously apparently protected the Fijians against purging, dieting, and body dissatisfaction.

CONCLUSION

All theories of gender-role development emphasize the importance of models. In both of these studies, researchers took advantage of a natural experiment to assess the effects of exposure to television on some aspect of gender roles, and in both cases, effects were evident, indicating that the impact of TV was sufficiently strong to be measurable over and above the impact of many other influences. Television may be an especially effective teacher of gender roles. North American children start watching TV when they are 2 years old, so TV provides more models than most young children encounter in real life.

—*Tannis M. MacBeth*

See also Notel, Unitel, Multitel Study; Research Methods, Natural Experiments

FURTHER READINGS

Becker, A. E., Burwell, R. A., Herzog, D. B., Hamburg, P., & Gilman, S. E. (2002). Eating behaviours and attitudes following prolonged exposure to television among ethnic Fijian adolescent girls. *British Journal of Psychiatry*, *180*, 509–514.

Kimball, M. M. (1986). Television and sex-role attitudes. In T. M. Williams (Ed.), *The impact of television: A natural experiment in three communities* (pp. 365–301). Orlando, FL: Academic Press.

NEWS, CHILDREN'S EXPOSURE TO

All forms of media have some effect on audiences who consume them. The nature and extent of the effect varies from one type of media to another, but all media impact their audiences in some manner. The news is not exempt from this universal media trait.

When children are exposed to news, whether print or broadcast, they experience a mix of effects. The overriding effect of children's exposure to news seems to be that they are better informed, more likely to understand how the world works, and better equipped to make sense of the challenges they will face in society than they would be without exposure to news.

It is possible for news coverage, particularly reports about violent, tragic, or otherwise disturbing events, to frighten, sadden, or confuse children. Like violence in entertainment media, violence in the news can, to some extent, desensitize children to violence, making them more accepting of it and, some would say, potentially more likely to behave violently. Others would disagree, saying that violence in the news is rarely presented in a way that is conducive to social learning of violent tendencies.

To maximize the benefit of children's exposure to news and to minimize potential negative effects, research has shown that parents should watch the news with their children, discussing and explaining what they see. Studies suggest that doing this will help children make more sense out of the news, put events into context, and probably increase their interest in news and current events.

A study conducted in 2002 by Stacy Smith of Michigan State University found children in the fourth, fifth and sixth grades understood television news better than younger children, but the older children also found some news stories more upsetting than their younger counterparts did. It was probably their superior ability to understand the news that caused the older children to find certain stories more upsetting. However, this research shows that children in both age groups reported finding at least some news reports to be upsetting. Other research shows that television viewing in general can be upsetting to children and that exposure to news is proportionally less upsetting than exposure to other types of violent or action-filled programming.

Some of the most insightful information about children's exposure to news can be found in data from a study of 14- and 17-year-olds from 29 countries conducted in the year 2000 by the International Association for the Evaluation of Educational Achievement (IEA). The IEA data suggest that children who are exposed to news, whether through television or newspapers, have a higher level of knowledge about civic events and issues than do children who are not exposed to news. In addition, the more exposure they have to news, both in newspapers and on television, the greater the level of their civic knowledge. However, the IEA study shows that exposure to television of all kinds is also positively correlated with an increase in civic knowledge. This pattern holds true for general television viewing up to 5 hours a day. For those who view more than 5 hours of television a day, the positive correlation does not persist.

The IEA study also shows that the strength of the correlation between exposure to news and level of civic knowledge is about equal for newspapers and television, meaning that regardless of how children are exposed to news, the same increase in civic knowledge occurs. Children, however, are much more likely to watch television news than to read a newspaper. Therefore, television news is probably involved more prominently in the association between exposure to news and increases in civic knowledge among children.

Taken collectively, these various research findings suggest that exposure to many kinds of media (including news) can frighten and disturb children but that media exposure is also positively correlated with increases in civic knowledge. In other words, the media may frighten, confuse, or disturb children, but these same media simultaneously help to inform children about the world around them. In addition, the research suggests that exposure to news, in particular, tends to disturb children less and inform them more than other kinds of media they might encounter, such as entertainment programming.

Many studies in psychology suggest the importance of parents being actively involved in their children's media consumption. Parents need to watch television (news included) with their children, discussing the meaning and implications of events seen there. The psychology literature also suggests that the news media can be used as educational tools and that learning can be augmented if news media are applied in the classroom as teaching tools.

A news report of a current event can serve as an ideal backdrop for a discussion with children about important issues of the day. Various universities, including Purdue University and North Carolina State University, have published research-based guides for parents who want to discuss with their children the events they see in news coverage.

Some researchers say terrorism and armed conflict are especially timely examples of news topics that parents should discuss and explain to their children. Judith A. Myers-Walls addressed this issue in North Carolina State University's *Forum for Family and Consumer Issues.* Myers-Walls suggests that parents should not avoid topics such as terrorism and conflict, even though those topics may be disturbing to children. Instead, parents should use news coverage as an opportunity to explain the reasons for and potential risks associated with violent events. Children who are exposed to the news as well as a thoughtful deconstruction of its meanings and implications are more likely have a better grasp of profound social issues as adults.

—*Marc C. Seamon*

See also Desensitization Effects; Mean World Syndrome; Media Education, Family Involvement in; Social Learning Theory/Social Cognitive Theory; Television, International Viewing Patterns and; Television Violence

FURTHER READINGS

Amadeo, J., Torney-Purta, J., & Barber, C. H. (2004). *Attention to media and trust in media sources: Analysis of data from IEA civic education study.* Retrieved from http://www.civicyouth.org/PopUps/FactSheets/FS_ Attention_To_Media_Trust_Sources.pdf

Myers-Walls, J. A. (2002). Talking to children about terrorism and armed conflict. *The Forum for Family and Consumer Issues, 7*(1).

Singer, M., Slovak, K., Frierson, T., & York, P. (1998). Viewing preferences, symptoms of psychological trauma, and violent behaviors among children who watch television. *Journal of the American Academy of Child and Adolescent Psychiatry, 37*(10), 1041–1048.

Smith, S. L., & Wilson, B. J. (2002). Children's comprehension and fear reactions to television news. *Media Psychology, 4*(1), 1–26.

NEWS, CHILDREN'S RESPONSES TO

As the main source of information on current events, television news presents many complicated challenges to adults and children alike. Through the news, children are presented a variety of complex issues, in both verbal and graphic forms, about the familiar and the foreign, the domestic and the international. More specifically, natural catastrophes, war, rioting, terrorist attacks, and so forth are crisis periods when children around the world may experience a heightened sense of chaos, lack of control over their lives, and a great need for information about their world as well as assistance in making sense of what is happening and assurance that the future will be better. Some researchers have also raised a concern that accumulated exposure to violent news may contribute to the Mean World Syndrome, in which children cultivate a negative perspective on the world as a mean and dangerous place.

What challenges does the news pose for children's understanding of their world and for their emotional well-being? Children hear about, see, and must cope with many troubling, often frightening events that were once known only to adults. In attempting to understand these events, children have to assimilate the fragments of information they receive from the media and try to make sense of them. They have to deal emotionally with the suffering of others and with gruesome portrayals of atrocities. Such stimuli pose demanding cognitive challenges even for adult viewers of the news, and they are particularly challenging for younger people. Furthermore, children's skill, interest, and experience in making sense of news reports varies with their age, developmental level, media competence, and personal life experience.

Research on the development of children's understanding of news has argued that their interest in and consumption of news is limited. Children, so it seems, rarely mention news programs as something they watch regularly, and overall, they rate news very low on their list of favorite topics. Yet, other studies have documented the fact that even young children are exposed to news quite often, as either incidental viewers or as part of a family gathering, and that this behavior may be growing as the nature of news has changed to a more available, dynamic, visual, and intensive type of coverage, particularly at times of social crisis. Interest in news has been related to increasing age, gender (more boys than girls following the traditional association of masculinity with the public sphere), and class (more interest among the educated and middle class).

Questions about the place news might have in children's lives have been developed through three complementary lines of inquiry.

EMOTIONAL DEVELOPMENT

The most extensive line of inquiry has attempted to understand the impact that news has on the emotional development of children, provoking reactions such as fear, anxiety, anger, physiological reactions, and sleep disturbance. Parents report that news programs are distressing to children, and their reactions have been consistent with developmental differences: Younger children are more fearful of news that looks and sounds scary, and over the years, they gradually become more fearful of news dealing with more abstract concepts of threat and danger (e.g., wars and disasters). Studies have also demonstrated that children experience negative emotional responses not only to the television coverage of traumatic events (such as the assassination of President Kennedy, the Challenger Space Shuttle disaster, the Oklahoma bombing, the Gulf War, 9/11 attacks on the United States, and the 2003 war on Iraq), but also to routine news depicting violence and disasters. In addition, studies also suggest that the danger's perceived proximity to the child and parental discourse and attitudes toward the event play significant roles in mediating children's fear and anxiety reactions. More specifically, it was found that younger children are consoled more efficiently by physical means (e.g., a hug, a favorite snack), whereas older children are more receptive to cognitive strategies (e.g., comments that the danger is far away or that the military is prepared to face it).

UNDERSTANDING OF NEWS

A second line of inquiry has examined children's understanding of news and the knowledge attained from watching, reading, and listening to news reports. In contrast to adults, children are more likely to comprehend televised news rather than other forms of news, research has found. Similar studies examined the development of children's ability to distinguish between television fact and fiction based on the acquisition of two complementary areas of knowledge and skills—those related to the real world and those related to the world of television. Preschoolers could distinguish news from other television genres and identify it as an adult genre of no interest to them. Kindergartners were already able to perceive news as dealing with important, real, and relevant issues that are "bad" and "sad" in nature, and their understanding seems to be shaped by the local media culture.

POLITICAL SOCIALIZATION

Finally, studies have sought to determine the contribution of news media to the political socialization of children and adolescents as well as to their developing sense of civic awareness. These studies have focused on documenting the central role television plays as part of the political environment in which children are being socialized and the potential that news has as a major information source through which children learn about politicians, political systems, and political agenda. In addition, news reports were found to influence children's attitudes in specific areas, such as development of stereotypes regarding minorities and enemies or political positions toward social and political conflicts. Younger children are more dependent on television; as they mature, newspapers are added as a source of information about news and current events on television. Television remains the central source of political information for young viewers from lower social economic classes.

It is interesting to note that those children and adolescents with more interest in news and current affairs, obtained in part via the media, tended also to discuss it more within their family. As a result, socializing agents reinforce one another. However, adolescents did not necessarily adopt their parents' habits of consuming news and political contents via the media, nor their parents' political attitudes.

No clear relationship has been found between the influence of news in shaping knowledge and attitudes and their practical application in various forms of political activities. However, several studies have demonstrated that given the opportunity, children may also become active participants in public discussion of current events through their posting of their feedback and opinions on news-related websites designed especially for them.

—*Dafna Lemish*

See also Mean World Syndrome; Media Education, Political Socialization and; News, Children's Exposure to; Violence, Effects of

FURTHER READINGS

Buckingham, D. (2000). *The making of citizens: Young people, news, and politics.* London: Routledge.
Cantor, J., & Nathanson, A. I. (1996). Children's fright reactions to television news. *Journal of Communication, 46*(4), 139–152.
Hoffner, C., & Heafner, M. J. (1993). Children's affective responses to news coverage of the war. In B. S. Greenberg & W. Gantz (Eds.), *Desert Storm and the mass media* (pp. 364–380). Cresskill, NJ: Hampton Press.
Lemish, D., & Götz, M. (Eds.). (in press). *Children and media in times of war and conflict.* Cresskill, NJ: Hampton Press.
Smith, S. L., & Wilson, B. J. (2002). Children's comprehension of and fear reactions to television news. *Media Psychology, 4*(1), 1–26.
Walma van der Molen, J. H., Valkenburg, P. M., & Peeters, A. L. (2002). Television news and fear: A child survey. *Communications, 27,* 303–317.
Walma van der Molen, J. H., & van der Voort, T. H. A. (2000). The impact of television, print, and audio on children's recall of the news: A study of three alternative explanations for the dual-coding hypothesis. *Human Communication Research, 26,* 3–26.

NEWS, PORTRAYALS OF CHILDREN AND ADOLESCENTS IN

A growing cadre of scholars across a range of academic disciplines have taken up the study of the representational politics guiding mediated portrayals of youth, much of it focusing on news coverage of children and adolescents. In a nutshell, their research has documented a tendency on the part of journalists to define youth as a problem (framing youth either *as risks* or *at risk* themselves) while simultaneously silencing young people in stories about them.

In his book, *Framing Youth,* Mike Males reports how newspapers and magazines systematically distort the truth about teenagers. For example, comparing *Los Angeles Times* coverage of youth violence in general and homicide in particular with the actual rate of such crimes committed by youth, Males provides evidence that the coverage is three times as extensive as would be warranted by actual youth arrests for violent crimes and five times as extensive as actual homicide involvement by youth. In addition, the coverage of youth violence is nine times more extensive than that of adult violence. Similarly, in their year-long study of local California newspapers' coverage of youth violence, John McManus and Lori Dorfman document not only that coverage of youth violence is excessive but also that such coverage is decontextualized in that it ignores broader social causes and solutions for youth violence.

Besides presenting youth as risks to the larger society, news coverage often frames youth as *at* risk from a range of social ills. In one of the only studies focusing on news coverage of adolescent girls, Sharon R. Mazzarella and Norma Pecora found that U.S. newspapers frame girls as a generation in crisis—a crisis consisting primarily of low self-esteem and poor body image. Moreover, newspapers create a scenario in which girls are the victims of these problems and desperately needing adult intervention to save them. These findings are supported in Lynne Y. Edwards's recent study examining U.S. newspaper coverage of girls and the Internet in which she found that newspapers frame girls as victims of both cyber-predators and of technology itself—in both cases needing protection from adults, notably law enforcement officials.

According to research conducted on behalf of the FrameWorks Institute, local television news coverage of teens also is characterized by its emphasis on teen lives as being dangerous and violent. By focusing on such topics as crime and car accidents, the study argues that television news helps perpetuate negative stereotypes about teens. This finding is even more pronounced regarding youth of color. In a study of California television coverage of juvenile crime, Travis Dixon, Daniel Linz, and Cristina Azocar (2000) document that African American and Latino youth are more likely to be portrayed as breaking the law than are white youth. Interestingly, this phenomenon has

not gone unnoticed by youth themselves. In a Children Now study, some 1,200 youth between the ages of 10 and 17 reported seeing white and Asian teens covered by TV news in a mostly positive manner and African American and Latino teens in a mostly negatively manner.

The tendency to link negative behavior with youth of color was underscored in coverage of the Columbine High School shootings in April 1999—coverage that featured headlines announcing: "If It Could Happen Here, Many Say, It Could Happen Anywhere," basically asking how could such an incident could happen in white, middle-class suburbia. The implication, according to Henry Giroux, is that this level of violent behavior is to be expected of urban, poor, or African American and Latino youth, but not of their white suburban peers. Giroux argues that white, middle-class children are afforded the assumption of innocence—in other words, we are shocked when they commit such crimes. When they do engage in such behavior, as in the case of Columbine, news coverage and public reactions are characterized by a wave of "soul searching" and the tendency to look for outside causes such as popular culture to explain what went wrong.

The highest profile case in a string of school shootings, Columbine generated extensive news coverage and prompted the nation to engage in a level of soul-searching regarding youth violence previously unmatched. In an analysis of network television news coverage during the week immediately following each of eight recent school shootings, the *Media Monitor* found that Columbine generated the highest amount of coverage, some 151 stories and just under 4 hours of airtime during that week. Interestingly, across the coverage of all eight school shootings, violent content in popular culture—including movies, music, television, video games, and so on—was often blamed. Similarly, in an analysis of newspaper coverage of Columbine from around the world, Erica Scharrer, Lisa Weidman, and Kimberly Bissell demonstrated the news media's tendency to blame other forms of popular culture for the shootings at Columbine High School. Such findings reflect American society's historical tendency to fear the links between youth and popular culture—a fear often played out in news coverage of youth.

Although the literature on news coverage of youth is growing, the vast majority of these studies focus on coverage of teenagers and not children. A Children

Now study found that children receive little attention in local TV news stories. When they are covered, however, it is most likely to be a crime story, and children are most likely to be presented as the victims. Moreover, the study found that children are quoted in less than 20% of the stories about them. Such stories are more likely to rely on quotes from adults including parents, doctors, law enforcement officials, and the like.

Journalists might reasonably be reluctant or unable to speak with young children directly; however, the failure to quote youth themselves is found even in stories about teenagers, according to numerous studies. This phenomenon has prompted Larry Grossberg to label youth as "the most silenced population in society" (1994, p. 25), with youth having little or no agency or voice in stories about their lives.

—*Sharon R. Mazzarella*

See also Adolescents, Media Portrayals of; African Americans, Media Images of; Children Now; Ethnicity Race, Stereotyping Latina/os, Media Images of

FURTHER READINGS

Aubrun, A., & Grady, J. (2001). *Aliens in the living room: How TV shapes our understanding of "teens."* Washington, DC: FrameWorks Institute. Retrieved from http://www.frameworksinstitute.org/products/youth.shtml

Children Now. (2001). *The local television news media's picture of children.* Oakland, CA: Author.

Dixon, T. L., Linz, D., & Azocar, C. (2000, June). *Overrepresentation and underrepresentation of African American and Latino juvenile lawbreakers on local television news.* Paper presented at the meeting of the International Communication Association, Acapulco, Mexico.

Edwards, L. Y. (2005). Victims, villains, and vixens: Teen girls and Internet crime. In S. R. Mazzarella (Ed.), *Girl wide web: Girls, the Internet, and the negotiation of identity* (pp. 13–30). New York: Lang.

Giroux, H. A. (2000). *Stealing innocence: Corporate culture's war on children.* New York: Palgrave.

Grossberg, L. (1994). The political status of youth and youth culture. In J. S. Epstein (Ed.), *Adolescents and their music: If it's too loud, you're too old* (pp. 25–46). New York: Garland.

Males, M. A. (1999). *Framing youth: 10 myths about the next generation.* Monroe, ME: Common Courage Press.

McManus, J., & Dorfman, L. (2000, April). *Youth and violence in California newspapers.* Berkeley, CA: Berkeley Media Studies Group. Retrieved from http://www.bmsg.org/pub-issues.php

Reese, D. (1998, July). *New study on children's perceptions of race and class on television.* Retrieved from http://www.kidsource.com/kidsource/content4/children.views.TV.pn.html

Scharrer, E., Weidman, L., & Bissell, K. (2003). Pointing the finger of blame: News media coverage of popular-culture culpability. *Journalism & Communication Monographs, 5*(2), 49–98.

Violence goes to school: How TV news has covered school shootings. (1999, July/August). *Media Monitor, 13*(3). Retrieved from http://www.cmpa.com/mediaMonitor/mm070899.htm

NOTEL, UNITEL, MULTITEL STUDY

What effects, if any, does TV have on viewers' attitudes and behavior? Does it affect their reading skills, creativity, vocabulary, aggressive behavior, gender-role attitudes, participation in other leisure activities, or use of other media? The Notel, Unitel, Multitel study offered an unusual opportunity in the form of a natural experiment that enabled researchers to avoid a major "chicken and egg" problem faced by researchers in examining such questions: how to determine whether viewers are affected by TV in the areas of interest, whether viewers who differ on these dimensions use TV differently, or whether both influences occur in a transactional relationship. This problem prompted the U.S. Surgeon-General's Commission to lament in 1972 that it was no longer possible to do a before-and-after TV study in a North American community because by then, virtually all communities had television access. The natural experiment represented by the Notel study did, however, enable researchers to make causal inferences with regard to the effects of television, provided that careful consideration was given to alternative possible explanations for the findings. Cook and colleagues (1990) contend that this type of research, which they call *untreated control group design with pretests*, usually produces interpretable causal results because it involves both pretests and posttests for nonequivalent control groups (in this case, Unitel, Multitel) as well as for the group (Notel) that is the focus of the natural experiment.

In July 1973, not long after the U.S. Surgeon-General's report was published, Tannis MacBeth Williams learned of a Canadian town that still did not have television reception but would be getting it soon, and she decided, with her faculty and graduate student colleagues, to take advantage of this exciting, unusual research opportunity. The details of the methodology and results of this research have been published as a book (Williams, 1986) and summarized in a chapter (MacBeth, 2001). This encyclopedia entry provides a brief overview of the project.

DESIGN OF THE STUDY

MacBeth and colleagues chose *Notel* as the pseudonym for the town initially without TV. If they had studied only Notel, however, they would not have known whether any changes that occurred following the introduction of TV to Notel were due to the availability of TV or to some other event that occurred during the period of the study. They needed at least one control community for comparison. Notel residents suggested a town about an hour's drive away, which the researchers called *Unitel* because it had had one channel, the Canadian Broadcasting Corporation's public network, CBC, for about 7 years. Notel was going to obtain that same channel (and only that) through the installation of a new repeating transmitter. Residents of Notel and Unitel agreed that the towns were otherwise similar. The researchers wondered, however, whether TV effects might vary depending on whether viewers could watch only one versus several channels, so they added a second control town. The place they called *Multitel* had had four channels for 15 years: CBC and the three private U.S. networks, ABC, CBS, and NBC. The three towns were similar in size, demographic variables such as socioeconomic status (SES), the cultural backgrounds of the residents, and the types of industry in the area. Each town had a population of about 700 but served an area four times as large through its schools and services.

One important feature of this study is that people in Notel were not self-selected; that is, they had not chosen to live there because TV was unavailable. Indeed, they had lobbied very hard to get a repeating transmitter installed by the CBC. Comparisons between families who choose to have or not to have a particular media technology are a problem because these two groups also differ on many other dimensions. These differences make it impossible to rule out the likelihood that effects apparently due to presence or absence of that technology are not really due to some other "third variable." This is a major problem for

researchers studying all new technologies, television in the 1950s and 1960s and, more recently, personal computer and Internet use. It usually takes years before a new technology penetrates a community to the point that almost everyone uses it. People of higher SES invariably acquire new technologies earlier than those of lower SES, so it is difficult to rule out SES as an alternative possible explanation of some of the results. This was not an issue in Notel in 1973. Residents knew what TV was and watched it when they were elsewhere, but most could not watch it regularly. The median number of hours watched per week in Notel before TV arrived (Phase 1) was zero. By comparison, the Phase 1 median for Unitel was 23.5 hours per week and for Multitel, 29.3 hours.

Some reports by others on the Notel, Unitel, Multitel study have described Notel as an isolated community in northern Canada. This is wrong. Like Unitel and Multitel, Notel is in southern Canada and was not isolated. This is important because the effects of various media in an isolated community that is accessible only by air or by sea, as is true of many small Canadian communities, may well be different from the effects in a nonisolated community. Notel would have had television sooner, but the transmitter that brought TV to Unitel 7 years earlier had been ineffective in Notel. Although it is only an hour's drive from Unitel, Notel is located in a valley in such a way that most residents could not pick up the transmitter's signal most of the time, although Unitel residents could do so. Notel, like Unitel, had highway and train service going in two directions. In anticipation of the installation of the new repeating transmitter in the late fall of 1973, almost all Notel residents had already obtained TV sets.

All three towns were studied just before Notel obtained television reception (Phase 1) and again 2 years later (Phase 2). The 2-year interval was chosen because it seemed long enough that any effects of TV would be clearly evident, but not so long that other major historical changes were likely to occur in Canadian society, either in general or in any of the three towns. Also, the longer the interval from Phase 1 to 2, the more likely it would be that residents would move away. Attrition is always a problem in longitudinal studies in which the same people are studied on more than one occasion, especially if there is differential attrition among the groups. In this study, overall attrition from Phase 1 to 2 was relatively low, 28.5%, and did not differ significantly for the three towns.

TOPICS AND PARTICIPANTS

The Notel researchers chose to study topics that had been identified in previous research as potentially influenced by television, either positively or negatively. Many of the studies in this project focused on children, either elementary or high school students, but some focused on adults. Unfortunately, resources to study preschool children were not available.

For most topics, the study included children and adults at more than one age level. With three towns studied in both Phase 1 and Phase 2, this provided a minimum of 12 data points for each topic, for each measure (e.g., physical aggression, fluent reading skill), with more than one measure used for most topics. For each topic, researchers were therefore looking for a pattern of results that made sense in relation to the availability of television.

For almost all topics, both cross-sectional and longitudinal comparisons were made. Comparisons between different people studied on the same occasion are cross-sectional, for example, comparisons among children in Notel, Unitel, and Multitel within Phase 1 and similar comparisons within Phase 2. The study also included longitudinal analyses of the same children, comparing their Phase 1 and 2 scores on the same or a similar measure, for example, Notel children's creativity scores in Phase 1 when they were in grade 4 or 7 with those same children's creativity scores 2 years later in Phase 2 when they were in grade 6 or 9. For this type of analysis, researchers also checked to see that the Phase 1 scores of children who were available to be restudied in Phase 2 did not differ from the Phase 1 scores of children who were not available in Phase 2 because of attrition. This was important because in some other longitudinal research on children and media, attrition from the first to subsequent measurements differed for those low versus high on the measure; for example, attrition was greater for children who initially were high rather than low in aggressive behavior because they left school or changed schools, perhaps in part because of their aggressiveness.

GENERALIZABILITY OF FINDINGS

Notel, Unitel, and Multitel are three small towns. How representative are they? Several aspects of the findings are reassuring in this regard. First, the study replicated results obtained by other researchers for urban samples in the United States and elsewhere. For example, boys were found to be on average more physically aggressive than girls; the mean WISC Block Design score for boys was higher than for girls; boys on average held more stereotypical attitudes about gender roles than did girls; women obtained higher person-orientation scores and lower thing-orientation scores than did men; ideational fluency and originality creativity scores were strongly and positively correlated; creativity and intelligence scores were relatively independent; and the TV viewing habits of children and adults in the three towns were comparable to those reported by others. Second, the mean performance of Notel, Unitel, and Multitel students on IQ tests that had been previously standardized on representative U.S. or Canadian samples was similar to the norms for those tests. Third, scores obtained with the gender-role attitude measure in Unitel and Multitel were in the same range as scores on this measure for an urban sample in Vancouver, Canada's third-largest city. Most important, the study results tend to confirm and extend, rather than to contradict, findings obtained in field and laboratory studies by other North American and Western European researchers.

CONCLUSION

In designing this research, the researchers hypothesized that TV influences its viewers in many ways, both positively and negatively, based on previous research and theory. The natural experiment provided by the imminent arrival of TV in Notel and comparisons with Unitel and Multitel provided an opportunity to measure the effects of TV over and above the many other influences that operate in naturalistic settings. In brief, TV had a negative effect on creativity; the acquisition of reading skills in the early elementary grades; participation in several types of community activities (e.g., sports) by adolescents and adults; students' attitudes regarding gender roles, which became more strongly and stereotypically sex-typed; children's physically and verbally aggressive behavior, for both boys and girls and for children initially low as well as those initially high in aggression. There was neither any supportive nor any contradictory evidence for the hypothesis that TV would have a positive impact on vocabulary, spatial ability, field independence, and fineness of information processing. There also was no positive or negative evidence regarding participation in certain kinds of community activities (e.g., religious, medical), although, as mentioned earlier, there was evidence of a negative impact for some other kinds of community activities, such as active participation in sports.

No single study is definitive. Laboratory experiments, field experiments, observational studies in field settings, and natural experiments such as the Notel, Unitel, and Multitel study provide complementary kinds of evidence regarding the effects of television and other media on attitudes and behavior. The results, when added to the converging evidence from other research over many years, indicate that TV does have measurable effects on its viewers. The hypothesis of no effects is no longer tenable. No researchers would argue that TV is the only or most important influence for any of the topics studied, but over and above the myriad other sources of influence, TV plays a role that is measurable on average, despite the many individual differences among viewers.

—*Tannis M. MacBeth*

See also Natural Experiments, Impact on Community Activities; Natural Experiments, Impact on Creativity and School Achievement; Natural Experiments, Impact on Gender Roles; Research Methods, Natural Experiments; and Violence, Natural Experiments and

FURTHER READINGS

Comstock, G. A., & Rubinstein, E. A. (Eds.). (1972). *Television and social behavior* (Vols. 1–5). Washington, DC: U.S. Government Printing Office.

Cook, T. D., Campbell, D. T., & Peracchio, L. (1990). Quasi-experimentation. In M. D. Dunnette & L. M. Hough (Eds.), *Handbook of industrial and organizational psychology* (2nd ed., Vol. 1, pp. 491–576). Chicago: Rand McNally.

MacBeth, T. M. (2001). The impact of television: A Canadian natural experiment. In C. McKie & B. D. Singer (Eds.), *Communications in Canadian society* (pp. 196–213). Toronto, Canada: Thompson Educational.

Williams, T. M. (1986). *The impact of television: A natural experiment in three communities*. New York: Academic Press.

O

OBESITY

Obesity is one of the biggest health threats many children face in the modern world. Its incidence has risen so dramatically in recent years that it has been called an epidemic. Obesity dramatically increases the risks of disease (in particular type 2 diabetes) and even death in both children and adults. It has been estimated that it is perhaps the biggest threat to public health and organized health care in many countries of the world.

Several studies have found a relationship between watching a lot of television at an early age and higher scores on the weight to height ratio (known as the *body mass index*) in adulthood. Much of this research is based on large cohorts of young people that have been followed over time. A curvilinear relationship between video game use and obesity has also been demonstrated. Several explanations between media use and obesity have been explored, although more research is needed to decide whether reducing media exposure makes any difference in fighting this major threat to children's health.

EXPLANATIONS AND HYPOTHESES

There are four possible explanations of the relationship between media exposure and obesity.

Displacement

The displacement hypothesis suggests that the pathway from television to obesity is indirect. Television viewing displaces more-active leisure activities, thus leading to a decrease in calorie-burning behaviors. Energy expenditure is reduced because behaviors requiring more energy are displaced by the sedentary behavior of TV viewing. There appears to be some but not much evidence of a direct relationship. TV viewing appears to be unrelated to activity levels. It is interesting to note that some sedentary media consumption behaviors (such as reading) do not appear to elicit concern.

Reduced Metabolism

Some authors believe that watching television induces a kind of passive physical state. One laboratory experiment showed, for instance, that rest metabolic rate was lower in children who watched television than in children who just rested. Video game use has been linked to *increased* metabolic rate because of the excitement it induces. If television viewing reduces metabolic rate, this means that viewing TV has a larger effect on body mass than many other nonactive behaviors.

Encouraging Energy Intake

Children are constantly exposed to advertising and marketing messages about food. Many messages encourage young people to consume high-energy foods with low nutritional value. There is some evidence that exposure to commercial messages increases the intake of unhealthy foods.

Increased Energy Intake

A number of studies show that eating snacks and drinking soft drinks are common behaviors in TV-viewing children. One study found that the daily intake of drinks and snacks while watching television amounted to about 19% of the average energy allowance in boys and about 14% in girls, although the actual numbers are likely to be culture specific. Snacking behavior accompanying television viewing thus appears to be the equivalent of an extra meal a day.

DISCUSSION

These four explanations of the relationship between media use (studied mainly with regard to television) and obesity (defined mainly as body mass index) are not mutually exclusive. To some extent, all four of them may influence body weight. Moreover, the relationship between body size and media use is only part of the problem. Even if media use does not increase weight, other effects remain possible. Television viewing has been associated with both snacking and meal skipping. This may explain why the relationship between television viewing and body mass index is smaller than might be expected: It is possible that those kids who eat many snacks when watching TV also skip many regular meals. Total caloric intake may, therefore, not be influenced by TV viewing, although nutritious food is displaced by less nutritious snacks and soft drinks. This could help explain the negative relationship between media use and health reported by many of the studies.

The number of published papers in this area is testimony to the fact that the study of media effects on obesity has become an emerging field. A number of issues still need to be resolved. First, both food consumption frequency and media use are difficult to measure accurately. Both the exposure and the outcome variables thus suffer from misclassification, which is bound to bias the results of any study considerably.

Second, this new field lacks interdisciplinary cooperation. Many epidemiologists have looked at television from a medical perspective, and many communication scholars have looked at obesity from a media research perspective. Both approaches sometimes lead to simplification of one side of the issue. Media scholars tend to be vague about defining determinants and outcomes while creating complex models that are difficult to prove empirically, but medical scholars tend to simplify the determinants and produce models based on stimulus-response theories of media effects.

Much work remains to be done to establish whether media use does lead to obesity and which processes explain such a relationship.

IS INTERVENTION OR PREVENTION NECESSARY?

Many authors suggest that reducing television viewing and computer game play could be an element of prevention (preventing the development of new cases of obesity) or intervention (reducing the number of existing cases of obesity). Both of these media consumption behaviors are expected to be major causes of widely reported decreases in activity levels of children in many countries. Reducing the time spent with these media should stop the displacement process and could have a place next to other types of intervention such as school-based programs or nutrition information campaigns. Some interventions have been successful, but overall the results are disappointing. Increasingly the solution to childhood obesity appears to be medication and even surgery.

—Jan Van den Bulck

See also Eating Disorders; Eating Habits, Media Influence on; Food Advertising, Influence of; Physiological Arousal; Product Placements, Food; Public Health Campaigns

FURTHER READINGS

Dietz, W. H., & Gormaker, S. L. (1985). Do we fatten our children at the television set? Obesity and television viewing in children and adolescents. *Pediatrics, 75*(5), 807–812.

Marshall, S. J., Biddle, S. J. H., Gorely, T., Cameron, N., & Murdey, I. (2004). Relationships between media use, body fatness, and physical activity in children and youth: A meta-analysis. *International Journal of Obesity, 28*(10), 1238–1246

Skidmore, P. M. L., & Yarnell, J. W. (2004). The obesity epidemic: Prospects for prevention. *Quarterly Journal of Medicine, 97*(12), 817–825.

Visscher, T. L. S., & Seidell, J. C. (2001). The public health impact of obesity. *Annual Review of Public Health, 22*, 355–375.

OBSCENITY

Obscenity is omnipresent in today's world. Even casual observers of American culture recognize that today's media are rife with depictions or references to acts of violence and explicit sexuality as well as profane language. In addition to such expressions or portrayals, there exists a massive pornography industry. In 2001, Frank Rich wrote in a *New York Times Magazine* article that Americans spend $10 billion to $14 billion per year on pornography, including pay-per-view movies on cable and satellite, phone sex, in-room hotel movies, sex toys, pornographic magazines, and pornographic websites. Although critics across the political spectrum—from the leading conservative Irving Kristol to the feminist Catherine McKinnon—are alarmed at what this says about the United States, its citizens, and its culture, defenders cite the First Amendment right to free speech in behalf of the unfettered dissemination of what often amounts to pornography. Studies indicate that children on the average view as many as 8,000 murders and 100,000 acts of violence during their elementary school years alone. The prevalence of images and messages of explicit sex and violence strikes many social critics as contributing to a wholesale culture of obscenity.

Popular culture now serves as a primary agent of socialization for children and adolescents, raising serious questions not only about individual programs or messages but also about their collective impact during crucial early periods of character formation and psychological development. Even a brief immersion in today's popular culture reveals the great extent to which obscene language and images have become everyday phenomena. Consideration of some relevant historical developments indicates how a culture of obscenity caught hold and came to dominate a life-world into which the young are introduced at earlier and earlier ages.

By the late 20th century and early 21st century, obscenity in visual images, language, and other forms (song lyrics, for instance) had escaped the boundaries of the pornography industry itself, which hitherto had been somewhat cordoned off from mainstream America. No longer the preserve of separate red light districts, so-called adult bookstores and movies went mainstream, and material once deemed pornographic appeared everywhere: daytime to prime-time television programs, music CDs, and Internet sites. The signs of a changed notion of the boundary between public and private were omnipresent: the appearance of lingerie shops in shopping malls; the display of models wearing only their underwear in full-page advertisements in the *New York Times,* on billboards, or on the sides of buses; and the crotch-grabbing and skimpily clad pop rock stars catering to preteens.

Parents who view the tenor of contemporary popular culture with dismay find that it is not only advertisers and other companies that help lower the standards of decency, but other parents as well. These parents, for instance, help host theme birthday parties where youngsters dress as pop stars, and they purchase violent video games as gifts for their own children, allow them to view uncounted violent scenes on television cartoons and DVDs, and permit them to dress in T-shirts with antisocial messages or depictions of scantily clad celebrities. Some parents' rationale for such acquiescence is that children desire these things, just as many retailers contend that they merely provide what consumers want. As a result, those who seek to limit what children are exposed to—inappropriate language, literal sexuality, and depictions of brutal or meaningless violence—confront a larger culture that no longer recognizes limits as valid.

BLURRING BOUNDARIES: ROOTS OF THE CULTURE OF OBSCENITY

Sociologist Philip Rieff wrote about the long-term historical transformation in the West from a religious culture to a therapeutic anti-culture. In earlier religious cultures, the renunciation of instinct was achieved in the name of a greater communal purpose, and sacrifice was made worthwhile by the cultural attainments and participation; this allowed for the sublimation of selfish impulses. In the contemporary era, a cult of impulse release undermined inherited notions of permission and restraint that are the foundation of culture. Whereas older religious traditions had a profoundly consoling aspect—helping to save the individual from excess and isolation—the new sensibility not only mandated self-expression and the unfettered pursuit of desire as the ultimate purpose of life but fostered the creation of endless new desires. Ostensibly therapeutic, the new anti-culture actually removed the conditions for satisfaction, which Rieff thought could be found only in the bond between the self and something beyond or outside it. Legitimating and exacerbating wants and needs, chronic therapy trumped the logic of outside commitments, thus simultaneously removing the sources of limitation and satisfaction of impulse.

Historian Rochelle Gurstein gives a detailed portrait of the decline of the "reticent" sensibility characteristic of 19th-century America and the rise of a culture of "exposure" in the early 20th century. During the Victorian era, Americans could appeal to notions of common sense, discretion, judgment, and the like because they could distinguish clearly the separation between private and public life. Gurstein, like political philosopher Jean Bethke Elshtain and others, argues that contemporary life has witnessed a merging of these two spheres, to the detriment of each. When brought into the full light of day, aspects of private life suffer from trivialization and desacralization, and public life loses its weight and integrity. For those who cannot put personal concerns aside for the common good, civic engagement becomes a mere excuse for the pursuit of self-aggrandizement. Impartial, shared moral standards give way to what philosopher Alasdair MacIntyre called *emotivism,* a perspective that makes subjective emotional preference the only criterion of judgment.

Christopher Lasch's notion of the "culture of narcissism" helped capture the strange predicament of the modern self. On the one hand, the self has sources of ostensible satisfaction at its disposal as never before because the notion that its impulses require taming no longer applies. On the other, its pathological inability to separate itself from objects and persons in the outside world means that the self can never attain satisfaction through engagement with anything truly other than itself.

One way to think about ways to recover a sense of proper, legitimate, and ultimately gratifying limits on the self and its instinctual designs is to revisit the issue of what makes something obscene. The question today is not only what should be considered adult-rated sexual material or pornography, which many would define through practices or ratings based on mere age appropriateness, but how to think about the deeper vulgarity, perversity, or vacuity of the culture at large.

THE DEFINITION AND COSTS OF OBSCENITY

In his book *Obscenity and Public Morality,* Harry Clor located the essence of obscenity in the transgression of the private/public boundary. Like Gurstein, who drew on his ideas, Clor argued that making public what properly belongs in the private realm constitutes an imposition on our sense of intimacy, often reducing intimate acts and understandings to their purely physical manifestations. Obscene materials are those that deliberately stir up lascivious impulses, gratuitously or graphically associate sexuality with extreme violence, or demonstrate violent harm of an individual with no real educational intent, for instance, in the service of science or art. MTV videos are one obvious example of this tendency to couple violence with sex.

By this standard, much of what passes for mainstream or popular fits into the category of obscenity. The cumulative effect of the culture of obscenity is objectification and dehumanization. The uniqueness and completeness—the integrity of the human person—and particular personal contexts in which one individual experiences a shared world of affection with another, or experiences pain and suffering, is lost. The limited human scale, mystery, and context of physical love and affection—as well as violence and death—is violated by the sheer quantity and repetition of depictions and references as well as the cold examining eye. The repetition of messages and images, as well as the too-close details, deadens the senses rather than stimulating them as promised. The culture of obscenity, rather than speaking to a lusty embrace of humanness, reduces human beings to objects, degrades profound aspects of human experience, and signifies an inability to experience real feeling rather than the superhuman capacity it advertises.

—Elisabeth Lasch-Quinn

FURTHER READINGS

Clor, H. M. (1969). *Obscenity and public morality: Censorship in a liberal society.* Chicago: University of Chicago Press.

Gurstein, R. (1996). *The repeal of reticence: A history of America's cultural and legal struggles over free speech, obscenity, sexual liberation, and modern art.* New York: Hill & Wang.

Lasch-Quinn, E. (2003). Socializing children in the culture of obscenity. In D. Ravitch & J. P. Viteritti (Eds.), *Kid stuff: Marketing sex and violence to America's children.* Baltimore: Johns Hopkins University Press.

Rieff, P. (1966). *The triumph of the therapeutic: Uses of faith after Freud.* New York: Harper & Row.

ONLINE MEDIA, AGENCY AND

In this day and age of avatars and conversational agents, it has become extremely important to understand the psychological locus and importance of perceived human agency in our mediated interactions. There are two ways in which agency is treated in the literature on communication technologies—(1) as robotic entities, either hardware or software related, that perform tasks for the user, often autonomously (e.g., interface agents that search for information on the Internet, conversational agents with whom users can carry on a dialogue), and (2) as online representations of offline human beings (e.g., avatars, screen names). Although technologically distinct, these two notions of agency may be psychologically indistinguishable to the user, given findings in recent research.

RESPONDING TO ONLINE AGENTS

As Nass, Lombard, Henriksen and Steuer (1995) demonstrate, human beings have an innate tendency to anthropomorphize technologies, both physically and psychologically. An individual's tendency to anthropomorphize is shown to predict his or her acceptance of computers in routinized (e.g., telephone operator), interpretive (e.g., novelist), and personal (e.g., judges) roles. Sundar (2004) showed that the level of psychological anthropomorphism even predicted a tendency to be loyal toward particular computer terminals. Reeves and Nass (1996) argue that even when technological interfaces do not expressly involve anthropomorphic cues or representations, human beings are hardwired to respond to communication technologies in social ways. Sundar and Nass (2000) call this tendency *source orientation* and demonstrate that users make social attributions directly to machines as if they are autonomous information and communication sources, without needing to invoke an underlying human agency such as the programmer or networker.

Sundar and Nass (2001) proposed a typology of online media sources by suggesting not just that traditional visible senders or gatekeepers of information are considered sources, but that the medium (technological source) and even the receivers (audience as source and self as source) can be construed as an independent source. In their experiment, they showed that users' perceptions of news content attributed to these different types of online sources were significantly different, implying that people are able to psychologically distinguish between professional journalists as gatekeepers and algorithms (as in Google News) as selectors of our information, and between themselves as source (e.g., portal sites) and other users as a collective source (e.g., collaborative filtering systems such as those used by Amazon.com wherein others' behavior is conveyed as an input for decision making).

However, user responses to these sources are based not always on effortful processing of source characteristics but on mental shortcuts *(cognitive heuristics)*, which can be triggered by simply invoking the name of the source. For example, Sundar, Knobloch-Westerwick, and Hastall (in press) show that the computer as a source can trigger the *machine heuristic,* emphasizing objectivity in information selection and absence of ideological bias. But the operation of such heuristics is largely dependent on the cues embedded in the interface as well as content (Sundar, 2006). If an online chat bot (short for *chatterbot,* a program designed to simulate intelligent conversation) has a visibly human presence on the interface and is Caucasian and female (e.g., Ramona on http://www.kurzweilai.net), then users are likely to factor her race and gender into their interactions with this bot and their perceptions of the content it delivers. In fact, anthropomorphic agents attempt to approximate real humans in their outward appearance, with the use of such design elements as animation, gesture, natural language communication, animation, and personality—ingredients that, according to Heckman and Wobbrock (2000), form the foundation of "a dangerous illusion," with potential for powerful persuasion through unethical, if not illegal ways.

PERSONAL AGENCY ONLINE

Aside from persuading users to assign human agency to nonhuman entities, modern computer-based media, especially online media, allow users to express and experience a greater sense of personal agency by allowing them to make a priori specifications of the kinds of content they would like to receive. Called customization, this feature allows each and every user to be unique and distinct (Kalyanaraman & Sundar, 2006). Sundar (in press) argues that the crux of the individualization in customized messages lies in the importance not so much of the self as receiver (because that is merely targeting—something that has been around for a long time in traditional media), but of the self as sender or source. The ability to influence the nature and course of an online interaction, be it prepackaged content or ongoing dialogue with another entity, underlies the seductive appeal of customization and goes to the heart of imbuing agency in the end user.

IMPLICATIONS FOR CHILDREN AND ADOLESCENTS

The powerful psychological appeal of agency in online media is particularly important to consider in the context of children and adolescents' interactions with media. Studies with adults, even technical professionals, have shown that users can be extremely gullible about anthropomorphic cues. Even in the absence of such cues, people are quite willing to attribute human-like traits to nonhuman interface features (Nass & Moon, 2000). Given this, children and adolescents are, if anything, more likely to succumb to this tendency. Media literacy campaigns would do well to educate this population about the pitfalls as well as the promise of interacting with online agents. Furthermore, designers of agents ought to factor in the greater vulnerability to persuasion of children and adolescents in their attempts to create satisfying, yet ethically unproblematic interactions online.

The rapid spread of customization is likely to give today's children and adolescents a much deeper sense of personal agency than any previous generation experienced. This has important implications for their assumptions about their right to choose in their offline lives, with implications for their cognitive and social development. Self-determination theorists Ryan and Deci (2000) have noted across dozens of studies that for intrinsic motivation to be evident, individuals need not only competence and self-efficacy but also a real sense of autonomy or at least an attribution of causality to themselves. A sense of agency can be a powerful motivator for action, be it immediate browsing behavior online, interactions with others, or other attempts at furthering one's learning.

—*S. Shyam Sundar*

See also Cognitive Skills, Computer Use and; Information Processing, Active vs. Passive Models of; Media Literacy, Key Concepts in

FURTHER READINGS

Heckman, C. E., & Wobbrock, J. O. (2000, June). *Put your best face forward: Anthropomorphic agents, e-commerce consumers, and the law.* Paper presented at the ACM Conference on Autonomous Agents (Agents 2000), Barcelona, Spain.

Kalyanaraman, S., & Sundar, S. S. (2006). The psychological appeal of personalized content in Web portals: Does customization affect attitudes and behavior? *Journal of Communication, 56*(1).

Nass, C., Lombard, M., Henriksen, L., & Steuer, J. (1995). Anthropocentrism and computers. *Behaviour and Information Technology, 14*(4), 229–238.

Nass, C., & Moon, Y. (2000). Machines and mindlessness: Social responses to computers. *Journal of Social Issues, 56*(1), 81–103.

Reeves, B., & Nass, C. (1996). *The media equation: How people treat computers, television, and new media like real people and places.* Stanford, CA: CSLI Publications and Cambridge University Press.

Ryan, R. M., & Deci, E. L. (2000). Self-determination theory and the facilitation of intrinsic motivation, social development, and well-being. *American Psychologist, 55*(1), 68–78.

Sundar, S. S. (2004). Loyalty to computer terminals: Is it anthropomorphism or consistency? *Behaviour & Information Technology, 23*(2), 107–118.

Sundar, S. S. (2006). Social psychology of interactivity in human-website interaction. In A. Joinson, K. McKenna, U. Reips, & T. Postmes (Eds.), *Oxford handbook of Internet psychology.* Oxford, UK: Oxford University Press.

Sundar, S. S. (in press). Self as source: Agency in interactive media. In E. Konijn, M. Tanis, S. Utz, & A. Linden (Eds.), *Mediated interpersonal communication.* Mahwah, NJ: Erlbaum.

Sundar, S. S., Knobloch-Westerwick, S., & Hastall, M. R. (in press). News cues: Information scent and cognitive heuristics. *Journal of the American Society of Information Science and Technology.*

Sundar, S. S., & Nass, C. (2000). Source orientation in human-computer interaction: Programmer, networker, or independent social actor? *Communication Research, 27*(6), 683–703.

Sundar, S. S., & Nass, C. (2001). Conceptualizing sources in online news. *Journal of Communication, 51*(1), 52–72.

ONLINE RELATIONSHIPS

Over the last decade, rapid advances in communication technology have contributed to a sustained body of scholarship in computer-mediated communication (CMC). The bulk of research attention has focused on comparing CMC with face-to-face (FtF) communication. For example, research has compared how CMC differs from FtF in several fundamental ways and discussed the unique aspects of CMC that result in impression-formation effects and the principles that govern online relationship building, among other topics. This program of research has been complemented by systematic conceptual development, even as the Internet has nurtured the examination of online social interaction in a variety of venues such as chat rooms, newsgroups, message boards, email, and websites.

Early research suggested that CMC could not approximate the warmth and feel of interpersonal communication, mainly because of the lack of nonverbal cues in the online context. However, increasing sophistication of communication technology has led researchers to recognize the numerous benefits proffered by CMC, including some that can help to develop online relationships. For instance, the process of communication can be synchronous (in real time, as in chat rooms) or asynchronous (e.g., email). The communicator can also take advantage of several advantages offered by these new technologies, depending on his or her own personality characteristics. For example, the relative anonymity offered by online venues can help a shy person ease into a conversation without suffering from the pressures of having to create an immediate "impression," as might happen in an FtF scenario. Furthermore, online venues can increase psychological affinity by bringing together communities of users with common interests and values. In addition, online relationships are not constrained by space or time. Finally, interactive features of new communication technologies enhance the quality of interaction—communicators can make use of multimedia features such as audio and video to provide a multifaceted dimension to communication. Also, they can easily send and receive messages to (and from) a large number of people without substantial cerebral or financial expenditure.

It is beyond the scope of the current entry to detail the wide body of work that has examined various aspects of online relationships; however, some important findings necessitate mention (see Bargh & McKenna, 2004, for an excellent review). Some early findings implied that CMC lacked the richness of (nonverbal) cues necessary to sustain relationships.

The landmark HomeNet project by Kraut and colleagues (1998) concluded that Internet use had severe negative consequences because it led to increased feelings of depression and loneliness and impaired existing relationships. However, a follow-up study by Kraut et al. (2002) concluded that the negative outcomes observed in the previous study were unfounded and that greater Internet use actually had psychological value. Experimental studies that have examined factors underlying relationship formation on the Internet between college students have shown that people who first met online expressed greater liking for their partners than people who met first FtF. Furthermore, these participants also tended to exhibit their "true" selves to a greater degree online (compared to FtF contexts). Other findings also suggest that people tend to lose their inhibitions in the online environment and are more likely to indulge in self-disclosure, which can aid formation and maintenance of relationships.

The use of new media and communication technologies for relationship formation appears to be especially trendy with young adults and college-age youth, as evident from the popularity of such online venues as MySpace and Facebook, as well as the rapid proliferation of blogs. In addition, reports from organizations such as the Pew Internet Center convey that many teenagers report using Instant Messaging (IM) services to form and sustain relationships, whereas traditional applications such as email are used for more formal purposes such as academic issues (at least among this segment). In addition to being synchronous and easy to use, IM programs also offer the benefit of including nonverbal cues like *emoticons* (or emotional icons) to help create the richness of interpersonal communication. However, although it appears that new technologies have contributed to the robustness of online relationships, several warning signs deserve scrutiny. For example, there is growing concern that many young users are divulging an inordinate amount of personal information and are rather injudicious in terms of exercising caution. According to several recent reports, sexual predators have taken advantage of adolescents they have met online. Thus, while technology will continue to enhance the quality of online relationships, it is also incumbent on society to adopt safeguards to protect this vulnerable segment of the population.

—Sriram Kalyanaraman

See also Chat Rooms; Computer-Mediated Communication (CMC); Computer Use, Socialization and; Email Pen Pals; Instant Messaging; Internet Relay Chat (IRC); Internet Use, HomeNet Study and; Internet Use, Psychological Effects of; Internet Use, Social; Personal Web Pages

FURTHER READINGS

Bargh, J. A., & McKenna, K. Y. A. (2004). The Internet and social life. *Annual Review of Psychology*, *55*, 573–590.

Bargh, J. A., McKenna, K. Y. A., & Fitzsimons, G. M. (2002). Can you see the real me? Activation and expression of the "true self" on the Internet. *Journal of Social Issues*, *58*(1), 33–48.

Kraut, R., Kiesler, S., Boneva, B., Cummings, J., Helgeson, V., & Crawford, A. (2002). Internet paradox revisited. *Journal of Social Issues*, *58*(1), 49–74.

Kraut, R., Patterson, M., Lundmark, V., Kiesler, S., Mukopadhyay, T., & Scherlis, W. (1998). Internet paradox: A social technology that reduces social involvement and psychological well-being? *American Psychologist*, *53*(9), 1017–1031.

McKenna, K. Y. A., Green, A. S., & Gleason, M. J. (2002). Relationship formation on the Internet: What's the big attraction? *Journal of Social Issues*, *58*(1), 9–31.

Walther, J. B., & Parks, M. R. (2002). Cues filtered out, cues filtered in: Computer-mediated communication and relationships. In M. L. Knapp & J. A. Daly (Eds.), *Handbook of interpersonal communication* (3rd ed., pp. 529–563). Thousand Oaks, CA: Sage.

P

PARASOCIAL INTERACTION

Donald Horton and R. Richard Wohl coined the term *parasocial interaction* in 1956 to describe the imaginary interactions between the audience and TV variety show hosts, noting the "seeming face-to-face relationship" that viewers developed with these personalities. Children and adolescents, like adults, develop strong parasocial relationships with a wide range of individuals whom they encounter only through the media, such as musicians, actors, and fictional characters. Parasocial relationships, or pseudo-friendships with media figures, are distinct from identification, which is defined as sharing or internalizing media characters' experiences.

Scholars suggest that parasocial relationships may reflect an innate motivation to form attachments to others, and they have likened the development of parasocial relationships to the process by which people form interpersonal relationships. Studies suggest that initial attraction to media figures motivates further efforts to "get to know" them, leading to increased confidence in predicting and understanding their behaviors, greater intimacy or parasocial attachment, and an increased sense of relationship importance. Parasocial bonds are deeply felt and have many of the characteristics of "real" relationships. Audience members mourn the deaths of celebrities whom they knew only through the media (e.g., Diana, Princess of Wales) and experience real emotional distress when fictional characters die or become unavailable due to the ending of a television series. Many teens, for example, were distraught when the cult series *My So-Called Life* was canceled, due to their parasocial attachment to the lead character.

Only a limited amount of research has examined parasocial interaction among youth. An early study showed that children who felt as though they knew TV characters were more likely to worry about the characters and to feel as though the characters had communicated with them during the show. Children form stronger attachments to same-sex characters, but this pattern seems to change in adolescence, when teens are more inclined to form romantic parasocial attachments. In general, girls tend to develop stronger parasocial attachments than do boys. Parasocial relationships provide a sense of companionship and pseudo-friendship, but there is mixed evidence (nearly all with adults) regarding whether they compensate for a lack of social connections. Parasocial relationships enable young people to participate vicariously in relationships, through imaginary interactions, as preparation for real-life social roles. Some evidence also suggests that parasocial relationships may make young people more willing to rely on media characters and celebrities for personally relevant information and guidance.

—*Cynthia A. Hoffner*

See also Media Celebrities

FURTHER READINGS

Cohen, J. (1999). Favorite characters of teenage viewers of Israeli serials. *Journal of Broadcasting & Electronic Media, 43*, 327–345.

Cohen, J. (2003). Parasocial breakups: Measuring individual differences in response to the dissolution of parasocial relationships. *Mass Communication & Society, 6,* 191–202.

Giles, D. G. (2002). Parasocial interaction: A review of the literature and a model for future research. *Media Psychology, 4,* 279–305.

Hoffner, C. (1996). Children's wishful identification and parasocial interaction with favorite television characters. *Journal of Broadcasting and Electronic Media, 40,* 389–402.

Hoffner, C., & Cantor, J. (1991). Perceiving and responding to mass media characters. In J. Bryant & D. Zillmann (Eds.), *Responding to the screen: Reception and reaction processes* (pp. 63–101). Hillsdale, NJ: Erlbaum.

Horton, D., & Wohl, R. R. (1956). Mass communication and para-social interaction. *Psychiatry, 19,* 215–229.

Murray, S. (1999). Saving our so-called lives: Girls fandom, adolescent subjectivity, and "My So-Called Life." In M. Kinder (Ed.), *Kids' media culture* (pp. 221–235). Durham, NC: Duke University Press.

Noble, G. (1975). *Children in front of the small screen.* Beverly Hills, CA: Sage.

PARENTAL ADVISORY LABELS AND RATING SYSTEMS

By the early 2000s, most electronic media had devised and implemented a content advisory system designed to let adults know about objectionable content. Ratings systems are designed to allow parents to choose media content for their children without prescreening it. Each industry developed a collection of labels denoting differing levels of age-appropriate content. Those labels are usually referred to as a *rating*. In addition to these ratings, many media have developed an additional set of *content descriptors,* symbols that denote specific types of objectionable content (e.g., violent or sexual content, substance use).

Although rating systems help media build goodwill with audiences, media industries have rarely offered ratings spontaneously. Throughout the 20th and early 21st centuries, each medium has heard public outcries about its indecent content. Threats of government regulation or legal action have usually preceded the development of rating systems. The First Amendment's free speech concerns offer protection to content producers, thus preventing government-mandated ratings. Still, most industries have introduced ratings to forestall battles with the U.S. Congress, media advertisers, and political action groups.

At present, each medium uses a different rating system, although the various systems have similarities. The motion picture and television industries use a rating system that distinguishes content suitable for all audiences from content for which parental guidance is suggested and content that is inappropriate for children. The movie rating system often includes brief phrases that describe the type of objectionable content. Television networks include a system of content descriptors that denote the type of objectionable content (e.g., *V* for violence). The recorded music industry uses a single sticker that warns parents about "explicit content," with no age-based ratings. No content descriptors are included on the sticker, so parents must investigate the recording to determine exactly what type of content is potentially objectionable.

Perhaps the most elaborate rating system is used by the video game industry's Entertainment Software Rating Board (ESRB). This is an age-based system, identifying games that are appropriate for all players, young children, children older than 10 years old, teens, mature players, or adults only. These ratings are featured in game advertisements, such as the tag line "rated E for everyone" in a television ad for a video game. The ESRB's content descriptors, however, distinguish this rating system from others. One or more of 32 separate phrases can appear next to a game's rating to identify the type of content included (e.g., "strong sexual content," "blood and gore").

Several systems exist for rating Internet content, most of which are built into the website's computer code. One common system has been implemented by the Internet Content Rating Association (ICRA). These systems include ratings about the level of violent, sexual, or other mature content. These codes are then read by the filter settings that come with most Web browsers (such as Internet Explorer) or filtering software packages (such as Net Nanny or Cyber Patrol). Adults can set these filters to allow varying levels of violent, sexual, or other content to be downloaded. Different settings can be saved for each computer user, so parents can use stricter filters for child Web surfers. Web pages or sites that do not meet these filter settings are then blocked from view.

An important proviso when considering any rating system is to know who rates the content in question. Only the film industry has an independent rating board that screens all content released and distributed by companies that belong to the Motion Picture Association of America (MMPA). MPAA rating boards review thousands of movies; by comparison, thousands of *hours* of content must be reviewed for television, recorded music, and Internet media. As a result, ratings for the latter industries are assigned by content producers (e.g., the studio that made the television show or the record company) using industry-established guidelines. In addition, many private foundations and advocacy groups have taken it upon themselves to create and market rating systems that reflect their particular concerns (e.g., a religious group's ratings of how much a particular program upholds its religious and moral beliefs). These alternative rating systems are sometimes distributed for free or are offered as subscription-based information services on the Internet.

To date, criticisms of parental advisory labels and rating systems have been grouped into three principal groups. First are those that call for each industry to make ratings more prominent in advertisements for media content. One such report, issued by the Federal Trade Commission, was critical of the small type size or low volume for announcements of ratings for advertised movies, video games, and recorded music. Second, many organizations such as the Kaiser Family Foundation have called on content producers to develop and implement a universal rating system that could be applied to all media (thus eliminating any potential confusion between the various symbol systems currently used). These calls include pleas for a universal set of informative content descriptors. Third, some organizations such as the National Institute for Media and the Family have questioned the accuracy of media rating systems. The National Institute established its own parent panels to rate movies and television shows and found that in many cases, its panel's rating differed widely from the one assigned by the media outlet or industry rating panel.

—*Ron Warren*

See also Movies, Rating Systems and; Rating Systems, Parental Use of; Regulation (various entries)

FURTHER READINGS

Federal Trade Commission. (2004, July). *Marketing violent entertainment to children*. Retrieved from http://www.ftc.gov/bcp/conline/edcams/ratings/reports.htm

Federman, J. (2002). *Rating sex and violence in the media: Media ratings and proposals for reform*. Menlo Park, CA: Kaiser Family Foundation.

Kaiser Family Foundation. (2004). *Parents, media, and public policy: A Kaiser Family Foundation survey*. Menlo Park, CA: Author.

Walsh, D. A., & Gentile, D. A. (2001). A validity test of movie, television, and video-game ratings. *Pediatrics, 107*, 1302–1308.

PARENTAL REGULATION OF CHILDREN'S MEDIA

Over the years, parents have been held increasingly responsible for helping their children to become critical media consumers. Parents most commonly do this by regulating their children's media use. For example, they may set rules for media use or actively mediate it.

SETTING RULES FOR MEDIA USE

Formulating rules is an example of a direct way in which parents can regulate children's media use. For example, when it comes to television viewing, four approaches to family rules can be distinguished:

Rules with regard to media use and other activities. A number of activities (such as doing homework or having dinner) are considered to be more important than television viewing. This means that parents will try to separate these activities from television viewing.

Rules concerning the amount and scheduling of media use. Parents may limit the amount of time that children can watch television. Furthermore, they may have rules about *when* their children are allowed to watch television (e.g., only on Sundays). Similar rules can be imposed with regard to Internet use. When the family is connected to the Internet via a telephone modem, parents can calculate the cost for the time the family is connected to the Internet.

Rules about program content. Parents may have regulations (implicit as well as explicit) about which program content children are allowed to watch. For example, they may prohibit children from watching violent or sexual content. Again, similar rules may also be observed in the regulations parents make about Internet use. In that case, parents may try to prevent their children from viewing explicit content by using software such as content filters.

No rules. In some families, parents do not have any regulations about television viewing. This situation often indicates that television viewing rules are so well internalized that children and parents no longer regard them as rules.

MEDIATION OF MEDIA USE

Actively mediating media use involves parents talking about media content, for example, telling their children to what extent television content is a reflection of real life. Children's media use can also be indirectly regulated by parental media use, a process that is called modeling. This implies that parental media use serves as a model for children's media use. Children will then imitate parental behavior. For example, when children watch the same television programs as their parents, it is called positive modeling. Today, it is more common to talk about reverse modeling whereby children's media use influences parental media use.

RESEARCH ON PARENTAL REGULATION OF MEDIA

In recent research, the concept of parental regulation of media use has shifted to focus on the concept of parental guidance. The starting point for this approach was an investigation of how parents cope with the television use of their children—whether parents try to cope with it by implementing certain restrictions, or whether they guide their children's television use by openly talking about it. Bybee, Robinson, and Turow (1982) distinguished three ways to guide children's television viewing: restrictive guidance, evaluative guidance, and unfocused guidance. *Restrictive guidance* implies that parents control the amount of time that children watch television as well as the type of programs that they watch (e.g., "My mother forbids me to watch certain TV programs"). *Evaluative guidance* refers to parents explaining certain aspects of the content to their children (e.g., "My mother tells me when someone in a TV show is doing something bad or something good"). *Unfocused guidance* implies that parents watch television together with their children and talk about the content with their children.

Currently, however, families are confronted with radical changes in the structure of the media environment (such as digitalization, Internet, and multimedia technology), changes that pose new challenges to family life. Researchers wondered whether parental guidance would change in this multimedia environment, so they expanded the research about parental guidance from television viewing to other media use (e.g., parental guidance of computer use). From this broader perspective, restrictive guidance implies controlling the use of television, computers, books, and comics. Evaluative guidance implies explaining the content and meaning of television programs, computer games, books, and comics. Unfocused guidance means that parents watch television together with their children, play a computer game together with their children, and read books and comics together with their children.

Interesting findings from this type of research are that evaluative and unfocused guidance are aimed at commitment and a good communicative link between parents and children. As such, the impact such guidance has on family life will surpass its impact on media use. Evaluative and unfocused guidance can help in creating a positive and caring family environment. Furthermore, silent coviewing, normally perceived as negative, can be seen as positive, especially for young children, who get a sense of security from such coviewing. In addition, researchers found that the outcome of the different forms of guidance depends on the subsystem (father-son, father-daughter, mother-son, or mother-daughter) using it. Mothers' attempts to restrict the reading of books decreases the level of conflict between boys and their mother, while it increases the level of conflict between girls and their mother. Furthermore, when a mother restricts television viewing, it leads to an increase in conflict between brothers and sisters. When a father is doing the same thing, it leads to a decrease in conflict between brothers and sisters. In conclusion, it can be said that the way parents guide their children's media use may predict the level of conflict in the family.

—*Veerle Van Rompaey*

See also Displacement Effect; Family Communication Patterns Model; Internet Use, Social; Kaiser Family Foundation; Media Education, Family Involvement in; Media Effects, History of Research on; Parenting Styles; Peer Groups (various entries)

FURTHER READINGS

Bybee, C., Robinson, D., & Turow, J. (1982). Determinants of parental guidance of children's television viewing for a special subgroup: Mass media scholars. *Journal of Broadcasting, 26*, 697–710.

Valkenburg, P. M., Krcmar, M., Peeters, A. L., & Marseille, N. M. (1999). Developing a scale to assess three styles of television mediation: "instructive mediation," "restrictive mediation," and "social coviewing." *Journal of Broadcasting and Electronic Media, 43,* 52–66.

Van den Bergh, B., & Van den Bulck, J. (1999). Media use, perceived parental media guidance, and supportive parent-child communication in fifth and sixth graders' communications. *The European Journal of Communication Research, 24*(3), 329–350.

Van den Bulck, J., & Van den Bergh, B. (2000). The influence of perceived parental guidance patterns on children's media use: Gender differences and media displacement. *Journal of Broadcasting and Electronic Media, 44*(Summer).

PARENTING STYLES

Popular opinion holds that media's effect on children is a matter of the quality of parenting. This mind-set blends two distinct concepts in the research on parenting. The first is *parenting practices*, which refers to specific situational behaviors designed to achieve child-rearing goals (e.g., punishing bad behavior or rewarding good behavior). *Parenting styles*, on the other hand, represent a more stable set of attitudes and beliefs that form the context of parenting practices. For example, a parent's belief in nonviolent conflict resolution might mean rewarding a child for verbally expressing anger (rather than using fists).

Hence, parenting style is a critical but indirect influence on child development. The concept rests on two dimensions: how responsive parents are to children's needs and desires and how demanding parents are of children's obedience. Diana Baumrind developed a typology of parenting styles. The first type is called *authoritative parenting* and emphasizes responsiveness and demandingness. This style involves high levels of nurturance, parent-child involvement, sensitivity, reasoning, control, and encouragement of the child's independence. Authoritative parenting practices include low to moderate levels of discipline, high levels of nurturing, and high expectations of children's behaviors. *Authoritarian parents* emphasize obedience and are characterized by high levels of discipline, restrictiveness, rejection, and power assertion. These parents show low levels of nurturing behaviors toward children but moderate to high expectations for children's behaviors. *Permissive parents,* the third type, are defined in opposition to authoritarian parents. Permissive parents demonstrate a great deal of warmth and acceptance toward children but low levels of parent-child involvement and discipline. A fourth category, *neglectful parents,* was added in the 1980s. These parents stress neither responsiveness nor demandingness and exhibit low levels of all parenting practices. The style is characterized by high indifference to children's needs and behaviors.

Most research on parenting has tried to link these four styles to child development outcomes. Authoritative parents were most likely to have preschool children who show self-motivation, have prosocial peer interactions, persist with tasks longer, initiate new activities more frequently, and achieve more in school. Children of authoritarian parents, on the other hand, were more inhibited in their preschool participation, felt a stronger sense of external control, and were more aggressive and disruptive in their peer-play activities. Children of permissive parents were less self-reliant and less motivated to achieve than other children.

There are no studies linking parenting styles to children's media use. However, a similar concept—*family communication patterns*—refers to the general tone of parent-child communication. Similar to studies of parenting style, this research identified two principal dimensions. The first, a communication orientation, refers to parental communication that emphasizes a mutual understanding of thoughts, feelings, and opinions. The second, a conformity orientation, stresses parental authority and a need to agree with each other than to express disagreeable thoughts. Parents who stress both a communication and conformity orientation roughly mirror those with an authoritative parenting style. Those who stress a conformity orientation roughly mirror authoritarian parents. Parents who stress neither a conformity nor communication orientation roughly mirror permissive parents. No family communication pattern has been defined that seems related to neglectful parenting styles.

Several studies have identified correlations between family communication patterns, media use, and media effects. Communication-oriented parents are more likely to critically discuss television content with their children. They are more likely to make both positive and negative statements about TV without dictating children's thoughts and reactions to content. These parents are also more likely to ask children questions about content, and their children are more likely to ask questions in return. Thus, these children are more likely to regard parent-child interaction about television as a discussion in which their thoughts are seriously considered. The result is that parents take an active role in shaping children's interpretation of media content. This is largely seen as beneficial as children develop their own interpretive strategies for media content.

Control-oriented children are more likely to watch their parents' preferred television shows (regardless of other factors). This illustrates the tendency for children of control-oriented parents to imitate the behaviors they see in authority figures. Some evidence exists that control-oriented children are more likely to view violent television. Mothers in these families use more commands, comments that direct children how to interpret content, and advice about television. This suggests a pattern of direct transfer between control-oriented parents and their children. Children who mirror their parents are more likely to meet the demandingness of a control-oriented family communication pattern and an authoritarian parenting style. Some research has indicated that this leads to more positive reinforcement and less critical reflection about media content.

These contrasts have implications for children's interpretation of violent content. Communication-oriented children were more likely to judge violence based on the violent character's motivation (e.g., a character punching someone who had just hit him first). Control-oriented children based their judgment on whether the act was punished or not (e.g., whether the violent character was taken to jail by police officers). When control-oriented children saw violence that was not punished, they were more likely to choose aggressive endings for stories presented after viewing violence. Furthermore, the discussion strategies used in communication-oriented homes were found to encourage perspective taking during violent programs (e.g., considering the violence from the victim's point of view). Perspective taking has been linked to more developed moral reasoning skills (e.g., empathy for victims of violence) in young children.

—*Ron Warren*

See also Adult Mediation Strategies; Family Communication Patterns Model; Media Effects, Family Interactions and; Parental Regulation of Children's Media

FURTHER READINGS

Baumrind, D. (1991). Parenting style and adolescent development. In J. Brooks-Gunn, R. Lerner, & A. C. Peterson (Eds.), *The encyclopedia on adolescence* (pp. 746–758). New York: Garland Press.

Brenner, V., & Fox, R. A. (1999). An empirically derived classification of parenting practices. *Journal of Genetic Psychology, 160,* 343–356.

Dumlao, R. (2003). Tapping into critical thinking: Viewer interpretations of a television conflict. *Studies in Media & Information Literacy Education, 3*(1).

Krcmar, M., & Vieira, E. T., Jr. (2005). Imitating life, imitating television: The effects of family and television models on children's moral reasoning. *Communication Research, 32,* 267–295.

PARENTS MUSIC RESOURCE CENTER (PMRC)

The Parents Music Resource Center (PMRC) was founded in May 1985 to raise awareness among parents about the profane, violent, and sexually explicit lyrics of some popular music that reached a mass audience of children and adolescents in the United States. Although a voluntary record labeling system was implemented in the 1980s by the record industry in response to PMRC pressure, the center failed to produce self-restraint within the record industry in the long term. During the 1990s, violent and erotic imagery resurfaced in heavy metal and particularly gangsta rap music videos and texts.

The founders of the PMRC included Susan Baker (wife of then-Secretary of the Treasury James A. Baker, III), Tipper Gore (wife of then-Senator and later Vice President Al Gore, Jr.), Pam Hower, and Sally Nevius, along with other influential Washington women. Leaders presented themselves as mothers worried about the moral development of children in a popular cultural environment that was awash with violent and obscene references. The PMRC assumed that pop music's lyrics and symbols were among the factors contributing to a rise in social problems, such as the increased prevalence of rape, suicide, and pregnancies among adolescents. The center insisted that parents needed to be warned about the music their children bought in huge quantities and listened to for hours on end.

Although popular music had always contained more or less vivid descriptions of romance and love, the PMRC was convinced that pop themes had become more profane and vulgar during the 1970s and early 1980s. The initiators acted on a common-sense notion that seeing and hearing explicit images or texts contributed to premarital sex, violence, alcohol and drug use, suicide, and satanism. Specifically, the genres of heavy metal and hip hop were singled out as proponents of lewd and vicious behavior and anti-Christian themes. The PMRC argued that children should be prevented from listening to what it called "porn rock" released by highly popular performers, for example, Prince's "Darling Nikki" from the *Purple Rain* album. Another concern was explicit imagery presented in such music videos as Van Halen's "Hot for Teacher," which depicts a female teacher doing a striptease for the boys in her class, and Motley Crue's "Looks That Kill," featuring scantly clad women captured and imprisoned in cages by men in leather garments.

With its close connections to the American political establishment, the PMRC was able to promote highly publicized Senate hearings starting on September 19, 1985. The PMRC urged the U.S. record industry to restrain use of explicit content and warn consumers with labels or printed lyrics visible on the outside packages of music products. Beach Boy Mike Love backed the PMRC, but Dee Snyder (Twisted Sister), Jello Biafra (Dead Kennedys), John Denver, and Frank Zappa, testifying on behalf of the musicians' community, criticized the proposal. They framed it as an infringement of the First Amendment of the U.S. constitution, securing the right of free speech, and feared that a system of labeling music would lead to censorship. Zappa went so far as to characterize it as "an ill-conceived piece of nonsense" that promised "to keep the courts busy for years dealing with the interpretational and enforcement problems inherent in the proposal's design."

No legislation was proposed, but on November 1, 1985, after negotiations with the PMRC, the Record Industry Association of America (RIAA) announced that members would voluntarily promote a labeling system for albums with explicit content, declaring "Parental Advisory: Explicit Lyrics." Initially, the PMRC seemed successful in curbing music found threatening to young people's development; some chains, notably Wal-Mart, declined to stock albums with the "Tipper sticker." With their sales in danger, record companies were cautious and began to avoid labeling, leading to disappointment and critique from

the PRMC. Some buyers may have been more reluctant to purchase labeled albums, but to fans of the PMRC's discredited artists, the stickers singled out exciting, forbidden music. Thus, the labels may have had an effect the PRMC never intended.

In the 1990s, the leverage of the center declined, and in 1993, its most prominent member, Tipper Gore, stepped back from her responsibilities as vice president. The parental advisory warning, standardized in 1990 and no longer a sticker but part of the album print itself, is still featured on album covers of music that the RIAA and its members consider "not for all ages."

—*Tom ter Bogt and Stephen Soitos*

See also Regulation, Music

FURTHER READINGS

Christenson, P. (1992). The effects of parental advisory labels on adolescent music preferences. *Journal of Communication, 42*(1), 106–113.

Craig, A., Anderson, C. A., & Carnagey, N. L. (2003). Exposure to violent media: The effects of songs with violent lyrics on aggressive thoughts and feelings. *Journal of Personality and Social Psychology, 84*(5), 960–971.

Gore, T. (1987). *Raising PG kids in an X-rated society.* Nashville, TN: Abingdon Press.

Nuzum, E. (2001). *Parental advisory: Music censorship in America.* New York: HarperCollins.

PEER GROUPS, FILE SHARING AMONG

Peer-to-peer (P2P) file-sharing networks are networks of computers that allow users to directly search for and download files (such as audio and video files) from other computers in the network. The popular but now defunct Napster was not a true P2P network because individual computers in the network searched a centralized server for music files and then downloaded those files from the computers that hosted them. Subsequent P2Psoftware, such as *Kazaa* and *LimeWire,* allows users to connect to one another directly, and there is no central entity routing transactions between computers.

When Napster was declared illegal in 2001, P2P file-sharing networks were developed because it was initially hoped that, lacking a central server, they would be too amorphous to prosecute. P2P file sharing can be used to download software, music, music videos, and movies, and it is very popular among teenagers and college students. Concerns related to the use of P2P networks by youth include illegal downloading of copyrighted material, inadvertent exposure to pornography, and exposure to banner ads, adware, and other malicious programs.

ACCESSING COPYRIGHTED DIGITAL ENTERTAINMENT

Because P2P networks allow users to exchange copyrighted material without paying for it, they have run afoul of the law. The Supreme Court ruled in June 2005 that operators of P2P networks are legally responsible for the copyright infringement on their networks. Most university campuses have banned P2P file sharing of copyrighted works. Although there is no systematic research on this topic, media and anecdotal reports suggest that children and adolescents continue to illegally download copyrighted material, especially music, on P2P networks such as *Kazaa* and *LimeWire*. One reason for youths' continued downloading of copyrighted material may be their lack of understanding of copyright law and the illegal nature of this activity. Even among those who know that downloading is illegal, many may be guided by the quintessentially adolescent view that "it can't happen to me" and continue to download, thinking that they will not be caught.

INADVERTENT EXPOSURE TO PORNOGRAPHY

Perhaps the biggest concern with regard to children and adolescents is their inadvertent access to pornography when searching for files on P2P networks. A report of the U.S. General Accounting Office (GAO) revealed that child and adult pornography could easily be found and downloaded from P2P networks. Of concern is their finding that such pornography is frequently retrieved when users search with innocuous keywords, such as cartoon characters or names of celebrities—keywords that are likely to be used by young children. Research indicates that pornography and related sexual media can influence sexual attitudes, moral values, and sexual activity of children and youth and can contribute to sexual violence. It is significant that the evidence indicates pornography

has an adverse effect on older adolescent boys and young men already at high risk for aggressive behavior. Research suggests that exposure to influential sexual media up through the college years is overwhelmingly negative, although only a small proportion of participants recalled a physical response (e.g., sexual arousal) to such exposure. Females experience more negative memories (e.g., crying and sadness) than males, who more often reported arousal or interest. Extrapolating from these findings, we can infer that young people's memories of influential sexual media may result from inadvertent exposure on P2P networks and may be overwhelmingly negative, especially for girls, with some enduring effects and a relatively low rate of sexual response.

EXPOSURE TO BANNER ADVERTISEMENTS AND ADWARE

Finally, P2P networks contain banner ads that are often sexual in nature and that promote personal ads or products such as condoms. Furthermore, because the software used to access these networks can be downloaded for free, it is often bundled with adware, which can both slow down (e.g., through pop-ups) and threaten the security of the computer. Young users are not aware of this, and research suggests that children, in particular, may have to be taught to become critical consumers of online advertisements.

—*Kaveri Subrahmanyam and Patricia Greenfield*

See also Advertising, Deceptive Practices in; Computer-Mediated Communication (CMC); Federal Trade Commission; Internet Pornography, Effects of; Music Genres, History of; Regulation, Music

FURTHER READINGS

Borland, J. (2005, June 27). *Supreme Court rules against file swapping.* Retrieved March 20, 2006, from http://news.com.com/Supreme+Court+rules+against+file+swapping/2100-1030_3-5764135.html

General Accounting Office. (2003). *File sharing programs: Peer-to-peer networks provide ready access to pornography.* Retrieved October 9, 2005, from http://www.gao.gov/new.items/d03351.pdf

Greenfield, P. M. (2004). Inadvertent exposure to pornography on the Internet: Implications of peer-to-peer file sharing networks for child development and families. *Journal of Applied Developmental Psychology, 25,* 741–750.

PEER GROUPS, IMPACT OF MEDIA ON

How do the media contribute to young people's relations with their peers? This entry addresses this simple but important question, focusing on a general psychological process that can be observed across different media. Although much previous research and political debate have focused on the media's supposed negative influence on young people, recent research has started to document some of the more positive developmental outcomes of media involvement. This entry describes ways in which adolescents actively use the media to negotiate an important developmental process, namely the establishment of a positive social identity within a network of friends.

Several studies indicate that adolescence is a period when group behavior is very apparent, and friendship groups have long been seen as valuable networks through which processes of identity and self-esteem can be negotiated. Interest in the media has been identified as an important starting point for the formation of friendship groups. Indeed, research has suggested that having common interests in activities such as watching television and listening to music are regarded by adolescents as "defining" qualities of friendship. In a recent survey of British adolescents' reasons for listening to music, conducted by the University of Leicester Music Research Group, many adolescents reported listening to music to convey a particular impression of themselves to potential friends.

Recently, research has begun to draw explicitly on theories of group behavior to examine the developmental benefits of group membership during adolescence. One prominent approach in this respect is Tajfel and Turner's social identity theory. The theory starts from the assumption that everyone belongs to social groups, whether these be large-scale social categories such as gender or race to which individuals are ascribed automatically, or smaller-scale groupings such as friendship groups, membership of which is usually earned. Central to the theory is the idea that individuals seek to evaluate their social group memberships positively; that is, they strive for positive *social identity*. A wealth of research has demonstrated that the need for positive social identity underpins a broad range of group-based phenomena, not least intergroup discrimination.

Several studies have demonstrated that friendship groups are an important basis for the development of social identity during adolescence and that this process itself can have positive consequences for development in other domains. For example, Tarrant and his colleagues recently demonstrated that adolescents who feel a strong sense of attachment to or identification with a friendship group report less difficulty in negotiating various developmental tasks, such as accepting bodily changes and establishing close interpersonal relationships. Such adolescents also tend to report higher levels of self-esteem than those less strongly identified with a friendship group.

In determining the impact of the media on peer group relationships, research on social identity has generally adopted one of two approaches. First, some researchers have investigated the processes by which adolescents' engagement with media is managed so as to distinguish, or *differentiate*, between different friendship groups. Second, and more recently, researchers have investigated whether engagement with media might be used productively to *promote better relations* between different groups; in other words, studies in this area have considered whether media might be used to bring different social groups together. Below is a brief overview of these two lines of research.

MEDIA AND INTERGROUP DIFFERENTIATION

In one study, Tarrant and colleagues presented British adolescents with a set of 26 interests and activities, which included several media-based items (e.g., computer games, music, television, film). The participants were asked to do two things with this set: First, they rated each interest and activity in terms of how socially valued it was by other individuals their age; and second, they estimated the degree to which their own friendship group (the in-group) and another group (the out-group) was associated with each. The results showed that participants' group estimates were consistently biased in favor of their own group; thus, media and other activities that were positively valued were associated to a greater degree with the in-group than with the out-group. The opposite tendency was observed for negatively valued media; these were associated to a greater degree with the out-group. Of particular interest in this study was the finding that this bias was positively correlated with social identification. That is, those participants who perceived the greatest difference between the two groups' orientation to the various interests and activities subsequently reported a stronger sense of attachment to their own group of friends.

These findings were interpreted by the researchers in terms of Kelley's seminal work on person perception. Kelley had previously demonstrated how individuals rely on trait information in forming judgments of others and demonstrated that personality traits can act as central descriptors by offering defining information about the likely characteristics of a person. Consistent with that research, it was argued that certain interests are valued more positively than others because they similarly convey central trait-like information. Thus, the affiliation of their own friendship group with positively valued media can be seen as one way in which the adolescents could convey a positive impression of that group, while at the same time distinguishing that group from other groups.

MEDIA AND INTERGROUP HARMONY

Although the second line of research has so far capitalized only on adolescents' strong interest in musical media, it seems likely that the underlying psychological processes will also be reflected in other media forms with which adolescents are engaged. A study by Bakagiannis and Tarrant presented a sample of British adolescents with differing information about their own group's and another group's musical interests. In one of the study's conditions, participants were informed that members of the two groups had highly similar interests. Compared to a control group whose members were told nothing about each group's musical interests, those participants who believed the two groups had similar interests displayed lower levels of intergroup discrimination when asked to describe their attitudes toward the two groups. In other words, the study showed that encouraging adolescents to believe their own social group and another group had a common media interest led to the formation of more favorable attitudes toward that group.

In addition to the obvious theoretical relevance of research on how different forms of media can promote positive relationships between social groups, such work has a clear practical application by contributing to broader social and political discussions concerning how intergroup harmony can be fostered in an increasingly multicultural society. The continued adoption of the social identity perspective in such initiatives will likely make an important contribution to our understanding of the underlying psychological processes.

—*Mark Tarrant*

See also Adolescents, Developmental Needs of, and Media; Peer Groups, Influences on Media Use of

FURTHER READINGS

Bakagiannis, S., & Tarrant, M. (2006). Can music bring people together? Effects of shared musical preference on intergroup bias in adolescence. *Scandinavian Journal of Psychology, 47,* 129–136.

Coleman, J. C. (1974). *Relationships in adolescence.* London: Routledge & Kegan Paul.

Kelley, H. H. (1950). The warm-cold variable in first impressions of persons. *Journal of Personality, 18,* 431–439.

Tajfel, H., & Turner, J. C. (1979). An integrative theory of intergroup conflict. In W. G. Austin & S. Worschel (Eds.), *The social psychology of intergroup relations* (pp. 33–47). Belmont, CA: Brooks/Cole.

Tarrant, M., MacKenzie, L., & Hewitt, L. A. (in press). Friendship group identification, multidimensional self-concept, and experience of developmental tasks in adolescence. *Journal of Adolescence.*

Tarrant, M., North, A. C., Edridge, M. D., Kirk, L. E., Smith, E. A., & Turner, R. E. (2001). Social identity in adolescence. *Journal of Adolescence, 24,* 597–609.

PEER GROUPS, INFLUENCES ON MEDIA USE OF

Adolescents spend a significant portion of their time using media, commonly for purposes of entertainment, identity formation, experiencing high sensation, coping, and youth culture identification. Information about how peers influence such media use comes from self-reports gathered from surveys and questionnaires or from studies using qualitative methods. Experimental studies are not represented in the literature. Thus, based on data in most studies, it is unclear whether peers influence media preferences, media preferences dictate the choice of peers, or the effect is reciprocal. Longitudinal studies are more helpful in addressing this question, but relatively few have been conducted. Nevertheless, the literature can help us understand the relationship between peers and media choices by examining media use over the developmental course and by identifying the social context of media use.

MEDIA USE OVER THE DEVELOPMENTAL COURSE

In about the seventh or eighth grade, when children enter their teens, their media habits change markedly. Television use drops substantially and is replaced with music listening, almost exclusively to popular music as opposed to classical. This trend continues until late adolescence, when music use equals TV exposure. At the same time, children undergo a transition in which the peer group grows in importance as a source of socialization, and the family diminishes. Several studies have documented that adolescents with stronger peer orientations tend to listen to more music, whereas more family-oriented adolescents watch more television. During summer holidays, when adolescents have fewer opportunities to interact with peers, television preferences tend to regress to content favored during childhood. Indeed, TV viewing is correlated with time spent with family; however, music listening is associated with time spent with peers and friends.

As children develop, the role of peers changes in media use decisions, as demonstrated in studies of motives for video game playing. For children in the eighth grade (13 to 14 years old) and, to a lesser extent, for college students, the opportunity to interact with friends predicts use of video games. However, social interaction does not predict video game use among children in fifth grade (10 to 11 years old). For fifth graders, competition and the desire to be strong are significant predictors of video game use.

THE SOCIAL CONTEXT OF MEDIA USE

Opportunities for peer interaction, or the lack thereof, are associated with preferences for different media among adolescents. In one study, television use was higher for high school seniors (about 18 to 20 years old) who reported never going on dates or who reported rarely or never going out in the evening for fun compared to those who had more frequent social contact with peers. Another study found that loneliness and shyness predicted frequency of television use among adolescent boys (10 to 17 years old). The same researchers observed that the number of friends predicted time spent watching TV alone. Contact with same-sex peers is especially important, and youth who lack such interaction may use media to alleviate feelings of loneliness and isolation.

The nature of the peer group itself also influences media choices. Several longitudinal studies by Keith Roe have documented media preferences of different peer groups among European samples. In one study, he found that low school achievement at age 13 was related to stronger orientation toward peers. This orientation toward peers was related to preferences for rock and punk music 2 years later. However, as academic achievement increased, so did preference for classical music. These relationships emerged even after controlling for socioeconomic status. Similar findings surfaced in Roe's study of VCR use. Based on these results, Roe argued that educational institutions function to polarize students, leading to the formation of pro- or anti-school attitudes. These attitudes spawn different subcultures, which are the basis for many media preferences. Other longitudinal research by Roe found that a preference for socially disvalued media was related to membership in subcultures that were experiencing downward social mobility. Indeed, adolescents who prefer heavy metal music tend to have doubts about their abilities to succeed academically and to have problems with family, whereas teens who prefer light music tend to be overly responsible, rule conscious, and conforming. However, at least one study found that a preference for heavy metal music was not associated with delinquency among peers.

Different peer groups are associated with the use of different media content. For example, one 1973 study found that adolescents 16 to 18 years old were more likely to see sexually explicit material in the presence of mixed company or same-sex peers than when they were alone with members of the opposite sex. For males and females, the more popular they were (i.e., the more close friends they had) and the more frequently they dated, the more likely they were to have seen sexually explicit material. Other studies have reported that VCR use often occurs among same-sex peers and often involves viewing socially devalued media. For example, Swedish adolescents' (15 to 16 years old) use of the VCR occurred overwhelmingly in the presence of a small group of friends and for underachieving, anti-school Swedish youth, VCR use was likely to include content such as pornography, violence, and horror. Other research has noted that movie viewing among adolescents is most likely to occur in the presence of friends or siblings rather than parents.

Social settings also impact the enjoyment of different media. In studies of music listening, researchers have generally found that adolescents experience the greatest positive emotion when listening in the presence of friends and less positive feelings when listening alone or with parents.

Identity formation is an important part of adolescent media use, and teens may watch media content that they do not necessarily enjoy in order to gain acceptance. For instance, Roe reports that in mixed company, female adolescents often acquiesced to male preferences for violence or action when renting videos, although males were less likely to comply with female preferences for sad or romantic films. Among male peers, violent or sexually explicit material was used as a test of male toughness, even though participants in the study reported dislike of such content. Furthermore, behavior of peers may impact the enjoyment of some content. In one study, experimenters coached confederates to either conform or act counter to gender stereotypical behavior during a horror film. Males reported greater enjoyment of the film when a female companion acted squeamish uring scenes of horror, but less when she was unresponsive to the violent content. Similarly, females reported less fear of the film when a male companion displayed toughness rather than weakness.

—John Davies

See also Adolescents, Developmental Needs of, and Media; Music, Group Identity and; Music Listening, Uses of; Peer Groups, Impact of Media on; Television, Motivations for Viewing of; Uses and Gratifications Theory

FURTHER READINGS

Krosnick, J. A., Anand, S. N., & Hartl, S. P. (2003). Psychosocial predictors of heavy television viewing among preadolescents and adolescents. *Basic and Applied Social Psychology, 25,* 87–110.

Larson, R., & Kubey, R. (1983). Television and music: Contrasting media in adolescent life. *Youth & Society, 15,* 13–31.

Larson, R., Kubey, R., & Colletti, J. (1989). Changing channels: Early adolescent media choices and shifting investments in family and friends. *Journal of Youth and Adolescence, 18,* 583–599.

Roe, K., (1995). Adolescents' use of socially disvalued media: Toward a theory of media delinquency. *Journal of Youth and Adolescence, 24,* 617–631.

PEER GROUPS, JOINT USE OF MEDIA IN

Children and adolescents prefer using media together with friends and their peer group. Habits of media use within a peer group differ depending on the media type (e.g., print versus electronic media) and are also related to age and gender. Media use also varies from one country to another. Some forms of media are more compatible with social activity than others, and some media types can serve as status symbols.

PEER GROUPS

Peer groups are characterized by common leisure interests, ethical values, and preferences concerning important in-group matters such as lifestyle and music. They often consist of young friends of both genders, and in most cases, they develop in school contexts. Peers are especially important for adolescents.

Being part of a peer group represents an important developmental step, so most adolescents belong to one. Within them, social skills are fostered because corporate guidelines have to be negotiated, cooperation and mutuality are practiced, and opinions and attitudes are constructed.

The self-classification to a group of people initiates a process of social comparison, where differences between members of the group members are emphasized, sharpening the individual's perception of his or her own attributes. Allocation to peer groups takes place in a socially, developmentally, and educationally selective way. Thus, the members of a peer group play an important and active role within a child or adolescent's development.

Although peer groups do not actually change their members' habits, the organization of leisure time is markedly affected. In this way, peer group members mutually influence preferences for using media types and subtypes. Social influence concerning attitudes toward special media types is itself an important feature of a peer group. The resultant valuations can be an auxiliary means to distinguish from out-group members or from parents. However, the influence of peer group members cannot totally eliminate media use patterns previously acquired in one's family of origin.

PRINT MEDIA

Unlike the use of most electronic media, reading books or journals is not normally a shared peer group activity. Even within a circle of good friends, reading together is uncommon. Peer groups play the role of rather informal agencies that indirectly foster literacy development. There is a significant relationship between the reading activities of the members of a peer group. The strength of this relationship increases with age and reaches its peak in adolescence. Reading-related communication within peer groups is also strongly associated with spending more time reading. Adolescents are highly influenced by their peers' choice of literature—the right choice of text can be a way of joining a peer group. Voluntary reading quantity is frequently affected by peers, so peer group interaction has an indirect influence on reading fluency and text comprehension. Text comprehension can be also enhanced by reading-related communication with the members of a group.

Children and adolescents who are affiliated with aggressive and school-dissociated peer groups show lower reading achievement. Students who self-select a school-dissociated peer group often experience reading habits as a differentiating feature between their own in- and the other's out-group. In this way, peer groups partially determine the development of the individual's reading-related self-concept.

Heavy readers tend to make friends in a peer group of heavy readers. Furthermore, having close friendships or partnerships with people who usually read a lot is a strong motivation to increase reading and to talk about literature.

ELECTRONIC MEDIA

Children and adolescents like playing electronic games, some of which are programmed to allow contests with others. These electronic games are used more often as a joint activity than TV watching, and a greater percentage of boys than girls say that they usually play such games with their friends. Boys who play electronic games frequently show a tendency toward a behavior type that can be described as ambitious skill-improving.

A completely different peer-group activity is the online relationship. This notable phenomenon is related to some user characteristics that should be mentioned here: As predictors of *close* online relationships, adolescent difficulties show just as much predictive power as alienation from parents. However, users of chat rooms and multi-user dungeons often make friendships that are in many ways similar to face-to-face relationships.

Although the Internet can be used to foster one's connection with the social world, high Internet use is associated with high emotional loneliness. One reason for this may be that high Internet use can take the place of face-to-face relationships. Girls in particular prefer communicative computer use such as email or chat rooms.

TV is a domestic medium, but peer coviewing and discussion of things such as anti-social television occurs more often than parental coviewing. The most popular programs are often watched in the company of friends. Especially 13-to-14-year-old children prefer watching TV together with friends because adolescents often watch television as a means of connecting to a peer group. Talking about TV-related questions is a popular leisure activity, and the percentage of children and adolescents who talk about television increases with age. Watching and discussing content frequently can lead to generally positive attitudes toward the mediated content.

Watching a video is mainly practiced in a peer group context, too. However, talking about videos occurs less than talking about TV programs; probably because peers have simultaneously talked while watching it.

—*Armin Castello*

See also Adolescents, Developmental Needs of, and Media

FURTHER READINGS

Harris, J. R. (2002). Beyond the nurture assumption: Testing hypotheses about the child's environment. In J. G. Borkowski, S. Landesman Ramey, & M. Brostol-Power (Eds.), *Parenting and the child's world: Influences on academic, intellectual, and social-emotional development* (pp. 3–20). Mahwah, NJ: Erlbaum.

Krosnick, J. A., Anand, S. N., & Hartl, S. P. (2003). Psychosocial predictors of heavy television viewing among preadolescents and adolescents. *Basic & Applied Social Psychology, 25*(2), 87–110.

Nathanson, A. I. (2001). Parents versus peers: Exploring the significance of peer mediation of antisocial television. *Communication Research, 28*(3), 251–274.

Rosebrock, C. (2004). Informelle Sozialisationsinstanz peer group. In N. Groeben & B. Hurrelmann (Eds.), *Lesesozialisation in der Mediengesellschaft. Ein Forschungsüberblick* (pp. 169–201). Munich: Juventa.

Singer, D. G., & Singer, J. L. (Eds.). (2001). *Handbook of children and the media.* Thousand Oaks, CA: Sage.

PERSONAL WEB PAGES

A recent Pew Internet & American Life Project study suggests that a substantial percentage of American youth create, or have created, online content. For example, the study found that almost two thirds of online youths between the ages of 12 and 17 have exhibited a semblance of technological savvy by creating such content as personal web pages that feature graphics, multimedia, and narratives (see Lenhart & Madden, 2005, for specific details). This is hardly surprising, considering that the Internet and the Web have permeated modern society, and concomitant technological advancements offer users several means through which they can easily create and disseminate information in the online world.

In addition to ease of creation, one major factor underlying the ubiquity of personal websites is the social currency that they deliver to the creator of such content. Personal web pages represent individualistic expression and render possible the accentuation of the self in easily distributable modes. Two points are especially noteworthy: the necessity of self-expression and the ability to express unique attributes of the self to a broad audience without encumbrance. As cultural psychologists have long argued, individuals have always had the innate desire to express their individualism in many ways. For instance, an inspection of a teenager's bedroom offers insights into the person's identity and the core values and beliefs espousing the individual's personality. The ability to express the self is evident in numerous venues—from cars to apparel. Thus, while personal web pages as a medium of self-expression are hardly innovative, several inherent characteristics of the Web make them somewhat unique. First, the capability to market the self to a large audience is enhanced exponentially (because any user with online access can potentially locate a particular page). Second, time, space, and geographic factors are removed, thereby facilitating self-expression. Third, individuals need not be restricted by financial constraints, as the cost of creating and maintaining a personal website is minimal. Fourth, the actual information that an individual wants to disseminate or express can be transmitted in several modes, or modalities (e.g., in addition to text, individuals can use other modes such as audio, video, graphics, or a combination of these modes). Finally, the unique technology of the Web can assist users with making their websites interactive (using such tools as chat rooms, feedback forums, message boards, etc.) and easily navigable (using creative hyperlinking strategies).

However, although the popular notion suggests that creators of personal websites manifest their personal identities in cyberspace, relatively little research attention has been paid to exploring personality perceptions of website creators. One innovative study by Vazire and Gosling (2004) applied frameworks from the interpersonal perceptions literature to examine whether personal websites result in impression formation effects. Vazire and Gosling imply that personal websites are an accurate reflection of identity claims—declarations that proclaim an individual's unique persona and convey how he or she would like to be viewed. Furthermore, they empirically demonstrate that information contained in personal websites are accurate reflections of individuals' "true" selves and hence result in observers evaluating (creators') personalities based on their websites. These findings provide research evidence supporting popular anecdotal claims that many individuals, especially adolescents and college-age youth, regard personal websites as an important means of social interaction.

Another recent ethnographic study jointly conducted by Yahoo!, OMD, and Teenage Research Unlimited (TRU) examined the influence of new media and communication technology on teenagers from several countries and found that teens embrace certain core values, namely, community, self-expression, and personalization (see Sass, 2005). That is, personalization or customization allows Web users to tailor their online content according to specific desires or likes and hence allow expression of their true selves. Furthermore, customization can also render a sense of belonging in Web users. The promise of customization has been touted by scholars in several disciplines, but one recent experimental study of college students offers convincing evidence that customization has enormous psychological value. Kalyanaraman and Sundar (2006) showed that college-age users exhibit a marked preference for personalized features and information because customization can enhance perceptions of relevance, involvement, interactivity, and novelty.

Of course, any current discussion of online content creation would be remiss without an acknowledgment of the growing importance of Web logs, or blogs. Essentially, blogs are online diaries, and they appear to be hugely popular with young adults. For example, about 40% of young adults with online access have created blogs. According to the Pew Internet & American Life Project report, blogs appear to be especially popular with young girls in the 15 to 17 age range, as a quarter of this segment with online access maintain their own blogs, compared to about 15% of boys in the same age range. Consistent with earlier discussions, Pew researchers found that young adults largely use blogs as a networking tool.

In conclusion, even as a growing number of young adults are becoming sophisticated in their use of new media, the continuing popularity of venues such as personal web pages will be contingent on the speed of technological advancement. For a generation that is accustomed to a large number of basic human needs being fulfilled through digital means, further innovations in interactive and customized technologies may be paramount in an even greater number of online users creating—and maintaining—Web-based content. However, technological progress may also be juxtaposed with online naiveté, as several scholars and policymakers have voiced concern that an increasing number of adolescents appear to be unaware of the potential detriments of revealing too much personal information on the Web.

—Sriram Kalyanaraman

See also Computer-Mediated Communication (CMC); Computer Use, Socialization and; Human-Computer Interaction (HCI); Interactive Media; Inter-activity; Internet Use, Psychological Effects of; Internet Use, Social; Online Media, Agency and; Online Relationships; Websites, Children's

FURTHER READINGS

Kalyanaraman, S., & Sundar, S. S. (2006). The psychological appeal of personalized online content in Web portals: Does customization affect attitudes and behavior? *Journal of Communication, 56,* 110–132.

Lenhart, A., & Madden, M. (2005). *Teen content creators and consumers.* Pew Internet & American Life Project. Retrieved November 25, 2005, from http://www.pew internet.org

Sass, E. (2005, September 28). OMD, Yahoo! find it's a brave you world, study reveals teen media habits. *MediaPost Publications.* Retrieved November 25, 2005, from http://publications.mediapost.com/index.cfm? fuseaction=Articles.showArticleHomePage&art_aid= 34610

Vazire, S., & Gosling, S. D. (2004). E-perceptions: Personality impressions based on personal websites. *Journal of Personality and Social Psychology, 87*(1), 123–132.

PHYSIOLOGICAL AROUSAL

Media effects researchers have studied physiological arousal in order to understand both the emotional and cognitive effects of media. Although they have focused on activation of the sympathetic nervous system, they have examined both cortical and autonomic arousal. Research on physiological arousal has been used to study the effects of both content and non-content elements of media. Recently, the construct of physiological arousal has been extended to new media environments in which researchers attempted to examine the excitatory potential of computer animation, the speed of image downloading, and video games. Physiological arousal has also been an important indicator of such emotional media experiences as "sense of being there" or "presence."

Like many aspects of mediated communication, the construct of arousal has been difficult to define. The complexity of its meaning has resulted in a broad range of theoretical and operational definitions. Most media effects researchers have tended to treat the concept of arousal mainly in physiological terms. This has probably been due to the basic tenet of psychophysiology that the system responsible for governing many of our psychological experiences will manifest itself in signals that can be recorded by physiological measurement. When applied to the context of mediated communication, this principle has led many researchers to believe that changes in an individual's affective state or covert behavior displayed during exposure to a media stimulus will be followed by corresponding changes in physiological activity. Although this conception of one-to-one relationship has generally been thought to oversimplify the relationship between individuals' psychological states and their proposed physiological manifestations, its promise has led many media effects researchers to adopt it as a logical alternative to verbal self-reports and behavioral measures.

CORTICAL AROUSAL

When defined physiologically, arousal generally means a heightened state of activation or excitement of both cortical and autonomic processes. Cortical arousal is a typical indicator of attention. It occurs when the reticular activating system (RAS) stimulates various regions of the cerebral cortex, and it is usually measured by recording the variations over time in the electrical potentials observed on the surface of the scalp. Early pioneers of cortical arousal focused on its impact on performance or behavioral intensity. Although activation in the RAS is believed to be the primary mechanism governing cortical arousal and thus provides a condition from which to infer the direction and intensity of a moment-to-moment shift in attention, activities of autonomic activation are also used for a similar purpose. For example, a sudden deceleration in cardiac reaction during exposure to a sensory stimulus is believed to indicate short-term attention, whereas a gradual increase in response to an ideational stimulus is associated with long-term attention to the stimulus.

AUTONOMIC ACTIVATION

Although cortical arousal has often been used to examine the attention-getting potential of certain visual elements of television messages, such as scene changes and movement, most media effects researchers have used autonomic activation as the primary physiological mechanism for arousal. Although there seems to be a minor disagreement over what physiological activities should be monitored for a proper measure of arousal, researchers of this kind primarily focus on activities in the sympathetic division of the autonomic nervous system (ANS). Commonly monitored autonomic indices of arousal include heart rate, blood pressure, pupil dilation, and skin conductance response, also known as *electrodermal activity.* Increases in these indices generally indicate a high level of arousal.

This emphasis on autonomic activities as primary measures of physiological arousal stems from Walter B. Cannon's (1927) general conceptualization of arousal as a system of energy mobilization. According to Cannon, physiological arousal is presumed to elicit

a signal directing the organism to mobilize resources so that an appropriate action can be made in the presence of a stimulus carrying significant information. The ultimate goal of this adaptive system is to approach stimuli that are appealing while avoiding threatening stimuli. So arousal and its physiological manifestation are viewed mainly as a part of the organism's defense mechanism. Cannon also suggested that various forms of physiological responses of arousal all originate in the sympathetic division of the ANS, which is the key to our emotional experiences. This notion of a unitary arousal system has resulted in the classic formulation of arousal as "undifferentiated" or "unspecified" activation of the autonomic system. If this is the case, multiple indicants of arousal should show a high level of covariance with each other as they are proposed to vary only in intensity along a single continuum ranging from deep sleep to high excitement. The cognitive appraisal of bodily responses determines the affective state or emotion the individual is experiencing.

One problem associated with this single-system explanation for arousal is the lack of association between different physiological measures that are assumed to behave in a similar pattern. This lack of correlation raises questions about the legitimacy of their uniform application to different contexts. The parasympathetic branch of the ANS is generally responsible for calming or reducing arousal, which typically occurs under the condition of a significant environmental change following either an expected or unexpected event. This phenomenon has allowed many attention researchers to use the direction of cardiac reaction, rather than other autonomic measures, as an important physiological indicator to distinguish between different mental states driven by different psychological events. In fact, Lacey observed this phenomenon years earlier and proposed what is commonly known as *directional fractionation*; it suggests a multidimensional, modular-specific function of the autonomic system. More recently, several researchers have proposed an alternative view that both systems may work in three different modes—simultaneously (coupled), independently (uncoupled), and mutually exclusive (reciprocal).

RESEARCH ON EFFECTS OF CONTENT ELEMENTS

In several studies, physiological arousal has been monitored as one of the primary outcome (i.e., effect) variables for both emotional and cognitive responses to media messages. The purpose was to isolate those message elements that were known to generate certain psychological effects. For example, violence is one of the most popular contents of television entertainment, and its emotional impact can be measured by indexing a viewer's physiological activities (e.g., heart rate or skin conductance response) as they unfold during the exposure. In a similar way, a researcher can examine the emotional impact of frightening movies or suspenseful television programs on children. In these examples, physiological data not only provide the researcher with valuable information about the potential effects of certain media contents, such as violence and suspense, but also help to determine the magnitude of the emotional reactions displayed by certain individuals. Early emotion researchers have focused on identifying emotion-laden media contents, such as violence, suspense, horror, and erotica. Depending on the content manipulated and the observed physiological characteristics, researchers use different qualifiers to label particular emotional states as *sexual arousal* or *fear arousal*.

RESEARCH ON EFFECTS OF NONCONTENT ELEMENTS

Recent arousal researchers have paid more attention to noncontent elements of media messages and their physiological correlates. Their general approach to investigating mediated communication is to define a media message as a constant stream of visual and auditory sensory stimuli. How these stimuli are registered, attended to, analyzed, and remembered in our brain determines the nature of our cognitive and emotional reactions to a message. In this line of research, various indices of physiological arousal are used as indicators of psychological parallels, such as attention and emotional arousal. Noncontent elements that have drawn a great deal of research interest because of their saliency and alleged impact on attention and arousal are motion, screen size, pacing, cuts, edits, negative videos, and so on. The general finding is that the presence of these so-called formal features, most noticeable in visual and auditory elements of media entertainment and information, capture our involuntary attention and produce strong emotional responses due to their status as novel, unpredictable, and significant stimuli. The system's increased sensitivity and the lower threshold to respond to these stimuli will be followed by markedly different activities in several

measures of physiological arousal. Increases in these activities are interpreted as an urgent call for the system to mobilize available resources. The ultimate goal of this drive is to facilitate the processing of information at hand by maximizing the efficiency of resource allocation to different tasks.

THEORIES RELATING AROUSAL AND MEDIA EFFECTS

Besides its role in helping researchers delineate the parameters of effective media content and forms, the most significant contribution of physiological arousal to media research has been the development of some major theories tying the concept of arousal with various forms of media effects. In those theories, physiological arousal has been conceptualized as an important intervening variable that mediates a certain media effect. For example, researchers have developed two general ideas to explain the critical role physiological arousal plays in intensifying emotional responses to media violence and sexuality. According to the so-called enhancement hypothesis, a high level of physiological arousal induced during media exposure intensifies the overall impact of an emotional content. An important implication of this hypothesis is that when an individual is aroused either by exposure to emotional media content or to a form element (e.g., motion), he or she will respond to the situation more dramatically and intensively, particularly when the situation calls for action. In other words, the high level of physiological arousal will enhance the action tendency (e.g., aggressive behavior) of an individual in response to a media stimulus (e.g., television violence). A similar effect can be observed when an individual enjoys music more, particularly when the music is accompanied by a heightened state of arousal.

Probably the most sophisticated theoretical mechanism relating physiological arousal to the action tendencies of an individual or other enhancement effects of media stimuli is the excitation transfer theory proposed by Dolf Zillmann. This theory is based on three basic premises related to the nature of physiological arousal. First, physiological arousal is diffuse and value neutral, meaning that its nature must be determined by the individual who experiences it. Once physiologically aroused, the individual surveys the environment in an effort to search for the locus of its happening. A successful attribution will then allow the individual to label the physiological state as a subjective experience of emotion that is consistent with the context. One ramification of this line of reasoning is that there is a possibility of misattribution or disassociation between the true cause and the subjective experience, and when this occurs, the individual can behave in accordance with the misattributed cause. Second, once elicited, physiological arousal decays gradually. This point is directly related to the premise that physiological arousal can be additive within the same individual, even when it occurs at different times. The residual arousal from a prior emotional experience can be transferred to a subsequent event so that the emotional reaction to the second event can be overly intensified. For example, an individual experiencing a high level of arousal after being exposed to a frightening movie may find a dramatic ending or a quick resolution amusing and enjoyable. This explains our paradoxical enjoyment of those media stimuli that contain the most horrific images or the greatest suspense when in fact aversion or anxiety seems to be the dominant emotional experience throughout the exposure.

The enhancing effect of physiological arousal can be most devastating when it occurs in the context of exposure to sexual material containing violent images. Increased arousal generated by the sexual material will be transferred to the violence, and viewers will react to the violence more aggressively than they would normally do. This happens when an individual misinterprets the extra level of arousal gained from the sexual material either as anger or hostility, which in turn leads to postexposure aggression.

—*Nokon Heo*

See also Arousal Theories; Excitation-Transfer Theory

FURTHER READINGS

Cacioppo, J. T., Berntston, G. G., & Crites, S. L. (1991). Social neuroscience: Principles of psychophysiological arousal and response. In E. T. Higgins & A. W. Kruglanski (Eds.), *Social psychology: Handbook of basic principles.* New York: Guilford.

Cannon, W. B. (1927). The James-Lange theory of emotion: A critical examination and an alternative theory. *American Journal of Psychology, 39,* 10–124.

Coles, M. G. H., Donchin, E., & Porges, S. W. (Eds.). (1986). *Psychophysiology: Systems, processes, and applications.* New York: Guilford.

Duffy, E. (1957). The psychological significance of the concept of "arousal" or "activation." *Psychological Review, 64,* 265–275.

Graham, F. K. (1979). Distinguishing among orienting, defense, and startle reflexes. In H. D. Kimmel, E. H. Van Olst, & J. F. Orlebeke (Eds.), *The orienting reflex in humans.* Hillsdale, NJ: Erlbaum.

Lacey, J. I. (1967). Somatic response patterning and stress: Some revisions of activation theory. In M. H. Appley & R. Trumbull (Eds.), *Psychological stress.* New York: Appleton-Century-Crofts.

Lang, A. (1994). What can the heart tell us about thinking? In A. Lang (Ed.), *Measuring psychological responses to media* (pp. 99–111). Hillsdale, NJ: Erlbaum.

Öhman, A. (1979). The orienting response, attention, and learning: An information-processing perspective. In H. D. Kimmel, E. H. Van Olst, & J. F. Orlebeke (Eds.), *The orienting reflex in humans* (pp. 443–472). Hillsdale, NJ: Erlbaum.

Schachter, S., & Singer, J. (1962). Cognitive, social, and physiological determinants of emotional state. *Psychological Review, 69,* 379–399.

Stern, R. S., Ray, W. J., & Davis, C. M. (Eds.). (1980). *Psychophysiological recording.* New York: Oxford University Press.

Zillmann, D. (1991). Television viewing and physiological arousal. In J. Bryant & D. Zillmann (Eds.), *Responding to the screen: Reception and reaction processes* (pp. 103–133). Hillsdale, NJ: Erlbaum.

PORNOGRAPHY, CHILD

See CHILD PORNOGRAPHY

PORNOGRAPHY, INTERNET

Among the hottest and most challenging of all political topics facing legislatures, courts, librarians, parents, and teachers today is how to balance the rights of adults to view sexual material online with the need to protect children from viewing these same materials. There is very little dispute that the government has a compelling interest in protecting children from possible harms caused by consuming Internet pornography. However, there is quite a bit of disagreement on what is the best way to accomplish that goal. Congress has tried twice to pass laws to curtail the availability of pornography to minors, but both laws have failed to pass constitutional muster. However, proponents of Internet filtering software won a victory in 2003 in *United States v. American Library Association.* The

Children's Internet Protection Act, or CIPA, mandates that libraries that receive federal funding for Internet access must install filters on their Internet-accessible computers; this act was found constitutional.

EXPOSURE TO AND USAGE OF ONLINE PORNOGRAPHY

Studies vary in their estimates of the exposure of children and adolescents to online pornography. According to a 2005 study released by Third Way, which bills itself as "a strategy center for progressives," not only is the largest group of consumers of online pornography youth 12 to 17 years of age, but the pornography industry itself estimates that 20% to 30% of its traffic comes from those under 18. Similarly, a report from the Pew Research Center suggests that while more parents are installing filters intended to protect their children than ever before, and 62% of parents actually check where their children have been online, only 33% of children believe their parents are checking on them. However, Lo and Wei (2005) found that 38% of their sample of 2,001 Taiwanese teens had been exposed to online pornography. Boys reported more exposure than girls, and all reported using Internet pornography more than other traditional forms of pornography such as books and comics.

How does this exposure to online sexual materials affect children? Mitchell, Finkelhor, and Wolak (2003) report that most studies examining questions like this report that exposure to nonviolent pornography has a negligible effect, whereas violent pornography may result in increased aggression toward women. Most such studies are done on college students or adults, they note, and no studies target children under the age of 14. These authors examined the amount of unwanted exposure to pornography experienced by children and found that roughly one in four children who use the Internet encounter unwanted sexual materials. About 6% of children in the study reported feeling some kind of distress from the unwanted exposure—thereby suggesting, noted the authors, that children experience a short-term harm as well as the long-term psychological or moral harm usually discussed.

In their study of Taiwanese teenagers, Lo and Wei (2005) found that the teens' exposure to online sexual materials correlated to increased acceptance of and participation in sexual promiscuity. They further suggested that online pornography effects were stronger than those attributable to traditional pornography.

FILTERS AND OTHER MEANS OF RESTRICTING ACCESS

Filtering software is the broad term for software installed on the user's computer that blocks sites based on the presence of objectionable content. Such filters are usually based either on blacklists of offensive sites or "whitelists" of acceptable sites. Some filters are content-based, scanning websites for offensive words or for large numbers of flesh-colored images.

CIPA, while deemed constitutional, does not mandate installation of a particular filtering software package on library computers. There are many options for filtered Internet access. The most common is a client-side application (on the home or library computer, not on the Internet service provider's server) that filters access. These filtering packages include such titles as CyberPatrol, CYBERsitter, and Net Nanny. They offer features such as individual profiles, so parents can customize their children's access, editable filter lists, and blocks for chats and newsgroups. Filtering software compares the content on a requested page to its list of blocked sites and returns a response consistent with that list.

Critics of filters point to their still-clumsy protocols, which result in both over- and underblocking, as well as the proprietary lists of blocked sites that most filtering software companies maintain. Resnick, Hansen, and Richardson (2004) reported that filtering software is far from a silver bullet protecting children from all objectionable content. They called for additional research into the strengths and weaknesses of filters, claiming that many previous examinations of filter over- and underblocking were methodologically flawed. Proponents claim that filtering is the least restrictive means of achieving the goal of keeping pornographic content away from children.

Server-side filtering is an option for parents who are concerned about underblocking of sexual content. These services, such as MayBerry USA and CleanWeb, filter content before it reaches a user's computer. The filter cannot be disabled or evaded, as objectionable content never reaches the computer.

Rating systems such as PICS (Platform for Internet Content Selection) are voluntary systems undertaken by website owners to rate their materials. All online content, not just sexual content, can be rated using PICS, and filters could theoretically be crafted to block certain ratings of content. The PICS standard is not universal—in fact, it is not intended to be so—which is both a strength and a weakness. Because it is not a government entity crafting the ratings, it is not censorship, but because anyone can craft a set of ratings, and such ratings are voluntary, it does not satisfy proponents of filtering.

In June 2005, Internet Corporation for Assigned Names and Numbers (ICANN) announced that it was supporting a new .xxx top-level domain name intended to provide a separate section of the Internet for online sexual content. This announcement was met with consternation from international governments and the online pornography industry alike. Issues raised range from the ghettoization of sexual materials, to the belief that the pornography industry will not voluntarily move to such a domain, to the creation of a virtual "red light" district. As yet, the controversy remains unresolved.

It should be noted that parental authority in the management of Internet access for their minor children has never been challenged. The Child Pornography Prevention Act of 1996 is intended to restrict the purveyors of online sexual content, and CIPA applies only to libraries.

—*Genelle Belmas*

See also First Amendment; Regulation (various entries)

FURTHER READINGS

Bohorquez, F., Jr. (1999). Note: The Price of PICS: The Privatization of Internet Censorship. *New York Law School Law Review, 43,* 523–565.

Doherty, K. (1999). www.obscenity.com: An analysis of obscenity and indecency regulation on the Internet. *Akron Law Review, 32,* 259–300.

Graham, I. (1999). Will PICS torch free speech on the Internet? In EPIC (Ed.), *Filters and freedom: Free speech perspectives on Internet content controls.* Washington, DC: EPIC.

Keller, K. (1999). "From little acorns great oaks grow:" The constitutionality of protecting minors from harmful Internet material in public libraries. *St. Mary's Law Journal, 30,* 549–613.

Lenhart, A. (2005). *Protecting teens online.* Retrieved December 9, 2005, from the Pew Internet & American Life website, http://www.pewinternet.org/pdfs/PIP_Filters_Report.pdf

Lo, V., & Wei, R. (2005). Exposure to Internet pornography and Taiwanese adolescents' sexual attitudes and behavior. *Journal of Broadcasting and Electronic Media, 49*(2), 221–237.

Mitchell, K., Finkelhor, D., & Wolak, J. (2003). The exposure of youth to unwanted sexual material on the Internet:
A national survey of risk, impact, and prevention. *Youth & Society, 34*(3), 330–358.

Nadel, M. (2000). The First Amendment's limitations on the use of Internet filtering in public and school libraries: What content can librarians exclude? *Texas Law Review, 78,* 1117–1157.

Resnick, P., Hansen, C., & Richardson, C. (2004). Calculating error rates for filtering software (Association for Computing Machinery report). *Communications of the ACM, 47*(9), 67–71.

Semitsu, J. (2000). Note: Burning cyberbooks in public libraries: Internet filtering software and the First Amendment. *Stanford Law Review, 52,* 509–545.

Third Way. (2005, July). *The porn standard: Children and pornography on the Internet.* Retrieved December 9, 2005, from http://www.third-way.com/news/THE_PORN_STANDARD.pdf

Wagner, R. (1999). Filters and the First Amendment. *Minnesota Law Review, 83,* 755–813.

Wardak, L. (2004). Note: Internet filters and the First Amendment: Public libraries after *United States v. American Library Association. Loyola University Chicago Law Journal, 35,* 657–725.

PORNOGRAPHY, MAGAZINES

Although written and pictorial depictions of sexually explicit behavior date back at least as far as recorded history, the roots of contemporary pornographic magazines can be found in the 1950s. Scholars have examined numerous dimensions of the content of pornographic magazines and have also studied the effects of exposure to and consumption of such publications. According to some surveys, nearly all adolescent males and the majority of females older than 16 years of age have seen some form of pornographic magazine content, and younger teens are also frequently exposed to such materials.

HISTORY OF PORNOGRAPHIC MAGAZINES

Numerous historians have noted that drawings of people engaged in hetero- and homosexual behavior adorned cave walls, statues, Grecian urns, and a multitude of ancient artwork. Short tomes of a sexual nature became increasingly common in the 18th century. For example, historians have noted that erotic stories were widely circulated among Civil War soldiers in the 1860s, as were early nude photographs of women. In short, as the means to produce media developed, content of a sexual nature soon followed.

Magazines depicting all manner of sexual behavior were available prior to the mid-20th century, although not on a mass market scale. Instead, small-scale publications were typically distributed "under the counter," from traveling salesmen out of the trunks of cars, or via equally clandestine means. Many observers credit the success of *Playboy* magazine with legitimizing so-called gentlemen's magazines when it began publication in 1953. Relaxed social mores and legal restrictions resulted in a burgeoning of more sexually explicit magazines beginning in the late 1960s. Magazines such as *Penthouse* and *Hustler* soon began publication and featured increasingly graphic depictions of nude females.

Sexually explicit magazines enjoyed continued success through the next two decades, with some of the largest magazines reporting peak circulation figures in the millions. However, most reported significant declines in circulation in the late 1990s due to the growth of freely available Internet pornography. Some magazines responded by continuing to increase the sexual explicitness of their photographs, as well as by focusing on various *paraphilias* (nontraditional sexual activities). A number of publishers, including the publisher of *Penthouse*, were forced to file bankruptcy to cope with declining sales. Nonetheless, other mainstays of the adult magazine industry, such as *Playboy*, were more successful in translating their success in print to the online environment.

CONTENT OF PORNOGRAPHIC MAGAZINES

By definition, contemporary pornographic magazines contain pictorial depictions of sexual content representing varying degrees of explicitness. However, examination of most of these magazines reveals an abundance of content in addition to these pictorials, such as cartoons, fiction of an erotic and nonerotic nature, viewer comments, and articles addressing an array of topics. This format is hardly coincidence: It helps provide constitutional protection under current obscenity laws.

Some surveys of pornographic magazines have identified thousands of unique titles available in major metropolitan cities in the United States. Despite the abundance of these magazines (or perhaps because of it), social scientists have failed to conduct systematic, comprehensive, baseline assessments of the content

of sexually explicit magazines. Nonetheless, some general conclusions may be drawn. Studies have demonstrated that the majority of sexually explicit magazines are intended for heterosexual male consumption. The majority of sexual content consists of photographs of nude females alone or of two or more people engaged in heterosexual activities such as oral sex and intercourse. Nonetheless, pornographic magazines catering to a variety of sexual interests, fetishes, and orientations are common.

One scholar examined factors suggesting that some adult-oriented magazines, such as *Playboy* and *Penthouse*, were directed toward upper-class readers, whereas others were aimed at a working-class audience, including magazines such as *Cheri*, *Gallery*, and *Hustler*. Moreover, the author noted numerous aesthetic characteristics of the photographs and models that distinguished the two categories. For example, the study noted that upper-class magazines emphasized youth and beauty in terms of models, their surroundings, and photograph composition. Working-class magazines contain models of greater ethnic variety and wider age range, and the photographs emphasized explicit depictions of the female genitalia. Research has also found that sexually explicit magazines reinforce racist ethnic stereotypes, such as portraying Latino women as sexually insatiable. In addition, a longitudinal review of *Playboy* magazine provided data to support the argument that pornographic magazines have grown increasingly explicit over time.

One additional aspect of pornography that has received considerable attention has been the presence of sexually violent content. Studies have found differing amounts of sexually violent content in pornographic magazines, leading some scholars to trivialize the presence of such content. Indeed, some studies have argued that the increased presence of such content throughout the 1970s was an aberration, and the presence of sexual violence in both photographs and cartoons is rare. Nonetheless, contemporary research continues to find sexually violent themes in sexually explicit magazines and videos and on the Internet.

EXPOSURE TO AND EFFECTS OF PORNOGRAPHIC MAGAZINES

Surveys of teens and young adults indicate that exposure to some form of sexually explicit photos and magazines is extremely common. One survey of teens and young adults ages 13 to 24 revealed that 100% of males age 16 and older, and nearly as many females, report having seen soft-core sexual content such as *Playboy* magazine. These figures are only slightly smaller for younger teens ages 13 to 15, as 92% of males and 84% of females report having seen similar content. What's more, the average age of first exposure to these magazines was 11 for males and 12 for females. Older teens reported having seen more sexually explicit magazines than younger teens. Males 16 to 18 years old reported seeing an average of 16.1 magazines, whereas those 13 to 15 years old reported seeing an average of 5.2 magazines. Across all age ranges, females reported seeing fewer magazines, with older teens reporting an average of 5.7 magazines and younger teens reporting 2.2 issues.

Although differences in survey techniques and questions make comparisons across time difficult, prior studies generally reported lower rates of exposure, suggesting that the use of pornographic magazines has increased over time. The increased popularity of the Internet has shifted the focus of concerns from pornographic magazines to websites, and recent survey data indicates that 70% of teens report having unintentionally seen pornography while searching for other content. These figures were higher for teens searching for health information. Such reports underscore critics' concerns over teenagers' exposure to pornographic content. Studies have noted that teens often look to the media as a source for sexual information. One of the overarching concerns regarding adolescents' exposure to pornographic magazines is that these images serve as inappropriate learning tools. Critics argue that many children are first exposed to human sexuality via adult-oriented magazines, videos, or Internet pornography. This exposure may be particularly harmful because it comes at a point in childhood development when young people are forming long-lasting impressions about sexual behavior. In addition to distorting children's views on sexuality, pornographic magazines may also have behavioral effects as well, causing children to imitate behaviors seen in adult magazines and videos.

Although the effects may be indirect, scholars have also examined pornography's harmful effects on the family. Research has demonstrated that exposure to pornography results in reduced marital satisfaction and reduced reproductive desire. In addition, increased attention has been given recently to pornography addiction, which can cause harm to children as parents withdraw emotionally from the family.

Pornography addiction can also result in actual physical withdrawal from the family environment as the parent spends increased time consuming sexually explicit content.

Social scientists have expended considerable effort examining the effects of pornography consumption, although ethical standards prohibit conducting such research on young teens and adolescents. Nonetheless, many studies have used college student populations as research participants, and many empirical studies report having participants as young as 18. Such research has linked the consumption of sexually explicit content with increased acceptance of rape myths and the increased trivialization of rape crimes. Numerous other harmful effects have been documented due to exposure to filmed depictions of sexually explicit content, including increased preference for nonstandard sexual practices such as bestiality and sadomasochism, decreased satisfaction with marital partners, and increased acceptance of pre- and extra-marital sexual relations. Research examining pornographic magazines has also found a significant positive correlation between state-by-state circulation rates of sexually explicit magazines and rape rates. Most contemporary pornography research examines Internet pornography and sex addiction.

—*R. Glenn Cummins*

See also Child Pornography; Desensitization Effects; Ethnicity, Race, and Media; Movies, Sexuality in; Obscenity; Physiological Arousal; Pornography (various entries); Sexual Information, Internet and; Sexualized Violence; Violence, Desensiti-zation Toward

FURTHER READINGS

Bogaert, A. F., & Turkovich, D. A. (1993). A content analysis of *Playboy* centerfolds from 1953 to 1990: Changes in explicitness, objectification, and models. *Journal of Sex Research, 30*, 135–139.

Brown, D., & Bryant, J. (1989). The manifest content of pornography. In D. Zillmann & J. Bryant (Eds.), *Pornography: Research advances and policy considerations* (pp. 3–24). Hillsdale, NJ: Erlbaum.

Bryant, J., & Brown, D. (1989). Uses of pornography. In D. Zillmann & J. Bryant (Eds.), *Pornography: Research advances and policy considerations* (pp. 25–55). Hillsdale, NJ: Erlbaum.

Donnerstein, E., Linz, D., & Penrod, S. (1987). *The question of pornography: Research findings and policy implications*. New York: Free Press.

Greenberg, B. S. (1994). Content trends in media sex. In D. Zillmann & J. Bryant (Eds.), *Media, children, and the family: Social scientific, psychodynamic, and clinical perspectives* (pp. 165–182). Hillsdale, NJ: Erlbaum.

Winick, C. (1985). A content analysis of sexually explicit magazines sold in an adult bookstore. *Journal of Sex Research, 21,* 206–210.

Zillmann, D., & Bryant, J. (Eds.). (1989). *Pornography: Research advances and policy implications.* Hillsdale, NJ: Erlbaum.

PORNOGRAPHY, MOVIES

The end of the 20th century brought the mainstreaming of pornography in the United States, as a once-underground business came into homes, offices, and hotel rooms aided by technological, legal, and political changes. At the same time, the pornography industry's products became increasingly graphic, explicit, and degrading, pushing society's boundaries.

The term *pornography* is sometimes used to describe all sexually explicit books, magazines, movies, and Internet sites, with a distinction made between soft-core (nudity with limited sexual activity not including penetration) and hard-core (graphic images of actual, not simulated sexual activity including penetration). In other uses, the term is juxtaposed to *erotica* (material that depicts sexual behavior with mutuality and respect), leaving pornography as the term for material depicting sex with domination or degradation. Laboratory studies of pornography's effects commonly use three categories: overtly violent, nonviolent but degrading, and sexually explicit but neither violent nor degrading.

Heterosexual pornography makes up the bulk of the commercial market. There is a significant amount of gay male pornography available, with a smaller amount of material produced commercially for lesbians. Pornography is distributed using all communication technologies: printing, photographs, film, telephones, video, DVD, and computers. *Playboy*, which debuted in December 1953, was the first sex magazine to break into mainstream distribution channels. In the 1960s and 1970s, pornographic films moved into public theaters. In the 1980s, video swamped other forms of pornography, with the number of new pornographic video titles released each year increasing from 1,500 in 1986 to 11,000 in 2001.

Computers emerged as a major vehicle for pornography in the 1990s, although the future legal status of online pornography is unclear after the Supreme Court threw out much of the Communications Decency Act, a controversial part of the 1996 telecommunications law that prohibited not only obscene but indecent material that could be viewed by children. For now, the Internet remains home to large amounts of pornography—stories, photographs, video, and interactive material.

The two main categories in today's pornographic movie industry are features and "wall-to-wall/gonzo." Features, shot mostly on video but occasionally on film, have a traditional three-act script with some plot and characters. The industry markets these as "couples' movies" that can appeal to women as well as the traditional male audience. Wall-to-wall movies are all-sex productions that have no pretense of plot or dialogue. Many of these movies are shot gonzo style, in which performers acknowledge the camera and often speak directly to the audience. The best-known production companies closest to the mainstream, such as Vivid and Wicked, specialize in features; however, the bulk of the market is wall-to-wall/gonzo movies. In addition, there are specialty titles—movies that feature sadomasochism and bondage, fetish material, transsexuals—that fill niche markets.

The majority of hard-core movies include oral, vaginal, and anal sex, almost always ending with ejaculation on the woman. In the wall-to-wall/gonzo movies, double penetration (anal and vaginal penetration by two men at the same time) and aggressive oral penetration of women are increasingly common, as are hair pulling, slapping, and rough treatment. As these movies push the limits of overt violence and brutality, pornography producers search for new ways to attract male viewers looking for increased stimulation.

In the 1973 *Miller v. California* decision, the Supreme Court established a three-part test for defining obscenity (material that appeals to the prurient interest; portrays sexual conduct in a patently offensive way; and does not have serious literary, artistic, political, or scientific value) and identified contemporary community standards as the measure of evaluation. Although a strict application of state and federal obscenity laws could lead to prosecution of much contemporary pornography, enforcement usually occurs only where there is political support from citizens. This prosecutorial discretion means material for sale openly in one jurisdiction may not be available in another. However, the availability of mail-order and computer pornography ensures that graphic, sexually explicit material can be obtained easily anywhere. The only exception is child pornography—material that is made either using children or, in the digital age, through the use of technology that makes it appear the sexual activity uses children. The former is illegal without question (*New York v. Ferber*, 1982) and available only underground; the legal status of the latter remains uncertain (*Ashcroft v. Free Speech Coalition*, 2002).

Until the 1970s, debates over pornography pitted liberal advocates of sexual freedom against conservative proponents of traditional sexual morality. That changed with the feminist critique of pornography, which emerged out of the struggle against sexual violence during the women's movement in the 1960s and focused on the way in which pornography eroticizes domination and subordination. Feminist critics argued for a focus not on subjective sexual mores but on the harm to women used in pornography and against whom pornography is used.

Much of the debate about pornography concerns the question of effects. Does pornography, particularly material that explicitly eroticizes violence or domination, result in sexual violence against women, children, and other vulnerable people? Pornography's supporters and some researchers argue there is no conclusive evidence. Other researchers contend the evidence points to some kind of effects with some groups of men. No one argues that pornography is the sole causal factor in rape; the question is whether the use of pornography can be considered a sufficient condition for triggering a sexual assault. Because experimental research on such topics using minors is more difficult and ethically problematic, there are few data specifically about pornography's effects on children and adolescents.

Many feminists have argued that attention to the experiences of men and women—both those who use pornography and those against whom pornography is used—makes the connection clear. Such accounts provide specific examples of how pornography can (1) be an important factor in shaping a male-dominant view of sexuality, (2) contribute to a user's difficulty in separating sexual fantasy and reality, (3) be used to initiate victims and break down resistance to sexual activity, and (4) provide a training manual for abuse.

It is difficult to make reliable estimates of children's use of, or access to, pornography, whether in traditional print, movie, or computer form. A 2004 United Kingdom study found that 57% of young people ages 9 to 19 have come into contact with pornography online, which seems a plausible, although perhaps conservative estimate. Whatever the actual percentage, as pop culture more generally turns toward pornographic conventions, the exposure of children and adolescents to pornographic images and values is best understood as a continuum; all are exposed to some level of the pornographic, and it is likely those various levels are mutually reinforcing. The complexity at this level makes it difficult to isolate the specific effects of any one medium or genre.

—*Robert Jensen*

See also Pornography, Regulation of; Pornography, U.S. Public Policy on

FURTHER READINGS

Dworkin, A. (1981). *Pornography: Men possessing women.* New York: Perigee. (Reprint edition, 1989, Plume)

Lane, F. S. (2000). *Obscene profits: The entrepreneurs of pornography in the cyber age.* New York: Routledge.

MacKinnon, C. A., & Dworkin, A. (1997). *In harm's way: The pornography civil rights hearings.* Cambridge, MA: Harvard University Press.

Strossen, N. (1995). *Defending pornography: Free speech, sex, and the fight for women's rights.* New York: Scribner.

Williams, L. (1989). *Hard core: Power, pleasure, and the "frenzy of the visible."* Berkeley: University of California Press.

PORNOGRAPHY, REGULATION OF

The regulation of sexual content has a long and varied history in the United States. Borrowing initially from English common law, American legislatures and courts have over the years developed ways to regulate sexual content; these evolved into a test that has been in place since 1973.

At the outset, however, it should be noted that the terms *pornography* and *obscenity* have different legal definitions. Once sexual material has been found to be legally obscene, it is no longer protected by the First Amendment. Pornographic material retains some First Amendment protection in that consenting adults may continue to create, purchase, distribute, and consume it. *Indecency* has yet a third definition; it is applied to the broadcast media and aimed toward protecting children. This article will focus primarily on the regulation of obscenity and child pornography.

EARLY ENGLISH LAW

As early as 1868, English courts were considering how to regulate sexual content. In *Regina v. Hicklin,* an English judge held that sexual materials should be considered in light of their effect on the most susceptible members of society. Furthermore, the material could be removed from its context and considered alone to determine its impact. This standard was applied in the United States from colonial times through the 1930s, and it was included in the 1873 Comstock Act, which made it illegal to send any "obscene, lewd, or lascivious" books through the mail. The Comstock Act was used to punish individuals offering contraception products through the mail.

ROTH TO *MILLER*

The U.S. Supreme Court's first attempt to define obscenity—that is, sexual material that receives no First Amendment protection—was in the 1957 case of *Roth v. United States.* In this case involving two plaintiffs who sold sexual materials and advertised them through the mail, the Court held for the first time that material deemed legally obscene was outside the protections of the First Amendment. The Court eliminated the *Hicklin* requirements involving the material's effect on the least susceptible person and the ability of the court to remove the material from its context. Instead, the Court advanced the first legal definition of obscenity: "whether, to the average person, applying contemporary community standards, the dominant theme of the material, taken as a whole, appeals to prurient interest" and is "utterly without redeeming social importance." (*Prurient* means lascivious or displaying inordinate interest in sex.)

This standard proved difficult to interpret and apply. Following several years of cases wherein the Court could not decide what was obscene and what was not (prompting the famous and oft-quoted Potter Stewart line from the 1964 case, *Jacobellis v. Ohio:* "But I know it when I see it, and the motion picture involved in this case is not that"), the Court refined the obscenity test in 1973 in *Miller v. California.*

This case, which involved a mass mailing to advertise pornographic books, provides the current test for obscenity. A work is considered to be obscene if (1) an average person, applying contemporary community standards, finds the work, taken as a whole, to appeal to the prurient interest; (2) the work depicts or describes, in a patently offensive way, sexual conduct described in the applicable state law; and (3) the work, taken as a whole, lacks serious literary, artistic, political, or scientific value. If all three elements of this test are met, the work is legally obscene and without First Amendment protection.

CHILD PORNOGRAPHY

Child pornography is a problem of special interest to courts and legislatures. The basic rule of thumb is that all child pornography, work featuring minors engaged in sexual activity, has no First Amendment protection. That is, the *Miller* test need not even be applied. In the 1982 case of *New York v. Ferber,* the Supreme Court said that states need not adhere to *Miller* to be able to punish child pornography. States have greater leeway in seeking out and punishing child pornographers because the stakes for the children involved are so high. In addition, the goal of eliminating the market for child pornography is compelling.

In 1990, in *Osborne v. Ohio,* the Court permitted the punishment of individuals for the possession of child pornography. Relying on its arguments in *Ferber,* the Court said that such penalties furthered the goal of reducing the market for child pornography products.

ANIMATED PORNOGRAPHY

In the 2002 case of *Ashcroft v. Free Speech Coalition,* the Court made a distinction between pornography that uses real children and that which uses animated cartoons that may resemble children. In so doing, the Court struck down the portion of the Child Pornography Prevention Act of 1996 (CPPA) that punished sexual materials that "appear to be" of minors or that "convey the impression" that they contain minors. Virtual child pornography, said the Court, does not harm children in the ways that real child pornography does—by its creation and perpetually through its distribution. If no children are harmed in the making of virtual child pornography, the Court said, the government may not penalize its creation.

Congress responded to this decision with the PROTECT (Prosecutorial Remedies and Other Tools to end the Exploitation of Children Today) Act of 2003. The act asserts that the majority of child pornography today exists on computer hard drives and that although it is cost-prohibitive to generate child pornography from scratch using computer technology, it is cheap to use images of real children and alter them so that they become unrecognizable as initially real. The act punishes digital, computer, or computer-generated images that are, or are "indistinguishable from," those of a minor engaging in sexually explicit conduct (tightening the language that was struck down in the *Free Speech Coalition* case). Tougher penalties were also added, and the act encourages voluntary reporting by Internet service providers of child pornography found on their servers.

The PROTECT Act became controversial (and was even attacked by Chief Justice William Rehnquist in 2004) because it includes a section that would single out and keep track of judges who issue lighter than maximum sentences ("downward departures") in child pornography cases. Judicial commentators have suggested that this congressional mandate was passed without consultation with the judiciary.

—*Genelle Belmas*

See also First Amendment; Internet Pornography, Effects of

FURTHER READINGS

Alexy, E., Burgess, A., & Baker, T. (2005). Internet offenders: Traders, travelers, and combination trader-travelers. *Journal of Interpersonal Violence, 20*(7), 804–812.

Bower, D. (2004). Holding virtual child pornography creators liable by judicial redress: An alternative approach to overcoming the obstacles presented in *Ashcroft v. Free Speech Coalition. Brigham Young University Journal of Public Law, 19,* 235–260.

Hardy, S. (2004). Reading pornography. *Sex Education, 4*(1), 3–18.

Hendriks, A. (2002). Examining the effects of hegemonic depictions of female bodies on television: A call for theory and programmatic research. *Critical Studies in Media Communication, 19*(1), 106–124.

Koppel, A. (2005). Does obscenity cause moral harm? *Columbia Law Review, 105*(5), 1635–1679.

Lambe, J. (2004). Who wants to censor pornography and hate speech? *Mass Communication & Society, 7*(3), 279–299.

Langevin, R., & Curnoe, S. (2004). The use of pornography during the commission of sexual offenses. *International Journal of Offender Therapy & Comparative Criminology, 48*(5), 572–586.

Martinson, D. (2005). Pornography and deceptive advertising: What is the role of government in a free society? *Social Studies, 96*(1), 30–33.

Wackwitz, L. (2001). Burger on Miller: Obscene effects and the filth of a nation. *Journal of Communication, 52*(1), 196–211.

PORNOGRAPHY, U.S. PUBLIC POLICY ON

There are a range of questions and opinions in the United States concerning the propriety and acceptability of pornography, based on distinctions such as type of material and age of consumer. Moral outrage toward the involvement of children and young adolescents in the production of sexually explicit materials is the norm, however. By law, children and adolescents below the age of 18 are not permitted any access to pornographic materials in any form, and both the actual distribution and the intended dissemination of such materials to underage consumers are illegal. The advent of the World Wide Web has made access to all forms of pornography simple and inexpensive. For the above reasons, federal regulation of the production and distribution of pornography has grown more and more conservative over time, so that there are more restrictions on accessing pornographic materials and on the inclusion of children in their production. Opposition typically focuses on issues of free speech, juxtaposing the harm access to pornography may cause with the harm restrictions might inflict. Restrictions on juvenile participation in the production of pornographic materials have general support.

DEFINITIONS

The following definitions are those currently in use by the U.S. federal government:

Pornography. The term *pornography* is defined as any material created in an effort to provoke sexual interest. This is an exceptionally broad definition and can legitimately embrace *Playboy* magazine and NC-17 rated films, Harlequin romance fiction, and music videos featuring scantily clad performers.

Child pornography. Child pornography refers to any visual depiction of sexually explicit conduct, within any medium and produced by any means, that (1) involves the actual participation of a minor, (2) involves a character indistinguishable from a minor, or (3) has been made to present the impression of direct participation by a minor. For the purposes of this definition, *sexually explicit conduct* was defined by the Prosecutorial Remedies and Other Tools to end the Exploitation of Children Today (PROTECT) Act as graphic sexual intercourse, bestiality, masturbation, sadistic or masochistic abuse, real or simulated, of any sort, or a similar presentation of human genitals or pubic areas. Examples can range from films of prepubescent children engaging in sexual acts with adults, to a webcam picture of a nude 17-year-old. The actual language of the PROTECT Act has recently come under fire, as it says that a visual depiction can be considered child pornography if it shows a person of legal majority but that person is "virtually indistinguishable" from an actual minor. The constitutionality of this reading is currently under review.

Obscene/Obscenity. The term *obscenity,* referring to that which is obscene, is defined as something that an average person, applying the current societal values, would find (1) appeals to sexual interests in a way that also produces feelings of shame or obsession, (2) presents in a blatantly outrageous way that which can be described as sexual activity, and (3) is without true worth according to the standards of any discipline. Examples will necessarily depend on the local community, but common practice has been to judge those standards based on as conservative a framework as possible. What this means is that whereas those living in an undergraduate all-male dorm may find a magazine or film-clip tame, the broader community of permanent residents may not, and it could therefore be defined as obscene.

U.S. POLICY

The current policy of the U.S. government is that whereas pornography in general is entitled to protection under the First Amendment, that protection is not to be extended to materials that are defined as obscene or as child pornography, also known as "kiddie porn." In recent years, the United States has leaned toward a zero-tolerance approach to child pornography. The U.S. Supreme Court under Chief Justice William Rehnquist in July 1990 held that a citizen's right to privacy does not extend toward any materials defined as child pornography.

Current efforts are focused on prosecuting those creating, distributing, and collecting child pornography, as well as requiring agencies and organizations receiving federal funds to block Internet access to sites considered obscene, harmful to minors, or hosting child pornography. On an international level, the Optional Protocol to the Convention on the Rights of the Child on the Sale of Children, Child Prostitution, and Child Pornography prohibits the sale of child pornography. Although the United States has yet to ratify the principle Convention on the Rights of the Child, it ratified this Optional Protocol in December 2002.

LEGISLATION AND ENFORCEMENT

The amount of federal legislation relating to pornography has grown in recent years, as has the number of agencies formed to prevent juvenile access to or participation in it.

Recent Legislation

Recent laws relating to children and adolescents and pornography include strictures against the creation of misleading Internet domain names in an effort to trick someone into viewing restricted materials; provisions for the seizure of property gained through child pornography-related activities; or bans on engaging in the production of child pornography outside U.S. boundaries for the purposes of eventual U.S. importation. The Children's Internet Protection Act requires schools and libraries that receive federal funds for computer purchase or Internet access to implement filtering systems to block obscene materials from juveniles. Two proposed measures are specifically related to children and adolescents. The Internet Safety and Child Protection Act of 2005, currently being referred to the U.S. Senate's Subcommittee on Select Education, proposes to tighten the age verification requirements of those who operate "adult" websites and to levy a tax equal to 25% of the site membership fees, with those funds going to law enforcement organizations and measures to fight Internet and pornography-related crimes that impact children directly. The revised Children's Safety Act of 2005 provides for establishing a Children's Safety Office under the Department of Justice, enhancing sentencing requirements, and providing more specified language regarding the definition of the phrase "the sexual exploitation of children," replacing it with "aggravated sexual abuse, sexual abuse, abusive sexual contact involving a minor or ward, or sex trafficking of children, or the production, possession, receipt, mailing, sale, distribution, shipment, or transportation of child pornography."

Law Enforcement Organizations

A large number of private, local, state, and federal organizations specifically target pornography as it relates to children and adolescents. These include the Association of Sites Advocating Child Protection, the Child Exploitation and Obscenity Section of the Department of Justice, the Customs Service's CyberSmuggling Center and its Child Exploitation Unit, the FBI's Crimes Against Children program, the Innocent Images National Initiative, and the National Center for Missing and Exploited Children.

—*Solomon Davidoff*

See also Child Pornography; Children's Internet Protection Act of 2000 (CIPA); Children's Online Privacy Protection Act of 1998 (COPPA); Internet Watch Foundation; Obscenity; Pornography (various entries); Regulation, Internet; Sex, Internet Solicitation of; Sexualization of Children; Sexualized Violence; Telecommunications Act of 1996; United Nations Convention on the Rights of the Child; Webcams

FURTHER READINGS

Cohen, H. (2003, October 15). *Child pornography: Constitutional principles and federal statutes.* Washington, DC: Congressional Research Service. Retrieved November 10, 2005, from http://www.firstamendmentcenter.org/pdf/CRS.childporn1.pdf

Cooper, S., Giardino, A, Vieth, V., & Kellog, N. (2005). *Medical, legal, and social science aspects of child sexual exploitation: A comprehensive review of pornography, prostitution, and Internet crimes.* St. Louis, MO: G. W. Medical Publishers.

Ferraro, M., & Casey, E. (2004). *Investigating child exploitation and pornography: The Internet, law, and forensic science.* Burlington, MA: Elsevier Academic Press.

Heins, M. (2001). *Not in front of the children: "Indecency," censorship, and the innocence of youth.* New York: Hill & Wang.

Jeffrey, D. (1997). In the name of protecting children. *Gauntlet: Exploring the Limits of Free Expression, 2*(14), 72–74.

PORNOGRAPHY, X-RATED MOVIES AND

Since the origins of motion pictures, sex and nudity have been common subjects for films. Today, a wide variety of titles are freely available in many local video retailers, and consumers can access vastly larger catalogues of movies through various online rental and sales outlets. Although data on the number of adolescents exposed to such content are limited, surveys indicate the teens are being exposed to pornographic films at a younger age.

HISTORY OF X-RATED MOVIES

Although hardly salacious, some of Eadweard Muybridge's first experimental forays into motion pictures in the late 19th century consisted of filmed depictions of nude male and female models engaged in mundane tasks. Early motion-picture devices such as the kinetoscope allowed viewers to peer into a viewing device to witness racy vignettes of a female stripping or performing a seductive dance.

More sexually explicit films remained taboo in the United States for the first half of the 20th century. The quality of the films was poor, and none had sound. Moreover, distribution systems for sexually explicit films were primitive, and exhibition was private and limited to small groups of men. These "blue movies" or "stag films"—named for their male audience—bore little resemblance to their contemporary counterparts. The more progressive social climate of the 1960s led to increased acceptance of sexually explicit content of all varieties, and adult theaters that publicly screened pornographic films became increasingly common. Two films, *Deep Throat* and *Behind the Green Door*, both released in 1972, have been credited with ushering X-rated films into the mainstream of American society and reducing social stigmas associated with pornographic films.

In the late 1970s, exhibition of sexually explicit films in private homes was made possible with the advent of affordable video cassette players. Numerous scholars cite the adoption of VCRs to support the oft-made claim that pornography drives the development of new communications technology. Similar claims have been made about virtually all mass media, starting with the printing press and continuing to modern-day DVDs, personal computers, and the Internet. Sexually explicit films are also available via cable systems by subscription and pay-per-view. Moreover, the rapid growth of broadband Internet technology is also fulfilling the promise of video-on-demand, making entire libraries of pornographic films available for download at a moment's notice.

Today, the adult film industry remains vibrant and profitable. The adult industry on the whole is estimated to make billions of dollars in profits each year, and cable operators alone make anywhere from $50 million to $500 million each year from adult programming. Moreover, the adult film and video industry is represented by its own association, which tracks sales and rentals of adult titles, holds a yearly convention and awards ceremony, and even publishes a member directory.

CONTENT OF X-RATED MOVIES

Examinations of sexually explicit content are made difficult by a multitude of labels and distinctions, some of which are grounded in fact and some of which are rather arbitrary. For example, feminist critics of sexually explicit content draw a distinction between pornography—which focuses on violence, domination, and conquest—and erotica—which focuses on consensual sexual behavior. Clearly, the labels leave abundant room for subjective judgment. With respect to films and videos, the most accepted dichotomy is between hardcore or triple-X films and soft-core erotica. As the name implies, hard-core films are characterized by much more graphic depictions of sexual acts, and they are generally less socially acceptable than soft-core films.

Although countless X-rated titles are widely available to consumers, little empirical research has comprehensively examined the content and themes that make up the adult film universe. The dominant content of adult videos is the depiction of males and females engaged in a variety of sexual acts, including vaginal intercourse, anal intercourse, and oral sex. Films focusing on masturbation most frequently feature females rather than males. Although not the majority, films focusing on other sexual behaviors such as bondage, sadomasochism, homosexual behavior, and transgender sexual behavior are common. Films focusing on illegal behavior such as child pornography are not distributed through traditional channels, although observers have noted that the development of the Internet has resulted in the spread of such materials. The majority of characters appearing in X-rated videos appear to be in their late teens through 30 years of age and are white.

Perhaps the dominant theme of X-rated films and videos is that of sex without commitment. Characters are rarely portrayed as married or in monogamous relationships, and they are sometimes portrayed as strangers or only recent acquaintances. Some scholars have noted the presence of sexually violent themes in X-rated films, although research surrounding the topic is conflicting. Some empirical data suggest that these themes are not the norm. Moreover, data have shown that depictions of sexual aggression with positive outcomes for the victim are rare. Similar studies argue that although sexually violent themes are not the norm, they are common nonetheless. Scholars have also analyzed pornographic films to demonstrate the presence of negative gender and racial stereotypes.

EXPOSURE TO AND EFFECTS OF X-RATED MOVIES

Scholars have devoted considerable attention to obtaining normative measures of exposure to sexually explicit content, including pornographic videos. Some of the most widely cited data were collected in the 1980s and indicate that nearly half of teens 13 to 15 years old, and 84% of teens 16 to 18 years old, reported having seen X-rated films containing explicit sexual content, although results suggest that exposure was not frequent. However, survey data indicated that the age of first exposure to such material decreased as a function of respondents' age, meaning that teens are exposed to pornographic films at a younger age. Contemporary data regarding exposure to sexual content focuses on sex in mainstream television, films, and magazines or Internet pornography. Thus, reliable up-to-date figures regarding exposure to pornographic videos are not available. Nonetheless, comparison of survey data dating from the 1970s suggests an increase in the number of adolescents who had seen pornographic films. Early surveys of young adults ages 17 to 24 indicated that a majority of male adolescents (53%) and an even greater majority of females (88%) reported having *never* seen a pornographic film at all, let alone more than one. Recent data regarding teens' exposure to Internet pornography indicate that exposure to pornographic content has increased, as 70% of teens 15 to 17 years old report *unintentional* exposure to pornographic content online. Clearly, the opportunity for exposure to sexually explicit content has grown.

An abundance of research has focused on assessing the potentially harmful effects of pornography on society, although virtually all such research has focused on adult exposure. Ethical standards governing social science research obviously prohibit testing the effects of exposure to pornography on children and young teens. However, much empirical research routinely uses college students as young as 18 years old to serve as research participants, and the same is true of research examining sexually explicit content. Thus, most results are generalizable to the young adult population.

One of the primary effects of the consumption of sexually explicit videos is desensitization and habituation. Exposure to pornography can also result in physiological habituation, such that viewers are no longer aroused by sexually explicit content that once elicited excitation. In addition, research has demonstrated that viewers will seek increasingly hard-core and atypical pornographic material after prolonged exposure to sexually explicit films, presumably to seek this excitatory state. Exposure to massive amounts of pornography has also resulted in increased estimations of the prevalence of nonstandard sexual behavior such as sadomasochism, bestiality, and nonexclusivity among sexual partners. Moreover, exposure to pornographic films has led some research participants to place less value on the institution of marriage and to report reduced reproductive desire. Finally, prolonged exposure to pornography has also been shown to result in decreased satisfaction with one's own intimate partner in terms of physical appearance, sexual curiosity, and sexual performance.

Some scholars have also expended considerable effort exploring the effects of sexually violent media content. Numerous studies have demonstrated that viewers who were exposed to pornographic films over an extended period of time viewed rape as a more trivial offense. Moreover, this effect has been found in studies examining both sexually violent and nonviolent pornography, as well as some R-rated action and horror films that dwell on female victimization.

Although most research has focused on the negative effects of exposure to pornographic films, select studies have examined potentially beneficial uses of pornography. Such work has focused largely on the treatment of sexual dysfunction, although scholars have also advocated the use of sexually explicit content as an educational tool.

—R. Glenn Cummins

See also Child Pornography; Desensitization Effects; Ethnicity, Race, and Media; Movies, Sexuality in;

Obscenity; Physiological Arousal; Pornography (various entries); Sexual Information, Internet and; Sexualized Violence; Violence, Desensiti-zation Toward

FURTHER READINGS

Brown, D. (2003). Pornography and erotica. In J. Bryant, D. Roskos-Ewoldsen, & J. Cantor (Eds.), *Communication and emotion: Essays in honor of Dolf Zillmann* (pp. 221–254). Hillsdale, NJ: Erlbaum.

Brown, D., & Bryant, J. (1989). The manifest content of pornography. In D. Zillmann & J. Bryant (Eds.), *Pornography: Research advances and policy considerations* (pp. 3–24). Hillsdale, NJ: Erlbaum.

Bryant, J., & Brown, D. (1989). Uses of pornography. In D. Zillmann & J. Bryant (Eds.), *Pornography: Research advances and policy considerations* (pp. 25–55). Hillsdale, NJ: Erlbaum.

Cowan, G., & Campbell, R. R. (1994). Racism and sexism in interracial pornography: A content analysis. *Psychology of Women Quarterly, 18*, 323–338.

Donnerstein, E., Linz, D., & Penrod, S. (1987). *The question of pornography: Research findings and policy implications.* New York: Free Press.

Garcia, L. T., & Milano, L. (1990). A content analysis of erotic videos. *Journal of Psychology & Human Sexuality, 3*(2), 95–103.

Linz, D., Donnerstein, E., & Penrod, S. (1988). Effects of long-term exposure to violent and sexually degrading depictions of women. *Journal of Personality and Social Psychology, 55*, 758–768.

Zillmann, D., & Bryant, J. (1984). Effects of massive exposure to pornography. In N. M. Malamuth & E. Donnerstein (Eds.), *Pornography and sexual aggression* (pp. 115–138). New York: Academic Press.

Zillmann, D., & Bryant, J. (Eds.). (1989). *Pornography: Research advances & policy implications.* Hillsdale, NJ: Erlbaum.

PRESCHOOLERS, MEDIA IMPACT ON DEVELOPMENTAL NEEDS OF

The preschool years, roughly defined as 2 to 6 years old, are unique in the development of children's interaction with media. As children mature, their access to and use of the media, as well as their content preferences and tastes, change dramatically. The underlying assumption of the various psychological approaches that center on the interaction of the individual child with the media is that, with experience, children's cognitive, emotional, and social skills develop over time. Stage theories assume that human development proceeds through universal chronological stages. Accordingly, they suggest that the preschool years are a unique stage of development with its own special behavioral and cognitive characteristics termed *pre-operational* by the Swiss psychologist Jean Piaget.

The pre-operational stage is characterized mainly by the acquisition of language. This allows representative thought, expanding the youngster's experiences beyond the "here and now" of the senses and motor activities that characterize the earlier stage of development. Thus, the child is able to think and talk about television experiences outside of the viewing situation. However, at this stage, the child is unable to perform many of the more advanced mental activities typical of older children at the next stage—concrete operations.

MEDIA USE

Preschoolers apply their developing cognitive skills to the media as to any other aspect of their lives. Such capabilities determine in large degree what they use and attend to as well as the kind of meaning they make of these experiences. Indeed, recent studies that explored young children's exposure to media reveal that use of all media increases when children move into preschool years: viewing television and videos/DVD levels off around 3 to 4 years old and then declines before peaking later in mid-childhood, whereas reading and computer use, which require special skills, continue to increase linearly until entering school. Interestingly, income is not related to most American children's amount of media use. This suggests that the infiltration of media in young children's life has become a universal phenomenon in developed societies.

Similarly, there are no significant gender differences in media use at this age, except for the use of video games, which are more popular among boys of all ages. Television and video/DVD viewing, reading, or computer use were found to be quite similar for both preschool boys and girls. However, viewing is related to parental education: Children of less educated parents watched more television. Higher parental education and income are also associated with having viewing rules for their children in regard to the amount of time and the kinds of programs viewed. Computer access, too, is related to families'

socioeconomic status, as youngsters growing up in families with higher income and education are more likely to own a computer and to have Internet access.

Television remains the most central medium for this age group, if one includes all technologies and forms of transmission (i.e., broadcast, cable, satellite, videotapes, DVD). The growing body of research on preschoolers in the developed world has found great variability in the amount of viewing time at this age; however, 2 to 3 viewing hours a day are often reported. The variance depends, among other things, on the measure used (e.g., parental reports, observations, computerized rating measures). For example, children who live in homes where the television set is constantly on were found to spend more time viewing television and less time reading in comparison to children where the television was turned on only to view particular programs.

VIEWING PREFERENCES

Research has found that, at an average age of 2½ years, many youngsters are capable of and willing to stay tuned to a program that interests them for a full half hour or even more. They have favorite programs and tend to know when and on which channel they are broadcast. This age coincides with the transition into the language-oriented pre-operational stage of cognitive development along with other physiological and social changes typical of this age group.

As toddlers grow into preschoolers, they gradually become more interested in and able to comprehend narratives as well as diverse magazine formats. However, they continue to need more time than adults to process television images and thus prefer slower paced programming; compared to older children, they enjoy lots of repetition. Preschoolers show a strong preference for programs produced specially for them that combine segments of animation, puppets, documentaries, and drama (e.g., *Sesame Street*). Such programs are designed with the understanding that preschoolers' attention span and viewing preferences develop gradually. Thus, magazines may adopt a "quilted" format that offers a variety of segments, providing each child the opportunity to interact according to individual needs and abilities. From about the age of 5 or 6, children start developing preferences for more fast-paced programs and more complicated content and start gradually to disassociate themselves from clearly educational and "safe" preschool programs.

ATTENTION TO TELEVISION

In contrast to some populist claims that preschoolers are "hooked" on or "hypnotized" by media, research has found that preschool viewers clearly demonstrate frequent changes in orientation, moving their focus back and forth between the screen and the surrounding environment. Attention to television continues to grow as a function of the child's development, personality, program content, and environment. The ability to sustain interest in the television program for longer stretches of time and to manipulate their own attention to television as well as to competing activities is gradually strengthened and modified. By the age of 6, the child's attention to television can be sustained for long periods of time and remains so until adolescence. Attention to television during this period increases for content that the child is capable of understanding and decreases for incomprehensible content or content that seems to belong to the adults' world.

From a research perspective, the child needs to demonstrate some form of attention to television as a necessary condition for any thought-related processes. This is by no means a simple process to understand, as attention to television is not easily defined. Preschoolers, while visually oriented toward the screen, may be daydreaming or otherwise disengaged. Or, they could be playing with toys in front of the television, occasionally glancing at it following an audio cue such as a loud siren, a familiar commercial, or a child's giggle. The context may have a role in attention; for example, a variety of activities may take place simultaneously with viewing (e.g., snacking, playing), interchangeably with viewing (e.g., drawing a picture on the coffee table during the talk show but watching during the commercial break), or independent from it (e.g., looking at a picture book on the couch while the rest of the family is viewing a drama series).

To be sure, when the child is busy with a variety of activities, he or she may be regularly and subconsciously scanning the audio channel of the operating television set to detect sounds that indicate content changes. Audio cues (e.g., an opening tune of a favorite program, sudden noise, familiar voice) or behavioral cues from people may lead to a shift in attention level and orientation to the screen. Attention to television is also directed by a process of viewing inertia, which explains how children's viewing may overcome moments of comprehension "breakups" or changes in content types. The longer the period of time that a viewer continues to view television, the higher the chance that this behavior will continue, regardless of the viewing difficulties encountered. This process works in the opposite direction as well: The longer the child's visual orientation is away from the screen, the lower the chance that he or she will return to it. This process has been found to exist regardless of content and viewer's age.

COMPREHENSION OF TELEVISION CONTENT

Preschoolers have a fairly good grasp of some audiovisual conventions and are able to discriminate between different program genres, including the distinction between programs and commercials. Yet, the research literature suggests that preschoolers have a very different understanding of television content and television as a medium than do older children and youth.

For example, one particular area of interest in the developmental psychology literature is changes in young children's ability to distinguish between real and fantasy dimensions of television. Most preschoolers are able to distinguish between real objects and televised images as well as between human actors and cartoon characters. They recognize the factuality of news, but only gradually make correct judgments about fictional dimensions of television entertainment as they mature. In general, they lack the understanding that television programs are staged and that television characters are portrayed by actors. They have only a partial understanding of the persuasive intent of television commercials, to which they are highly attracted.

An integrative review of the developmental literature suggests that preschoolers and kindergartners differ from older children in their cognitive abilities to understand television and that with maturation, they gradually acquire abilities in the following areas: (a) the understanding of story lines and narratives, including the ability to reconstruct events, understand sequence, distinguish between central and incidental information, connect causes to consequences, and the like; (b) the understanding of characters such that they are able to describe characters not only by exterior appearance, but also by personality traits, motivations, feelings, personal history, and social orientation, as well as the contexts in which they interrelate with others; (c) the understanding of audiovisual language, including the ability to identify and to understand the codes and conventions of audiovisual expressions, such as special effects, shooting angles, slow and fast motion, and the like; (d) the understanding that all forms of television are a production, even realistic genres, and that each television text involves actions by many professions and roles. Generally, preschoolers do not understand that television is an industry that functions within a complicated system of economic, social, political, legal, and human constraints that influence its content in various ways. Nor do they understand the interrelationships between television and reality, including TV's selective nature, its role in creating as well as representing certain parts of reality, and its contribution to the construction of our worldview.

FEAR REACTIONS TO TELEVISION

Contrary to what might be expected, preschoolers do not become less easily frightened as they grow older. Rather, what seems to happen is that they are less bothered by some stimuli that concerned them in the past, while other stimuli that had never elicited reactions in the past do so as they mature. More specifically, preschoolers are typically scared of animals, supernatural forces (such as ghosts, witches, and monsters), and things that look anomalous or move unexpectedly. They might be more afraid of something that looks dangerous but in fact is not than something that does not look dangerous but in fact is. This process will be reversed during school years. Thus, young children react more fearfully to imaginary programs (e.g., cartoons, monsters) than to real dangers (e.g., news reports about an anticipated natural disaster). In addition, cognitive comforting strategies such as explanations that "this is not real" or "this is happening very far away" are less effective than behavioral comforting strategies, such as a hug or offering a snack.

—Dafna Lemish

See also Developmental Differences, Media and; Television, Attention and; Television, Child Variables and Use of; Television, Viewer Age and

FURTHER READINGS

Anderson, D. R., & Pempek, T. A. (2005). Television and very young children. *American Behavioral Scientist, 48*(5), 505–522.

Calvert, A. L., Rideout, V. J., Woodland, J. L., Barr, R. F., & Strouse, G. A. (2005). Age, ethnicity, and socioeconomic patterns in early computer use. *American Behavioral Scientist, 48*(5), 590–607.

Cantor, J. (2001). The media and children's fears, anxieties, and perceptions of danger. In D. G. Singer & J. L. Singer (Eds.), *Handbook of children and the media* (pp. 207–221). Thousand Oaks, CA: Sage.

Collins, W. A. (1983). Interpretation and inference in children's television viewing. In J. Bryant & D. R. Anderson (Eds.), *Children's understanding of television: Research on attention and comprehension* (pp. 125–150). New York: Academic Press.

Dorr, A. (1983). No shortcuts to judging reality. In J. Bryant & D. R. Anderson (Eds.), *Children's understanding of television: Research on attention and comprehension* (pp. 190–220). New York: Academic Press.

Lemish, D. (1997). Kindergartners' understandings of television: A cross-cultural comparison. *Communication Studies 48*(2), 109–126.

Valkenburg, P. M., & Cantor, J. (2000). Children's likes and dislikes of entertainment programs. In D. Zillman & P. Vorderer (Eds.), *Media entertainment: The psychology of its appeal* (pp. 135–152). Mahwah, NJ: Erlbaum.

Van Evra, J. (2004). *Television and child development* (3rd ed.). Mahwah, NJ: Erlbaum.

PRIMING THEORY

Cognitive and social psychologists have used priming paradigms since the early 1970s to study how humans process information and how that remembered information affects our behavior. As applied to the media, priming refers to the effects of the content in the media on people's later behavior or judgments. Priming has been used extensively to study the short-term effects of media violence and stereotyped portrayals of minorities and the long-term effects of political coverage on evaluations of a candidate.

Priming procedures were first used to explore the representation of information in memory. Some theories of memory, such as network models of memory, assume that information is stored in memory in the form of nodes and that each node represents a unique idea (e.g., there is a "Big Bird" node in memory). Furthermore, these nodes are connected to related nodes in memory by associative pathways (e.g., "Big Bird" is linked to *Sesame Street* or "Cookie Monster" or "the Muppets" but probably is not directly linked to "President Herbert Hoover"). Also, it is believed that each node has what is called an *activation threshold*.

If the node's level of activation exceeds its threshold, the node fires, and energy flows down network pathways from the node to other related nodes. For example, if the Big Bird node fires, activation spreads to related nodes, such as Cookie Monster. Once a related node is activated (in this example, Cookie Monster), it then requires less additional activation for it to fire. This means that the concept has been primed.

Cognitive psychologists have shown that the activation level of a node will dissipate over time if no additional source of activation is present. Eventually, given no more activation, the activation level of the node returns to its resting state, and it is no longer considered to be activated. In tasks that involve judgments or evaluations of a social stimulus, the priming effect will last up to 15 to 20 minutes and possibly up to 1 hour.

Social and developmental psychologists began using priming procedures in the late 1970s to study person perception, stereotyping, and attitude activation. For example, Graham and Hudley (1994) had middle school boys read a set of 10 sentences. For half of the boys, 8 of the 10 sentences dealt with negative outcomes that were under the control of the child in the sentence. For the other boys, 8 of the 10 sentences described the same outcome, but the child in the sentence was not responsible for the outcome. After completing this priming task, participants took part in what they thought was a second, unrelated study. In that study, participants were asked to imagine that they were at a water fountain and another student knocked into them, and they got water all over their shirt. The scenario was set up so that it was ambiguous whether the bump was deliberate or not. As predicted by priming theory, the boys who had read the sentences where the child was responsible for the negative outcome were more likely to judge that the child intentionally got them wet at the water fountain than were the boys who read the sentences where the child was not responsible for the negative outcome. In research of the priming effect, typically, the ambiguous information is biased toward the primes.

Research on priming has demonstrated two important characteristics of priming effects. First, the strength of a priming effect is a dual function of the *intensity* and the *recency* of the priming event. As for intensity, a stronger prime will result in higher activation levels in the target item, and its effect on the target will dissipate more slowly than a weaker prime.

The strength or intensity of the prime can refer to the frequency of the prime (e.g., a single exposure to a gun versus five exposures to a gun in quick succession) or the duration of the priming event. Recency simply refers to the time lag between the prime and the target (e.g., the time between seeing a gun on TV and seeing an ambiguous behavior that could be interpreted as hostile). Recent primes are stronger than temporally distant primes.

—*David R. Roskos-Ewoldsen*

See also Aggression, Movies and; Aggression, Television and; Cognitive Script Theory; Cuing and Priming; Media Effects, Models of

FURTHER READINGS

Berkowitz, L. (1984). Some effects of thoughts on anti- and prosocial influences of media events: A cognitive-neoassociationistic analysis. *Psychological Bulletin, 95,* 410–427.

Graham, S., & Hudley, C. (1994). Attributions of aggressive and nonaggressive African-American male early adolescents: A study of construct accessibility. *Developmental Psychology, 30,* 365–373.

Higgins, E. T., Bargh, J. A., & Lombardi, W. (1985). Nature of priming effects on categorization. *Journal of Experimental Psychology: Learning, Memory, & Cognition, 11,* 59–69.

Josephson, W. L., (1987). Television violence and children's aggression: Testing the priming, social script, and disinhibition predictions. *Journal of Personality and Social Psychology, 53,* 882–890.

Price, V., & Tewksbury, D. (1997). New values and public opinion: A theoretical account of media priming and framing. In G. A. Barnett & F. J. Boster (Eds.), *Progress in communication sciences: Advances in persuasion* (Vol. 13, pp. 173–212). Greenwich, CT: Ablex.

Roskos-Ewoldsen, D. R., Klinger, M., & Roskos-Ewoldsen, B. (2006). Media priming. In R. W. Preiss, B. M. Gayle, N. Burrell, M. Allen, & J. Bryant (Eds.), *Mass media effects research: Advances through meta-analysis.* Mahwah, NJ: Erlbaum.

Roskos-Ewoldsen, D. R., Roskos-Ewoldsen, B, & Carpentier, F. D. (2002). Media priming: A synthesis. In J. B. Bryant & D. Zillmann (Eds.), *Media effects in theory and research* (2nd ed., pp. 97–120). Mahwah, NJ: Erlbaum.

Srull, T. K., & Wyer, R. S. (1979). The role of category accessibility in the interpretation of information about persons: Some determinants and implications. *Journal of Personality and Social Psychology, 37,* 1660–1672.

PRIX JEUNESSE FOUNDATION

PRIX JEUNESSE is the premier international children's television organization. Through its biannual competition, its networking and coordination efforts, and its outreach programs, the foundation strives to promote quality children's programming around the world.

The PRIX JEUNESSE Foundation was established in 1964 as a coordinated effort between the German government and German broadcasting corporations. Since its inception, the foundation has created ties with other global organizations, such as UNESCO, the Goethe Institute, the European Broadcasting Union, and the Centre International pour l'Enfance et la Jeunesse (CIFEJ) to increase its reach.

ACTIVITIES OF PRIX JEUNESSE

The most important function of PRIX JEUNESSE has always been the biannual festival, the PRIX JEUNESSE INTERNATIONAL. The purpose of this competition is threefold: to highlight exceptional work that is being done in children's television programming worldwide, to provide a forum for discussion of important issues in children's television, and to provide an arena for global networking within the children's television community. The competition is open to broadcasters across the globe, and winning its coveted award has become the highest honor in children's television programming.

The PRIX JEUNESSE INTERNATIONAL is held every other year in Munich, Germany, where members of the global children's television community from industry, advocacy, and academia meet to view the submissions, discuss them in small groups, and judge the entries. The small discussion groups have become a core element of the festival. The discussions allow participants from around the world to better understand how people with various backgrounds react to the programs and to recognize new trends or innovations in programming that they can take back to their home country. The key outcome of this festival is the creation of a "market of great ideas."

To foster the dissemination of these ideas, the foundation has created the PRIX JEUNESSE Suitcase. The foundation works with festival participants to "pack" a Suitcase for them to take back to their home country as a training tool. Although the content of each Suitcase varies depending on the needs of the audience, it always includes a sampling of the best and most innovative entries from the festival. In addition to providing packaged training materials, PRIX JEUNESSE has also developed several training programs. These workshops are given in coordination with local media organizations and focus on the current needs of the organization, country, or region.

Finally, PRIX JEUNESSE functions as a global lobbyist for quality, innovative children's programming through creating and fostering regional networks. Regional partners include the Asia-Pacific Broadcasting Union (ABU), PRIX JEUNESSE IBEROAMERICANO, the African Radio and Television Union (URTNA), and the Arab States Broadcasting Union (ASBU). PRIX JEUNESSE works to connect the people and activities of these regional organizations through joint initiatives. For example, PRIX JEUNESSE recently worked with producers from Serbia, Montenegro, Albania, Macedonia, and Kosovo to create a Balkan children's TV magazine co-production to be aired in all of the countries. The 15-minute weekly magazine for 9-to-14-year-olds emphasizes the importance of mutual understanding and began airing in October 2004.

—*J. Alison Bryant*

See also Media Advocacy; Media Education, International; Television, International Viewing Patterns and; United Nations Convention on the Rights of the Child

FURTHER READINGS

Kleeman, D. K. (2001). PRIX JEUNESSE as a force for cultural diversity. In D. G. Singer & J. L. Singer (Eds.), *Handbook of children and the media* (pp. 521–532). Thousand Oaks, CA: Sage.

Kleeman, D. K. (in press). Advocates for excellence: Engaging the industry. In J. A. Bryant (Ed.), *The children's television community*. Mahwah, NJ: Erlbaum.

WEBSITE

PRIX JEUNESSE website: http://www.prixjeunesse.de

PRODUCT PLACEMENTS, ALCOHOL

The placement of different brands of alcohol in movies has a long tradition, and product placements of alcohol also appear frequently in rap songs. Although concerns have been raised about the impact of such placements on adolescent drinking, research is needed to explore the influence of product placements on adolescents' attitudes toward drinking, their perceptions of the normative appropriateness of drinking and the prevalence of drinking, and whether placements influence adolescent drinking behavior.

One early example of product placement of alcohol in movies is the 1945 movie, *Mildred Pierce*, in which Joan Crawford—who received the best actress Academy Award for this role—drank Jack Daniel's whiskey. Perhaps a better known example is Katharine Hepburn's discarding Humphrey Bogart's—he received the best actor Academy Award for this role—Gordon's Dry Gin into the river in *The African Queen* (1951). The placement of alcohol products in the media is widespread. A content analysis of the top 10 movies each year of the 1990s found that the two most popular placements in these movies were for soft drinks and beer. In 1997–1998, there were over 230 paid placements of alcoholic products in movies and more than 180 different paid placements in TV series. In 2005, the first product placement on Broadway was for Jose Cuervo tequila in the Neil Simon play, *Sweet Charity*. Simon agreed to changes in the script so that the placement could occur. Likewise, recent studies of popular music have found that close to half of all rap songs mentioned specific brands of alcohol.

Why have product placements become so prominent? One reason is that audiences seem to like product placements because they make the TV show or movie seem more realistic. Indeed, early product placements simply involved a company providing its product to production companies for use in movies. More recently, product placements have developed into a form of paid advertising, where the company pays for the product to be used in a movie or TV show; more prominent product placements cost more than simple background placements of the product. Indeed, the practice should be called *brand* placement because the investment in placements is not to increase the use of the product category; rather, companies hope the placement will increase the use of their brand of the product. For example, sales of Red Stripe beer reportedly increased 50% after it appeared in the movie, *The Firm*. A second reason why placements may be so popular is the practice allows advertisers to target very specific audiences because the demographics of who attends which kinds of movies are well understood. Third, compared to paid advertisements, product placements are cheap.

The concern about alcohol product placements involves their effect on children's and adolescents' likelihood of drinking alcohol. A 1998 survey found that 50% of all high school seniors reported drinking at least once in the past month, and 31.5% of the seniors had engaged in binge drinking (defined as five or more drinks in a single drinking episode). However, as the American Medical Association notes in a 2001 report on underage drinking, there is a distinct lack of research on the influence of product placements on adolescent drinking.

Research does suggest that people are less approving of placement of alcohol and tobacco in movies and on TV than they are of other types of product placements. But adolescents, in general, like product placements more than adults. In addition, adolescents who watch lots of movies tend to be more brand conscious and pay more attention to product placements in the media. Finally, adolescents tend to perceive that other people are influenced by product placements but that they are immune to the effects of placements.

—*David R. Roskos-Ewoldsen*

See also Adult Mediation of Advertising Effects; Advertising, Effects on Adolescents of; Advertising, Effects on Children of; Advertising, Health and; Alcohol Advertising, International; Product Placements (various entries)

FURTHER READINGS

American Medical Association. (2001). *Partner or foe? The alcohol industry, youth alcohol problems, and alcohol policy strategies.* Chicago: Author.

Federal Trade Commission. (1999). *Self-regulation in the alcohol industry: A review of industry efforts to avoid promoting alcohol to underage consumers.* Washington, DC: Author.

Gould, S. J., Gupta, P. B., & Grabner-Krauter, S. (2000). Product placements in movies: A cross-cultural analysis of Austrian, French, and American consumers' attitudes toward this emerging international promotional medium. *Journal of Advertising, 29,* 41–58.

Nelson, M. R., & McLeod, L. E. (2005). Adolescent brand consciousness and product placements: Awareness, liking, and perceived effects on self and others. *International Journal of Consumer Studies, 6,* 515–528.

Yang, M., Roskos-Ewoldsen, B., & Roskos-Ewoldsen, D. R. (2004). Mental models for brand placement. In L. J. Shrum (Ed.), *The psychology of entertainment media: Blurring the lines between entertainment and persuasion* (pp. 79–98). Mahwah, NJ: Erlbaum.

PRODUCT PLACEMENT, CIGARETTES

Hollywood has known for a long time about the power of product placements in the movies—the positioning of name-brand products, either for payment or free of charge, to increase sales. In fact, during the 1930s and 1940s, tobacco companies paid movie stars thousands of dollars to endorse their brands. In the 1970s and 1980s, the practice became widespread among Hollywood studios, despite their denials: According to internal documents from the Brown & Williamson company, Sylvester Stallone guaranteed use of their brand of cigarettes in at least five films (including *Rambo* and *Rocky IV*) for a total fee of $500,000. The Philip Morris Company reportedly paid $350,000 to place Lark cigarettes in the James Bond movie, *License to Kill*, and another $42,500 to place Marlboros in *Superman II*.

Direct payments for product placements of cigarettes supposedly ended in 1989, when the top 13 tobacco firms adopted the following guidelines to avoid federal regulation: "No payment, direct or indirect, shall be made for the placement of our cigarettes or cigarette advertisements in any film produced for viewing by the general public." The 1998 Master Settlement Agreement reached between tobacco companies and 46 states forbids this practice. Nevertheless, given the prevalence of cigarette smoking in current Hollywood movies, questions remain about whether product placement of cigarettes is occurring, to what extent, and why. In fact, the tobacco industry has been taking advantage of loopholes in the agreement by providing free promotional items to movie studios and to actors and actresses. In the past, the industry was known to have provided free cigarettes for use in adult films like *Who Framed Roger Rabbit?*, *Grease*, and *Die Hard*. It also sent monthly mailings of free cigarettes to 1,888 actors and celebrities who smoke.

Smoking in Hollywood movies continues unabated. A content analysis of the top 25 box office hits from 1988 to 1997 found that 85% of the films contained tobacco use, with 28% containing recognizable brands. Actor endorsement of cigarette brands increased from 1% among the films produced between 1988 and 1990, before the voluntary ban on paid product placement by the tobacco industry, to 11% after the ban (1991 to 1997). Some critics assert that smoking in the movies is the single most powerful influence on young people today, accounting for more than half of all new teen smokers. In one study, smoking in the movies tripled the odds that a teen would try smoking, independent of whether his or her parents smoked.

Although smoking advertisements are banned on TV, smoking continues to be advertised via movie trailers. Ten movies in 2002 had a brand presence in the movie and smoking in the trailer. The TV ads for these 10 movies reached 93% of all 12-to-17-year-olds in the country, and 81% of all 12-to-17-year-olds saw at least one of these trailers three or more times.

—*Victor C. Strasburger*

See also Cigarette Advertising, Effects of; Product Placements, Alcohol

FURTHER READINGS

Sargent, J. D., Dalton, M. A., Beach, M. L., Mott, L. A., Tickle, J. J., Ahrens, B. M., & Heatherton, T. F. (2002). Viewing tobacco use in movies: Does it shape attitudes that mediate adolescent smoking? *American Journal of Preventative Medicine, 22*, 137–145.

Strasburger, V. C. (2006). Alcohol and drug exposure. In S. L. Calvert & B. J. Wilson (Eds.), *Handbook of child development and the media*. Malden, MA: Blackwell.

WEBSITE

Smoke Free Movies: www.smokefreemovies.ucsf.edu

PRODUCT PLACEMENTS, FOOD

A product placement refers to the practice of placing a particular brand of a product in a movie. Many people recall a small boy leaving a trail of Reese's Pieces from a shed where an alien was hiding to the boy's house (indeed, people are probably more likely to remember the name of the candy than the boy's name—Elliot). The consumption of Reese's Pieces increased by about 67% within a few months of the opening of the movie, *E.T.* Of course, generic candy (or even a fruit such as grapes) could have been used to draw the alien into the house.

Product placements are becoming increasingly popular; a recent content analysis of prime-time television found that, on average, there were close to 30 brand appearances per hour of prime-time programming. Indeed, products are placed in video games as well. Donkey Kong does not use just any banana—he uses Chiquita bananas.

One reason product placements are so popular may be that brand placement overcomes the problem of "zapping." A person is less likely to run to the kitchen when Reese's Pieces are being placed on the ground by a little boy during a movie than when a commercial is run for Reese's Pieces. Second, brand placements have a longer lifetime than typical advertisements. With the release of the 20th anniversary *E.T.*, Hershey's placement of Reese's Pieces may continue to be effective 20 years after the initial placement.

Much of the academic research has focused on the influence of product placements on memory of brands placed within movies or TV shows. The initial research was mixed. Sometimes, people showed very good memory of placements whereas other times, they recalled very few placements. More recently, researchers have started looking at implicit memory of product placements. Implicit memory involves demonstrating an effect of earlier exposure to a brand without explicitly asking people to remember what they saw earlier. For example, people may be asked to complete a series of word problems where they fill in missing letters to complete a word. This is called a word fragment completion task. For example, to test if people had implicit memory of Sprite in the movie, *The Client*, they were presented with a series of word puzzles including "S__ RI__ E." Research found that people who had seen the movie were more likely to complete the word fragment with SPRITE than people who had not seen the movie. Product placements consistently result in improved implicit memory for the products placed in a movie or video game.

The concern with food product placements is that they may be contributing to the alarming increase in childhood and adolescent obesity seen in the United States. Statistics suggest that as many as 15% of youth in the United States are obese. Rates of obesity are increasing at alarming rates. For example, the percentage of

obese 6-to-11-year-olds increased from about 4% in the 1960s to 15.3% in 2000. The Surgeon General predicts that obesity may replace smoking as the leading cause of preventable deaths in the United States.

Unfortunately, it is difficult to ascertain the influence of brand placement because much of the data on brand placement is proprietary. Despite the resounding success of the Reese's Pieces story, the empirical research on brand placement is less encouraging, suggesting that the practice may not be as effective at increasing sales as some would like to believe. However, research does suggest that adolescents who watch more movies are more brand conscious and pay more attention to product placements. Likewise, food advertising influences young children's brand preferences and pestering behavior in grocery stores, which in turn may influence dietary choices and future brand preferences. In addition, several studies have found that product placements influence people's choice behavior. If people are going to get a soft drink, they are more likely to choose a particular brand of soft drink if they have seen in a movie than if they have not seen the brand placed in the movie.

—*David R. Roskos-Ewoldsen*

See also Advertising, Effects on Adolescents of; Advertising, Effects on Children of; Advertising, Health and; Advertising, Purchase Requests and; Eating Habits, Media Influence on; Food Advertising (various entries); Product Placements, Alcohol; Product Placements, Cigarettes

FURTHER READINGS

Auty, S., & Lewis, C. (2004). Exploring children's choice: The reminder effect of product placement. *Psychology & Marketing, 21,* 697–713.

Gould, S. J., Gupta, P. B., & Grabner-Krauter, S. (2000). Product placements in movies: A cross-cultural analysis of Austrian, French, and American consumers' attitudes toward this emerging international promotional medium. *Journal of Advertising, 29,* 41–58.

Kaiser Family Foundation. (2004). *The role of media in childhood obesity.* Retrieved from www.kff.org

Nelson, M. R., & McLeod, L. E. (2005). Adolescent brand consciousness and product placements: Awareness, liking, and perceived effects on self and others. *International Journal of Consumer Studies, 6,* 515–528.

Yang, M. (2004). *The effectiveness of brand placements in the movies: Levels of placements, explicit and implicit memory, and brand choice behavior.* Unpublished doctoral dissertation, University of Alabama, Tuscaloosa.

Yang, M., Roskos-Ewoldsen, D. R., Dineua, L., & Arpan, L. (in press). The effectiveness of "in game advertising": Comparing college students' explicit and implicit memory for brand names. *Journal of Advertising.*

Yang, M., Roskos-Ewoldsen, B., & Roskos-Ewoldsen, D. R. (2004). Mental models for brand placement. In L. J. Shrum (Ed.), *The psychology of entertainment media: Blurring the lines between entertainment and persuasion* (pp. 79–98). Mahwah, NJ: Erlbaum.

PROFANITY, TRENDS IN

If all human societies in history share a minimum number of social customs and institutions, the designation of certain words as taboo speech (and the subsequent intentional and contextual use of such speech) clearly qualifies as one such commonality. Because its form is largely dependent on cultural context, cursing—a predominant form of taboo speech—is a concept difficult to define. Generally speaking, cursing is the use of words that audiences are likely to find offensive. What people find to be offensive may, however, depend on their perception of the speaker and the context in which the curse was uttered. The controversy surrounding the increasing use of curse words on American television programs speaks to the delicate nature of this issue. The use of profanity in U.S. television programs is increasing despite implementation of the current television ratings system.

CONTEXT

English-language curses are generally either scatological, sexual, racist, or blasphemous in nature, although exceptions do exist. As with many other types of uttering, swearing is used for a multitude of purposes, including emphasizing certain messages; establishing one's claim to group inclusiveness; reinforcing class, gender, race, and age inequities; relieving tension and achieving catharsis; attacking someone verbally; and eliciting a response from one's audience. Historically, curses have circulated more within the private sphere (e.g., conversations with friends) than the public sphere (e.g., social gatherings, church, and school). With the advent of a pervasive electronic environment (particularly cable TV), however, the curse word has made a strong appearance in the public sphere, as well. The availability of televised profanity to young audiences, in particular, has triggered a nationwide campaign to clean the airwaves of curses. The age- and content-based television ratings system implemented in 1997 was a major step in this direction, but parent groups and many legislators criticize the existing ratings system for its inability to stem the rising wave of profanities uttered on TV.

TRENDS IN THE USE OF PROFANITY

Studies undertaken over the past 30 years have shown an ascending trend in the use of profanities, both in people's everyday conversations and in the television programs they watch. According to the Parents Television Council, the frequency of curses uttered in all media has increased fivefold in the past 10 years. In 2001, Kaye and Sapolsky found that nearly 9 out of 10 prime-time programs contained swear words. Profanity was encountered on both unrated programs and programs rated for "parental guidance," proving that the ratings system is not working as originally intended. Most swearing on TV was done by characters over the age of 21. When under-21 characters did curse, their utterance was either neutral or positive. Another 2001 study indicated that swearing on the airwaves occurred most often in male-to-male interactions, with a tendency to use mild curse words in interactions with the opposite sex.

—*Razvan Sibii*

See also Adult Mediation of Violence Effects; Aggression, Television and; Arousal Theories; Catharsis Theory; Desensitization Effects; Forbidden Fruit Hypothesis; Gender Roles on Television; Parental Advisory Labels and Rating Systems

FURTHER READINGS

Hughes, G. (1991). *Swearing: A social history of foul language, oaths, and profanity in English.* Cambridge, MA: Blackwell.

Kaye, B. K., & Sapolsky, B. S. (2004). Offensive language in prime-time television: Four years after television age and content ratings. *Journal of Broadcasting & Electronic Media, 48*(4), 554–569.

Kaye, B. K., & Sapolsky, B. S. (2004). Watch your mouth! An analysis of profanity uttered by children on prime-time television. *Mass Communication and Society, 7*(4), 429–452.

Krcmar, M., & Sohn, S. (2004). The role of bleeps and warnings in viewers' perceptions of on-air cursing. *Journal of Broadcasting & Electronic Media, 48*(4), 570–586.

PROMOTIONAL TIE-INS

Promotional tie-ins are a form of marketing promotion in which two or more brands or companies agree to participate in a joint strategy to increase value for both brands regarding exposure or sales, while providing each partner with targeted communication efforts that many times exceed the opportunities provided via traditional advertising alone. Many companies use this as a special form of advertising and marketing to reach the important target audience of children and teenagers, who have become an increasingly powerful consumer segment.

Strategies aimed toward these younger audiences typically involve identifying the most popular characters from children's movies, TV shows, books, and video games and attempting to maximize this popularity via the successful co-merchandising of products that bear the names or images of the characters. This usually occurs as a partnership between an entertainment company and another type of company, which supplies either character-themed merchandise or an entertainment item itself (e.g., a DVD or video game) as a premium to customers who buy its products. Thus, the entertainment company gets the benefit of increased exposure, "hype," or sales, while the co-promoting company gets the benefit of enhanced exposure and an increase in both volume and sales of its own products. Product licensing and promotional tie-ins account for a business that is well over $100 million annually. For example, since the first *Star Wars* movie in 1977, the six films under the name have generated almost $9 billion in merchandise sales and product promotions.

One familiar promotional strategy relating to children typically involves giving away character-themed merchandise (e.g., a *Teenage Mutant Ninja Turtle* action figure) with the purchase of children's meals at a particular fast-food restaurant. The vast range of premium character-themed merchandise goes far beyond just action figures and includes all sorts of specialty products such as hats, T-shirts, watches, posters, cups and glasses, lunch boxes, and sometimes even discounts to the movie being promoted. The implementation of such promotional strategies geared toward children, quite commonplace today, is not a new occurrence in the world of entertainment and marketing. Indeed, the drastic increase in sales of raccoon-tail hats and other similar items propelled by Disney's Davy Crockett TV shows in the 1950s remains one of the most successful promotional tie-in efforts ever.

Because of its prevalence in marketing toward children and adolescents, the fast-food industry typically is the most visible or best-known co-developer of these promotions. McDonald's, Burger King, Wendy's, Taco Bell, KFC, Pizza Hut, Domino's, and Little Caesar's all have pursued promotional tie-ins for movies such as *Star Wars*, *The Flintstones*, *Rugrats*, *Ghostbusters*, *The Lion King*, *Spider Man*, *Batman Returns*, and so on, as well as for some items somewhat less obvious to adults, such as Nintendo or Sega video games and the Scholastic Goosebumps mystery book. Major players on the entertainment side generally include the major motion picture and TV studios, children's programming companies such as Sesame Workshop or Nickelodeon, and the many other companies involved in producing non-TV and non-movie entertainment for children (e.g., video games, books, music).

However, many promotional tie-in marketing strategies extend beyond simply partnering with a fast-food chain. Packaged food and beverage companies that market to children certainly have shown their interest in this strategy as well, including Coca-Cola, Pepsi-Cola, Hershey, Frito-Lay, Kellogg's, and Quaker. The use of the promotional tie-in strategy commonly may go beyond the realm of products geared toward children, as some companies have seen the value of trying to reach the parents of the intended younger target. For example, in a promotional effort that included several children's food products, Walt Disney Pictures' *Aladdin* also partnered with CPC International to include the sale of Hellmann's mayonnaise and Mazola corn oil in the promotion and worked communications company AT&T into the mix. Furthermore, other partnerships have included promotional tie-ins with hotel chains and theme parks/recreation areas.

Because companies spend millions of dollars on promotional tie-in campaigns and continually want to determine the most effective ways to do so, the social questions that typically arise when describing children as a target audience for advertisements also have surfaced in this area as well. While many companies continue to pursue market research to gain insight into the minds and desires of children, media (advertising) critics and some governmental leaders have questioned not only the ethics associated with promotional tie-ins in and of themselves but also the effects that such continuous, deliberate marketing efforts have on younger people.

For example, in addition to examining the possibility of banning food advertising on TV aimed at children and in the midst of criticism of the BBC and Sesame Workshop for recent sponsorship agreements and promotional tie-ins with McDonald's, the United Kingdom's Food Standards Agency also continually monitors and produces research regarding the effects of food promotions to kids. In the United States, the advocacy group Dove Foundation recently asked Burger King to remove *Star Wars, Episode III: Revenge of the Sith* icons from its kids' meals because the meals were targeted toward the segment of children 4 to 9 years old (which is usual), but the movie was rated PG-13. Also in the United States, the Children's Online Privacy Protection Act (COPPA), enforced by the Federal Trade Commission (FTC), regulates the content of child-oriented websites regarding promotional tie-in efforts such as sweepstakes and contests, as well as general promotional practices such as data collection and spamming.

—*Frank E. Dardis*

See also Advertising, Health and; Disney; Electronic Games, Rates of Use of; Electronic Media, Children's Use of; Food Advertising to Children; Media Entertainment; Movie Viewing, Adolescents'; Movie Viewing, Children's; Multimedia Toys; Relationship Marketing

FURTHER READINGS

Darvin, B. (2005, March/April). A kid's-eye view on character tie-ins. *KidScreen*, p. 81.

Horovitz, B. (2005, May 24). Group asks Burger King to halt "Star Wars" deal [Electronic version]. *USA Today*. Retrieved March 28, 2006, from http://www.keep media.com/pubs/USATODAY/2005/05/24/865899?cxtI D=10026

Miller, C. (1993, January 18). Disney launches huge ethnic campaign for "Aladdin." *Marketing News, 27*(2), 12.

Schreiber, D. (2003, December 1). Fat free TV anyone? *Television Business International, 15*(7), 1.

PUBLIC HEALTH CAMPAIGNS

Public health campaigns are developed for a multitude of reasons, and they are implemented in many different ways. They are often created to increase awareness of recently discovered diseases and conditions, such as West Nile virus; to maintain awareness of well-understood health risks, such as AIDS; to impart knowledge about how to avoid various health risks, such as heat stroke; to promote behaviors with healthful benefits, such as quitting smoking or exercising regularly; and to prevent risky behaviors, such as

START THE DAY WITH A GOOD BREAKFAST

In 1862, Abraham Lincoln established the U.S. Department of Agriculture (USDA), which was elevated to Cabinet level in 1889. The department published its first dietary recommendations in 1894. During the early 20th century, the USDA distributed "food guides" with recommendations on food groups, diets for people of various ages, and appropriate times of day for meals and snacks. During World War II, the department circulated materials on canning and gardening and encouraged Americans to plant "victory gardens." Today, the USDA provides numerous resources with information on nutrition, food preservation, and food safety.

SOURCE: U.S. Department of Agriculture, Office of Home Economics (n.d.).

unprotected sex. Public health campaigns often include advertisements placed in mass media such as television and radio, press releases sent to news organizations, informational brochures, and educational programs offered in schools and other community organizations.

Many organizations that produce and disseminate public health campaigns—for instance, the Centers for Disease Control and Prevention (CDC)—also include a wealth of information on their websites to support their campaigns. As a result, more recently, mass media campaigns have been created to increase awareness and direct audiences to the Web for further information, much in the same way that campaigns have led audiences to phone in or write to an organization for further information.

In running an effective campaign, the target audience and the issue of concern are crucial and often inseparable. Different campaign strategies are necessary for particular issues and audiences. For example, the anti-littering campaign "Don't mess with Texas" was enormously successful, with its effectiveness was largely due to strong state pride and regional history. It's unlikely that a similar campaign would do as well in another state. Furthermore, a single audience is likely to respond in different ways to ads placed in different media or to different kinds of appeal (for instance, fear, humor, or straightforward information), and both campaign intent and the way the issue is framed can determine the choice of media and audience-specific strategies. Knowing an audience and an issue also helps in determining the best frequency—how often messages should be disseminated and programmed—because a campaign should include enough ads to make it meaningful and memorable but not so many as to make it overbearing or tedious.

Framing an issue may require a great deal of research, especially when the intent is to cause behavioral change. Because most campaigns attempt to impart knowledge that will change attitudes and, in turn, the audiences' actions, behavioral change is often the main indicator of campaign success, even if the stated goal is simply to raise awareness or change opinions. Communication research raises complex issues about using knowledge and attitudes to influence behaviors, and it provides relevant strategies for imparting information effectively to influence the underlying aspects of behavior.

For instance, social learning theory and protection–motivation theory focus on two components known to predict important decisions—self-efficacy and the advantages of action as opposed to inaction. According to these theories, people must understand that the benefits of taking action outweigh the costs, and they must believe that they are capable of taking the action. The health belief model builds on this by adding that people must also believe they are vulnerable to the costs of inaction. For example, an AIDS campaign based on these theories would state who is at risk (e.g., all who share needles or have unsafe sex), specify their probability of developing the condition, describe the benefits of action and costs of inaction (e.g., life versus death), and convey the ease of taking preventive action (e.g., using new needles or wearing condoms).

Another example is the theory of reasoned action, which focuses on behavioral intent. It says the most important factor in determining behavior is intention to act, which in turn is based on attitudes, beliefs about others' wishes regarding the behavior, and motivation to comply with those wishes. For instance, campaigns designed to decrease littering often express the costs (e.g., dirty environment), benefits (e.g., clean environment), and ease of action (e.g., using a trash can) in an attempt to instill an anti-littering attitude (e.g., littering is dirty, and litterers are lazy), and they also attempt to create a perception of social norms (e.g., most people hold anti-littering attitudes) to encourage the belief that littering will lead to becoming an outcast.

Although vast amounts of theory and research are available regarding the factors that influence public health campaign effectiveness, much of this knowledge goes unused in their creation. For instance, the recent campaign, "Keep Your Body Healthy," from the National Institute on Drug Abuse connects the dangers of using drugs with contracting HIV/AIDS. However, many of the spots, including "Jack and Jill," simply note a possible relationship between drug use and casual sex. This particular public service announcement (PSA) tells a story of two youths having casual sex as a result of taking drugs; one of the two adolescents contracts HIV from the other during intercourse. Never in the spot does it mention the prevalence of HIV among youth, the possibility of contracting HIV from another, the harm HIV can cause, the ease with which one could avoid engaging in casual sex, or the likelihood that drug use leads to casual sex. Moreover, it also fails to mention that condom use can prevent HIV infection. So, all in all, the spot leaves many questions in viewers' minds about the tentative connection between drug use and HIV/AIDS that the ad sets up. Given such a weak argument, many adolescents could likely dispute the ad successfully, and this, in turn, would yield little, if any, influence on their future behaviors.

Beyond reception, memory and decision making are also important. According to the above theories, even though people may be persuaded by a message or set of messages, they need to recall the information learned and apply it in order for the campaign to be successful. In addition, it cannot be assumed that people will always use their knowledge and attitudes in a well-reasoned, logical manner. Because of this, an updated version of the theory of reasoned action, named the theory of planned behavior, includes *perceived behavioral control,* noting that the model only predicts well-thought actions.

Recent anti-smoking campaigns, for instance, rely on viewers to pay strict attention to their ads in order to follow the logic; they also include a very large number of facts designed to persuade youth not to use tobacco. Ads often contain information taken from "big tobacco" marketing plans, and one ad depicts a tobacco company board meeting, framing it as a 1970s-style sitcom called "Fair Enough," complete with a laugh track. Another spot shows employees following New Yorkers around the city with big, orange arrows and comments such as "Problems with Self-esteem," "Emotionally Insecure," "Probably Leads a Fairly Dull Existence," and "Grooming not a Strong Priority." The spot ends by explaining that the descriptions were taken from the tobacco company's consumer profiles, and the announcer says, "now that's customer appreciation for you." As you can see, the ad not only contains a lot of information but also offers an incredibly complex message. Although creative and attention getting, the ads may not have much impact on adolescent smoking. In particular, many youth don't "plan" to start smoking, but rather pick up the habit at times when they're not looking ahead to the long-term effects.

To explain how decisions are made without much thought, Fazio's MODE model suggests that such choices depend mainly on the strength of a connection between the concept at hand and positivity or negativity. For instance, adolescents' choice whether or not to experiment with illicit drugs, when made without a lot of thought, would depend on whether the concept of drug use immediately brings to mind good or bad thoughts. Recently, researchers have begun to apply Fazio's theory to anti-drug campaigns, and the studies show that ads designed to grab and hold youths' attention are not as effective as those that simply connect drugs with negativity again and again. Although this research is just beginning, initial results imply that traditional attention-getting strategies, for instance, those that say "using drugs supports terrorism," may not be as effective in reducing drug use as more subtle techniques that simply link drugs with negative sentiments.

—*Carson B Wagner*

See also Advertising Campaigns, Prosocial; Social Learning Theory/Social Cognitive Theory; Television, Prosocial Content of

FURTHER READINGS

Ajzen, I. (1991). The theory of planned behavior. *Organizational Behavior and Human Decision Processes, 50,* 179–211.

Bandura, A. (1977). *Social learning theory.* Englewood Cliffs, NJ: Prentice Hall.

Cialdini, R. B., Reno, R. R., & Kallgren, C. A. (1990). A focus theory of normative conduct: Recycling the concept of norms to reduce littering in public places. *Journal of Personality and Social Psychology, 58*(6), 1015–1026.

Fazio, R. H. (1990). Multiple processes by which attitudes guide behavior: The MODE model as an integrative framework. *Advances in Experimental Social Psychology, 23,* 75–109.

Flora, J. A. (2001). The Stanford community studies: Campaigns to reduce cardiovascular disease. In R. E. Rice & C. K Atkin (Eds.), *Public communication campaigns* (3rd ed., pp. 193–213). Thousand Oaks, CA: Sage.

McGuire, W. J. (2001). Input and output variables currently promising for constructing persuasive campaigns. In R. E. Rice & C. K. Atkin (Eds.), *Public communication campaigns* (3rd ed., pp. 22–48). Thousand Oaks, CA: Sage.

Salmon, C. T. (1989). *Information campaigns: Balancing social values and social change.* Newbury Park, CA: Sage

Wagner, C. B. (2001). *Unobtrusive measures and unreasoned action: Anti-drug ads and attitude strength.* Unpublished doctoral dissertation, University of Colorado at Boulder.

PUBLIC SERVICE ANNOUNCEMENTS (PSAs)

Since the advent of electronic media, there has been a proliferation of public service announcements (PSAs), including campaigns aimed at children and adolescents. However, the notion that mass media can be used for the society's betterment is hardly a recent development. As early as the late 1700s in the United States, print media were used to promote smallpox inoculation, slavery abolition, and women's rights, and in the years since, media have been mobilized to address myriad issues concerning the environment, energy, wildlife, health, international issues such as apartheid and nuclear weaponry, and social issues such as racism, sexism, and abortion. Attempts have taken many forms beyond advertising, from fiction books like *Uncle Tom's Cabin* to propaganda films and televised entertainment, but due to the persuasive nature of the form, over time, PSAs have become perhaps the most important mass media instrument in social marketing.

The purpose of social marketing is to persuade the public to think, feel, or act in accordance with the goals of the sponsoring agency, be it public or private, and PSAs concern issues both personal and social in nature. Often, when social marketing aims at issues generally supported by the public and policymakers, it is referred to as a *public service campaign*, but when it concerns topics and viewpoints not widely backed, it is labeled an *advocacy strategy*. Regardless of issue or viewpoint popularity, at a larger level, the domain of PSAs might be best comprehended in terms of social marketers' aims, or rather in what ways PSAs are intended to persuade.

Concerning the foci of influence, it is widely accepted that PSAs center around awareness and knowledge, attitudes and feelings, or behavior and intent, and various contents, forms, and argumentation styles are used to elicit such responses. Although researchers often measure differences in knowledge, awareness, attitudes, and affect as a result of PSA consumption, recording behavioral differences is not as easy. This is especially true when the behavior under consideration is far removed from the immediate viewing context, as are many of the behaviors that PSAs attempt to change, such as discouraging illicit drug use and promoting safe sex, a proper diet, or regular check-ups with a physician. As a result, attention is focused on measuring antecedent responses such as knowledge and attitudes, and it is assumed that related behaviors will follow. This theoretical response chain is widely recognized as the knowledge-attitude-behavior hierarchy of effects (K-A-B).

Although the categories of effects are widely agreed upon, classifying the ways in which PSAs attempt to influence cognitions, affect, and instincts or craving is not so clear-cut. Many state that social marketing attempts to make an impact in terms of either promotion or modification. For instance, PSAs can promote ideas and attitudes that help lead adolescents to practice safe sex, or they can be designed to modify existing behaviors such as underage smoking. However, other have argued that we should consider prevention separately from promotion. In other words, promoting engagement—for example, "Remember to brush three times a day!"—and promoting abstinence—for example, "Just say no to drugs!"—are theoretically different strategies; it might be better to term the latter *prevention* as opposed to "promoting abstinence."

This distinction might be better clarified with a discussion of William McGuire's inoculation theory, which says, in short, that PSAs promote knowledge, attitudes, and behaviors that will help people avoid succumbing to arguments favoring antisocial behaviors and in turn will help them resist engaging in such activities. Efforts are targeted toward at-risk populations, or those who are likely to encounter situations that favor antisocial behaviors, and the objective is to reach those audiences before they encounter the situation. However, PSAs may inadvertently direct attention toward topics that may otherwise not be a consideration, and in doing so, PSAs run the risk of promoting

the antisocial behavior itself, especially if viewers come to disagree with the arguments presented.

For instance, it has been shown that anti-drug PSAs can arouse adolescents' curiosity toward using illicit drugs. As such, even with a prevention focus, PSAs may raise issues among viewers who might otherwise never have thought of them, and in such instances, social marketers may do better to gain a deeper understanding of the issue at hand and promote ideas or activities that would lead audiences in a different direction entirely. An excellent example of a public service campaign influenced by this notion is Freevibe's "What's your anti-drug?", which promotes pastimes such as soccer, skateboarding, computers, drawing, reading, and school. But, because these PSAs frame the question with reference to illicit drugs, they may still pique adolescents' curiosity.

Regardless of a PSA's intent, however, an intimate understanding of the issue and the audience toward whom the ads are targeted is an invaluable tool in producing effective messages. Sufficiently conceptualizing the audience has implications even at the first point of contact, so that a message is not immediately dismissed as irritating, unclear, uninteresting, or lacking in credibility.

An excellent example of a program of research that has systematically studied the confluence of audience and issue regards adolescent sensation seeking and drug use, pioneered by Palmgreen, Donohew, and Harrington (2001). Sensation-seeking levels show a positive correlation with drug-taking risk, and their research has demonstrated that it is better to target high-sensation-seeking youths by provocatively stressing the dangers of drugs in high-sensation media outlets and programming. On the other hand, for low-level sensation seekers, it is better to focus on peer resistance and coping skills in a more serious manner and to insert the PSAs into less sensational programming. In sum, it is best to match as closely as possible the PSA and the context in which it is shown with various audience types, and this strategy also helps to avoid unintentionally introducing audiences to issues they may not (yet) be facing.

—*Carson B Wagner*

See also Public Health Campaigns

FURTHER READINGS

Atkin, C. K., & Freimuth, V. S. (2001). Formative evaluation research in campaign design. In R. E. Rice &

C. K. Atkin (Eds.), *Public communication campaigns* (3rd ed., pp. 125–145). Thousand Oaks, CA: Sage.

McGuire, W. J. (2001). Input and output variables currently promising for constructing persuasive campaigns. In R. E. Rice & C. K. Atkin (Eds.), *Public communication campaigns* (3rd ed., pp. 22–48). Thousand Oaks, CA: Sage.

Paisley, W. J. (2001). Public communication campaigns: The American experience. In R. E. Rice & C. K. Atkin (Eds.), *Public communication campaigns* (3rd ed., pp. 3–21). Thousand Oaks, CA: Sage.

Palmgreen, P., Donohew, L., & Harrington, N. G. (2001). Sensation seeking in antidrug campaign and message design. In R. E. Rice & C. K. Atkin (Eds.), *Public communication campaigns* (3rd ed., pp. 300–304). Thousand Oaks, CA: Sage.

Salmon, C. T., & Murray-Johnson, L. (2001). Communication campaign effectiveness: Critical distinctions. In R. E. Rice & C. K Atkin (Eds.), *Public communication campaigns* (3rd ed., pp. 49–68). Thousand Oaks, CA: Sage.

Sundar, S. S. (1999, Oct. 14). Statement before the subcommittee on criminal justice, drug policy, and human resources of the United States House of Representatives: Hearing on the Office of National Drug Control Policy (ONDCP) national youth anti-drug media campaign. Washington, DC.

Wagner, C. B. (1998). *Social cognition and anti-drug PSA effects on adolescent attitudes.* Unpublished master's thesis, Pennsylvania State University.

Wartella, E., & Middlestadt, S. (1991). The evolution of models of mass communication and persuasion. *Health Communication, 3*(4), 205–215.

WEBSITE

FreeVibe: www.whatsyourantidrug.com

PUBLIC TELEVISION

See EDUCATIONAL TELEVISION, PROGRAMMING IN; SESAME WORKSHOP

PURCHASE INFLUENCE ATTEMPTS

Children have an important influence on a variety of purchasing decisions, with respect to both child-related purchases such as toys, snacks, or sweets and everyday household purchases such as breakfast products and desserts. As children grow older, they even gain a say in their parents' choice of restaurants, holiday destinations, or cars.

Children seem to exert influence on their parents in two ways: direct and indirect. Children exert direct influence when they actively ask for or demand a product. Indirect (or passive) influence is the situation in which parents take account of the wants and preferences of their children when shopping. Many parents have a list in their head of the favorite brands of children, which they take into account when shopping. Research on children's purchase influence attempts has predominantly focused on the development and the consequences of children's purchase request behavior.

DEVELOPMENT OF PURCHASE INFLUENCE ATTEMPTS

From the moment of birth, children have particular preferences for tastes, colors, and sounds and communicate their wants and preferences to their parents. However, the initial expression of wants and preferences is primarily reactive: The child indicates when the stimulus offered is pleasant or unpleasant.

Once children reach 2 years of age, they begin to express their wants and preferences more actively. During this period, children discover that they have their own will and begin to experiment with it. Children now begin to ask for products that they like, especially when the products are in their immediate vicinity, for example, in a store or on television. During early childhood, the frequency of children's purchase influence attempts steadily increases, then starts to decrease again when children reach about 7 years of age. Around this age, children begin to make purchases independently, and they tend to exert more indirect or passive influence on their parents than younger children do.

Purchase Influence Style

As children mature, they display a growing ability to apply sophisticated influence techniques. Very young children quite often ask for products—and whine as well as show anger to persuade their parents to provide them. In contrast, older children tend to use more sophisticated persuasion techniques, such as negotiation, argumentation, soft-soaping, arousing sympathy, and even white lies. In addition, boys are generally more persistent in their requests for advertised products than girls are. They more often rely on forceful or demanding strategies when trying to persuade their parents, whereas girls are more likely to rely on tact and polite suggestions.

Types of Products Requested

In general, children ask for products that they consume themselves or in which they have a special interest, such as toys or products that come with a premium. The types of requests that children make to their parents change as they get older. Up to the age of 3 years old, children ask mainly for food, whereas 3-to-5-year-olds also start to ask for toys. Children up to the age of 7 or so primarily ask for candies, toys, and snacks. At about 9 years of age, children begin to ask for useful products, such as clothes, school stationery, and sport items. Finally, adolescents tend to ask for products with a social function, such as clothing and music equipment.

CONSEQUENCES OF CHILDREN'S PURCHASE INFLUENCE ATTEMPTS

The consequences of children's purchase influence attempts can generally be divided into intended and unintended consequences. Intended consequences include children's influence on family purchases—in other words, the extent to which children's requests result in actual purchase by the parent. Unintended consequences include the extent to which children's purchase influence attempts result in conflicts between parents and children.

Influence on Family Purchases

The influence of children on family purchasing has been increasing steadily since the 1970s, but since the 1980s it has grown dramatically. Children's increased influence on family purchases can be explained by various sociological changes over the past decades. Parents have higher incomes and better educational levels. In addition, they have fewer children and have them at a later age. There are more divorced parents, single-parent families, and families in which both parents work. These factors all contribute to the tendency for parents to indulge their children's wishes more often, to feel guilty more often, and to do what they can to ensure that their children want for nothing.

It has been estimated that children influence about one third of family purchases. However, a number of factors have been identified that interact with parental yielding to children's purchase influence attempts. First, research has demonstrated that children exert the greatest influence on products that they will use, including toys, clothes, and candies, or that they will enjoy, such as theme parks. Second, various studies have shown that parents yield to older children's request more often than to younger children's requests. Finally, children from families with a high income and from single-parent families tend to have more influence on family purchases.

Parent-Child Conflict

Children can be very persistent when asking for something. This can sometimes lead to conflicts between parents and children, for example, when they are in a supermarket or a toy store. Such parent-child conflicts have been shown to occur more frequently with younger than with older children. A first explanation is that younger children more often have difficulty delaying gratification than older children have. If young children see something as attractive, they focus all their attention on the enticing aspects of this stimulus and find it difficult to resist, which may increase the chance of parent-child conflict.

Second, the decrease in parent-child conflict as a result of influence attempts may be a result of children's growing ability to apply sophisticated persuasion techniques. As described above, young children quite often ask, whine, and show anger to persuade their parents. Older children, in contrast, tend to use more sophisticated persuasion techniques, such as negotiation, flattery, and white lies. Such sophisticated persuasion strategies generally lead to less parent-child conflict than the persuasion strategies of younger children do.

—*Moniek Buijzen and Patti M. Valkenburg*

See Also Adult Mediation of Advertising Effects; Advertising, Effects on Children of; Advertising, Intended vs. Unintended Effects of; Advertising, Parent-Child Conflict and; Advertising, Regulation of; Food Advertising to Children; Obesity

FURTHER READINGS

Buijzen, M., & Valkenburg, P. M. (2003). The unintended effects of television advertising: A parent-child survey. *Communication Research, 30,* 483–503.
Buijzen, M., & Valkenburg, P. M. (2003). The effects of television advertising on materialism, parent-child conflict, and unhappiness: A review of research. *Journal of Applied Developmental Psychology, 24,* 437–456.
Valkenburg, P. M. (2004). *Children's responses to the screen: A media psychological approach.* Mahwah, NJ: Erlbaum.

R

RADIO, HISTORY OF

Since the 1920s, children and adolescents have enjoyed tuning into radio. Over the years, they have listened to a wide range of programs, from radio versions of their favorite comic books to disc jockeys spinning popular Top 40 tunes. The radio industry has continually created content with children and adolescents in mind. Radio has been used as a means both to educate this age group and to advertise to this lucrative demographic. Radio programming for children and adolescents can be divided into two distinct periods: the golden age of radio before the arrival of television and radio after the emergence of TV.

RADIO'S GOLDEN AGE

Although experimentation with radio technology dates back to the 19th century, the medium was not used as a means of broadcasting content to a mass audience until the early 1920s. Over the next two decades, the radio audience grew rapidly, reaching a majority of U.S. homes by the mid-1930s. During this period, a number of innovations were introduced, including the creation of national radio networks and the adoption of advertising as the industry's main source of revenue. By the mid-1930s, radio was the most popular mass medium, simultaneously entertaining millions of households throughout the United States.

During radio's golden age, a period stretching roughly from the early 1930s to the mid-1940s, listeners had access to a wide range of programming content. A radio station's daily broadcast often featured a variety of 15-minute programs, including vaudeville-inspired comedy and variety shows, dramas and plays, daytime and evening serials, quiz and trivia shows, news and educational programs, and musical performances.

Through this period, many radio stations and networks offered programs targeted specifically at children. These shows, aired during the hours after school and on weekends, were popular with children. Reacting to children's desire to hear stories rather than music, the radio networks often created serial programs, ending each episode with a cliffhanger designed to bring the listener back to the next episode. Many popular programs, for example, *Little Orphan Annie*, *Captain Midnight*, and *Superman,* were based on comic books, a medium already popular with children. Other program formats popular with children at the time include comedies, mysteries, and plays.

Along with shows created especially for them, children enjoyed listening to programs created for adult audiences. Adult programs like *Myrt and Marge*, *Eno Crime Clues*, and *Rudy Vallee* were as popular with children as programs designed specifically for the age group. In the end, it appears as though the time of day a program was aired was more important for children's listening habits than the audience the producers intended to target.

During the golden age of radio, programs were created with funds from a national radio network or from a corporate sponsor. Shows containing no advertisements were considered sustaining programs and were created by radio networks to fill the radio day, while sponsored programs were funded with advertising dollars. Corporations hoping to advertise their products to children and their parents often sponsored children's programs during this time period. Programs advertised a wide range of products including food items and household goods. For instance, *Tarzan* promoted a chocolate milk beverage and *Fu Manchu* advertised a hand lotion.

RADIO AFTER TELEVISION

With the advent of television, radio underwent an identity crisis. Popular programs, such as *The Lone Ranger* and *The Life of Riley*, jumped from radio to television, leaving radio to find new content to fill the airwaves. Faced with the need to adapt or die, the industry shifted from comedies and dramas to a format system largely dominated by music. Replacing actors with disk jockeys, radio stations began specializing in genre music and experimenting with nonmusical formats such as talk radio and news programming. Children and adolescents embraced the change, particularly radio's focus on different styles of music. In the 1950s, teenagers were drawn in large numbers to rock and roll, and radio gave them what they wanted. Over the decades since, children and adolescents have continued to tune into to a wide range of music from Top 40 to country to rap.

In the 1990s, several stations and networks designed specifically for children emerged on the radio scene. Across the country, several cities introduced stations devoted solely to children, while Fox Broadcasting introduced a syndicated radio program. On a national level, several networks were launched, including Children's Media Network's Kid Star and Children's Broadcasting Corporation's Radio AAHS. By the end of the decade, both networks had failed, but a third children's network, ABC's Radio Disney, remained successful. Started in 1996, Radio Disney targets children between the ages of 2 and 11 years with a mix of pop music and songs from movie soundtracks. It also incorporates news and safety tips into the 24-hour programming feed.

Although the majority of young radio listeners today are tuning into music, they also listen to talk radio and educational programs. Adolescents are also taking an active role in the creation of radio shows. National Public Radio regularly features segments created by adolescents, including *Teenage Diaries* and news segments provided by Youth Radio, which also offers program content to a network of radio stations and distributes shows through the Internet.

Eighty years after it was first introduced, broadcast radio still captures the attention of children and adolescents. Once a medium that entertained young listeners with dramatic and comedic programs, today it offers young listeners a world of music and information.

—Charlene Simmons

See also Radio, International

FURTHER READINGS

Eisenberg, A. L. (1936). *Children and radio programs.* New York: Columbia University.

McCormick, M. (1996, November 9). Children's radio continues to liven up airwaves. *Billboard*, p. 58.

Sharrer, E. (2004). Children's programs. In C. Sterling (Ed.), *The museum of broadcast communications encyclopedia of radio* (pp. 319–323). New York: Fitzroy Dearborn.

Swartz, J. D., & Reinehr, R. R. (1993). *Handbook of old-time radio.* Metuchen, NJ: Scarecrow.

Taylor, C. (2000, March 25). Radio Disney tunes in young listeners and turns youth pop craze on its ear. *Billboard*, p. 78.

RADIO, INTERNATIONAL

Within today's media landscape, radio is regarded as a rather old medium. It has made its way into the people's everyday lives almost everywhere in the world. According to the latest edition of the UNESCO *Statistical Yearbook,* in 1999 an estimated 2.4 billion radio receivers were in use throughout the world. On average, there were 418 radio receivers for every 1,000 people, with clear differences between developing countries (245 radio receivers per 1,000 inhabitants) and industrialized countries (1,061 per 1,000 inhabitants).

Due to different political, economic, and cultural conditions, radio systems differ substantially among countries. At the same time, some common trends can be observed on the international level. One of these trends is that listening to the radio has become a secondary activity that engages listeners throughout the day; in the evening, when most people start to watch television, radio's reach goes down. Another trend, closely connected to the first one, is that music has become the core content of radio. Finally, most radio channels are formatted along strict principles that fix the distribution of word and music, the style of music, the way to address the listeners, and so on. The overall strategy is to provide reliable companionship throughout the day. There are different formats, mainly music dominated (e.g., AC or Adult Contemporary; CHR or Contemporary Hit Radio), but also including dedicated talk radio or culture-oriented channels.

With respect to the organization of radio, most countries have developed dual radio systems including a more or less balanced combination of public service broadcasters (funded by fees, taxes, donations, or advertising) and private broadcasters, including both commercial and noncommercial stations. Commercial radio is funded mainly by advertising revenues and thus follows the strategy of serving as a convenient companion throughout the day. Noncommercial radio includes a wide range of more or less institutionalized stations that are run for idealistic reasons, with the subcategory of so-called community radios being a particularly important part of many countries' radio landscape.

Compared to television, radio is easy to handle on the production side as well as on the recipient's side. Therefore, this medium is ideal for local and regional communication, for the community sector, and for nonprofit initiatives seeking expression on a public forum. Radio is still particularly important as a means of communication and education in developing countries. For example, in Africa, radio is regarded as the most valued, most credible, and most important news medium. More than 90% of the African population listens to the radio. This is due to several reasons. First, radio is highly compatible with the oral cultures in Africa. In providing local music and local language, radio supports identity formation and integration. Furthermore, unlike press media, it requires neither literacy on the part of listeners nor costly distribution systems on the part of broadcasters.

However, radio is not exclusively the medium of the neighborhood. Radio is also a highly international medium. After a long history in which international radio was used as a means of political influence, especially during World War II and the Cold War, today, many countries offer an international service distributed via shortwave or via satellite. Examples include BBC World Service, Radio France International (RFI), Radio Televisao Portuguesa Internacional (RTP), Deutsche Welle, and Voice of America. Such international radio broadcasts have often been—and still are—particularly important whenever dictatorial regimes try to restrict national media diversity. In these situations, national media lose credibility, and radio listeners look for independent information from alternative sources.

The BBC World Service is one of the most renowned international radio stations. It offers programming in 33 languages throughout the world. Although paid for by the British government, its programming is politically independent. News programs of BBC World Service are regularly rebroadcast by regional stations. In many countries, BBC World Service is the only news medium trusted by the population to be outside government influence. Beyond news, a broad range of education, entertainment, and sports is offered.

In the last decade, radio has been considerably affected by the advent and fast diffusion of the Internet, with the two media developing a close coalition. Via the Internet, people in any country of the world can listen to radio stations from any other country in the world, including general channels, thematic channels, Internet-only stations, and traditional stations that distribute their programs simultaneously via the Internet. Radio via the Internet can be produced and distributed for quite low cost and is available globally. However, not all people in all parts of the world enjoy the obligatory prerequisites for listening to this kind of radio—computer and Internet access. So far, even in industrialized countries, the use of Internet radio is quite low. In Germany, only 6% of the users of online media said they listen to Internet radio at least once a week.

There are a variety of initiatives regarding children's programming at both the international and national levels. The World Radio Forum (WRF) encourages partnerships between organizations and private companies to develop radio for, by, and with young people. The WRF champions child rights and aims to articulate values important for children and their communities. It has launched the Radio Manifesto, which defines children's needs and priorities with regard to radio, provides an international forum for those lobbying for children's and youth programming, and outlines standards for appropriate child-centered and youth-based programs.

Within the framework of the overall principle of "media activities and good ideas from, with, and for children," UNICEF tries to increase children's interest in their peers in other countries and to overcome barriers between cultures. As one part of its activities, a UNICEF radio service for children has been founded. The programming focuses on children's rights. The overall range of topics is broad; for example, on February 24, 2006, there were items on AIDS, violence against children, and camel riding in Pakistan, as well as the diary of a girl living in Iraq.

BBC's Afghan Education Project (AEP) has developed Radio Education for Afghan Children (REACH) to help address the educational needs of Afghan children ages 6 to 16 years who have missed most or all of their schooling. It is hoped that, by listening to the weekly radio programs at home, children will be exposed to Afghanistan's traditions, culture, and history, as well as receiving information about present-day concerns such as mine awareness and health education.

On the national level, some Internet-based initiatives try to promote the idea and availability of children's radio. For example, the *Radio4kids* website in the United Kingdom sets out "to thoroughly review and monitor the provision of radio offered to children in the UK." The core aims of this initiative include to promote the concept and idea of radio being produced by children for children, to campaign for the eventual setting up of a national radio station that showcases young people's work, and to provide guidance and training to teachers and others involved with children to help produce, edit, and submit material to potential broadcasters.

—*Uwe Hasebrink*

See also British Broadcasting Corporation (BBC); Media Effects; Radio, History of; Radio, Listeners' Age and Use of

FURTHER READINGS

Jankowski, N., & Prehn, O. (Eds.). (2002). *Community media in the information age: Perspectives, findings, and policies.* Cresskill, NJ: Hampton Press.

McNeill, S. (2004, April 20). *Identity and cultural diversity.* Speech presented to the Fourth World Summit on Media for Children and Adolescents in Rio de Janeiro. Retrieved February 25, 2006, from http://www.midia tiva.tv/index.php/midiativa/content/view/full/821

Oehmichen, E., & Schröter, C. (2004). Die OnlineNutzer Typologie. *Media Perspektiven, 8,* 386–393.

Wittmann, F. (2003). Medienlandschaft Westafrika: Chancen und Barrieren der Kommunikationsflüsse. Retrieved from http://www.medienheft.ch/kritik/biblio thek/k20_WittmannFrank.html).

UNESCO. (1999). *Statistical yearbook 1999.* Retrieved March 28, 2006, from www.uis.unesco.org/TEMPLATE/ html/CultAndCom/Table_IV_S_3.html

WEBSITES

Information on Radio Initiatives for Afghan Children: http://www.comminit.com/experiences/pds22004/experiences-511.html
Radio 4 Kids: http://www.radio4kids.co.uk/index2.html
World Radio Forum: http://www.worldradioforum.org/index.shtml

RADIO, LISTENERS' AGE AND USE OF

Research on radio uses deals with what listeners seek from radio stations and what these listeners receive in return. Age is one important factor in how people use radio, with children using radio more frequently as they get older, especially for listening to music. The study of radio use (as contrasted with radio effects) assumes the ultimate power of the listener and falls under the umbrella of the conditional effects of the media. In particular, uses and gratifications theory looks at what people do with media, rather than what the media do to people.

Uses and gratifications theory was first developed in the early 1940s by such researchers as Herta Herzog and Paul Lazarsfeld (http://www.britannica.com/bcom/eb/article/6/0,5716,48556+1+47446,00.html?query=lazarsfeld%20paul) as they studied radio listeners. It was an early response to research on the direct effects of media, which assumed that all media had powerful and uniform effects.

A 1951 study showed that children had different uses for adventure stories based on their integration into groups of peers. Those in peer groups used the stories as a source of games, while those outside of peer groups used the stories for fantasies. The researcher concluded that different people can use the same communication message for very different purposes. Contemporary theorists such as Alan Rubin have isolated two categories of motives for media use: instrumental (learning, social) versus ritual (escape, habit, relaxation).

About the same time, another study looked at the listening habits of the young radio audience at a time when serialized dramas for children were still available on network radio. In the 1950s, however, very young audiences were beginning to discover television (e.g., *Howdy Doody, Captain Kangaroo*). While the youngsters may have left radio for TV, their adolescent brothers and sisters were drawn to radio, where they could hear rock and roll music and performers such as Elvis Presley.

Since the advent of television in the 1950s, radio has become of less interest to children, so research has focused more on television, especially on its potential for harming children. Television attracts all categories of young people and provides them with the widest range of satisfactions. Even proprietary media research (e.g., by media research companies such as Arbitron and Nielsen) regularly reports radio listening data only for children ages 12 and older, typically because advertisers assume younger children gravitate to television. Children age 2 years and older are counted as television viewers.

Music is the only other medium that ranks close to television, particularly for adolescents, because it can be both the focus of attention and a background medium, has both social and individual uses, and suits a diversity of moods. Radio competes with recorded music, and its use has declined as technology creates alternative delivery systems. In recent years, adolescents have shown much greater interest in recorded audio media and other digital personal media (e.g., iPODs, other MP3 players) that allow music to be downloaded and stored rather than accessed via live broadcasts.

Academic research on radio is somewhat limited in recent years because of attention to television and the Internet, although concern about music lyrics produced notable work in the 1980s and early 1990s. Peter Christenson found age correlates with the amount of radio listening and whether or not listening is done alone or with others. His work confirms earlier research that found a key difference between television and radio with regard to youth: Young people tend to use music and radio to get away from parents, possibly because parents are more willing to permit the unsupervised use of these media than of television. Parents who ban computers and television from bedrooms do not often forbid radio listening. Christenson founds that benefits of radio listening (e.g., music, information, distraction, background noise) do not differ by age or gender. He also confirmed 1972 reports that about a third of sixth graders listen to radio 2 or more hours per day. By the third grade, 80% of children have a favorite station, up from 50% at the previous grade level. He concluded that preteens are "eavesdropping" on the teen world via radio and recorded music, causing occasional concern to parents. In the 1980s, research explored the public policy implications of music lyrics at a time of heightened interest before the labeling of CDs. One study found that African American children consumed 25% more radio than white peers, twice the 12% difference between the groups' television use.

Specialized research is still important to the radio industry. A recent Arbitron survey found that about 90% of 6-to-11-year-olds tuned into their favorite radio stations 8 to 9 hours each week. Many children develop surprising loyalty to stations and formats. The Arbitron study showed just how important the preteen market is to advertisers. A subsequent study made phone calls to parents and kids who had completed listening diaries from the first survey. The study revealed that children have very distinct listening and format preferences that can be targeted to deliver specific messages. In Los Angeles, for example, 67% of girls ages 6 to 11 years preferred a Top 40 station, whereas 71% of the boys in the same age range preferred a rhythmic contemporary hits radio (CHR) station.

Arbitron's study found that in households with young children, listening to the radio is still a family activity after school. The most likely locale for tuning in to a child's favorite station is the family car, where 85% most often listen to the radio. According to the study findings, children chose the radio station either all of the time (34%) or some of the time (38%). The study showed that kids like radio commercials and are receptive to radio ads that are fun and informative. They are also likely to respond to the products and services being advertised and frequently ask their parents to make purchases on their behalf.

—*Douglas A. Ferguson*

See also Bedrooms, Media Use in; Radio, History of

FURTHER READINGS

Christenson, P. G. (1994). Childhood patterns of music uses and preferences. *Communication Reports, 7*(2), 136–144.

Christenson, P. G., & DeBenedittis, P. (1986). "Eavesdropping" on the FM band: Children's use of radio. *Journal of Communication, 36*(2), 27–38.

Fetto, J. (2002). Young listeners. *American Demographics, 24*(11), 11.

RATING SYSTEMS, PARENTAL USE OF

Most electronic media industries employ a rating system to identify content that parents might find objectionable for children. Ratings systems usually include a set of symbols that identify age levels for which content might be appropriate; many also include letters or phrases that identify the specific type of mature content. The ostensible purpose of these systems is to allow parents to gauge media content without having to prescreen it. At the same time, creation of these ratings systems builds some goodwill for media industries with their audiences, advocacy groups, and government regulators.

Parents' use of media ratings systems has, according to the Kaiser Family Foundation, been relatively stable. About half of all parents in their surveys say they have used those ratings, but only one quarter reported using them frequently to guide children's viewing choices. Kaiser's surveys have also reported similar rates of adoption for video game ratings and the advisory stickers used to label explicit content in recorded music. However, the adoption rate for movie ratings remains higher; about three quarters of parents report using movie ratings. This might be due to the fact that the Motion Picture Association of America (MPAA) film ratings have been available longer (since 1968). Two generations of parents have grown up with and understand these ratings.

Effective use of any media ratings system depends on parents knowing their meaning. This has been less of a challenge with older ratings systems like the MPAA ratings. More recently developed systems, such as the television ratings adopted in 1997, fostered some confusion among parents. National surveys conducted in the first 3 years of that rating system found that although a majority of parents said they were aware of the ratings, many could not accurately identify the meaning of all the symbols. Follow-up studies conducted in the early 2000s showed that about half of parents were at least fairly well informed about the ratings symbols' meanings. However, one study conducted by the Annenberg Public Policy Center found that children were more aware and knowledgeable about the ratings than were their parents. To date, there are no available studies that test parents' knowledge of other media ratings systems.

Perhaps a larger question, however, concerns parents' knowledge of less visible ratings, such as those used for Internet content. The system developed by the Internet Content Rating Association (ICRA) is currently the most widely used. These ratings are designed to be used by Internet browsers as a filter on downloaded content. Widely used browsers, such as

Internet Explorer and Netscape, allow users to set filtering levels by changing the browser's internal settings. Brief words or phrases are used to describe the various filtering levels for sex, nudity, violence, and language. For example, Internet Explorer's options for nudity range from "no nudity" to "provocative frontal nudity." Some phrases are accompanied by a brief description or example, but the majority are not. Parents who wish to actively use these ratings must learn how to set the browser's settings and visit the ICRA's website for information about them. To date, no published study has presented data about whether parents do this or simply accept the browser's default settings (meaning the filter is off).

Uncertainty about a medium's rating system has obvious implications for its use. Focus group studies conducted by researchers at Michigan State University and the University of Pennsylvania confirmed parents' confusion over the television ratings system. Some, for example, thought that the TV-Y7 rating meant that the show was intended for children 7 years and younger; others believed that the show should be viewed only by children older than 7 years. Furthermore, many of those parents interviewed expressed disagreement with the standards used to assign ratings to television shows. A study by David A. Walsh and Douglas Gentile, published in the journal *Pediatrics*, documented this disagreement. Those researchers assembled panels of parents who were asked to rate television shows, movies, and other content. Each was asked if the content would be suitable for toddlers, children, and teens. While the parent panels agreed with the industry ratings in a majority of cases, many instances of disagreement were noted, with the parents rejecting material that media producers and film raters had approved for children.

Parents who are confused or disagree with a ratings system must evaluate content on their own. This judgment might be made after prescreening the material in question, but this is seldom possible given the thousands of movie, television, and recording titles targeted toward young audiences each year (not to mention the vast number of websites accessible to children). Two factors might guide parents' choice of ratings use or reliance on their own media knowledge. The first is parents' existing attitudes about a medium's potential harmful effects on children. The more a parent believes television can encourage bad behavior, for instance, the more television ratings might be used to restrict children's viewing. This is also the case for the second factor, parents' current level of media supervision. Two studies found that ratings were more likely to be used by parents who already restricted children's viewing. Both reasoned that those parents might be using ratings to confirm their intuitive judgment about content. Hence, ratings systems (no matter how simple or convenient) do not seem to encourage new viewing restrictions from parents.

—Ron Warren

See also Internet Content Rating Association (ICRA); Motion Picture Association of America (MPAA); Television Rating Systems, Parental Uses of

FURTHER READINGS

Abelman, R. (1999). Preaching to the choir: Profiling TV advisory ratings users. *Journal of Broadcasting & Electronic Media, 43,* 529–540.

Greenberg, B., Rampoldi-Hnilo, L., & Mastro D. (Eds.). (2000). *The alphabet soup of television program ratings.* Cresskill, NJ: Hampton Press.

Kaiser Family Foundation. (2001). *Parents and the V-chip: How parents feel about TV, the TV ratings system, and the V-chip.* Menlo Park, CA: Author.

Walsh, D. A., & Gentile, D. A. (2001). A validity test of movie, television, and video-game ratings. *Pediatrics, 107,* 1302–1308.

Warren, R. (2002). Preaching to the choir? Parents' use of TV ratings to mediate children's viewing. *Journalism & Mass Communication Quarterly, 4,* 867–886.

RAVES

Originating in Europe during the 1980s, raves became popular in major coastal American cities during the early 1990s, subsequently spreading to other metropolitan areas. The participation of youth in these events transcends the boundaries of any one nation.

In the beginning, typical raves were late-night dance parties that featured electronic music, occurring in rented or "borrowed" settings. The music was a mixture of digitally created sounds and previously recorded music. Distinct genres included house, jungle, trance, techno, breakbeat, hardcore, and downtempo. Disc jockeys (DJs) spun music, compiling their own unique show, which featured a combination of music, sounds, beats, and lights to create an entire setting for an intense and unique dance scene. DJs attracted a following like any other musical performer, and their artistic styles were promoted by organizers who book events at different venues and nightclubs.

Use of drugs, particularly ecstasy and other "club drugs," became associated with these events, and a variety of drug-related paraphernalia (e.g., pacifiers, lollipops, and glow sticks) emerged in these settings. Although the prevalence and type of drug use was not well measured at early events, the popular view was that this was a social setting where drug use was prevalent and accepted. Incidents of drug-related overdoses were featured on the front pages of major newspapers, and a few deaths brought a public outcry for action by authorities. In addition, other medical concerns—overheated venues, lack of sufficient hydration following vigorous physical exercise associated with dancing, and the availability of illegal substances of unknown content—resulted in the emergence of safety networks formed by young people themselves. One such network is DanceSafe, a U.S. and Canadian national coalition of organizations in which volunteers promote health and safety among partygoers. In addition, this coalition addresses questions about drugs, pill testing, drug use, and safety of individuals, as well as informing consumers about various legal actions being taken across the United States relating to these events.

Gradually, the original ad hoc rave scene gave way to electronic music dance events (EMDEs) offered in established nightclubs. Although nightclubs provided a more business-oriented setting, the association with drug use on premises continued. In 2003, the U.S. Senate passed the Illicit Drug Anti-Proliferation Act (also known as the Rave Act), which specifically prohibits an individual from "knowingly opening, maintaining, managing, controlling, renting, leasing, making available for use, or profiting from any place for the purpose of manufacturing, distributing, or using any controlled substance, and for other purposes." Thus, businesses are under increasing pressure to control their environments and to eliminate drug use on premises. However, little attention has been given to how this might be accomplished.

Attendees at EMDEs are generally young (ages 18 to 25), ethnically diverse, and of both genders. Especially important, these events attract both college students and young working people, thus providing a social setting with an interface between classes. Events are sometimes advertised to attract specialized populations such as gay/lesbian events or special theme nights (e.g., 80's night or holiday parties). Advertising for the events occurs in newspapers, over the Internet, through flyers, and sometimes via word of mouth.

The amount of illicit drug use that occurs at EMDEs has been investigated in few scientific studies. These studies tend to provide more knowledge about recent history of drug use among attendees than about drug use on premises. Recent research from a small set of events suggests that the attendees use drugs prior to the event and that very few attendees convert from no drug use to drug use on the premises (based on biological assays and self-reports). Nonetheless, this research suggests that the proportion of attendees who leave the EMDEs and are positive for drug use is high for many events. There is considerable variation in the proportion across different types of events, however.

In the past, raves were particularly associated with the use of ecstasy. However, the overall rates of ecstasy use in the general population have declined since 2003, and the proportion of attendees of club events who are found positive for ecstasy use has been under 10% in recent studies (compared to 30% in studies prior to 2003). Other forms of amphetamines remain popular at these events (e.g., methamphetamine, speed, and crystal meth). In addition, alcohol is commonly used by attendees of EMDEs and is served at most of the events.

A number of risky behaviors associated with EMDEs are of concern from a public health standpoint. Although drug overdoses are not common, they can occur. An environmental mix of drug use, overheated venues, and lack of hydration, coupled with the physical exertion of dancing, can create health problems. Other social and behavioral risks associated with drug use include sexual risk taking, violence, and driving under the influence of alcohol or drugs. In addition, risks of legal consequences for drug sales or possession are also of concern.

To date, prevention efforts have focused on providing information to individuals through volunteer organizations. Laws have been used to pressure businesses to police and enforce a no-drugs policy on premises. However, many club drugs come in pill form, and these drugs are easy to conceal and to consume. Finally, it is not clear what characteristics of events (e.g., genre of music being played, type of venue) and attendees (e.g., age, gender, educational or occupational status) are associated with increased risk of drug use and subsequent harmful outcomes. These emerging findings suggest that more deliberate investigation of this environment is needed to clarify both the need for preventive interventions and possible targets for these interventions.

—Brenda A. Miller and Debra Furr-Holden

See also Anti-Drug Media Campaigns; Music Genres, Dance/House/Techno; Music Genres, Heavy Metal

FURTHER READINGS

Arria, A., Yacoubian, G., Fost, E., & Wish, E. D. (2002). Ecstasy use among club rave attendees. *Archives of Pediatrics and Adolescent Medicine, 156*, 295–296.

Leinwand, D. (2002, November 13). Cities crack down on raves. *USA Today,* pp. 1–2.

Miller, B. A., Furr-Holden, C. D., Voas, R. B., & Bright, K. (2005). Emerging adults' substance use and risky behaviors in club settings. *Journal of Drug Issues, 35*(2), 357–378.

Yacoubian, G. S., Boyle, C. L., Harding, C. A., & Loftus, E. A. (2003). It's a rave new world: Estimating the prevalence and perceived harm of ecstasy and other drug use among club rave attendees. *Journal of Drug Education, 33*(2), 187–196.

WEBSITES

Ishkur's Guide to Electronic Music: http://www.di.fm/edmguide/edmguide.html

READING, HISTORY OF

Insofar as it is defined as the ability to make sense of certain patterns of signs, the activity of reading has always been a hallmark of human life. Modern scientists interpret the human-made notches found on unearthed prehistoric bones as ample proof of the early human's ability to and inclination toward inscribing meaning onto objects, thus conserving that object for later appraisals. The phenomenon of reading is intimately connected to that of writing, and the histories of the two modes of communication are intertwined. In its early stages, reading was always done aloud, and the transition to silent reading did not occur until the 7th century AD. Early efforts at teaching children to read used texts written for adults, and not until the 18th century was there a significant amount of literature specifically for children.

Table 1 International Literacy Rates, 2002

Country	Adult Literacy Rate (males)	Adult Literacy Rate (females)	Youth Literacy Rate (males)	Youth Literacy Rate (females)
Albania	99 percent	98 percent	99 percent	99 percent
Bangladesh	50	31	58	41
Brazil	86	87	93	96
Burundi	58	44	67	65
Cambodia	81	59	85	76
China	95	87	99	99
Ecuador	92	90	96	96
Ghana	82	66	94	90
India	68	45	80	65
Indonesia	92	83	99	98
Iran, Islamic Rep.	84	70	96	92
Israel	97	93	100	99
Latvia	100	100	100	100
Portugal	95	91	100	100
Romania	98	96	98	98
Russian Federation	100	99	100	100
South Africa	87	85	92	92
Spain	99	97	100	100
Syrian Arab Republic	91	74	97	93

SOURCE: Data from World Bank, *Economic Outcomes: 2005 World Development Indicators*. Retrieved from http://devdata.worldbank.org/eoutcomes.pdf

NOTE: The World Development Indicators database, from which these figures are taken, does not contain relevant data about the United States. According to the *CIA World Fact Book*, in 1999, 97% of the U.S. population could read and write. Data available at: http://www.cia.gov/cia/publications/factbook/geos/us.html

However, beginning with the second half of the 20th century, children's literature became big business, with writers such as J. K. Rowling (author of the *Harry Potter* books) enjoying impressive financial gains from the selling of their books, toy branding rights, and movie copyrights.

DEFINITION AND EARLY HISTORY

Reading can be defined as the activity of assigning meaning to abstract signs created by a human being through the undertaking of writing. One could trace the beginnings of writing (and therefore of reading as well) to about 4000 BC, when the activity of Sumerian scribes underwent a major change. Prior to that time, abstract signs (e.g., the crude drawing of a house) were understood by virtue of their visual similarity to the object they represented. After 4000 BC, people began to interpret a sign by virtue of the standardized sound associated with it. One was now reading a language, rather

than deciphering a series of graphical representations of objects. Reading, at this point, was done exclusively aloud. The responsibilities of a scribe included recording commercial agreements, speeches, and royal proclamations, as well as reciting such recordings when prompted. Reading was speaking with the aid of a written text.

CONTINUOUS WRITING AND THE TENDENCY TO READ ALOUD

The ancient Sumerian, Phoenician, and Hebrew scribes did not use vowels in their writings, but they separated individual words using punctuation and spaces. Working with an alphabet developed by the Phoenicians, the Greeks changed both of these conventions, inserting vowels in the text, but dropping the separation. Also picked up by the Romans in the second century, this unbroken kind of writing became known as *scriptura continua*. Contemporary studies of language and reading (both ethnographical and clinical) show that continuous writing requires more cognitive work on the part of the reader than broken text does. Coupled with investigations into children's ability to read silently, these studies point to a strong connection between the manner in which writing is organized and displayed and the manner in which people read the text. Children have thus been found to be partial to using scriptura continua, as this kind of writing closely resembles the oral speech to which they are already accustomed. The lack of word separation, however, prevents them from quickly acquiring the ability to recognize a word by merely glancing at it, without initially adding individual letter-sounds. Because of such difficulties, children who are learning to read will do so aloud—a maneuver that allows them the luxury of hearing language, in addition to seeing it on paper.

WORD SEPARATION AND THE ABILITY TO READ SILENTLY

The seventh century AD saw the reintroduction of word separation in Indo-European languages, initially undertaken by Irish and Anglo-Saxon scribes. For the next 10 centuries, discontinuous writing spread throughout the rest of Europe. At this historical juncture, the activity of reading aloud slowly began to give way to silent reading. Scriptura continua had made it necessary for the readers' eyes to wander along the text ahead of their voice so they could identify "readable" units of language. The spaces between words, however, afforded readers more flexibility in terms of eye movement across the pages. Quickly jumping from word to word was now possible, and the advantage of hearing your own reading aloud diminished in importance. Today, the structure of the written language continues to influence the manner in which reading was undertaken, even though similar languages with different scripts do exist and are often mutually comprehensible.

TEACHING CHILDREN

Although most human societies in history gave much thought to educating their youth, the manner in which this process was conceived of differed widely. Ancient cultures such as the Romans, the Greeks, and the Hebrews tended to focus their educational efforts on preparing children to become worthy members of a specific community (political, military, or religious in nature). Most educational materials, therefore, were not designed specifically for children but, rather, for a general citizenry. When people began to formally teach children in sixth-century Britain, Christian monks used primarily religious texts written for an adult audience. For entertainment purposes, children read historical narratives and fables (e.g., the *Iliad, Aesop's Fables*). During the 15th and 16th centuries, the rise of a Western European middle class brought about an increased interest in juvenile education, and lesson books specifically prepared for children began to appear.

EARLY CHILDREN'S LITERATURE

It was only after the widespread translation and publication of Charles Perrault's 1698 collection of fairy tales, however, that a genuine "children's literature" came into being in Europe. Perrault's stories—Sleeping Beauty, Puss in Boots, Little Red Riding Hood, and Cinderella, along with others that would become famous around the world—were arguably the first texts written primarily for the entertainment of children (and not for their instruction). For 50 years, however, such fairy tales barely trickled into Europe's countries, and the vast majority of children had no access to them. That situation began to change in 1744, when John Newbery opened a press and a bookstore in London specifically meant to cater to children's literary needs. The widely popular products of Newbery's enterprises (e.g., the *Little Pretty Pocket Book*) were followed, at the beginning of the 19th century, by the publication of the Grimm brothers' fairy tales and, in 1845, by the translation in English of stories by Hans Christian Andersen, to this day the most popular children's writer. The rest of the century witnessed an explosion of children's literature, spurred by the work of such authors as Lewis Carroll (*Alice's Adventures in Wonderland,* 1865), Frank Baum (*The Wizard of Oz,* 1900), Robert L. Stevenson (*Treasure Island,* 1883), and Mark Twain (*The Adventures of Tom Sawyer,* 1876, and *The Adventures of Huckleberry Finn,* 1884).

LITERACY RATES

The Puritan culture of colonial America stressed the importance of education as a way of acquiring necessary knowledge, such as the ability to read the Bible. The widespread informal teaching sessions conducted by New England women in their houses, and the subsequent establishment of formal educational institutions, accounted for higher rates of literacy in the New World than in Europe. Due to historical disagreements about the definition of literacy, as well as the dearth of statistical data, little information exists on the exact literacy levels of pre-19th-century America. Existing estimates are based on analyses of signatures on old documents, a method that accounts for the lack of data on early children's, women's, or minority's literacy rates. By 1650, it is thought that 60% of white, male Americans were able to read. In 1840, the U.S. census included a question about illiteracy, but the resulting data suffer from the bias of self-reporting. In 1979, only 0.6% of the U.S. population was reported to be illiterate, which accounted for just under 1 million people. According to the United Nations, in 2003, the United States was ranked 10th in the world in terms of literacy rates.

In 2000, at the U.N. Millennium Summit, the world's countries agreed to make efforts to achieve universal primary education by 2015. At the time of that decision, according to World Bank estimates, 115 million children (62 million of whom were girls) did not benefit from any type of formal education. Almost half of those children lived in sub-Saharan Africa. The 2015 target has been widely criticized, and politicians and public policy specialists doubt that it can be achieved.

—*Razvan Sibii*

See also Books for Children; Cognitive Script Theory; Digital Literacy; Literacy; Reading, Literacy and; Reading, Patterns of

FURTHER READINGS

Fischer, S.R. (2003). *A history of reading*. London: Reaktion Books.

Kaestle, C. F., Damon-Moore, H., Stedman, L. C., & Tinsley, K. (1991). *Literacy in the United States: Readers and reading since 1880*. New Haven, CT: Yale University Press.

Manguel, A. (1996). *A history of reading*. New York: Viking.

Saenger, P. (1997). *Space between words: The origins of silent reading*. Stanford, CA: Stanford University Press.

READING, IMPACT OF TV ON

Since television's emergence as a mass medium, there has been a concern that it would affect reading among children, and since the early 1950s, a considerable body of research has addressed the issue. However, from the beginning, there has been little agreement among researchers as to the strength, direction, or even the existence of such a relationship.

DISPLACEMENT THEORY

The main theoretical perspective informing research in this area is displacement theory, which basically states that TV viewing takes time away from reading and other activities beneficial to children's development. However, the earliest studies in both the United States and Europe failed to find consistent evidence for such an effect. Rather, it appears that other mass media and play activities are television's main competitors and that children who neglect reading because of TV would neglect reading for something else if TV were not available. Moreover, far from displacing reading, some early studies even indicated that TV might actually be stimulating it by awakening interest in new subjects.

FROM BIVARIATE TO MULTIVARIATE RESEARCH

Although there has never been consistent evidence that television displaces reading, by the 1980s, a substantial number of studies had reported negative correlations between reading achievement and TV viewing. However, many of these studies were based on cross-sectional data employing bivariate analyses that failed to control for possible mediating variables; as a result, it is impossible to address the question of causality. This led to the search for more sophisticated research designs making it possible to analyze different groups of children, different types of television content, and different areas of academic achievement. The results of such research considerably refined the nature of the relationship by identifying significant mediating factors such as age (TV does not inhibit reading achievement among young children but does do so among teenagers), gender (in general boys watch more TV and have lower reading scores than do girls), cognitive development (among same-age younger children, the cognitively more developed watch more TV than the cognitively less developed, whereas the opposite is the case among older children and adolescents), and academic achievement (with curvilinear differences between high, average, and low academic achievers). Socioeconomic status differences, too, influence both TV-viewing frequency and reading achievement.

SOURCE: © Baby Blues Partnership, Kings Features Syndicate.

LONGITUDINAL STUDIES

In an attempt to bring some coherence to these disparate sets of results, some researchers have created large-scale, longitudinal designs employing multivariate analyses. In one such study, Rosengren and Windahl concluded that TV viewing could be both a positive and a negative influence, depending on the type of content viewed, the context surrounding the viewing, and the developmental stage of the viewers. In another study, Keith Roe tested the efficacy of the various approaches by comparing *negative models* (TV viewing leads to lower reading test scores), *positive models* (more viewing leads to higher reading test scores), and *school models* (school-based factors such as motivation and academic self-concept better explain reading test scores than do external factors such as media use). Although the results provided support for each perspective, the negative model appeared to be stronger than the positive model, while the strongest and most parsimonious results were provided by the school model. These and other studies also reaffirmed the importance of age, gender, and socioeconomic status in mediating the postulated relationships.

IMPACT OF TELEVISION: STILL NO CONSENSUS

Nevertheless, taken as a whole, the contradictory nature of the available evidence still leads researchers reviewing the field to draw directly conflicting conclusions. For example, in one of the most extensive reviews, Susan Neuman concluded that there is no reliable, replicable evidence for the postulated (negative) effects relationship. According to her, the critical factor is less the medium of communication than the family learning environment. Conversely, following their review, Koolstra and van der Voort, while admitting that the evidence is mixed and inconclusive, nevertheless came to the conclusion that a negative effect on children's reading as a result of TV exposure remains the most plausible working hypothesis. The results of their own studies indicated a weak TV-induced deterioration in children's attitudes toward, and ability to concentrate on, reading. Meanwhile, following a recent longitudinal study of German children, Ennemoser concluded that despite some evidence for a causal relationship between television and reading achievement, the underlying mechanism of the television effect remains unclear, with conventional hypotheses unsuited to its complexity.

Clearly, the case is still under examination, and the jury is still out.

—*Keith Roe*

See also Cognitive Development, Media and; Digital Literacy; Educational Television, Effects of; School-Age Children, Impact of the Media on; Social Class; Television, Child Variables and Use of; Television, Viewer Age and

FURTHER READINGS

Ennemoser, M. (2003). Television effects in kindergarten and elementary school grades: Causes, explanatory hypotheses, and differential effects. *Nervenheilkunde, 22*(9), 443–456.

Huston, A. C., Wright, J. C., Marquis, J., & Green, S. B. (1999). How young children spend their time: Television and other activities. *Developmental Psychology, 35*(4), 912–925.

Koolstra, C. M., & van der Voort, T. W. A. (1996). Longitudinal effects of television on children's leisure-time reading: A test of three explanatory models. *Human Communication Research, 23*(1), 4–35.

Mutz, D. C., Roberts, D. F., & Vanvuren, D. P. (1993). Reconsidering the displacement hypothesis: Television's influence on children's time use. *Communication Research, 20*(1), 51–75.

Neuman, S. B. (1991). *Literacy in the television age.* Norwood, NJ: Ablex.

Raeymakers, K. (2002). Young people and patterns of time consumption in relation to print media. *European Journal of Communication, 17*(3), 369–383.

Roe, K., Eggermont, S., & Minnebo, J. (2001). Media use and academic achievement: Which effects? *Communications: The European Journal of Communication, 26*(1), 39–58.

Rosengren, K. E., & Windahl, S. (1990). *Media matter: TV use in childhood and adolescence.* Norwood, NJ: Ablex.

Vandewater, E. A., & Bickham, D. S. (2004). The impact of educational television on young children's reading in the context of the family. *Journal of Applied Developmental Psychology, 25*(6), 717–728.

Wright, J. C., Huston, A. C., Murphy, K. C., St. Peters, M., Scantlin, R., & Kotler, J. (2001). The relations of early television viewing to school readiness and vocabulary of children from low-income families: The early window project. *Child Development, 72*(5), 1347–1366.

READING, LITERACY AND

Literacy is defined as the cognitive processing of text information, a motivational attitude toward reading, and the integration of texts into everyday life. Cognitive processing involves comprehending words and sentences, creating meaning from them, and integrating the contents into existing knowledge. Motivational attitude means expecting to benefit from reading, as well as the cognitive or a aesthetic processes involved, and making reading choices based on interests. Readers integrate text content into everyday life by connecting what they read to their own experiences, making subjective or objective evaluations, or transforming the text into priming for behavioral action.

THE READER'S COGNITIVE APPRENTICESHIP

Literacy is much more than the ability to recognize letters and to assign phonemes to them. Reading provides access to the cultural conventions people use to communicate and to understand their social environment. Cultural techniques are acquired through guided participation. Like the process of learning crafts, reading is taught to children through presentation and participation, that is, when a parent reads aloud to the child. In the beginning, the parent serves as a model for handling books appropriately (modeling) and then encourages and assists the child in retelling a picture story (coaching, scaffolding). As time goes by, the parent decreases the amount of assistance given to the child (fading). Later in the process, adults can encourage the child to talk about reading experiences (articulation) and think about different reading strategies (reflection). The learning processes of articulation and reflection are often found in academic reading instruction. To foster reading progress, there should be a close fit between the child's reading abilities and the support offered by the expert.

PARENTAL STRATEGIES IN STORY READING

Parents with different cultural backgrounds act differently when reading to preschoolers. The frequency of reading depends on ethnicity, child's age, number of siblings, and parents' education. Some researchers distinguish between parental "describers" and "comprehenders." Describers encourage the child to label and describe pictures, while comprehenders make sure that children draw conclusions beyond description and include personal experiences in the conversation about pictures and stories. Describers are often found in groups like the social underclass in the United States, families of immigrants from Turkey or Suriname in the Netherlands, and the Maori in New Zealand. At the age of 6, the children of comprehender families perform better in vocabulary tests and understanding of stories. Other characteristics of parental reading strategies may also affect these findings. For this reason, some researchers recommend that parents offer a broad range of ways to read, rather than training children in a single style. Then parents can use strategies that fit the child's reading development, the demands of the book, and the reading situation. For example, reading aloud in preschool, where many children may be sharing one book, involves a specific way of reading (performance-oriented style); detailed information about the book is offered at the beginning, followed by reading that is rarely interrupted with comments and explanations. There is also evidence that the willingness of the child to take an active part in the reading situation influences the parental reading style.

DEVELOPMENTAL REQUIREMENTS FOR LITERACY

To visually record letters, words, and sentences, the eye alternates rapidly between focus and movement. In the first developmental stage, young readers engage with pictures, graphics, and symbols and interact with attachment figures. Later, distinct visual characteristics of written text stabilize, and a phonological representation of single characters gradually evolves. As a further precursor of literary language (language as used in writing rather than its oral form), children begin to understand the alphabetical principle of speech—the correspondence between graphemes (bits of text) and phonemes (bits of sound). After the development of this logographic strategy, a further alphabetic strategy follows, in which even unknown words can be read through an active application of the grapheme-phoneme correspondence.

At the age of 3 to 5 years, sensitivity to language sounds increases. This gain strongly depends on the ability to segment language by identifying spoken words and sentences. The focus of attention shifts from the meaning of language to its structure. This phonological awareness can influence the development of literary language. A child's phonological awareness develops in the context of the family; children growing up in unfavorable socioeconomic conditions show less elaborated phonological awareness. As a precursor of reading competence, the synthesis of terms is an essential ability. This happens when single phonemes are linked with meaningful words.

A further developmental step occurs when a child is able to record larger units in the reading process—first, morphemes, and later, words. A permanent matching with the individual semantic system is presumed in this process. The availability of mental models regarding different topics and the quality and quantity of relevant knowledge facilitate the acquisition of central text messages and the ability to distinguish them from other contents.

The comprehension of literary texts requires certain competences. Literary texts instruct readers to construct a situational model that enables them to make inferences about meaning. Readers must be able to recognize clues in the text that signal the need for inference related, for example, to beliefs, desires, and opinions of people. Specialized knowledge about typical scripts, narrative schemes, and literary genres must also be available. Many empirical studies address the ability to distinguish between fiction and reality and to understand irony.

PROMOTION OF LITERARY LANGUAGE ACQUISITION

Phonological Awareness

To encourage phonological awareness, exercises can be used to give insight into the structure of language. Phonological awareness is enhanced by conscious listening as well as by rhyme exercises or exercises that give practice in identifying words and sentences.

Phonemic Awareness

Narrowly defined, phonological awareness consists of phonemic awareness. The term *phonemic awareness* summarizes competences in apperception, identification, and modification of phonemes. To encourage phonemic awareness, specific exercises in the pedagogical context can be effective, such as the isolation of phonemes, the recognition of identical phonemes in different words, the apperception of differences between phonemes, word synthesis through combining phonemes, and the segmentation of words through taking away, adding, or changing phonemes.

The systematic interrelations between spoken and written language and the basics of the alphabetical principle are taught by specific instruction on the relation between graphemes and phonemes.

Reading Fluency

Greater reading fluency often is associated with a better understanding of the text. Reading fluency can be improved through listening and active reading, especially when feedback is given frequently and when the intervention has small-scale objectives.

Strategies for Building Text Understanding

A better text understanding can be achieved through a flexible use of successful reading strategies. Examples include activating the reader's own knowledge before beginning, formulating hypotheses on the basis of headings, monitoring word understanding while reading, reflecting text understanding, forming short paragraph summaries, testing of the hypotheses from headings at the end of the passage, and connecting text contents with the reader's own knowledge.

Cultural Communication

Various studies—for example, the Organization of Economic Cooperation and Development's survey of adolescent reading in many countries—have proved that cultural communication at home is the most important determinant of the amount of time spent reading, the diversity of materials read, attitudes toward reading, and reading competence. Investigations of reading in schools show a medium effect on the development of oral language and a moderate effect on reading development. Positive results have been achieved by giving working adults the opportunity to read out their favorite texts to pupils in the school setting.

An important research result about literature instruction is that every pupil should get the chance to develop his or her own text understanding and to talk about individual texts with peers. In some countries, an explicit goal of education is to help children learn to communicate thoughts and feelings provoked through lecture in conversations with their classmates. Book clubs have often been founded to further this aim. Pupils may use conversations about self-chosen readings to discuss cultural standards, values, and styles of discourse. It can be especially useful for adolescents who belong to ethnic minorities to include culture-specific forms of discourse (e.g., *signifying* as a form of talk in African American communities) into literature instruction.

READING MOTIVATION

In the transaction with (anticipated) text features, an evaluation of the text takes place based, on the one hand, on specific text category knowledge and, on the other, on an individual's reading self-concept. The latter develops as a consequence of successes and failures in reading. The resulting text-specific reading motivation helps explain individual reading competence, as opposed to basic cognitive competence. By factor analysis, three main parts of the construct of reading motivation can be identified: the above-mentioned reading self-concept, intrinsic reading motivation (individual range of interests), and extrinsic factors (potential indirect sources of enforcement). Motivational difficulties in acquiring written language skills are rarely discussed. In elementary school, a motivational decrease regarding text-based tasks can already be found. Reading motivation declines continually in the course of the school years up to adolescence.

The pleasure found in literary reading (the reading of novels, short stories, poetry, or plays) is much higher during adolescence than it was earlier, as teenage readers have learned to interpret texts and to ask interpretive questions. Besides easy access to books and sufficient time to read, motivation depends on the connection children see between their personal daily experiences and the content of the reading; in addition, children must be convinced that they can take an active role in their own cognitive development. Therefore, factors that enhance reading motivation in secondary school are real world interaction, interesting texts, autonomy, and collaboration with peers.

Reading motivations change in the course of development. For preschoolers, reading opens new and fantastic worlds. In elementary school, the readers themselves feel like heroes, while reading offers adolescents an opportunity to reflect on themselves. The systematic search for adequate interpretations of texts and relations to other texts does not begin until college for the most part. Young women often report a clearly higher level of reading motivation than young men do. This may be due to the fact that women are more likely to use literature to cope with critical life situations.

—*Armin Castello and Michael Charlton*

See also Literacy; Reading, History of; Reading, Patterns of

FURTHER READINGS

Kamil, M. L., Mosenthal, P. B., Pearson, P. D., & Barr, R. (Eds.). (2000). *Handbook of reading research* (Vol. 3, pp. 425–788). Mahwah, NJ: Erlbaum.

Neumann, S. B., & Dickinson, D. K. (Eds.). (2002). *Handbook of early literacy research.* New York: Guilford Press.

Polselli Sweet, A., & Snow, C. E. (Eds.). (2003). *Rethinking reading comprehension.* New York: Guilford Press.

READING, PATTERNS OF

Reading is a vital ingredient in the human experience and the intellectual development of children and adolescents. Reading develops a capacity for focused attention and imaginative growth that enriches young

Reading aloud to young children is one of the most important ways to foster reading literacy. Reading and discussing what is read with children not only builds language and reading skills but also strengthens family relationships.

SOURCE: © Red Barn Studio, istockphoto.com; used with permission.

aesthetic reading (reading for pleasure). *Efferent* (from the Latin word *efferre,* to carry away) reading is purposeful reading, which students are taught day after day in schools. Efferent readers connect cognitively with the text and plan to take something useful from it—such as answers for a test. According to Rosenblatt, the efferent reader's focus is on what will remain after the reading—such as information to be acquired or the solution to a problem. In contrast, the aesthetic reader's attention is on what he or she is experiencing during the reading event—that is, on what Rosenblatt describes as his or her relationship with that particular text. Aesthetic reading is done for the joy of it, and readers are absorbed in the experience of making meaning from verbal signs. Thus, aesthetic readers connect emotionally to the material.

people. This entry examines the effect of dominant reading patterns and readership trends among children and adolescents, reasons for low reading levels, and the concept of *aliteracy* among children and adolescents.

Over the years, researchers have concluded that young people who read more books tend to have the highest level of participation in other activities. Louise M. Rosenblatt, an influential scholar of reading, maintains that the act of reading is a dynamic "transaction" between the reader and the text. In her 1978 book, *The Reader, the Text, the Poem,* she notes that the reader's recognition of verbal symbols transforms the text into something more than an object composed of paper and ink. Thus, according to Rosenblatt, the meaning of any text lies not in the work itself but in the reader's interaction with it.

Rosenblatt classified reading patterns into two types: efferent reading (reading for information) and

DECLINE IN READING AMONG CHILDREN AND ADOLESCENTS

In 1984, while Daniel J. Boorstin was the librarian of the U.S. Congress, he wrote an epochal report, *Books in Our Future*, in which he defined *aliteracy* as "having the ability to read but no interest in doing so." Boorstin said that aliteracy was widespread in the United States, and several articles in the report alluded to the growing number of nonreaders. Based on pertinent statistics—among them only about half of all Americans read regularly—he referred to the "twin menaces" of illiteracy and aliteracy.

According to the report *A Nation at Risk: The Imperative for Educational Reform, 1983,* issued by the National Commission on Excellence in Education, about 23 million American adults were functionally illiterate—they would not pass the simplest test of reading, writing, and comprehension—and about 13% of

American 17-year-olds were functionally illiterate. The educational process itself was identified as one cause; for example, the report noted that American students spend less time on homework than students in many other nations. The report concentrated primarily on American secondary education. A close examination of U.S. secondary schools found that the curricula no longer had a central purpose unifying all of the subjects.

The National Association of Secondary School Principals expressed concern in 1998 that by almost every measure, voluntary reading declines after elementary school because teachers consider students to be competent readers by the sixth grade and place the burden on them to continue to improve their skills and to choose to read without encouragement.

There is also strong research evidence that reading scores begin to decline when students leave the elementary grades. This decline in reading scores appears to correspond to the relative reduction in support for young adolescents' reading development. A study conducted by researchers at Indiana University compared results of the Iowa Test of Basic Reading Skills from 1944–1945, 1976, and 1986. Sixth-grade scores increased from 6.2 to 6.6 whereas 10th-grade scores dropped from 10.2 to 9.7. The decline of reading time in the secondary school day can also be attributed to the perception many have that young adolescents are already adequately proficient in reading and, thus, studying other areas—foreign language or computers—is a better use of their time. Yet, 40% of 9-year-olds scored below the basic level in reading on the 1994 National Assessment of Educational Progress.

Research indicates that children who are heavy television viewers (more than 3 hours per day) show the greatest decline in reading ability. A growing number of policymakers and educators around the world are concerned about low levels of reading among children and adolescents. They believe aliteracy is potentially as alarming as illiteracy because it affects students' potential for success in higher education.

REASONS FOR LOW READING LEVELS

The significant decline in reading among children and adolescents can be attributed to technological change in modern society. Young people and emerging adults are less interested in reading because they are more engaged by television and the rich multimedia content, interactivity, and ease of use of computer games and Internet communication. Children and adolescents are more responsive to these visually powerful media

environments, in which reading is at best sparse or not critical for enjoying the medium or the message. With the rise of television and interactive media such as the Internet, popular media content has shifted away from words to images. Thus, aliterate children and adolescents can read, but they tend to avoid the activity. As more children and adolescents avoid reading, they become less informed, active, and independent minded.

There may be other reasons for low levels of reading. Faced with multiple media choices and increased pressures on their time, children and adolescents may be less inclined to read. They may prefer the visual to the verbal, choosing an entertainment-oriented medium such as television or computer games. Thus, for many young people, reading is a passive, outdated, and boring way to spend the time. A 2006 study by the American College Testing (ACT) program, an independent nonprofit body that tests college-bound students, concluded that reading in American high schools does not adequately challenge students. The study noted that many high school graduates lack the reading skills needed to succeed in college and in workforce training programs. The ACT study's findings suggest that many high school teachers are not incorporating higher-level reading materials—the types of texts that students will encounter in college and in the workforce—into their classes. The study was based on responses from 1.2 million 2005 high school graduates who took the ACT college admission and placement exam.

The ACT study identified being able to read complex texts as the "clearest differentiator" between students who are ready for college-level reading and those who are inadequately prepared. Students who are ready for college-level reading are better poised for success than are aliterate students. They are more likely to enroll in college in the fall following high school graduation, earn higher grades in college social science courses, earn higher first-year college grade point averages, and return to the same college for a second year. The ACT study found that just 51%— the lowest percentage in more than a decade—of the test takers met the ACT college readiness benchmark for reading. The percentage of students prepared for college-level reading peaked at 55% in 1999 and has declined since then.

WIDESPREAD DECLINE IN READING AMONG ADULTS

Children and adolescents learn from adults, and recent studies indicate a prevalent decline in reading among adults. A 1999 Gallup Poll found that only 7% of Americans were voracious readers, reading more than a book a week, while some 59% said they had read fewer than 10 books in the previous year. According to the poll, the number of people who do not read at all has been rising for the past 20 years.

A significant part of the learning society and intellectual culture is embedded in literature. Literary reading (the reading of novels, short stories, poetry, or plays) is in dramatic decline with fewer than half of American adults now reading literature, concluded a 2002 survey conducted by the U.S. Census Bureau for the National Endowment for the Arts. The study also documents an overall decline of 10 percentage points in literary readers from 1982 to 2002, representing a loss of 20 million potential readers. The rate of decline has been increasing and, according to the survey, nearly tripled from 5% to 14% between 1992 and 2002.

The survey asked nearly 17,000 adults if, during the previous 12 months, they had read any novels, short stories, poetry, or plays that were not required for work or school. The rate of decline is steeper in some demographic groups. While literary reading declined among all age groups, the three youngest groups saw the steepest drops. The rate of decline for the youngest adults, ages 18 to 24, was 55% greater than that of the total adult population. According to the results of the study, women read more literature than men, but literary reading by both genders is declining. Only slightly more than one third of adult males now read literature. Reading among women is also declining significantly, but at a slower rate. Among ethnic and racial groups surveyed, literary reading decreased most strongly among Hispanic Americans, dropping by 10 percentage points. Literary reading declined among whites, African Americans, and Hispanics.

—*Debashis "Deb" Aikat*

See also Media Genre Preferences; Reading, Impact of TV on; Reading, Literacy and; Television, International Viewing Patterns and; Television, Viewer Age and

FURTHER READINGS

Boorstin, D. J. (1984). *Books in our future* (Report to the Congress of the United States, Joint Committee on the Library of Congress). Washington, DC: Government Printing Office.

Ferguson, R. L. (2006, March). *Reading between the lines: What the ACT reveals about college readiness in reading.* Retrieved March 14, 2006, from http://www.act.org/path/policy/pdf/reading_report.pdf

Hill, K. (2004, June). *Reading at risk: A survey of literary reading in America.* Retrieved March 14, 2006, from http://www.nea.gov/pub/ReadingAtRisk.pdf

Rosenblatt, L. M. (1978). *The reader, the text, the poem: A transactional theory of the literary work.* Carbondale: Southern Illinois University Press.

Rosenblatt, L. M. (1978). *Literature as exploration.* New York: Appleton-Century-Crofts. (Original work published 1938)

REALITY TV

Although its history reaches back to the early days of television, reality-based programming, or reality TV, did not gain substantial popularity until the dawn of the 21st century. More than 100 new reality programs have aired since the summer of 2000, and the genre continues to dominate as the newest staple of the American TV diet. Because this phenomenon is so recent, there is little research on the effects of these programs on adolescents, despite evidence of their popularity. Nielsen ratings for the 2004–2005 television season indicated that of the 10 most frequently viewed programs among 12-to-17-year-olds, four were reality-based (*American Idol, Survivor, Extreme Makeover–Home Edition,* and *Nanny 911*). Still, given the popularity of reality TV among young people, concerns over its potential impact have understandably been raised.

DEFINING REALITY TV

There is no clear industry standard or definition of reality TV. As a result, conceptualizations often err on the side of inclusiveness, capturing all programming claiming to present reality, including news programming, talk shows, and sporting events. Focusing solely on the programs that have emerged as part of the burgeoning reality TV phenomenon, for example, *Survivor, The Bachelor, American Idol,* and the like, Nabi and colleagues defined reality TV programming as programs in which real people play themselves without a script, with events—contrived or otherwise—placed in a narrative context. They further specify that reality programs show people in their own home or work environments rather than on a set and that such programs are created primarily for viewer entertainment. As their research indicated that most people find reality programming to be only somewhat real, the element of being "unscripted" rather than "real" is likely the more defining feature of the genre.

Despite the unifying elements that bridge the range of reality programs, there are substantial differences among such programs, suggesting that several reality TV subgenres may exist. Nabi and colleagues identified five subtypes: romance (e.g., *The Bachelor*), drama (*Real World*), game show/competition (*Survivor*), talent (*American Idol*), Crime (*Cops*), and informational (*Trading Spaces*), and this list is likely to expand and shift as new programs are developed. However, because any one program may contain qualities reflective of multiple subgenres, the boundaries among these categories may be somewhat fluid.

WHY PEOPLE WATCH REALITY TV

In exploring why people watch reality TV and what sorts of people are attracted to such programming, Nabi and colleagues found that viewers are particularly drawn in by the suspenseful/unscripted nature of reality programs as well as the appeal of viewing others' interpersonal dynamics. However, the contrived elements and potentially manipulative editing detract from its appeal. They also found that people who tend to be impulsive experience a greater range of gratifications when viewing reality TV. In related research, Reiss and Wiltz examined the association of 16 basic human motives with reality TV viewing, concluding that the motivation to attain social status or to feel self-important are most strongly related to reality TV consumption, followed by the desire for vengeance.

Considering different subgenres of reality programming, Nabi and colleagues found that people may enjoy reality programming for some of the same reasons they enjoy fictional dramatic programming. For example, they may experience positive emotions or be transported into the narrative. However, viewers seem to enjoy different subtypes of reality TV for different reasons. This study found that people enjoyed reality-crime programs for what they learned, but that they enjoyed reality-romance programs for the interpersonal insights gained. Given different underlying reasons for enjoyment, it is reasonable to expect different program types to engender different effects, although there is, in fact, very little research on the actual influence of reality TV.

EFFECTS OF REALITY TV VIEWING

Before the explosion of reality TV after 2000, crime-related programs, such as *Cops*, served as the focus for academic research on the effects of reality program viewing. Studies suggested that such programs overrepresented violent crime, crimes solved, non-whites as offenders, and whites as law enforcement officers. Research has also found that such misrepresentations can influence the way audiences think about crime in society. For example, Oliver and Armstrong found that Caucasians who were frequent viewers of reality crime programs were more likely to exaggerate crime prevalence estimates than those who watched less of this type of programming, suggesting that frequent viewers might be more likely to see the world as a dangerous and scary place. In related research, Eschholz and colleagues found that viewing programs like *Cops* strengthened confidence in law enforcement agencies, especially for white viewers.

Given the dearth of research on the effects of reality programs generally, it is unsurprising that the effects of such programs on adolescents are confined to mere speculation at this point. Critics have voiced concerns that exposure to reality programs might negatively alter young people's expectations in terms of, for example, romantic relationships, sexual behavior, body image, alcohol consumption, gendered behavior, and the like, which in turn might pose physical and psychological risks to young viewers. Furthermore, as reality programs starring adolescents proliferate (e.g., *The Scholar*, *Brat Camp*, *Gene Simmons' Rock School*), concern over the effect of program participation has also been raised. It is important to point out that these are long-standing worries regarding television programming generally, not solely reality TV. To the extent that reality TV programs are both perceived as more realistic and also misrepresent reality, such concerns may be well-founded. However, it is important to recognize that if constructed with positive intentions, reality TV has the potential to serve as a positive influence, promoting cooperation and healthful behaviors. Thus, the content of individual reality programs, rather than the genre itself, will ultimately determine the extent to which concerns about the effects of reality TV viewing on adolescents are justified.

—*Robin Nabi*

See also Television, Motivations for Viewing of

FURTHER READINGS

Balkin, K. F. (2004). *Reality TV*. San Diego, CA: Greenhaven.

Eschholz, S., Balckwell, B. S., Gertz, M., & Chiricos, T. (2004). Race and attitudes toward the police: Assessing the effects of watching "reality" police programs. *Journal of Criminal Justice, 30,* 327–341.

Fishman, M., & Cavender, G. (1998). *Entertaining crime: Television reality programs*. New York: Aldine de Gruyter.

Nabi, R. L., Biely, E., Morgan, S., & Stitt, C. (2003). Reality-based television programming and the psychology of its appeal. *Media Psychology, 5,* 303–330.

Nabi, R. L., Stitt, C., Halford, J., & Finnerty, K. (in press). Emotional and cognitive predictors of the enjoyment of reality-based and fictional television programming: An elaboration of the uses and gratifications perspective. *Media Psychology*.

Oliver, M. B., & Armstrong, B. (1998). The color of crime: Perceptions of Caucasians' and African-Americans' involvement in crime. In M. Fishman & G. Cavender (Eds.), *Entertaining crime: Television reality programs* (pp. 19–35). New York: Aldine de Gruyter.

Reiss, S., & Wiltz, J. (2004). Why people watch reality TV. *Media Psychology, 6,* 363–378.

Salamon, J. (2004, September 29). Underage and way overexposed. *New York Times*, p. 14.

REGULATION, ELECTRONIC GAMES

The phenomenal growth of electronic gaming technology, both in popularity and sophistication, has been paralleled by calls for increased regulation of the medium due to concerns about the potential harmful effects of game play on children. Politicians, parent advocacy groups, and other critics of electronic games have been particularly concerned about the interactive depictions of violence and sexuality in popular titles. Over time, pro-regulation forces have attempted to shield children from games by introducing anti-game legislation and by pressuring the industry and retailers to self-regulate, with mixed success.

EARLY ATTEMPTS TO REGULATE

The first significant attempts to regulate electronic games occurred at the local level in the early 1980s. These early efforts focused on restricting arcades out of concern that they encouraged truancy and delinquent behavior among children and teens. A small group of detractors such as PTA mother Ronnie Lam also voiced concerns about violence and sex in early games, but the graphics were so poor and abstract that few even noticed.

ELECTRONIC GAMES GO TO WASHINGTON

By the early 1990s, a more realistic generation of electronic games had become popular with children and adolescents, sparking much controversy. *Mortal Kombat*, a colossally successful fighting game featuring gobs of blood and gruesome finishing maneuvers, delighted fans but shocked parents and politicians,

The Entertainment Software Rating Board (ESRB) has developed and launched a national ad campaign that includes public service announcements like the one above, which appear in print, online, and on radio and TV. The campaign, featuring the slogan "OK to Play?," urges parents and others to use both rating symbols and content descriptors in order to make informed computer and video game purchase decisions. The ESRB provides ratings and advertising guidelines for more than 1,000 electronic games per year. Ratings are determined by a consensus of at least three trained evaluators who review videotaped footage of the game as well as a questionnaire filled out by the game's publisher. In addition to the ratings for age groups, there are more than 30 content descriptors that refer to violence, sex, language, nudity, substance abuse, gambling, humor and other potentially sensitive subject matter.

who launched a crusade against electronic games. Beginning in 1983, Senators Joseph Lieberman and Herb Kohl spearheaded hearings investigating the industry. They called representatives from the major game manufacturers in front of Congress and demanded that something be done to protect children from exposure to certain types of content. In addition to the ghastly violence in *Mortal Kombat*, the sexual portrayals in the full-motion video game, *Night Trap,* were singled out during the hearings. Under threat of governmental intervention and possible censorship, game producers came up with their own solution. They created an organization known as the Entertainment Software Association (ESA) to represent their interests and through it proposed a game ratings system.

SELF-REGULATION AND THE ESRB

The Entertainment Software Rating Board (ESRB), according to the organization website, is a "self-regulatory body for the interactive entertainment software industry." It independently rates video and computer games. The ESRB ratings system was received favorably by Senators Lieberman and Kohl and has been praised for being the most comprehensive media ratings scheme. ESRB ratings now appear on the boxes of all major games, with two parts to each rating. The first part, the *ratings symbol*, suggests the age-appropriateness of a game. Common ratings symbols include E for Everyone, T for Teen, and M for Mature. The second part, *content descriptors*, indicate specific types of content in a game, usually the one(s) that triggered the ratings symbol. The ESRB has more than 30 common content descriptors indicating multiple varieties of violent, sexual, language, and drug-related content. This ratings system gives parents information to help them decide which games are appropriate for their children.

RECENT REGULATORY ACTION

Attempts to regulate electronic games did not end with the creation of the ESRB, due to highly publicized events such as the 1999 Columbine school shootings, which some blamed on computer game play, and also on the emergence of controversial new titles, particularly the *Grand Theft Auto* series. In these games, which rose to popularity in the early 2000s, players assume the role of a carjacking criminal who can be made to perform antisocial behaviors ranging from killing police to beating prostitutes to death after having off-screen sex with them. The severity and breadth of objectionable content in the *Grand Theft Auto* series focused attention on other areas that should be regulated, such as the marketing of games to children and retailer enforcement of the ratings system.

Enforcement of the ratings system has received a great deal of recent attention. Since 2003, several U.S. states (e.g., Illinois and California) have introduced legislation that would make the selling of violent or sexually explicit games to minors a crime. However, most of these bills have been challenged by the ESA and struck down by courts on grounds that they violate free speech rights.

An alternative approach is increased self-regulation. The Interactive Merchants Trade Association (IMTA) represents almost all major game retailers, and member stores have recently pledged to restrict the sale of M-rated games to minors. The success of this initiative has been questioned, however. The National Institute on Media and Family releases a yearly report card with information about the effectiveness of game regulation, and it continually gives low scores to retailer ratings enforcement (although the 2004 report card indicated some improvement over the previous year).

THE ONGOING CONTROVERSY

A key issue in the ongoing battle over electronic game regulation concerns whether or not games are entitled to free speech protection. In many countries, violent game titles have been censored or banned outright, but this seems unlikely to happen in the United States. As pointed out in work by James Ivory, the willingness of federal courts to restrict the sale of games has diminished over time, due to the technological advances of the medium. While the early electronic game *Pong* may have been little more than the video equivalent of a ping pong match, most current games incorporate narrative, music, and other components of books and films. The addition of these artistic elements aligns games with protected forms of speech and has been made possible by advances in game technology over time.

Technological advances of electronic games are emerging as another important issue that could impact future regulation. In summer 2005, hidden sexually explicit scenes were discovered in *Grand Theft Auto: San Andreas*, prompting Senator Hillary Clinton and others to call once again for more controls on violent and sexually explicit games. It is significant that the sex scenes were not caught by the ESRB, which likely would have rated the game Adults Only instead of Mature if they had seen that material. This brought attention to the fact that the huge interactive landscapes of many contemporary electronic games may not be possible to fully and accurately rate using existing techniques. As electronic games continue to evolve and become even more sophisticated, the means by which they are regulated will likely need to evolve as well, making the regulation of electronic games an ongoing process in need of attention.

—*Paul Skalski*

See also Aggression Electronic Games and; Electronic Games, Effects of; Electronic Games, Violence in

FURTHER READINGS

Gonzalez, L. (2004). *When two tribes go to war: A history of video game controversy.* Retrieved August 20, 2005, from http://www.gamespot.com/features/6090892/p-5.html

Ivory, J. (2003, July). *Protecting kids or attacking the First Amendment? Video games, regulation, and protected expression.* Paper presented to the Law Division at the 86th annual convention of the Association for Education in Journalism and Mass Communication.

Kent, S. L. (2001). *The ultimate history of video games.* Roseville, CA: Prima.

King, B., & Borland, J. (2003). *Dungeons and dreamers: The rise of computer game culture from geek to chic.* Emeryville, CA: McGraw-Hill.

Ninth annual Mediawise video game report card. (n.d.). Retrieved August 20, 2004, from http://www.mediafamily.org/research/report_vgrc_2004.shtml

REGULATION, INDUSTRY SELF-REGULATION

Media industry self-regulation evolves as a response to external criticism and is often implemented as a way to preclude threats of legislation. Public and legislative concern about media reflects society's normative ideal of what media should and should not do in our culture. Particularly where children and adolescents are concerned, there is tremendous interest in mitigating the potentially negative effects of media content and media use and encouraging the positive contributions media can make. But, while calls for government oversight are made, First Amendment guarantees of free speech and free press prohibit most direct government interference in content-based decisions. Pressuring media to self-regulate is a way to

address concerns without having to raise the specter of constitutional issues.

Self-regulation, by definition, puts media industry personnel in charge of overseeing their own media products. Skeptics must be persuaded the industry is making a genuine effort to address the collective concerns of the public. Self-regulation may also, however, be more agile than government regulation in response to changes in the industry such as new technological developments.

Ratings systems are the most evident form of self-regulation that addresses issues with which parents are concerned. The movie industry has age-based ratings. The music industry has warning labels attached to the packaging of recordings with explicit lyrics. Television programs are rated with a combination of age-based and content-based distinctions. Video games are assigned age-based ratings, and some basic content information is available on packaging. Each of these systems is administered either by individual media producers or by an industry trade association. None of the systems uses psychologists or child development experts to help assign ratings. Each of the ratings systems is unique, which makes it difficult for parents to keep track of what each rating truly means. There has been some movement to create a uniform ratings system that could be applied across different forms of media, but so far this service is available only through for-profit companies.

The other prominent media self-regulatory systems apply to the advertising industry and are encouraged by the Federal Trade Commission. Of particular interest regarding children and adolescents is the Children's Advertising Review Unit (CARU), a division of the Council of Better Business Bureaus. This group was formed in the mid-1970s at the request of the advertising industry. Their primary function is to review advertising directed at children under 12 and to ensure that it is true and accurate and takes into account the level of cognitive development of its target audience. Some areas of advertising that receive scrutiny include food products (especially junk food), alcoholic beverages, and violent or explicit media content, especially movies, music, and video games.

Other forms of self-regulation are less well known. Many media organizations have codes of ethics, or a list of standards and practices by which they are to abide. Specific news outlets, from the *Cedar Rapids Gazette* to the *New York Times* have policies designed to address day-to-day challenges. Professional organizations like the American Society of Media

Photographers spell out more generalized principles for their members. The difficulty with such codes is that they are often so general as to be useless in particular situations, or so specific that they don't address a wide range of controversial material. These internal codes are also not made widely available to the public, as media organizations fear they may face legal sanctions for violating their own written standards.

Some organizations have hired full-time media critics. Ken Auletta, columnist for the *New Yorker* and author of multiple books on media issues, is among the best known. Most other critics work for major print media, rather than for electronic media outlets. There are a few programs on radio and television that focus on issues in the media industries, including National Public Radio's *On the Media*. The responsibility of media critics is to report on industry issues and praise ethical media actions as well as criticize ethical lapses.

Another option some media organizations have adopted is to hire an ombudsman. Ombudsmen can be found in newsrooms across the United States, South America, Europe, and parts of Asia and the Middle East. Ombudsman positions are paid for by the organization, but generally, people serving as ombudsmen have a contractual promise that they will not be fired during the duration of their service. The ombudsman is to serve as an internal critic of ethical decision making and as a contact person for members of the public concerned about the organization's content. In the United States, ombudsman positions are primarily in newspaper newsrooms. Very few broadcast organizations have adopted this model of self-regulation. In addition, an ombudsman is intended to oversee ethical issues in news coverage, not in entertainment content.

Other venues for audience members to voice their concern are more widely available. Letters to the editor are an effective way for consumers of print media to express concern about particular content that may be problematic to parents. Most media organizations also have mechanisms for audience feedback via the Internet. Email and bulletin board postings have made it much easier for parents to let their views be known directly to media organizations.

Although relatively common in Europe, Asia and Africa, news councils in the United States are rare. The three existing councils are regional. A national news council existed briefly in the 1980s, but it ceased operation due to lack of media support. A news council is made up of a group of media industry insiders and members of the general public. People who feel they have been treated unfairly by a media organization can bring their complaint to the news council. Both sides present the facts of the case as they see them, and after deliberation, the council votes on whether the media organization violated its professional responsibilities. There are no sanctions, except the negative publicity the media organization endures about the council's actions. This model of self-regulation has generally been applied to news-related issues rather than entertainment content.

Media industries have also partnered with other professional organizations to establish guidelines for the portrayal of certain issues. For example, bench-bar-press guidelines have been established through the cooperation of judges, lawyers, law enforcement personnel, and members of the media. These guidelines address the appropriateness of information to be released regarding criminal cases. Other areas of concern have been the responsible portrayal of alcohol consumption, smoking, sexual behavior, violence, and drug use.

—Jennifer L. Lambe

See also Advertising, Regulation of; Children's Advertising Review Unit (CARU); First Amendment; Food Advertising, Regulation of; Media Education, Family Involvement in; Media Matters Campaign; Motion Picture Association of America (MPAA); Parental Regulation of Children's Media; Regulation (various entries); Television Ratings Systems, Parental Uses of

FURTHER READINGS

American Academy of Pediatrics. (n.d.). *Media matters: A national media education campaign.* Retrieved November 17, 2005, from http://www.aap.org/advocacy/mediamatters.htm

Bertrand, C. J. (2002). *Media ethics and accountability systems.* New Brunswick, NJ: Transaction.

Bushman, B. J., & Cantor, J. (2003). Media ratings for violence and sex: Implications for policymakers and parents. *American Psychologist, 58*(2), 130–141.

Krasnow, E. G., Longley, L. D., & Terry, H. A. (1982). *The politics of broadcast regulation.* New York: St. Martin's Press.

REGULATION, INTERNET

Children are avid users of the Internet. The amount of time they spend in front of a computer screen increases with age. Children use the Internet both at school and at home. Households with children are more likely to have access to the Internet than those without children. Parents and educators embrace the educational and entertainment values of the Internet. However, they are equally concerned about what children might encounter online. Two concerns stand out: children's exposure to sexually explicit materials and the loss of privacy. Although the government firmly supports self-regulation on the Internet, given the compelling interest of protecting minors, it has made continuous efforts to regulate the Internet along these two directions. Some of the efforts have succeeded while some have failed.

SEXUALLY EXPLICIT MATERIALS ON THE INTERNET

The Communications Decency Act of 1996 was Congress's first attempt to regulate the content of the Internet to protect minors. As part of the 1996 Telecommunications Act, the Communications Decency Act was signed into law on February 8, 1996, making it a crime to knowingly transmit indecent or obscene communication by computer to a minor under 18 years of age. Soon after the law was passed, two separate three-judge panels in 1996 found the law unconstitutional. On June 26, 1997, the U.S. Supreme Court struck down the law. It found that the act's "indecent transmission" and "patently offensive display" provisions violate the First Amendment's protection of free speech. The law was also found to be full of vagueness in key terms, lacking definitions of both *indecency* and *patent offensiveness*.

The Child Online Protection Act (COPA), which was Congress's response to the failure of the previous law, has narrower applications. The act applies only to Web communications and commercial websites. It prohibits commercial websites from knowingly transmitting pornographic materials on the Internet to minors (people under 17 years of age). The Child Online Protection Act was also challenged. In 1999, a U.S. District Court declared the law unconstitutional. In May 2002, the U.S. Supreme Court reviewed the ruling and returned the case to the Circuit Court for further review. In March 2003, the Third Circuit Court again struck down the law as unconstitutional on the ground that it is likely to be overbroad, which will hinder adults' access to this material. On June 29, 2004, the Supreme Court upheld the ruling of the Circuit Court. However, the Court acknowledged that given the rapid pace of Internet development, it is likely that filtering will be able to protect children online in the future. The Court referred the case back to the District Court for further investigation and action.

The Children's Internet Protection Act represents a third attempt by Congress to limit children's exposure to sexually explicit materials on the Internet. Passed on December 15, 2000, the law addresses concerns about children's access to the Internet in schools and libraries. Under the act, schools and libraries that receive discounts (e-rate programs) for their Internet access must take measures to block or filter any pictures that are obscene, contain child pornography, or are harmful to minors. Schools are required to adopt a policy to monitor children's online activities. The law was challenged by the American Library Association in 2001, and a lower court found the application of the act to libraries unconstitutional. However, on June 23, 2003, the U.S. Supreme Court reversed that decision, ruling that public libraries must purchase filtering software and comply with all portions of the act.

In 2002, Congress passed Dot Kids Implementation and Efficiency Act, and it was signed into law on December 4, 2002. The purpose of this law is to provide a safe online environment for children, promote positive experiences, and prevent children from being exposed to harmful materials. The act requires NeuStar, a private technology company, to create a second-level domain, a *kids.us,* which will be used for websites geared toward children younger than 13. Websites that are willing to register for the domain must abide by certain rules to ensure the child-friendly nature of the sites. NeuStar is responsible for reviewing the content of the websites before registration and for continuously monitoring the content.

CHILDREN'S PRIVACY

In 1996, the Center for Media Education issued *The Web of Deception*, reporting that websites for children were using various tactics to collect personal information from children without seeking prior parental permission. The Federal Trade Commission conducted its own study in 1998 and concluded that children's privacy was not protected on the Internet. The Children's Online Privacy Protection Act, which was passed by Congress in 1998 and took effect in April 2000, applies to all commercial websites that target children under 13 and to websites that knowingly collect personal information from children. The act requires website operators to (a) post privacy policy on their homepages as well as pages where personal information is collected; (b) collect only the necessary information that will allow children to participate in online activities; (c) ask for verifiable parental permission before they collect personal information from children; and (d) allow parents to review and delete personal information that is collected about their children. The Federal Trade Commission is responsible for the enforcement of the law. So far, the commission has fined a number of Web operators in violation.

With the fast development of the Internet, children are facing an ever more sophisticated online environment. New issues and concerns emerge frequently, such as host-selling online. The government is facing continuous challenges of protecting children's interests online.

—*Xiaomei Cai*

See also Center for Media Education (CME); Children's Online Privacy Protection Act of 1998 (COPPA); Federal Trade Commission; Websites, Children's

FURTHER READINGS

Center for Media Education. (1996). *The web of deception.* Retrieved November 20, 1998, from http://www.cme .org/children/marketing/deception.pdf

REGULATION, MOVIES

In their early years, movies did not have First Amendment protection in the United States, and states established film censorship boards. However, in the latter half of the 20th century, First Amendment protection was extended to films, and industry self-regulation became the norm. The Motion Picture Association of America (MPAA) established an age-based ratings system in 1968. Despite its flaws, the MPAA's ratings system has served as a model for other media, especially television and video games. Regardless of the medium, the burden on parents is growing as technology speeds forward, making it increasingly difficult for them to monitor what their children consume. Industry

Table 1 Court Rulings Related to Internet Regulation

Ashcroft v. American Civil Liberties Union, 542 U.S. 656 (2004).
Child Online Protection Act, 47 U.S.C.S. §231 (1998).
Children's Online Privacy Protection Act, 15 U.S.C.S. §6501 (1998).
Children's Internet Protection Act, 47 U.S.C.S. §902 (2000).
Communications Decency Act, 47 U.S.C.S. §223 (2000).
Dot Kids Implementation and Efficiency Act, 47 U.S.C.S. §901 (2002).
Reno v. American Civil Liberties Union, 521 U.S. 844 (1997).
United States v. American Civil Liberties Union, 540 U.S. 93 (2003).

self-regulation—or self-categorization—can only place labels on content; it is up to parents to stay informed and decide what's appropriate for their children.

THE EARLY YEARS

In the early days of the movie industry, government censors and industry regulators battled for control of screen content. Pennsylvania was the first state to institute a film censorship board in 1911, and other states followed suit. Spurred on by the U.S. Supreme Court's 1915 decision in the *Mutual Film Corporation v. Industrial Commission of Ohio* case, which deemed film a "business pure and simple" and denied movies the First Amendment protection granted to print media, the push was on for a federal film censorship board.

The studio heads hired Will Hays, a former postmaster general under President Warren G. Harding, to "clean" the screen and to promote industry self-regulation over state and federal censorship boards. Hays fought censorship boards successfully throughout the 1920s, and, in 1930, the Hays Code—a list of content prohibitions and sensitive areas—of self-regulation was written. However, with the country in the grips of the Depression and box office revenue declining, filmmakers ignored the code, instead infusing greater levels of sex and violence into films to lure people back into theaters. Social reformers, Catholic leaders, politicians, and—for the first time—researchers (as part of the Payne Fund Studies published in 1933) decried the dangerous influences of films on the audience. In 1934, with the threat of a federal censorship board renewed, the Hays Code became the Production Code, and Joseph Breen was named head of the Production Code Administration (PCA). Under Breen, many popular films from the early 1930s were taken out of circulation, and new productions needed a "seal of approval" to play in mainstream theaters. For a brief period of time, the PCA and Breen wielded considerable power in Hollywood.

FROM PRODUCTION CODE TO RATINGS SYSTEM

On November 1, 1968, the Motion Picture Association of America (MPAA) replaced the Production Code with an age-based ratings system, but the code's slow death actually began shortly after World War II. In 1952, the U.S. Supreme Court heard the *Burstyn v. Wilson* case, which dealt with producer Joseph Burstyn's attempt to show Italian director Roberto Rossellini's, *The Miracle,* believed by some to be sacrilegious, in the United States and declared film a "significant medium for the communication of ideas." First Amendment protection for motion pictures would soon follow.

Replacing the code with ratings reflects a philosophical change on the part of regulators, a movement from content prohibition to content categorization. Instead of altering content to receive a seal of approval, filmmakers could now submit their work and have it rated accordingly. The MPAA gives the responsibility of rating films to the Classification and Ratings Administration (CARA), a board originally composed of mental health professionals and educators, but now made up of parents. The original ratings in 1968 were G (general audience), M (mature), R (restricted for under 16), and X (no children under 18).

Since its inception, the ratings system has undergone several changes. The age limit for R was raised from 16 to 17. Believing that the M rating may cause confusion, the MPAA changed it to GP (general audiences, parental guidance suggested), and finally to PG (parental guidance suggested). The MPAA also started including rating descriptions—brief explanations of why a film received its rating—first for R and subsequently for films in all rating categories. The most recent category changes were the creation of PG-13 (parents strongly cautioned) in 1984, and the replacement of X with NC-17 (no children 17 and under) in 1990. While the NC-17 rating has had little impact on film content and regulation, the PG-13 rating's effect has been significant. The MPAA claims that ratings are intended for parents with minor children only, and MPAA research indicates they are satisfied with the system, but the question of how to rate content is a controversial one that still exists today.

CRITICISMS OF THE RATINGS SYSTEM

As in the 1930s, politicians, conservative critics, and academics have recently been vocal critics of the ratings system. A primary charge against the MPAA is that ratings operate under a double standard in that violent content is treated more leniently than sexual content, despite research suggesting greater potential harm associated with viewing media violence. Studies examining ratings descriptions of R- and NC-17-rated films, and comparing content from R-rated and NC-17-rated or unrated versions of the same films support the belief that the ratings system allows children easier access to graphic violence than graphic sex.

Another criticism is that powerful studios and influential people get preferential treatment by the MPAA. Anecdotally, the 1984 creation of the PG-13 is unofficially attributed—in part at least—to *Indiana Jones and the Temple of Doom*, which was judged too violent for PG, but, because it was a Steven Spielberg-George Lucas action film, did not receive an R rating.

RATINGS CREEP

Perhaps the strongest criticism of the ratings system is "creep," the slippage over time of increasingly adult content into less restrictive rating categories. Research into ratings creep has focused primarily on descriptive language used by the MPAA and others. One study looked at MPAA rating descriptions and non-MPAA websites that offer movie content information to find evidence of ratings creep. In a separate study, researchers focused on ratings creep in descriptions for PG-13-rated films, primarily because this unrestricted category includes a majority of the top-grossing films of all time and accounts for a growing percentage of films rated and released each year. In just the 3-year period examined, descriptions of PG-13-rated films indicated an increase in adult content overall, showed marginal gains in sexual content, and demonstrated more intense violent content. In short, the current PG-13-rated movie may contain more sex and more graphic violence than one that received the same rating a few years ago.

—*Ron Leone*

See also First Amendment; Motion Picture Association of America (MPAA); Movies, Sexuality in; Movies, Substance Abuse in; Movies, Violence in; Parental Advisory Labels and Rating Systems; Parental Regulation of Children's Media; Rating Systems, Parental Use of; Regulation, Industry Self-Regulation; Regulation, Television; Television Rating Systems, Parental Uses of

FURTHER READINGS

Black, G. D. (1994). *Hollywood censored: Morality codes, Catholics and the movies.* New York: Cambridge University Press.

Leone, R. (2002). Contemplating ratings: An examination of what the MPAA considers "too far for R" and why. *Journal of Communication, 52*(4), 1–17.

Leone, R. (2004). Rated sex: An analysis of the MPAA's use of R and NC-17 ratings. *Communication Research Reports, 21*(1), 68–74.

Leone, R., & Osborn, L. (2004). Hollywood's triumph and parents' loss: An examination of the PG-13 rating. *Popular Communication, 2*(2), 85–101.

Lewis, J. (2000). *Hollywood v. hard core: How the struggle over censorship saved the modern film industry.* New York: New York University Press.

Thompson, K. M., & Yokota, F. (2004, July 12). Violence, sex, and profanity in films: Correlation of movie ratings with content. *Medscape General Medicine, 6*(3), 1–19. Retrieved July 13, 2004, from http://www.medscape .com/viewarticle.480900_print

Wilson, B. J., Linz, D., & Randall, B. (1990). Applying social science research to film ratings: A shift from offensiveness to harmful effects. *Journal of Broadcasting & Electronic Media, 34,* 443–468.

WEBSITES

Motion Picture Association of America: www.mpaa.org

REGULATION, MUSIC

Two main issues currently surround the regulation of music and the music industry: explicit lyrics referring to sex, violence, or substance abuse and Internet file sharing. This entry addresses the background of each issue and what legal steps have been taken to regulate them.

The Recording Industry Association of America (RIAA) is the trade group representing the U.S. recording industry. Its mission is to foster business and legal climates that support and promote its members' creative and financial vitality. RIAA members mostly consist of record companies who manufacture and distribute about 90% of all commercially sold sound recordings produced in the United States. The

"The Parental Advisory is a notice to consumers that recordings identified by this logo may contain strong language or depictions of violence, sex or substance abuse. Parental discretion is advised."

Figure 1   Parental Advisory Label and Language

SOURCE: Parental Advisory, 2003. Retrieved October 13, 2005, from http://www.riaa.com/issues/parents/advisory.asp

mission of the RIAA thus involves two overarching goals: protecting the artists' First Amendment rights and protecting the intellectual property rights of artists and record companies.

REGULATION OF MUSIC LYRICS

The uproar over music lyrics may seem recent, but in fact, the banning of music goes back hundreds of years. Yet, with the rise of heavy metal in the early to mid-1980s, and later with the rise of hip hop and rap in the late 1980s, concerns of obscenity, pornography, and indecencies were brought to the forefront.

In 1985, the RIAA agreed with the National Parent Teacher Association and the Parents Music Resource Center to include warning labels on albums containing explicit lyrics that depicted sex, violence, or substance abuse (see Figure 1). It was hoped the decision would facilitate intelligent decision making on the part of parents regarding their children's album selections. Although the recording companies and the artists decide which albums should be labeled, the RIAA contends that the practice of "parental advisory" labeling is widely adhered to within the recording industry.

In addition to the parental advisory label, it is now common for artists and record companies to record two versions of an album—an explicit version and an edited version—allowing options for parents and consumers without censoring the speech of the artists. Certain retail stores sell only the edited versions of albums. Other stores have policies forbidding the sale of explicit versions to consumers under 18 years old.

The advent of widespread online music retailing has made the regulation of explicit content somewhat problematic. The RIAA outlines voluntary guidelines for online retailers as it does for record companies, but because online music distributors are typically not affiliated with the record companies or the artists, online retailers make their own decisions about whether or not to follow the RIAA's Parental Advisory Policy.

As online distribution of music became commonplace in the mid-to-late 1990s, the issue of property rights climbed to the forefront of music regulation. This phenomenon led to the second important issue surrounding the regulation of the music industry: consumer file sharing.

ONLINE PIRACY

The Digital Millennium Copyright Act of 1998 makes it a crime to circumvent antipiracy measures built into commercial software, outlaws the manufacture or sale of code-cracking devices for illegally copying software, limits Internet service providers from copyright infringement liabilities for transmitting information over the Internet, and requires webcasters to pay licensing fees to record companies. Despite the best intentions of this act, enforcement remains problematic because illegal file sharing involves millions of transactions per day.

The now-famous Napster case marked the true beginning in the fight against illegal file sharing. On December 7, 1999, RIAA on behalf of its members filed suit charging Napster with "contributory and vicarious copyright infringement." Napster, an online file sharing venue where members traded millions of sound recordings free of charge, had stated it was simply a conduit allowing people to share personal files. On February 12, 2001, after an initial appeal by Napster, the Ninth Circuit Court of Appeals sided with the District Court and the RIAA, ruling Napster to be in violation of copyright laws.

The Napster case was not the end of litigation against online file sharing. Suits against Aimster and Verizon soon followed. Despite these courtroom victories, the RIAA was not always successful in its quest to stop consumer file sharing. In April 2003, a U.S. district court in Los Angeles ruled in favor of Grokster and Morpheus and against the RIAA because these file-sharing companies allow users to swap music files directly rather than going through a central server,

which had been Napster's downfall. Judge Stephen Wilson likened the scenario to selling videocassette recorders (VCRs): The manufacturers of VCRs cannot be held liable for copyright infringements carried out by those who purchase VCRs. The RIAA has since redirected its efforts against Internet piracy from peer-to-peer (P2P) software providers to individual users, taking legal action against numerous consumers.

The recording industry loses an estimated $4.2 billion to piracy each year worldwide. *Piracy* generally refers to the duplication and distribution of sound recordings without permission from the record company. Online piracy specifically refers to the unauthorized uploading of a copyrighted sound recording and making it available to the public, or downloading a sound recording from an Internet site, even if the recording is not resold. In a speech to the New York State Bar Association and International Bar Association on October 23, 2003, addressing the legal issues involved in peer-to-peer file sharing, John G. Malcolm, deputy assistant attorney general of the U.S. Department of Justice's Criminal Division, stated,

> We do not believe . . . that new technologies, including the Internet, should be exempted from existing laws and societal norms simply because they are novel or easy to use . . . Can (we) take whatever we want, whenever we want it without paying for it just because we now have the means to do so?

In response to the illegal file-sharing trend, most major record labels have developed plans for subscription-based online sales. Internet file-sharing companies such as the iTunes Music Store, Pressplay, and RealPlayer have made copyrighted songs and albums legally available for online purchase in an à la carte format. The battle wages on, however, as digital technologies become more efficient and sophisticated. The latest trend is that of cellular phone ring tones; cell phone users may download (for a price) original music recordings from many popular albums, replacing the standard telephone ring. Consumers can install different ring tones to identify different callers, creating a scramble among record companies, artists, webcasters, and lawmakers to see who can best regulate and profit from the ever-changing phenomenon that is digital technology.

—Michelle Arganbright

See also Music, Transgressive History of; Music Lyrics, Effects of

FURTHER READINGS

Barnet, R. D., & Burriss, L. L. (2001). *Controversies of the music industry*. Westport, CT: Greenwood.

David, M., & Kirkhope, J. (2004). New digital technologies: Privacy/property, globalization, and law. *Perspectives on Global Development and Technology, 3*(4), 437–449.

Garrity, B. (2004). Digital dough divides biz. *Billboard, 116*(51), 1–2.

Heilman, D. (2001). *A tug-of-war over intellectual property.* Retrieved Oct. 13, 2005, from http://www.computeruser.com/articles/2005,1,2,2,0501,01.html

Krasilovsky, M. W., & Shemel, S. (1995). *This business of music.* New York: Billboard Books.

Malcolm, J. G. (2003). *Privacy and intellectual property—legal issues related to peer-to-peer file sharing over the Internet* (Testimony). Retrieved Oct. 13, 2005, from website: http://www.cybercrime.gov/Malcolmtestimony102303.htm.

Recording Industry Association of America. (2003). *About us.* Retrieved Oct. 13, 2005, from http://www.riaa.com/about/default.asp.

Recording Industry Association of America. (2003). *Antipiracy.* Retrieved Oct. 13, 2005, from http://www.riaa.com/issues/piracy/default.asp

Rosen, H. (2001). Press conference statement. Retrieved Oct. 13, 2005, from www.riaa.com/news/newsletter/press2001/021201_2.asp

WEBSITES

Recording Industry Association of America: www.riaa.com
For information on specific legal cases, see http://www.riaa.com/news/filings/default.asp

REGULATION, RADIO

Radio is a category of electronic media under the jurisdiction of the Federal Communications Commission (FCC), an independent administrative agency established by Congress in the Communications Act of 1934. Previously, Congress had established the Federal Radio Commission (FRC) in the Radio Act of 1927 to allocate broadcast radio frequencies. The 1934 act replaced the FRC with the FCC and expanded the regulatory authority of the agency.

Radio broadcasts use the electromagnetic spectrum, which is federally regulated as a national public resource. The FCC has exclusive authority from Congress to allocate the AM and FM bands of the spectrum by dividing them into assignable commercial and noncommercial frequencies and allotting them to individual stations intended to serve particular geographic locations, such as an area surrounding a small town or major city. Through licensing proceedings, the FCC assigns AM and FM radio frequencies to station operators called *licensees,* who are required by law to serve the public interest in exchange for the privilege of using the electromagnetic spectrum to broadcast.

The FCC regulates the structure of broadcast radio by such means as licensing application and renewal proceedings and also by enforcing such rules as those that limit the number of AM and FM radio stations that a single company can legally control in a local broadcast market. In addition, the FCC enforces some content regulations, including rules prohibiting broadcast obscenity and most tobacco advertising and a rule that seeks to shield children from indecent and profane broadcasts. With broadcast and cable television, the FCC enforces rules that regulate aspects of children's programming and advertising; there are no similar rules for radio broadcasters.

OBSCENITY, INDECENCY, AND PROFANITY IN RADIO BROADCASTS

Provisions in the Communications Act prohibit "obscene, indecent or profane language by means of radio communications," and the FCC is authorized to promulgate rules enforcing these provisions. Obscenity, as a constitutionally defined category of sexual expression, is devoid of First Amendment protection and banned in all media including electronic media like radio. Indecency and profanity, which are categories of nonobscene expression defined by the FCC, are protected by the First Amendment, and courts have placed constitutional limits on the extent to which the FCC can regulate these types of content on the airwaves. Current FCC rules allow nonobscene indecency and profanity in radio and television broadcasts but only during designated hours of the day when children are not likely to be part of the audience.

The U.S. Supreme Court has defined *obscenity* as material that contains patently offensive descriptions or depictions of sexual conduct and, when taken as a whole, appeals to prurient interest and lacks serious literary, artistic, political, or scientific value. The "prurient interest" requirement is judged from the perspective of a reasonable person applying contemporary community standards. The FCC enforces the ban on broadcast obscenity at all times on regulated electronic media, including radio.

The FCC has defined *indecency* as "language or material that, in context, depicts or describes, in terms patently offensive as measured by contemporary community standards for the broadcast medium, sexual or excretory activities or organs." The FCC has defined *profanity* as "including language that denot[es] certain of those personally reviling epithets naturally tending to provoke violent resentment or denoting language so grossly offensive to members of the public who actually hear it as to amount to a nuisance." FCC rules allow radio and television broadcasters to air nonobscene indecency and profanity only during the "safe-harbor" time period from 10 p.m. to 6 a.m. each day. The FCC can fine a broadcast radio station up to $32,500 per incident for broadcasting indecency or profanity outside the safe-harbor time period. The FCC does not have authority to regulate indecency or profanity on satellite, cable, or the Internet.

In 1995, in *Action for Children's Television v. F.C.C.*, the U.S. Court of Appeals, D.C. Circuit, approved the FCC's indecency definition. The court found the FCC could constitutionally use the safe-harbor approach to regulate broadcast indecency based on the strong governmental interest in shielding children from indecent broadcasts. Previously, in the 1978 case of *F.C.C. v. Pacifica Foundation,* the U.S. Supreme Court had upheld the constitutionality of FCC regulation of nonobscene indecency in radio broadcasts. In that case, the Court upheld a warning issued by the FCC to a radio station that had broadcast comedian George Carlin's "seven dirty words" monologue during daytime hours. In warning the station, the FCC found the radio broadcast indecent under the agency's definition. In its ruling, the Court concluded that broadcasting had become "uniquely pervasive" in the lives of the public and "uniquely accessible to children, even those too young to read." The Court concluded that the "special treatment of indecent broadcasting" was justified by the ease with which children could access broadcast material as compared to other media content.

BROADCAST RADIO AND ADVERTISING OF HARMFUL PRODUCTS

In the Federal Cigarette Labeling and Advertising Act, Congress banned advertising for cigarettes and little cigars as of January 1, 1971, for all electronic media under the jurisdiction of the FCC. Later that year, the U.S. Supreme Court upheld a federal court judgment finding the ban constitutional under the First Amendment. In 1986, Congress passed the Comprehensive Smokeless Tobacco Health Education Act and included smokeless tobacco in the tobacco advertising ban for electronic media. The ban on tobacco advertising in regulated electronic media includes AM and FM radio broadcasts.

On the other hand, current federal restrictions on gambling advertising apply to broadcast television but not to radio. No federal legislation or FCC rule currently prohibits or specifically restricts alcoholic beverage advertising on regulated electronic media including radio. Whether and when to air such advertising is largely within the discretion of broadcast radio licensees, although an argument could be made that alcoholic beverage advertising during radio programs with high levels of underage listeners would violate the public interest standard.

—*R. Michael Hoefges*

See also Children's Television Act of 1990; Federal Communications Commission (FCC), Advertising and

FURTHER READINGS

Action for Children's Television v. Federal Communications Commission (ACT III), 58 F.3d 564 (D.C. Cir., 1995).

Carter, T. B., Franklin, M. A., & Wright, J. B. (2003). *The First Amendment and the fifth estate.* New York: Foundation Press.

Federal Communications Commission. (2005, June). *About the FCC: A consumer guide to our organization, functions, and procedures.* Retrieved from http://www.fcc.gov/aboutus.html

Federal Communications Commission v. Pacifica Foundation, 438 U.S. 726 (1978).

In the matter of industry guidance on the (Federal Communications) Commission's case law interpreting 18 U.S.C. §1464 (indecency policy statement), 16 F.C.C.Rcd. 7999, *et seq.* (2001).

REGULATION, TELEVISION

The Communications Act of 1934 as amended requires that broadcast licensees serve the public interest, convenience, and necessity. Since the 1960s, this has consistently been interpreted to include meeting the special needs of the child audience. Historically, regulators have focused on shielding children from violent and sexually explicit programming, ameliorating the effects of advertising, and guaranteeing the provision of educational programming. Although the U.S. Congress sets the framework for regulating television, the Federal Communications Commission (FCC) decides how the public interest standard should be interpreted in particular situations and handles day-to-day enforcement.

REGULATION OF SEXUALLY EXPLICIT MATERIAL

Federal law prohibits the broadcast of obscene, indecent, or profane material. Although the transmission of obscene material (commonly thought of as hard-core pornography) has not occurred on television, the broadcast of indecent and profane material has been a cause of concern for decades. The FCC defines *indecency* as "language or material that depicts or describes, in terms patently offensive as measured by contemporary community standards for the broadcast medium, sexual or excretory activities or organs." *Profanity* is defined as "certain of those personally reviling epithets naturally tending to provoke violent resentment or denoting language so grossly offensive to members of the public who actually hear it as to amount to a nuisance."

Because indecent and profane materials are protected speech under the First Amendment, at least for adult consumption, the FCC has limited its enforcement of the indecency and profanity provisions to times of day when children are not likely to be in the broadcast audience, that is, between the hours of 6 a.m. and 10 p.m. Broadcasters who air prohibited material during those hours are subject to administrative sanctions including fines in the amount of $32,500 per utterance. In mid-2006, Congress was considering proposals that would raise the maximum fines for such violations to as much as $500,000 per utterance. It is important to note that as of 2005, these rules apply only to broadcast television. Subscription television services such as those carried on cable systems or direct broadcast satellite systems may transmit indecent or profane programming at any time.

REGULATION OF VIOLENT PROGRAMMING

As of 2005, there are no laws or regulations against the broadcast of violent programming on television. However, in 1996, Congress required the television industry to develop a program ratings code that would enable parents to determine the content of programs. These program ratings are listed in television program guides and appear in the corner of viewers' television screens at the beginning of each program. Also in 1996, Congress required that all new television sets be equipped with a device that would allow parents to exclude programs with certain ratings from being seen in the home. This *V-chip* reads the television program codes as they are being transmitted to the television receiver. Parents can then set the V-chip to exclude any program with a particular rating code—one indicating violent content, for example. The ratings code and V-chip can also be used to help parents censor programs with sexual material.

REGULATION OF ADVERTISING DIRECTED TOWARD CHILDREN

Recognizing that children's cognitive development might make it difficult for them to fully understand the purpose and intent of advertising, the FCC in 1974 issued a policy statement exhorting broadcasters to limit the number of commercials aimed at children. The statement also encouraged programmers to place *bumpers*—announcements helping children to understand a program change was coming—between program material and commercials. The commission also warned against using children's television show hosts to sell or promote products during a television program.

In the Children's Television Act of 1990, Congress set strict advertising limits on programs directed toward children age 12 and younger. According to the act, no more than 12 minutes of commercial material per hour may appear in children's programs on weekdays; on weekends, the limit is 10.5 minutes of commercial material per hour. Responding to concerns that some children's cartoons based on toy lines (e.g., G.I. Joe, the Smurfs) may in fact be no more than long commercials for the toys, Congress also prohibited the broadcast of "program-length commercials," leaving a definition of the term to the FCC. The commission has defined program-length commercials as "a program associated with a product in which commercials for that product aired." Thus, commercials for G.I. Joe action figures may not be aired during the *G.I. Joe* program, for example.

In a recent action, the FCC banned the practice of including website addresses in children's television programs if those addresses lead children to sites promoting the sale of products or services. All of the described limits on commercialization in children's television programs apply to both broadcast and cable network programming. Failure to abide by these limitations may lead to fines against the offending station or network.

PROVISION OF EDUCATIONAL PROGRAMMING FOR CHILDREN

The Children's Television Act of 1990 requires all broadcast television licensees to serve the educational and informational needs of children, defined by the FCC in this context as children 16 years of age and younger. FCC regulations currently require television licensees to air at least 3 hours of educational programming per week. Such programming must be *core* programming, which means that it must be at least 30 minutes in length and regularly scheduled at times when children are likely to be watching television, which the FCC defines as between 7 a.m. and 10 p.m. For purposes of the act, educational programming is defined broadly as "content that serves children's cognitive/intellectual or social/emotional needs." The FCC considers compliance with these requirements when the station's licenses are up for renewal every 8 years. A licensee that does not adhere to these requirements conceivably could lose its broadcast license. The educational programming requirements described here apply only to broadcast television licensees; they do not apply to cable television networks.

—*Michael A. McGregor*

See also Advertising, Regulation of; Children's Television Act of 1990; Federal Communications Commission (various entries); Telecommunications Act of 1996; Television Rating Systems, Parental Uses of; V-Chip (Violence Chip)

FURTHER READINGS

Federal Communications Commission, Implementation of Section 551 of the Telecommunications Act of 1996, 13 F.C.C.R 8232, 11 C.R. 934 (1998).

Federal Communications Commission, Industry Guidance on the Commission's Case Law Interpreting 18 U.S.C. § 1464 and Enforcement Policies Regarding Broadcast Indecency, 16 F.C.C. 7999 (2001).

Federal Communications Commission, Policies and Rules Concerning Children's Television Programming, 6 F.C.C.R. 2111, 68 R.R.2d 1615 (1991).

Federal Communications Commission, Policies and Rules Concerning Children's Television Programming, 11 F.C.C.R. 10660, 3 C.R. 1385 (1996).

RELATIONSHIP MARKETING

Relationship marketing is often used interchangeably with other terms, such as *one-to-one marketing, behavioral marketing, database marketing,* and *customer relationship marketing,* all of which mean more or less the same thing. The strategy is at the heart of a new digital marketing paradigm that emerged during the 1990s with the rapid growth and commercialization of the Internet. Among its early and influential proponents were Don Peppers and Martha Rogers, whose 1993 book, *The One to One Future* spawned a series of handbooks, seminars, articles, and conferences and quickly became a valued resource for online marketers. Relationship marketing is based on the principle of developing unique, long-term relationships with individual customers to create personalized marketing and sales appeals based on their individual preferences and behaviors. It has become a core strategy for marketers targeting teenagers, not only on the Web, but also through cell phones, video games, and other digital media.

Online marketers employ a variety of techniques to get to know each customer as intimately as possible. One method is the use of incentives, such as games, surveys, discounts, and prizes, to get individuals to supply personal information about themselves. For example, a survey can collect name, address, and email address, along with information about income level, attitudes, fears, and behaviors. While this is also a common direct marketing practice in "offline" media, such forms of data collection can become more intrusive in online and other interactive media, where the response time is quick and the incentives (e.g., free email, discounts, and other kinds of instant gratifications) can be hard to resist. Another method is the covert tracking of online behavior. Unlike TV ratings, which generally use anonymous aggregate numbers to reveal the viewing behavior of key demographic groups, online usage data can track how individuals respond to and interact with advertising. A burgeoning industry has developed to provide an array of *personalization technologies,* including *cookies,* which have been integrated into the basic design of interactive marketing. Through these various techniques, marketers compile a detailed profile of each customer, including not only demographic data but also his or her response to and interaction with advertising messages. The information can then be used to create and refine online ads and buying opportunities especially tailored to the psychographic and behavioral patterns of the individual. In some cases, the profiles are also sold to third parties.

In 1998, in response to a lobbying effort by children's advocacy and privacy groups, Congress passed the Children's Online Privacy Protection Act, which restricts the collection of personal information by Web operators from children under the age of 13. As a result, many online children's marketers were forced to curtail the growing practice of database marketing targeted at individual children. However, no government protections have been established for adolescents. Consequently, most of the websites aimed at teenagers make extensive use of data collection, profiling, and targeted advertising.

—*Kathryn C. Montgomery*

See also Advertising, Exposure to; Advertising, Market Size and

FURTHER READINGS

Connon, D. A. (2002, May/June). The ethics of database marketing. *Information Management Journal, 36*(3), 42–45.

Gordon, I. H, (1998). *Relationship marketing: New strategies, techniques, and technologies to win the customers you want and keep them forever.* New York: John Wiley.

Montgomery, K. C. (2001). Digital kids: The new online children's consumer culture. In D. G. Singer & J. L. Singer (Eds.), *Handbook of children and the media.* Thousand Oaks, CA: Sage.

Montgomery, K., & Pasnik, S. (1996). *Web of deception: Threats to children from online marketing.* Washington, DC: Center for Media Education.

Peppers, D., & Rogers, M. (1993). *The one to one future: Building relationships one customer at a time.* New York: Currency Doubleday.

Peppers, D., & Rogers, M. (2004). *Managing customer relationships: A strategic framework.* Hoboken, NJ: John Wiley.

Pitta, D. A. (1998). Marketing one-to-one and its dependence on knowledge discovery in databases. *The Journal of Consumer Marketing, 15*(5), 468.

Shani, D., & Chalasani, S. (1993). Exploiting niches using relationship marketing. *The Journal of Business and Industrial Marketing, 8*(4), 58–67.

Turow, J. (1997). *Breaking up America: Advertisers and the new media world.* Chicago: University of Chicago Press.

WEBSITES

Association for the Advancement of Relationship Marketing: http://www.aarm.org

RELATIONSHIPS, ONLINE

See ONLINE RELATIONSHIPS

RESEARCH METHODS, CHILDREN AND

Children and teenagers represent a very special clientele when it comes to research; they are still developing and are challenged by the various influences on their identity development as they seek to find their place in life; to learn about themselves by dealing with others; to interact with and position themselves within the family, the peer group, and other institutions; and to perceive their gender and act according to their role. Often, they turn for help to the available media. The theoretical concept of development tasks may be used as a framework for research involving young people. The development of young people is no longer viewed as occurring in strictly separate stages but rather is seen as an individual process that takes place amid various complex social demands. Media research with children, therefore, refers to three related but distinct processes Valkenburg identifies as imaginative play, daydreaming, and creativity. Above all, the research on children requires a wide range of methodologies, all of which must be interpreted according to age-related ways of perception and processing, allowing for an analysis of how the child makes meaning from different perspectives and with various methods and instruments. Procedures must be flexible and adequate for every situation while allowing young research participants to promote their own points of view, fostering a specific child-oriented need and topic structure. Children may still find it difficult to concentrate on the experimental task for long and may express their concerns accordingly; in addition, they are seldom aware of the consequences of their media use.

A variety of methods are needed to re-enact, analyze, and document children's media use. Cognitive, emotional, and social stages of media processing can be distinguished only analytically because they are always intertwined in the process of actual media interaction, and children do not talk about them as if they were separate stages. Only a combination of various methods—qualitative and quantitative—allows for an adequate approach to the field of research and particular investigations. The complex way in which children deal with media requires that analysis reflect a variety of methods and perspectives. Triangulations in research make this possible by specifically combining research perspectives and methods that are suitable for considering various aspects of a problem.

In media research involving children, questioning and observation are the predominant methods. Questioning—especially with the help of main thread interviews—is the only direct approach to gain insight into the child's self-assessment, even though it is quite demanding for the researcher. When children are interviewed directly, the researcher is confronted with problems arising from the limited ability of children to express themselves verbally, which makes the communication between researcher and subject more difficult. A direct interview first and foremost requires the interviewer to show empathy and sensitivity in working with children; of course, test materials, test conditions, and specific demands suitable for work with children are needed. It seems reasonable to take the advice of Yarrow (1960), who suggests that the interviewer assign to the child an expert role.

With small children, it is appropriate to search for an age-specific approach to avoid anxiety and inhibition as well as to facilitate subconscious deductions and connections. The use of cartoons and drawings is recommended, and with preschool children, the introduction of a hand puppet may prove useful for mediation between researcher and subject. This may create a less asymmetric level and avoid socially expected answers. In addition, the hand puppet may facilitate subconscious deductions and connections. Puppets are familiar toys children use predominantly to express topics of self- and social assessment in a role play; "playing pretend"—a constituent of child role-play, especially at kindergarten age—may enable children to convey thoughts, feelings, desires, and hopes that underlie their actions.

A second and equally important empirical method is that of participant observation. One of its benefits is that it does not rely on verbal material; also, children are more adept than adults at ignoring the observer. An observation is, therefore, a reasonable alternative and extension to interviews or questionnaires. One disadvantage is a certain arbitrariness in choosing and defining observation units theoretically; consequently, it is important to ensure an intersubjective reenactment by making sure others can understand what the observer did. In addition, observation techniques require a lot of training for the observer.

In combination with observing everyday play situations designed as initiated role-play, participant observation may be a suitable approach to understanding the impact of media use on young children's behavior. Following the observation, the researcher may fall back on the most prominent form of play in social interaction with children of the same age—role-play—to access the underlying approach to meaning-making and meaning attribution. This is helpful when complex, multilayered mental experiences are to be described. Subjectively experienced spatial-temporal contexts related to the child's reaction to the place should be registered comprehensively during the survey. On top of that, the role-play method makes possible a wide range of natural patterns of behavior and nonverbal modes of expression.

In using children's drawings, extra attention should focus on nonverbal meaning contexts and explicit evaluation of the child's aesthetic responses to media, such as their favorite media figure on TV. Drawings provide an in-depth psychological insight into children's meaning-making that cannot be gained from methods such as interviews and participant observation of play situations. The analysis of drawings provides insight into basic and unconscious processing of media experiences. The symbolic content of drawings and their "hidden meaning," expressed through the choice of depicted objects and their relationships as well as stylistically determined features such as color, line, and form of objects, allow the researcher to deduce the meaning children may have gained from the content of media, their perceptive and intellectual abilities (through choice of forms and themes), their emotional condition at the time of drawing (type of line, graphic expression, disposition, character), and their developmental stage.

Experiments are carried out primarily with young children, who are not yet able to verbally express experiences and attitudes. For instance, Grimm (1999) describes measurement of a baby's reaction to audiovisual stimuli by evaluating sucking behavior with specially designed dummies that constantly measure sucking intensity. Such results can be analyzed later on with respect to the stimulus presentation. Another research area involves topics linked with social taboos that provoke socially acceptable answers; studies focusing on violence or pornography, for example, might use physiological measurements.

Experiments try to control all the variables that influence children's media actions, with the goal of revealing the influence/impact of media supply, social settings, the perception situation, and sociodemographic factors. Nevertheless, classic sociological experiments are often criticized for having little ecological validity; in other words, results from a lab situation may not be transferable to everyday life. Research trials in the field of qualitative research on children and the media should take place in contexts that are as natural as possible, and variations should be of an everyday nature. The field of child media research looks primarily at cognitive aspects; an example is Troseth's 1999 study, which investigated whether 2-year-olds profited from video sequences in a real-life orientation task.

Studies concerning interaction patterns, for instance, with computer games, and their new meaning in relation to children's use call for innovations in research. Process- and situation-centered methods must be combined to measure cognitive processes during media use. Methodological suggestions and comments on available procedures can be found in studies on selective use of television and in research papers on the perception of online offers. An important method in this context is thinking aloud, a specific form of asking questions in order to evaluate orientation and decision tasks during the viewing of media. A combination of various procedures can be used in this context. For instance, Bucher and Barth (1998) combined observation (video recording) of the subjects, screen recording, and thinking aloud in their experimental study of perception patterns during online communication.

Screen- and video recording seem adequate methods to monitor the behavior of children when they work with interactive elements of computer programs, allowing for an analysis of decision tasks, possible options, and the final decision. Aufenanger (2003) pointed out that this method is able to record children's navigation in hypermedia and their commentaries as well. For school-age children, the main thread interview (in this case without a hand puppet), the group interview, group discussion (for those who are already able to take another's perspective), and participant observation seem suitable methods. Children 6 years of age and older also qualify for representative or standardized questionnaires as they are already literate. However, children up to the age of 10 years have to be assisted with questionnaires, or the questions must be asked verbally and the questionnaire filled in for them. Besides the questionnaire, a combination of concepts, self-assessment, protocol, or notes may prove useful.

Young children are not yet adjusted to temporal aspects of the world, and their animistic-anthropomorphic way of thinking is influenced strongly by momentary desires. Their ability to distinguish between fiction and reality is still based on unspecified ideas. To maintain a comprehensive concept of the world, main thread interviews and representative/standardized interviews with their parents and teachers are advisable. An advantage of involving parents and teachers in the field of child media research is that the respective educational concept receives a central importance. The attitudes of parents and teachers also influence the children's interactive competence.

Future research should not simply embark on the quest for effective methods because their usefulness depends on being seriously grounded in theory. For instance, Valkenburg suggests more elaborated theoretical models, in which child factors (e.g., developmental level, intelligence) and different environmental agents (e.g., media exposure, family influences) all operate as interacting determinants of children's development creativity.

—*Ingrid Paus-Hasebrink*

See also Media Effects, History of Research on; Research Methods (various entries)

FURTHER READINGS

Ammons, R. B. (1950). Reaction on a projective doll-play interview of white males two to six years of age to difference in skin color and facial feature. *Journal of Genetic Psychology, 70,* 323–341.

Aufenanger, S. (2000). Die Vorstellung von Kindern im virtuellen Raum. *DISKURS, 1,* 25–27.

Aufenanger, S. (2003). *Wie Kinder die neuen Medien verstehen* [How children understand new media]. Retrieved November 23, 2005, from http://snm03.snm-hgkz.ch/tiki/tiki-index.php?page=wie+Kinder+die+neuen+Medien+verstehen

Bucher, H.-J. & Barth, C. (1998). Rezeptionsmuster der Onlinekommunikation. *Media Perspektiven, 10,* 517–523.

Denzin, N. K. (1989). *The research act.* Englewood Cliffs, NJ: Prentice Hall.

Grimm, J. (1999). *Fernsehgewalt. Zuwendungsattraktivität, Erregungsverläufe, sozialer Effekt. Zur Begründung und praktischen Anwendung eines kognitiv-physiologischen Ansatzes der Medienrezeptionsforschung am Beispiel von Gewaltdarstellungen.* Opladen/Wiesbaden: Westdeutscher Verlag.

Havighurst, R. J. (1972). *Developmental tasks and education*. New York: McKay.

Paus-Haase, I., & Keuneke, S. (1999). Symbolangebote und kindliche Ästhetik. Zur spezifischen Welt- und Selbstwahrnehmung auf der Basis von Medieninhalten. In N. Neuß (Ed.), *Ästhetisches in der Welt von Kindern* (pp. 235–250). Frankfurt: GEP-Buch.

Paus-Haase, I., Süss, D., & Lampert, C. (2001). Kinder als prägende Akteure neuer Kommunikationskulturen. Reflexion adäquater methodischer Zugriffe. In U. Maier-Rabler & M. Latzer (Eds.), *Kommunikationskultur zwischen Kontinuität und Wandel. Universelle Netzwerke für die Zivilgesellschaft* (pp. 317–332). Konstanz: UVK.

Paus-Hasebrink, I. (2005). Forschung mit Kindern und Jugendlichen. In I. Mikos & C. Wegener (Eds.), *Qualitative Medienforschung. Ein Handbuch* (pp. 222–231). Konstanz: UVK & UTB.

Petermann, F., & Windmann, S. (1993). Sozialwissenschaftliche Erhebungstechniken bei Kindern. In M. Markefka & B. Nauck (Eds.), *Handbuch der Kindheitsforschung* (pp. 125–139). Berlin: Luchterhand.

Sader, M. (1995). Rollenspiel. In U. Flick et al. (Eds.), *Handbuch qualitative Sozialforschung. Grundlagen, Konzepte, Methoden und Anwendungen* (pp. 193–198). Weinheim: Beltz Psychologie Verlags Union.

Troseth, G. L. (1999, September 1–5). *Getting a clear picture: Young children's understanding of a televised image.* Paper presented at the IXth European Conference on Developmental Psychology, Island of Spetses, Greece.

Valkenburg, P. M. (2001). Television and the child's developing imagination. In D. G. Singer & J. Singer (Eds.), *Handbook of children and the media* (pp. 121–134). London: Sage.

Yarrow, L. J. (1960). Interviewing children. In P. E. Mussen (Ed.), *Handbook of research methods in child development* (pp. 561–602). New York: John Wiley.

RESEARCH METHODS, CONTENT ANALYSES

The method of content analysis extends back into the 18th century, when the method of counting words in hymns and sermons was used to uncover heresy. It has since been used for a variety of purposes. Historically, although content analysis is embedded in the social sciences, communications researchers have focused primarily on the manifest content of communications exchanges; these analyses typically have not been concerned with behaviors beyond those strictly related to message producing and handling. In terms of television, the primary purpose of content analysis has traditionally been to identify, document, and trace major dimensions of the programming. For example, researchers have assessed the nature and measured the extent of violent acts on broadcast television programs. Content analysis has been used to measure and assess content of other types of media, such as newspapers, magazines, and, more recently, video games and the Internet. Recently, data gathered through content analyses have also been used in combination with other data, such as survey data, to relate content variables to other variables, such as personality characteristics, attitudes, and violent or sexual behaviors.

The major steps of a content analysis involve identifying the variables to be counted (e.g., physical violence against women), determining the unit of analysis (e.g., per hour or scene, page, song, or game level), deciding on a sample and sampling procedure (e.g., one week of prime-time television or one Internet site), training coders and assessing reliability (i.e., via percentage agreement or kappa calculation), and coding the sample. The process can be complex; variables and units of analysis must be well-defined to achieve acceptable reliability among coders—something as simple as counting the number of red shirts in a single television program can be surprisingly difficult (e.g., is a tank top a shirt? Where is the line between maroon and red? If the shirt is on a chair, but not presently being worn, should it still be counted?). Reliability and validity are important aspects of content coding. Researchers juggle defining a variable narrowly enough that coders will consistently make the same judgments about the material (i.e., be reliable) and making sure that the broader viewing audience would be likely to interpret the data in the same manner (i.e., be valid).

As a research method, a content analysis can evolve according to the complexity of research questions. Some analyses have now begun to include contextual elements surrounding the depiction or activity in question as a way to explore whether certain attributes of the message tend to be more meaningful to viewers than others. Other studies grapple with more philosophical concerns, such as how to accurately consider the ways individual interpretations of the material in question may vary by age, class, gender, or culture. Because the process involves counting, content analyses are most often regarded as a quantitative research method; however, content analysis is also closely associated with qualitative research, particularly narrative methods.

—*C. Lynn Sorsoli*

See also Food Advertising, Content in; Media Effects, History of Research on; Sex in Television, Content Analysis of

FURTHER READINGS

Krippendorff, K. (2004). *Content analysis: An introduction to its methodology* (2nd ed.). Thousand Oaks, CA: Sage.

Kunkel, D., Cope, K. M., Farinola, W. M., Biely, E., Rollin, E., & Donnerstein, E. (1999). *Sex on TV: A biennial report to the Kaiser Family Foundation.* Washington, DC: Kaiser Family Foundation.

Neuendorf, K. A. (2001). *The content analysis guidebook.* Thousand Oaks, CA: Sage.

RESEARCH METHODS, ETHICAL ISSUES IN

All research involves a wide range of ethical issues, which have to be taken into account at every stage of the research process. These concern not only specific issues related to young participants, such as ensuring their privacy, but also issues related to the methods used to gain access to the data or field, the quality of the collected material (e.g., how questions are worded), and the later analysis. Five main issues are often examined in the literature on ethics and research: the aspects of power, informed consent and choice, confidentiality, independence, and the reporting and disseminating of findings. All these issues are also crucial when conducting research online, for example, via email interviews or observations; this type of research also raises additional ethical challenges.

In research, the issue of power is always present, and this becomes even more evident when conducting research with children. The adult researcher may be perceived as an authority figure whose viewpoints dominate the research situation. Informed consent means that all participants, whatever their age, must be informed about and understand the purpose of the study, what their role is, and how the collected data will be used and presented. In addition, participants should always have the choice of withdrawing from a study anytime during the research process. However, it is not enough just to inform children that their participation is voluntary. Every researcher must reflect on whether the child actually has the opportunity to say no to a teacher or an adult researcher and is not feeling parental or peer pressure. For example, is a lack of

motivation to participate an indication of unwillingness to take part in a study? The third issue, confidentiality, involves concealing the young informant's identity. Children's rights to privacy and confidentiality must be taken into account when, for example, presenting the results and deciding where the data are to be stored. The fourth question requires that researchers address the ethics of funding and consider the independence of a study from commercial business and other nonacademic interests. In this connection, the question of when and if the young participants should get some sort of reward for taking part in a study must be answered. Payments can be used as a tool for persuasion and thereby pressure the child to participate. As for reporting and disseminating the findings, several ethical issues are encountered including the possibility of giving personal feedback to the participants and whether they will be able to comment on the findings. Additional aspects to be examined are in what forums the findings are published and whether conclusions are based on the collected data or merely supporting the researcher's views.

—*Ulrika Sjöberg*

See also Media Effects, History of Research on; Media Effects, Models of; United Nations Convention on the Rights of the Child

FURTHER READINGS

Alderson, P., & Morrow, V. (2004). *Ethics, social research, and consulting with children and young people.* Essex, UK: Barnardo's.

Buchanan, E. A. (Eds.). (2004). *Readings in virtual research ethics: Issues and controversies.* London: Information Science Publishing.

Malcolm, H. (2005). Ethical considerations in researching children's experiences. In S. Greene & D. Hogan (Eds.), *Researching children's experiences. Approaches and methods* (pp. 61–86). London: Sage.

Morrow, V., & Richards, M. (1996). The ethics of social research with children: An overview. *Children & Society, 10,* 90–105.

RESEARCH METHODS, ETHNOGRAPHY

Ethnography is a research method that stresses direct observation of people in typical social environments.

Its goal is to build a detailed, holistic description of individuals' behaviors, attitudes, and interpretations of other people. This is done by joining a group under study as a participating member, often for weeks or months. Thus, the researcher gathers information on the group's activities (e.g., television viewing in a typical family's home) within the context of day-to-day living. A second goal of ethnography is to present the group's experiences in their own words and images. Usually, the ethnographer is not an original member of the group, so he or she must bridge the barriers against constructing this insider's perspective. This means that the language, routines, and cultural values of the group must be described in detail by a virtual stranger.

A few researchers have applied the ethnographic method to studies of media and children's daily lives. Two studies, one by Jennifer Bryce and Hope Leichter and one by Amy Jordan, used ethnographic methods to study family media use. Their studies showed that families operate as a system of interrelated components (e.g., parents, children, home organization, media) that create daily routines and a shared sense of reality. The researchers showed that families' media use reflected their attitudes about the use of time. Middle- and upper-class families defined time as a precious resource. Rules for watching television were reflected by pointing out "good" and "bad" uses of time. Jordan revealed that media were often used to punctuate parts of the day, initiating or ending the family's various routines. One example was the use of electronic tapes and books at bedtime to console children and help them sleep.

Other proponents argue that ethnography's strengths lie in the unstructured nature of observations, permitting researchers to show family life (and media's place in it) as it is lived. This can be as simple as tracking media use in the home or as complex as exploring the way the people's interpretations of media content show up in their ideas about "normal" family life. Ideally, the result is a realistic picture of media and social life. However, it is hard to get people to consent to participate in ethnographies. Once the ethnographer is admitted to the group, it is hard to know if what he or she sees is "real" and not altered for appearance's sake. This complicates the goal of faithfully describing media's role in daily life. Furthermore, ethnographers looking so closely at these activities can sometimes overlook broader social forces that shape them (e.g., media corporations' influence on available media choices).

—*Ron Warren*

See also Media Effects, History of Research on; Media Effects, Models of

FURTHER READINGS

Bryce, J. W., & Leichter, H. J. (1983). The family and television: Forms of mediation. *Journal of Family Issues, 4*, 309–328.

Jordan, A. B. (1992). Social class, temporal orientation, and mass media use within the family system. *Critical Studies in Mass Communication, 9*, 374–386.

Lindlof, T. R., & Taylor, B. C. (2002). *Qualitative communication research methods* (2nd ed.). Thousand Oaks, CA: Sage.

RESEARCH METHODS, EXPERIMENTAL STUDIES

Experiments test the causal relationship between at least one factor (or independent variable) and at least one potentially affected (dependent) variable. Like experiments in the natural sciences, experiments in the social sciences and in media research rely on the comparison of outcomes that follow from different starting conditions. These starting conditions constitute the experimental treatment and are designed to differ from each other in a systematic fashion and only in respect to the independent variable, whose impact on the dependent variables is to be assessed. Participants (e.g., media users) are confronted with these differing starting conditions, and one or several empirical methods are used to measure the dependent variables (e.g., questionnaires, observational methods, physiological measures). These data are then compared between participants who were exposed to different starting conditions. Substantial (i.e., statistically significant) differences in the dependent variables represent empirical evidence for a causal effect of the independent variable on the dependent measures. Alternative explanations for group differences in the dependent measures (e.g., gender, age, media literacy) are ruled out because participants are randomly assigned to starting conditions. This randomization is expected to form groups that are (in average values) very similar (or, given a sufficient number of individuals per group, equal) to each other. Therefore, alternative explanations for differences in the dependent variables cannot be valid because in the ideal case, any conceivable alternative factor is distributed identically across experimental conditions.

EXAMPLE: EFFECTS OF VIDEO GAMES

In research on adolescents and the media, the impact of violent media on aggression is frequently tested experimentally. Bushman and Anderson (2002) randomly assigned their participants to play either a violent video game or a nonviolent game for 20 minutes (experimental treatment). Subsequently, the participants were asked to read three stories that included a potential interpersonal conflict and were required to write down a completion for each story, addressing the actions, thoughts, and feelings of the protagonists. After the experiment, trained coders went through the participants' writings and counted the number of aggressive actions, thoughts, and feelings that were mentioned. This number reflects the salience of aggression in the participants' mind at the time they wrote the texts (i.e., immediately after the experimental treatment). Players of a violent video game produced more aggressive story elements than players of a nonviolent game, which the authors regard as experimental demonstration of the causal relationship between game violence and aggressive thinking (as a component of aggressive behavior tendencies).

EXPERIMENTAL DESIGN

Experiments are the best choice to test short-term causal effects in media research. Careful planning is needed, however, to create methodologically sound experimental designs that are in line with one's theoretical assumptions. Video games, for instance, are interactive and—in contrast to films—open to participants' individual modifications, which is a potential problem for valid experimentation. Other limitations have to be kept in mind as well (e.g., differences between experimental laboratories and real life; neglected long-term effects); combining experiments with other approaches (e.g., panel studies) may amplify the evidence for theoretical assumptions.

—*Christoph Klimmt*

See also Aggression, Television and; Electronic Games, Cognitive Effects of; Electronic Games, Violence in; General Aggression Model (GAM); Media Effects; Media Effects, History of Research on; Research Methods (various entries); Social Learning Theory/ Social Cognitive Theory; Violence, Experimental Studies of

FURTHER READINGS

Brewer, M. B. (2000). Research design and issues of validity. In H. T. Reis & C. M. Judd (Eds.), *Handbook of research methods in social and personality psychology* (pp. 3–16). Cambridge, UK: Cambridge University Press.

Bushman, B. J., & Anderson, C. A. (2002). Violent video games and hostile expectations: A test of the general aggression model. *Personality and Social Psychology Bulletin, 28,* 1679–1686.

Davis, S. F. (Ed.). (2003). *Handbook of research methods in experimental psychology.* Malden, MA: Blackwell.

Klimmt, C., Vorderer, P., & Ritterfeld, U. (2004). Experimentelle Medienforschung mit interaktiven Stimuli: Zum Umgang mit Wechselwirkungen zwischen "Reiz" und "Reaktion" [Experimental media research with interactive stimuli: Dealing with interaction between "stimulus" and "response"]. In W. Wirth, E. Lauf, & A. Fahr (Eds.), *Forschunglogik und design in der Kommunikationswissenschaft Band 1* (pp. 142–156). Köln: von Halem.

RESEARCH METHODS, FIELD STUDIES

Field studies refer to studies that are conducted in a natural setting such as school, home, or play area. The use of field studies is especially seen in two traditions of media research. The first focuses on media effects by, for example, observing whether viewing of violent contents encourages aggressive modes of behavior. The second tradition is that of cultural studies, in which field studies are conducted to examine such topics as the way media are used and embedded in various social and cultural contexts in people's daily life.

Television has received the most attention in field studies conducted on children's use of media. Besides the effects of television on aggressive behavior, as well as the effects of advertising, the main focus has been on how young viewers interact with (e.g., emotionally) and interpret TV programs, usually applying a cognitive-developmental perspective, and on their social uses of television. In an example of such research, Tannis MacBeth Williams and colleagues studied the effects of television in a Canadian town before and after TV arrived in the households. The researchers observed an increased number of aggressive acts by second graders in classrooms and on the playground.

The work of Michelle A. Wolf in the United States examines how younger children (4 to 12 years old)

make sense of television programs by observing and interviewing the children and by letting them produce their own television programs at a day-care/summer camp facility. Several aspects are discussed, including the influence of personality on content preferences, children's ability to distinguish between reality and fiction, and their understanding of television's narrative conventions. Another study on television has been conducted by the Australian researcher Patricia Palmer, who analyzed younger children's (8 to 9 and 11 to 12 years old) relationship with television in their homes, using interviews, drawings, observations, and surveys. The project looks at how television content is discussed and defined by children (taking into account age and gender), what they actually do in front of the TV set, and the social uses of television within the family and among friends. A more recent field study has been done by Danish media researcher Jesper Olesen, who observed and compared children's (10 to 12 years old) use of television and video with the family and peers at home. The study shows how the two types of viewing contexts influence the child's viewer position. Children are regarded as experienced viewers when watching with friends, but different rules apply in the family, where the child is assigned a subordinate position as adults evaluate the child's experience in terms of age and developmental stage.

Although the most common methods used in field studies are observations, interviews, and field notes, changing perspectives in child and childhood research have evolved recently, with implications for the methods used in field studies. Children today are seen as reliable informants of their own experiences. The need to perceive young people as active researchers is also stressed in terms of, for example, having a say in the nature and focus of research. By, for instance, providing children with different visual means in research, such as video cameras, new opportunities are given to the children to construct visual representations of their lives, and new types of knowledge result.

—*Ulrika Sjöberg*

See also Media Effects; Notel, Unitel, Multitel Study; Research Methods, Ethnography; Research Methods, Natural Experiments

FURTHER READINGS

Olesen, J. (2000). Childhood, media, and viewer positions. In B. Van den Bergh & J. Van den Bulck (Eds.), *Children and media: multidisciplinary approaches* (pp. 67–88). Leuven-Apeldoorn: Garant.
Palmer, P. (1986). *The lively audience. A study of children around the TV set*. North Sydney: Allen & Unwin Australia Pty Ltd.
Williams, T. M. (Ed.). (1986). *The impact of television: A natural experiment in three communities*. Orlando, FL: Academic Press.
Wolf, M. A. (1987). How children negotiate television. In T. R. Lindlof (Ed.), *Natural audiences: Qualitative research of media uses and effects* (pp. 58–94). New Jersey: Ablex.

RESEARCH METHODS, LONGITUDINAL STUDIES

Longitudinal studies examine change over time. Studies that measure the *same* people, organizations, media, or other entity repeatedly over time are longitudinal, such as a study of the same children who are sixth graders this year and were fifth graders last year. Studies that measure *new* individuals or entities at different time points are cross-sectional, for example, a study of this year's sixth graders compared to last year's sixth graders.

How change occurs over time is critical to many theories and questions regarding children, adolescents, and the media. Taking a developmental perspective involves noting how the children change over time in their relationship with the media. For example, as children age, how do their reactions to violent movies change?

Theories that aim to explain processes or understand causality also benefit from attempting to model how the process changes over time. Take, for example, the question of whether exposure to risky sex in media portrayals affects the likelihood of teens engaging in risky sex. If a researcher collects data at one time point and finds a correlation between media exposure and risky sex behavior, the process is unclear. Did exposure to risky sex portrayals lead adolescents to model that behavior? Or, did a propensity to engage in risky sex lead teens to seek out media likely to contain sexual content? With longitudinal data, it may be possible to test both hypotheses to see which explanation best fits the data.

To conduct a longitudinal analysis, a researcher needs at least two waves or rounds of data; four or more are better for understanding the process of change. The data could be generated from, for example, repeated observations, surveys, physiological measures, or analyses of media content over time.

Longitudinal studies also require a measure of time that makes sense in the context of the study, such as seconds, weeks, years, sessions, age, or grade. It is important is to measure around the time when the researcher expects change to be detectable. Some analysis methods require the same time interval between measurements (e.g., every 3 months). Other methods allow unique intervals per person, such as the time elapsed since each child's natural exposure to a media message. Some methods also allow explanatory variables to vary over time.

There have been advances recently in the methods available to analyze longitudinal data and the statistical packages that include those techniques. Multilevel modeling can examine simultaneously the predictors for change over time within individuals, differences between individuals, and differences in groupings of individuals. For example, a national study examined the effects of alcohol advertising exposure over time, individual characteristics, and levels of alcohol advertising present in each market to understand which factors contributed to drinking over time. Another analysis method is event history analysis (also known as survival analysis and failure rate analysis), which examines when specific events occur to individuals and what predicts them. For example, when do youth begin and subsequently cease complying with a campaign message?

—*Leslie Snyder*

See also Media Effects, History of Research on

FURTHER READINGS

Singer, J. D., & Willett, J. B. (2003). *Applied longitudinal data analysis: Modeling change and event occurrence.* New York: Oxford University Press.

RESEARCH METHODS, META-ANALYSES

Meta-analysis, also known as research synthesis, is a quantitative technique used to analyze the research literature in a particular domain. Although the goals are similar to a qualitative literature review, meta-analyses use established procedures to search, code, and quantitatively analyze all of the relevant studies. For example, Anderson has used meta-analyses to examine the effects of violent video games on children by coding and analyzing all published research studies to date that test the impact violent video games.

VALUE OF META-ANALYSIS

Syntheses of the research evidence are useful for a number of reasons. Meta-analyses can answer research questions in a more reliable manner than basing an answer on any one study. Given that every study has flaws and that the particular flaws are different for different studies, looking at the entire body of work avoids the biases in any single study.

In addition, meta-analysis avoids researcher biases that may affect qualitative literature reviews. It is particularly useful when there is a large body of research addressing a particular question or theoretical relationship. Research syntheses may uncover patterns of findings—when relationships are stronger and when they are weaker—that have not been discussed in prior reviews or remain controversial. For example, a meta-analysis by Groesz, Levine, and Murnen of the effect of experimental exposure to thin media images on body satisfaction found small differences between girls and women under 19 and those over 19, but a greater effect among girls and women with a history of body image problems or who scored high on body dissatisfaction prior to the experimental exposure.

Meta-analysis also focuses attention on the size and direction of effects, rather than statistical significance. Understanding the size of an effect may impact theory, inform public policies, be used to set realistic goals for applied programs, provide a benchmark for the evaluation of future programs, and inform the number of research participants needed in future studies. For example, the results of a study by Anderson in which the average effect of violent video games on aggressive behavior was $r = .26$, coupled with the amount of violent game playing that is taking place, suggest an urgent need to inform the public about the impact of such games. In the Groesz et al. study, the average effect size of experimental exposure to thin body-ideal media images on body satisfaction was $r = .15$, supporting the theory that television and fashion magazines promote a standard of beauty that leads many people to feel bad about their bodies and suggesting a need to develop effective media literacy programs to reduce the impact of such exposure.

Finally, meta-analyses are useful in identifying the methodological shortcomings present in a research area. Often, theoretically relevant studies fail to report adequately the statistics necessary for meta-analyses. Sometimes, the research synthesis points to a need to use a different type of study design to triangulate an answer to a research question. Anderson's violent video game meta-analysis concluded that there is a strong need for longitudinal studies in the area to complement the existing experiments and correlational studies.

DESIGN OF A META-ANALYSIS

The first step in conducting a meta-analysis is to design the study. What is the research question? What systematic procedure will be used to search for relevant studies? This may include searching particular electronic databases, using reference sections of other articles, and contacting researchers in a professional organization. What criteria will be used for deciding which studies are relevant? This typically involves inclusion of key variables, reporting of key statistical information, and study design criteria. The research team must also design the codebook and coding sheet. The second step is to conduct the search and gather the relevant studies. Next, one codes the accumulated studies, using a content analysis procedure. Finally, the data are analyzed. The effect sizes reported in the studies need to be converted into a common statistic, such as *d* or *r*; meta-analysis books provide summaries of common conversion formulas.

Meta-analyses are applicable only to the quantitative studies in an area. The approach does not take into account theoretical papers or qualitative studies. To be included, studies need to report the effects for the same constructs and relationships.

—*Leslie Snyder*

See also Body Image in Girls and Young Women; Electronic Games, Effects of; Electronic Games, Violence in; Media Effects, History of Research on; Media Effects, Models of

FURTHER READINGS

Anderson, C. A. (2004). An update on the effects of playing violent video games. *Journal of Adolescence, 27,* 113–122.
Groesz, L. M., Levine, M. P., & Murnen, S. K. (2002). The effect of experimental presentation of thin media images on body satisfaction: A meta-analytic review. *International Journal of Eating Disorders, 31,* 1–16.
Lipsey, M. W., & Wilson, D. B. (2001). *Practical meta-analysis.* Thousand Oaks, CA: Sage.
Rosenthal, R. (1994). Parametric measures of effect size. In H. Cooper & L. V. Hedges (Eds.), *The handbook of research synthesis* (pp. 231–244). New York: Russell Sage Foundation.

RESEARCH METHODS, NATURAL EXPERIMENTS

When researchers want to document some aspect of media effects, their goal is to determine whether there is a causal relationship between media use and users' responses or behavior. The design of the research is crucial in determining whether causal inferences can be made. In their classic monograph and its more recent revisions, Campbell and his colleagues explained the distinction between *true* or *randomized* experiments and *quasi-experiments,* including both *natural experiments,* which are the focus of this entry, and *field experiments.*

In true experiments, which are usually conducted in laboratory rather than real-world settings, participants are randomly assigned to the various treatment group conditions, so causal inferences about the treatment effects *can* be made. But it is rarely possible for the researchers to manipulate more than a few independent variables relevant to the potential cause-effect relationship of interest, so true randomized experiments usually test hypotheses about the independent and interactive effects of only a small number of manipulated variables. Therefore, they cannot answer the question of whether the potential causal effect occurs under real-life conditions involving many more relevant factors. Depending on the research methods used to study natural experiments, one of their strengths is that they may be able to answer both the *can* (causal influence) and the *does* (real-life) ecological validity questions regarding media effects.

WHAT IS A NATURAL EXPERIMENT?

In natural experiments, which are sometimes called *found* experiments, researchers do not manipulate the group differences they study. Instead, they take advantage of a naturally occurring change to assess its effects. For example, a preexisting group with access to some form of media (e.g., television, Internet, mobile phone) may be compared with another preexisting group without similar access. Or a preexisting group may be studied before a medium (e.g., television reception) first becomes available and then again after some period of use. Ideally, this group experiencing change in access to the medium of interest will be contrasted with other similar (control) groups whose exposure did not change over the same interval, in a "before and after" study.

CAUSAL INFERENCES IN NATURAL EXPERIMENTS

The first condition for making a causal inference, the knowledge that the media cause preceded its effect in time, is usually easily met in natural experiments. This timing difference is probably what interested the researchers in studying the situation.

The second condition for causal inference is that the media exposure (treatment condition) and its effect on users (e.g., on their school achievement, or aggression) must covary. This is usually measured statistically, but statistical errors sometimes occur. For example, there may be a difference in the study's sample that does not exist in the population it represents (often described as a Type I error), or conversely, the statistics used may fail to detect in the sample a true pattern of covariation that does exist in the population (Type II error). Or if there is enough statistical power in a very large sample, then a trivial relationship that is not important either for policy or for theoretical reasons may nevertheless be statistically significant. These three potential false conclusions about covariation include six threats to statistical conclusion validity identified by Cook and colleagues in 1990 and described in detail by MacBeth (1998) in relation to quasi-experiments on the effects of television. One of these six threats, the reliability of measures, applies in natural media experiments primarily to measures of the possible media effects. It applies much less to the measures of media use because one of the advantages of natural experiments is that media exposure is specified as part of the design (e.g., presence versus absence of television or some other medium).

The third necessary condition for making causal inferences in natural experiments is that there are no plausible alternative explanations for the effects, for example, on aggressive behavior, other than the impact of the medium. Cook et al. described the following

nine possible alternative, third-variable explanations, or threats to internal validity. The relationship between the presumed media cause and its effect might instead be due to some other *historical* event that took place between the pretest and posttest. This could be either a general societal change affecting all of the groups, or a local historical change specific to one or more of the groups, or both. A presumed causal relationship might be due instead to participants becoming older, wiser, or changing in other ways (i.e., due to *maturation*). This can be addressed by studying more than one age level in each of the groups. If there are no age/school grade differences in all groups at both the pretest and posttest, then maturation can be ruled out as a cause of any other pre–post differences.

Testing effects due to acquiring test-specific knowledge or becoming "test-wise"—that is, better at doing the type of test or other measure of the possible media effect used in the study—also need to be considered. Pretest–posttest differences due to a *change in the measuring instrument* and *statistical regression toward the mean* are other alternative possible explanations (threats to internal validity) to consider and rule out, along with *selection*. This refers to the possibility that differences among the treatment conditions are due to different types of people in the group, that is, preexisting group differences. This is absolutely crucial in studies of new media, because their penetration into the population varies systematically with socioeconomic status (SES). New media are almost always acquired first by the better educated and more affluent, and such families also vary systematically in other ways (e.g., interests, work, leisure activities, attitudes) from less well-educated or affluent families. Having pretest measures is essential for ruling out the problem of selection. They enable researchers to assess whether the groups in the natural experiment differ at the pretest, not only in demographic variables such as SES but also in the behaviors of special interest (e.g., school achievement, aggression).

Whenever the same individuals are studied longitudinally, that is, on two or more occasions, there is some attrition, or dropout, between the first and subsequent points of data collection. This internal threat to validity of *mortality* should ideally be low, and similarly low for all of the groups in the study. *Interactions with selection* may also occur, for example, selection–maturation, in which the groups may contain different types of people (e.g., varying in SES) who may mature at different rates in the behavior of interest (e.g., school achievement). Finally, there may be *ambiguity about the direction of causal influence*, but as was noted earlier, this is more likely to be true for correlational studies and is not usually a problem with quasi-experiments.

When all nine alternative plausible explanations of the effects can be ruled out as threats to the internal validity of the natural or other quasi-experiment, then the relationships can be assumed to be causal.

Researchers studying natural experiments also must be concerned with threats to *construct validity,* that is, alternative interpretations of the measures and manipulations. For research on media effects, this involves being sure that the behavior studied (e.g., aggression) is not really something else (e.g., rough-and-tumble play) and that media exposure is as purported. MacBeth discusses Cook et al.'s 11 possible threats to construct validity in relation to the design of natural experiments regarding media effects (especially TV).

Finally, media researchers studying natural experiments must be concerned about *external validity,* that is, the extent to which the findings obtained for their samples can be generalized to other times, places, and people. Cook et al. lists five such threats, which MacBeth (1998) discusses in relation to natural experiments on TV effects, along with the techniques suggested by Cook et al. for increasing external validity.

Of the four categories of concern, internal and statistical conclusion validity are similar in promoting causal relationships, whereas construct and external validity are similar in dealing with generalization from causal relationships. Cook et al. emphasizes (a) that trade-offs among the four are inevitable, (b) that internal validity is most important for making causal inferences, and (c) that this is best accomplished in natural and other quasi-experiments through research design rather than statistical adjustments.

DESIGNS OF MEDIA NATURAL EXPERIMENTS

Cook et al. (1990) describes four designs of natural experiments, discussed by MacBeth in relation to media research focusing on television. The first three types of design—one-group posttest design, one-group pretest–posttest design, and posttest-only design with nonequivalent groups—do not usually permit causal inferences. The fourth design, untreated control group designs with pretests, involves both pretests and posttests for nonequivalent control groups as well as for the group that is the focus of the natural media

experiment. This design usually does produce interpretable causal results.

—Tannis M. MacBeth

See also Natural Experiments (various entries); Notel, Unitel, Multitel Study

FURTHER READINGS

Campbell, D. T., & Stanley, J. C. (1966). *Experimental and quasi-experimental designs for research.* Chicago: Rand McNally.

Cook, T. D., Campbell, D. T., & Peracchio, L. (1990). Quasi-experimentation. In M. D. Dunnette & L. M. Hough (Eds.), *Handbook of industrial and organizational psychology* (2nd ed., Vol. 1, pp. 491–576). Chicago: Rand McNally.

MacBeth, T. M. (1998). Quasi-experimental research on television and behavior: Natural and field experiments. In J. K. Asamen & G. L. Berry (Eds.), *Research paradigms, television, and social behavior* (pp. 109–151). Thousand Oaks, CA; Sage.

Phillips, D. P. (1986). The found experiment: A new technique for assessing the impact of mass media violence on real world aggressive behavior. *Public Communication and Behavior, 1,* 259–307.

RESEARCH METHODS, QUALITATIVE

Qualitative research methods, in the realm of social sciences, are research methods that are usually but not exclusively employed to understand people's context-mediated behaviors and cognitions through the generation of descriptive data. Furthermore, a major goal of qualitative research methodology is to understand how the research participants make meaning of themselves or the phenomenon being researched. In addition, qualitative research methods are characterized by a distinct set of data collection and analytical tools that are aimed at understanding the experiences of research participants by focusing on their words and by observing their actions in the natural setting.

RESEARCH QUESTIONS

The choice to employ qualitative research methods is governed by the type of research question that the researcher is attempting to answer. Unlike quantitative research methods, where researchers are looking for variance or correlations between variables or specific phenomena, researchers using qualitative methods usually are more interested in understanding the processes behind a phenomenon. An example of a research question that is best suited to qualitative research methods is, "How do adolescents decide what clothes to purchase for school?"

DATA COLLECTION

The two major forms of data collection employed by qualitative methodologists are interviews and observations in context. Interviews, usually intended to help the researcher understand how participants derive meaning from a phenomenon by listening to or reading their words, are conducted by the researcher administering an interview protocol consisting of a group of questions geared toward answering a research question. A structured interview protocol, where all participants are given the opportunity to answer the exact same question, gives the researcher the opportunity to compare the phenomenon and generalize across all participants. Semistructured or unstructured interview protocols are geared toward research intended to examine how individual participants make meaning of a phenomenon in the distinct context in which they find themselves. The other major form of data collection in qualitative methodology, observation in context, is also used to understand how participants derive meaning from a phenomenon. Furthermore, observations (like interviews) are also intended to serve as descriptions of the behaviors and actions that are associated with the phenomenon. Interviews and observations can be used exclusively or collaboratively to help the researcher best answer the research question.

DATA ANALYSIS

A number of analytical strategies are associated with qualitative methods, including case studies, portraiture, and discourse analysis. Different strategies are more or less appropriate depending on the research questions and research purposes; however, all involve culling the data and extracting major themes from it. Some researchers have preexisting themes in mind, based on prior research, when they inspect the collected data. Other researchers choose to let the themes emerge from the observation or interview data they have collected. The key feature of such analysis is that the themes are inextricably linked to specific data sources (i.e., excerpts of interview transcripts or observation notes).

QUALITATIVE RESEARCH AND YOUTH

The value of qualitative research methods in research on youth is their success in helping adult researchers both understand and display the meaning youth make about their experiences in school or their choices in engaging media. For example, Jane Brown and colleagues have used qualitative approaches to understand the ways in which adolescents incorporate media into everyday life. Assuming that the artifacts that a teen uses to decorate a bedroom reflect the personal factors of importance to the occupant, Brown uses the "room touring" method to learn the place of media. The teen describes the contents of the bedroom while the peer or media interviewer asks the teen why the various artifacts are included and what are their sources. These qualitative procedures have allowed exploration of the influence of media on sexuality in teens and the role of media in identity formation.

—*Daren A. Graves*

See also Adolescents, Developmental Needs of, and Media; Electronic Media, Children's Use of; Internet Use, Social; Media, Meanings of; Research Methods, Room Touring

FURTHER READINGS

Maxwell, J. A. (1996). *Qualitative research design: An interpretive approach.* Thousand Oaks, CA: Sage.

Miles, M. B., & Huberman, A. M. (1984). *Qualitative data analysis: A source book of new methods.* London, UK: Sage.

Steele, J. R., & Brown, J. D. (1995). Adolescent room culture: Studying media in the context of everyday life. *Journal of Youth and Adolescence, 24*(5), 551–576.

Struass, A., & Corbin, J. (1990). *Basics of qualitative research: Grounded theory procedures and techniques.* Newbury Park, CA: Sage.

RESEARCH METHODS, QUESTIONNAIRES AND SURVEYS

The survey is one of the most widely used methods of media research because it is flexible, can be relatively inexpensive, and can be used to gather a lot of information from a broad array of people in a short period. Surveys are used both to describe current patterns of behavior (e.g., frequency of television viewing, favorite television shows) and to examine relationships between variables (e.g., TV viewing and violent behavior). It is more difficult to establish causal relationships between variables with surveys than it is with experiments because surveys conducted at one time point (cross-sectional) cannot establish time order or control for all possible alternative explanations.

Five kinds of surveys are used frequently in both academic and media market research: mail, Internet, telephone, personal (face-to-face) interview, and group administration. Each kind of survey has advantages and disadvantages in terms of cost, amount and kind of information that can be gathered, potential interviewer bias, and response rates.

Surveys sent in the mail and over the Internet are least expensive and can cover wide geographic areas. Response rates (the percentage of eligible respondents who complete the questionnaire) typically are low, however, unless incentives and follow-up mailings are included. Because no interviewer is present, it is also difficult to know if the target respondent was actually the one who completed the questionnaire.

Surveys conducted over the telephone are also relatively inexpensive, but response rates are dropping as people grow wary of marketing calls disguised as survey research. Personal interviews conducted in respondents' homes are the most expensive survey method in terms of both time and money, but the flexibility of the interview is increased, along with the number and sensitivity of questions that can be asked. The potential for interviewer bias in face-to-face interviews can be reduced by having respondents complete the entire questionnaire or the most sensitive parts on a portable computer after the interviewer has introduced them to the study (this is called computer-assisted personal interviewing).

Group administration of questionnaires in work settings or school classrooms can be an efficient way to gather information if random samples are not required. Response rates typically are high, and more questions can be asked than in a mail or telephone survey. It may be difficult to control interaction among respondents in such a situation, however, which could introduce bias.

Survey researchers take special care in constructing questions and ordering them in the questionnaire so respondents can answer easily and not be influenced by preceding questions. Effective questionnaires include short, persuasive introductions and clear instructions for each question. Pretests are often conducted to make sure that each question in the questionnaire is relevant to the respondents and the project's goals. Good questions are simple and short, minimize the respondent's impulse to answer in a socially desirable way (e.g., reporting they watch public television more than they actually do), and ask for information that the respondent is capable of providing (e.g., number of hours spent watching television yesterday rather than over the past month).

—*Jane D. Brown*

See also Research Methods, Qualitative

FURTHER READINGS

Dillman, D. (2000). *Mail and Internet surveys: The tailored design method* (2nd ed.). New York: John Wiley.

Wimmer, R. D., & Dominick, J. R. (2003). *Mass media research: An introduction*. Belmont, CA: Wadsworth.

RESEARCH METHODS, ROOM TOURING

Room touring is a qualitative research method developed to learn more about how adolescents use media in their everyday lives, especially in their own bedrooms. In a room tour, the adolescent takes the interviewer on a tour of his or her bedroom, pointing out visual images and objects, including media, and discussing their personal significance and use.

The technique draws on the idea that an adolescent's bedroom can play an important role in the process of self-definition and that media materials are often used in the process. Research in the 1980s found that American adolescents spent almost 13% of their awake time in their bedrooms and often used media as a way to learn more about themselves and to regulate their moods. Later, in the 1990s, national surveys found that adolescents' bedrooms had become little media centers equipped with many kinds of media, including music systems, televisions, and computers hooked up to the Internet.

Jane Brown and her students conducted a series of small studies with adolescents in which room touring was one of the methods used to learn about the media's role in adolescents' identity development. The researchers found that for many teens, the bedroom is a safe, private space in which experimentation with possible selves can be conducted. In one study, girls reported often bringing their friends to their rooms to talk, to read magazines, and to listen to music. One 15-year-old said, "My room's like my personal place. It's what I want it to be . . . I can just make it like me."

Brown and her colleagues concluded that tours of an adolescent's bedroom can suggest the complexity of a teen's identity structure and approach to the world as well as which sources of influence, including mass media, are important in the teen's life and construction of self. In some of their studies, they took still pictures or videotaped the walls of the rooms as the adolescent commented into a handheld tape recorder. They described one boy's room:

> Jack, an African American, explained the mélange of pictures of both Black and White girls that adorned his walls: "If they look good I just put them up on the wall." The young women . . . were interspersed with pictures of GI Joe (drawings done when he was 10 or 11 years old and "GI-Joe crazy"), a drawing of *Lady and the Tramp* ("I just seen that in a magazine and I drew it."), and a *Star Wars* drawing. (Brown et al., 1994, p. 818)

Other images included a picture of Arsenio Hall (because "he dresses") and labels from brand-name clothing.

One challenge of room touring is categorizing the vast array of images and artifacts in the room. Brown et al. concluded that most of what they saw could be grouped into one of six categories: (1) appropriation (using a cultural image in a personal way, e.g., as Jack had when he drew his own images from popular movies); (2) social connections (maintaining ties with a loved one, e.g., pictures of relatives or friends); (3) fantasy (imagining being someone or with someone, e.g., Jack fantasizing about magazine models); (4) social differentiation/integration (being different from or similar to someone, e.g., Jack emulating Arsenio Hall's style); (5) personal art; and (6) bricolage (compilations of disparate images and items).

—*Jane D. Brown*

See also Adolescents, Developmental Needs of, and Media; Bedrooms, Media Use in; Cultural Identity

FURTHER READINGS

Brown, J. D., Dykers, C. R., Steele, J. R., & White, A. B. (1994). Teenage room culture: Where media and identities intersect. *Communication Research, 21*(6), 813–827.

Brown, J. D., White, A. B., & Nikopoulou, L. (1993). Disinterest, intrigue, resistance: Early adolescent girls' use of sexual media content. In B. S. Greenberg, J. D. Brown, & N. Buerkel-Rothfuss (Eds.), *Media, sex, and the adolescent* (pp. 177–195). Creskill, NJ: Hampton Press.

Csikszentmihalyi, M., & Larson, R. (1984). *Being adolescent: Conflict and growth in the teenage years.* New York: Basic Books.

Roberts, D. F., Foehr, U., & Rideout, V. (2004). *Kids and media in America.* New York: Cambridge University Press.

Steele, J. R., & Brown, J. D. (1995). Adolescent room culture: Studying media in the context of everyday life. *Journal of Youth and Adolescence, 24*(5), 551–576.

S

SCHEMA THEORY

Schema theory states that the human mind is organized by a series of stable processing tools, known as schemas. A schema consists of generalized knowledge about a particular topic and the associations among that topic and other relevant information. For example, a gender schema refers to the general knowledge that an individual has about the meaning of being male or female. Consider a person who believes that men are more commonly doctors, whereas women are nurses; men are aggressive, whereas women are nurturing; and men like to go hunting, whereas women like to go shopping. All of these pieces of information, along with their associations with various domains of life, create a general picture of what this individual thinks about men and women. This general picture forms what is known as a schema: a cognitive structure that serves as a framework for understanding all information that is relevant to gender.

It is important to consider how the media influence the development of schemas, especially for children and adolescents. Schemas are thought to be formed by repeated exposure to consistent information. Applying this idea to media research, researchers have studied how media exposure affects the formation of schemas. Given the increasing amount of media exposure among children and adolescents, schema theory can play an important role in understanding the impact of media on youth. For example, individuals who view large amounts of television programming that contains frequent messages that are consistent with traditional gender stereotypes are more likely to form a gender schema that contains these stereotypes.

Schemas serve as a shortcut during the processing of information. Schemas guide *attention* by orienting individuals toward information that is relevant to them; *processing*, by providing a framework for understanding information in a way that is consistent with prior beliefs; and *remembering*, by providing a link with information already stored in memory. These shortcuts can increase efficiency in the processing of information. However, schemas can also lead to biased processing. Studies have shown that individuals are more likely to remember something inaccurately if it is inconsistent with a preexisting schema. For example, the man with the gender schema described earlier may "remember" that his female acquaintance is a nurse when she is actually a doctor.

Individuals vary in the content of their schemas. For example, consider a person who believes that women are successful at a wide range of jobs and carry a lot of responsibility in society. These pieces of information feed into this individual's gender schema and create a very different framework for understanding information about gender than is accessible to a person with the gender schema described previously. Individuals also vary in the types of schemas that they create. For example, an individual who is interested in politics and pays a lot of attention to political information will create a political schema for organizing thoughts and information about politics. However, a person who is uninterested in politics will not create such a schema.

In addition to schemas about aspects of the world, individuals also form schemas for parts of their own self-concept, known as self-schemas. For example, a gender self-schema is a schema that organizes information about how gender matters to a person's life and identity. A woman who has a gender self-schema is more likely to believe that being female is an important determinant of the things she does and how she is treated than a woman without a gender self-schema. Self-schemas have been studied for various domains of self-concept, such as appearance, weight, and race.

Much research on how the media influence individuals' thoughts and emotions has focused on individual differences in how people process information relayed by the media. These individual differences are thought to be related to differences in schema type and content. For example, individuals with a well-developed schema for violence have been shown to perceive more violence in a television show than individuals without such a schema. In fact, perception of violence in a television show was demonstrated to relate more strongly to preexisting differences in schemas than to variability in how many violent acts were actually viewed. Individual differences in schemas have also explained how individuals respond to political advertisements. Researchers found that among individuals who have political schemas, some individuals focus more on political issues, whereas others focus more on the character of politicians. These preexisting schemas were shown to bias what individuals remembered after viewing the same political advertisements. Individuals with an issue schema were more likely to remember the issues discussed in the ad, whereas those with a character schema were more likely to remember the character traits that were portrayed.

The media are also thought to influence human thoughts and emotions by activating self-schemas. Much of this research has focused on self-schemas related to physical appearance. For example, it has been shown that young women who formed a self-schema for their appearance, especially one focused on the desire to achieve an idealized body image, became emotionally upset or anxious when they were exposed to information in the media that activated this ideal, such as super models in magazine ads or commercials. Women who did not have an appearance self-schema did not demonstrate this emotional arousal. Therefore, schemas are useful for explaining differences in how individuals respond to information in the media.

At noted above, exposure to repeated messages in the media may promote the development of certain schemas. Children and adolescents are considered to be particularly susceptible to the influence of the media on the development of their schemas, primarily because they have fewer life experiences to guide their schema formation and therefore are more open to the messages transmitted through the media. Researchers have found that active discussion with children about the messages in the media can serve to foster critical analysis of such messages, thereby blocking some of the effect of media messages on the formation of schemas.

—*Daniel W. Brickman,*
Marjorie Rhodes, and Brad J. Bushman

See also Body Image in Girls and Young Women; Cognitive Development, Media and; Schema/Scripts, Aggressive; Schema/Scripts, Gender; Schema/Scripts, Sexual

FURTHER READINGS

Hargreaves, D., & Tiggemann, M. (2002). The effect of television commercials on mood and body dissatisfaction: The role of appearance-schema activation. *Journal of Social & Clinical Psychology, 21*(3), 287–308.

Markus, H. (1977). Self-schemata and processing information about the self. *Journal of Personality & Social Psychology, 35*(2), 63–78.

Nathanson, A. I., Wilson, B. J., McGee, J., & Sebastian, M. (2002). Counteracting the effects of female stereotypes on television via active mediation. *Journal of Communication, 52*(4), 922–937.

Potter, W. J., Pashupati, K., Pekurny, R. G., Hoffman, E., & Davis, K. (2002). Perceptions of television: A schema. *Media Psychology, 4*(1), 27–50.

Shen, F. (2004). Chronic accessibility and individual cognitions: Examining the effects of message frames in political advertisements. *Journal of Communication, 54*(1), 123–137.

SCHEMAS/SCRIPTS, AGGRESSIVE

Despite plentiful evidence of a link between exposure to media violence and aggression, it is unclear what theoretical mechanism accounts most elegantly for the data. Although both physiologically based theories (e.g., excitation transfer) and predominantly cognitive theories have been supported, both offer a better explanation for short-term increases in aggression than for the long-term effects that have been found. A cleaner and perhaps more intuitive explanation comes from the sociocognitive literature. Specifically, schemas, scripts, and mental models are frequently cited as a causal explanation for the link between exposure to media violence and increases in long-term aggression.

Overall, schema theory states that knowledge is organized around particular concepts. A schema contains the features or attributes that are associated with a category. For example, person schemas include information about people or categories of people that includes their skills, competencies, or values and perhaps exemplar members. Event schemas are processes, practices, or ways in which we typically approach tasks and problems. Role schemas contain sets of expectations, that is, how we expect an individual occupying a certain role to behave.

In the literature on mass media, emphasis is often placed on scripts, a specific type of schema that refers to our knowledge of how a sequence of events proceeds, or perhaps should proceed, including the behaviors and actions involved. One oft-cited example is the restaurant schema. A script for an event, for example, a conflict with a peer, can be acquired quite quickly. For example, preschoolers develop scripts surrounding social interaction even for behaviors that 3-year-olds don't engage in (e.g., alcohol use). In addition, young children can develop these scripts after only one exposure to information about the event. Last, children as young as 5 years of age tend to draw on their own existing mental scripts (e.g., a trip to McDonald's) in encoding and later recalling a story about a trip to McDonald's.

How is this related to media exposure and aggression? Children are thought to develop scripts quickly, especially when little competing information is available. In addition, repeat exposure to a depicted script may act as a reinforcement, making the script more robust, more easily accessible, and more readily activated. That is, if a child encounters a situation, say a conflict, for which he or she has a script available, the child may draw on that information to know what to do. The behaviors chosen and ultimately enacted may come from that script, and that script may have been established through exposure to conflicts in the mass media.

Mental models, another framework used to understand long-term increases in aggression after exposure to media violence, are perhaps the broadest term used to describe the conceptual architecture of the mind.

Mental models are cognitive representations of events and situations, including the characters in those situations, the interrelations among the characters, the causal relationships between people and occurrences, and the sequence and timing of events. Mental models are, therefore, what we abstract from our experiences and store in memory as an example of some thing or some situation. Indeed, the abstraction moves beyond an exemplar and becomes, in our minds, the thing itself. Like scripts and schemas, this cognitive architecture is used to guide incoming information, to reason and problem-solve, and to assist in or direct recall.

In each case, the argument is made that through exposure to mediated models of aggression, viewers learn elaborated schemas, scripts, and mental models for aggression, including when to use them, how to enact them, and whether and under what circumstances they are right. In other words, viewers develop complex webs of imagery surrounding the construct of violence. The long-term effect of media exposure on aggression, then, is typically associated with the observational learning of schemas about aggression and scripts for problem solving that include aggression. The heavier the media usage, the more dense, complex, and easily activated the web.

Using these cognitive architectures as a theoretical framework, past media research has found a link between exposure to violent television and several outcomes associated with aggression. For example, Huesmann and Guerra found that children who watched more television violence were more likely to see aggression as normative than were those who did not watch as much violent television. Similarly, Krcmar and Curtis were interested in the effect of violent television on children's moral judgments about aggression. In this study, children ages 5 through 12 watched near-identical videos in which the main characters had a verbal conflict. The clip was then edited either to show the conflict coming to blows or to make it appear that the characters walked away from the conflict. Those who saw the physically violent version were more likely to use aggressive mental models later to judge an unrelated story involving aggression. Interestingly, however, 20% of the children in the control (i.e., nonviolent version) condition reported having seen punching and kicking in the stimulus tape. The authors concluded that children develop fairly ritualized models of cartoon violence that may have caused them to see violence even when it did not occur and to judge violence as more acceptable.

Schema theory has also been used to explain why exposure to television violence may be associated with less advanced moral reasoning. In a study by Krcmar and Valkenburg, the researchers found that children who watched more fantasy violence in series like *Superman, X Men*, and *Power Rangers* were more likely to judge justified violence in moral dilemmas as right. The authors argued that with a well-developed script for superhero and fantasy violence, one that would have developed through more exposure to cartoon violence, children would be more likely to perceive justified violence as correct. Because fantasy violence tends to portray violence as perpetrated by a hero for the greater good, it makes sense that heavy fantasy-violence viewers would agree with the idea that violence can be good when there appears to be a cause. Similarly, children who are exposed to media violence are more likely than their light-viewing counterparts to attribute hostility to others' actions.

Last, scripts and schema theory are used to explain the effect of exposure to media violence on behavioral aggression itself. For example, Huesmann argues that as children age, these initial scripts—acquired through exposure to real models in the form of family interactions or mediated models in the form of television violence—become more complex and also can be activated in a more automatic, less conscious way. This process results in increased aggression and also decreases their likelihood of filtering out inappropriate behavior such as aggression.

—*Marina Krcmar*

See also Aggression, Advertising and; Schema Theory; Violence, Effects of

FURTHER READINGS

Chen, Z. (1999). Schema induction in children's analogical problem solving. *Journal of Educational Psychology, 91*(4), 703–715.

Domke, D., Shah, D. V., & Wackman, D. B. (1998). Media priming effects: Accessibility, association, and activation. *International Journal of Public Opinion Research, 10*, 51–74.

Garnham, A. (1997). Representing information in mental models. In M. A. Conway (Ed.), *Cognitive model of memory* (pp. 149–172). Cambridge, MA: MIT Press.

Huesmann, R. L., Moise-Titus, J., Podolski, C. L., & Eron, L. D. (2003). Longitudinal relations between children's exposure to TV violence and their aggressive and violent behavior in young adulthood: 1977–1992. *Developmental Psychology, 39*(2), 201–221.

Huston, A. C., Wright, J. C., Fitch, M., Wroblewski, R., & Piemyat, S. (1997). Effects of documentary and fictional television formats on children's acquisition of schemata for unfamiliar occupations. *Journal of Applied Developmental Psychology, 18*(4), 563–586.

Josephson, W. L. (1987). Television violence and children's aggression: Testing the priming, social script, and disinhibition predictions. *Journal of Personality and Social Psychology, 53*, 882–890.

Paik, H., & Comstock, G. (1994). The effects of television violence on antisocial behavior: A meta-analysis. *Communication Research, 21*, 516–546.

Potter, James, W. (2004.) *Theory of media literacy: A cognitive approach*. Thousand Oaks, CA: Sage.

Roskos-Ewoldsen, D. R., Roskos-Ewoldsen, B., & Killman Carpentier, F. (2002). Media priming: A synthesis. In J. B. Bryant & D. Zillmann (Eds.), *Media effects in theory and research* (2nd ed., pp. 97–120). Mahwah, NJ: Erlbaum.

Shrum, L. J., Wyer, R. S., & O'Guinn, T. C. (1998). The effects of television consumption on social perceptions: The use of priming procedures to investigate psychological processes. *Journal of Consumer Research, 24*, 447–458.

Tuckey, M. R., & Brewer, N. (2003). How schemas affect eyewitness memory over repeated retrieval attempts. *Applied Cognitive Psychology, 17*(7), 785–800.

Wyer, R., & Srull, T. (1989). *Memory and cognition in its social context*. Mahwah, NJ: Erlbaum.

Zillmann, D. (2000). Mood management in the context of selective exposure theory. In M. E. Roloff (Ed.), *Communication yearbook* (Vol. 23, pp. 103–123). Thousand Oaks, CA: Sage.

SCHEMAS/SCRIPTS, GENDER

According to gender schema theory, children's preexisting beliefs about men and women, or their gender schemas, shape their attention to novel and familiar stimuli, their interpretation of current situations, their memory of past events, and their decisions regarding their own behavior. Because media portrayals of gender and gender roles are often highly stereotypical, concern has been raised about the role of media exposure in children's development of stereotypical gender schemas. Empirical evidence suggests that exposure to stereotypical portrayals of men and women on television does in fact lead children and adolescents to adopt similarly stereotyped attitudes about gender.

Content analyses have documented the nature of media portrayals of men and women. Early studies focused on the mere presence of male and female characters, finding that male characters outnumbered female characters in most media genres, in many cases appearing twice as often as women. More recent research suggests that this bias toward male characters is gradually decreasing over time. Many researchers argue that content analyses must extend their focus beyond the mere presence of characters to consider the traits that are most frequently attributed to men and women and the occupations and roles that men and women are shown holding. These studies show that women are more often portrayed as deferent, weak, romantic, and emotional, whereas men are more often portrayed as active, aggressive, athletic, and intelligent. In addition, men are more frequently shown in positions of responsibility, as solving problems, expressing opinions, or rescuing other characters, whereas women are most frequently shown deferring to male characters. In terms of occupation, men are more likely than women to be portrayed as holding a high-status position, including those in science and technical fields. Many female characters on television are portrayed without any clear reference to their occupation; when a woman has a profession, it is often gender stereotyped, for example, teachers or secretaries.

These stereotypical portrayals generally extend across all media genres, including genres specifically targeted to young viewers. Content analyses have documented gender-stereotypical portrayals in magazines, movies, television programming and commercials, music videos and video games, picture books and educational software aimed at preschoolers, children's television, comics and cartoons, and award-winning children's literature. Although content analyses support an overwhelming bias toward stereotypical portrayals of gender, it must be noted that counterstereotypical characters and programs can also be found in most of these genres as well. For example, the animated program *Rugrats*, a favorite among young children, includes among its characters fathers who are frequently verbally supportive and affectionate toward their children and a girl who frequently bosses, orders, and threatens her male peers. Similarly, although men are more frequently cast as scientists or engineers than women are, many contemporary movies showcase female scientists who are capable and hold high-status positions. Because of the presence of both stereotypical and counterstereotypical

portrayals of gender, different children may be exposed to vastly different sets of gender schemas through their media use.

Media use has been linked to children's beliefs and attitudes about men and women and their choices for their own behaviors. Although associations have emerged with other genres (e.g., magazines and movies), the overwhelming majority of research in this area has been conducted with television. Among children and adolescents, frequent television viewing is associated with holding stereotypical beliefs about men and women, including what traits they demonstrate, what behaviors they are likely to enact, and what occupations they are likely to hold. Television viewing has also been linked to children's endorsement of stereotypical attitudes about what men and women *should* do. For example, in a noteworthy longitudinal study, Michael Morgan found that adolescent girls who watched more television showed an increase in their endorsement of sexist attitudes over a one-year time frame. In addition, television viewing has been linked to children's and adolescents' own occupational aspirations. Experimental studies lend support to correlational findings by documenting short-term effects of media exposure on gender-role beliefs, attitudes, and preferences.

Associations between media use and the development of gender schemas, however, may not be unilateral, and recent work has explored how effects might vary based on the ethnicity, gender, and developmental stage of the viewer or on the nature of the content being viewed. Recent research has replicated findings among diverse populations documenting associations with the gender-role attitudes specifically among Latina/o and African American youth. Although many studies report effects for both genders, several studies have documented stronger associations among girls. Developmental stage is also a critical factor in the development of gender schemas, and although minimal research has explicitly examined age effects, there is preliminary indication that developmental stage might moderate media effects on gender schemas. Specifically, children who had recently achieved gender constancy (the notion that *male* and *female* are permanent, unchangeable categories) were found to be more affected by stereotypical media portrayals than younger children. Similarly, adolescents who are constructing their identity and contemplating multiple selves might be especially susceptible to schemas about gender roles and occupations.

It also appears that different forms of media may differentially impact schema development. Considering the differential impact of different genres, one study found that adolescents' stereotypical attitudes about women and work were associated with their exposure to sports and action-adventure programming but not with exposure to other genres. In other cases, media use was actually associated with *less* stereotypical schemas. Specifically, exposure to counterstereotypical programming has been linked to endorsement of less stereotypical attitudes about gender.

Furthermore, adult intervention may have the potential to minimize the effects of exposure to stereotypical media. A recent experiment found that when adults criticized the stereotypical portrayals young children were watching on television, children subsequently adopted more flexible attitudes about gender roles.

—*Deborah Schooler*

See also Advertising, Gender and; Gender Roles (various entries); Magazines, Adolescent Boys'; Magazines, Adolescent Girls'; Schema Theory; Schemas/Scripts, Sexual; Sex in Television, Content Analysis of

FURTHER READINGS

Nathanson, A. I., Wilson, B. J., McGee, J., & Sebastian, M. (2002). Counteracting the effects of female stereotypes on television via active mediation. *Journal of Communication, 52*(4), 922–937.

Rivadeneyra, R., & Ward, L. (2005). From Ally McBeal to Sabado Gigante: Contributions of television viewing to the gender role attitudes of Latino adolescents. *Journal of Adolescent Research, 20*(4), 453–475.

SCHEMAS/SCRIPTS, SEXUAL

Scripting theory posits that individuals use sets of ordering rules, called scripts, to interpret, predict, or produce the scenes around them. Sexual scripts, in particular, provide information about the appropriate sequences of events involved in sexual encounters, the prevalence of certain sexual behaviors among one's peers, or the expected roles of men and women in sexual situations. Media sources present a concentrated sample of sexual scripts, and accordingly, scripting theory is especially useful for examining media influences on the sexual socialization of children and adolescents. The sexual scripts presented are often contradictory in nature and frequently focus on *gendered* sexual roles. Recent correlational and experimental data suggest that exposure to scripted media content may influence adolescents to adopt scripted attitudes and beliefs.

Content analysis has been used to document the types of sexual scripts most prevalent in the mass media consumed by children and adolescents. Sex is frequently portrayed as recreational, involving passion, pleasure, and minimal risk. The television programs most watched by children and adolescents depict sex as a game and as a fun pleasurable activity for people of all ages. Contemporary women's magazines, a third of whose consumers are adolescents, portray sex as casual and fun, with both men and women cast as primarily sex-driven beings. Moreover, on both television and in magazines, sex is typically portrayed as risk free.

Genres targeted specifically to teens present a slightly different set of scripts. Scripts in teen-oriented genres are often more contradictory in nature, treating sexuality as ubiquitous and of central importance while simultaneously highlighting sexual risk and promoting abstinence. The television programs most highly rated among adolescents contain the most frequent references to sex. At the same time, programs featuring adolescent and college-age characters are the most likely to address sexual risk. Similarly, teen-oriented magazines, for example, *Seventeen*, convey the contradictory messages that girls should look sexy and attract sexual attention from boys but should refrain from engaging in sexual activity.

A large portion of sexual scripts deal with the different sexual roles of women/girls and men/boys. Beliefs about how men and boys should act include being actors and initiators in sexual relationships, seeing women as sexual objects, enhancing masculinity by pursuing sexual relationships, experiencing sexual feelings as uncontrollable, being demanding in sexual situations, not having homosexual feelings, and not becoming emotionally attached to women. Beliefs about how women and girls should act include being sexually passive, being physically attractive to interest men, being manipulative rather than direct, setting sexual limits, appearing sexually chaste, and not having sexual desire. Media representations of these gendered sexual scripts are plentiful. For example, music videos often feature one or two male performers, shown to be wealthy and powerful, surrounded by a mass of scantily clad women who serve primarily as sexual objects. Video games present a similar set of gendered sexual scripts; men are depicted as active and violent agents, and women are depicted as sexual objects.

The repeated presentation of these specific messages about sexuality provides young viewers with scripts about the sequence of events in a sexual encounter, the roles of each partner in those encounters, and the expected consequences of sexual activity. In a cyclical process, available scripts can then be used by viewers to aid in interpreting media content. Although no such research has been conducted with youth samples, research with undergraduate women indicates that viewers use the scripts they have developed from prior media exposure to interpret novel ambiguous sexual situations. The majority of sexual references on television take the form of innuendo, and given their limited sexual experience, it is likely that young viewers will call on these scripts even more frequently than adults when interpreting sexual content.

Children and adolescents may also be using these scripts to interpret their real-life experiences. Survey research has documented associations between adolescent consumption of sexually explicit media and beliefs about the prevalence of certain sexual behaviors among other adolescents. For example, adolescent viewers of daytime talk shows and soap operas tend to overestimate the number of their peers who are sexually active. Beliefs about peer norms have been shown to be a reliable indicator of adolescent sexual behavior. Accordingly, adoption of beliefs that exaggerate the proportion of one's peers who are sexually active may partially account for associations between consumption of sexually explicit media and adolescent sexual behavior.

Recent research indicates that exposure to media saturated with traditional sexual scripts about men and women may contribute to adolescents' sexual attitudes and behaviors. In a recent experiment, African American high school students who watched script-laden music videos subsequently reported more stereotyped attitudes about the sexual roles of men and women than students who watched videos that were less scripted. Survey research has further demonstrated associations between adolescents' regular viewing of scripts about male and female sexual roles and their sexual health outcomes, especially among girls. Specifically, girls who watched more television portraying men as sex-driven reported more sexual experiences and more vulnerability to sexual risk, whereas girls who watched more television featuring girls and women as sexual limit-setters reported fewer sexual experiences, less vulnerability to sexual risk, and more consistent condom use.

—Deborah Schooler

See also Schema Theory; Schemas/Scripts, Gender; Sex in Television, Content Analysis of

FURTHER READINGS

Tolman, D. L., Kim, J. L., Schooler, D., & Sorsoli, C. L. (under review). *Rethinking the associations between television viewing and adolescent sexual health: Bringing gender into focus.*

Ward, L. M. (1995). Talking about sex: Common themes about sexuality in the prime-time television programs children and adolescents view most. *Journal of Youth and Adolescence, 24*(5), 595–615.

Ward, L. M., Hansbrough, E., & Walker, E. (2005). Contributions of music video exposure to black adolescents' gender and sexual schemas. *Journal of Adolescent Research, 20*(2), 143–166.

SCHOOL-AGE CHILDREN, IMPACT OF THE MEDIA ON

According to a recent study by the Kaiser Family Foundation, children between 8 and 18 years old are exposed to about 8½ hours of media daily, an increase of 1 hour from 1999. (Although *school-age* in this entry generally refers to children ages 6 to 12, the Kaiser Foundation study involved the broader age range.) Their exposure is actually packed into about 6½ hours a day, however, with the other hours accounted for by *media multitasking,* the use of several types of media simultaneously. The media involved in their daily consumption include books and magazines, radio, television, cable, computers, Internet access, music videos, video games, and handheld devices. Many children have quickly become accustomed to having pagers, cell phones, DVD and CD players, and MP3s as well. According to the Kaiser Foundation report, bedrooms are now actual media centers, with large numbers of children having TVs, video games, VCR or DVD players, computers, cable TV, radios, or MP3s in their bedrooms. Even more have at least one computer at home and Internet access, even if it is not in their bedrooms. Youngsters communicate with peers through email, chat rooms, and instant messaging, and they surf the Internet, download music, and watch TV.

Significant benefits and positive outcomes are associated with this media exposure. Internet access can provide important and current information on a range of topics. In moderation, television viewing and computer use can complement and supplement what and how children typically learn in a classroom. The analytic and critical thinking skills developed in school can help them understand and assess TV content, and TV's appeal and capacity for conveying complex information visually in interesting and stimulating formats can supplement classroom learning. TV viewing and computer game-playing can be social activities, and electronic communication can increase contacts with friends and family members and meet many of the same needs that extended phone conversations did in the past. Ready access to music is enjoyable and relaxing.

Possible negative short-term and long-term effects, however, are also of concern. As children learn best through active involvement, social and verbal interactions, and experimenting, one concern is that much of children's media use is too passive and the activity is too one-way. There are concerns about the effects of heavy media use on children's physical health and well-being. Some worry that children who spend many hours in front of a screen, whether with the Internet, playing games, or watching television or music videos, are less likely to exercise and more likely to be less fit or even obese or to have more health problems than those children who spend fewer hours with media and who engage in other more varied and active pursuits. There is also a good deal of research to document media users' increased exposure to depictions of alcohol use, tobacco use, violence, casual sex, stereotyping, and other content that can affect and negatively influence their developing beliefs, attitudes, and behavior. Heavy media use has also been associated with anxiety, sleep disruptions, poor school performance, isolation, and fear, as well as aggressive behavior.

Children who use these media constitute a heterogeneous group. Differences among media users such as age, gender, level and patterns of media use, motivation or purpose for media use, socioeconomic background, family makeup, cognitive ability, educational level, and past experiences significantly affect the potential short-term and long-term impact of their

experiences with the media. In addition, there are also variations in the format and content of the media forms themselves and in the context in which media are used. Children can use various media alone, for example, or with peers or family. They can also use media in their own bedrooms or in a more public part of the house, and these different contexts further affect which media they use, how much time they spend with various media, and the content to which they are exposed. Finally, children use media for many different reasons at any given time, including information seeking, diversion, social interaction, mood management, and escape from difficult situations, all of which also affect the potential impact of the media. Interactions among all of these variables further complicate the picture.

There is also differential access to the media. Some children have far fewer media resources at home and less access to electronic devices. The important notion of a digital divide refers to the unequal access among children to media and concern that the children who are media have-nots will not be able to keep pace with others who have a huge variety of media from which to choose.

AGE DIFFERENCES

Age and gender differences in how media are used and which forms are chosen affect the type of information that children receive and how it may affect them. The degree to which children can understand and remember what they see on television, for example, is affected by their developmental level. Whereas younger children are more affected by highly salient material such as action, animation, color, and music, school-age children are more interested in things that are consistent with their abilities, situations, and experience, and they are also able to process complex and language-based information and material more efficiently than younger children.

Some of the most important developmental differences in children's use of media include their ability to understand content, to recognize some of the formal features and techniques of television, and to distinguish between what is realistic and what is fantasy, between what is normal or real and what is contrived or embellished. School-age children, for example, are better able to understand replays and flashbacks than younger children. They no longer see them as new occurrences of an event, nor are they as confused by them. They are better able to understand advertising, including the purpose of advertising and how it can influence buying behavior. Distinguishing reality from fantasy can be a difficult task even for adults, however, as the line is often blurred between reality and media content. Media characters are sometimes treated as real people. For instance, Martin Sheen, who played President Bartlett on NBC's *The West Wing,* was asked for his political opinions during the U.S. presidential campaign, and people who pose as doctors in commercials or celebrities who pitch a product lend weight to the product being advertised. A family's pattern of media use, relationships within the family, and coviewing with family members also affect how seriously children will take media content or how much they will identify with media figures.

VIOLENCE AND AGGRESSIVE BEHAVIOR

There has been concern for many years about the association between exposure to violent content and children's development of more aggressive behavior or decreased sensitivity to violence. Many studies have demonstrated an association between exposure to violence in television portrayals, movies, music videos, magazines, and video games, on the one hand, and changes in some children's attitudes and behavior; however, not all children who view violence or who play violent games become more aggressive. Cognitive ability, amount of viewing, past experience, age and gender, perceived reality, and the number of alternative sources of information determine the impact of such content. Children who view television violence as realistic, for example, and those who have less information about alternative behaviors are more likely to see violence and aggressive behavior as acceptable ways to resolve issues or solve problems. Similarly, children who watch many hours of violence and aggression and who have few alternative real-life social interactions from which to learn may also be more affected by such violence.

Television violence has also been associated with increased fear and anxiety in school-age children. Fantasy violence, graphic news coverage, violent sports, and other portrayals often trigger anxiety and fear rather than increased aggressive behavior. As school-age children tend to fear more those things that *could* happen, such as an abduction, exposure to such content can lead to separation anxiety, sleeping problems, nightmares, and poor focus in school.

SCHOOL PERFORMANCE

The relationship between media use and school performance and academic achievement is another cause of concern. A considerable amount of research indicates few significant negative effects on light or moderate users of media and some well-documented positive effects. Children increasingly use media, particularly computers and the Internet, to obtain information, do research, and supplement their learning from more traditional avenues such as libraries. For school-age children who have few alternative resources or sources of information, light to moderate TV viewing and computer use at school and in libraries can help them gain information to which they would not otherwise have access and can trigger interest in subject areas to which they were not exposed previously. Heavy media use, on the other hand, is usually associated with negative outcomes, regardless of whether other resources are available or not. The causal direction in these associations is less clear, however. It is possible, for example, that children who are having serious problems in school or whose progress has already been limited may seek out more media use as an alternative source of information or as a way to avoid their difficulties.

MEDIA IMPACT

Amount of media use appears to be one of the most important variables in determining the impact on children and adolescents. Children have increasing access to information not available to children in a pretechnological age, and it is now more difficult for parents to control their children's media use. Children also now have greater access to information that previously was restricted to adults, but this greater access does not mean that they have full comprehension of the material. Their ability to process and understand such information is still affected and limited by their developmental stage, their cognitive ability, and their past experiences.

Despite the high rates of exposure to media that most children experience, and the frequent cautions in the literature for parents to monitor their children's media experience, studies repeatedly point to low levels of such supervision and monitoring by parents. Parents need to ensure that their children are not misunderstanding and misinterpreting media content and that they are exposed to appropriate materials for their age and developmental level. Talking with children about content, exploring their perceptions and ideas, and helping them to see the possible impact it can have, can be helpful in mitigating a negative influence on children.

A considerable amount of research, then, suggests that the impact of media is greatest when viewers take it seriously to get information, especially when they see the content as realistic and when they have fewer alternative sources of information. Media influence appears to be less significant when various media forms are used in moderation and primarily for diversion or entertainment and when a child has many other activities and sources of information. These factors, however, are also influenced by age, gender, cognitive ability, and family variables, which in turn affect children's use of media, choice of games, and their attention to, comprehension of, and recall of material to which they are exposed. Which media are used, and when, why, how, where, and how much they are used, determine the impact on children's physical, social, psychological, intellectual, and emotional development. Media literacy programs that inform children *about* the media, however, and increased parent education about media use and its effects can lead to children's enjoyment of the most positive aspects of the media while at the same time decreasing potential negative effects and impact.

—*Judith Van Evra*

See also Computer Use (various entries); Media Exposure; Media Genre Preferences; Movie Viewing, Adolescents'; Movie Viewing, Children's; Music Videos, Effects of; Violence, Effects of

FURTHER READINGS

Kaiser Family Foundation. (2005). *Generation M: Media in the lives of 8–18 year olds.* Retrieved from http://www.kff.org/entmedia/entmedia030905nr.cfm

National Institute on Media and the Family. (2002). *Media use.* Retrieved from http://www.mediafamily.org/facts/facts_mediause.shtml

Singer, D. G., & Singer. J. L. (Eds.). (2001). *Handbook of children and the media.* Thousand Oaks, CA: Sage.

Subrahmanyam, K., Kraut, R., Greenfield, P., & Gross, (2000). The impact of home computer use on children's activities and development. *The Future of Children: Children and Computer Technology, 10*(2), 123–144.

Van Evra, J. (2004). *Television and child development* (3rd ed.). Mahwah, NJ: Erlbaum.

SCHOOLS, ADVERTISING/ MARKETING IN

Given the extensive presence of commercial interests in today's schools, it may be hard to believe that at one time, schools were thought of as commercial-free settings focused on teaching and learning. Evidence of corporate presence and direct sales appeal to children and teens grew relatively slowly for several decades, but advertising and marketing have exploded in the past 30 years. This entry looks at that history and at the various forms of school-related marketing present today: product sales, direct advertising, indirect advertising, and market research.

HISTORY OF COMMERCIALISM IN SCHOOLS

The noncommercial nature of schools began to change in the 1920s—quietly at first—when public relations frontiersman Edward L. Bernays brought Ivory Soap–sponsored soap-carving competitions into classrooms. The advertising and marketing presence steadily grew in the early 1930s, as the American Bankers Association, tarnished by the stock market crash of 1929 and the ensuing Depression, worked to restore its image by introducing educational materials into public schools. The marketing pace notably quickened in 1937 when the National Association of Manufacturers distributed its *Young America Magazine* to 70,000 schools. The association promoted the magazine as a way to bring American industry's true story into places needing it most: schools and homes. Junior Achievement arrived in schools by the late 1940s. Designed by American industry as a way to interest children and teens in entrepreneurialism, it further solidified and legitimized corporate presence in the public school classroom.

Public-private partnerships entered the school commercial landscape in 1979, when schools signed on with major corporations in the technology field. With the stated goal of creating computer literacy and a technologically astute workforce, 51% of public schools were participating in these partnerships by 1979.

Meanwhile, Whittle Communications launched the concept of ad panels and wallboards in school hallways and lunchrooms. Featuring product advertising and a celebrity message, these panels and wallboards rapidly grew in school prominence. In 1989, Whittle Communications introduced Channel One television programming into classrooms, thus moving Whittle from hallways and bulletin boards directly into the instructional day. This move provided the major gateway for the diversity of advertising and marketing approaches that have followed.

CURRENT ADVERTISING AND MARKETING PRACTICES

A U.S. General Accounting Office report in September 2000 created a four-category framework for reviewing in-school advertising and marketing practices: (1) product sales, (2) direct advertising, (3) indirect advertising, and (4) market research. Each category includes a variety of practices described here.

Product Sales

The common feature within this category is the sale of a product to gain revenue for the school.

Exclusionary Contracts

One of most prevalent and publicized practices, *cola contracts* are made with major soft drink companies; an individual school, a school district, or district consortia enters into an exclusionary, multiyear contract with the corporation. Sales quotas are set, and the contracting school, district, or consortium is given a contract-signing payment and guaranteed a certain monetary figure for meeting the quota. Coke and Pepsi are the most prevalent and publicized corporations establishing these contract arrangements. Other contract arrangements are made with fast-food companies to sell food on the school grounds or in the school cafeteria. McDonald's and Taco Bell are two of the corporate entities that establish these kinds of arrangements.

Beyond food and drink, a variety of companies contract on an exclusionary basis in areas such as school pictures, yearbooks, class rings, graduation caps and gowns, and gym uniforms. Nike and Reebok are among the most familiar names in this latter category.

Cash and Credit Rebate Programs

Some schools and districts collect a given store's receipts and, in return, receive a share, perhaps 1%, of the receipt total toward school equipment or supplies.

Credit card and Internet shopping adopt a similar principle, with the school being designated at the time of the purchase. Creative newer entries in this category include Dialing for Schools and Driving for Education. In the first, a long-distance telephone service provider agrees to pay the school or district a specified percentage of the revenue generated by local resident and business sign-ups. In the second, a local car dealership offers schools major educational equipment or materials in exchange for proof-of-driving certificates, obtained by having a parent or other participating adult go to the car dealership showroom for a new-car test drive.

Fund-Raising Activities

A third product sales category encompasses a wide range of fund-raising activities. An army of students fan out across the community, selling the product (e.g., candy, magazines, gift wrap) to their parents, relatives, neighbors, and friends. The school or group receives a percentage of the sales revenues.

Direct Advertising

The many approaches in this category all directly advertise to students in school. One of the most prominent venues is advertising on the school grounds and on school equipment (e.g., billboards, marquees, message boards, school buses, and the athletic stadium scoreboard). Company-donated book covers contain assorted ads as do assignment books, posters, and school bus kiosks. In a second venue, school publications (newspaper, yearbook, sports programs) sell ad space to create revenue. A third venue—and one of the most controversial—encompasses media-based advertising. Channel One contracts with schools who agree to show their news program (10 minutes of news, 2 minutes of commercials) on 90% of all school days in 80% of all classrooms. The school receives a satellite dish, two central VCRs, internal wiring, and a television set for each classroom. In a similar contractual pattern, Star Broadcasting beams Top 50 "hot rock" or "hot country" and ads into the schools' hallways, lunchroom, and lobbies. The Word of Mouse ad concept provides ad-laden mouse pads to all the computers in a school system, while newspapers-for-schools programs bring papers and their ads into the classroom.

A fourth avenue of direct advertising is the corporate sample in which a company provides a product sample (e.g., candy, snack food, or personal hygiene product).

Indirect Advertising

Corporate-sponsored educational materials are the most prevalent practice in this category. Companies supply teaching units or educational materials covering a broad range of topics to a school or classroom. Corporate-sponsored contests and incentives are the second most prevalent entry in this category (e.g., a national pizza company giving pizza coupons for reading a specified number of books). Other indirect methods include textbook branding (e.g., using specific product names in mathematics problems), corporate-sponsored teacher training (held in the training-providing company on its equipment) and corporate grants or gifts, the latter being the least commercial method of all.

Market Research

This category has three basic aspects: polls and surveys, Internet panels, and Internet tracking. The panels conduct polls and surveys of tastes, preferences, and demographics online while Internet tracking collects data on individual student "hits" on given websites. These research methods are rapidly growing in sophistication and variety.

The appeal of the school advertising/marketing venue is the unique opportunity to reach all children and teens in the target demographic. Early marketing holds corporate potential for establishing long-term brand loyalties as well as influencing major current family purchases.

—*Edward L. Palmer*

See also Commercial Television and Radio in Schools; Commercial Television in Schools: Channel One; Food and Beverage Advertising in Schools

FURTHER READINGS

Consumers Union. (1995). *Captive kids: Commercial pressures on kids at school.* Yonkers, NY: Consumers Union Education Series.

Ewen, S. (1996). *PR!: A social history of spin.* New York: Basic Books.

Stead, D. (1997, January 5). Corporations, classrooms, and commercialism: Some say business has gone too far. *New York Times,* Section 4A, pp. 30–33ff.

U.S. General Accounting Office. (2000, September). *Public education: Commercial activities in schools.* Washington, DC: Author.

SELECTIVE EXPOSURE

Selective exposure refers to the choice of and continued attention to media presentations for the primary purpose of attaining useful information and mood-altering entertainments. Selective exposure is usually measured in the periods of time that children, adolescents, and adults spend watching television; using computers; listening to the radio and aural recordings of any kind; or reading books, magazines, and the newspaper. The choice of entertainment for the purpose of mood and emotion enhancement has been a central object of exploration. The formation of media preferences in children and adolescents has received much attention in recent selective-exposure research. The pursuit of presentations with informational utility for adolescents has been examined also.

CONCEPTUALIZATION OF SELECTIVE EXPOSURE

Selective exposure to media content refers to the selection of essentially one presentation for attentive processing over a period of time of arbitrary duration. Such selection implies the de facto rejection of simultaneously available alternative presentations.

This conceptualization incorporates the premise that human information processing is limited to one integrated chain of events at a time and that in view of the diverse media content offered at all times, people are compelled to exercise choices. In practical terms, people who turn to media content are confined to selecting particular presentations for attentive processing because they cannot attentively trace and make coherent meaning of a multitude of concurrently featured material. The selection may be liberally altered, however, such that people can occasionally or frequently switch between different presentations. In such cases, selective exposure to presentations is accumulated across all segments of time during which attention is given to the perception and processing of the media presentations under consideration.

MEASUREMENT OF SELECTIVE EXPOSURE

The assessment of the people's choice of media presentations has a long-standing history, especially in the political arena, and the questionnaire survey has been the primary research tool. People are asked to relate their media preferences as best they can recall and are willing to reveal. This technique of assessment was eventually incorporated in a broader approach known as uses and gratifications research. As a significant feature, this approach entails queries about the motives that people believe are driving their media preferences.

Selective-exposure research has taken issue with the validity of introspective accounts of people's exposure motives, and it has established alternative techniques for determining these motives. Focus is on the sampling or the manipulation of exposure motives and on the direct observation of selective-exposure behavior. Although the time of deliberate attention to selected presentations constitutes the primary measure of selective exposure (e.g., the time of listening to specific musical selections or of watching particular television programs), tests on information attained from presentations are used as alternative measures or validating supplements. The expression of exposure desire (i.e., people's indication that they want to see or hear particular media presentations) has also been used as a measure.

SELECTIVE-EXPOSURE THEORY AND RESEARCH

As a part of his theory of cognitive dissonance, Leon Festinger proposed that media messages that appear to challenge an established belief would foster an aversive experience of dissonance and that to avoid the anticipated aversion, people would avoid exposure to such messages. He also proposed that, in contrast, people would be inclined to seek out belief-bolstering messages because these messages offer gratifying confirmation.

The theory of cognitive dissonance generated a considerable amount of research. Much of it challenged rather than supported the derived selective-exposure hypotheses, however, mostly because belief-challenging messages offered useful information and were selected despite their likely creation of dissonance. The theory proved greatly influential nonetheless. Among other things, it led to the sweeping proclamation of negligible media influence, as anything challenging people's views and calling for adjustments would be selectively bypassed.

With the proposal of a mood-management theory, Dolf Zillmann shifted attention from the consideration of the selective-exposure implications for attitude changes concerning political and health issues to the mood-altering capacity of entertainment. His theory assumes that entertainment choices may be rather random initially but then are shaped by reactions of pleasure or displeasure that result from chosen exposure. More specifically, the theory projects that people in a bad mood who experience alleviation or a change to good mood after exposure to specific material will be inclined to expose themselves again to similar material. In contrast, people in a bad mood who experience no mood improvement or even a turn for the worse will be inclined to avoid exposing themselves again to similar material. More generally and irrespective of prior mood, it is expected that mood improvement from exposure to particular media presentations will increase the likelihood of future exposure to these presentations, whereas mood worsening from exposure will diminish the likelihood of future exposure. The frequent experience of consistent mood change from exposure to an apparent class of presentations then fosters a degree of preference or disdain as an enduring choice-guiding disposition. This disposition is affective and does not depend on the cognitive elaborations such some decision models propose. Allowances are made, however, for the recognition of the affective nature of preferences and for their cognitive endorsement or modification.

Selective-exposure research has determined three characteristics of media presentations that effectively serve mood enhancement as projected by mood-management theory: (a) for mood improvement generally, material that has the capacity to elevate experienced positive mood above and beyond that of prevailing states; (b) for relief from aversively experienced states of hyper- or hypo-arousal, exposure material that has the capacity to reverse level of arousal; and (c) for negative states, material that has little or no semantic affinity with the circumstances that created the prevailing states.

Generally speaking, mood-management theory has received considerable support from research on entertainment preferences. Some challenges of the pleasure-based premise of the theory are apparent, however. They come primarily from findings concerning the appeal of tragic drama and the lure of destructive violence in horror and in reality programs, including the news. Theories of informational utility have been invoked to complement mood-management considerations. These theories emphasize principal dimensions of salience, such as the magnitude, likelihood, and immediacy of threats to, or rewarding opportunities for, personal welfare. In addition, selective-exposure research has started to explore the apparent appeal of information about the endangerment and victimization of others per se, especially when such information is pictorially conveyed. Counterhedonistic media choices of this kind have been explained as an evolutionary remnant of environmental screening.

Although selective-exposure theorizing is partial to exposure-decision models that require little cognitive elaboration, it is open to reflective models, such as Icek Ajzen's theory of reasoned, planned behavior. Cognitive models of this kind are well suited to explaining why, for instance, people decide to seek out counterhedonistic, even acutely distressing messages, in the interest of informed citizenship. Similarly, they can explain why people delay exposure to gratifying presentations to pursue more essential but less enjoyable objectives first. The consideration of rationally imposed delays in yielding to hedonistic exposure motives, addressed as telic hedonism in mood-management theory, is particularly important in avoiding the derivation of faulty predictions from the theory.

—Dolf Zillmann

See also Adolescents, Developmental Needs of, and media; Choice in media use; Depression, Media Use and; Media Genre Preferences; Mood Management Theory; Music Listening (various entries); Selectivity; Tweens, Media Preferences of

FURTHER READINGS

Ajzen, I. (1991). The theory of planned behavior. *Organizational Behavior and Human Decision Processes, 50,* 179–211.

Atkin, C. K. (1985). Informational utility and selective exposure to entertainment media. In D. Zillmann & J. Bryant (Eds.), *Selective exposure to communication* (pp. 63–91). Hillsdale, NJ: Erlbaum.

Festinger, L. (1957). *A theory of cognitive dissonance.* Evanston, IL: Row, Peterson.

Freedman, J. L., & Sears, D. O. (1965). Selective exposure. In L. Berkowitz (Ed.), *Advances in experimental social psychology* (Vol. 2, pp. 58–98). New York: Academic Press.

Knobloch, S., Callison, C., Chen, L., Fritzsche, A., & Zillmann, D. (2005). Children's sex-stereotyped self-socialization through selective exposure to entertainment: Cross-cultural experiments in Germany, China, and the United States. *Journal of Communication, 3,* 122–138.

Knobloch, S., Dillman Carpentier, F., & Zillmann, D. (2003). Effects of salience dimensions of informational utility on selective exposure to online news. *Journalism & Mass Communication Quarterly, 80*(1), 91–108.

Rosengren, K. E., Wenner, L. A., & Palmgreen P. (Eds.). (1985). *Media gratifications research: Current perspectives.* Beverly Hills, CA: Sage.

Zillmann, D. (1988). Mood management: Using entertainment to full advantage. In L. Donohew, H. E. Sypher, & E. T. Higgins (Eds.), *Communication, social cognition, and affect* (pp. 147–171). Hillsdale, NJ: Erlbaum.

Zillmann, D. (2000). Mood management in the context of selective exposure theory. In M. E. Roloff (Ed.), *Communication yearbook* (Vol. 23, pp. 103–123). Thousand Oaks, CA: Sage.

SELECTIVITY

Selectivity is the process of selecting media content. The concept is most commonly used to refer to intentional exposure to media content. Intentionally avoiding certain types of content can also be considered a form of selectivity. The processes governing selectivity also explain why some content appears to be selected or avoided unintentionally.

IMPORTANCE OF SELECTIVITY RESEARCH

Both public scrutiny of and research on the contents of the media often lead to concerns about the potential effects of media messages on children, in particular when explicit sexual, violent, or offensive content is involved. Nevertheless, content analyses of the media do not tell us all we need to know to decide whether the media have an effect. Media can have effects on people only if those people were *exposed* to the messages we are concerned about. Quantitative content analyses usually fail to make a distinction between content broadcast and content received. On the other hand, some theories have been based on the assumption of nonselectivity. Much research on cultivation theory, for instance, assumes that television viewers "watch by the hour" and are nonselective.

WHAT EXPLAINS EXPOSURE TO MEDIA CONTENT?

Three processes influence exposure to media content. First, individual characteristics explain certain media behaviors. Children cannot watch television when they are at school. Second, structural factors explain media behaviors. Even the biggest fan of a particular monthly magazine cannot read new issues of the magazine every week. Finally, uses and gratification processes guide media use. Children expose themselves to certain types of media content because they gratify particular needs.

Individual Characteristics

The most important factor at the individual level is availability. A person can only watch television shows or listen to radio programs when he or she is available when they are being broadcast. Digitalization and miniaturization of devices may change the importance of this factor in the future as far as physical availability is concerned. Some research suggests that recording devices or exposure-on-demand systems are less powerful than may have been expected. People still tend to expose themselves to most media messages when those messages are provided through the regular channels.

When a child or adolescent is busy (either in a school environment or during leisure activities), that person is mentally unavailable.

The second individual factor is awareness of the media and of alternatives. Television viewers often end up watching programs they are not particularly interested in because they are unaware of more interesting programs on other channels. This is explained partly by lack of knowledge, partly by habit: People go to the same websites for news or have a limited repertoire of television channels from which they choose.

Structural Factors

Availability is also an important characteristic of what the media supply. If there are no magazines, books, or websites about a particular hobby, an enthusiast of that hobby will not be able to read about it. In countries where mainstream TV channels do not broadcast soft pornography, children have no access to such programs.

The fact that other people influence viewing behavior is often overlooked. For anyone not living alone, media exposure is a result of group pressures and group influences. Behavior of the individual is, thus, not independent from the behavior of the other members of the family, creating (in theoretical and statistical terms) a multilevel problem. This is particularly true in the case of children because of parental mediation: Whether children and adolescents are exposed to certain media messages is strongly influenced by the extent to which their parents are willing and able to influence their media use behaviors.

Preferences

Research on television viewing appears to suggest that individual and structural factors explain most media exposure. From 25% to 50% of the viewers of one episode of a series watch the next episode. This might suggest that exposure to TV is almost random; however, in reality, the inconsistencies are mainly explained by variation in the other factors, such as availability. Some have argued that selectivity should not be studied at the level of an individual television program but at a more general level, such as that of genre. Selectivity does not imply that people should watch only one program, listen to only one type of music, or always read the same newspaper. It is likely that even if the actual message selected differs, the gratification sought is still the same.

Although the main gratification sought from television is not derived from some particular type of content but from mere exposure to the medium, this fact is often overlooked. This gratification-seeking explains apparently pointless channel hopping: Viewers sometimes prefer watching anything to not watching at all.

ACTIVE SELECTION OR PASSIVE AVOIDANCE?

Selection of media content is a multifaceted issue. Some children expose themselves to certain types of media because they actively seek them out. Others are exposed as a result of structural and individual factors with little active involvement, as is the case when children who watch one program simply continue to watch the next program that is on that channel (a process known as the *lead-in* effect). Similarly, some children actively try to avoid certain types of media content, whereas others are never exposed to certain types of content through no active choice of their own. It is a mistake to assume that exposure is always the result of some conscious act. Few authors seem to have realized that uses and gratifications research should not be limited to "gratifications sought" and "gratifications found." Four types of selective behavior exist:

intentional exposure, unintentional exposure, unintentional avoidance, and intentional avoidance.

—*Jan Van den Bulck*

See also Information Processing, Active vs. Passive Models of; Selective Exposure; Uses and Gratifications Theory

FURTHER READINGS

Goodhardt, G. J., Ehrenberg, A. S. C., & Collins, M. A. (1987). *The television audience, patterns of viewing, an update.* Aldershot, UK: Gower.

Hawkins, R. P., Pingree, S., Hitchon, J., Gorham, B. W., Kannaovakun, P., Kahlor, L., Gilligan, E. Radler, B., Kolbeins, G. H., & Schmidt, T. (2001). Predicting selection and activity in television genre viewing. *Media Psychology, 3*(3), 237–263.

Van den Bulck, J. (1995). The selective viewer: Defining (Flemish) viewer types. *European Journal of Communication 10*(2), 147–177.

Webster, J. G., & Wakshlag, J. J. (1983). A theory of television program choice. *Communication Research 10*(4), 430–446.

SENSATION SEEKING

Sensation seeking is a psychological concept with biological foundations; it has been defined by Marvin Zuckerman (1994) as "the seeking of varied, novel, complex, and intense sensations and experiences, and the willingness to take physical, social, legal, and financial risks for the sake of such experience" (p. 27). Sensation seeking seems to reach its peak for most people during adolescence, rendering it a key concept in the study of media use and effects among younger audiences. Research on media and sensation seeking among children and adolescents has mostly centered in two areas: entertainment and targeted health campaigns.

MEASURING SENSATION SEEKING

Although sensation seeking is almost always measured using self-report techniques, empirical evidence supports the common assumption that sensation seeking is accompanied by higher levels of physiological arousal. More recent theorizing has found high sensation seekers to have a *high positivity offset* and a *low negativity bias.* Positivity offset is the degree to which one's appetite system is more active than one's aversive system in a neutral environment. Negativity bias is the speed with which the aversive system responds to negative stimuli of increasing intensity. Usually, although not always, sensation seeking is measured with a version of Zuckerman's Sensation Seeking Scale, which consists of four subscales: experience seeking, thrill and adventure seeking, disinhibition, and boredom susceptibility. However, some scholars criticize this scale, contending, for one thing, that the four subfactors have inconsistent relationships with various media-related factors.

ENTERTAINMENT MEDIA

Some research in this area has looked at the relationship between sensation seeking and the ways in which adolescents use a particular medium, such as television. Some research claims that young viewers who are very high sensation seekers do not use television, probably because of the medium's inability to truly stimulate and create high levels of arousal.

A large proportion of the research on sensation seeking and entertainment has focused more specifically on what differences exist in media genre preferences between high and low sensation seekers. Studies have found that high sensation seeking is related to consumption of horror (especially for those enjoy watching gory scenes), violent films, heavy metal music, and violent media content and to watching action and music videos, daytime talk shows, stand-up comedy programs, documentaries, and cartoons; on the other side, it is related to watching fewer newscasts and drama series. High sensation seekers also find violent cartoons funnier and action and adventure programs more interesting. Additional research has found that the disinhibition subfactor may be positively related to enjoyment of violent content (except violent drama), but thrill and adventure seeking may be negatively related to enjoyment. In other work, alienation was found to mediate the link between sensation seeking and use of violent media; that is, sensation seeking was related to alienation, which was in turn related to use of violent media.

Further empirical inquiry has examined the moderating effect of sensation seeking in responses to violent media content among adolescents and children. A study found that youth were more aggressive when they were at higher than their normal levels of sensation seeking and at higher than their normal levels of violent media use.

HEALTH CAMPAIGNS

The second major line of research on sensation seeking, young people, and the media involves health communication campaigns. Because high sensation seekers are risk takers, they also tend to engage in risky health behaviors more frequently, especially the use of illicit drugs and gateway drugs such as cigarettes, alcohol, and marijuana. Thus, Philip Palmgreen and others have developed a program called SENTAR (sensation-seeking targeting) to reach young audiences with advertisements addressing a variety of risky health behaviors. Advertising campaigns with high sensation value can be developed that are more likely to effectively persuade this target population.

This approach has been tested using public service announcements that address several risky behaviors, such as marijuana use, cocaine use, and heroin use in high sensation-seeking adolescents. Other studies have found that high sensation seekers remember these targeted ads more and that the ads are effectively reaching this population. Research also indicates that high sensation-seeking adolescents process these types of ads with a combination of sympathetic distress and argument-based processing as opposed to low sensation-seeking adolescents, who use a strictly argument-based process.

There is evidence that the popular Drug Abuse Resistance Education (DARE) program, in which police officers lead classroom-based sessions on drugs, seemed to work better for high sensation seekers. While these people still used more drugs than low sensation seekers, high sensation seekers who participated in DARE had a greater percentage difference when compared to non-DARE schools than was exhibited for low sensation seekers.

Overall, sensation seeking is an important variable when considering young people and the media. Empirical evidence indicates that sensation seeking is an important indicator of what types of media young people will seek out. It is also a critical consideration in testing the diffusion and effectiveness of public health campaigns targeted at adolescents.

—*Kenneth A. Lachlan and David K. Westerman*

See also Adolescents, Developmental Needs of, and media; Media Genre Preferences; Public Health Campaigns; Public Service Announcements (PSAs)

FURTHER READINGS

Aluja-Fabregat, A., & Torrubia-Beltri, R. (1998). Viewing of mass media violence, perception of violence, personality, and academic achievement. *Personality and Individual Differences, 25,* 973–989.

Clayton, R. R., Cattarello, A., & Walden, K. P. (1991). Sensation seeking as a potential mediating variable for school-based prevention intervention: A two-year follow-up of DARE. *Health Communication, 3,* 229–239.

Donohew, L. (1990). Public health campaigns: Individual message strategies and a model. In E. B. Ray & L. Donohew (Eds.), *Communication and health: Systems and applications.* Hillsdale, NJ: Erlbaum.

Everett, M. W., & Palmgreen, P. (1995). Influences of sensation seeking, message sensation value, and program context on effectiveness of anticocaine public service announcements, *Health Communication, 7,* 225–248.

Greene, K., Krcmar, M., Walters, L. H., Rubin, D. L., & Hale, J. L. (2000). Targeting adolescent risk-taking behaviors: The contributions of egocentrism and sensation-seeking. *Journal of Adolescence, 23,* 439–461.

Palmgreen, P., & Donohew, L. (2003). Effective mass media strategies for drug abuse prevention campaigns. In Z. Sloboda & W. J. Bukoski (Eds.), *Handbook of drug abuse prevention: Theory, science, and practice* (pp. 27–43). New York: Plenum.

Palmgreen, P. Donohew, L., Lorch, E. P., Hoyle, R. H., & Stephenson, M. T. (2001). Television campaigns and adolescent marijuana use: Tests of sensation seeking targeting. *American Journal of Public Health, 91,* 292–295.

Stephenson, M. T. (2003). Mass media strategies targeting high sensation seekers: What works and why. *American Journal of Health Behavior, 27,* S233–S238.

Tamborini, R., & Stiff, J. (1987). Predictors of horror films attendance and appeal: An analysis of the audience for frightening films. *Communication Research, 14,* 415–436.

Zuckerman, M. (1994). *Behavioral expressions and biosocial bases of sensation seeking.* New York: Cambridge University Press.

SESAME WORKSHOP

All children deserve a chance to learn and grow. To be prepared for school. To better understand the world and each other. To think, dream and discover. To reach their highest potential.

—Sesame Workshop

Sesame Workshop, first established as the Children's Television Workshop in 1968, is a nonprofit organization of writers, artists, researchers, and educators who create educational content for children from birth through age 12; that content is delivered through multiple media: television, radio, books, magazines, computers, film, video, and community outreach. Sesame Workshop is best known for *Sesame Street,* a pioneering program designed by producers, researchers, and educators to harness the power of media to address school readiness for underserved preschoolers. Other programs produced by Sesame Workshop addressed educational gaps in mathematics (*Square One TV*), literacy (*The Electric Company* and *Ghostwriter)*, science and technology (*3-2-1 Contact* and *Cro*), and resiliency (*Dragon Tales*).

Sesame Workshop creates innovative, engaging content for children in more than 120 countries worldwide, partnering with local experts to ensure its programs and products are both culturally relevant and educationally sound. The content created provides access to all kinds of learning—spanning the entire range of children's developmental needs. These topics range from the academic basics of literacy, mathematics, and science to health and life skills such as coping with emotions, conflict resolution, sharing, respect, and inclusion. The content is uniquely delivered in real-life contexts; subjects have included overcoming the stigma of AIDS in South Africa; educating girls in Egypt; promoting cross-cultural respect and understanding among children in the Middle East; and in this post-9/11 world, helping U.S. children demystify differences and value diversity.

To maintain the highest standards of curriculum design, as well as incorporate recent findings of research, all content is developed through a dynamic process. This process involves educators, researchers, and producers who collaborate throughout the life of a project to ensure that everything created is both engaging and developmentally appropriate. This unique, ongoing integration of curriculum development, formative research (i.e., research conducted to inform production decisions regarding the appeal and comprehension of content in relation to the intended target audience), and summative research (i.e., research conducted to assess the educational impact of the content) into the process of production is known as the Sesame Workshop Model.

Sesame Workshop uses children's natural attraction to media in ways that serve their best interests and their highest potential. As a nonprofit organization, Sesame Workshop puts the proceeds it receives from the sales of licensed products right back into the development of *Sesame Street* and other programs and initiatives for children in the United States and around the world.

The Sesame Workshop experience shows that "small things"—a hand puppet, a kind word, a song—can make a big difference. Small beginnings have profound possibilities, especially when their effects are multiplied by a global community committed to making meaningful, measurable, lasting differences in children's lives, now and for generations to come.

—*Rosemarie T. Truglio*

See also Children's Television Act of 1990; Television, Prosocial Content and

SEX, INTERNET SOLICITATION OF

The Internet can be used for a variety of sexual purposes, including sexual enlightenment or advice, erotic matter and pornography, sex shops, and webcams showing sexual activity. In addition, the Internet, with its chat rooms and online forums, its game sites and dating sites, has become a popular contacts market where it is possible to seek and find partners for flirting, love affairs, or sex, whether on a virtual or real-life basis. Although much of this activity involves consenting adults, some sexual solicitation is directed at children and adolescents and leads to the victimization of young people. There is no empirical knowledge yet available on how intensively young people (male and female) in different age groups and cultures participate in the Internet as active searchers for sexual contact. However, they do initiate such activity, which may lead to problematic relationships even when it does not lead to criminal victimization.

The terms *virtual sex* or *cybersex* are used to describe sensual interactions between two or more people that take place online (via email, instant messaging, online chat, webcam, etc.), are intended to achieve sexual excitation and satisfaction, and are often accompanied by masturbation. Some Internet users consciously restrict their erotic online contacts to cybersex. Others are mainly interested in real sexual encounters.

Surveys carried out in the United States reveal that a significant percentage of both male and female adult users are involved in sexual solicitation on the Internet. From the standpoint of clinical psychology, the vast majority of these users are adults of sound mind who have positive experiences of consensual sexual activities that they engage in online with other adults. However, a minority of those practicing cybersex have psychological difficulties or disorders. People with deviant sexual preferences, such as a sexual interest in children, may take advantage of the anonymity and opportunity for a virtual identity switch that the Internet affords to act out their deviant patterns. It is also possible for them to assert the legitimacy of their behavior in online forums with people who have similar preferences.

PREVALENCE OF SEXUAL SOLICITATIONS AND INTERNET SEX CRIMES

In a 2000 U.S. survey by Finkelhor, Mitchell, and Wolak, a representative sample of young users (between 10 and 17 years old) of the Internet were surveyed. About 19% of them declared they had received unwanted sexual solicitation in the previous year. In the majority of cases, the children and young people ignored the messages, and neither online nor offline contacts resulted. However, 5% of those surveyed said they had also received a distressing sexual solicitation (i.e., the solicitation made them feel very or extremely upset or afraid). One third of the surveyed youth who had received a solicitation were male, and two thirds were female. According to the youth, adults (age 18 and older) made 24% of all solicitations and juveniles 48% (the age of the solicitor was unknown in the remaining 28% of all solicitations).

The 2003 National Juvenile Online Victimization Study was conducted in the United States between July 1, 2000, and July 1, 2001, by Wolak, Mitchell, and Finkelhor, to help in determining the scope of Internet sex crimes against minors. An examination of law enforcement activities at the local, county, and state levels turned up 2,577 arrests for Internet sex crimes against minors during that period. The perpetrators were almost always male (99%), non-Hispanic white (92%), and more than 25 years old (86%); nearly all (97%) acted alone in the crime, and many (67%)

possessed child pornography. Internet sex crime arrests could be divided into three separate groups:

- 36% of the arrests were associated with possession of, exchange of, or trade in child pornography but not its production.
- 39% of the arrests were for harm to individual, identifiable minors. In these cases, the perpetrators made contact with the victims via the Internet to abuse them online or offline. The perpetrators questioned young people in chat or email situations about their sexual fantasies and experience, sent them explicit sexual propositions, or encouraged them to take part in sexual telephone calls, exchange of photos, or a videoconference in which they appeared naked. Where a meeting offline had been arranged on the Internet, in extreme cases, the outcome had been rape and murder. In half the cases, the perpetrators arrested were strangers to the child; in the other half, they were people from the child's real social setting (such as family members or friends of their parents).
- 25% of the arrests were achieved by means of undercover investigations in which police officers claimed to be minors on the net in chat rooms and contact exchanges. Here the detectives act as decoys for adults who are online to achieve sexual contact with children. Although there is no actual harm to a child in these cases, the attempt at child abuse is itself a crime in the United States.

It is important that detectives playing the child's role should not themselves introduce sexual subjects or proffer sex but should simply observe whether these come from the potential perpetrator, whose identity is then pursued. These undercover detective practices are permitted by law in certain countries (such as the United States) but not in others (such as Germany).

In view of the frequently alarmist reports in the media on the perils of the Internet, it must be emphasized that the Internet cases are offset by many millions of cases of sexual abuse of children offline each year in the United States. It is thus hardly justified to represent the Internet as an outstanding danger zone. Moreover, prevention and countermeasures are particularly effective in the context of Internet crime; for example, a girl who receives sexually suggestive emails via Internet can tell her parents, who can get help from Internet providers and prosecution authorities to follow the digital trail and trace the originator of the message.

OTHER RISKS OF ONLINE ACTIVITY

Besides the danger of becoming the victim of an Internet-related sex crime, young people engaging in sexualized contacts via the Internet with their contemporaries are exposed to other risks. Pushy behavior and harassment can increase under the protection of anonymity, and adolescents can be perpetrators as well as victims of such activity. It is a particularly common event in many chat rooms for women and girls (and anybody using a feminine nickname) to be faced with unwanted sexual remarks and propositions. To avoid them, children and teenagers should limit their visits to chat rooms and online platforms that have moderators and rules of use to prevent (and, if necessary, prosecute) inappropriate behavior. At the same time, young people need to be taught about what is appropriate as online behavior toward other young people (both outside and within the sexual context).

Even if an online sexual approach from one young person to another has followed an enjoyable course, dangers can still arise in the transfer to offline contact. Exchanging confidences online with unknown people can very quickly generate feelings of closeness and bonding. The perception of closeness or even of being in love may well lead to unwisely trusting behavior at the first real meeting. It is, therefore, recommended that a first rendezvous after online flirting take place only with the knowledge of significant others (perhaps in their presence or in a public setting), so that the risk of an unpleasant surprise is reduced and the situation can be kept under control. Young people and their parents need to be well-informed as to the appropriate precautions.

If the first face-to-face encounter is a pleasant event, the relationship is likely to proceed faster than usual to sexual activity. One reason is that feelings of closeness and of longing have already been developed in the course of the preceding online communication and may weaken the resolve to practice only safe sex. Another factor may be shortage of time. Because Internet acquaintances often live at quite a distance from each other, personal meetings tend to be rare and brief, leaving less scope for slow, reflective development of the relationship. In view of this, sex education should include not only the facts of life but those of Internet affairs and relationships.

There is a further risk in using the Internet for erotic or sexual purposes: Unfaithfulness and two-timing are more likely. Adults are not the only ones to end up in marital crisis because of their partners' cybersex adventures. Young people, too, can suffer greatly when steady boyfriends or girlfriends practice online infidelity—flirting with other girls or boys online, exchanging erotic photos, and setting up sexual situations. Many people take the partner's affair as a real and serious betrayal of the real-life relationship, even when it has remained purely a cyberaffair. Other couples define cybersex as unreal games and permit such play to partners. Ubiquitous cybersex opportunities force couples into negotiation of the relevant rules and boundaries for their relationship.

Finally, because online sexual encounters provide immediate rewards, adolescents (as well as adults) with escapist tendencies can get dependent on them.

OPPORTUNITIES FOR ADOLESCENTS

Amassing sexual experience is one of the developmental tasks for young people as they grow into adults. Many factors, both internal and via social contact, determine their sexual socialization. The media are often perceived as a potential danger or disruption to this process—in instances, perhaps, where children and adolescents are confronted with sexual material they do not yet understand. However, it is also possible for the media to contribute very positively to the process of sexual socialization; for example, media may be a vehicle for vital and accurate sexual information and may provide a safe space in which adolescents can explore and express their sexuality in age-appropriate ways.

From this point of view, the potential of the sexual contact on offer on the Internet can be seen as good. Those young people whose social environment restricts their opportunities for healthy development on the sexual front can find them on the Internet. They can share sexual fears, fantasies, and feelings with their contemporaries, acting them out symbolically in cybersex. For example, young gays and lesbians are often very isolated if they live in rural areas; Internet forums and chat rooms may provide an opportunity to explore their sexual identity with other youngsters of the same mind and obtain social support.

Computer-mediated communication also lowers the threshold of inhibition, making it easier for people to give a relaxed and self-assured impression, which can make sexual approaches less scary for adolescents than they otherwise tend to be. The Internet can even be a realm where sexual experimentation can take place in relative safety (especially for girls). The sexual interactions typical of online chats or role-play games on MUDs (multi-user dungeons or domains) require that things otherwise often left unsaid be put into words, with the result that a high degree of intimacy is achieved. Obviously, it would be mistaken to idealize these constructive aspects of cybersex, but they are frequently reported. The quality of cybersex is not a matter of the medium but of the sexual and social competence of those involved.

—*Nicola Döring*

See also Chat Rooms; Chat Rooms, Social and Linguistic Processes in; Instant Messaging; Internet Use, Addiction to; Internet Use, Age and; Multi-User Dungeons/ Domains (MUDs); Sex, Media Impact on; Sexual Information, Internet and; Sexualization of Children

FURTHER READINGS

Boies, S. C., Cooper, A., & Osborne, C. S. (2004). Variations in Internet-related problems and psychosocial functioning in online sexual activities: Implications for social and sexual development of young adults. *Cyberpsychology & Behavior, 7,* 207–230.

Carvalheira, A., & Gomes, F. A. (2003). Cybersex in Portugese chatrooms: A study of sexual behaviors related to online sex. *Journal of Sex and Marital Therapy, 29*(5), 345–360.

Cooper, A. (Ed.). (2002). *Sex and the Internet: A guidebook for clinicians.* Philadelphia: Routledge.

Cooper, A., Scherer, C., Boies, S. C., & Gordon, B. L. (1999). Sexuality on the Internet: From sexual exploration to pathological expression. *Professional Psychology: Research and Practice, 30,* 33–52.

Dombrowski, S. C., LeMasney, J. W., Ahia, C. E., & Dickson, S. A. (2004). Protecting children from online sexual predators: Technological, psychoeducational, and legal considerations. *Professional Psychology: Research & Practice, 35,* 65–73.

Döring, N. (2000). Feminist views of cybersex: Victimization, liberation, and empowerment. *CyberPsychology & Behavior, 3*(5), 863–884.

Döring, N. (2002). Studying online love and cyber romance. In B. Batinic, U.-D. Reips, & M. Bosnjak (Eds.), *Online social sciences* (pp. 333–356). Seattle, WA: Hogrefe & Huber.

Finkelhor, D., & Hashima, P. (2001). The victimization of children & youth: A comprehensive overview. In S. O. White (Ed.), *Law and social science perspectives on youth and justice* (pp. 49–78). New York: Plenum.

Finkelhor, D., Mitchell, K., & Wolak, J. (2000). *Online victimization: A report on the nation's youth* (National Center for Missing & Exploited Children Bulletin). Retrieved from http://www.unh.edu/ccrc/

Griffin-Shelley, E. (2003). The Internet and sexuality: A literature review 1983–2002. *Sexual and Relationship Therapy, 3,* 255–270.

Griffiths, M. (2001). Sex on the Internet: Observations and implications for Internet sex addiction. *Journal of Sex Research, 4,* 333–342.

McKenna, K., & Bargh, J. (1998). Coming out in the age of the Internet: Identity "de-marginalization" from virtual group participation. *Journal of Personality and Social Psychology, 75*(3), 681–694.

Quale, E., & Taylor, M. (2001). Child seduction and self-representation on the Internet. *CyberPsychology & Behavior, 4*(5), 597–608.

Quale, E., & Taylor, M. (2003). Model of problematic Internet use in people with a sexual interest in children. *Cyberpsychology & Behavior, 6*(1), 93–106.

Salyers Bull, S., Mcfarlane, M., Lloyd, L., & Rietmeijer, C. (2004). The process of seeking sex partners online and implications for STD/HIV prevention. *AIDS Care, 16*(8), 1012–1020.

Wolak, J., Mitchell, K., & Finkelhor, D. (2003). *Internet sex crimes against minors: The response of law enforcement* (National Center for Missing & Exploited Children). Retrieved from http://www.unh.edu/ccrc/

Young, K. S., Griffen-Shelley, E., Cooper, A., O'Mara, J., & Buchman, J. (2000). Online infidelity: A new dimension in couple relationships with implications for evaluation and treatment. *Sexual Addiction & Compulsivity, 1–2,* 59–74.

SEX, MEDIA IMPACT ON

Sexual content typically has been defined as any depiction of sexual activity, sexually suggestive behavior, or talk about sexuality or sexual activity. It has been estimated that the typical American adolescent encounters about 10,000 to 15,000 sexual references, jokes, and innuendoes in the media each year.

Despite ongoing criticism of the media's increasingly frequent and explicit sexual content, less than 1% of published research studies have investigated the association between media exposure and sexual beliefs and behaviors. Much of the research has focused on documenting what kind of sexual content is in various kinds of media, while only a few studies have linked that content with subsequent effects on sexual behavior. Most of the studies of sexual content have focused on television, with an emphasis on prime-time shows, music videos, and soap operas; fewer studies have examined magazines, feature films, music, advertising, videogames, and the Internet.

The Kaiser Family Foundation has sponsored a biennial study of sex on television since the late 1990s. These studies have shown that sexual content is prevalent, varies slightly by genre, and has increased in frequency. In general, television's sexual content is not typically visually graphic but is dominated by either verbal innuendo or less explicit physical acts; most of the sexual action and language occurs outside marital relationships; discussion and depiction of sexual planning and consequences are rarely portrayed; and women's physical beauty and men's strength and physical prowess are emphasized. In short, television frequently portrays spontaneous, glamorous sexual behavior outside long-term relationships. The typical depiction of sexual activity has been classified as recreational rather than relational.

Sexual images and messages are more explicit in some mainstream magazines, especially women's and men's health and fitness magazines. Women's magazines encourage women to focus on increasing their sexual desirability to gain the attention of men. The work of relationships is depicted as the exclusive domain of women, while men are expected always to be ready for sex.

In the early part of the 21st century, the average adolescent in the United States spends more than 40 hours per week with some form of mass media. Many have access to the media in the privacy of their own bedrooms, and many spend more time with the media than with their parents. Simultaneously, school systems are increasingly reluctant to provide comprehensive sex education. Given this heavy frequency of media use, relatively less time spent with parents, school reticence, and increased access to sexual content in the media, it is reasonable to expect that children and adolescents might be learning about sex from the media. Adolescents often cite the media as one of their top sources of sexual information.

Early correlational studies and a few experimental studies in which exposure to sexual content was varied found that more frequent exposure to sexually oriented television genres such as soap operas and music videos was associated with more permissive attitudes about premarital sex among adolescents. Two longitudinal studies also showed that exposure to sexual content in the media was related to earlier sexual behavior. Collins et al. (2004) conducted a telephone survey of a representative sample of 12-to-17-year olds and found that increased exposure to sexual content on television increased the likelihood of a teen having sexual intercourse within the following year. Brown et al. (2006) found that greater exposure to a diet of sexual content across four media (television, movies, music, magazines) in early adolescence predicted earlier initiation of sexual intercourse 2 years later. Thus, the pattern of findings indicate that exposure to sexual media content is indeed linked to sexual outcomes.

Although most concern has focused on the idea that the media cause young people to have sex earlier than they might otherwise, it is likely that young people also seek sexual information in the media as they enter puberty and sexual feelings and relationships become more relevant. It may well be that as sexual content in the media becomes more salient, young people seek it out and then learn and are affected by what they see, hear, and read. It is important to remember, too, that all teens will not be affected in the same way or to the same extent. In the Brown et al. (2006) study, the linkage between sexual media diet and sexual behavior was stronger for the white adolescents than it was for the African American youth. The African American teens apparently were more influenced by perceptions of their parents' expectations and their friends' sexual behavior than by what they saw or heard in the media. Media effects do not occur in a vacuum, and audiences come to the media with other information and norms that influence how they interpret and apply what they find in the media. This is the basic premise of the media practice model, which has been used to help explain how the media are used by adolescents as they develop a sense of who they are as sexual human beings.

Three other theories have been used to understand how the media have an effect on sexual beliefs and behavior. Cultivation theory suggests that the consistency of the portrayal of sexual content in the media will cultivate common beliefs about sexual norms and patterns of sexual behavior, especially among frequent media users. Cognitive social learning theory suggests that young people will imitate the kind of sexual behavior they see in the media especially if the characters are seen as similar to them and as attractive and if they do not suffer negative consequences. Experimental studies examining short-term effects of sexual media stimuli support the ideas of priming theory: that the media may activate semantically related concepts that gradually form stereotypical sexual schemas in adolescents' minds.

The study of the sexual effects of the media is relatively young compared to research on other kinds of media effects, such as the effect of TV violence on aggressive behavior. More studies are needed to sort out the direction and pattern of effects on sexual beliefs and behaviors. Very little is known, for example, about the sexual effects of the Internet. The Internet provides unprecedented access to much more explicit sexual content than what has been provided in mainstream media, so it will be important to learn more about how young people are using and responding to such content.

—*Jane D. Brown and Amy Shirong Lu*

See also Adolescents, Developmental Needs of, and Media; Bedrooms, Media Use in; Sex in Television, Content Analysis of; Sex in Television, Incidence and Themes

FURTHER READINGS

Brown, J., L'Engle, K., Pardun, C., Guo, G., Kenneavy, K., & Jackson, C. (2006). Sexy media matter: Exposure to sexual content in music, movies, television, and magazines predicts black and white adolescents' sexual behavior. *Pediatrics, 117*(4), 1018–1027.

Collins, R., Elliott, M., Berry, S., Kanouse, D., Kunkel, D., & Hunter, S., & Miu, A. (2004). Watching sex on television predicts adolescent initiation of sexual behavior. *Pediatrics, 114*(3), E280–E289.

Escobar-Chaves, S., Tortolero, S., Markham, C., Low, B., Eitel, P., & Thickstun, P. (2005). Impact of the media on adolescent sexual attitudes and behaviors. *Pediatrics, 116*(1), 303–326.

Kunkel, D., Biely, E., Eyal, K., Cope-Farrar, K., Donnerstein, E., & Fandrich, R. (2003). *Sex on TV (3): A biennial report.* Menlo Park, CA: Kaiser Family Foundation.

Rich, M. (2005). Sex screen: The dilemma of media exposure and sexual behavior. *Pediatrics, 116*(1), 329–331.

Strasburger, V. (2005). Adolescents, sex, and the media: Ooooo, baby, baby—a q & a. *Adolescent Medicine Clinics, 16*(2), 269–288.

Ward, L. (2003). Understanding the role of entertainment media in the sexual socialization of American youth: A review of empirical research. *Developmental Review, 23*(3), 347–388.

SEX IN TELEVISION, CONTENT ANALYSIS OF

Quantitative content analyses conducted over the past two decades have documented the form and frequency of sexual content on television programming, finding that the programs most watched by youth are saturated with references to and depictions of sexual behavior (often physical flirting, passionate kissing, or intimate touching). Indeed, more than 80% of the prime-time television programs most popular among adolescents contain references to or depictions of sexual behavior. These analyses have further demonstrated that, over time, the amount of sexual content on television has increased, as have discussions of sexual risk and safer-sex topics. Qualitative content analyses find that television's sexual content includes multiple thematic messages about the value, consequences, and nature of sexual activity. For example, sex is frequently depicted as recreational in nature, and men and women are typically depicted as having different sexual roles.

Recent analyses find that roughly one third of television programs contain at least one depiction of sexual behavior, reflecting an increase from one quarter of programs in the late 1990s. Among programs rated favorably by adolescents, this rate climbs to 50%, with the average 1-hour program containing three scenes with depictions of sexual behavior. The vast majority of these depictions consist of precursory sexual behaviors, such as physical flirting, passionate kissing, or intimate touching. Although explicit depictions of sexual intercourse are rare, intercourse is frequently implied by the use of cinematic techniques familiar to young audiences. For example, a couple may be shown lying in bed, partially clothed immediately following a scene with passionate kissing and touching. More than 10% of all prime-time television programs contain such instances of implied intercourse, and as many as 20% of the programs most popular among adolescents contain instances of implied or depicted intercourse. These sexual behaviors occur, most commonly, between unmarried partners.

In addition to quantifying the frequency of sexual behaviors, content analysis has been used to evaluate the messages *about* sexuality conveyed via sexual dialogue. The television programs most watched by adolescents are specifically saturated with sexual talk; at the episode level, as many as 80% of programs popular among teens contain talk about sex, compared to less than 70% of all network prime-time programs and about 60% of the full range of television programming. Closer inspection of individual episodes reveals that sexual talk appears frequently and consistently in the programs children and adolescents watch most. Rather than appearing only once or twice in an episode, sex talk typically occurs in more than a quarter of all character interactions, so that a child might expect to hear anywhere from 10 to 30 comments about sexuality while watching her favorite half-hour program; a teen might hear as many as 45 such comments.

In light of children's and adolescents' frequent exposure to sexual content on television, concern has been raised regarding the relative infrequency with which sexual risk and safer-sex practices are acknowledged. Content analyses of youth-oriented television programs aired in the 1990s revealed that fewer than 15% of programs with sexual content addressed the potential risks associated with sexual activity or described the safer-sex practices that could be involved in preventing risk. Risk and prevention messages were conceptualized to include partners' choice to delay intercourse, the use of safer-sex practices (e.g., condoms), or depictions of the negative consequences of sex (e.g., an unwanted pregnancy). Content analysis of more recently aired programs shows a shift toward more frequent acknowledgment of sexual risk and safer-sex practices. About 25% of programs with sexual content addressed risk and prevention themes, and programs featuring teen characters were the most likely to contain such messages.

The content of sexual dialogue further tends to endorse a specific set of messages about sexuality. First, dialogue is used to convey meaning about the value of sexuality. Consistent with findings that sexual behavior on television occurs most frequently among unmarried partners, dialogue about sexuality commonly puts forth the value of recreational sex. Sex is discussed as a game or competition between women and men and as a fun, exciting, and pleasurable activity for everyone. Less common but still present are messages about the relational nature of sexuality, and these include discussion of the emotional connections between partners and the intimacy associated with sexuality. Second, dialogue is used to convey different sexual roles of heterosexual men and women. Men are portrayed as sex-driven and concerned primarily with women's appearance. Women, on the other hand, are often portrayed as passive gatekeepers of men's sexual advances. When they are portrayed actively in pursuit of sexual activity—which happens frequently—such behavior is punished more often than not. Specifically, a content analysis of prime-time dramas featuring teen and college-age characters found that depictions of sexual activity initiated by female characters were significantly more likely to

result in negative consequences (including rejection, unwanted pregnancy, or formal punishment) than similar incidents initiated by male characters.

Gay and lesbian characters have recurring roles in several of the programs most popular among children and adolescents, such as *Will & Grace*, *Buffy the Vampire Slayer*, *Dawson's Creek,* and *The Simpsons*, and they have smaller roles in many more programs. Although larger-scale (and quantitative) content analyses have not addressed same-sex sexual behavior or dialogue about homosexuality, a small set of studies have subjected television content to critical analysis for themes about and representations of homosexuality. Comedies such as *Will & Grace* and *The Simpsons* have received attention for their regular inclusion of homosexual characters and frequent references to same-sex desire. At the same time, these programs have been criticized for portrayals that stereotype homosexual characters or that divorce same-sex behavior from same-sex desire.

—*Deborah Schooler*

See also Advertising, Sexuality in; Movies, Sexuality in; Research Methods, Content Analyses; Schemas/Scripts, Sexual; Sex, Media Impact on; Sex in Television, Incidence and Themes; Sex in Television, Perceived Realism of; Sexual Content, Age and Comprehension of; Soap Operas, Sexuality in

FURTHER READINGS

Kunkel, D., Cope, K. M., & Biely, E. (1999). Sexual messages on television: Comparing findings from three studies. *The Journal of Sex Research*, *36*(3), 230–236.

Ward, L. M. (1995). Talking about sex: Common themes about sexuality in the prime-time television programs children and adolescents view most. *Journal of Youth and Adolescence*, *24*(5), 595–615.

SEX IN TELEVISION, INCIDENCE AND THEMES

Systematic content analysis research has been conducted since the 1970s to identify patterns of sexual messages on entertainment television programming and to illuminate the media's role in the process of sexual socialization. The pervasiveness of television and its repeated messages make it an important socializing agent with regard to sex. Many young people report that they rely on television for information about sexual issues and norms. To date, content analyses have provided information regarding the extent of sexual messages on entertainment programs and the context within which such messages are embedded. Content analyses have been conducted on both the overall entertainment television landscape (usually excluding sports, news, and children's programming) and programming that is more relevant and appealing to young people. Different content analyses often define and measure sex in diverse ways, making it difficult to compare findings across studies. Still, several conclusions can be drawn about the presentation of sex on entertainment television.

THE INCIDENCE OF SEXUAL CONTENT ON TELEVISION

Sexual messages on television have increased over the years. Most recently, content analyses have revealed that nearly two thirds of all programs include some sexual content. The percentage of programs that include messages about sex is even higher in prime-time programming, where between 71% and 85% of programs have been found to include such content. Studies have found about 10 to 15 instances of sexual imagery, language, or behavior per hour of prime-time programming.

Examining specific genres of television programming, researchers have found that soap operas tend to include the highest rates of sexual content, followed by comedies, which usually present sex in a humorous context. Movies tend to include more, and more explicit, sexual content than original television programming, and programs on cable networks tend to portray more sex than broadcast programs. Interestingly, programs that adolescents view most tend to include an especially high incidence of sex, with up to four out of five shows including at least one scene with sexual content. Nearly one third of interactions per hour of prime-time programming viewed by teens include sexual messages.

Researchers have lately been examining the specific sexual media diets of adolescents, acknowledging that television is part of a constellation of media content to which youth are exposed. A recent study found that 11% of television content specifically viewed by adolescents contained sexual content. About half to three quarters of music videos, a genre

specifically produced for and targeted at adolescents, have consistently been found to include sexual imagery, often combining sexuality with violence.

Researchers are in agreement that the majority of sexual portrayals on television are in the form of talk about sex, and fewer are depictions of sexual behaviors. Although explicitness has increased through the years, sexual behaviors on television tend to be more implicit, relying mostly on innuendo in the form of sexual suggestiveness and light physical contact. The most common sexual behavior on television is kissing. Sexual intercourse, although portrayed less frequently, has been increasing significantly over the years. It is now included in nearly 15% of entertainment programs. Sexual intercourse is particularly common in soap operas and prime-time shows viewed by adolescents.

THE CONTEXT OF SEXUAL CONTENT ON TELEVISION

Contextual variations in the content of television programs are likely to lead to different effects on viewers. Therefore, beyond the frequency with which sex is portrayed on television, it is important to consider the nature of such portrayals. Content analyses have focused on the characters who engage in sexual behaviors, primarily examining their age and gender, as well as the relationships between those engaging in intercourse. Other contextual elements that have received attention in content analyses include the mention of risks associated with sexual behaviors and the consequences depicted for these behaviors.

Characters Engaged in Sexual Intercourse

Sexual intercourse, arguably the most salient sexual behavior for adolescents on television, is portrayed in nearly one in seven entertainment programs. Sexual intercourse acts portrayed on television occur most often between adults who are acquainted with but are not married to one another (see Ward, 2003, for a review). Less than 5% of characters who engage in intercourse across all television programming, and 10% of those in soap operas, are teens. Except for soap operas, in which characters tend to portray negative or balanced attitudes toward sexual activities, characters express mostly positive attitudes toward sex and a recreational orientation, treating sex as a casual activity meant to bring pleasure and enjoyment to the individual. In prime-time programming viewed by teens, characters' physical attractiveness is of importance.

Risks and Consequences Associated With Sexual Behaviors

Few mentions of the risks associated with sex, such as unintended pregnancy or the contraction of sexually transmitted diseases, occur on television programming, although their incidence has been slightly increasing over the years. Still, when risks are addressed, their treatment is mostly superficial. This is true across the entertainment television landscape as well as in specific programming such as prime-time shows, soap operas, and shows heavily viewed by teenagers. Most acts of sexual intercourse on television—and on television programming viewed by teens—result in no clear positive or negative consequences. When consequences of intercourse are portrayed, positive outcomes are more common than negative ones, especially on genres such as soap operas. Only about one fifth to one third of consequences mentioned on television refer to negative outcomes such as unintended pregnancy or HIV and STD contraction. Although one study found considerably more interactions about sexuality that resulted in or noted negative consequences, most of these consequences were emotional or social in nature and only few were physical, a finding consistent with past studies.

—*Keren Eyal*

See also Movies, Sexuality in; Sex in Television, Content Analysis of; Sexual Risk and Responsibility, Portrayals of; Soap Operas, Content Analyses of; Soap Operas, Sexuality in

FURTHER READINGS

Kunkel, D., Biely, E., Eyal, K., Cope-Farrar, K., Donnerstein, E., & Fandrich, R. (2003). *Sex on TV 3: A biennial report to the Kaiser Family Foundation*. Menlo Park, CA: Kaiser Family Foundation.

Pardun, C. J., L'Engle, K. L., & Brown, J. D. (2005). Linking exposure to outcomes: Early adolescents' consumption of sexual content in six media. *Mass Communication & Society, 8*, 75–91.

Ward, L. M. (2003). Understanding the role of entertainment media in the sexual socialization of American youth: A review of empirical research. *Developmental Review, 23*, 347–388.

SEX IN TELEVISION, PERCEIVED REALISM OF

Television programs are filled with both visual and verbal sexual content. Sexual behaviors, innuendo, and discussions appear in a wide range of programs. Although a number of studies have examined the relationship between viewing sexual content and beliefs about social reality, fewer studies have investigated the ways in which the perceived reality of television's sexual content is related to children's and adolescents' sexual attitudes and behaviors. Most of these have focused on older adolescents, specifically college undergraduates. These studies have looked at the ways in which perceived reality mediates the impact of different types of sexual content, as well as the extent to which attitudes, gender, experience, and age influence perceptions of the realism of sexual content.

Research in perceived reality is based on the assumption that exposure to television content alone does not determine the impact of that content. Children and adolescents actively select and interpret television content and assess its reality by referring to their own experiences, observations, and knowledge of the world. If the content of television is viewed as being realistic, it may be given greater importance. If the content is viewed as being unrealistic, however, this may limit its influence on audiences.

A MEDIATING EFFECT

Perceived reality can mediate the effects of viewing sexual content on perceptions of sexual activities and attitudes. In one study, Ward and Rivadeneyra showed undergraduates clips of sexual situations (discussions of sexual encounters and relational conflicts) taken from popular situation comedies. The more viewers found the clips realistic, identified with the characters, and felt the actions could happen in their own lives, the higher their estimates of males' and peers' sexual experience. This was most noticeable for female participants. The type of content, however, can affect perceived realism judgments.

Taylor had college undergraduates watch video clips of popular television programs containing either visual depictions of sexual behaviors (pre- and post-intercourse scenes) or verbal discussions of sexual activity. He found that, regardless of group, adolescents who believed that the content was highly realistic were more likely to endorse sexually permissive attitudes and were more accepting of sexual intercourse and oral sex in casual relationships.

Among the adolescents who watched the visual depictions, perceived realism did not significantly affect their beliefs about peers' sexual behaviors. However, among those viewing the verbal discussions, higher levels of perceived realism was linked to increased beliefs about the number of female, but not male, peers who were sexually active. This may reflect differences between the visual depictions, which involved fairly stereotypical heterosexual behaviors, and the verbal clips, which involved women who were encouraging a friend to be sexually active or describing their own sexual experiences. The impact of the perceived reality of verbal sexual content may be of particular importance given that content analyses have found that television programs include discussions of sex far more often than visual depictions and that these appear in the situation comedies that younger children watch.

In addition to affecting perceptions of others, perceived realism can also affect satisfaction with individuals' own sexual activities. Baran found that high school and college students' satisfaction with their virginity decreased as their identification with sexually active characters and perceptions of the accuracy of media portrayals of sexual behavior increased.

FACTORS INFLUENCING PERCEIVED REALITY

Researchers have also examined the factors influencing perceived realism. Adolescents' motivations for media use can affect realism judgments. Those who watch television to "learn about the world" have a higher perceived reality. Attitudes about sexual relationships can also affect perceived reality. In one study, adolescents who endorsed a recreational orientation toward relationships (relationships are a game or competition between men and women) were more likely to believe that sexual content was realistic. Conversely, those who endorsed a more traditional orientation (sex belongs primarily in marital relationships) gave lower ratings of perceived realism to sexual content.

Experience, including experience with the ethnic groups depicted, can also increase the audience's ability to judge the realism of television's sexual content. For example, Latina/o participants in one study gave higher ratings of perceived reality to programs showing primarily white characters. Sexual experience is also an important factor. Adolescents with limited sexual experience have a limited basis for comparison

and may therefore be limited in their abilities to make critical judgments about sexual content.

Developmental age also influences the ability to make perceived reality judgments. Although extensive research has been conducted on the impact of cognitive development on realism judgments for other types of content, sexual content has received less attention. Granello, however, conducted a series of focus groups with girls ages 12, 16 to 17, and 21, examining their views of the dating relationships and behaviors in the television program, *Beverly Hills 90210*. The youngest girls believed the program showed teenagers "as they really" were. Girls in the 17-year-old group thought that although the show was not representative of their own lives, it was a realistic depiction of life in California. The 21-year-olds thought the program was unrealistic.

These studies suggest that perceptions of the reality of sexual content influence television's effects. Adolescents' perceived reality judgments are apparently complex and determined by a variety of motivational and experiential factors.

—*T. Makana Chock*

See also Developmental Differences, Media and; Fantasy–Reality Distinction; Gender Roles on Television; Individual Differences, Media Preferences and; Media Effects; Media Effects, Models of; Movies, Perceived Realism of; Sex, Media Impact on; Sex in Television, Content Analysis of; Sex in Television, Incidence and Themes; Sexual Risk and Responsibility, Portrayals of; Soap Operas, Effects of

FURTHER READINGS

Baran, S. J. (1976). Sex on TV and adolescent sexual self-image. *Journal of Broadcasting, 20,* 61–68.

Granello, D. H. (1997). Using *Beverly Hills, 90210* to explore developmental issues in female adolescents. *Youth & Society, 29*(1), 24–53.

Taylor, L. D. (2005). Effects of visual and verbal sexual television content and perceived realism on attitudes and beliefs. *Journal of Sex Research, 42*(2), 130–138.

Ward, L. M., Gorvine, B., & Cytron, A (2002). Would that really happen? Adolescents' perceptions of sexual relationships according to prime-time television. In J. D. Brown, J. R. Steele, & K. Walsh-Childers (Eds.), *Sexual teens, sexual media* (pp. 95–123). Mahwah, NJ: Erlbaum.

Ward, L. M., & Rivadeneyra, R. (1999). Contributions of entertainment television to adolescents' sexual attitudes and expectations: The role of viewing amount versus viewer involvement. *Journal of Sex Research, 36*(3), 237–262.

SEXUAL CONTENT, AGE AND COMPREHENSION OF

Research into the impact of sexually oriented media messages on children and adolescents' sexual expectations, attitudes, and behaviors has always been closely related to the issue of how young viewers may understand these messages. Effects researchers have realized that viewers' ability to process, understand, and evaluate sexual content is likely to change throughout adolescence, and therefore, they have acknowledged that media effects may be different at different levels of maturity. For that reason, a number of studies have asked questions about whether and how young viewers comprehend sexually oriented contents; in most of these investigations, the concept of comprehension was understood in a broad sense, as beliefs about the content and reactions to its sexual nature. More specifically, a young viewer's response to sexual contents has been examined through studies that focus on one or two of four principal notions: (1) children and adolescents' comprehension of sexual innuendo, (2) their interpretations of what sexual messages may mean, (3) their emotional reactions to these contents, and (4) their judgments about the realism of the messages.

YOUNG VIEWERS' RESPONSES TO SEXUAL CONTENT

Comprehension

A notable example of the studies that explicitly focused on the issue of comprehension is the study of Silverman-Watkins and Sprafkin, using an observational learning perspective in which media effects are presented as a three-stage process of exposure, acquisition, and acceptance. The researchers focused on the second stage, examining whether children and adolescents understood references to sexuality in television programs. Their results indicated that 12-to-16-year-olds were able to work out the actual meaning of sexual allusions relatively well; a conclusion that was supported by a recent British qualitative study in 9-to-17-year-old schoolchildren. The comprehension scores were different, however, when a distinction is made between diverse types of sexual topics and when comprehension was examined in separate age groups. In the Silverman-Watkins and Sprafkin study, comprehension scores for allusions to intercourse were lower than scores for references to discouraged sexual practices (e.g., homosexuality). Furthermore, both pre- and postpubescent 12-year-olds experienced more difficulty in understanding sexual innuendo than 14- and 16-year-olds. In a more recent study, a group of 8-to-10-year olds was contrasted with viewers between 10 and 12; the latter category understood sexual jokes and innuendos, whereas the younger group reacted rather uncomfortably to the clips they were shown. Additional support for these conclusions was provided by Greenberg and his colleagues; they described that 14- and 15-year-old television viewers easily learned terms previously unheard of on the subjects of prostitution and homosexuality.

Interpretation

The second type of investigation examined how young viewers interpret sexually suggestive messages, including characteristics that contribute to individually different interpretations. Thompson and his colleagues, for instance, noted that the communication style in high school students' families was directly related to the cognitive activity with which they processed a music video about teenage pregnancy. Further studies concluded that inconsistent interpretations emerged in viewers of a different gender, race, or maturity level. Kalof found gender differences in how young viewers constructed the meaning of sexuality and power based on a Michael Jackson video. In a sample of 12-to-15-year-old females, girls who reached puberty earlier than average were more likely to interpret sexually oriented television messages as favorable toward teenage sex. Brown and Schulze reported that white females were more likely to believe that Madonna's "Papa Don't Preach" was about a girl who chose to keep her unborn child, whereas most black males in the study thought that the girl expressed her hopes not to be left by her boyfriend. Another study revealed that readings of sexual contents may also differ according to the sexual schemas and scripts that are used to interpret sexual episodes. Meischke explored how female college students understood the implicit fade-to-black part of a sexual act in an R-rated movie; they found that when the girls' interpretations related to the sexual act itself, they tended to rely on elements of the story. When their interpretations had to do with safe-sex behaviors, however, viewers were more likely to fall back on generalizations about sexual behaviors in real life and in the movies rather than on observations of the plot.

Emotional Reactions

Cantor, Mares, and Hyde analyzed undergraduates' descriptions of a memorable encounter with sexual media in research that represents the category of studies that focuses on viewers' emotional reactions to sexual contents. They found that when respondents' memories went back to the period between 5 and 12 years of age, the reactions were often expressed in terms of guilt or confusion. Accounts of memories that dated from adolescence, on the other hand, regularly included feelings of anger or disgust. Brown, White, and Nikopoulou's study on 11-to-15-year-old girls' reactions produced comparable conclusions. Three distinctive styles of dealing with sexually suggestive media messages were revealed. A reaction of indifference and uninterest was typical of younger girls who did not regard media references to sexuality as relevant for their own lives. This type of reaction mostly occurred in prepubertal girls, who often preferred contents that reflect the value they attach to family and friends. A response of interest and even fascination was characteristic of adolescent females who actively search for information on sexuality, enjoy fantasizing about love and intimacy, and are attracted by behavioral models as presented in the media. These girls make use of mediated portrayals of sex and romance to construct a set of norms, perceptions, and values required for proper participation in adult romantic and sexual life. Finally, a reaction of resistance was typically found in females who had reached the stage of late puberty. These girls had learned about sexuality from experience in the dating arena and, often because of that, had reservations about the level of realism in sexual portrayals.

In Granello's interview study with female viewers of *Beverly Hills 90210*, a similar set of reactions was found. They could not be ascribed to similar ages, however. The 12-year-old respondents' particular interest in friendships between the female characters, their negligible consideration of story lines about male-female relationships, and the fairly small attention they paid to the physical appearance of the male characters corresponded to what the Brown, White, and Nikopoulou

study described as the youngest viewers' reaction of uninterest. However, whereas Brown and her colleagues observed fascination as well as resistance in girls younger than 15, Granello detected these reactions only in 17- and 21-year-olds, respectively. The 17-year-old viewers of *Beverly Hills 90210* showed great curiosity about the sexual information that was presented and were thrilled by the attractiveness of the male characters; the 21-year-old women had clear doubts about the realism of the portrayals and called the male characters "boys" rather than "real men."

Judgment

Some of these studies either implicitly or explicitly have referred to a fourth dimension in comprehension research: young viewers' judgment about the realism of sexual portrayals. Both the research of Brown and her colleagues and of Granello pointed out that adolescents' realism beliefs declined as adolescents got older and their levels of sexual experience rose. Another study revealed that 19-to-24-year-old readers of teenage magazines had developed a clear disbelief in the content of sex-related articles, whereas the 13-to-18-year-olds reported only some reservations. This conclusion has been challenged, however. One study found that college students with higher levels of sexual experience believed that scenes from situation comedies such as *Roseanne* were more likely to happen in their own lives. According to Rehkoff's investigation, respondents in a committed relationship were more likely to perceive televised portrayals as realistic.

Summary

In summary, the overall trends indicate, first, that young viewers between the ages of 10 and 14 gradually start to comprehend sexual allusions. Furthermore, young girls' (but not necessarily young boys') emotional reactions to sexually oriented contents appear to follow a process of three stages. Parallel to these stages, skepticism about the realism of sexual media portrayals is likely to increase. Some studies suggest these processes largely to be driven by changes in adolescents' maturity. Other research, however, specified that developmental trends in young viewers' interpretations and reactions are not inevitably connected to their level of sexual experience.

AGE AND COMPREHENSION IN IMPACT STUDIES

Some of these conclusions occasionally return in studies examining the link between exposure to sexual contents and teenagers' attitudes, expectations, and behaviors. Findings about different responses when viewers differ in gender, sexual experience, and maturity have been adopted in impact studies. In a recent study by Eggermont, the association between television exposure and perceptions of peers' sexual activity was stronger in 12-year-old viewers at a more advanced level of pubertal development. Ward reported that experienced male students were more likely than inexperienced male students to accept stereotypes about sexual relationships. Studies also demonstrated that effects of sexually oriented media messages occur more consistently in female viewers than in male viewers.

Some effects studies, looking to take viewers' responses into account, include measurements of such concepts as perceived realism, identification, and viewing motives, known collectively as *viewer involvement*. According to Baran's studies, beliefs about the sexual competence of media characters and their sexual satisfaction are associated with negative attitudes toward remaining a virgin and less satisfaction with one's own sexual experiences. Ward and Rivadeneyra reported that realism perceptions significantly predicted greater levels of sexual experience. In women, they found that stronger identification was related to stronger endorsement of recreational attitudes about sex.

—Steven Eggermont

See also Adolescents, Developmental Needs of, and Media; Developmental Differences, Media and; Media Effects, Family Interactions and; Music Videos, Effects of; Schemas/Scripts, Sexual; Sex, Media Impact on; Sex in Television, Perceived Realism of; Sexual Risk and Responsibility, Portrayals of; Sexualization of Children; Soap Operas, Sexuality in

FURTHER READINGS

Baran, S. J. (1976). How TV and film portrayals affect sexual satisfaction in college students. *Journalism Quarterly, 53*, 468–473.

Baran, S. J. (1976). Sex on TV and adolescent self-image. *Journal of Broadcasting, 20*, 61–68.

Brown, J. D., & Schulze, L. (1990). The effects of race, gender, and fandom on audience interpretations of Madonna's music videos. *Journal of Communication, 40*, 88–102.

Brown, J. D., White, A. B., & Nikopoulou, L. (1993). Disinterest, intrigue, resistance: Early adolescent girls' use of sexual media content. In B. S. Greenberg, J. D. Brown, & N. L. Buerkel-Rothfuss (Eds.), *Media, sex, and the adolescent* (pp. 263–276). Cresskill, NJ: Hampton Press.

Buckingham, D., & Bragg, S. (2004). *Young people, sex and the media: The facts of life?* Hampshire, UK: Palgrave Macmillan.

Cantor, J., Mares, M. L., & Hyde, J. S. (2003). Autobiographical memories of exposure to sexual media content. *Media Psychology, 5*, 1–31.

Granello, D. H. (1997). Using *Beverly Hills 90210* to explore developmental issues in female adolescents (A qualitative analysis). *Youth and Society, 29*, 24–53.

Greenberg, B. S., Linsangan, R., & Soderman, A. (1993). Adolescents' reactions to television sex. In B. S. Greenberg, J. D. Brown, & N. L. Buerkel-Rothfuss (Eds.), *Media, sex, and the adolescent* (pp. 196–224). Creskill, NJ: Hampton Press.

Kaiser Family Foundation and Children Now. (1996). *The family hour focus groups: Children's responses to sexual content on TV and their parents' reactions*. Oakland, CA: Kaiser Family Foundation.

Kalof, L. (1999). The effects of gender and music video imagery on sexual attitudes. *The Journal of Social Psychology, 139*, 378–385.

Meischke, H. (1995). Implicit sexual portrayals in the movies: Interpretations of young women. *Journal of Sex Research, 32*, 29.

Rehkoff, R. (2004). *The role of TV viewing in emotional satisfaction: Romantic expectations and romantic TV*. Paper presented at the 2004 ICA Conference, New Orleans.

Silverman-Watkins, L. T., & Sprafkin, J. N. (1983). Adolescents' comprehension of televised sexual innuendos. *Journal of Applied Developmental Psychology, 4*, 359–369.

Thompson, M., Walsh-Childers, K., & Brown, J. D. (1993). The influence of family communication patterns and sexual experience on processing of a movie video. In B. S. Greenberg, J. D. Brown, & N. L. Buerkel-Rothfuss (Eds.), *Media, sex, and the adolescent* (pp. 248–263). Cresskill, NJ: Hampton Press.

Treise, D., & Gotthoffer, A. (2002). Stuff you couldn't ask your parents: Teens talking about using magazines for sex information. In J. Brown, K. Walsh-Childers, & J. Steele (Eds.), *Sexual teens, sexual media* (pp. 173–189). Mahwah, NJ: Erlbaum.

Ward, L. M. (2002). Does television exposure affect emerging adults' attitudes and assumptions about sexual relationships? Correlational and experimental confirmation. *Journal of Youth and Adolescence, 31*, 1–15.

Ward, L. M. (2003). Understanding the role of entertainment media in the sexual socialization of American youth: A review of empirical research. *Developmental Review, 23*(3), 347–388.

Ward, L. M., Gorvine, B., & Cytron, A. (2001). Would that really happen? Adolescents' perceptions of sexual relationships according to prime-time television. In J. Brown, K. Walsh-Childers, & J. Steele (Eds.), *Sexual teens, sexual media* (pp. 95–123). Mahwah, NJ: Erlbaum.

Ward, L. M., & Rivadeneyra, R. (1999). Contributions of entertainment television to adolescents' sexual attitudes and expectations: The role of viewing amount versus viewer involvement. *Journal of Sex Research, 36,* 237–249.

SEXUAL INFORMATION, INTERNET AND

Although the Internet is a source of information about sex for many teens, little is known about the nature of that information. What is known suggests that information is somewhat limited and sometimes difficult to access, although this may be changing as more sex information geared toward teens is appearing on the Internet. Observational studies indicate that most teens employ relatively simplistic search strategies when seeking information on the Internet about health topics, including sex. Although information about sex is also gleaned from Internet pornography and exchanged through email, instant messages, and chat rooms, this entry focuses on static informational content provided on the World Wide Web. Although concerns about misinformation and sexual predators have led researchers to look at communication of sex information via the Internet, findings are only speculative at this point.

Nearly 9 in 10 adolescents (ages 12 to 17) have access to the Internet, and about three quarters of them have access at home. Nationwide surveys suggest that somewhere between one quarter and half of these online teens have sought out sexual health information via the Internet for themselves or for friends, with older teens and females searching significantly more often. In part, Internet use is likely an extension of the established tendency for teens to use independent reading to learn about many topics related to sex so that they can avoid judgments by parents, clergy, teachers, or peers. In addition to these considerations of privacy and confidentiality, teens also consider it easier and more convenient to access information on the Internet rather than from alternative expert sources such as consulting a physician; accessing information

through the Internet is considered easy and convenient by most teens.

Few content analyses have explored sexual information available on the Internet, and existing studies may be of limited utility in understanding what is currently available due to the high rate of change in available content and search methods. The explosive expansion of the World Wide Web during the early part of the 21st century means that descriptions of content are rapidly outdated. Furthermore, the proliferation of pornographic content on the Web makes the systematic analysis of sexual information for teens difficult. For example, an early study of sexual information on the Web found that when young adults searched for information about STD symptoms, only 4% of web pages resulting from their searches were sex education pages; most were classified as pornography.

The few published content analyses of sexual information for teens available online suggest that sexual information for teens is available on the Internet but that it is generally incomplete and sometimes difficult to navigate. Most websites designed to provide sexual information to teens are produced by advocacy groups (e.g., the Sexuality Information and Education Council of the United States) or government groups (e.g., the Department of Health and Human Services). Many websites fail to clearly identify their affiliation or to provide detailed information about their authors and their credentials. Information on such sites focuses largely on sexual health, particularly on the prevention of sexually transmitted infections and unwanted pregnancy. Information about negotiating sexual behaviors with a partner, strategies for communicating about sex, and nuanced messages about the role of sex in relationships are generally lacking. Furthermore, content analyses suggest that the information about sex on the Internet may be difficult to access due to characteristics of the websites on which it is located. For example, most sites in published studies lacked an internal search mechanism or site map.

To understand what sexual information is actually accessed by teens, it is important to know how teens use the Internet to find information. Information science researchers have conducted numerous observational studies of adolescents to better understand their information-seeking behaviors. Most focus on searches for educational material, but the few studies that have observed youth searching for health information (including sexual health information) have yielded similar results. The studies show that most adolescents use general purpose search engines (e.g., Yahoo!) and follow only the top 10 search results; they have difficulty formulating search queries due to misspellings and problems with the level of specificity; within a web page, they search less systematically than adults; they struggle with medical terminology; and they rarely evaluate the source of web pages. In addition to actively seeking sexual information online, survey data and focus group studies suggest that most teens have inadvertently stumbled across pornography online, often via unsolicited email or misleading links.

Unfortunately, little research has systematically measured the effects of Internet sexual information on teenage behavior. At present, surveys and focus groups are the only methods that researchers have used to measure teenagers' perceived reception of health information (only some of which is sexually related). Teenagers claim that they are able to find answers to their health questions nearly all of the time using the Internet and that the information they view is useful. However, their optimism may be overstated. Researchers have consistently found that although teens perceive the Internet as easy to use, in practice, they have difficulty using it appropriately and effectively.

According to a study by the Kaiser Family Foundation, the majority of teenagers who have looked up health information online said that they talked to a friend or parent about what they found. A small but significant number (14%) mentioned that they visited a doctor because of what they saw online. Nearly 40% said that they changed their behavior in some way because of what they came across. Of course, these patterns were observed for health information in general and may not apply to sexual information in particular.

—*Laramie D. Taylor and*
Derek L. Hansen

See also Internet Blocking; Internet Use, Positive Effects of; Internet Use, Rates and Purposes of; Sexual Information, Teen Magazines and

FURTHER READINGS

Chelton, M. K., & Cool, C. (Eds.). (2004). *Youth information-seeking behavior: Theories, models, and issues.* Lanham, MD: Scarecrow Press.

Keller, S. N., LaBelle, H., Karimi, N., & Gupta, S. (2002). STD/HIV prevention for teenagers: A look at the Internet universe. *Journal of Health Communication, 7,* 341–353.

Rideout, V. (2001). *Generation Rx.com: How young people use the Internet for health information.* Menlo Park, CA: Kaiser Family Foundation. Retrieved April 25, 2006, from http://www.kff.org/entmedia/20011211a-index.cfm

SEXUAL INFORMATION, TEEN MAGAZINES AND

Magazines are an important source of information about sex for young people, but the quality of that information is questionable. Lifestyle magazines designed for adolescent girls provide a substantial amount of sexual health information, but they focus more on sexual decision making in romantic relationships. Although no comparable magazines exist for a male audience, their nearest corollary, the so-called Lad magazines (e.g., *Maxim, Stuff,* and *FHM*), contain information about sexual pleasure and almost none about sexual health.

When teens and young adults are asked to indicate their first or predominant source of information for specific topics related to sex, they say that independent reading, including magazines, is a more important source of information than parents, peers, or schools. The same studies suggest that this is true for both young men and young women and for the sexually experienced as well as the less experienced. This importance is likely to reflect a number of factors, including teens' desire for privacy and need to avoid censure or punishment by parents, educators, or clergy. Getting information from magazines also allows teens to avoid revealing their relative ignorance of sexual matters to same-sex peers or romantic partners. Independent reading may also be perceived as a more reliable source of information; indeed, this seems to be justified, as learning about sex from independent reading has been found to be positively correlated with factual knowledge about sex, whereas learning from parents is negatively correlated with such knowledge.

Young people recognize their need to learn about sex. National surveys using representative samples of young people including teens have found that most want to receive more information about sexual health in general as well as specific sexual health topics, including symptoms, testing, and treatment of STDs; how to use condoms correctly; how sex, personal empowerment, and happiness fit together; and how to communicate with partners about sensitive sexual issues.

Magazines designed for and marketed to teens contain abundant information about sex, as do magazines that, although designed for young adults, are often read by teens. Several content analyses have examined the sexual content in magazines for teen girls (e.g., *YM, Seventeen,* and *Teen*). They generally find that the sexual information in such magazines is abundant but often problematic. Information about sexual health is not infrequent—on average, nearly half of all articles and columns dealing with sexual content focus on sexual health, and nearly 70% contain at least some mention of a sexual health topic. Common topics include pregnancy (especially unplanned pregnancy), contraception, STDs, and reproductive health care. Mention of abortion or childbirth is rare. Sexual health content increased slightly during the 1980s and 1990s. The quality of this information, however, is somewhat unclear. Existing analyses suggest that information about contraception and STDs tends to be general (e.g., one should use the former and avoid the latter) rather than specific and detailed.

Information about other sexual topics, however, increased dramatically over the same time period. Some of the more prevalent topics include sexual decision making, virginity, sexual attraction, and sexual techniques. Information about sexual decision making in magazines for adolescent girls tends to stress sexual restraint in the face of male sexual desire—girls are encouraged to be certain that they are emotionally ready for sex before relenting to the putatively relentless demands for sex from male romantic partners. At the same time, girls are encouraged to be sexually attractive and to seek out romantic partners.

Women's lifestyle magazines that are popular among older adolescents (e.g., *Cosmopolitan, Glamour*) contain an increasing amount of detailed information about sex, as well as information tailored to a presumably more sexually mature audience. Such magazines are more likely, for example, to discuss specific sexual techniques, cheating and monogamy, enhancing sex appeal, and planned pregnancy than are teen magazines. Unlike in teen magazines, sexual decision making is not an important topic in women's magazines.

In contrast to magazines marketed to adolescent girls, no lifestyle magazines are targeted at adolescent boys. Lad magazines are a genre that is targeted primarily at college-age men but nevertheless features a decidedly adolescent tone. Unlike magazines targeted at women and girls, Lad magazines contain very little information pertaining to sexual health. Instead, the most common topics addressed are women's sexual

pleasure, improving the male sex life, unorthodox sexual behaviors and locations, and general sexual satisfaction. Furthermore, even information about women's sexual pleasure in these magazines is framed in terms of male sexual outcomes; information about what women want is presented as an effective way of getting more frequent or varied sex. Finally, although serious dating relationships are presented as the normative context for sexual behavior, these relationships are also portrayed ambivalently.

As discussed above, what little research is available on sexual information in magazines designed for and read by teens focuses on the specific topics included in such information. No published empirical research has addressed the quality or accuracy of the information contained in these magazines.

—*Laramie D. Taylor*

See also Magazines, Adolescent Boys'; Magazines, Adolescent Girls'; Sexual Information, Internet and

FURTHER READINGS

Andre, T., Dietsch, C., & Cheng, Y. (1991). Sources of sex education as a function of sex, coital activity, and type of information. *Contemporary Educational Psychology, 16,* 215–240.

Bielay, G., & Herold, E. S. (1995). Popular magazines as a source of sexual information for university women. *Canadian Journal of Human Sexuality, 4,* 247–261.

Kaiser Family Foundation, Hoff, T., Green, L., & Davis, J. (2003). *National survey of adolescents and young adults: Sexual health knowledge, attitudes, and experiences.* Menlo Park, CA: Kaiser Family Foundation.

Taylor, L. D. (2005). All for him: Articles about sex in American Lad magazines. *Sex Roles, 52*(3/4), 153–163.

Walsh-Childers, K., Gotthoffer, A., & Lepre, C. R. (2002). From "just the facts" to "downright salacious": Teens' and women's magazine coverage of sex and sexual health. In J. D. Brown, J. R. Steele, & K. Walsh-Childers (Eds.), *Sexual teens, sexual media: Investigating media's influence on adolescent sexuality* (pp. 153–171). Mahwah, NJ: Erlbaum.

SEXUAL MINORITIES, PORTRAYALS OF

When sexual minorities are portrayed in the mass media, these portrayals generally exclude children or adolescents, either questioning their sexuality or identified as homosexual. Although occasionally high school students or other under-18-year-old characters are depicted as gay, lesbian, bisexual, or transgendered (GLBT), various fears about mixing adolescence and homosexuality have prevented a more full exploration of this topic.

Much research in this area has instead focused on how the growing number of mostly adult sexual-minority portrayals in media serves as a source of information for children or adolescents who might be questioning their assumed heterosexuality. In specific, portrayals of sexual minorities in the media are considered to be an important tool of socialization for GLBT adolescents. Unlike other traditionally under-represented groups, for example, racial or religious minorities, GLBT individuals assume their identity in late adolescence and largely apart from an intact support network. For this reason, many sexual minorities turn to mass media for portrayals of individuals that might reflect their same sexual orientation. Research has discovered, for instance, that after the character played by a young actor on a popular daytime soap opera "came out" as gay, the (heterosexual) actor playing the part received letters from teenagers who commented that his character was the only person they could talk to about their own sexual orientation. Research has shown that, in addition to individuals using media portrayals of sexual minorities as role models, parents and family members who are dealing with the realization that a family member may be gay use media stereotypes to find about a community they typically do not encounter overtly.

Because media portrayals of sexual minorities are often the first experience of a GLBT individual that an adolescent experiences, much research has focused on critical readings of the growing number of GLBT characters in fictional and reality-based media. In general, the range of portrayals is considered to be extremely limited. Content analysis of media texts has found that sexual minorities are depicted largely as villains or victims and are often relegated to a type of "problem status." Homosexuality, in other words, is something to be dealt with, and not simply a normalized part of a character's overall identity.

Other studies have stressed that sexual minorities are relegated to supporting characters and rarely assume a leading role. Moreover, many of the homosexual characters are played by heterosexual actors, providing few real-life role models for questioning youth. Although the number of sexual minorities depicted in film and television dramatically increased in the 1990s, with programs such as *Ellen*, *Will & Grace*, and *Dawson's Creek*, these representations tended to be comedic, one-dimensional, or largely asexual.

Studies have shown that young people generally consider the mass media to be as valuable as parents or peers when it comes to acquiring sexual education, so the lack of actual sexual portrayals of GLBT characters in the media is problematic. In particular, GLBT teens portrayed in the media are largely denied the opportunity to engage in the same sexual situations as their heterosexual counterparts. Because the ensemble casts of youth programs typically feature only one sexual minority character, the romantic possibilities for that character are dramatically limited in comparison with heterosexual friends.

Beyond script logistics, research has also focused on how advertisers' fears of public backlash over explicit homosexual content have made programmers and producers shy away from events like two men kissing. While two women are frequently allowed to engage in sexual contact (presumably for the enjoyment of male viewers), scholars have noted that kisses between men are not only rare but also rarely romantic. For instance, when Jack McFarland kissed Will Truman on the sitcom *Will & Grace*, the lip-lock, although involving two gay men, was strictly platonic. While films like *Philadelphia* and *The Birdcage* enjoyed commercial box office success, research has focused on how even these GLBT-friendly films portray a sanitized and extremely cautious version of gay life to mass audiences. Many times, in films such as *Brokeback Mountain*, the lead homosexual characters are played by heterosexual actors who routinely discuss the challenges of "playing gay" on screen, thereby reinforcing stigmas against homosexuality even while the film itself offers a sympathetic portrayal of GLBT characters.

Nonadvertiser-supported television is able to push boundaries in terms of sexual content; however, programs like Showtime's *Queer as Folk* are not always widely available to young audiences. Industry analysis of media portrayals makes clear that in comparison with advertising-supported media, subscription or other revenue-based networks are able to more fully address the experiences of GLBT characters. On *Queer as Folk*, for example, the character of Justin began the series as a 17-year-old who was involved sexually with an older man. Throughout the series, viewers saw Justin confronting homophobia at home and in school, exploring his newfound gay identity, and submersing himself in an urban gay subculture.

Research on the portrayals of sexual minorities has also found that reality programs are more likely to depict multidimensional GLBT characters. The MTV program *The Real World*, as an example, not only has regularly featured GLBT cast members, but also has often explored the intersections of sexuality, race, and class. Pedro Zamora, a Latino male who was HIV-positive, broke new ground in commercial television during the program's third season. This is particularly notable as the television reality counts primarily teens and preteens as its core audience.

Whereas academic scholarship has focused primarily on the lack of positive portrayals of sexual minorities in the media, conservative policy groups like Focus on the Family and the Christian Coalition of America have campaigned against GLBT characters and story lines. Recently, the Rev. Jerry Falwell suggested that the children's program, *Teletubbies,* contained a hidden homosexual agenda represented by the purple Teletubby, Tinky Winky. Dr. James Dobson of Focus on the Family also implicated SpongeBob SquarePants, Jimmy Neutron, and Barney in a similar scheme of promoting homosexuality to children. Interest groups that promote positive portrayals of GLBT characters, such as the Gay and Lesbian Alliance Against Defamation (GLAAD), also regularly conduct research that aims to have an effect on producers of media content.

As homosexuality gains acceptance in wider social contexts, it is hypothesized that the portrayals of GLBT characters in media will develop more fully.

—*David Gudelunas*

See also Gender Identity Development; HIV/AIDS, Media Prevention Programs and; Parasocial Interaction; Sex, Media Impact on; Sex in Television, Content Analysis of; Sex in Television, Perceived Realism of; Socialization and Media

FURTHER READINGS

D'Augelli, A. R., & Patterson, C. J. (Eds.). (1995*). Lesbian, gay, and bisexual identities over the lifespan.* New York: Oxford University Press.

Gross, L. (2001). *Up from invisibility: Lesbians, gay men, and the media in America.* New York: Columbia University Press.

Gross, L., & Woods, J. D. (Eds.). (1991). *The Columbia reader on lesbians and gay men in media, society, and politics.* New York: Columbia University Press.

Russo, V. (1981). *The celluloid closet: Homosexuality in the movies.* New York: Harper & Row.

SEXUAL RISK AND RESPONSIBILITY, PORTRAYALS OF

While a large body of research funded by the Kaiser Family Foundation has shown that televised portrayals of sex and sexuality are common across the television landscape, this same research has also indicated that portrayals of sexual risk and responsibility topics (e.g., abstinence, condom use, safe sex) are noticeably lacking. Thus, while watching television, young people are learning incomplete scripts for sexual behavior. Many adolescents have multiple sexual partners and report using condoms inconsistently, if at all. Sexual risk-taking among adolescents is a public health concern. Although there are numerous explanations for sexual risk-taking behavior, media portrayals of "unsafe sex" have been implicated, and it is important to examine portrayals of sexual risk and responsibility messages on television in this connection.

The media play an important role in the sexual socialization of adolescents. Research demonstrates that adolescents' attitudes can be influenced by sexual portrayals on television and that they can learn from these depictions as well. The media provide adolescents with scripts for sexual encounters. Adolescents can learn everything from how to ask someone on a date to when it is appropriate to engage in sexual intercourse and what sexual precautions, if any, one should take.

However, research suggests that only 5% of all scenes containing sexual content contain any messages about sexual risks and responsibilities. Sexual risk and responsibility topics can be grouped into three broad categories: messages about sexual precaution, depictions of the risks or negative consequences of sex, and messages pertaining to sexual patience. The most frequently occurring of these three topics concerns sexual precautions, such as the use of a condom or other contraceptive strategy or mentions of "safe sex." Depictions of the risks/negative consequences of sexual behavior (e.g., worry about or actual occurrence of STDs, pregnancy) occurred in 2% of all scenes with sexual content. Portrayals that incorporate a theme related to sexual patience are found in only about 1% of scenes with sexual content. Examples in this category include abstinence, virginity, or simply waiting until one feels ready for a sexual relationship.

It should be noted that not all scenes with sexual content are necessarily at the level where sexual health and safety messages are appropriate. These concerns are most salient in scenes or programs that present advanced sexual content. Programs that have content related to sexual intercourse (an actual or implied depiction or a discussion of sexual intercourse) seem the most relevant context for this type of information. It is encouraging to note that, in fact, 25% of all programs with this type of advanced sexual content do contain messages related to sexual risk or responsibility.

Another salient context for including safer-sex messages is programs that are popular with teenagers. These programs tend to have significantly higher levels of sex when compared to the amounts found in industry-wide programming. However, close to half of teen shows with advanced sexual content feature a sexually responsible message. This indicates some sensitivity on the part of television producers to the need to expose adolescents to these important messages. However, this still leaves more than half of these shows without any mention of sexual risk or responsibility.

The context of a media portrayal is known to be an important variable in the effects process, so in addition to understanding the frequency with which these messages are portrayed on television, it is also important to understand *how* they are portrayed. Unfortunately, research indicates not only that safe-sex references are infrequent but also that they tend to be a minor or inconsequential part of the entire scene; they are almost as likely to be portrayed with a negative, dismissive tone as with a positive one.

In summary, although sex on television is frequent, mentions of sexual risk and responsibility topics are rare and when these important topics are raised, they are often treated in a way that minimizes their importance. The concern is that young people may internalize and model an incomplete sexual script or one that dismisses the importance of sexual risk and responsibility concerns.

—Kirstie Farrar

See also Movies, Sexuality in; Public Health Campaigns; Public Service Announcements (PSAs); Schemas/Scripts, Sexual; Sex, Media Impact on; Sex in Television, Content Analysis of; Sexual Information, Internet and

FURTHER READINGS

Cope, K. M., & Kunkel, D. (2002). Sex in teen programming. In J. Brown, J. Steele, & K. Walsh-Childers, (Eds.), *Sexual teens, sexual media* (pp. 59–78). Mahwah, NJ: Erlbaum.

Farrar, K. M., Kunkel, D., Biely, E., Eyal, K., & Donnerstein, E. (2003). Sexual messages during prime-time programming. *Sexuality and Culture, 7*(3), 7–37.

Kunkel, D., Biely, E. N., Eyal, K., Farrar, K. M., Fandrich, R., & Donnerstein, E. (2003). *Sex on TV III: A biennial report to the Kaiser Family Foundation*. Menlo Park, CA: Kaiser Family Foundation.

SEXUALIZATION OF CHILDREN

The sexualization of children is a broad concept that refers to the representation and treatment of children as objects of eroticism or sex. Such representation and treatment ranges from fashion and advertising to juridical issues of child pornography, child prostitution, sex trafficking, statutory rape, and child sexual abuse. The sexualization of children is a phenomenon that has attracted legal and social attention but remains controversial. Some legislation protects children from certain forms of sexualization, yet the boundaries between pornographic and nonpornographic activities and representations remain gray, and their impacts continue to be debated.

Legally, the sexualization of minor children is governed in most countries by criminal and civil codes that define the legitimacy of sexual acts involving children below a certain age. This age of consent varies widely, from as low as 12 up to 21. The sexual abuse of children is thus a concept that is varyingly interpreted, with even the word *child* or *minor* defined according to a nonstandard range of criteria.

This lack of consensus has given rise to controversy about the sexual exploitation of children. Laws governing the sexual exploitation of children have emerged over the past century, addressing various aspects of childhood sexuality and the sexualization of children; but there are ongoing public debates about what constitutes normalcy, delinquency, and abuse. In general, the sexual activity of minors is illegal, as is the sexual activity of adults with minors, which is always understood to be coercive. Similarly, the use of minors for purposes of prostitution or sex trafficking is a felony in most countries. These are all instances of the sexualization of children.

The United Nations has recognized the sexualization of children in these forms as a human rights issue. The United Nations Convention on the Rights of the Child (Article 34) contains clear language prohibiting the sexual exploitation of children and includes protocols on the sale of children, child prostitution, and child pornography.

The issues are less clear regarding the sexualized representation of children. In April 2002, the U.S. Supreme Court ruled in *Ashcroft v. Free Speech Coalition* that the representation of children engaged in sex acts is legally permissible as long as real children are not used in the portrayals. However, this ruling is being contested; in April 2003, the Protect Act of 2003 was signed into law, and one of its provisions is for increased penalties for child exploitation and child pornography, including those using virtual imagery.

The sexualization of children outside the realm of pornography is also a pressing social concern. The fashion industry has been widely criticized for promoting hypersexual clothing for children, as have advertising and marketing campaigns featuring sexualized minors. Icons of popular culture, including pop singers and actors, are also held responsible for disseminating sexually charged content to children.

Most academic research on the topic characterizes such representations as a risk, both to the children and to society. Two recent studies conclude that such representation conveys to children the idea that sexual displays are condoned by adults and contributes in general to the victim-blaming myth that children *want* to be sexually used by adults. Other studies have noted the similarities between mainstream images of sexualized children and pornography, finding that such images normalize and sanction adult sexual interest in minors.

Research on the effects of such representation also finds that exposure to such media content increases sexual activity among minors, can lead to sex work, and is used by pedophiles for purposes of arousal.

One analysis of these images points out the contradiction between the legislation and social concern about child sexual abuse and the widespread exhibition of sexualized children's bodies in advertising, films, beauty pageants, and other mediated forums.

This ambivalence has brought up related legal questions, such as Is all visual representation of children's nudity de facto sexual? Current studies seek to delineate a distinction between sexual and nonsexual representations of children's bodies, as well as the private/public distinctions that might shape their interpretations.

A related body of research views the furor over sexualized imagery and the attendant harms to children as a kind of moral panic, arguing that children's sexuality can and should be publicly represented in healthy and progressive ways.

—*Meenakshi Gigi Durham*

See also Advertising, Sexuality in; Chat Rooms; Child Pornography; Children's Internet Protection Act of 2000 (CIPA); Children's Online Privacy Protection Act of 1998 (COPPA); Obscenity, Pornography, Internet; Pornography, U.S. Public Policy on; Sex, Internet Solicitation of; Sexualized Violence; United Nations Convention on the Rights of the Child

FURTHER READINGS

Cover, R. (2003). The naked subject: Nudity, context, and sexualization in contemporary culture. *Body and Society* 9(3), 53–72.

Davis, N. J. (1999). *Youth crisis: Growing up in a high-risk society*. Westport, CT: Praeger.

Driscoll, C. (2002). *Girls: Feminine adolescence in popular culture and cultural theory*. New York: Columbia University Press.

Higonnet, A. (1998). *Pictures of innocence: The history and crisis of ideal childhood*. London: Thames & Hudson.

Howitt, D. (1996). *Paedophiles and sexual offences against children*. New York: Wiley.

Kilbourne, J. (1999). *Deadly persuasion: Why women and girls must fight the addictive power of advertising*. New York: Free Press.

Kincaid, J. R. (1998). *Erotic innocence: The culture of child molesting*. Durham, NC: Duke University Press.

Levine, J. (2002). *Harmful to minors: The perils of protecting children from sex*. Minneapolis: University of Minnesota Press.

Merskin, D. (2004). Reviving Lolita: A media literacy examination of sexual portrayals of girls in fashion advertising. *American Behavioral Scientist, 48*(1), 119–129.

Tucker, L. (1998). The framing of Calvin Klein: A frame analysis of media and discourse about the August 1995 Calvin Klein jeans advertising campaign. *Critical Studies in Mass Communication, 15*(2), 141–157.

UNICEF. (2002). *Convention on the rights of the child.* Retrieved September 1, 2005, from http://www.unicef.org/crc/crc.htm

Walkerdine, V. (1997). *Daddy's girl: Young girls and popular culture*. Cambridge, MA: Harvard University Press.

Wesley, J. K. (2002). Growing up sexualized: Issues of power and violence in the lives of female exotic dancers. *Violence Against Women 8*(10), 1182–1207.

SEXUALIZED VIOLENCE

Violent pornography is widespread and easily accessible through films, magazines, and the Internet. *Forbes* magazine recently estimated the pornographic industry to be worth more than $56 billion. Pornography involving violence (i.e., sexualized violence) is thought by many to be highly offensive, abhorrent, and out-of-place in civilized society. Recent analyses reveal that sexual violence abounds in the pornographic industry, with violence being shown in about 25% of pornographic videos and magazines and in about 42% of pornography on the Internet. Although there is a paucity of research concerning the effects on children and adolescents of viewing violent pornography, the available research suggests that such exposure may result in problems in sexual development and may increase the risk of their acting in sexually violent ways.

Outside the research community, various individuals have claimed that pornography is a cause of violent behavior. One notable example is serial killer Ted Bundy, who killed at least 28 women or girls before his capture and subsequent execution in a Florida State Prison in January 1989. In an interview with Dr. James Dobson on the night before his execution, Bundy described his exposure as a 13-year-old to soft-core pornographic material in a dumpster near his home. Bundy claimed that after this first experience with pornography, he immediately became addicted, seeking depictions of more graphic and explicit violent behavior on television and in other materials. He blamed pornographic violence in the media for turning him into a killer.

Although Bundy was adamant about the destructive effects of viewing sexualized violence on television, research has revealed a less than clear picture. To discover exactly how violent pornography influences children and adolescents is a very difficult task. Controlled experimental studies that expose children to violent pornography and then observe their subsequent behavior would be unethical and have not been conducted. Therefore, the influence of violent pornography on children and adolescents has been examined using two related approaches. The first involves correlational studies that examine pornography use in sex offenders (both adult and juvenile). As many convicted sex offenders are first exposed to violent pornography early in their youth and begin to offend about the same time, these studies are relevant to the current discussion. The second involves a wide range of experimental studies that focus on the effect of viewing violent pornography on adults (mostly college-age men).

Mike Allen and colleagues have conducted a number of meta-analyses that combine the results of all the studies conducted on the effect of viewing pornography. These studies revealed that convicted sex offenders are more likely than noncriminals to perform a sexual act, such as masturbation, consensual sex, or criminal sex, after viewing pornography. Interestingly, physiological studies have found that sex offenders are more aroused after viewing violent pornography than nonoffenders, yet are less aroused after viewing pornography depicting consensual sex. The picture is less clear with regard to pornographic use among juvenile sex offenders. Although there is very little research on this topic, recent studies estimate that about 30% to 89% of juvenile sex offenders regularly view pornographic materials. On average, those who view pornography are likely to start viewing about 11 to 12 years old. Interestingly, when asked if viewing pornography influenced their sexual deviance, 90% felt that it had no effect on their behavior. It should be noted that the above studies dealt with all forms of pornography and unfortunately did not specify if the pornography was violent or not.

A review of experimental studies with adults revealed that participants hold more favorable attitudes concerning sexual aggression after viewing violent pornography in the laboratory. They are more likely to endorse rape myths (e.g., "Women incite men to rape") and have less sympathy for victims of sexual aggression. Furthermore, participants exposed to sexual pornography are more likely to be aggressive in a laboratory setting than those not exposed. In a typical study, participants are randomly assigned to a group (i.e., control, pornography, or violent pornography) and view a video according to their group assignment. Later, participants are told that they will be participating in another supposedly unrelated study, usually involving a teacher/learner paradigm where they are able to "punish" another participant, often with supposed electrical shocks or blasts of noise. Related factors, such as initial level of aggression and previous experience with pornography, are typically taken into account to try to ensure that these factors do not influence results. These studies may not apply to real-life experience, but they do allow researchers to study the effects of viewing violent pornography in a controlled situation.

So, how does viewing violent pornography influence sexual aggression and attitudes? When aroused after viewing any kind of pornography, an individual is likely to want to act on those feelings. Most people feel that it is acceptable to engage in consensual sexual relations after viewing pornography; in fact, many couples use pornography as a tool to enhance their sexual relationship with one another. However, this becomes a problem when a person is aroused by viewing violent sex, as it is certainly not socially acceptable and usually is illegal to engage in the kind of behavior that is being portrayed. This is where a dilemma comes in, one of control issues versus self-gratification.

Children and adolescents who view violent pornography are probably more at risk than adults who view such material. The Internet allows many children and adolescents access to violent pornography, which previously would have been difficult for them to obtain. Exposure to such pornography may interfere with the course of natural sexual development and may inappropriately accelerate sexual relationships. As specified earlier, controlled experimental studies have not examined this issue due to ethical reasons. However, there is a vast amount of research studying the effects of exposure to violent TV on children and adolescents. These studies reveal that exposure to violent TV at a young age can have a fairly large impact on immediate and future aggression, both in attitudes and behavior. Similarly, viewing violent pornography may prime an individual to behave in a sexually violent way in the short term and may create a network of sexually violent scripts to guide behavior in the long term.

Although the research on the effects of violent pornography on children and adolescents is limited, research from a variety of fields suggests that youth are highly at risk after viewing such material. The best way to protect children and adolescents is to limit *any* exposure.

—*Sarah M. Coyne*

See also Child Pornography; Cognitive Script Theory; Cuing and Priming; Pornography (various entries); Priming Theory

FURTHER READINGS

Allen, M., D'Allessio, D., & Brezgel, K. (1995). A meta-analysis summarizing the effects of pornography II: Aggression after exposure. *Human Communication Research, 22,* 258–283.

Allen, M., D'Alessio, D., & Emmers-Sommer, T. M. (2000). Reactions of criminal sexual offenders to pornography: A meta-analytic summary. In M. Roloff (Ed.), *Communication yearbook* (Vol. 22, pp. 139–169). Thousand Oaks, CA: Sage.

Dobson, J. (2000). *Life on the edge.* Nashville, TN: W Publishing Group.

Malamuth, N. M., Addison, T., & Koss, M. (2000). Pornography and sexual aggression: Are there reliable effects and can we understand them? *Review of Sex Research, 11,* 26–91.

Zolondek, S. C., Abel, G. G., Northey, W. F., & Jordan, A. D. (2001). The self-reported behaviors of juvenile sexual offenders. *Journal of Interpersonal Violence, 16,* 73–85.

SITCOMS

Situation comedies, often referred to as sitcoms, have been a major staple program type for television networks; sitcoms are the only genre represented in the Top-10 rated programs every year since 1949. The sitcom is an extremely popular genre both for viewing audiences and for television advertisers. The context is light and often humorous, and the characters are generally easy to identify with. Although the content of sitcoms has varied over the decades, the genre has remained a constant favorite. Much research has been conducted on the type of messages that are contained in sitcom content, which includes a variety of images that are important in terms of their impact on children and adolescents. The domestic situation comedy, or family sitcom, has a long history of depicting and transmitting images of American families into viewers' homes. Sitcoms also are a source of gender images and sibling relationships.

SITCOM FORMAT AND AUDIENCE

The format of sitcoms generally features a recurring cast. Each half-hour episode establishes a situation, a complication arises, confusion and humor develop among the characters, and then the situation is usually resolved before the episode ends. Unlike dramatic series, which are often open-ended, conflict does not commonly carry over between episodes in sitcoms. In most situation comedies, character development is usually downplayed in favor of plot twists and humorous situations, making the characters relatively simple and predictable. Characters generally remain largely consistent through an entire series and may often seem a bit silly and contrived. Shows such as *I Love Lucy* from the 1950s, *Happy Days* from the 1970s, and *Seinfeld* from the 1990s all fit into the genre of sitcoms.

Sitcoms are among the most watched programs for families, especially those shows that appeal to children as well as adults. Shows such as *Full House* and *The Cosby Show* have been among the most popular sitcoms on television for children, according to the Nielsen ratings. Specifically, *The Cosby Show* was the highest rated program from 1985 through 1990 as a result of its appeal to children and adults alike. From 1989 through 1995, *Full House* was consistently rated within the top 30 programs on television due to its popularity with young audience members. More recently, sitcoms such as *Malcolm in the Middle* have also been popular largely among child viewers.

Analysis of the advertising revenue and program content on television broadcasting channels indicates that advertisers pay premium prices to air their ads during sitcoms. The reasons are generally thought to be that advertisers prefer programs that are light and not challenging in order to set a positive mood for their selling messages; in addition, sitcoms often appeal to broad audiences. It is to the benefit of advertisers that sitcoms remain a popular genre among audiences.

SITCOM CONTENT

Portrayals of Families

Between 1947 and 1990, 85% of families on television were shown in a comedy format during prime time. The number of fictional television series featuring a family as the primary story vehicle nearly doubled from 1950 to 1990, with more than half of those shows in each decade falling into the sitcom category. Plots of this type, depicting fictional families, are believed to carry with them implicit lessons about family life and family member roles for their viewing audiences. Although it may be speculative to draw conclusions from content to effects, exposure to such programming has been shown to change the way viewers think about real-life families, specifically in regard to ideas about marriage, family, and divorce. The portrayal of family roles in television programs may be especially influential for children, based on their limited experience with various family types, level of television exposure, and susceptibility to the influence of role models. Their expectations about

their real-life family may be affected by this televised information. In a study conducted by Olson and Douglas of second, sixth, and tenth graders, the majority of respondents said that all real-life families were like those in the family series they watched most often (*The Cosby Show* and *Family Ties* were identified with the most regularity) and that the emotions of the characters were portrayed realistically in these shows.

Gender Roles

Studies indicate that depictions of gender roles have fluctuated over time, with peaks in character happiness or satisfaction and family stability ratings at the highest during the 1950s and mid-1980s. More recent domestic comedies contain less positive depictions of varying gender roles, specifically displaying more male dominance and less satisfaction and stability in families. Recent depictions of families indicate that characters are more distressed and less desirable. As another sign of shifting gender roles on sitcoms, Erica Scharrer examined long-running and top-rated domestic sitcoms from the 1950s through the 1990s in an exploratory content analysis, finding that modern television fathers and working-class television fathers are more likely to be portrayed foolishly than sitcom fathers of the past or fathers of higher socioeconomic classes. Sitcom fathers are often presented as the target of a growing number of jokes and in situations that make them look increasingly foolish, such as on the sitcom *Home Improvement*. This research demonstrates that joke telling by sitcom characters, often directed toward the father characters, can potentially be viewed as a shift of power between the sexes on these programs.

Sibling Interactions

Sibling interactions on sitcoms have also undergone an apparent transformation over the years, according to research by Larson. Child characters in 1950s situation comedies such as *Leave It to Beaver*, *Ozzie and Harriet*, and *Father Knows Best* interacted less often than children in 1980s programs such as *The Cosby Show*, *Growing Pains*, and *Family Ties*. This is partly due to the fact that advertisers had not yet developed children as a target market in the earlier years. However, the 1950s characters were shown more positively when interacting with each other, whereas in programs of the 1980s, greater amounts of conflict were present among sitcom siblings.

—Andrea M. Bergstrom

See also Family, Television Portrayals of; Fathers, Media Portrayals of; Mothers, Media Portrayals of

FURTHER READINGS

Brown, K., & Cavazos, R. (2005). Why is this show so dumb? Advertising revenue and program content of network television. *Review of Industrial Organization, 27*(1), 17–35.

Campbell, R., Martin, C., & Fabos, B. (2005). *Media and culture: An introduction to mass communication.* New York: Bedford Press.

Dorr, A., Kovaric, P., & Doubleday, C. (1990). Age and content influences on children's perceptions of the realism of television families. *Journal of Broadcasting and Electronic Media, 34,* 377–397.

Larson, M. S. (1989). Interaction between siblings in primetime television families. *Journal of Broadcasting and Electronic Media, 33,* 305–315.

Olson, B., & Douglas, W. (1997). The family on television: Evaluating gender roles in situation comedy. *Sex Roles: A Journal of Research, 36*(5–6), 409–438.

Scharrer, E. (2001). From wise to foolish: The portrayal of the sitcom father, 1950s-1990s. *Journal of Broadcasting and Electronic Media, 45*(1), 23–41.

Skill, T., Robinson, J. D., & Wallace, S. P. (1987). Portrayal of families on prime-time TV: Structure, type and frequency. *Journalism Quarterly, 64,* 360–367.

SOAP OPERAS, CONTENT ANALYSES OF

Daytime serial dramas, or soap operas, emerged from radio programming of the 1940s and 1950s and became a popular genre among housewives and retirees. The pace of these serial dramas is often quite slow, with more talk than action and with a focus on interpersonal relationships. Over recent decades, the content of soap operas has become edgier, attracting adolescents and college students. Because of their increasing popularity, devoted viewers, and expanding audiences, researchers have begun to examine the specific nature of their content and to ask whether it is appropriate for younger viewers.

This question drives many content analyses of daytime soap operas. For these analyses, researchers record a selection of soap opera programming, typically 1 week, and then systematically analyze the programs for the presence of specific behavior or themes. Alternatively, some analyze soap opera digests that offer summaries of each day's episodes. The intent of either approach is to document the frequency or prevalence of specific actions, themes, or attributes. In general, findings paint the soap opera world as one dominated by white, middle- to upper-class, attractive professionals. Nonwhites accounted for only 3% to 5% of all soap opera characters in early analyses and nearly 15% in more recent studies. Unlike all other TV genres, however, men and women typically appear in equal numbers on soaps, although women tend to be younger than men. The majority of soap opera characters (75%) are between 20 and 50, with only 1% of major characters over age 65.

A common focus of soap operas is romantic and sexual relationships. Indeed, recent findings from Dale Kunkel and his colleagues show that soaps are the genre for which the highest percentage of programs (96%) contain sexual content. As such, the bulk of the existing content analyses focus on sexual content. For these analyses, researchers first develop a list of sexually intimate behaviors, such as passionate kissing, unmarried intercourse, and prostitution, and then analyze multiple episodes to document the number of times these behaviors are displayed visually or mentioned verbally. Additional characteristics of sexual content are sometimes noted, including sex, age, race, and marital status of the participants; nature of the relationship between participants (e.g., strangers, married); and tone of the interaction. Several common findings emerge. First, sexual references are more often verbal than visual. Verbal references to unmarried intercourse are particularly common; references to prostitution, homosexuality, and STD prevention are less frequent. When sexual content is visual, it tends to be passionate kissing or erotic touching; physical representations of sexual intercourse are rare. Second, findings indicate that verbal or visual sexual references have increased from about 2 per hour in the early 1980s to 5 to 8 by the late mid-1990s. A 2003 programming analysis put this rate at 5.1 scenes per hour. Finally, such content occurs more frequently in reference to unmarried intercourse than married intercourse.

A second focus of soap opera content analyses is the prevalence of substance use, particularly alcohol, described as the most frequently used drug on television. Studies have investigated the frequency with which alcoholic drinks are consumed or discussed, settings and circumstances under which such behavior occurs, reasons alcohol is consumed, and any apparent consequences of drinking. Several findings have emerged. First, alcohol portrayals are quite common, but they are less frequent on daytime soaps than in prime-time programming. Studies report that incidents of alcohol use appear 1.5 to 3 times per half hour in American soaps and 6.4 times per hour in British soaps, where many scenes take place in pubs. Second, in terms of context, the majority of drinking characters are male, and much drinking takes place in the home (in American soaps). Third, drinking is most frequently depicted as serving social facilitation purposes (e.g., wine with dinner, cocktails at a party), and such behavior is either reinforced or meets no consequences. Drinking to escape reality is the second most common reason for drinking, especially among alcoholics. This is typically frowned on and meets with concern; drinking to intoxication is often negatively reinforced. Yet overall, soap opera drinking is somewhat common yet typically moderate and problem free, with minimal depiction of the consequences of drinking, especially any negative health consequences.

A third issue frequently analyzed is the nature of portrayals of health and mental health problems, which are major themes on soap operas. Here, findings indicate that these portrayals tend to focus more on the extreme than on the mundane. Homicide, suicide, shootings, and rape occur more frequently in soaps than in real life. Mary Cassata and colleagues found that 41% of all health-related occurrences are accidents and that accidents account for about 65% of soap opera fatalities. Closer analyses of soap opera crime indicate that deceit, murder, and premarital/extramarital sex are the most frequently occurring moral issues. Reproductive issues are also exaggerated. Pregnancy and delivery complications are common, and most deliveries are premature or occur in unusual locations. Findings also indicate a high rate of psychiatric disorders. One study found that psychiatric disorders were the second most commonly occurring health-related condition. Unfortunately, distortions of mental health experiences do occur, including an overrepresentation of women among the mentally ill (75%), minimal depiction of effective treatments, and frequent associations with criminal behavior (among male characters).

Given that soap operas are characterized as being heavy on talk and low on action, a final domain of content analyses has focused on examining soap opera

conversations. Here the goal is to examine topics of conversation, participants, and appropriateness of the conversations. More than half of all dyadic conversations are reported to be mixed sex, and participants are most often personal friends, blood relatives, marriage partners, or coworkers. Common topics of conversation include business matters, family relationships, health, and romantic relationships, with small talk peppered within and across most conversations. Small sex differences have also emerged: Male characters are more likely to discuss professional relationships, business matters, and deviant behavior, and female characters are more likely to discuss family and romantic relationships, health, and domestic matters. Character gender has been shown to affect patterns of advising and ordering, as well. Together, these content analyses illustrate the unique and somewhat conflicting nature of soap operas, whose conversations often touch on the mundane but whose plot twists and story lines demonstrate a thirst for drama and flair.

—*L. Monique Ward and Dana S. Levin*

See also Research Methods, Content Analyses; Sex in Television, Content Analysis of; Soap Operas, Effects of; Soap Operas, Sexuality in

FURTHER READINGS

Fine, M. G. (1981, Summer). Soap opera conversations: The talk that binds. *Journal of Communication, 31,* 97–107.

Fruth, L., & Padderud, A. (1985). Portrayals of mental illness in daytime television serials. *Journalism Quarterly, 62,* 384–387, 449.

Greenberg, B. S., & Busselle, R. W. (1996). Soap operas and sexual activity: A decade later. *Journal of Communication, 46,* 153–160.

Lowry, D. T., & Towles, D. E. (1989). Soap opera portrayals of sex, contraception, and sexually transmitted diseases. *Journal of Communication, 39,* 76–83.

Wallack, L., Breed, W., & de Foe, J. R. (1985). Alcohol and soap operas: Drinking in the light of day. *Journal of Drug Education, 15*(4), 365–379.

SOAP OPERAS, EFFECTS OF

Soap operas have existed almost as long as radio and television have. The term *soap opera* is, however, not used all over the world; in Latin America, the most popular corresponding program genre is the *telenovela*, and in Asia, it is drama serials. The narrative of soap operas differs from that of *telenovelas* and Asian drama serials in several ways; one of the most conspicuous differences is that the soap opera consists of an ongoing, "open" story that may continue for many years whereas *novelas* and drama serials last for only a limited number of episodes. Although U.S. serials are distributed widely around the world, there is even wider global circulation of serials made in certain other cultures, especially in Latin America and most of all in Brazil. Australia, the United Kingdom, and several Asian countries (e.g., South Korea) are great exporters of soap operas, as well.

Recently, local and internationally exported soap operas, *telenovelas,* and drama serials, often attracting large audiences, have become more and more common around the world, not least because of the explosive spread of cable and satellite television in the 1980s and 1990s. In several countries, men and young people are an increasingly large part of the audience for these fictional serials, which previously were viewed mainly by women. Many soaps, *telenovelas,* and drama serials have also become increasingly daring, sometimes showing in a single or a few episodes more about sex, divorce, deceit, revenge, power struggle, shady economic transactions, crime, and so on than a person experiences in her or his whole life.

RESEARCH ON YOUTH AND SOAP OPERAS

Although there has been extensive research on adult viewers of soap operas, especially women, relatively few studies exist on soap operas and children or adolescents. A survey of research studies around the world shows clear cultural differences not only between soap operas, *telenovelas*, and drama serials, and the contents of such programs produced in different countries, but also in children's or young people's reception and meaning-making of the programs. The research contributions described in this entry should, therefore, be regarded as case studies, the findings of which cannot be empirically generalized across borders.

The research approach of these studies in Asia, Australia, Europe, and Latin America is often of a qualitative and short-term character, especially within the tradition of reception studies, in which children or adolescents tell from their own perspectives how they read and are influenced by the programs. Some studies, especially in the United States, aim to analyze specific influences of soaps (e.g., on young people's beliefs) from a cultivation, effect, socialization, or similar perspective. How much, and in what directions, the serials influence young people in the long term cannot be inferred from existing research.

EFFECTS OF SOAP OPERA VIEWING

Even if everyone makes something different out of the programs, the reception studies give rise to some general conclusions. First, these studies confirm that many young people in many countries watch soap operas/*telenovelas*/drama serials, often from an early age. Besides getting pleasure, excitement, and sometimes laughter from viewing these fictional serials, children and young people report that the programs give them ideas, advice, and insight into life and people—especially with reference to interpersonal relations and interactions—that can be useful now and when getting older. In addition to learning, the programs have a range of social functions: Young people identify and parasocially interact with certain characters, situations, and values; distance themselves from others; check out how characters' behavior works; or think about how they themselves would behave in corresponding situations. They also talk about the serials with others. Therefore, several researchers conclude, by watching, learning from, and talking about these TV fictions, young people are working with their social identity and exploring ways of coping with issues in their own lives, at present and later on. Some children say that the serials also influence them in other ways.

The cultivation and effect studies often focus on soap opera viewing and adolescents' perceptions of personal relations, gender roles, sexual behaviors, marriage, motherhood, social issues (e.g., divorce, abortion, crime), occupations, and the like. Several studies have found relations between how these phenomena are represented in the television world and adolescents' notions of the same phenomena in social reality, thus supporting hypotheses that the glamorous/exaggerated/distorted television portrayals nourish false beliefs and unrealistic expectations about the social world. On the other hand, it is often impossible to assume one-sided causality because people with certain views and motivations also actively select and watch material of interest to them. (For example, those with idealized views of marriage may selectively choose romanticized media content.) Generally, what young people choose to watch are programs and elements that relate to their own lives, so their readings of the programs and what they learn from them are often deeply rooted in the contexts in which they live. Often, then, there is a reciprocal relation between what people seek from the media and how media may reinforce and develop perceptions, a process that is also modified by the viewer's own practice and peers and adults in her or his own environment.

There are significant age differences in children's and young people's meaning-making, and research shows how factors such as gender, personality, peers, family integration, and social class reflect different needs and play a role in the interpretation and cultivation processes. For instance, media researcher Maya Götz finds an age-typical development of enthusiasm for soap operas in Germany. For children ages 6 to 9, regular reception of a daily soap is integrated into the family routine as a "bedtime story" and an opportunity to exchange views on the more adult world. Increasingly, among preteens ages 10 to 13, the daily soap becomes an information resource, a kind of "window on the adult world." Slightly older children, ages about 12 to 15, recognize in the characters parts of themselves as well as their newly developing philosophy of life, while distancing themselves from other philosophies or personalities portrayed; they often identify with a particular character. It is primarily 14-to-15-year-old girls who develop a particular emotional involvement with soaps and admit to being "addicted" to them. In such cases, daily viewing of the soap opera becomes a vehemently demanded, zealously guarded retreat that young adolescent girls create for themselves (mostly watching the soap alone) in order to remain in contact with their own feelings and knowledge about relationships. Among older adolescents, ages 16 to 19, there is a lighter appropriation of the genre, together with a more distant attitude. The family now tends to be increasingly reintegrated into the sharing of enthusiasm for the soap, although the fantasies and emotional participation are remembered and continued.

SOAP OPERAS FOR EDUCATION AND SOCIAL CHANGE

In many countries, especially in Africa, Asia, and Latin America, producers attempt to take advantage of the functionality of media in tackling social ills and motivating young people. The goal is to use the format of radio and TV drama, soap operas, *telenovelas*, docu-soaps, and other entertaining genres for education to raise debate and contribute to solving health and other problems in society. The use of entertainment-education in an integrated manner and often in the form of multimedia initiatives has been growing significantly over the past decade, notably in addressing health-related issues such as HIV/AIDS. The ideal communicative scenario in this respect is communication for social change, that is, to deal with the challenge of providing an information- and dialogue-rich enabling environment where the media contents contribute to empowering the audiences in facing health-related and other social issues in everyday life.

One of hundreds of such programs is the youth-oriented South African drama series *Yizo Yizo*. The show has extremely high audience ratings and aims to reflect reality (ordinary black South Africans living in townships) rudely and toughly (portraying children's experiences of formal schooling, including violence, sexual harassment and rape, and drug abuse). Research indicates that the series succeeds to a great extent in revealing the depth and complexity of social crises and raising debate and action in society. This entertainment series represents an approach to citizenship and communication for social change that seriously challenges the contents of many soap operas and reality TV programs invented in richer countries.

—*Cecilia von Feilitzen*

See also Cultivation Theory; Entertainment-Education, International; Media Effects; Reality TV; Soap Operas, Content Analyses of; Socialization and Media

FURTHER READINGS

Alexander, A. (1985). Adolescents' soap opera viewing and relational perceptions. *Journal of Broadcasting and Electronic Media, 29,* 295–308.

Brooker, W. (2001). Living on *Dawson's Creek*: Teen viewers, cultural convergence, and television overflow. *International Journal of Cultural Studies, 4*(4), 456–472.

Buckingham, D. (1987). *Public secrets:* EastEnders *and its audience*. London: British Film Institute.

Buerkel-Rothfuss, N. L., & Mayes, S. (1981). Soap opera viewing: The cultivation effect. *Journal of Communication, 31,* 108–115.

von Feilitzen, C. (Ed.). (2004). Young people, soap operas, and reality TV. In *Yearbook 2004*. Göteborg, Sweden: Nordicom.

Gillespie, M. (1995). *Television, ethnicity, and cultural change*. London: Routledge.

Götz, M. (2002). *Alles Seifenblasen? Die Bedeutung von Daily Soaps im Alltag von Kindern und Jugendlichen* [Only soap bubbles? The significance of daily soaps for children and adolescents]. Munich, Germany: KoPäd.

Klitgaard Povlsen, K. (1995). *Beverly Hills 90210 i Danmark* [Beverly Hills 90210 in Denmark]. Copenhagen, Denmark: Copenhagen University.

Larson, M. S. (1996). Sex roles and soap operas: What adolescents learn about single motherhood. *Sex Roles, 35*, 97–110.

McKinley, E. G. (1997). *Beverly Hills 90210: Television, gender, and identity*. Philadelphia: University of Pennsylvania Press.

Rivadeneyra, R., & Ward, L. M. (2005). From Ally McBeal to Sabado Gigante: Contributions of television use to the gender role attitudes of Latino adolescents. *Journal of Adolescent Research, 20*(4), 453–475.

Segrin, C., & Nabi, R. L. (2002). Does television viewing cultivate unrealistic expectations about marriage? *Journal of Communication, 52*(2), 247–263.

Ward, L. M., & Rivadeneyra, R. (1999). Contributions of entertainment television to adolescents' sexual attitudes and expectations: The role of viewing amount versus viewer involvement. *Journal of Sex Research, 36*, 237–249.

SOAP OPERAS, SEXUALITY IN

Television soap operas have been a broadcast entertainment staple for 50 years, and radio soaps began two decades earlier. At least 23 million adult Americans are daily viewers of one or more TV soaps, and as many as 30 million claim to be regular viewers. Add to those figures a few million teen and preteen viewers and the massive reach of soaps is evident. The general trend from a variety of research perspectives has identified an increase in overall sexual content, particularly sexual intercourse, an increase in visual depictions of sex, and a strong emphasis on sexual activities among unmarried partners.

Across different analyses of sexual content in television soap operas, there is considerable symmetry in what has been called *sex*. Typically, sex includes depicted behaviors or verbal references to intercourse, some form of foreplay, erotic kissing, and more recently, incidents of homosexuality, in addition to such criminal sexual activities as prostitution and rape.

Sexual behavior, so defined, was first reported for the 1976, 1979, and 1980 seasons by Greenberg, Abelman, and Neuendorf. They found about two sexual activities per hour in their samples. What was then called petting, including long and passionate kisses, was most prominent, accounting for half of all incidents. The second most frequent activity was implied intercourse between individuals not married to each other. By the third study, implied intercourse was the most frequent activity.

Lowry and Towles (1989) compared the 1979 and 1987 seasons and found a radical change in the distribution of implied intercourse between married and unmarried partners. In the 1979 study, 31% of such acts were between married partners; that dropped to 3% in their follow-up study.

A 1985 study by Greenberg and D'Alessio analyzed 10 episodes of the three top-rated soaps. There were 3.7 coded sex incidents/references per hour, a sharp increase from the earlier study reports of 2 per hour. Intercourse (2.3 per hour) and long kisses (1 per hour) accounted for 9 of every 10 references. Intercourse was twice as likely among unmarried couples as among marriage partners, and one in five of the former was married to someone else. The coded sex acts were mostly verbal (70%), and all but a handful of the visual ones were long kisses.

By 1994, using the same coding scheme, sexual activity increased from 3.7 per hour to 5 per hour in the same three soaps and to 6.6 per hour across all five soaps analyzed in a study by Greenberg and Busselle. For the two soaps added to the sample because of their high ratings that season, the levels of sexual activity were extreme—11 per hour (*Days of our Lives*) and 7 per hour (*The Young and the Restless*). References to unmarried intercourse alone (2.4 per hour) now exceeded all sex acts found in the pre-1985 studies. In this study, rape acts were frequent, 1.4 per hour, based on then new concerns with date rape. In 50 episodes, there were five discussions of safe sex. A notable difference in the decade between the studies was the increase in visual depictions of sexual intercourse. In the 1985 study, there was one such visual incident; in the later study, one in four of all sex incidents visually simulated intercourse.

Heintz-Knowles (1996) studied the full set of nationally televised soaps. Her overall findings suggest more visual behaviors than earlier; most sexual activity among those with established relationships, rather than one-night stands; no increase in discussion

of safe sex; the omission of date-rape story lines; and sexual activity improving the participants' relationships with each other, at least temporarily.

Four studies by Kunkel and his colleagues (1999, 2001, 2003, 2005) examined soap sex in the broader context of all TV genres. In their first composite week (for the 1997–1998 season), 85% of their soap sample programs had some sexual content, a larger proportion than any other of the seven genres examined (movies were second at 83%). Of the soaps containing sexual elements, 11% also contained some risk/responsibility portrayal concurrently. If it was talk about sex, soaps averaged 4+ incidents per hour; only comedies had a higher average (5.9). If it was sexual behavior, soaps averaged 2.2 per hour, compared with 2.7 in comedies and 1.5 in dramas.

The 2001 study (of the 1999–2000 season) placed soaps third—behind movies and situation comedies—in the percentage of episodes that contained sexual content: 80% of all soaps had sex content compared with 89% of movies and 84% of sitcoms. Thus, soaps did not decrease nor did movies increase; sitcoms jumped dramatically. In contrast, only 7% of soaps contained any reference to sexual risks or responsibilities, compared to 13% of movies and 5% of sitcoms. Talking about sex remained similar with 4.1 incidents per hour, but soap opera discussions were now exceeded by sitcoms (7.3) and dramas (4.3). Sex behaviors for soaps were 2.4 per hour, still exceeded only by sitcoms (3.1).

Their analysis for the 2001–2002 season put soap operas soundly in first place in one category: 96% of its episodes had sexual content, compared with 87% in movies and 73% in sitcoms. Talking about sex was consistent with prior studies, at 4.1 incidents per hour, and sex behaviors continued to increase, now to 2.6 per hour. Sitcoms led in both sex talk (7.4) and sex behaviors (3.7).

Their 2005 report found that 70% of all shows have sexual content and that the number of scenes per program involving sex reached 5 per hour. Among soaps, 85% of its episodes had sexual content, whereas only 13% of those episodes contained portrayals of risk or responsibility.

—*Bradley S. Greenberg and Tracy Worrell*

See also Sex in Television, Content Analysis of; Sex in Television, Incidence and Themes; Soap Operas, Content Analyses of

FURTHER READINGS

Berr, J. (2005, May 15). Soap operas face real melodrama as ratings, advertising start to slip. *Ventura County Star (California),* Business and Stocks, p. 3.

Greenberg, B. S., Abelman, R., & Neuendorf, K. (1981). Sex on the soap operas: Afternoon delight. *Journal of Communication, 31*(3), 83–89.

Greenberg, B. S., & Busselle, R. (1996). Soap operas and sexual activity: A decade later. *Journal of Communication, 46*(4), 153–160.

Heintz-Knowles, K. E. (1996, September). *Sexual activity on daytime soap operas: A content analysis of five weeks of television programming.* Menlo Park, CA: Kaiser Family Foundation.

Kunkel, D., Biely, E., Eyal, K., Cope-Farrar, K., Donnerstein, E., & Fandrich, R. (2003). *Sex on TV–3* (A biennial report of the Kaiser Family Foundation). Santa Barbara: University of California, Santa Barbara.

Kunkel, D., Cope, K., Farinola, W., Biely, E., Rollin, E., & Donnerstein, E. (1999). *Sex on TV: Content and context.* Menlo Park, CA: Kaiser Family Foundation.

Kunkel, D., Cope-Farrar, K., Biely, E., Farinola, W., & Donnerstein, E. (2001). *Sex on TV–2* (A biennial report of the Kaiser Family Foundation). Menlo Park, CA: Kaiser Family Foundation.

Kunkel, D., Eyal, K, Finnerty, K., Biely, E. & Donnerstein, E. (2005). *Sex on TV–4* (A biennial report of the Kaiser Family Foundation). Menlo Park, CA: Kaiser Family Foundation.

Lowry, D. T., & Towles, D. E. (1989). Soap opera portrayals of sex, contraception, and sexually transmitted diseases. *Journal of Communication, 39*(2), 76–83.

SOCIAL CLASS

Although many studies have referred to social class as an important factor in media use, most include it merely as a background variable, with surprisingly few devoting much specific, detailed attention to it. Consequently, knowledge of this relationship, although extensive, is shallow with regard to the ways in which these variables actually interact.

SOCIAL CLASS AND SOCIAL STATUS

The first problem to be addressed is the definition of social class itself. In one of the few in-depth analyses of social class and media use among children and adolescents, Rosengren and Windahl (1989) noted that it is possible to trace operationalizations of the concept to the work of either Karl Marx or Max Weber. In the Marxist view, the economic structure of a society divides people into different classes, a class being composed of those occupying comparable places in the system of production. Weber also defined social classes in economic terms but based his definition on the means at a person's disposal to operate in any given market. To the notion of class, Weber added that of status, referring to the social prestige assigned to a person by others. Thus, in this tradition, the term *social* (or *socioeconomic*) status is more commonly used. However, social class and social status should not be regarded as mutually exclusive concepts. Whereas social *class* may be seen as defining the main socioeconomic framework within which mass media use takes place, social *status* prescribes more precise ways in which the media are used by different status groupings.

In mass communication research, there has been no uniformity in the use of these concepts. The Marxist variant is found mostly in European research, whereas the Weberian perspective, although also frequently employed in Europe, has left a deeper mark on American research. As a result of this lack of uniformity, various indicators of class or status have been employed, such as income, occupational status, and level of education.

In addition to Marx and Weber, Pierre Bourdieu's concept of *cultural capital* has also been applied to the social foundations of media use. Cultural capital is defined as symbolic wealth socially regarded as worthy of being sought and possessed. According to this theory, the cultural capital children receive from home will affect their chances of success at school and thereby also the opportunities for later achieving status and a favorable position within the process of production. Cultural capital has also been found to be directly related to amounts and types of media use. A person's level of education has been found to be a good indicator of social status, thus conceived.

Rosengren and Windahl also stressed the need to differentiate between the concepts of *class of origin* and *class of destination* because the cogency of these contexts varies across the life span. Thus, whereas the social class of children is defined by that of their parents (class of origin), that of adults tends to be based on their own educational and occupational achievement (class of destination). For adolescents, the situation is more equivocal because they find themselves in a transitional context. As they grow older, the influence of their class of origin steadily diminishes; as they approach the end of their educational careers, they become increasingly aware of their probable destination in the status hierarchy, including whether or not their trajectory is socially mobile in an upward or downward direction. Via the process of *anticipatory socialization* (the process of adopting the values and orientations of a group to which one aspires but does not yet belong, with the aim of aiding one's transition into membership of that group), this perceived future can affect current behavior such as media uses and preferences. These indeterminate and transitory elements of adolescents' social class location may at least partially account for the weak correlations with adolescents' media use often reported in the literature.

RESEARCH EVIDENCE

Early studies of children's TV viewing did not find social class to be a significant factor. However, as the medium diffused more widely, evidence of social class variations in TV use began to be consistently reported, primarily in Europe but also in the United States. Later studies refined the bivariate relationship, stressing the importance of such variables as age, gender, ethnicity, school achievement, and parents' media use as mediating factors. In particular, a strong interaction between social class and gender has been found, with the patterns of media use of middle-class girls very different and much more structured than those of working-class boys. Moreover, significant differences have been found in the degree of linearity in the relationship between children's media use and social origin, with the educational status of the mother proving to be a stronger and more linear predictor than the occupational status of the father. The concept of media use, too, needs to be differentiated because the existence and strength of relationships has been found to differ across various media, with some of the strongest and most consistent being found with respect to adolescents' music use.

Theoretical developments since the 1990s have to some extent diverted the focus of research away from generalizing concepts such as social class toward theories of individuation and personalized lifestyles. However, concepts such as lifestyle and social class may fruitfully be combined in models postulating that individual lifestyle choices are made within, and structured by, broader (changing) class contexts. Moreover, the case for ignoring class is rather weak, given the fact that studies in the United States and Europe continue to identify it as a significant factor. Deepening our understanding of the complexities of this relationship, however, will require more sophisticated, multivariate research designs because the research indicates that the effects of social class or status on children's and adolescent's media use may be mostly indirect.

—*Keith Roe*

See also Knowledge Gap; Literacy; Socialization and Media

FURTHER READINGS

Bourdieu, P. (1984). *Distinction: A social critique of the judgment of taste.* New York: Routledge.

Jordan, A. B. (1992). Social class, temporal orientation, and mass media use within the family system. *Critical Studies in Mass Communication, 9*(4), 374–386.

Merton, R. K. (1968). *Social theory and social structure.* New York: Free Press.

Roe, K. (1994). Media use and social mobility. In K. E. Rosengren (Ed.), *Media effects and beyond* (pp. 183–204). New York: Routledge.

Roe, K. (2000). Socio-economic status and children's television use. *Communications: The European Journal of Communication, 25*(1), 3–18.

Rosengren, K. E., & Windahl, S. (1989). *Media matter: TV use in childhood and adolescence.* Norwood, NJ: Ablex.

Skogan, K. (1998). A touch of class: The persistence of class cultures among Norwegian youth. *Young: The Nordic Journal of Youth Research, 6*(2), 15–37.

SOCIAL LEARNING THEORY/ SOCIAL COGNITIVE THEORY

Social learning theory and social cognitive theory were developed by Albert Bandura in an effort to explain how individuals learn from the environment. Both theories provide a useful framework for understanding how the media influence behavior. This entry describes the main elements in social learning theory and social cognitive theory and their direct application to understanding the influence of the media on development.

Traditional learning theories suggest that people learn about societal expectations by performing behaviors and receiving direct positive or negative feedback from the environment. For example, learning theories suggest that girls and boys learn to play with different types of toys because they receive different feedback from parents, peers, and teachers when they play with the "right" toys (e.g., boys with trucks and girls with dolls) than when they play with the "wrong" toys (e.g., boys with dolls and girls with trucks.) From these sorts of experiences, individuals learn which behaviors work and which behaviors don't work in their environment.

The development of social learning theory marked a theoretical advance by suggesting that humans need not experience every cause and effect in order to learn; rather, they can learn by observing others. For example, children do not have to directly experience different feedback to learn about gender expectations; they can learn by observing the actions of others and the consequences they receive. Bandura termed this process *observational learning.*

Bandura further expanded his theory of learning in his description of social cognitive theory by focusing on the active role of human cognition in the process of observational learning. Bandura suggests that people are not passive recipients of knowledge transmitted by their environments; rather, they actively seek out and process information. This means that every individual does not learn from every event in the environment; people, to some extent, choose what they see and to what they pay attention.

Social cognitive theory suggests that three interacting components determine which events result in observational learning: *personal characteristics,* such as attentional skills, interest, or prior beliefs; *behavioral actions*, including the choices people make to be in certain places or to look at certain things; and *environmental events*, or the things that happen to take place in the person's environment. Figure 1 depicts how these three factors interact to influence whether observational learning takes place.

Once these three components interact to produce an opportunity for observational learning, social cognitive theory suggests that four steps must take place for an observed event to influence an individual, or for learning to take place. These include (1) *observation,* or whether the person views an event, (2) *processing*, how the person understands the presented information, (3) *remembering,* whether the information is encoded in long-term memory, and (4) *internalizing*, whether the information is accepted by the individual such that it creates, or reinforces, a belief. Social cognitive theory suggests that all of these steps must be completed in order for an observed event to influence later behavior.

Bandura suggests that individuals engage in the process of observational learning with models presented through the media. For example, children can learn about gender-appropriate toys by watching a TV show

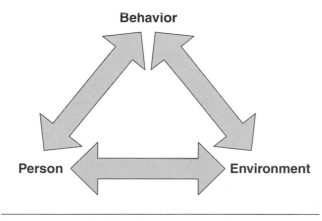

Behavior

Person   **Environment**

Figure 1   The Three Factors That Influence
                    Observational Learning

in which a child is treated negatively for playing with a wrong toy. Furthermore, social cognitive theory suggests that humans have the capacity to generalize the patterns of actions and consequences that they observe in one situation to other similar situations. Therefore, in our example, children who view such an event on television easily apply what they see to other toys, games, and activities. Furthermore, the models in the media provide a source of information for *vicarious verification,* a process by which individuals check the accuracy of their own beliefs through comparison with others. For example, if adolescents think that certain behaviors might be OK but aren't quite sure, they can be encouraged to believe that the behaviors are OK by checking their thoughts against the thoughts expressed by models on television.

According to social cognitive theory, information presented in the media will influence behavior only if an individual engages in all phases of observational learning. For example, consider a TV program in which a young boy bullies other children but does not get in trouble. A boy who engages in observational learning with this character as a model has the potential to learn that bullying behavior will not be punished. However, this learning could be interrupted at any stage. The boy may quickly change the channel because he is not interested (failure to *observe*). The boy may watch the program but not recognize the meaning (failure to *process*). He may understand the events taking place but be quickly distracted causing him to forget the plot (failure to *remember*). Finally, if the boy remembers the program but has a strong prior belief that bullies always get in trouble, he may reject the message of the scene (failure to *internalize*).

However, social cognitive theory also provides guidance for understanding how the media can manipulate messages to make successful observational learning more likely. In our example, the boy is more likely to learn the message that bullies do not get punished if such messages are contained in shows the child is interested in (making *observation* more likely); if the message is presented clearly (making *processing* more likely); and if the show focuses on the main theme, repeats the message many times, and is free of distracters (making *remembering* more likely). Finally, the media can influence whether an event is *internalized* by directly impacting beliefs. For example, if a child repeatedly views shows in which bullies do not get punished, and the shows contain varied plots and characters all with the same message, the child's initial belief that bullies always get punished may come into question, making internalization more likely.

In summary, social cognitive theory suggests that the available models represented in the mass media provide many opportunities for observational learning through the demonstration of behavioral actions and consequences, as well as through the modeled expression of thoughts, emotions, and attitudes.

—Marjorie Rhodes, Daniel W. Brickman, and
Brad J. Bushman

See also Media Effects; Schema Theory; Socialization and Media

FURTHER READINGS

Bandura, A. (1976). *Social learning theory.* Englewood, NJ: Prentice Hall.

Bandura, A. (1989). Human agency in social cognitive theory. *American Psychologist, 44*(9), 1175–1184.

Bandura, A. (2001). Social cognitive theory of mass communication. *Media Psychology, 3*(3), 265–299.

SOCIALIZATION AND MEDIA

Research on media socialization of children and youth is concerned with different ways that media play a part in the psychosocial development of the adolescent. Socialization is understood as an interaction between the individual and his or her environment. Children do not adapt themselves to their environment passively; rather, they actively construct an understanding of the world through interactions with their environment, and they actively shape their environment. Media are used to accomplish developmental tasks. In today's media society, the acquisition of media competence has become one of the important developmental tasks. Media socialization is influenced by parents, peers, the individual himself or herself, and the social environment, in a process that both opens up possibilities for and creates restrictions on the use of media and their contents.

INTERDISCIPLINARY APPROACHES

Basic theories of media socialization are rooted in different disciplines, for example, developmental

psychology, sociology of childhood, media research, and pedagogy. Developmental psychology shows that different developmental tasks have to be accomplished in certain stages due to biological, social, or individual necessities. Earlier theories considered the sequence of the developmental tasks to a greater extent as socially determined, such as the moment of the separation from parents or of the first intimate relationships. Today, it is rather emphasized that there are different processes that are equivalent in modern individualist societies. Media are used by children to accomplish such developmental tasks. They make use of media to become independent by developing their own media preferences, which may not coincide with those of their parents and may instead be anchored in their peer culture. Media contents are browsed for role models that contribute to the development, for example, representations of gender roles or of lifestyles.

Sociological theories emphasize the relationship between societal development and the changing role of the media. In the current media society, media permeate all life spheres of children from the earliest days on, continually changing families, schools, and other areas in which children grow up and are formatively influenced.

Media research examines the presence of media devices in places such as children's rooms, schools, and youth centers; how much time is spent with the media; what the goals of the media use are; and what effects emerge. It concludes that there are considerable differences by social class and gender in media access. Access gaps can deepen social differences further in the society, and they also influence the chances of development of the individual.

Finally, pedagogy is concerned with the relationship between parents, teachers, and others who influence the socialization of children by intentional media education. The main area is the development of media competence and the prevention of negative influences by media. More recent approaches emphasize also the possibilities of the media as resources for children.

CONTEXTS OF MEDIA SOCIALIZATION

In early childhood, the primary socialization takes place in the family. The media usage of children is influenced to a great extent by the mediation of the parents as well as by parents' own media usage as role models. Studies show that children's rooms have been increasingly equipped with media over the past decades; as a result, children are developing a relative autonomy regarding the media in their everyday life. Television has become a medium used by families to form relationships among family members, for example, in the case of mother and daughter watching soap operas together and fathers and sons viewing sport programs; to give another example of family togetherness, siblings play a computer game together while parents discuss a newspaper article. Thus, media strengthen the substructures within the family and frequently contribute to the transmission of gender-specific media behavior and thereby to role-related behavior.

In school, media are used primarily as a learning aid. Reflection about media effects, however, rarely occurs in spite of several projects on media pedagogical concepts over the years. Media play an important role in the informal exchanges of peers during school and their leisure time. For example, the mobile telephone is used to communicate during school breaks, and a TV program or experiences with a new computer game are intensively discussed. Those who do not possess a computer or who are not allowed to watch television run the risk of being excluded by peers at school.

Media themselves and the world of consumption constitute an increasingly important agent of media socialization. The economy is addressing children and youth as customers more and more directly. Studies show that children spend a relatively high share of their pocket money on media, boys mainly on computer games and girls on mobile telephones. Through advertising on TV music channels, which are intensively used by youth, adolescent brand loyalty is fostered. Thus, media are of significance in the socialization of children as consumers.

RISKS OF MEDIA CONSUMPTION BY CHILDREN

Cultural commentators such as Neil Postman and Dave Grossman take pessimistic views, arguing that media are responsible for the disappearance of childhood. They postulate that media destroy the protected space of childhood by confronting children much too early with all aspects of the world, including consumption, violence, and constant entertainment. Children may encounter many topics for the first time in the media, which results in a distorted representation of reality. Several studies have demonstrated a relationship between the aggressiveness of children and their consumption of violence in media. Recent studies have examined adolescents' addiction to television and the Internet. On the Internet, game clans and communication forums such as chat rooms or newsgroups can lead to media addiction.

MEDIA AS RESOURCES FOR PSYCHOSOCIAL DEVELOPMENT

Authors of the cultural studies approach emphasize that children use the media creatively to guide themselves, to develop their identity, and to test different identity representations. Transient but intensive devotion to horror films, computer games, or soap operas or to collecting objects like Pokemon is understood not as a risk, but rather as a resource that allows children to acquire their identity and position in the society as independent members. Not only reading, writing, and arithmetic, but also dealing with television and new media are cultural techniques. Children use them to compensate for deficits in other spheres. Thus, an intensive association with a media figure can compensate for family situations such as parental divorce or separation as well as for problems in relationships with teachers or peers.

CHANGES IN MEDIA SOCIALIZATION

Studies that examine historical changes in everyday media usage conclude that children become capable of using the media independently and are addressed directly as consumers at an ever earlier age. Furthermore, total time of media usage is increasing. At the same time, media are more frequently used not exclusively, but rather parallel to other activities. This is promoted by the mobility of the media and the multimedia capability of devices. Globalization leads to worldwide spread of children's and youth culture, for example, Harry Potter, Japanese manga, and anime such as *Dragenball*. Along with this, the marketing of new items moves more quickly and levels off sooner. Thus, society's general acceleration is reflected in an acceleration of the changing media habits of children and the youth. Although the children's commitment to fan cultures becomes more changeable, some basic patterns remain: gender differences and differences of social backgrounds in early media socialization.

—Daniel Süss

See also Developmental Differences, Media and; Media Education, Family Involvement in; Peer Groups, Impact of Media on; Youth Culture

FURTHER READINGS

Grossman, D., & DeGaetano, G. (1999). *Stop teaching our kids to kill.* New York: Crown.

Livingstone, S., & Bovill, M. (Eds.). *Children and their changing media environment: A European comparative study.* Mahwah, NJ: Erlbaum.

Postman, N. (1982). *The disappearance of childhood.* New York: Delacorte Press.

Süss, D. (2004): *Mediensozialisation von Heranwachsenden* [Media socialization of adolescents]. Wiesbaden: VS Verlag.

SPONSORED EDUCATIONAL MATERIAL (SEM)

Hundreds of sponsored educational material (SEM) units are corporately produced and distributed annually to school classrooms. The topics span a broad range including SEMs on the environment, nutrition, health and safety, economics, history, money management, health insurance, and a variety of specific product units such as car-care products, specific energy producers, meat and livestock advocacy, and so on.

SEM comes in a variety of forms—poster kits, teaching packets of print materials, multimedia kits with videotapes, software, CD-ROMs, and print materials. Units vary in the range of materials provided. For example, three of the most extensive (Intel, Exxon Foundation, and the American Forest Foundation) contain 290 to more than 400-page teachers' guides as well as videos, CD-ROMs, student activities booklets, research assignments, data files, posters, and simulation games. Those treading the lighter side contain only a poster and a small teachers' guide. Consumers Union took on the daunting task of classifying this wide array of materials and evaluating those that contained an accompanying teaching guide (thereby classifying their materials as instructional curricula). This entry examines the general nature and approach of SEM within each of the major topical categories, the degree to which SEM units are balanced or biased and incomplete, and the overall implications of these findings for school curricular materials.

GENERAL NATURE AND APPROACH OF SEM

Environment

Companies providing environmental units range quite broadly, from entities such as the American Coal Foundation and the American Forest Foundation to Exxon, McDonald's, Procter & Gamble, Dow Chemical, Chlorine Institute, Steel Can Recycling Institute, and the Council for Wildlife Conservation & Education, Inc. Examples from the nature and flavor of respective presentations follow.

American Coal Foundation. Its materials have the goal of helping seventh-to-ninth-grade classes "learn more about America's most abundant energy source—coal." The unit indicates that coal is abundant, inexpensive, and poses very few environmental problems. CO_2 emissions and global warming are presented as a potential Earth benefit.

American Forest Foundation. This program for grades K–8 seeks to help children think seriously about complex environmental issues, both local and global. It supports the concept of managed forestry while indicating that trees, forests, forest products, and responsible conservation or land-use are vitally important.

Exxon Education Foundation. The extensive set of resources is designed for middle school and high school. Materials seek to help students understand the scientific principles supporting world energy choices and the social implications accompanying those choices.

McDonald's. Targeting 7-to-12-year-olds, McDonald's enlisted the Field Museum of Natural History to help create student understanding of environmental issues and encourage them to become active participants, both currently and in the future.

Procter & Gamble. Billed as "Planet Patrol" for fourth to sixth graders, the unit prompts students to consider environmental impact in their product use and product decisions. The curriculum teaches that the company is environmentally responsible and that disposable diapers are positive for the environment because they can be composted.

Dow Chemical. Developed by the American Chemical Society, this unit targets high school chemistry classes with the goal of increasing scientific literacy by demonstrating chemistry's societal impact. It contains the basic message that everything around us is composed of chemicals and students should understand how chemicals work and how they impact students' lives and society in general.

Chlorine Institute. This unit for middle school children sets out to develop student interest in this chemical element and parlay it into an interest in element-based building-block chemistry.

Steel Can Recycling Institute. For grades 5 to 8, this unit sensitizes students to the importance of recycling all renewable materials and the special value in using and conserving steel, which is characterized as one of the most environmentally friendly materials.

Council for Wildlife Conservation & Education, Inc. Designed for middle and high school, the council's unit outlines its success in bringing back endangered species from the brink of extinction and implementing measures to assure their health and long-term viability.

Nutrition

The following three examples provide a cross-sectional view of SEMs—Dole Food Company, Kellogg's, and Mars, Inc.

Dole Food Company. Designed in partnership with the Society for Nutrition Education, this "5 a Day Adventures" curriculum teaches middle schoolers the benefits of eating five or more servings of fruits and vegetables daily.

Kellogg's. Partnering with the American Health Association and the American Academy of Pediatrics, the company developed two units for elementary school children ("Eat to the Beat" on choosing healthful foods and "Kids get going with breakfast" with tips on good breakfast-eating habits). A third unit for middle and high school students provides information about using the food pyramid to build a healthful diet.

Mars. With World Cup Soccer and Scholastic, Inc., this elementary school unit aims to connect food and fitness with "100% Smart Energy to Go." Mars bars are characterized as such energy.

Health and Safety

State Farm. The insurance company produced three units—two for elementary school children and one for grades K–12. The topics range from "Inside/Out" (what influences our health) to "Smoke Detectives" (fire prevention and safety) to "Movers and Shakers" (earthquake information and preparedness). All units have extensive support materials.

Upjohn Corporation. Their "Secret of Life" unit for middle school children introduces them to concepts of genetics. It was designed to coordinate with a *Science and Children* PBS series.

National Energy Foundation. Entitled "Safety Watcher," this unit educates elementary school children on electrical safety.

Economics, History, and Money Management

Visa. Its high school student orientation is designed to help build strong financial and consumer skills.

California Beef Council. For grades 6–8, this unit explores the image and legend of the American cowboy.

CONTENT BALANCE OR BIAS/INCOMPLETENESS

Like the range of topics, the SEM units sprawl quite widely across the balance or bias spectrum. Within the conservation units cited, five of the nine (55.5%) were found to be strongly biased, whereas two (22.2%) were moderately biased and two were balanced. The highly exemplary units were Dow Chemical and the American Forestry Foundation, both notably objective and noncommercial.

Among the nutritional units cited, Dole proved exemplary, whereas the others (80%) were considered highly biased. And in the economics, history, and money management area, both units cited were evaluated as moderately biased. Overall, 80% of all units evaluated contained bias or incomplete information, and more than 50% were deemed either commercial or highly commercial. This scorecard suggests that the stellar examples cited are a precious few and that among the many SEMs, product promotion and bias are far more the rule.

—Edward L. Palmer

See also Advertising, Health and; Advertising Campaigns, Prosocial; Commercial Television and Radio in Schools; Public Service Announcements (PSAs); Schools, Advertising/Marketing in

FURTHER READINGS

Consumers Union. (1995). *Captive kids: Commercial pressures on kids at school.* Yonkers, NY: Consumers Union Education Series.

U.S. General Accounting Office. (2000, September). *Public education: Commercial activities in schools.* Washington, DC: Author.

SPORTS TELEVISION

Sporting events represent an important source of programming for the television industry. Countless live sporting events and spin-off programs (e.g., talk shows, preview and postgame shows, sports news, and highlight shows) are aired each day. Specialized sports networks available on cable abound and include golf, football, outdoor sports, college sports, soccer, and racing of all varieties, to name but a few. In addition, premium channels in most markets allow viewers—for an extra charge—to see all of the games played in major league baseball, and the National Basketball Association (NBA), Women's National Basketball Association (WNBA), National Football League (NFL), National Hockey League (NHL), and the Premiere league. Finally, pay-per-view television allows viewers to watch WWE wrestling and nearly all title fights in the world of boxing.

One way to estimate the importance of sports programming to the television industry is to examine the amount of money networks spend to buy the rights to these events. Table 1 provides the costs of most of the rights for most major sporting events during the 2002–2003 season—more than $5 billion were spent for the television rights for 1 year, and that excludes the cost of the WNBA, boxing, wrestling, and a host of

other sports such as college football. NBC paid $793 million for the rights to the 2004 Summer Olympics held in Athens, Greece, and NBC will pay $894 million for the rights to the 2008 Summer Games in Beijing. According to *USA Today,* NBC, MSNBC, and the other NBC networks aired more than 800 hours of Olympic programming during the 2004 games. These games garnered an audience of more than 200 million viewers and set a ratings record as the most-watched non-U.S. Summer Olympics in history.

Further evidence of the importance of sports programming to the television industry can be found in the Nielsen ratings. During the 2003–2004 television season, the three most widely viewed TV specials focused on the Super Bowl. In fact, according to the Nielsen ratings, sports programs held 4 of the top 5 slots and 6 of the top 10 television specials for the year.

These high levels of viewership for the 2003–2004 television season are not an anomaly. Nielsen's list of the highest rated programs of all time is filled with sports programming. In fact, 55% of the 40 most widely viewed programs of all time were sports programs. This list includes NFL games and women's Olympic figure skating, with World Series baseball games and NBA games not too much further down the list.

Most televised sporting events do not attract ratings audiences as large as the most popular prime-time network programs. Researchers recognize that the Nielsen ratings consistently underestimate the audience of sporting events because of measurement error. This error in audience estimation stems from the fact that Nielsen system has not traditionally taken into consideration the fact that many TV viewers watch sporting events with friends and in public places. Thus, anyone not watching TV at home is lost in the ratings assessment process.

While estimates vary, somewhere between 10% and 20% of all TV viewing is done outside the home. In the Nielsen system, which employs 8,000 families to represent the U.S. viewing audience, that percentage could mean a huge swing in the ratings, an increase of as much as 12 rating points. In fact, Nielsen and other rating companies have begun to employ portable people meters to combat this problem. These devices work like a cell phone and transmit audio sounds back to Nielsen so they can keep track of all media usage home or away, without reliance on the memory of the Nielsen family member. Although sports programming might not attract an audience as large as prime-time network programs, the ratings for sporting events are consistently

Table 1   Approximate TV Rights Expenditures for 2002–2003

Sport	Network(s)	Cost/Millions
National Football League games	ESPN	$600
	ABC	$550
	Fox	$550
	CBS	$500
Major league baseball	Fox	$417
	ESPN	$141
Winter Olympics	NBC	$555
NCAA basketball games	CBS	$565
National Basketball Association games	NBC	$350
	TNT/TBS	$178
NASCAR	Fox	$200
NASCAR	NBC/TBS	$200
Professional Golf Association	ABC/CBS/NBC	$162
National Hockey League games	ESPN/ABC	$120
IRL/Indy 500	ABC	$28
U.S. Open tennis	CBS	$38
Wimbledon tennis	NBC	$22
	TBS	$8
Figure skating	ABC	$12
Triple crown horse racing	NBC	$10

Total Television Rights for 2002 = $5.2 Billion

SOURCE: TN media analysis of Nielsen data, cited in Downey, K. (2001). "Sports TV get pricier and pricier. Here's why." Retrieved June 31, 2005, from http://www.media lifemagazine.com/news2001/apr01/apr09/4_thurs/news1thursday.html

as high as programs on cable. With the employment of portable people meters, advertisers may find sports programming is more competitive than previously known.

Given the proliferation of sports programming available, the question becomes, How much time do people spend watching sports on TV? According to Robinson and Godbey's (1997) study of leisure time in the United States, 37.8% of Americans' leisure time is spent watching television. Adults watch television an average of 87.6 minutes per day, which is more than any other activity, save their main job and sleeping. Roberts and Foehr found that the average 8-to-18-year-old, however, watches more than 3 hours per day.

A *Sports Illustrated* poll reported that 84% of Americans watch sports on television at least once a week, and 71% of those polled considered themselves fans. A 2001 nationwide study, commissioned jointly by the Amateur Athletic Foundation of Los Angeles and ESPN, reports that 93% of all children in the United States, ages 8 to 17, report using some form of sports

media. Seven in 10 children interact with sports through the media a couple of times a week or every day, and 88% of those use television for their sports information, preferring it over radio, print, and the Internet. Although children said "big three" professional sports—NBA, NFL, and major league baseball—were the sports they interact with most through the media, the Olympic Games are watched by more children (84%) than any other type of sports television programming, according to figures from Statistical Research, Inc. (2001). These numbers come even at a time when broadcast TV audiences are on the decline, and there are more choices than ever on cable.

Social critics have argued that television is changing the nature of our culture. Given that an estimated $6 billion is wagered legally and illegally on the Super Bowl and 6% of the nation's workforce calls in sick on the following Monday, it is easy to make an argument that sports may, at times, be detrimental to society. Some critical scholars and social theorists have argued that sports proficiency is less a way out of poverty than it is a way to maintain the status quo. These critics suggest televised sporting events are used by the power elite as a vehicle for inculcating sexist, racist, nationalistic, and violent ideas in viewers; they are not simply entertainment for the masses.

Although sports and TV are inextricably intertwined, many sports purists and social critics have argued the relationship has had detrimental effects on the sports, extending the length of games to incorporate advertisements, artificially breaking the flow of games, and even changing the techniques employed by athletes during the games—so they are more likely to end up in the nightly highlight shows. Further examples of these changes abound: Instant replay, the shootout in hockey, the television timeout in football and basketball, the revised championship point system in NASCAR, modification of league configurations, and the creation of playoff systems all appear to be changes made to accommodate television and advertisers. This is to say nothing about the changes that have occurred in the notion of student athletes competing in intercollegiate activities.

Because so much time is spent viewing sports television, it is incumbent on future scholars to examine the impact of coviewing of sports on family interaction. According to Statistical Research (2001), 70% of children between the ages of 8 and 17 usually watch sports television with others. About 55% report watching with their fathers, 23% with their mothers, and 14% with both their parents. These coviewing opportunities need to be examined carefully by mass communication scholars because they provide parents excellent opportunities for discussing moral issues found in competition; the games also provide an excellent vehicle for promoting media literacy.

There are many reasons why sports programming is so popular with television audiences. Sporting events are an excellent source of drama. The contests are typically zero-sum games with unpredictable outcomes. The rules provide predictable structures and rituals that give viewers a sense of familiarity and understanding of the event. However, forces outside the control of participants (e.g., weather, luck, injuries, and officiating) can directly or indirectly affect the outcome. The games contain villains and heroes, like all good drama. Finally, they provide audience members the feelings of involvement, identification, and participation in the activity that are missing from most other forms of television content. Sports programs, unlike many other genres of programming, are designed to feel like a live event in which viewers can immerse themselves as if they were in the stadium or arena. The advent of new technologies such as high-definition television and interactive television will only enhance the live experience.

—James D. Robinson and Kymberly Higgs

See also Coviewing; World Wrestling Entertainment (WWE)

FURTHER READINGS

Besser, C. N. (2005, June 27). PPM is the next big score for sports TV. *Advertising Age,* p. 22.

Bidding for the Olympics on TV [Electronic version]. (2003, April 21). *USA Today.* Retrieved from http:// www.usatoday.com/sports/olympics/2003-04-21-tv-rights_x.htm#fees

Bourdieu, P. (1984). *Distinction: A social critique of the judgment of taste.* Cambridge, MA: Harvard University Press.

Bourdieu, P. (1988). Program for a sociology of sport. *Sociology of Sport Journal, 5,* 153–161.

Bourdieu, P. (1991). Sport and social class. In C. Mukerji & M. Schudson (Eds.), *Rethinking popular culture: Contemporary perspectives in cultural studies* (pp. 357–373). Berkeley: University of California Press.

Downey, K. (2001). Sports TV get pricier and pricier: Here's why. *Media Life.* Retrieved June 31, 2005, from http://www.medialifemagazine.com/news2001/apr01/apr09/4_thurs/news1thursday.html

Edgerton, G., & Ostroff, D. (1985). Sports telecasting. In B. C. Rose (Ed.), *TV genres: A handbook and reference guide* (pp. 257–286), Westport, CT: Greenwood Press.

Gough, P. (2004, August). NBC sets new Olympic record: 200 mil viewers [Electronic version]. *Hollywood Reporter.* Retrieved January 31, 2005, from http://www.hollywoodreporter.com/thr/television/brief_display.jsp?vnu_content_id=1000620967

Nielsen Media Research. (2004). All time highest-rated television programs. In E. Gopel (Ed.), *The world almanac and book of facts 2005.* New York: World Almanac Books.

Nielsen Media Research. (2004). Top 10 television specials, 2003–2004. In B. Brunner (Ed.), *Time almanac 2005.* Upper Saddle Ridge, NJ: Pearson Education.

Roberts, D., & Foehr, U. (2004). *Kids and media in America: Based on a Kaiser Family Foundation study.* New York: Cambridge University Press.

Robinson, J., & Godbey, G. (1997). *Time for life: The surprising ways Americans use their time.* University Park: Pennsylvania State University Press.

Showalter, S. (1986). It's a whole new ball game [Electronic version]. *Media & Values, 36.* Retrieved January 30, 2005, from http://www.medialit.org/reading_room/article201.html

Statistical Research, Inc. (2001). *AAF/ESPN children and sports media study.* Westfield, NJ: Author.

A super national holiday. (February 2, 2002). *The Week.* Retrieved from http://www.theweekmagazine.com/article.asp?id=84

STICKY MARKETING

Sticky marketing refers to employing tactics that make people willingly expose themselves to a promotional message again and again. Specifically, the term is usually used to refer to web pages; a sticky web page is one that people choose to return to repeatedly, thereby increasing the likelihood that they will learn, be persuaded, and perhaps even purchase something. Sticky marketing enables targeting, personalization, and interaction with surfers, who may then become patrons. Children may be quite receptive to sticky marketing techniques, which has led policymakers to implement restrictions relating to websites targeted at children.

There are numerous ways to make a site sticky; the most effective ones do so in a way that is integrated with the company's brand image and other promotional messages. For example, a website may offer visitors the opportunity to email a web page to a friend, thereby creating the potential to increase the site's reach. It can provide customized content in the form of a horoscope, local weather, or updated headlines. It can provide free email or downloadable programs, such as screensavers or wallpaper. It can create a forum where people may chat or post messages; again, not only does this increase the likelihood of repeat visits from the original user, it also increases the likelihood that new users will discover the site. Anything that brings a visitor back to a web page is a form of sticky marketing: It makes visitors "stick" to the page. In this sense, the brand associated with the site gains credibility and longevity.

Research shows that young children are unable to understand the consequences of revealing their personal information and that vast amounts of such information from children have been collected by marketers. Concern over this led the Federal Trade Commission (FTC) in 1998 to present Congress with a report on the subject that ultimately led to the passage of the Children's Online Privacy Protection Act (COPPA), which took effect in April 2000.

The act requires commercial websites directed at children to obtain parental consent for collection of personal data from any child under the age of 13 and prohibits disclosure of that information to other commercial entities. It also stipulates that there can be limited collection of personal data during participation in online contests and games, as well as from home pages, pen pal services, email services, message boards, and chat rooms. These are all sticky marketing tactics.

—*Lara Zwarun*

See also Branding; Children's Online Privacy Protection Act of 1998 (COPPA); Internet Bulletin Boards

FURTHER READINGS

The Children's Online Privacy Protection Rule. 64 Fed. Reg. 312 (November 3, 1999). Retrieved from http://www.ftc.gov/ogc/coppa1.htm

Electronic Privacy Information Center. (2000). The Child Online Privacy Protection Act, 15 U.S.C. §§6501-6506, P.L. No. 105-277, 112 Stat. 2681-728. Retrieved from http://www.epic.org/privacy/kids

Shukla, A. (2000. March 1). *Sticking to basics: Business 2.0.* Retrieved November 1, 2005, from http://www.business2.com/b2/web/articles/0,17863,527710,00.html

SUBSTANCE USE

See DRUG USE, DEPICTIONS OF

SUPER-PEER THEORY

There are a number of theories regarding exactly *how* the media have an impact on children and teenagers. One of the more cogent and recent ones is the super-peer theory, which applies particularly to adolescents. Although the influence of *peers* on adolescents has been accepted for many decades, the influence of the *media* on adolescents remains controversial. Many studies have documented the importance of peers in determining the initiation of such behaviors as cigarette smoking, drug use, and sexual intercourse. But one question has traditionally remained unanswered: Where do the peers get their notions that smoking cigarettes or drinking beer or having sex will make them "cool"? The super-peer theory hypothesizes that the media can exert influence in the same way as teens' peers do, but in an even more powerful way, hence the "super" peer.

When sex, drug use, and violence are so prevalent on the TV and movie screens, it makes teenagers think that everyone but them is having sex, drinking alcohol, smoking marijuana, or getting into fights. Teenage sitcoms routinely show young people obsessed with sex. Movies are more explicit in showing not only sexual activity but teens drinking, smoking, and even committing violence. So, for example, one survey of teenagers found that they felt that TV encouraged them to have sex. Other studies have found that teenagers routinely overestimate the number of their peers who are having sex, probably, in part, because of media influence. In another study, pregnant teens were twice as likely as nonpregnant teens to think that TV relationships are real and that TV characters would not use birth control.

When considering high-risk adolescent behavior (sex, drugs, violence, suicide), the concept of *normative behavior* is extremely important. Teens want to blend in with each other, and so they seek to do whatever is considered the norm. If they think that all of their friends are sexually active, or smoking marijuana, or drinking alcohol, they are more likely to try it themselves. The media present teens with innumerable "friends" and attractive adult role models who are engaging in high-risk behaviors. For example, the average teen views nearly 15,000 sexual references on TV each year, yet less than 170 deal with responsible sexuality. The increasing number of ads for Viagra, Cialis, and Levitra makes it seem that adults are thinking about sex all of the time, so why shouldn't teenagers? The 2,000 beer and wine ads that the average teen sees annually make drinking alcohol appear normal and macho. And, of course, the prevalence and acceptability of media violence make aggressive behavior seem like a common solution to everyday problems. As a result, teens are led into thinking the media world is the "real world," and they should behave accordingly.

—*Victor C. Strasburger*

See also Media Effects

FURTHER READINGS

Brown, J. D., Halpern, C. T., & L'Engle, K. L. (2005). Mass media as a sexual super peer for early maturing girls. *Journal of Adolescent Health, 36*(5), 420–427.

Strasburger, V. C. (2004). Children, adolescents, and the media. *Current Problems in Pediatric and Adolescent Health Care, 34*(2), 51–113.

Strasburger, V. C. (in press). Why teenagers do the things they do: The powerful influence of the media. *Primary Care Clinics.*

SURGEON GENERAL'S SCIENTIFIC ADVISORY COMMITTEE ON TELEVISION AND SOCIAL BEHAVIOR

With a $1 million budget, the Surgeon General's Scientific Advisory Committee on Television and Social Behavior was born in 1969 and operated out of the National Institute of Mental Health.

Consisting of 12 social scientists appointed by then-Surgeon General William Stewart, the committee was charged with determining the impact of television violence on young people. Completed in January 1972, the committee's five-volume technical report consists of 40 scientific papers and fills more than 2,300 pages.

Media content and control. Volume 1 examines television content, content creation, and media usage patterns. Most of this volume's reports scrutinize and discuss how television violence portrayals have changed over time; the volume also contrasts portrayals in the United States with television programming in Great Britain, Sweden, and Israel. Between 1967 and 1969, 8 of 10 prime-time entertainment programs contained violence, at a rate of about 8 incidents per hour. Nearly 96% of the cartoons contained violence, and the rate of those violent acts was much higher than the rate observed in prime-time programming.

Television and social learning. Volume 2 focuses on how preadolescent children learn from television; it was based on Albert Bandura's (1965) work on observational learning. The findings support the notion that children can and do learn aggressive behavior from television. Whether these findings can be generalized beyond the laboratory was beyond the scope of the investigations, and that was the primary criticism levied by the industry against these highly regarded studies.

Television and adolescent aggressiveness. Volume 3 answers questions about the aggressive behavior of adolescents and their media usage. Positive and significant correlations between preference for violent programming and aggressive behavior, as well as time spent viewing violent programming and aggressive behavior, were observed. Although the correlations were low to moderate—accounting for only about 10% of the variance—the relationships remained even after controlling for factors such as socioeconomic status and performance at school. Although TV violence alone cannot account for aggressive behavior in adolescents, the notion that adolescent aggressiveness and viewing TV violence are related was supported.

Television in day-to-day life. Volume 4 focuses on family viewing patterns, program preferences, and the amount of time audiences spent with television during the 1970s. This volume also examines the uses people have for television as well as a variety of demographic variables including age, socioeconomic status, and race. Comparisons of the time spent with TV and other leisure on a daily basis, as well as audience attitudes toward programming and commercials, were also included in this volume.

Television effects: Further explorations. Perhaps the most discussed portion of this section of the report is the discussion of Feshbach and Singer's (1971) work on TV violence and catharsis. Although this theory is not widely believed today, catharsis suggests that audience members can vent their aggressive feelings through the release they experience while watching violence on television. This is a classic example of the value of critique and the public nature of scholarship.

A sixth volume titled "Summary and Conclusions" was also produced by the advisory committee. Unfortunately, the conclusions reported in the summary were not based on the technical report, and some of the researchers complained their results were not presented fairly or accurately. These alleged misrepresentations were problematic because the summary was available before the technical report and because several eminent scholars, including Albert Bandura and Leonard Berkowitz, had been excluded from the advisory committee.

The technical report concludes that children's programming is more violent than prime-time programming and that children spend a great deal of time watching television. The research examined the impact of variables that might affect the relationship between

exposure to violence and aggressiveness; in most cases, these variables did not eliminate the small to moderate relationship observed between violent programming and aggressive actions. Finally, the preponderance of evidence presented supports the position that viewing violence increases the likelihood of aggressive behavior. Children can and do imitate the aggressive behavior viewed on TV and can become disinhibited or desensitized to violence.

*—James D. Robinson, Kimberly Bell, and
Jeanine W. Turner*

See also Aggression, Television and; Family Environment, Media Effects on; Media Effects; Television, Child Variables and Use of; Television, Motivations for Viewing of; Television, Viewer Age and; Television Violence; Television Violence, Susceptibility to

FURTHER READINGS

Bandura, A. (1965). Influence of models' reinforcement contingencies on the acquisition of imitative responses. *Journal of Personality and Social Psychology 1,* 589–595.

Boffey, P. M., & Walsh, J. (1970, May 22). Study of TV violence: Seven top researchers blackballed from panel. *Science, 68,* 949–952.

Bogart, L. (1972). Warning, the Surgeon General has determined that TV violence is moderately dangerous to your child's mental health. *Public Opinion Quarterly, 36,* 491–521.

Feshbach, S., & Singer, R. D. (1971). *Television and aggression: An experimental field study.* San Francisco: Jossey-Bass.

T

TALK SHOWS, CHILDREN AND ADOLESCENTS

As young people construct their identity, they are faced with specific developmental tasks that require a high degree of competence in daily life. In this process of development, they draw on resources in their media environment. In constructing their self-concept, young people take into account reality as they perceive it. Media such as talk shows provide important symbolic material that young people can use in the process of developing a personal and social identity.

Numerous convincing studies suggest that although the talk show is not the favorite genre of adolescents (those older than age 12), it nevertheless is of some importance in shaping their view of reality. For example, Davis and Mares (1998) investigated the influence of viewing talk shows on adolescents' perception of social reality through a survey of 282 U.S. high school pupils between the ages of 13 and 18 years. The questionnaire included the subjects' self-assessment concerning the frequency of certain behavior patterns shown in talk shows and individual judgments on certain social behavior patterns. Issues raised included running away from home, illegal weapons in schools, teenage pregnancy, adolescent sex, and adultery. Participants who said they viewed many talk shows often overestimated the frequency of deviant behaviors (regularly shown on the talk shows) in daily life, as researchers had predicted. However, two further hypotheses could not be verified. Frequent viewers of talk shows were no more likely than infrequent viewers to trivialize social issues related to

these behaviors, and frequent viewers did not appear indifferent or insensitive to people experiencing problems in these areas.

This kind of empirical evidence is supported by studies conducted in Germany. In 1997, Bente and Fromm found programs that involve emotional TV viewing—the genre to which daily talk shows belong—share characteristics such as personification, authenticity of the show, intimacy, and emotionalization. These aspects are crucial in the development of a young person's identity. The question that arises, therefore, is how influential these shows are. In a large-scale study conducted in Germany, Paus-Haase et al. (1999) examined the extent to which watching daily talk shows affected the perception of reality and the understanding of what it means to be a person among adolescents (between 12 and 17) who are more frequent viewers. This study was designed as a multistage inquiry including (a) a product- and perception-related quantitative analysis consisting of representative interviews with 657 adolescents concerning their viewing of talk shows, their reasons for watching them, and their perception of the topics and presenters as well as various aspects of how they perceive reality; and (b) qualitative analyses that involved group discussion with a total of 120 subjects and individual interviews with 53 participants who declared themselves either fans of a talk show or occasional viewers.

Although daily talk shows do not explicitly address adolescents, numerous young viewers show considerable interest in them, this study found. In part, this is because of their special design, which uses various modes of production to convey authenticity, tackle serious everyday life issues, and portray intense arguments. Some of these shows reached regular shares of up to 30% in the market segment of 12-to-17-year-old viewers. Young people choose what talk shows to watch on the basis of the issues that interest them. Surprisingly, topics that are considered to raise the ratings of shows, such as sex or crime, prove to be less popular among adolescents. They seem to be most interested in topics that are discussed relatively seldom, such as music and what it is like to be a young person. Topics dealing with body care, beauty, and fashion are significantly more popular with girls than boys. Girls seem to display a stronger interest in most other categories as well, with the exceptions of society or politics and male topics such as professional sports. The ways in which young people approach these issues differ greatly depending on gender, education, and several other factors, such as family structure and the number and quality of peer group relations. These various approaches are dependent on two major functions a talk show may have for young people: providing guidelines for everyday life management, and providing entertainment and amusement. However, some adolescents disapprove of talk shows in general, and 25% of young people between 12 and 17 say that they do not watch talk shows at all.

Based on the empirical findings of the qualitative studies described above, central interpretative dimensions can be identified, involving four basic patterns of reception. Each of these patterns is located on a continuum between two contradictory poles and is expressed in different degrees: naïve versus reflected reception, involved versus distanced reception, search for entertainment versus search for orientation, and positive assessment versus negative assessment of the shows.

Against the background of these four dimensions, six reception patterns were found. The first pattern can be described as *oppositional reading* and refers to an attempt to satisfy a desire for entertainment; this pattern is exclusively encountered in young men with more formal education and exceptional talents, who behave in a relatively grown-up manner and refuse a naïve or involved reception based on their ability to reflect and their strong concept of masculinity.

The second pattern is a critical and competent *search for orientation and self-awareness*; this pattern is found with boys and girls between the ages of 12 and 15 years who attend secondary school (gymnasium in Germany) and show a high degree of competence in dealing with media. Based on their age, they demand an orientation for upcoming developmental tasks. They

are, however, able to distance themselves from reality constructions in talk shows; this occurs due to their reflexive reception (ability to distance themselves) even though they are involved in the program. In addition, they appear to be firmly rooted in their families, peer groups, and school and personal friendships.

The third reception pattern is again a *search for orientation and self-awareness*, this time, however, in the form of naïve reception by girls faced with a variety of problems. This form of reception refers only to girls between the ages of 15 and 17 who are faced with problems in the family and watch talks shows rather naïvely. The educational background of these respondents is not meeting their challenges. Most of these girls had been socialized in the former German Democratic Republic (GDR) and had problems coming to terms with the structural changes that have taken place in the decade after German unification. They tend to live in problematic family circumstances, and their options as to what to do with their leisure time are severely limited. The uncertainty that characterizes their lives places additional pressure on girls during prepuberty and puberty, a time when they strive to build their self-confidence and play an active role in family discussions as well as in school and in peer groups. Against this background, girls use talk shows as advisers in concrete problem situations—usually in connection with their family—and as orientation aids in difficult personal situations (drugs, criminality, sexuality, first love, beauty, and body image).

The fourth pattern is the *naïve-idealizing reception* by younger girls who are faced with problems. Daily talk shows function as an alternative concept to their daily environment, as a fairy tale in a complex reality. These girls watch the shows in an exceptionally naïve and idealizing manner; of those young people presented in this study, they appear to be most likely to be influenced by talk show contents. Their constructions of reality as well as their values are strongly influenced by the topics, guests, and presenters of daily talks. The girls with this reception pattern were, with one exception, 12 years old and residents of the former GDR; thus, they are faced with problems similar to those described in the third pattern, particularly with regard to their families. Furthermore, due to their young age, they encounter daily talk shows with additional naiveté, and they are faced with developmental tasks of early puberty in which they need the loving support of their parents. They view talk show presenters as saviors or knights in shining armor.

The fifth pattern refers to recipients who drift between the two opposite ways of approaching daily talk shows—amusement and orientation. Young people in this category are characterized by a high ambivalence in dealing with such programs; they are young men (15 to 17 years of age) who drift between a naïve and reflected as well as between an involved and distanced reception. On the one hand, as is typical for their gender, they want to amuse themselves with daily talk shows. On the other hand, however, they look for orientation in a focused manner. These boys are lacking stability and orientation in the most important developmental phase, puberty. Their fluctuating pattern of reception reflects internal tensions in connection with their environmental conditions.

The sixth and final pattern, displayed by boys and girls of different ages, involves an alternation between the poles of involvement and distanced reception, between male and female ways of dealing with daily talk shows. These youngsters also oscillate between a rather masculine and feminine self-representation in their actions and attitudes. Boys, in particular, encounter a lack of understanding in their peer groups; in those groups, they have to be cool, and it is considered unmanly to watch daily talk shows for orientation. Based on their ambivalent self-constructions of gender, these young people look for examples and topics in daily talk shows that enable them to perceive themselves as rather masculine at one time and rather feminine at another.

Theunert and Schorb (2000) investigated daily talk shows within the context of demographically relevant information in Germany. According to this survey, 18% of 210 subjects between 12 and 17 years old reported that they get information from talk shows. Another survey method—a dialogue based on these results—involved 10 adolescents who discussed these issues in a 2-day seminar with representatives from politics and television people from the field of information programming. According to main findings of this survey, young females seem to believe that talk shows give them important information. One out of three girls thinks that the information she gets from talk shows is relevant to daily life and helps her deal with problems. In comparison to adolescents from Western Germany, adolescents from former Eastern Germany are represented significantly more, with 38%.

—Ingrid Paus-Hasebrink

See also Adolescents, Developmental Needs of, and Media; Developmental Differences, Media and; Family Environment, Media Effects on; Gender Identity Development; Research Methods, Questionnaires and Surveys

FURTHER READINGS

Bente, G., & Fromm, B. (1997). *Affektfernsehen. Motive, Angebotsweisen und Wirkungen* [Affect-oriented television: Motives, presentation modes, and effects]. Opladen, Germany: Leske & Budrich.
Davis, S., & Mares, M.-L. (1998). Effects of talk show viewing on adolescents. *Journal of Communication, 48*(3), 69–86.
Havighurst, R. J (1972): *Developmental tasks and education*. New York: McKay.
Paus-Haase, I., Hasebrink, U., Mattusch, U., Keuneke, S., & Krotz, F. (1999). *Talkshows im Alltag von Jugendlichen. Der tägliche Balanceakt zwischen Orientierung, Amüsement und Ablehnung* [Talk shows in the everyday life of adolescents: The precarious balance between orientation, amusement, and rejection]. Opladen, Germany: Leske & Budrich.
Theunert, H., & Schorb, B. (2000). Nicht desinteressiert, aber eigene Interessen. Jugend, Politik, Fernsehinformation [Not without interest, but with specific interest. Adolescents, politics, TV-information]. *Medien und Erziehung, 44*(4), 219–228.

TEENAGER, HISTORY OF

Used to denote young people between 13 and 19 years old, the concept of "the teenager" developed in the United States during the 1940s. Since the 1600s, it had been common to refer to youths as being in their "teens," but it was only during the mid-20th century that the term *teenager* entered the popular vocabulary. The American advertising and marketing industries were crucial in popularizing the concept. U.S. marketers used the *teenager* to denote what they saw as a new market of young, affluent, and leisure-oriented consumers, a market created by the economic boom that followed World War II.

THE RISE OF YOUNG PEOPLE'S SPENDING POWER

A distinctive commercial youth market first emerged during the 19th century. During the Victorian era, a gradual increase in young workers' leisure time and disposable income laid the basis for an embryonic youth market, with cities in America and Europe seeing the development of mass-produced goods, entertainments, and fashions targeted at the young.

The youth market expanded further during the 1920s and 1930s. In Britain, despite a general economic downturn, young workers' disposable income gradually rose, and they were courted by a growing range of commercial interests, including dance halls and magazine publishers. In the United States, the economic boom of the 1920s also ensured a budding youth market. The expansion of American colleges and universities allowed for the development of a recognizable campus culture among young, relatively well-to-do students who represented an attractive market for a variety of entertainment and consumer industries, including dance halls, clothing stores, cinemas, and cafeterias.

The American youth market was hard-hit by the economic depression of the 1930s. During the 1940s, however, young people's incomes were revitalized by the labor demands of the wartime economy. According to some estimates, American youth accounted for a collective spending power of about $750 million per year by 1944. This level of disposable income helped crystallize notions of teenagers as a uniquely autonomous social group and also provided the basis for a further expansion of the commercial youth industries and their associated media.

THE DEVELOPMENT OF THE TEENAGE MARKET

During the 1950s, the scope and scale of the U.S. youth market underwent significant growth. This was partly a result of demographic trends. A wartime increase in births and a postwar baby boom saw the American teen population grow from 10 to 15 million during the 1950s, eventually hitting a peak of 20 million by 1970. A postwar expansion of education, meanwhile, further accentuated notions of youth as a distinct social group, with the proportion of U.S. teenagers attending high school rising from 60% in the 1930s to virtually 100% during the 1960s. The vital stimulus behind the growth of the teenage market, however, was economic. Peacetime saw a decline in full-time youth employment, but a rise in youth spending was sustained by a combination of part-time work and parental allowances, with some estimates suggesting that teenage Americans' average weekly income rose from just over $2 in 1944 to around $10 by 1958.

A huge range of media and products were geared to the 1950s teenager, with consumer industries interacting with and reinforcing one another as they courted young consumers. Exemplifying the growth of the teen market was the rise of rock and roll, a genre of popular music tied much more closely than its predecessors to processes of mass marketing, media dissemination, and youth demand. The success of *Seventeen* magazine also testified to the growth of the American teen market. Conceived as a magazine for college girls, *Seventeen* was launched in 1944, and by 1949, its monthly circulation had soared to 2.5 million. Marketers such as Eugene Gilbert also helped promote the commercial potential of young people's spending power. Gilbert launched his career as a specialist in youth marketing in 1945, and by 1947, his market research firm, Youth Marketing Co., was flourishing. Gilbert was acknowledged as an authority on the teenage market, and during the 1950s, his book, *Advertising and Marketing to Young People* (1957), became a manual for teen merchandising.

THE DISSEMINATION OF TEENAGE LIFESTYLES

The growth of the mass media was a crucial factor in the dissemination of the concept of the teenager. The proliferation of teen magazines, films, and TV shows such as *American Bandstand* (syndicated on the ABC network from 1957) ensured that teen-oriented styles and music spread quickly throughout the United States. The global circulation of U.S. media also allowed the fashions and entertainment of teenage America to spread worldwide.

As in the United States, demographic shifts underpinned the growth of the European teen market. In Britain, for example, a postwar baby boom saw the number of people under 20 years old grow from 3 million in 1951 to more than 4 million by 1966. As in America, economic trends were also important. In Britain, for instance, buoyant levels of youth employment enhanced youth's disposable income and ensured a ready market for teen-oriented films, music, and fashions. European youth styles also fed back into the development of American teenage culture. During the mid-1960s, for example, the United States was captivated by a British pop music "invasion" spearheaded by the Beatles and the Rolling Stones.

THE TEENAGER IN THE 21st CENTURY

During the 1980s and 1990s a rise in youth unemployment, coupled with the declining size of the Western youth population, threatened to reduce levels of teen spending. By the beginning of the 21st century, however, demographic shifts and economic trends indicated that youth would continue to be a lucrative commercial market. Despite a long-term decline in Western birthrates, the youth population was set to increase during the new millennium as the echo of the baby boom worked its way through the demographic profiles of America and Europe. On both sides of the Atlantic, moreover, market research indicated that teenagers' spending power was still growing.

Teenage tastes also increasingly appealed to other age groups. For example, manufacturers, retailers, and advertisers increasingly targeted teenage fashions at pretecns (especially girls), who were encouraged to buy products ostensibly geared to older consumers. Teenage lifestyles also crept up the age scale. By the end of the 1990s, many consumers in their 20s and even 40s or older were favoring tastes and lifestyles associated with youth culture. The teenage market, therefore, was no longer the preserve of adolescents but had won a much broader cultural appeal.

—*Bill Osgerby*

See also Adolescents, Media Portrayals of; Advertising, Market Size and; Advertising, Materialism and; Branding; Childhood, Media Portrayals of; Consumerism; Globalization, Media and; Magazines, Adolescent Boys'; Magazines, Adolescent Girls'; Youth Culture

FURTHER READINGS

Abrams, M. (1959). *The teenage consumer.* London: Press Exchange.

Austin, J., & Willard, M. (Eds.). (1998). *Generations of youth: Youth cultures and history in twentieth-century America.* New York: New York University Press.

Fass, P. (1978). *The damned and the beautiful: American youth in the 1920s.* Oxford, UK: Oxford University Press.

Fowler, D. (1995). *The first teenagers: The lifestyle of young wage-earners in interwar Britain.* London: Woburn.

Gilbert, E. (1957). *Advertising and marketing to young people.* New York: Printer's Ink.

Hollander, S. C., & Germain, R. (1993). *Was there a Pepsi generation before Pepsi discovered it? Youth-based segmentation in marketing.* Chicago: American Marketing Association.

Osgerby, B. (1998). *Youth in Britain since 1945.* Oxford, UK: Blackwell.

Osgerby, B. (2004). *Youth media.* London: Routledge.

Palladino, G. (1996). *Teenagers: An American history.* New York: Basic Books.

Rollin, L. (1999). *Twentieth century teen culture by the decades: A reference guide.* Westport, CT: Greenwood Press.

TELECOMMUNICATIONS ACT OF 1996

The Telecommunications Act of 1996 was widely hailed as the most comprehensive piece of telecommunications legislation in 60 years. The law was the most comprehensive and substantial piece of legislation involving the communications industry since the Communications Act of 1934, which created the Federal Communications Commission. Recognizing the quickly changing nature of communications technology and the vast potential of digital technologies, Congress sought to restructure much of the law governing the telecommunications industry. The act affected the telecommunications industry along a number of fronts, including content, competition, and ownership. Although the law had an immediate effect on the industry, most notably in terms of radio station ownership, parts of the act have yet to come to full fruition.

INDUSTRY DEREGULATION

One stated purpose of the act was to reduce or remove barriers among the various parts of the telecommunications industry to increase competition in the marketplace, ultimately for the benefit of the consumer. For example, the act attempted to increase competition in the delivery of cable television content by repealing legislation preventing telephone operators from delivering video content into customer homes. Likewise, the act also repealed legislation preventing cable operators from delivering phone service into homes. Nonetheless, critics have proclaimed that despite these opportunities, industry economics and infrastructure continue to prohibit direct head-to-head competition in most local markets.

The most immediate effects of the Telecommunications Act of 1996 were felt in the area of station ownership, as the act relaxed long-established ownership caps, both for television and radio stations. With respect to television, the act allowed individual groups to own stations reaching up to 35% of the U.S. population, up from 25%. Moreover, the law also eliminated a 12-station cap on the number of television stations one group could own. The act also eliminated national radio station ownership caps and relaxed local radio ownership caps. This deregulation led to a wave of acquisitions and mergers within the broadcast industry, as group owners quickly began to purchase stations across the country. Critics argue that the effects of this corporate consolidation are a lack of diversity on the airwaves and the loss of local input regarding station programming. Despite the act's favorable attitude toward deregulation, the FCC has continued to closely examine broadcasters' efforts to provide programming for children. The FCC drew criticism in 2005 from the broadcast industry for carrying children's programming requirements to digital television.

TELEVISION RATINGS AND THE V-CHIP

Congress also used the Telecommunications Act to respond to growing concern over potentially objectionable television content. To allow parents increased control over the types of television content their children could view, the law mandated that all television sets sold in the United States be equipped with *V-chips*, devices that could block programming based on an electronic ratings system. Moreover, the act also ordered broadcasters to develop a ratings system to work in conjunction with the V-chip. The development of a television ratings system was the subject of some debate, and the initial ratings system offered by broadcasters to satisfy the requirements of the act was eventually modified. Critics took issue with the original age-based television ratings system, which suggested that programs were suitable for children of certain ages. Numerous parent and activist groups argued that such ratings gave parents little information regarding the nature of television content; the result of their complaints was the inclusion of content labels to denote the presence of sex, violence, objectionable language, and so on. This modified television ratings system is in use today by most television networks. Despite the presence of television ratings, the V-chip has yet to enjoy widespread use among parents. Research has suggested that the vast majority of parents do not actively use the V-chip to prevent their children from being exposed to objectionable content.

This failure is largely attributed to lack of familiarity with the ratings themselves and difficulty understanding how to activate the V-chip technology.

—*R. Glenn Cummins*

See also Children's Television Act of 1990; Motion Picture Association of America (MPAA); Movies, Rating Systems and; Rating Systems, Parental Use of; Regulation (various entries); Television Rating Systems, Parental Uses of; V-Chip (Violence Chip)

FURTHER READINGS

Aufderheide, P. A. (1999). *Communications policy and the public interest: The Telecommunications Act of 1996.* New York: Guilford.

Price, M. E. (Ed.). (1998). *The V-chip debate: Content filtering from television to the Internet.* Mahwah, NJ: Erlbaum.

TELEVISION, ADDICTION TO

People throughout the industrialized world typically devote about 3 hours a day to watching television. In many societies, this easily constitutes half of all a person's leisure time or, calculated another way, 9 full years of a 75-year life span. Nine years is even more remarkable if we consider that we sleep roughly one third of the life span and are therefore only left with 50 waking years not watching TV.

The term *addiction* has been extended to a whole host of nondrug behaviors, from gambling and sexuality to video gaming, television viewing, and Internet use. Some experts define addiction as biological dependence on a substance. If the addicted person no longer ingests the substance, he or she may experience unpleasant and often disorienting biological withdrawal symptoms. In this sense, applying the term *addiction* term to the use of electronic media or even gambling and sexual activity may be both wrong and misleading.

Others would argue that because all pleasurable experiences have a biological component, the traditional notions of biological addiction could still apply to sex, gambling, television viewing, or Internet use—even though with no substance involved—if a person becomes extremely dependent on that form of pleasure and feels horrible if no longer engaged in the behavior. This entry, however, focuses on television addiction as a dependence on television that is not defined in part as biological dependence.

Even apart from biological factors, however, television viewing can be self-perpetuating and can produce psychological dependency that is of considerable significance. Furthermore, heavy and prolonged viewing go hand in hand with television dependence, and a considerable range of effects, from obesity to foreshortened attention span, have been hypothesized or shown to result from heavy and prolonged viewing. Thus, understanding how television dependence develops and is reinforced is of real import.

Most people believe television viewing can be addictive. North American surveys have found that roughly 10% of adults believe that *they* are addicted, but 65% to 70% report believing that *others* are addicted. And many millions experience misgivings about how much they view. In a 1990 Gallup poll, 42% of adult Americans reported believing that they spent "too much time watching television."

Part of what holds people's attention to television is the "orienting response." First described by Ivan Pavlov in 1927, the orienting response is an instinctive visual (or auditory) reaction to any sudden or novel stimulus in the environment. Byron Reeves of Stanford University and Esther Thorson at the University of Missouri and their colleagues first used the EEG in 1985 to test whether the simple formal features of television (cuts, edits, zooms, pans, sudden noises, and so on) might activate the orienting response, thereby causing attention to be drawn to the screen. Reeves and Thorson and their team concluded that the formal features of cuts, edits, and movement did indeed command involuntary responses, which may have developed as a result of the evolutionary importance of detecting movement. They noted that it is the form rather than the content of television that is unique.

Music videos and other forms of advertising that frequently use rapid intercutting are thus particularly apt to hold attention. The orienting response may best explain typical viewer reports such as, "If a television is on, I just can't keep my eyes off it," "I don't want to watch as much as I do but I can't help it. It makes me watch it," and "I feel hypnotized when I watch television."

Dependence on the medium appears to develop for many as a result of a need to escape negative feelings or to help fill time or an emotional vacuum. In repeated studies by Robert McIlwraith (1998) of the Department of Psychiatry at the University of Manitoba, the 10% of university students and adults who call themselves TV addicts on surveys are significantly more likely than the 90% of self-reported nonaddicted viewers to report using television to cope with negative moods such as loneliness, sadness, anxiety, and anger. McIlwraith also finds self-proclaimed addicted viewers to be significantly more neurotic and introverted. On a measure called the Short Imaginal Processes Inventory (SIPI), he finds the TV addicts to be more easily bored and distractible and to have poorer attentional control than the nonaddicted. The addicted also often report using TV to distract themselves from unpleasant thoughts and to fill time. A 1990 study by Robert Kubey and Mihaly Csikszentmihalyi compared light viewers (who watch less than 2 hours a day) and heavy viewers (more than 4 hours). Heavy viewers reported feeling significantly worse when alone and when in unstructured situations such as waiting in line or when "between" activities.

APPLICATION OF THE *DSM–IV* SUBSTANCE ABUSE CRITERIA

The official diagnostic manual used by psychotherapists throughout North America, the American Psychiatric Association's *Diagnostic and Statistical Manual of Mental Disorders,* Fourth Edition (*DSM–IV*; 1994), no longer uses the term *addiction.* Instead, the term used is *substance dependence.* Using the *DSM–IV* for the purpose of illustration, Kubey (1996) has suggested that if television were a substance (as it could be because light particles are taken into the body when people view), many people who watch television could be given a diagnosis of dependence. Indeed, Dr. Allen J. Frances, who oversaw the most recent revision of the manual, concluded, "Under the broader definition, many kinds of compulsive behavior could be considered addictive, including obsessive sex or compulsive television viewing" (Goleman, 1990, p. C8).

Kubey suggested that some people's behaviors with television parallel as many as five of the seven *DSM–IV* criteria used for diagnosing substance dependence (only three of these criteria must be applicable in the same 12-month period to make a diagnosis of dependence). As with substances, with regard to television viewing, (1) people do spend a great deal of time using it; (2) people use it more often than they intend; (3) people make repeated unsuccessful efforts to reduce use; (4) people withdraw from or give up important social, family, or occupational activities; (5) people report "withdrawal"-like symptoms of subjective discomfort when use stops.

HOW DEPENDENCE MAY DEVELOP

Within moments of sitting or lying down and pushing a TV set's power button, many viewers will report feeling more relaxed than they did before. Because relaxation occurs quickly, people readily learn to associate viewing with relaxation. The association is positively reinforced through simple operant conditioning because viewers remain relaxed throughout viewing, *and* it is negatively reinforced via the stress and dysphoric rumination that sometimes occur during idle time without TV or once the set is turned off.

The quick onset of relaxation is particularly telling when compared to that produced by certain drugs that are known to be habit forming or addictive. As Alvin Swonger and Larry Constantine (1976) have written, "The attribute of a drug that most contributes to its abuse liability is not its ability to produce tolerance or physical dependence but rather its ability to reinforce the drug-taking behaviors" (p. 235). This is why both the speed of a drug's effect and how quickly it leaves the body are often critical factors in whether or not dependence develops. And, of course, reinforcement need not be experienced at all consciously for it to occur or to be a powerful motivator of behavior.

Some tranquilizers that are fast-acting, for example, or whose "half-lives" are very short—half the drug leaves the body more rapidly compared to other drugs—are much more likely to cause dependence precisely because the user is more prone to become aware that the drug is working or that its effects are wearing off. When this happens, the tendency to turn to the drug again for relief will be that much greater.

Relative to other means available to bring about relaxation (and distraction), television is among the quickest and certainly among the cheapest. Unlike conversation or games, one does not need anyone else to watch TV, and viewing provides faster and cheaper relaxation than does the use of drugs or alcohol.

DO TELEVISION VIEWERS EXPERIENCE WITHDRAWAL?

If the television habit is so easy to develop and holds so many millions so readily, do people experience anything akin to withdrawal if they stop viewing? More than 40 years ago, Gary Steiner (1963) collected fascinating individual accounts following a household's loss of a television set due to malfunction—this was back in the days when many families still had only one set: "The family walked around like a chicken without a head." "It was terrible. We did nothing—my husband and I talked." "Screamed constantly. Children bothered me and my nerves were on edge. Tried to interest them in games, but impossible. TV is part of them."

In experiments where families have voluntarily stopped viewing, or been paid do so, typically for a week or a month, increased tension among family members has been described, and many families could not complete the agreed period of abstinence. Charles Winick's (1988) review of studies of families whose television sets were in repair led him to the following conclusion:

> The first three or four days for most persons were the worst, even in many homes where viewing was minimal and where there were other ongoing activities. In over half of all the households, during these first few days of loss, the regular routines were disrupted, family members had difficulties in dealing with the newly available time, anxiety and aggressions were expressed . . . People living alone tended to be bored and irritated . . . By the second week, a move toward adaptation to the situation was common. (pp. 221–222)

Is viewing addictive? If we only mean by the term that one can easily develop dependence on the activity, the answer would be yes. But to be more properly classified as a true dependence or addiction, some would argue that an activity must also be harmful, interfering with the quality of the rest of one's life. And so, on this score, the answer is "it depends." Most people can watch television without their viewing interfering with the rest of life. In its easy provision of relaxation and escape, in small doses, television can probably be beneficial. For lonely people without other resources, it may be a godsend. But when the viewing habit interferes with the ability to grow, to learn new things, to lead an active life, then viewing indeed becomes an obstacle in life and perhaps deserves the label of addiction. To be sure, with the incredible ubiquity of electronic media, self-control over media habits is more of a challenge today than it was even in the recent past.

STRATEGIES TO REDUCE VIEWING

There are ways that individuals or families can achieve better control of their viewing habits if that is their goal. These are also listed in Kubey and Csikszentmihalyi's article on so-called television addiction in *Scientific American* in February 2002.

Among the suggestions they (and others) have made are these: Raise awareness (keep a log of how much you or family members view), promote alternative activities (individuals or families can make a list of activities that might be done at home instead of viewing), exert will power (recognize that almost as soon as one turns the set off, it becomes much easier to attend to other activities), enforce limits (for oneself and especially for children), view selectively (use a TV guide to pick those programs, and *only* those programs, that one will watch that day), employ the VCR (don't let program schedules interfere with your schedule), make television less available or go "cold turkey" (some have substantially reduced their viewing by ending a cable subscription, reducing the number of TVs in the household, or moving a TV to a room where it is less comfortable to view).

—*Robert Kubey*

See also Television, Motivations for Viewing of; TV-Turnoff Week

FURTHER READINGS

American Psychiatric Association. (1994). *Diagnostic and statistical manual of mental disorders* (4th ed.). Washington, DC: American Psychiatric Association.

Goleman, D. (1990, October 16). How viewers grow addicted to television. *New York Times,* pp. C1, C8.

Kubey, R. (1996). Television dependence, diagnosis, and prevention: With commentary on video games, pornography, and media education. In T. MacBeth (Ed.), *Tuning in to young viewers: Social science perspectives on television.* Thousand Oaks, CA: Sage.

Kubey, R., & Csikszentmihalyi, M. (1990). *Television and the quality of life: How viewing shapes everyday experience.* Hillsdale, NJ: Erlbaum.

Kubey, R., & Csikzentmihalyi, M. (2002, February). Television addiction is no mere metaphor. *Scientific American, 286,* 74–80.

McIlwraith, R. (1998). "I'm addicted to television": The personality, imagination, and TV watching patterns of self-identified TV addicts. *Journal of Broadcasting and Electronic Media, 42,* 371–386.

Steiner, G. (1963). *The people look at television.* New York: Alfred A. Knopf.

Swonger, A. K., & Constantine, L. (1976). *Drugs and therapy: A psychotherapist's handbook of psychotropic drugs.* Boston: Little, Brown.

Winick, C. (1988). The functions of television: Life without the big box. In S. Oskamp (Ed.), *Television as a social issue.* Newbury Park, CA: Sage.

TELEVISION, ATTENTION AND

The mass media often depict children sitting zombie-like in front of the television, mesmerized by images and sounds. While early theorizing about children's attention to television conformed to this view, a large body of research suggests that infants and children play an active role in their consumption of television content. Younger children use formal features—such as sound effects and animation—as indicators of program comprehensibility. As children get older, they rely less on formal features and make decisions to pay attention largely on the basis of television content. Programming that is neither too challenging nor too simple for a child will garner the highest levels of attention.

REACTIVE AND ACTIVE THEORIES OF ATTENTION

Jerome Singer's reactive theory of attention proposes that children's attention to television is largely controlled by nonmeaningful, formal features of television programming, such as sound effects and camera movement. According to Singer, children's attention to television is passive and involuntary, and comprehension flows automatically from attention. In contrast to the reactive theory of attention, Daniel Anderson and colleagues contend that children's visual attention to television is primarily driven by comprehension; that is, children judge the comprehensibility of content and then decide whether or not to pay attention.

To test the active and reactive theories of attention, researchers conducted an experiment where one group of children watched an episode of *Sesame Street* with toys available, while a second group watched the show without toys. In comparison to children who watched with toys, children in the no-toys group spent close to twice the amount of time visually oriented to the screen. However, there were no differences between the groups in terms of comprehension, suggesting that increased visual attention to television does not automatically result in increased comprehension.

In another study designed to test the active theory of attention, the comprehensibility of *Sesame Street* segments was manipulated by (1) replacing the original dialogue with a Greek translation, (2) replacing the original dialogue with backward speech, and (3) randomly rearranging scenes. A fourth condition consisted of unedited (normal) segments. Children spent the most time visually oriented to the normal segments while the backward dialogue received the least amount of attention. The fact that children's attention to *Sesame Street* varied across conditions, even though the visual formal features were the same, suggests that comprehensibility is indeed a factor in guiding children's visual attention to television.

Subsequent research directly compared the extent to which formal features and comprehensibility guide children's attention to television. In one experiment, health-related television segments were manipulated to create two formats (child and adult) and three levels of comprehensibility or difficulty. The child format presented the health information using animation, children's voices, and upbeat music whereas the adult format presented the same information using live photography, adult male voices, and subtle background music. Difficulty was manipulated by changing the editing pace, the amount of repetition, and linguistic complexity. The child format elicited significantly greater attention among kindergartners than the adult format. Children's attention to television did not vary as a function of segment difficulty. These results suggest that formal features play a more important role in driving children's attention to television than comprehensibility; however, some researchers have argued that children use formal features to judge the comprehensibility of television content.

FEATURE-SIGNAL HYPOTHESIS

Although there is little, if any, direct research support for the reactive theory of attention, research does suggest that certain categories of formal features reliably elicit attention from children. Specifically, movement, women's and children's voices, sound effects, music, laughter, and applause are generally associated with increased attention to television, whereas men's voices, long zooms, and still pictures are associated with a reduction in attention. Daniel Anderson and Elizabeth Lorch (1983) interpreted these findings within the framework of the active theory of attention, arguing that children use formal features as indicators of comprehensibility. Children pay attention to formal features that signal content intended for children, in other words, content that they are likely to understand. In this view, attention to formal features is not simply the result of an orienting response to perceptually salient stimuli; formal features are meaningful in the sense

that they provide information about program comprehensibility. Other researchers, however, contend that while older children's attention to television may be guided by the information formal features provide, perceptual salience is an important predictor of young children's attention to television.

MODERATE-DISCREPANCY HYPOTHESIS

Most researchers agree that there is a curvilinear relationship between attention and content difficulty. This moderate-discrepancy hypothesis suggests that the relationship between attention and comprehensibility can be captured by an inverted-U-shape. Content that is either too difficult for children to understand or overly simple will receive minimal attention, while content that is moderately challenging will garner the most attention.

Recent research on children's attention to television, such as that by Patti Valkenburg and Marjolein Vroone, supports the moderate-discrepancy hypothesis. Television segments designed for adults (news and adult-targeted commercials) received significantly less attention than segments designed for children. In addition, the easiest child segment resulted in high levels of attention from the youngest children (6-to-18-month-olds) but relatively low levels of attention among older children (36-to-58-month-olds). In contrast, the most difficult child segment resulted in high levels of attention among older children but minimal attention from younger children. Valkenburg and Vroone's results also support developmental theories of attention to formal features. Scenes that resulted in the greatest attention among 6-to-18-month-olds contained a large number of salient formal features, such as applause, laughter, and strange sounds. In contrast, the 3- and 4-year-olds paid more attention to scenes with fewer salient formal features and appeared to direct their attention on the basis of television content. Valkenburg and Vroone also found support for Anderson and colleagues' hypothesis that children use formal features as indicators of comprehensibility. Across all age groups, even among infants, the initial scenes of adult-oriented content resulted in significant decreases in attention, whereas the initial scenes of child-oriented content led to dramatic increases in attention.

—Ariel R. Chernin and
Deborah L. Linebarger

See also Cognitive Development, Media and; Formal Features; Information Processing, Active vs. Passive Models of; Television, Viewer Age and

FURTHER READINGS

Alwitt, L. F., Anderson, D. R., Lorch, E. P., & Levin, S. R. (1980). Preschool children's visual attention to attributes of television. *Human Communication Research, 7,* 52–67.

Anderson, D. R., & Lorch, E. P. (1983). Looking at television: Action or reaction? In J. Bryant & D. R. Anderson (Eds.), *Children's understanding of television* (pp. 1–33). New York: Academic Press.

Anderson, D. R., Lorch, E. P., Field, D. E., & Sanders, J. (1981). The effects of TV program comprehensibility on preschool children's visual attention to television. *Child Development, 52,* 151–157.

Campbell, T. A., Wright, J. C., & Huston, A. C. (1987). Form cues and content difficulty as determinants of children's cognitive processing of televised educational messages. *Journal of Experimental Child Psychology, 43,* 311–327.

Huston, A. C., & Wright, J. C. (1983). Children's processing of television: The informative functions of formal features. In J. Bryant & D. R. Anderson (Eds.), *Children's understanding of television: Research on attention and comprehension* (pp. 35–67). New York: Academic Press.

Lorch, E. P., Anderson, D. R., & Levin, S. R. (1979). The relationship of visual attention to children's comprehension of television. *Child Development, 50,* 722–727.

Rice, M. L., Huston, A. C., & Wright, J. C. (1982). The forms and codes of television: Effects of children's attention, comprehension, and behavior. In D. Pearl, L. Bouthilet, & J. Lazar (Eds.), *Television and behavior: Ten years of scientific progress and implications for the eighties* (pp. 24–38). Washington, DC: U.S. Government Printing Office.

Singer, J. L. (1980). The power and limitations of television: A cognitive affective analysis. In P. H. Tannenbaum (Ed.), *The entertainment functions of television* (pp. 31–65). Hillsdale, NJ: Erlbaum.

Valkenburg, P. M., & Vroone, M. (2004). Developmental changes in infants' and toddlers' attention to television entertainment. *Communication Research, 31,* 288–311.

TELEVISION, CHILD VARIABLES AND USE OF

Television use can refer to the amount of television watching and the kinds of programs viewed; the reception of programs (interpreting, understanding, experiencing, interacting with them); the role of television in the individual's everyday life and lifestyle; and people getting access to the medium and taking part in TV production. This entry discusses the amount of television viewing by children and adolescents around the world. Variables that affect viewing include the degree of media access young viewers have; their age, gender, and socioeconomic background; parental influence; and the availability and scheduling of children's programming.

METHODOLOGY

Television use is often studied in quantitative surveys by means of measures such as reach (proportion of viewers of the whole population); viewing time (hours, minutes); share (of the total audience and of the total viewing time, respectively); and rating (defined as average reach) during a day or a week, during parts of the day, and for different programs and program categories. Although such figures appear exact, they vary greatly because of differences in data collection methods (diaries, questionnaires, face-to-face or telephone interviews, electronic people meters, etc.). The formulation of questions, the kind of sample (simple random sample, quota sample, etc., of individuals or households), and the number of nonresponses also play important roles. As a consequence, the resulting viewing figures are for the most part not statistically representative; that is, average figures represent the people in the specific survey, not the people in the selected population or the whole country. Comparisons between countries are therefore not reliable. Even figures generated by the same method, for example, the often-used people meter, are not internationally comparative but reflect more methodological than cultural differences. (In this case, quota samples are used, and in many nations, households in the countryside, with low socioeconomic status, and so on, are excluded.)

Moreover, television use is not regularly measured in most countries in the world, especially among children. For these reasons, the common question "How much do children use television (and other media) around the world?" cannot be answered with precision.

AMOUNT OF VIEWING

With the spread of satellite television since the end of the 1980s, there was more than a 100% increase in

TV access during just one decade. Although not all countries have a domestic broadcaster, all are now reached by one or more satellite channels. However, not all households in the world have a television set or can receive the channels. In large rural regions where there is no or little electricity, especially in low-income countries in Africa, Asia, and Latin America, battery-operated radio is the most used medium among both children and adults. Where television (or video) sets are few, viewing usually occurs outside the home (e.g., in cafés or village centers).

In richer countries, where the majority of children live in multimedia environments that often overflow with media devices, television is the most used medium by the average child. Despite conflicting reports, most show that with the infusion of more and more digital media, TV viewing has not decreased among children; rather, overall media use has increased as use of the Internet and video or computer games has been added.

At the same time, research indicates that the use of television (and other media) in countries with multimedia access is becoming increasingly differentiated. Although some children use media less than the average amount (despite access), other children are game or Internet enthusiasts, keen book readers, extreme television or video fans, and so on. However, in all these and still other media style groups, television is nevertheless on average the dominating medium. The absolute majority of children in these countries use television almost every day.

Children in richer countries are also increasingly using two or more media simultaneously (viewing, reading, listening to music, using the Internet, etc.). A U.S. study in 2003–2004 of 8-to-18-year-olds showed that simultaneous media use occurred for about a quarter of the time spent watching television. The same was true of the time spent on all media. This means that during the nearly 6 hours per day that this age group spent using all media, they were exposed to 8 hours of media messages.

VARIABLES AFFECTING TV VIEWING

The amount of television use depends on factors such as access to television; the child's age, gender, personality, needs, interests, and so on; the parents' sociocultural and socioeconomic position; parental viewing patterns; parental mediation of viewing; time in terms of weekdays versus weekends and seasons of

the year; time of day when different kinds of television programs are shown; and the cultural, religious, political, and economic context of TV viewing. Some of these aspects are briefly commented on below.

Access

More television sets and channels result in increased television viewing. Thus, within the same country, the average child with many available TV channels watches more than children with fewer available channels, and children in homes with several TV sets watch on average more than children with only one set at home. In 2004, about 90% of 9-to-14-year-olds in Sweden had access to more than one TV at home, and the majority of 8-to-18-year-olds in the United States in 2003–2004 had a TV set in their own bedroom, while less than half of younger children had a TV set in the bedroom. Television sets are common in North America, Australia, and New Zealand, most countries in Europe, richer Asian countries, richer Arab countries, and several Latin American countries. The majority of children in most African, many Asian, and certain Latin American countries do not have access to TV at home or elsewhere, although the differences between cities and rural areas in the same country are often great. Bearing in mind that less than 20% of the 2 billion children on the globe live in the richer countries while more than 80% live in the so-called developing countries, there are very good reasons to talk about a television divide beside the more common expressions of digital and information divides.

Age

The majority of children in countries where television is widespread watch television more or less every day from the age of 2 to 3 years old. A U.S. study from 2003 found that about two fifths of those under 2 watched TV every day. Viewing then increases with age—in some countries, up to the early teens, after which a slight decrease occurs (e.g., in Argentina, Chile, Israel, the Netherlands, South Korea), whereas in other countries, there is no such decrease (e.g., in Australia, Czech Republic, Denmark, France, Germany, Lebanon, Philippines, Spain, South Africa, Switzerland, and the United Kingdom). Some studies of TV use in the United States report a decrease among teens while others do not. Reported average daily viewing times in the countries mentioned here vary for younger children between about 1½ and about 3 hours and for school-age children (up to the early teens) between about 1½ and 3½ hours. Because of methodological biases such as those described above, the figures cannot indicate in which countries children watch most. Average figures also hide large individual variations—from very light to very heavy viewers.

Gender

In some countries where television is widespread, boys watch slightly more television than girls, but in other countries with much television, there are no such gender differences. Some studies also suggest that in countries such as India and Tunisia, where girls' activities outside the home are restricted, girls may be more likely than boys to use media at home and may watch television more often. Gender differences in TV use are more noticeable when it comes to kinds of programs watched.

Socioeconomic Background

In countries with few media, children of low-income parents often use television (and other media) less because they do not have access to TV sets. In countries with many media, children of low-income parents on average devote more time to television (and to video and video games) than children of high-income parents. Children of high-income parents use print media, computers, and the Internet more often than children of low-income parents.

Parental Influence

Parents' TV behavior serves as an example that influences their children's viewing to a great extent—both amount of TV viewing and preferences for different TV programs.

Research on the impact of parental rules on children's TV viewing are conflicting, and the older the child, the fewer the rules. Even if there are rules, they are not always followed. In many countries, such as in Egypt, middle-class parents do not have time to regulate their children's viewing, and working-class parents often have a more generous attitude to television. For instance, poor families in Buenos Aires watch a great deal of television without guilt because television plays a compensating role in the sense that TV viewing is one of their very few opportunities for entertainment.

However, children whose parents do impose rules spend less time watching television than do other children. *Active mediation* in terms of talking to children about television is also usually more successful than *restrictive mediation* (rules) and simple *coviewing* by parents in reducing children's television use and modifying its influences.

With more and more television sets in the home, children are less likely to be supervised, and parents' coviewing, rule setting, and active mediation diminish.

Programming

In countries that produce diverse high-quality children's programs that are shown at appropriate times, younger children most often watch these programs, and their viewing of adult programming is more a consequence of the child's wish to be with the family in front of the television. Children also often prefer locally produced children's programs to imported cartoons. However, even in countries with a rich supply of good children's programming, an interest in adult programs, mainly entertainment and fiction, appears when growing children begin to orient themselves more toward the peer group, often around the age of 7 to 9. Good programs directed specifically at the *tweens* (from 8 or 9 to 12 or 13 years old) also attract viewers in that age group.

However, a great many TV stations and channels around the world do not offer much in the way of children's programming, or if they do, it consists primarily of imported cartoons. Or, children's programs may be scheduled for times when few children have the opportunity to gather in front of the screen because they are in preschool or school (their programs are scheduled only at times not attractive for adults). As a consequence, the great majority of children with access to television all over the world watch adult programming from an early age, in the afternoon, evening, and often late at night. Boys are generally more interested in sports, "nasty" comedies, and action, whereas girls are more interested in relationship dramas (e.g., soap operas, so-called reality TV) and calmer amusement than boys are. Children watch the news and other informative programming to a much lesser degree.

—*Cecilia von Feilitzen*

See also Asia, Media Use in; China, Media Use in; Digital Divide; Europe, Media Use in; India, Media Use in; Japan, Media Use in; Latin America, Media Use in; Television, International Viewing Patterns and

FURTHER READINGS

Agrawal, B. C. (2000). Children's media use in India—A current scenario. *News from ICCVOS, 4*(1), 3–4.

Goonasekera, A., Huang, C., Eashwer, L., & Guntarto, B. (2000). *Growing up with TV: Asian children's experience*. Singapore: Asian Media Information and Communication Centre.

Lamb, R. (1997). *The bigger picture: Audio-visual survey and recommendations*. New York: United Nations Children's Fund.

Livingstone, S., & Bovill, M. (Eds.). (2001). *Children and their changing media environment: A European comparative study*. Mahwah, NJ: Erlbaum.

Morduchowicz, R. (2002). The meanings of television for underprivileged children in Argentina. In C. von Feilitzen & U. Carlsson (Eds.), *Children, young people and media globalisation* (pp. 135–148). Göteborg, Sweden: Göteborg University, Nordicom.

Nordicom-Sveriges Mediebarometer 2004 [The Media Barometer 2004]. (2005). Göteborg, Sweden: Göteborg University, Nordicom.

Rideout, V., Roberts, D. F., & Foehr, U. G. (2005). *Generation M: Media in the lives of 8-18 year-olds*. Menlo Park, CA: Kaiser Family Foundation.

Rideout, V. J., Vandewater, E. A., & Wartella, E. A. (2003). *Zero to six: Electronic media in the lives of infants, toddlers, and preschoolers*. Menlo Park, CA: Kaiser Family Foundation and Children's Digital Media Center.

von Feilitzen, C. (2001). Children's amount of TV viewing: Statistics from ten countries. In C. von Feilitzen & U. Carlsson (Eds.), *Children and media: Image, education, participation* (pp. 69–73). Göteborg, Sweden: Göteborg University, Nordicom.

von Feilitzen, C. (2004). *Mer tecknat . . . ? Animerade TV-program–marknad, utbud, barn, föräldrar* [More cartoons . . . ? Animated TV Programs—Market, output, children, parents]. Stockholm: Våldsskildringsrådet, nr 31 (in Swedish).

Walters, R., & Zwaga, W. (2001) *The younger audience: Children and broadcasting in New Zealand*. Wellington, New Zealand: Broadcasting Standards Authority & Palmerston North: Dunmor Press Ltd.

TELEVISION, HISTORY OF CHILDREN'S PROGRAMS ON

Concern about the quality of children's television has waxed and waned throughout television's history. When children's advocates (usually parents and educators, and occasionally lawmakers) are outspoken about the need for television that nurtures and educates young people, broadcasters create a wider array of programming for them. During periods when this issue goes unaddressed, it is usually accompanied by children's programming that is formulaic and static. Today, the Internet, TiVo, satellite, and various cable options are part of children's television experience. Even in this complex television environment, it is still possible to predict the general landscape of children's programming. A common thread in television's history is that when broadcasters treat children as a unique audience with specific needs and abilities, their programming is more diverse in content, format, and scheduling; when programming is produced for children without this consideration, their shows become increasingly uniform.

THE EARLY YEARS OF CHILDREN'S PROGRAMMING

When television was introduced to consumers, one method used by broadcasters to attract people to the new medium was to offer children's programming. During the first years of broadcast television, from 1948 to 1952, a relatively large percentage of television shows were specifically devoted to children and aired during periods when children were most likely to watch, on weekday evenings between 6 and 8 p.m.

As television sets proliferated in homes throughout the 1950s, the hours devoted to children's programming dropped, and its time slot changed from early evenings to Saturday mornings. This development may have resulted in part from economic changes. As television sets increasingly penetrated U.S. homes, broadcasters no longer felt the need to promote television sets to a wary public. Instead, they could attract money from advertising sponsors by competing for the millions of viewers who already had sets. During early evening prime-time hours, broadcasters hoped to maximize the number of viewers by replacing shows specifically for children with family programming designed to appeal to the entire household.

By the late 1950s and early 1960s, broadcasters established what became the standard format of a children's show: a 30-minute production appearing once a week, usually on Saturday mornings when adults were least likely to watch and when children were free to view with fewer time constraints.

During this period, the content of children's shows changed from live-action adventures to animated fare. This shift grew out of the newly developed, low-cost animation techniques of William Hanna and Joseph Barbera, the exhaustion of the archives of older live-action films that were broadcast as reruns, and the desire to provide content for the growing numbers of color televisions being sold at low cost.

DIVERSITY IN PROGRAMMING

Given the popularity of low-cost animation, combined with the Saturday morning time slot now staked out exclusively for children, it is not surprising that the 1960s were characterized by a decline in the diversity of formats, content, and scheduling of children's programming. Toward the end of the decade, the percentage of animated shows, shows airing once a week, and shows without child characters increased. There was also a trend toward fantasy and action-adventure themes with mostly male, often superhuman animated characters as the main protagonists.

By the end of the 1960s, the uniformity of children's programming, the advertisements that accompanied shows, and the prevalence of violent themes had provoked the consternation of policy-makers and concerned citizens. Organizations such as Action for Children's Television (ACT) sought to limit advertising and violence in children's programming, and in 1970, the group filed a petition with the Federal Communications Commission (FCC) to ban commercials from children's programs. ACT was able to obtain limited concessions in subsequent years, such as prohibition of advertising specific products and reducing the amount of time spent on commercials during children's shows.

The shift in attention toward children's television at the end of the 1960s and into the 1970s sparked a trend toward more diverse program formats and content, as well as increased funding for educational

programming with the establishment of the Corporation for Public Broadcasting and the Public Broadcasting Service. The percentage of other formats (live-action, puppetry, or some combination of the two) increased during this period, as did the presence of recurring child actors, the variety of content beyond action-adventure themes, and the number of shows airing at times other than Saturday morning. Memorable shows that began during this time include the *After School Specials* on ABC, *Sesame Street, The Electric Company,* and *Make a Wish.*

During the 1970s, a technique known as a video mosaic format became prevalent. It incorporated a number of segments into an extended program lasting for an hour or more. By placing short "information spots" between shows, broadcasters carried viewers from one show to the next. Examples of these short information spots included *Multiplication Rock, Schoolhouse Rock,* and *In the Know.* These spots were short and aired at irregular times, but they also allowed networks to diversify their fantasy-based, action-adventure format to some extent. Another device within this mosaic format involved human or animated hosts acting as bridges between shows. A station's Saturday morning children's lineup now came to resemble one long show.

THE IMPACT OF PUBLIC POLICY

Children's television programming was transformed again during the early 1980s, when renewed government preference for deregulation was accompanied by the dramatic growth of cable television and the increased number of VCRs in American homes. The diversity in formats and scheduling of children's programming increased somewhat with the growth of cable channels devoted primarily to children. However, while the number of shows increased, there was little change in content, with the majority still being animated action-adventure shows.

The 1980s trend toward deregulation allowed broadcasters to use children's shows essentially as a tool to sell merchandise. Immediately after a show such as *Teenage Mutant Ninja Turtles* or *Power Rangers* aired, a commercial featuring toys based on its characters could be inserted. In response to the increasing number of such programs, ACT and other advocacy groups continued to lobby lawmakers regarding the need for a system of oversight of children's television.

Although some children's shows created during the 1980s and 1990s deviated from the standard fare, such as *Ghostwriter, 3-2-1 Contact,* and *Blue's Clues,* the public outcry over children's exposure to television advertisements and violence reemerged. ACT and others called on policymakers to rein in broadcasters. In 1990, the Children's Television Act was passed, requiring stations to provide 3 hours of educational programming per week in order to have licenses renewed. In 1992, the networks announced they would limit gratuitous violence and include onscreen advisories prior to strong programming.

In 1996, lawmakers introduced a new version of the Telecommunications Act, requiring the installation of an electronic device (a V-chip) in televisions that allowed families to block violent shows. The legislation also called on networks to create a ratings system that would designate specific content depicting degrees of violence and other controversial content.

—*David Ian Cohen*

See also Action for Children's Television (ACT); Advertising on Children's Programs; Cartoons, History of; Children's Television Act of 1990; Children's Television Charter; Media Effects, History of Research on; Sesame Workshop; Telecommunications Act of 1996; Television Rating Systems, Parental Uses of; Television Violence, Susceptibility to

FURTHER READINGS

Fisch, S., & Truglio, R. (2001). *"G" is for growing: Thirty years of research on children and* Sesame Street. Mahwah, NJ: Erlbaum.

Ingliss, R. (2003). *The window in the corner: A half-century of children's television.* London: Peter Owen.

Palmer, E. (1987). U.S. children's television in crisis: Problems of tradition, vision, and value. In M. E. Manley-Casimir & C. Luke (Eds.), *Children and television: A challenge for education* (pp. 165–184). New York: Praeger.

Signorielli, N. (1991). *A sourcebook on children and television.* Westport, CT: Greenwood Press.

Turow, J. (1981). *Entertainment, education, and the hard sell: Three decades of network children's television.* New York: Praeger.

Woolery, G. (1983). *Children's television: The first thirty-five years.* Metuchen, NJ: Scarecrow.

TELEVISION, INTERNATIONAL VIEWING PATTERNS AND

Patterns of television viewing can be defined by the frequency and duration of use, by the distribution of viewing episodes over the day, by the number and types of channels watched, by the genres and programs preferred, and by the social situation in front of the screen. From an international comparative perspective, these characteristics are variable because of differences between television systems and between cultural and social patterns of television viewing. Currently, we cannot rely on systematic and comprehensive comparative research on these differences, in particular for children and adolescents. Therefore, this entry examines evidence from studies covering different regions of the world and addresses some differences in viewing patterns.

The most obvious and prominent indicator of television viewing is related to the time devoted to this medium. The international data on viewing time per individual, as compiled in the annual publication, *Television 2005: International Key Facts*, are marked by some methodological differences in how viewing behavior is measured. Although most of the industrialized countries use people meter systems for audience research, there are subtle differences in the definition of *viewing,* the populations studied, whether watching videos or recorded TV programs is included, and so on. In general, however, the daily viewing time for adults in most industrialized countries is more than 3½ hours (210 minutes). The United States has a particularly high viewing time (almost 300 minutes in 2004, see Table 1); in Europe, Italy and some Central and Eastern European countries show the highest figures. Remarkable exceptions are the Nordic countries (Denmark, Finland, Norway, and Sweden) as well as Austria and Switzerland; the average viewing time in these countries is below 3 hours per day.

Substantial differences can be observed regarding the viewing times of children. Here it is particularly important to note the different age groups defined as *children.* Within the selected group of industrialized countries shown in Table 1, the average viewing time of children varies between 221 minutes (Hungary) and 88 minutes per day (Sweden). A difference of more than 2 hours per day per child indicates a massive difference in the respective children's everyday lives and activities,

Table 1 Viewing Time per Individual in 2004 (in minutes per day)

	Adults		Children	
	Age group	Minutes per day	Age group	Minutes per day
Hungary	18+	268	4–14	221
Turkey	20+	233	5–11	211
United States	18+	297	2–11	196
Russia	18+	217	4–12	171
Italy	15+	245	4–14	163
Poland	16+	246	4–15	161
Spain	16+	221	4–12	151
United Kingdom	16+	228	4–15	144
Japan	20+	223	10–19	132
France	15+	212	4–10	129
Germany	14+	215	3–13	93
Sweden	15+	159	3–14	88

SOURCE: Selected data from IP (2005). *Television 2005. International Key Facts,* p. 34. Paris/Cologne: IP.

and this must be considered whenever we deal with international comparisons of children's and adolescents' lives. Why children in some countries spend much more time with television than their peers elsewhere is hard to answer. Some have suggested that part of the explanation lies in the difference between the rather visually oriented Catholic cultures compared to the rather verbally oriented Protestant cultures. Others have pointed to the contrast between heavily commercialized television systems and systems with a strong position of public service broadcasters. However, these arguments do not explain all the differences to be observed.

Differences with regard to viewing patterns also occur when people watch television. In almost all countries, television reaches its maximum audience in the evening. However, there are differences regarding the exact time. Whereas Belorussian or Macedonian television viewing reaches its peak at 8 p.m., the respective times in other countries are later: 8:30 p.m. in the Czech Republic and Slovakia; 8:45 p.m. in Finland, Hungary, Lithuania, and Switzerland; 9 p.m. in Austria, Germany, and Denmark; 9:15 p.m. in France, Italy, and the United Kingdom; 9:30 p.m. in Flanders, Japan, and Portugal; 9:45 p.m. in Turkey and the United States; 10 p.m. in the Netherlands; and finally 10:30 p.m. in Greece and Spain. These observations refer to intercultural differences in the organization of the day, which also influences the everyday

lives of children and when they watch television. Another difference between countries concerns whether watching television is mainly concentrated in the evening, as is the case, for example, in Nordic countries and Germany; or whether there is a second prime time around 1 p.m., as is the case in Italy and Spain; or whether there is yet another strong peak in the morning, for example, in Japan and Finland. Children's patterns of television viewing rely heavily on the institutional time schedules of their country, that is, when they return from school, when parents return from work, when families normally have their dinner, and so on.

Beyond these structural conditions, children's patterns of viewing behavior are also influenced by the number of channels available to them. In countries with a small number of broadcast channels and a low distribution of cable and satellite, few children's programs are shown on the general channels. Their television environment is very different from that of children in multichannel environments. For example, in the United States, Japan, and the United Kingdom, many children can select from several dedicated children's channels at any time of the day. This larger choice does not necessarily mean that children use a wide range of channels; rather, they develop a favorite repertoire of channels to which they devote most of their viewing time. Another consequence of multichannel environments is an increasing fragmentation of viewing behavior within families; because members of each age group have programs all day that are specifically targeted to them, they watch their own programs rather than viewing programs together.

Regarding children's preferences in television programs, there is a striking commonality across almost all countries: Children like cartoons. Because cartoons can be transferred to other cultures more easily than any other kind of television program, children's programming is a highly globalized market sector. Most children who watch television know some Walt Disney figures or, more recently, some figures from the Japanese anime productions (e.g., Pokémon). This does not mean that these global programs have the same meaning for children in different cultural settings. To the contrary, many studies have shown that children take these programs as symbolic material. Against the background of their social and cultural conditions, and given their current developmental tasks, they play with this material, construct their identity, and learn about options to cope with certain situations. The results of this process might differ substantially among children from different countries.

—*Uwe Hasebrink*

See also Europe, Media Use in; Television Rating Systems, Parental Uses of

FURTHER READINGS

Hasebrink, U., & Herzog, A. (2004). Mediennutzung im internationalen Vergleich [International comparisons of media use]. In Hans-Bredow-Institut (Ed.), *International handbuch medien* (pp. 136–158). Baden-Baden, Germany: Nomos.

IP International Marketing. (2005). *Television 2005. International key facts.* Paris/Cologne: Author.

Livingstone, S., & Bovill, M. (Eds.). (2001). *Children and their changing media environment: A European comparative study.* Mahwah, NJ: Erlbaum.

TELEVISION, MORAL MESSAGES ON

Television is a medium with great potential to influence the lives of children and adolescents. However, the bulk of prior research regarding the impact of television viewing on children and adolescents has focused on possible negative influences of television. For example, ample research suggests that watching violence on television contributes to aggressiveness in children and adolescents. Research has also reported links between television content and adolescents' sexual behaviors and attitudes. It seems that policymakers, educators, and the general public also tend to focus on the negative effects of television viewing. Yet, not all television content is negative; positive moral messages can be found in a significant amount of television content. Although research regarding moral messages on television is limited, it suggests that exposure to such messages tends to have a moderate effect on the attitudes and behaviors of children and adolescents. These associations, however, are often mediated by other factors such as characteristics of the child, the context in which the message occurs in the television program, and factors in the environment in which the child views the program.

CONTENT OF MORAL MESSAGES

There are differing opinions on what might be considered moral messages on television. Social scientists tend to divide morality into justice-based morality, with its focus on issues of fairness and equality, and prosocial morality or a morality of care, which emphasizes kindness and helping. Thus, ideas or behaviors presented on television that embody the values of justice or care might be considered moral messages. These messages might appear in the form of proscriptions or prohibitions. Proscriptions are "thou shalts," which encourage behaviors that should be engaged in (such as helping others), whereas prohibitions are "thou shalt nots," which discourage actions that should not be performed (such as causing harm to others).

Analyses of the content of television programming suggest that television might portray as many moral messages as it does immoral messages (i.e., messages that promote or condone things such as violence and dishonesty). Ironically, some programs intended to convey moral messages—cartoons, for example—also contain significant violent content. Programs targeted at preschoolers contain the highest proportion of moral messages, followed by those directed to children and adolescents, with adult programs having the lowest ratio of moral to immoral messages. In addition, programs broadcast earlier in the day tend to have a higher moral to immoral messages ratio than those later in the day. Thus, programs most noted for incorporating moral messages are early morning shows for preschoolers such as *Barney*, *Mister Rogers' Neighborhood*, and *Sesame Street*, which convey moral messages such as the importance of honesty, kindness, and fairness. Interestingly, some programs originally intended for adults that became popular with children (such as *The Cosby Show* and *7th Heaven*), also have a strong emphasis on moral messages.

EFFECTS OF MORAL MESSAGES

There are several possible mechanisms by which exposure to moral messages on television might positively impact children and adolescents. First, moral messages might be conveyed through modeling of moral behaviors. Psychologist Albert Bandura originally provided evidence of modeling by showing that when children see adults on television acting violently toward an inflatable doll, the children tend to act violently toward the same doll when given the opportunity. This mechanism of modeling may also facilitate the learning of moral behaviors. For example, children may learn the importance of sharing by observing people on a television program who are engaged in sharing. Research has found some support for this idea. For instance, in one experiment, a group of children was shown a prosocial program where a boy risked his life to save a puppy, while another group of children was instead shown a neutral program with no modeling of moral behavior. Then, both groups of children were asked to play a game in which they could earn points by repeatedly pushing a button; the more times they pushed the button, the more points they earned. However, they were also told to listen to puppies in a distant kennel and push a help button when the puppies seemed distressed. Children who had seen the prosocial program were more likely to push the button to help the puppies than children who watched the neutral program. In short, it seems that characters on television may teach moral messages by example.

Another possible mechanism is that programs might actually verbally promote moral prescriptions and prohibitions. For example, parents in a television program might talk to their child about the importance of being honest and not cheating on a test in school. Also, in some programs for young children, it is common for the characters to address the viewer directly when promoting a moral message. The few studies that have directly examined this mechanism have found some support for its effectiveness in conveying moral messages, although the results are less consistent than those for modeling. In line with this, research on parenting suggests that parental modeling of moral behaviors is more consistently and strongly linked to children's learning and behaviors than verbalizations such as preaching moral values or prompting moral action.

MEDIATING FACTORS

Researchers have identified several factors that might mediate the effects of televised moral messages on children and adolescents. First, some individual characteristics of children affect the way they respond to moral messages. For instance, age seems to be a mediator, in that younger children tend to be more strongly influenced by moral messages on television that older children and adolescents. Gender and ethnicity are typically not mediators of the effects of moral messages. Second, the context in which a moral message is conveyed in a program seems to moderate its effect. For instance, televised moral messages tend to have weaker effects in situations where they compete with immoral messages. As an example, the modeling of prosocial behavior on television seems to more strongly influence prosocial behaviors of children when it is presented in a positive context, rather then in a context intermixed with aggression. Last, the environment in which the child watches the television program can mediate the effects of televised moral messages. For example, when watching televised moral messages is accompanied by additional instruction from adults, such as teachers or parents, there tends to be a stronger positive effect on children.

Given these findings, more attention should be paid to possible positive effects of television programs on child development. However, an important caveat is that although television seems to have the capacity to influence children and adolescents in positive ways, television is only one of many factors involved in the socialization of the upcoming generation.

—*Sam A. Hardy and Glenda B. Claborne*

See also Advertising Campaigns, Prosocial; Aggression, Television and; Electronic Games, Moral Behavior in; Television, Morality and Identification With Characters on; Television, Prosocial Behavior and; Television, Prosocial Content of; Television Violence

FURTHER READINGS

Fisch, S. (2005). Children's learning from television: It's not just violence. *TeleVizion, 18*, 10–14.

Lovelace, V. O., & Huston, A. C. (1983). Can television teach prosocial behavior? In J. N. Sprafkin, C. F. Swift, & R. Hess (Eds.), *Rx Television: Enhancing the preventive impact of TV* (pp. 93–106). New York: Haworth Press.

Mares, M., & Woodard, E. H. (2001). Prosocial effects on children's social interactions. In D. Singer & J. Singer (Eds.), *Handbook of children and the media* (pp. 183–203). Thousand Oaks, CA: Sage.

Mares, M. L., & Woodard, E. (2005). Positive effects of television on children's social interactions: A meta-analysis. *Media Psychology, 7*, 301–322.

Rosenkoetter, L. I. (2001). Television and morality. In D. Singer & J. Singer (Eds.), *Handbook of children and the media* (pp. 463–473). Thousand Oaks, CA: Sage.

TELEVISION, MORALITY AND IDENTIFICATION WITH CHARACTERS ON

Moral development is often conceptualized as having two components: moral judgments and moral reasoning. Moral judgments involve children's judgments about how right or wrong particular behaviors are, and moral reasoning is their ability to offer explanations for their judgments. At a young age, children's moral schemas are simple and egocentric. As they mature, children develop more complex moral schemas that take into account the needs and concerns of those in their social environment and eventually the larger society.

Although theories differ with regard to the processes that underlie moral development, most agree that children's social interactions—with parents, peers, and others—play a key role. Television is also an important socializing agent in the lives of children and adolescents. The medium offers a wide variety of models interacting with others in a variety of contexts, thus providing salient moral lessons regarding what is right and wrong.

Research shows that exposure to particular types of television content is associated with less advanced moral reasoning about the type of behaviors depicted (e.g., violence, sexual behaviors). For example, adolescents heavily exposed to TV shows featuring sexual indiscretions such as adultery judged similar behaviors as less bad than those with less exposure. Similarly, children who viewed more fantasy violence were more likely to believe that aggression was an acceptable solution. In addition, several studies found that exposure to violent fantasy and reality-based programs was associated with less advanced moral reasoning about violence. Evidence suggests that the link between TV violence and moral reasoning may be mediated by perspective taking with more violence exposure associated with less advanced perspective taking, which in turn leads to less advanced moral reasoning.

Typically, research on television's role in moral development has considered television in general or particular types of content (e.g., violence, sexual content), but it has not explicitly examined identification with television characters. Identification is one outcome of television viewing that is believed to mediate audience responses. In the media literature, the term *identification* has been used in many ways, but two definitions seem to have been employed most often. First, identification sometimes refers to the process by which an individual puts him- or herself in the place of a character and vicariously participates in the character's experiences during a program. Second, many scholars have recognized that the process of identification can extend beyond the viewing situation. The phrase *wishful identification* has been used to describe this type of response, a psychological process through which an individual desires or attempts to become like another person. For example, in one study, the most common form of celebrity attachment reported by adolescents was *identificatory attachment*, or the desire to be like or become the celebrity.

Research indicates that identification with media characters can have significant social and psychological consequences. Much evidence shows that audience members often make changes in their appearance, attitudes, values, activities, and other characteristics in order to become more like admired celebrities or media characters. Identification with media characters also affects adoption or rejection of specific behaviors or life goals. Not surprisingly, the characters whom viewers report wanting to be like possess a variety of desirable attributes. One reason that fantasy violence may affect moral judgments and reasoning lies in the nature of the violent portrayals, with much of the violence committed by attractive characters with whom young viewers are inclined to identify. In addition, violent narratives tend to focus on the characters who commit violence, rather than on the victims. Particularly problematic are the TV heroes or "good" characters who use aggression; content analyses confirm that this is common on television. Several studies found that children and adolescents, especially males, identified more strongly with characters and celebrities whom they perceived as more aggressive. There is evidence that identification with aggressors increases the adverse consequences of viewed violence. Nonetheless, this type of effect is not inevitable. One study found that increasing involvement with the victim, by encouraging children to take his perspective, reduced the adverse perceptual and behavioral effects of the violent program, especially for boys.

Identification with media characters and celebrities can also have positive moral consequences for viewers if the media models exhibit prosocial behaviors. One study found that children as early as first grade were able to identify the prosocial lessons in television situation comedies and that those who viewed more prosocial sitcoms—especially children with a better understanding of the lessons—engaged in more prosocial behavior. Many young people select prosocial media characters and celebrities as favorites. One study found that children's wishful identification with favorite characters was associated with perceiving them as having positive social characteristics (e.g., kind, helpful). As young people mature, they become more likely to take moral judgments into account when responding to media portrayals. There is evidence, for example, that adolescents sometimes explicitly reject antisocial characters as role models, regarding them instead as examples of how *not* to behave.

—*Cynthia A. Hoffner*

See also Adolescents, Developmental Needs of, and Media; Television, Moral Messages on

FURTHER READINGS

Adams-Price, C., & Greene, A. L. (1990). Secondary attachments and adolescent self-concept. *Sex Roles, 22,* 187–198.

Bryant, J., & Rockwell, S. C. (1994). Effects of massive exposure to sexually oriented primetime television programming on adolescents' moral judgments. In D. Zillmann, J. Bryant, & A. Huston (Eds.), *Media, children, and the family: Social scientific, psychodynamic, and clinical perspectives* (pp. 183–195). Hillsdale, NJ: Erlbaum.

Caughey, J. L. (1986). Social relations with media figures. In G. Gumpert & R. Cathcart (Eds.), *Inter/media: Interpersonal communication in a media world* (3rd ed., pp. 219–252). New York: Oxford University Press.

Cohen, J. (1999). Favorite characters of teenage viewers of Israeli serials. *Journal of Broadcasting & Electronic Media, 43,* 327–345.

Hoffner, C., & Buchanan, M. (2005). Young adults' wishful identification with television characters: The role of perceived similarity and character attributes. *Media Psychology, 7,* 325–351.

Hoffner, C., & Cantor, J. (1991). Perceiving and responding to mass media characters. In J. Bryant & D. Zillmann (Eds.), *Responding to the screen: Reception and reaction processes* (pp. 63–101). Hillsdale, NJ: Erlbaum.

Krcmar, M., & Cooke, M. C. (2001). Children's moral reasoning and their perception of television violence. *Journal of Communication, 51,* 300–316.

Krcmar, M., & Valkenburg, P. M. (1999). A scale to assess children's moral interpretations of justified and unjustified violence and its relationship to television viewing. *Communication Research, 26,* 609–635.

Krcmar, M., & Vieira, E. T., Jr. (2005). Imitating life, imitating television: The effects of family and television models on children's moral reasoning. *Communication Research, 32,* 267–294.

Nathanson, A. I., & Cantor, J. (2000). Reducing the aggression-promoting effect of violent cartoons by increasing children's fictional involvement with the victim: A study of active mediation. *Journal of Broadcasting & Electronic Media, 44,* 125–142.

Rosenkoetter, L. I. (1999). The television situation comedy and children's prosocial behavior. *Journal of Applied Social Psychology, 29,* 979–993.

TELEVISION, MOTIVATIONS FOR VIEWING OF

In its early years, the study of mass communication focused on media content as a prime cause of media effects. Research, however, failed to provide evidence of strong and uniform effects. Scholars began to speculate that the media might have no effects on those who have no use for it. The uses and gratifications perspective of media research is an audience-centered approach. Instead of focusing on what media *do to* people, it focuses on what people *do with* media. According to uses and gratifications, people's reasons for using television, or television viewing motivations, are important because they directly influence how much television people watch as well as the content that they select.

Research to identify the motivations behind television viewing began in the 1970s. Greenberg (1974) asked British schoolchildren to write essays about why they liked to watch television. These essays revealed eight general reasons for watching television: to pass time, to forget, to learn about things, to learn about myself, for arousal, for relaxation, for companionship, and as a habit. Rubin (1977) continued this line of research with U.S. schoolchildren. Based on his research, as well as other explorations with a variety of adult samples, nine general reasons for watching television emerge: for relaxation (e.g., to unwind), for companionship (e.g., to overcome feelings of loneliness), out of habit (e.g., a customary, regular activity), to pass time (e.g., to occupy empty time), for entertainment (e.g., enjoyment), to facilitate social interaction (e.g., for conversational topics), for information (e.g., to learn things), for arousal (e.g., excitement), and to escape (e.g., to get away from daily pressures). Typically, passing time and entertainment motives are children's strongest reasons for watching television; watching to learn and to escape are the motives children rate lowest.

Research on children and adolescents confirms that television viewing motivations are linked to television viewing levels and program choices. In general, the more motivated children and adolescents are to watch television for any reason, the more they watch television. Different types of motives, however, are associated with watching different types of programs. Watching television to learn is correlated with watching children's programming; watching to pass time is linked to watching comedies, but not news. Watching for escape is connected to watching more comedy and less children's educational programming and news.

Another central tenet of uses and gratifications theory is that people's personal characteristics and social situations influence the reasons that they have for watching television. There are few gender differences in children's television viewing motives. Evidence suggests that girls are more likely to watch for companionship reasons than boys. Age, however, has a significant impact on motives. In general, younger children are more motivated to watch television. This finding probably reflects the expanding range of experiences that opens up as children become older. An interesting study by Zohoori (1988) compared the television viewing motives of native-born and immigrant U.S. children. The researchers found that immigrant children are significantly more likely to watch television for information reasons: to learn about others and themselves. Immigrant children might see television as a tool to help them learn about their new country and culture.

It is quite useful to understand individual television viewing motivations, but scholars have uncovered some different underlying dimensions to the larger set of motives. Finn and Gore (1988), for example, found it useful to characterize television viewing motives as serving either *social compensation* or *mood management* needs. Social compensation refers to using television as a substitute for social interaction. The researchers argued that habit, passing time, companionship, and escapist motives reflect the use of television as a way to deal with deficiencies in one's social environment. Mood management refers to using television to regulate mood and physiological arousal. Relaxation, arousal, entertainment, and information motives reflect the use of television to increase or reduce environmental stimuli.

Rubin's (1984) analysis of television viewing motives, levels of television exposure, and program selection has led to a distinction between *instrumental* and *ritualistic* television viewing. Instrumental television viewing is watching television to gain information. It is associated with watching television news and information programs, but not very high television viewing levels. In general, consistent with their motives to learn, instrumental viewers plan what they watch and pay attention to the programs. Ritualistic television use, on the other hand, grows out of watching television out of habit, to pass time, and for entertainment. It is associated with high levels of television use and watching a range of different noninformational programs. Consistent with the habit and pastime motives, ritualistic viewers do not plan what they are going to watch and don't pay a lot of attention to the programs.

IMPORTANCE OF MOTIVATIONS FOR TELEVISION VIEWING

It is important to identify and understand television viewing motives for two major reasons. First, there is evidence that viewing motives have an impact on the effects of media content. Knowing why someone is watching can help explain how they will be affected by what they are watching. Research has shown that news viewers are more likely to learn from the news if they are watching for informational reasons than if they are watching for entertainment. If they watch for entertainment reasons, however, they are more likely to form parasocial relationships (or a sense of personal connections) with the new personalities. Social reality effects, such as agenda setting and cultivation, for example, also differ based on people's reasons for watching television.

A second reason to understand viewing motives is that teaching children to be aware of their own reasons for watching television is part of media literacy training. Children need to develop receivership skills, including an understanding of why they are watching television. Teaching children to consider their own motives can help them think about selecting programs that will satisfy their motives, consider other ways to satisfy those motives without television, and evaluate whether their choices have gratified their motives. Children should also be instructed how to match their motives and their program choices. For example, children who are motivated to learn about nutrition should be helped to select appropriate instructional media rather than learn from entertainment programs or commercial messages. An instructional focus on awareness of viewing motives should make children more critical consumers of television and mitigate possible negative media effects.

—*Elizabeth M. Perse*

See also Agenda Setting; Cultivation Theory; Media Effects; Media Effects, Models of; Uses and Gratifications Theory

FURTHER READINGS

Anderson, J. A. (1980). The theoretical lineage of critical viewing curricula. *Journal of Communication, 30*(3), 64–70.

Carveth, R., & Alexander, A. (1985). Soap opera viewing motivations and the cultivation process. *Journal of Broadcasting & Electronic Media, 29,* 259–273.

Finn, S., & Gore, M. B. (1988). Social isolation and social support as correlates of television viewing motivations. *Communication Research, 15,* 135–158.

Greenberg, B. S. (1974). Gratifications of television viewing and their correlates for British children. In J. G. Blumler & E. Katz (Eds.), *The uses of mass communications: Current perspectives on gratifications research* (pp. 71–92). Beverly Hills, CA: Sage.

Katz, E., Blumler, J. G., & Gurevitch, M. (1974). Utilization of mass communication by the individual. In J. G. Blumler & E. Katz (Eds.), *The uses of mass communications: Current perspectives on gratifications research* (pp. 19–32). Beverly Hills, CA: Sage.

McCombs, M. E., & Weaver, D. H. (1985). Toward a merger of gratifications and agenda-setting research. In K. E. Rosengren, L. A. Wenner, & P. Palmgreen (Eds.), *Media gratifications research: Current perspectives* (pp. 95–108). Beverly Hills, CA: Sage.

Perse, E. M. (1990). Media involvement and local news effects. *Journal of Broadcasting & Electronic Media, 34,* 17–36.

Perse, E. M (1994). Television viewing motives scale. In R. B. Rubin, P. Palmgreen, & H. E. Sypher (Eds.), *Communication research measures: A sourcebook* (pp. 371–376). New York: Guilford.

Rubin, A. M. (1977). Television usage, attitudes, and viewing behaviors of children and adolescents. *Journal of Broadcasting, 21,* 355–369.

Rubin, A. M. (1979). Television use by children and adolescents. *Human Communication Research, 5,* 109–120.

Rubin, A. M. (1984). Ritualized and instrumental television viewing. *Journal of Communication, 34*(3), 66–77.

Rubin, A. M., & Perse, E. M. (1987). Audience activity and television news gratifications. *Communication Research, 14,* 58–84.

Zohoori, A. R. (1988). A cross-cultural analysis of children's television use. *Journal of Broadcasting & Electronic Media, 32,* 105–113.

TELEVISION, OCCUPATIONAL PORTRAYALS ON

Television is an important source of information about occupations for children. Children learn about jobs not only from interacting with people in various occupations but also from the portrayals of the occupations they see in the media. Television's portrayal of occupations, however, is governed by dramatic rather than educational considerations. Only those jobs that serve a dramatic or useful function in a story or are part of a program's action are regularly portrayed on prime time. The work of law enforcement officers, doctors, and lawyers is often more exciting, suspenseful, interesting, and prestigious than that of farmers and laborers. Consequently, television consistently overrepresents these types of occupations while it underrepresents blue-collar occupations.

Children often want to emulate television characters who are shown working in glamorous jobs that pay well, yet are not too demanding. In a cultivation theory study using data from the Monitoring the Future Survey, Nancy Signorielli (1993) found that those high school seniors who watched more television wanted to have glamorous and exciting jobs that would pay them handsomely. At the same time, these same students did not want to work very hard, and they sought jobs with lots of built-in vacation time. In short, these high school seniors reported visions of their future employment that mirrored the way occupations and work are presented in broadcast, network, prime-time television programs.

A consistent finding is that the television world of work is dominated by male characters and that fewer women than men can be categorized by occupation. In prime-time programs of the 1990s, Nancy Signorielli and Aaron Bacue (1999) found that 4 out of 10 female characters either did not work or were in an unspecified occupation. By comparison, fewer than one quarter of the male characters could not be classified in an occupation or were portrayed as not working.

Early content analyses consistently found that occupational role portrayals were stereotyped in terms of who was cast in the roles. Male characters were frequently found in various high-status professional or law enforcement jobs. Their female counterparts, on the other hand, were found in a narrower range of occupations often perceived as less prestigious, glamorous, and interesting—roles such as secretaries, nurses, teachers, and household workers.

More recent content analyses have found more equal representations of men and women in occupations. For example, David Atkin (1991), in an analysis of television series broadcast between 1966 and 1990, found more single women in professional and managerial positions and fewer in secretarial jobs. In the early 1990s, on broadcast prime-time television, about one fourth of the women were in professional and white-collar jobs (including entertainment) and one fifth in blue-collar positions. Yet, at the same time, women are still cast in roles as homemakers, home care workers, and unskilled laborers to a greater degree. Men, on the other hand, are typically portrayed as professionals and managers or in jobs relating to police work.

Content studies of programs seen in the 1970s found that race was an important predictor of employment and occupation. Minority characters were less likely than whites to have an identifiable job. Regardless of gender, white characters were more likely than minority characters to be portrayed as working outside the home. In addition, white male characters were more likely than female and minority characters to be portrayed as professionals and white-collar workers.

Minorities, on the other hand, are seen in less prestigious, blue-collar jobs with many in service occupations. Moreover, male characters, regardless of race, are most frequently portrayed in police and criminal roles. Minorities, regardless of gender, were most frequently cast in service or clerical positions.

An analysis of prime-time programs in the 1990s continued to show differences in occupational portrayals by race as well as gender. Nancy Signorielli and Susan Kahlenberg (2001) found that more white than minority characters were characterized as working and that the labor force depicted in TV programming does not provide an accurate representation of the U.S. labor force. This study found that television overrepresents professionals in every category—men, women, whites, and people of color. On the other hand, white-collar (managerial, clerical) and blue-collar (service, labor) workers are distinctly underrepresented when compared with their numbers in the U.S. labor force. In fact, white-collar workers, especially men of color, are relatively scarce on television.

Blue-collar jobs are equally underrepresented, especially among characters of color. Except for law enforcement, most blue-collar jobs are more mundane, less glamorous and interesting and, as a result, deficient in their storytelling potential. Law enforcement jobs, however, are some of the most overrepresented on television. Unlike actual police, most officers on television spend their days catching and arresting dangerous criminals, breaking down doors, and engaging in high-speed car chases with suspects. Consequently, these jobs are transformed to have good storytelling material, and they have become fundamental to the story lines of action-adventure, crime, and dramatic programs, some of the staples of prime time.

Nancy Signorielli (2005) conducted a study of prime-time occupational portrayals from the late 1990s into the first few years of the 21st century. Women, particularly black women in programs with mostly minority characters, have the least diversity and prestige in terms of the jobs in which they are cast. Similarly, white women in programs with all white characters are the least diverse in terms of jobs. Men's occupations, on the other hand, are equally diverse in most types of programs; the exception is the lack of law enforcement-related jobs in programs with mostly minority characters (which often are situation comedies and so do not typically lend themselves to law enforcement jobs).

Overall, television's network prime-time programs continue to present a rather narrow and limited view of occupations. Exciting and glamorous occupations continue to dominate, whereas everyday jobs are rarely seen. Interestingly, the distribution of jobs for women and people of color has improved. Female characters in the 21st century are not automatically relegated to traditionally female jobs although they are still depicted as employed less often than male characters. Similarly, men and women of color are more likely to be seen as having an occupation, particularly in programs, often situation comedies, with mostly minority characters.

—*Nancy Signorielli*

See also Cultivation Theory; Gender Roles on Television

FURTHER READINGS

Atkin, D. (1991). The evolution of television series addressing single women, 1966–1990. *Journal of Broadcasting & Electronic Media, 35,* 517–523.

Elasmar, M., Hasegawa, K., & Brain, M. (1999). The portrayal of women in U.S. prime time television. *Journal of Broadcasting & Electronic Media, 43,* 20–34.

Greenberg, B. S., & Collette, L. (1997). The changing faces on TV: A demographic analysis of network television's new seasons, 1966-1992. *Journal of Broadcasting & Electronic Media, 41,* 1–13.

Norcott, H. J., Seggar, J. F., & Hinton, J. C. (1975). Trends in TV portrayal of blacks and women. *Journalism Quarterly, 52*(4), 741–744.

Signorielli, N. (1993). Television and adolescents' perceptions about work. *Youth & Society, 24,* 314–341.

Signorielli, N. (2005). *Minorities in prime time: A look at occupations and occupational prestige.* Paper presented at the annual conference of the National Communication Association, Boston.

Signorielli, N., & Bacue, A. (1999). Recognition and respect: A content analysis of prime-time television characters across three decades. *Sex Roles, 40*(7/8), 527–544.

Signorielli, N., & Kahlenberg, S. (2001). Television's world of work in the nineties. *Journal of Broadcasting & Electronic Media, 45*(1), 1–19.

TELEVISION, PROSOCIAL BEHAVIOR AND

Television can have a variety of effects on the social behavior of its viewers depending on the content of the programming, characteristics of the viewer, and the context of the viewing environment. Although much attention has been focused on the effects of violent or antisocial content, many have noted the positive benefits of viewing programs designed to teach positive life lessons. Prosocial lessons are those that are designed to enhance children and adolescents' social, emotional, and moral development. Research indicates that children can just as effectively learn prosocial behavior from prosocial content as they do antisocial behavior from antisocial content. Various factors influence the degree to which prosocial content on television influences children's social behavior. Effects are strongest when the behavior that is modeled is salient, clearly portrayed, and can be easily incorporated into a child's everyday interactions. Furthermore, adults and teachers who use materials to extend children's learning can maximize the positive benefits of viewing television designed to teach children important social lessons.

Marie-Louise Mares and Emory Woodard systematically examined 34 studies that focused on the effects of prosocial acts on television on children and adolescents' social behavior. Mares and Woodard focused on four categories of prosocial behavior that have been studied most extensively: altruism, positive interaction, self-control, and antistereotyping.

ALTRUISM

Studies of altruism often include programs that focus on sharing, donating, and comforting others in times of need. Mares and Woodard found that compared to other forms of prosocial content, portrayals of altruism appear to have the strongest effects on children's behavior. One reason is that the studies are set up as controlled laboratory experiments that ask children to explicitly transfer behavior from the screen to the lab. Studies of altruism typically find that when children view portrayals of a model acting generously (e.g., donating prize tokens to charity), they are more likely to donate tokens that are given to them to charity compared to children who watch a model behave selfishly (e.g., cashing in winnings for a big prize) or in a neutral manner.

POSITIVE INTERACTIONS

Several studies of positive interactions (e.g., friendly play, conflict resolution) have been conducted in naturalistic settings. For example, Lynette Friedrich and Aletha Huston-Stein found that children who had viewed *Mr. Rogers' Neighborhood* exhibited more friendly behavior in the school playground compared to those who viewed neutral content. Studies of *Barney and Friends* indicate that children learn about cooperation and friendship through viewing the show.

SELF-CONTROL AND PERSISTENCE

Studies of self-control include programs that focus on resistance to temptation, obedience to rules, and persistence at a task. The self-control studies are often set up as lab experiments similar to the studies on altruism. Many studies conducted in the 1970s indicated that children who view models who are able to resist temptation (e.g., resisting playing with a forbidden toy, eating forbidden food) are more likely to demonstrate self-control compared to children who view models who indulge in forbidden activities. In a more recent study, children who viewed 20 episodes of *Dragon Tales,* a show designed to encourage children to pursue challenges, more frequently chose to pursue challenging tasks, compared to those who were not exposed to the series.

REDUCTION OF STEREOTYPES

Finally, studies that fell into the antistereotyping category included studies on acceptance and celebration of cultures. Early evaluations of *Sesame Street* found that Caucasian preschoolers had more positive attitudes toward African Americans and Latino Americans after viewing *Sesame Street* over the course of the 2-year study. A more recent study of the Israeli-Palestinian production of *Sesame Street* showed that viewing led to an increase in prosocial problem solving and more positive attitudes toward children of the other group.

CHARACTERISTICS OF THE CONTENT

Children are more likely to learn from prosocial messages when the portrayals can be transferred to children's own lives. For example, researchers at Sesame Workshop found that children learned more prosocial behaviors from content that likely occurred often in a preschool setting (e.g., including other children in games) than content that is likely to occur less frequently (e.g., comforting in times of loss). Furthermore, children tend to behave in more prosocial ways when they view content based on reality compared to a fictional story.

There is some evidence that when prosocial behavior is combined with violent or antisocial behavior within a particular lesson, the message backfires. Linda Silverman found that 3-year-old children became less cooperative after watching *Sesame Street* segments that contained conflict followed by resolution of the conflict. Marsha Liss and Lauri Reinhardt found that the combination of prosocial and antisocial acts in the cartoon series, *Superfriends*, led to more aggressive behavior than either antisocial or prosocial depictions alone.

CHARACTERISTICS OF THE VIEWER

Demographic factors might influence how children are affected by prosocial depictions. Whereas the effectiveness of prosocial depictions seems not to vary by gender or race or ethnicity according to Mares and Woodard, there is some evidence that prosocial television had a stronger effect on children from middle- to upper-class homes compared to children from low-income families.

Age also seems to be an influential factor. The effect of prosocial content seems to increase between the ages of 3 and 7, peak at age 7, and then decline. There is some thought that until age 7 or so, children have not fully developed the cognition to incorporate content from television and understand how to transfer such behavioral patterns to their own lives.

CHARACTERISTICS OF THE CONTEXT

Children who view programs with an adult coviewer gain more from the educational experience of viewing than children who view alone. Furthermore, supplementary materials in classroom settings also seem to influence effects. For example, in a study of *Freestyle,* Jerome Johnston and James Ettema found the strongest effects in an experimental condition that included viewing plus extra classroom activities compared to viewing at home alone. Similarly, the effectiveness of *Barney and Friends* in teaching manners was enhanced by teacher-led discussion and activities.

COMPARISON TO THE EFFECTS OF VIOLENCE

Susan Hearold reviewed 230 studies on television and social behavior that were published prior to 1978. She concluded that prosocial effects were stronger and more enduring than antisocial effects, both in the laboratory and in more natural conditions. Mares and Woodard's more recent analysis of prosocial effects could be compared to Haejung Paik and George Comstock's analysis of violent or aggressive television. These two more recent meta-analyses found equal effect sizes for the two types of content.

—*Jennifer A. Kotler*

See also Advertising Campaigns, Prosocial; Cognitive Development, Media and; Developmental Differences, Media and; Media Effects; Television, Prosocial Content and

FURTHER READINGS

Fisch, S. (2004). *Children's learning from educational television:* Sesame Street *and beyond.* Mahwah, NJ: Erlbaum.

Hearold, S. (1986). A synthesis of 1043 effects of television on social behavior. In G. Comstock (Ed.), *Public communication and behavior* (Vol. 1, pp. 65–133). New York: Academic Press.

Mares, M. L., & Woodard, E. (2005). Positive effects of television on children's social interactions: A meta-analysis. *Media Psychology, 7,* 301–322.

Paik, H., & Comstock, G. (1994). The effects of television violence on antisocial behavior: A meta-analysis. *Communication Research, 21,* 516–546.

TELEVISION, PROSOCIAL CONTENT AND

While numerous studies document the vast number of violent acts on television, less attention has been focused on television that teaches positive social lessons. Nevertheless, there is evidence that children can learn many positive life lessons from viewing programs intended to teach. The important life lessons can vary from the intrapersonal to the interpersonal but are often categorized as *prosocial* because they are designed to enhance children's and adolescents' social, emotional, and moral development. Several studies have examined the prevalence and kinds of prosocial acts that have been found in children's, family, and general audience programming. Most of these studies were conducted in the early 1970s and 1980s. Many televised programs as well as commercials contain prosocial behavior.

Interpersonal kinds of content that have been examined are positive interactions, altruism, and reduction of stereotypes. Content analyses conducted by Bradley Greenberg and colleagues found that altruistic acts such as sharing and helping were the most common prosocial acts and occurred about 14 times per television hour in Saturday morning and prime-time programming. Similarly, Liebert and Poulous (1975) found 11 altruistic acts and 6 sympathetic behaviors per hour of television. Reduction of stereotypes or at least gender equality among male and female characters has also been found in several studies. For example, a study of *Teletubbies* and *Barney & Friends* found that both male and female characters hug, show affection, play together, and take turns.

The intrapersonal kinds of content that have been examined are such attributes as self-esteem, self-control, and delay of gratification. Liebert and Poulous found that instances of self-control or delay of gratification occurred less than once per hour. Whereas programs such as *Dragon Tales* contain messages to children about task persistence, overall, most programs with prosocial themes tend to focus on interpersonal skills.

TELEVISION POLICY AND PROSOCIAL CONTENT

The Children's Television Act requires that stations air at least 3 hours of educational television. Many stations are meeting that requirement by airing programs considered to contribute to children's social development. Kelly Schmitt found that 75% of shows designated as educational were indeed prosocial in nature. Most of the prosocial lessons were found in preschool programs, about three quarters of which contained a social lesson.

When children watch such educational television, they are exposed to largely prosocial skills, rather than academic or cognitive types of skills. Furthermore, when children were asked to describe what the educational programs were about, the vast majority discussed prosocial themes. In talking about prosocial shows, children were clearer and showed greater engagement than when they talked about more academic and cognitive programs. Amy Jordan notes that the greater recall of prosocial content could be due to the fact that children already knew such content whereas academic lessons might be new and thus more difficult to articulate.

OTHER PROGRAMMING

Researchers suggest that it is important to assess other types of programming that children view, not just shows specifically made for them, given that children and adolescents spend much of their time with other types of programming. Content analyses of family sitcoms shown during the 1980s found that communication between family members tended to be positive rather than negative or conflict based. Similarly, George Comstock and Krystyna Strzyewski analyzed prime-time television programming during the 1987–1988 season and found that characters typically resolved interpersonal problems in constructive (e.g., discussion) rather than destructive ways.

FAVORITE PROGRAMMING

Greenberg and colleagues analyzed the favorite programs of a sample of fourth, sixth, and eighth graders. They found that these programs contained an average of 44.2 acts of prosocial behavior in an average hour. The prosocial behavior included displays of altruism and empathy and discussion of feelings. The researchers also found that the violence was just as frequent, however.

A recent study conducted by Deborah Weber and Dorothy Singer analyzed the favorite programs and videos viewed by children age 2 and under. They found many occurrences of prosocial behavior, including sharing, helping, and manners. For example, in the video *Sesame Street: Learning to Share,* there were 45 instances of positive social behaviors.

COMMERCIALS

Commercials also contain examples of prosocial behavior. In one study, prosocial behavior appeared in 59% of all children's commercials. Friendly behaviors were the most common forms of prosocial behavior, with 42% of all commercials containing examples of affection between characters. Helping and teaching were common altruistic behaviors, appearing in 21% of all commercials. Mary Strom Larson analyzed 595 commercials in children's programming and found that commercials depicting only girls showed almost all cooperative interactions (i.e., 85% of the time). Mixed boy and girl commercials primarily portrayed cooperative interactions (51%), compared to boys-only commercials, which contained primarily competitive interactions.

—*Jennifer A. Kotler*

See also Cognitive Development, Media and; Media Effects; Television, Prosocial Behavior and

FURTHER READINGS

Calvert, S. L., & Kotler, J. A. (2003). Lessons from children's television: Impact of the Children's Television Act on children's learning [Special issue]. *Journal of Applied Developmental Psychology, 24,* 275–335.

Greenberg, B. S., Atkin, C. K., Edison, N. G., & Korzenny, F. (1980). Antisocial and prosocial behaviors on television. In B. S. Greenberg (Ed.), *Life on television: Content analysis of U.S. TV drama.* Norwood, NJ: Ablex.

Hearold, S. (1986). A synthesis of 1043 effects of television on social behavior. In G. Comstock (Ed.), *Public communication and behavior* (Vol. 1, pp. 65–133). New York: Academic Press.

Larson, M. S. (1993). Family communication on prime-time television. *Journal of Broadcasting & Electronic Media, 37,* 349–357.

Mares, M. L., & Woodard, E. (2005). Positive effects of television on children's social interactions: A meta-analysis. *Media Psychology, 7,* 301–322.

Powell, K. A., & Abels, L. (2002). Sex-role stereotypes in TV programs aimed at the preschool audience: An analysis of *Teletubbies* and *Barney & Friends. Women and Language, 25*(2), 14–22.

Schmitt, K. L. (1999). *The three-hour rule: Is it living up to expectations?* (Report No. 30). Philadelphia: University of Pennsylvania, Annenberg Public Policy Center.

Stout, D. A., Jr., & Mouritsen, R. H. (1988). Prosocial behavior in advertising aimed at children: A content analysis. *Southern Speech Communication Journal, 53*(2), 159–174.

TELEVISION, VIEWER AGE AND

Age is generally regarded as one of the most fundamental structuring factors with regard to the television audience. However, it should be noted that age in itself is not an explanatory variable but rather a convenient indicator of various kinds of development that are normal in human beings as they pass through the life span. These include biological-sexual development, cognitive development, and social development.

Any discussion of the relationship between young children and TV use should include an understanding of cognitive development (i.e., the ways in which we learn to think and process information). During the course of cognitive development, children become less dependent on immediate perception, and their ability to deal with multiple dimensions expands, providing them with greater means and resources for using the media. Consequently, levels of TV viewing tend to increase throughout childhood, although there are significant variations according to factors such as gender, ethnicity, and socioeconomic background. There is also evidence that because they tend to be hungrier for all kinds of information, up until the age of about 9 or 10 years, those children who are cognitively more developed watch more TV than their less-developed peers. However, they also tend to start losing interest in TV earlier as it no longer provides them with adequate cognitive or informational gratifications.

Studies differ with regard to the exact moment at which mean levels of TV viewing peak in childhood, some reporting it as early as 9 and others at 11 years of age or even later. Moreover, there is evidence that the arrival of music television channels has increased the age at which the peak occurs, although, more recently, this has been at least partly offset by the growth in popularity of computer game playing (especially among boys) and online chatting (especially among girls). What is certain is that between 9 and 13 years old, children experience a radical shift in program preferences as they become more selective and their tastes more differentiated. The result is a move away from more child-oriented to more adult-oriented patterns, accompanied by a move away from conventional TV channels to more specialized ones. Thus, genres such as action-based programs, films, and music (indeed, anything that provides a window on the world in general and adult life in particular) increase in popularity at the expense of children's programs and cartoons. However, program preferences remain heavily structured by gender so that, at this age, it is not too much to claim that boys and girls inhabit different media worlds.

With the onset of puberty, biological-sexual and social development become of central importance for television use. The striving for independence lessens orientations to the family, and as more and more time is spent outside the home, the importance of the peer group increases. Concomitantly, levels of TV viewing tend to fall significantly as other forms of media—above all, music, but also, more recently, the Internet—come to better fulfill the sets of needs and motives of individuals and the groups to which they belong. However, because females enter puberty on average 2 years earlier than males, it is once again essential to control for gender when analyzing these

processes. Ethnicity, socioeconomic background, and even nutritional factors (height and weight gain are excellent indicators of the timing of puberty) also affect the timing and rate of pubertal development.

During adolescence, with the exception of music television, mean levels of TV viewing continue to fall, with the result that older adolescents and young adults manifest very low mean levels of TV use (indeed, they are low users of most media). With the advent of early adulthood, television use is increasingly affected most by life stage and social context factors. As the process of founding one's own household, living with a partner, and perhaps starting a family unfolds, more time tends to be spent at home. As a result, levels of TV viewing increase, steadily rising to a new life-stage peak in later life.

Building on the early work of Brown, Cramond, and Wilde (1974), Rosengren and Windahl (1989) proposed a theoretical model for the relationship between human development and media use termed a *uses and development model,* which they combined with uses and gratifications theory. According to this perspective, certain developmental events and processes (cognitive, social, sexual-biological, or a combination of all three) create different sorts of resources (biological, cognitive, mental, or material) as well as various needs and requirements, including attitudes, interests, values, and tastes. These make possible and bring about certain types of media use, and these in turn bring about certain media effects and consequences.

In short, the model postulates that the need structure of the individual changes continuously as he or she passes through different developmental stages. Thus, for example, with age, certain motives will gain importance as others lose. The preschooler does not approach the screen for the same reasons as does a 10-year-old, and neither does so for the same reasons as a 15-year-old; nor do boys always approach the screen for quite the same reasons as girls. Consequently, when discussing the relationship between age, development, and television use among children and adolescents, it is essential to avoid generalizations by always carefully specifying the age, gender, and other social characteristics of the group in question.

—*Keith Roe*

See also Adolescents, Developmental Needs of, and Media; Cognitive Skills, Computer Use and; Developmental Differences, Media and

FURTHER READINGS

Brown, J. R., Cramond, J. K. & Wilde, R. J. (1974). Displacement effects of television and the child's functional orientation to media. In J. G. Blumler & E. Katz (Eds.), *The uses of mass communications.* Beverly Hills, CA: Sage.

Roe, K. (1998). Boys will be boys and girls will be girls: Changes in children's media use. *Communications: The European Journal of Communication, 23*(1), 5–26.

Rosengren, K. E., & Windahl, S. (1989). *Media matter: TV use in childhood and adolescence.* Norwood, NJ: Ablex.

Rubin, A. M., & Rubin, R. B. (1981). Age, context, and television use. *Journal of Broadcasting, 15*(1), 1–13.

TELEVISION RATING SYSTEMS

As part of the 1996 Telecommunications Act, Congress gave television industry representatives a year to develop a system to rate television programming. Establishing a ratings system was necessary to make the V-chip (violence chip) provision of the 1996 act possible. The rating assigned to each episode is transmitted electronically along with the program, allowing parents to use the V-chip to block shows they don't want their children to view. If the broadcast industry had failed to produce a workable rating system after a year, Congress left open the possibility of an outside body developing a way to rate programming.

The television rating system, developed by the National Association of Broadcasters, the National Cable Television Association, and the Motion Picture Association of America, is referred to as the *TV Parental Guidelines.* In addition to transmitting ratings electronically to enable V-chip operation, the ratings are provided in TV listings and are flashed on the screen for the first 15 minutes of each program. Broadcast and cable networks began applying the rating system in 1997.

There are two components to the program ratings. The first provides an age-based recommendation as to the appropriateness of each episode of a TV show. It is comparable to the motion picture rating system. The second part of an episode's rating provides labels to indicate specific content parents might find to be objectionable.

Six age designations are used. They include TV-Y, programs suitable for all children; TV-Y7, for children 7 years and older because at this age, children

are more likely to be able to distinguish between reality and make-believe; TV-G, programs suitable for a general audience although not specifically tailored to children; TV-PG, when parental coviewing is advisable for younger children; TV-14, unsuitable for preteen and younger audiences; and TV-MA, programming solely for an adult audience. Very few programs are assigned this last rating.

The age-based rating system was the only component of the TV content ratings when it was initially implemented. Quickly, however, there was concern that these ratings did not provide sufficient information for parents to make informed decisions about their children's viewing choices. Within a year, content categories were added to the age-based labels. The content categories are V (violence), S (sexual situations), L (coarse or crude language), D (suggestive dialogue, usually sexual), and FV (fantasy violence). The content categories are used as an addition to the age-based designations.

To avoid First Amendment challenges likely to accompany direct government involvement in program content, the ratings are assigned either by the program producers who create the TV shows or by the networks that air them. Each episode is rated independently, so a particular television program's rating can vary from week to week. News programming and sportscasts are not rated, but all other types of programming are. Although the ratings system is officially voluntary, all of the broadcast networks rate their programming, as do the vast majority of cable channels.

Proponents argue that the rating system, in combination with the V-chip, gives parents a useful tool to protect children from content the parents decide is inappropriate. But critics challenge the effectiveness of the ratings system and V-chip. The operation of the V-chip requires parents to overcome several technological hurdles. In addition, the usefulness of the system is constrained by the limitations of the ratings themselves.

One concern is that programmers purposefully assign less "mature" ratings to programs to avoid scaring potential advertisers. On the other hand, observers have noted that producers may actually produce programming with higher levels of sex and violence because they can simply rate the programming and leave parents with the responsibility to make sure those shows are screened out. Along the same lines, critics argue that flashing the ratings on the TV screen at the beginning of each program may attract some children to programs containing inappropriate content.

The exclusion of news and sports programming from the ratings system also limits the extent to which parents can dependably block programming with objectionable elements. Although the nature of these programs is such that ratings aren't practical, news programs and sporting events can contain high levels of violence and other objectionable content. Even parents who set the V-chip to block everything but the mildest programs would not have been able to keep out of their homes the now-infamous Super Bowl halftime show where Janet Jackson's wardrobe "malfunctioned" and exposed her nipple.

Given that program producers and networks assign their own ratings, the consistency of how each category is applied also comes into question. For example, does TV-PG reliably mean the same thing on NBC as it does on TBS? Does TV-PG even reliably mean the same thing on different programs airing on the same network? Content analysis of programming has shown the age-based ratings are used fairly consistently to distinguish the appropriateness of specific programs. The content descriptors, however, are much less dependable. In many instances, content descriptors aren't even being used to indicate the presence of violence, sex, or adult language. Even in children's programming, the FV (fantasy violence) indicator is often omitted.

Parents who disagree with ratings assigned to a particular program can appeal to the TV Parental Guidelines Monitoring Board. The board has 24 members, 6 each from the broadcast industry, the cable industry, and the creative community (writers, actors, etc.); 5 from child advocacy, medical, religious, or educational organizations; and the chair, who is the current president of the Motion Picture Association of America (MPAA).

—*Jennifer L. Lambe*

See also Adult Mediation Strategies; First Amendment; Forbidden Fruit Hypothesis; Motion Picture Association of America (MPAA); Parental Advisory Labels and Rating Systems; Parental Regulation of Children's Media; Rating Systems, Parental Uses of; Regulation, Television; Telecommunications Act of 1996; V-Chip (Violence Chip)

FURTHER READINGS

Federal Communications Commission. (2004). *FCC parents' place: TV ratings.* Retrieved from http://www.fcc.gov/parents/tvratings.html

Kunkel, D., Maynard Farinola, W. J., Farrar, K., Donnerstein, E., Biely, E., & Zwarun, L. (2002). Deciphering the V-chip: An examination of the television industry's program rating judgments. *Journal of Communication, 52*(1), 112–138.
Parental Choice in Television Programming, U.S. Code 47, Chapter 5, Subchapter 3, Section 303 (1996).
TV Parental Guidelines Monitoring Board. (n.d.). *The TV parental guidelines.* Retrieved from http://www.tvguidelines.org/

TELEVISION RATING SYSTEMS, PARENTAL USES OF

In January 1997, the nation's telecasters introduced a television program rating system in the United States. Under considerable congressional pressure, the industry volunteered to provide onscreen information as to the suitability of programs for different age groups. Two ratings categories were adopted for children's programs (one for all children and one for children 7 and above), and four categories were created for non-children (TV-G for general audiences, TV-PG where parental guidance was recommended, TV-14 for shows intended for viewers 14 and older, and TV-MA for mature audiences). In October 1997, under further pressure, the rating system added content labels for sex, violence, suggestive dialogue, and adult language. Television networks have no common standard for assigning ratings to television programs. Each network or production unit creates and applies its own definitions.

A series of national surveys of parents of 2-to-17-year-olds by the Kaiser Family Foundation, taken in 1998, 1999, 2001, and 2004, provide the most comprehensive description of public acceptance and use of the TV ratings. One year into the ratings, 57% of the national sample of parents said they had not seen or read anything that explained the ratings and what they meant, although four fifths had heard of them. More telling, 18% of the parents had never heard anything about such ratings, and 27% who were aware of them reported that they never or hardly ever used them. These parents also exaggerated their understanding of the system. The study indicates that among parents who say they understand the ratings *very well*, only one fourth are actually well informed when tested as to the symbols' meanings. One year later, half of the parents still did not use the TV ratings information, although more than 80% said they used the movie ratings.

In its 2001 survey, the Kaiser Family Foundation reported parental use still at near the halfway mark (56%), but that figure was much higher than the 7% of parents who used the V-chip in their TV monitor. Half of the parents surveyed said they used the parental advisories on CDs and music tapes, and 59% used the information on video games. In this study, 3 years after the ratings system was initiated, two thirds could not spontaneously name a specific TV rating, 69% could not correctly indicate what TV-Y meant, 53% could not explain TV-MA, 95% could not explain the content label D, and only 52% could correctly state that S stood for sexual content. Furthermore, half the parents sampled did not agree that the ratings accurately reflected the shows' content.

Findings in its 2004 survey do not alter these earlier findings substantially: Even among parents who have used the ratings, 60% believe they are not accurate *some* or *most* of the time.

This latter issue of relative accuracy was addressed by Kunkel and his colleagues in a 2001 study. They systematically examined 1,147 TV programs for "high-risk" violent and sexual behaviors, for example, extensive, serious, explicit violence or intercourse, sexual assault, and explicit nudity. About 10% of the shows the researchers looked at qualified as high-risk violent and 4% as high-risk sexual. Only one fourth of the high-risk violent shows contained a rating as strong as TV-14. There was no V label on fully 65% of the general audience programs that the research scheme identified as containing violent-risk content. In the subset of children's programming, more than two thirds of all high-risk violent shows carried a TV-Y label—suitable for children of all ages. Half of the high-risk sexual shows had a TV-14 rating, but 80% of these shows contained no S designation. The research findings argued for the lack of symmetry between the TV ratings provided by the industry and the actual program content.

In a 2001 study, Greenberg, Eastin, and Mastro found that for parents who wished to know the ratings in advance of looking at the onscreen information, such publications as *TV Guide* did not provide age-based ratings for 27% of program listings, and content information was present for only one fourth of those shows with age-based ratings. In a follow-up study, they compared published show ratings with what actually appeared in a videotaped sample of shows. Nearly one in five shows (18%) were rated both in print and onscreen but had different ratings, typically with a more youth-oriented rating in the published print version than in what was seen during the show's airing.

Abelman (2001) profiled parents more or less likely to use the television ratings and found that the most likely users were those parents least likely in need of mediation assistance. These are parents who work together in creating rules about TV, use reasoning and explanation, appeal to the child's pride, and have children who are low to moderate TV watchers and high academic achievers. Parents least likely to be using the ratings do not work together with their children and offer little supervision or discipline other than unfocused coviewing; their children are the heaviest TV watchers. Furthermore, these parents do not believe that TV has significant positive or negative effects. Between these two groups are parents who use more restrictive forms of TV mediation (e.g., program banning, time constraints) with children who are moderate to high TV consumers. These parents are most concerned with the behavioral impact of TV.

Hofschire (2001) summarized experimental research on ratings to determine the relative merits of two propositions: that such information would increase the likelihood of choosing less acceptable shows (forbidden fruit) or would decrease such choices (tainted fruit). Although citing some support for both, she concludes that participants preferred media content that had advisories or more restrictive ratings.

—*Bradley S. Greenberg*

See also Adult Mediation Strategies; Forbidden Fruit Hypothesis; Parental Advisory Labels and Rating Systems; Parental Regulation of Children's Media; Rating Systems, Parental Use of; Television Rating Systems; V-Chip (Violence Chip)

FURTHER READINGS

Abelman, R. (2001). Profiling parents who do and do not use the TV advisory ratings. In B. S. Greenberg (Ed.), *The alphabet soup of television program ratings* (pp. 217–240). Cresskill, NJ: Hampton Press.

Greenberg, B. S., Eastin, M. S., & Mastro, D. (2001). Comparing on-air ratings with the published ratings: Who to believe. In B. S. Greenberg (Ed.), *The alphabet soup of television program ratings* (pp. 39–50). Cresskill, NJ: Hampton Press.

Greenberg, B. S., Eastin, M. S., & Mastro, D. (2001). The ratings distribution in 1998, according to *TV Guide*. In B. S. Greenberg (Ed.), *The alphabet soup of television program ratings* (pp. 19–38). Cresskill, NJ: Hampton Press.

Hofschire, L. (2001). Media advisories and ratings: What the experimental research tells us. In B. S. Greenberg (Ed.), *The alphabet soup of television program ratings* (pp. 241–250). Cresskill, NJ: Hampton Press.

Kaiser Family Foundation. (1998). *Parents, children, and the TV rating system: Two Kaiser Family Foundation Surveys*. Menlo Park, CA: Author.

Kaiser Family Foundation. (1999, May). *Parents and the V-chip*. Menlo Park, CA: Author.

Kaiser Family Foundation. (2001). *Parents and the V-chip*. Menlo Park, CA: Author.

Kaiser Family Foundation. (2004). *Parents, media, and public policy*. Menlo Park, CA: Author.

Kunkel, D., Farinola, W., Cope, K., Donnerstein, E., Biely, E., Zwarum, L., & Rollin, E. (2001). Assessing the validity of V-chip rating judgments: The labeling of high-risk programs. In B. S. Greenberg (Ed.), *The alphabet soup of television program ratings* (pp. 51–68). Cresskill, NJ: Hampton Press.

TELEVISION VIOLENCE

The phenomenon of television violence has received much attention and debate. Its definition, implications, and rationale have been questioned and studied by policymakers, media scholars, and practitioners. Television violence has remained at the center of debates over television policy, particularly in reference to children and children's programming.

The difficulty in defining television violence lies in the breadth of the definition. Some consider violence to include only physically violent actions. Such a definition is easily quantifiable but overlooks other actions and behavior with potentially powerful consequences. Verbal threats and the implication of physical violence are important, particularly in terms of violence portrayed on television, where the violent act may not be actually depicted. It is also important to consider the possibility of psychological violence, such as verbal abuse and degradation.

Television violence is, therefore, defined as the transmission of violence, broadly defined, through the medium of television. In 1998, the National Television Violence Study (NTVS), a multiyear attempt to quantify the presence of violence on cable television, defined television violence as falling into any of three categories: credible threats, behavioral acts, and harmful consequences. This definition encompasses physical acts as well as the possibility of verbal and implied violence. Visual cues such as scars, bandages, blood, or hospitals can denote violence without actually showing it.

Public concern over television violence stems from the portrayal of both fiction and nonfiction. Nonfiction televised material and journalism tend to depict actual violent events such as wars, insurgency, and civil disputes. Television journalists covering war now have the capacity to report from the war zone, enabling the presentation of gun-fighting, people being killed or maimed, and the aftermath of such violence. Televised nonfictional violence can also be seen in *Cops*-style reality dramas, in which real people are dramatically portrayed in their interactions with law enforcement. Critics of nonfiction violence suggest that presentations are exaggerated and sensationalistic. Reality-based entertainment programs are open to such criticism; however, journalists argue that their work merely represents events in the real world.

Televised portrayals of fictional violence cannot as easily claim to represent reality. Instead, fictional accounts tell stories and dramatize events. Fictionalized violence is often less realistic than real violence. Cartoons and prime-time dramas alike employ unrealistic and inconsistent violence in their programs. For instance, some characters are blown back 10 feet by gunshots whereas others get up and continue fighting after having been shot multiple times. In addition to this, fictional characters using violence are sometimes portrayed in unrealistic or antisocial ways. For instance, heroic protagonists are often rewarded for using violence against their enemies.

The NTVS states that violence on television has been linked repeatedly with antisocial and aggressive behavior (NTVS, p. 5). Their conclusion is substantiated with findings such as:

- Nearly 40% of the violent incidents on television are initiated by characters who possess qualities that make them attractive role models.
- Fully 71% of violent scenes contain no remorse, criticism, or penalty for violence at the time that it occurs.
- Less than 20% of the violent programs portray the long-term damage of violence to the victim's family, friends, and community.

- At least 40% of the violent scenes on television include humor.
- Less than 5% of violent programs feature an antiviolence message. (NTVS, p. 26)

The significance of television violence for American youth lies in its implications, based principally on two factors. First, television usage is nearly ubiquitous among children in the United States today. Nearly all American children live in households with televisions, and the average child watches between 3 and 4 hours of television each day. Second, television as a medium is thought to influence through its portrayals. Children are thought to be more profoundly affected by televised violence than the general population. Scholars cite children's lesser ability to distinguish between reality and fiction, lack of understanding of consequences, and inexperience in the world as particularly meaningful. Children may adopt unsuitable role models and develop inappropriate problem-solving and conflict resolution practices as a result of their viewing violence and its glorification on television.

Wilson and colleagues found that these problematic consequences are exacerbated in children's programming, which research finds to be more violent than programming for adults. For instance, Woo and Kim note that professional wrestling, for which children and teens make up a significant portion of the audience, portrays violent and antisocial behavior both within and outside of actual match time. Inside the ring, wrestlers are practicing sport; however, their outside-the-ring behavior can suggest that disputes are appropriately resolved with violent fighting. In addition, televised wrestling makes heroes out of those wrestlers whose behavior is most antisocial. In a different study, Wilson et al. found that violent content is more likely to be featured in children's programming than in any other type of program.

It is generally believed that violence is prevalent on television because it is profitable for broadcasting companies. Violence, sex, and humor, are among the most powerful attention-grabbing tools available to broadcasters. Programming, therefore, favors violence, sex, and humor to acquire as large a share of the audience as possible.

Public concern over television violence has contributed to formal and informal remedies. Formally, the Federal Communications Commission has established numerous statutes to mediate between broadcasters'

First Amendment rights and public concern. For instance, television programs are now required to display ratings similar to those required by the Motion Picture Association of America to determine the age-appropriateness of content. In addition, parents are being empowered to play a larger role in their children's television viewing, supervising what is being watched and parenting in appropriate ways that offset the potential negative consequences of television violence.

—*Mark Finney*

See also Cartoons, Violence in; News, Children's Exposure to; News, Children's Responses to; Television Violence, Susceptibility to; Violence, Effects of; Violence, Extent of and Responses to

FURTHER READINGS

Federman, J. (Ed.). (1998). *National Television Violence Study* (Vol. 3). Thousand Oaks, CA: Sage.

Gentile, D. A. (2003). *Media violence and children: A complete guide for parents and professionals*. Westport, CT: Praeger.

Gunter, B., Harrison, J., & Wykes, M. (2003). *Violence on television: Distribution, form, context, and themes*. Mahwah, NJ: Erlbaum.

Hamilton, J. T. (1998). *Television violence and public policy*. Ann Arbor: University of Michigan Press.

Kelly, P. T. (1996). *Television violence: A guide to the literature*. New York: Nova Science.

Larson, M. S. (2001). Interaction, activities, and gender in children's television commercials: A content analysis. *Journal of Broadcasting & Electronic Media, 45*(1), 41.

MacBeth, T. M. (1996). *Tuning in to young viewers: Social science perspectives on television*. Thousand Oaks, CA: Sage.

Wilson, B. J., Smith, W., Potter, W. J., Kunkel, D., Linz, D., Colvin, C. M., & Donnerstein, E. (2002). Violence in children's television programming: Assessing the risks. *Journal of Communication, 52*(1), 5–35.

Woo, H.-J., & Kim, Y. (2003). Modern gladiators: A content analysis of televised wrestling. *Mass Communication & Society, 6*(4), 361–378.

TELEVISION VIOLENCE, SUSCEPTIBILITY TO

Within the field of communication, television violence is perhaps one of the most frequently and exhaustively researched topic, and for good reason. Several content analyses, particularly those conducted by George Gerbner and colleagues (beginning in 1967) and the National Television Violence Study indicate that violent images are pervasive on television and that children's television tends to be especially violent. In fact, one study by George Gerbner, Larry Gross, Michael Morgan, and Nancy Signorielli found that children's programming, dominated by cartoons, featured an average of 20 violent acts per hour. A more recent study by Dale Kunkel and colleagues found that 6 out of 10 shows designed for children feature aggression, with more than five violent scenes per show. As noted by Barbara Wilson and colleagues, it is surprising that programs targeting children 12 and younger feature more violence than other types of programming do.

Violence is quite prevalent on television programs targeting young people, and we also know that young people spend a significant portion of their lives with television. Research conducted by the Kaiser Family Foundation indicates that young people ages 8 to 18 spend an average of 3 hours a day watching television. Taking these research findings into consideration, researcher Alethea Huston and colleagues have estimated that by the time a child graduates from elementary school, he or she will have witnessed more than 8,000 murders and more than 100,000 other acts of violence on network television. Indeed, this figure is even higher if the child has access to cable television, DVDs, videocassettes, and video games.

Fortunately, researchers have contributed much knowledge to our understanding of television violence and its effects on young people (and adults) by conducting a wide range of research, including experiments, surveys, field research, and longitudinal analyses. When examined as a whole using meta-analytic methods, the existing research on television violence points rather convincingly to three potential outcomes: (1) learning aggressive attitudes and behaviors, (2) becoming desensitized, and (3) developing fear. However, the body of research in this area also reveals that not everyone is affected by television violence in the same way; that is, certain young people are more susceptible to violent content than others. In fact, a viewer's susceptibility to television violence is influenced by a range of factors, including viewer demographics, viewer traits and states, and contextual characteristics of the televised violent portrayals.

WHO IS MOST SUSCEPTIBLE?

Although all viewers, young and old, are vulnerable to television violence, research has indicated that some children and adolescents are more susceptible than others. Over the years, researchers have pointed to several factors (often referred to as "individual differences") that heighten a young person's susceptibility to the effects of television violence.

Age

Researchers investigating television violence have historically positioned young children as a unique audience, regarding this group as highly susceptible to the negative effects of viewing violence. This heightened level of susceptibility is often attributed to children's lower stage of cognitive development. There are many specific reasons why television typically has a larger effect on young children. For example, young children are more likely to identify with and imitate aggressive television characters than are older children and adults. The degree to which children perceive a violent portrayal as realistic and identify with aggressive characters has also been found to heighten their susceptibility to violent portrayals. In addition, because children younger than 8 years old cannot discriminate between fantasy and reality, they are vulnerable to learning and adopting as reality the attitudes and behaviors portrayed in television. Moreover, young children have trouble following story plots, so they are apt to be drawn to high-action programming (which often means violent programming) without considering the motivations or consequences of violence on the screen. In fact, in their analysis of the existing studies on the effects of television analysis, Haejung Paik and George Comstock found an inverse relationship between the age of the viewer and the magnitude of the effect of television violence on aggression; that is, as age increased, effects decreased. Clearly, young children appear to be especially susceptible to television violence.

Gender

Early studies on the effects of television violence have indicated that boys are far more vulnerable than girls. In fact, as noted by Paik and Comstock's analysis of surveys and experimental studies, television violence tends to have a stronger effect on males than females. This finding is partly due to the fact that boys tend to pay more attention to violence. One study by S. B. Levine suggests that boys seem more drawn to violent shows and are more agitated by them, where as girls tend to be repelled by them and saddened. However, in recent years, research has suggested that girls are increasingly susceptible to aggressive television portrayals; this is partly attributed to societal change and the increase in aggressive female characters on television. Clearly, more research is needed to shed greater light on gender and susceptibility to television violence.

Other Demographic Variables

Research has found that youth from minority groups and those from lower-class families watch more television and therefore are exposed to more televised violence. However, there is very little research to indicate that these groups are more or less affected by their viewing than others. In other words, within every social class and ethnic group, viewing television violence heightens the likelihood of behaving aggressively. More research is needed to help determine whether certain socioeconomic groups and ethnic groups are more vulnerable than others.

Intelligence

Many studies have indicated that children with lower intelligence levels watch more television in general and watch more violent television. Research has also suggested that children with low IQ are more likely to behave aggressively as grown-ups. However, as noted by researchers Brad Bushman and L. Rowell Huesmann, the relationship between television violence and aggressive behaviors is not simply the result of low-IQ youth watching more television violence and behaving more aggressively. Rather, research has indicated that television violence affects both high-IQ children and low-IQ children.

Aggressive Traits

Traits are used to describe a person's characteristic patterns of behaving, thinking, and feeling. Research has found that characteristically aggressive young people are more likely to be influenced in the short term by viewing violence than those without aggressive traits. For example, Brad Bushman and others have found that people who are naturally aggressive are more likely to have aggressive thoughts, feel angry, and behave aggressively immediately after watching violence on television. However, in contrast with the short-term effects found in experimental studies, longitudinal studies (those that examine people over a long period of time) have found that both low-aggression and high-aggression children are affected by television violence. In other words, characteristically aggressive young people may be more susceptible to violent television in the short term, however, all children, regardless of aggressive traits, are susceptible to violent television in the long term.

Aggressive States

Whereas *traits* are generally stable and long lasting, *states* are best understood as temporary and fluctuating. Research into the effects of television violence has found that when viewers are in a state of arousal, frustration, or anger, they are at greater risk of a negative effect. For example, research suggests that the effects are strongest on people who have been aroused or provoked just prior to exposure to violent television.

HIGH-RISK PORTRAYALS OF TELEVISED VIOLENCE

Characteristics of viewers play an important role in determining their susceptibility to violent messages on television. However, it is important to note that not all violent portrayals are equal; in fact, various types of violent messages pose more risk to viewers than others. The National Television Violence Study (NTVS) has contributed much to our understanding of violent portrayals that increase the risk of harmful effects on viewers, especially children. According to the NTVS researchers, a high-risk portrayal that poses the greatest risk of learning aggression features (1) a perpetrator who is attractive, (2) violence that seems justified, (3) violence that goes unpunished, (4) violence that results in minimal consequences to the victim, and/or (5) violence that seems realistic to the viewer. Characterizations in which the perpetrator of violence is attractive are especially problematic because viewers may identify with such a character, which may in turn increase the likelihood of a negative effect. Likewise, violent depictions that pose the highest risk of desensitizing viewers to the seriousness of violence feature repeated exposure to graphic or extensive violence as well as humorous violence. Finally, violent depictions that are most likely to lead to fear among viewers are those that involve an attractive victim, appear realistic, are repeated, go unpunished, and seem unjustified. Although certain types of violent depictions are more likely to lead to certain types of effects, the NTVS researchers also note that some contextual features, such as showing the negative consequences of violence, can actually lower the likelihood of harmful outcomes.

RISK FACTORS AND MEDIATING FACTORS

An important overall finding from the research on susceptibility to television violence is that not all youths are affected equally or in the same way by viewing media violence. The risks associated with television violence depend not only on the nature of television audience, but also on the nature of the violent portrayals. Factors that appear to most influence the effects of television violence on viewer aggression include characteristics of the viewer (such as age, gender, aggressive traits, and aggressive states) and characteristics of the violent portrayal (including characteristics of perpetrators, degree of realism and justification for violence, and depiction of consequences of violence). Out of all these factors, the age of the viewer seems to pose the greatest risk of negative outcomes; that is, young children are especially susceptible to televised violence because of their limited ability to understand television. Evidence that other individual, environmental, and content factors enhance the negative effects of exposure to media violence is less clear. However, along with research on the many factors that heighten a young person's susceptibility to television violence, there is also a body of literature on the forces that help to counteract the harmful effects of television violence. Parental coviewing of television, reducing children's exposure to violent television, encouraging the entertainment industry to create more responsible portrayals of violence, and teaching young people critical viewing skills (i.e., media education) can help to make children less susceptible to the negative effects of television violence.

—Angela Paradise

See also Aggression, Television and; Cartoons, Violence in; Developmental Differences, Media and; Media Effects; Television Violence; Violence, Effects of

FURTHER READINGS

Bushman, B. J., & Huesmann, L. R. (2001). Effects of televised violence on aggression. In D. G. Singer & J. L. Singer (Eds.), *Handbook of children and the media* (pp. 223–254).

Gerbner, G., Gross, L., Morgan, M., & Signorielli, N. (1980). The mainstreaming of America: Violence profile no. 6. *Journal of Communication, 30*(3), 10–29.

Huston, A. C., Donnerstein, E., Fairchild, H. H., Feshbach, N. D., Katz, P. A., Murray, J. P., Rubinstein, E. A., Wilcox, B. L., & Zuckerman, D. (1992). *Big world, small screen: The role of television in American society.* Lincoln: University of Nebraska Press.

Kunkel, D., Farinola, W., Cope, K., Donnerstein, E., Biely, E., & Zwarun, L. (1998). *Rating the TV ratings: One year out.* Menlo Park, CA: Kaiser Family Foundation.

Levine, S. B. (1995). A variety of measures could combat media violence. In C. Wekesser (Ed.), *Violence in the media* (pp. 142–147). San Diego, CA: Greenhaven.

National Television Violence Study. (1998). *National Television Violence Study* (Vol. 3). Santa Barbara: University of California, Center for Communication and Social Policy.

Paik, H., & Comstock, G. (1994). The effects of television violence on anti-social behavior: A meta-analysis. *Communication Research, 24,* 516–546.

Potter, W. J. (1999). *On media violence.* Thousand Oaks, CA: Sage.

Roberts, D. F., Foehr, U. G., & Rideout, V. (2005). *Generation M: Media in the lives of 8-18 year-olds* (A Kaiser Family Foundation Study). Retrieved November 2, 2005, from http://www.kff.org/entmedia/upload/Generation-M-Media-in-the-Lives-of-8-18-Year-olds-Report.pdf

Wilson, B., Smith, S., Potter, W. J., Kunel, D., Linz, D., Colvin, C., & Donnerstein, E. (2002). Violence in children's television: Assessing the risks. *Journal of Communication, 52*(1), 5–35.

THIRD-PERSON EFFECT

The third-person effect, originally proposed by W. Phillips Davison in 1983, consists of a perceptual component and a behavioral component. The perceptual component is the view that media messages have a greater effect on others than on oneself. Davison speculated that this belief would have behavioral consequences; for example, it might make people more willing to monitor or regulate media content to protect vulnerable others. Most research on the third-person effect has been done with adults. A handful of studies have examined this phenomenon among children and adolescents, and two studies have explored parents' beliefs about the effects of television on their own and other children.

Support for the third-person perception has been found for many types of media content, including product and political advertising, rap music, pornography, and media violence. Results suggest that the third-person perception is strengthened when the media message is negative or when persuasion by the message is perceived as less socially desirable, but that it is reduced or reversed for positive media content (e.g., public service announcements), as long as audience members consider it desirable to be influenced by the message. In a study of parents' beliefs about television violence effects, third-person perceptions (that their own child would be less affected than others' children) were larger for socially undesirable aggression-related effects than for effects on perceptions of social reality. In another study, children judged themselves as less affected than other children by cigarette advertisements (a third-person perception) but saw themselves as more influenced by anti-smoking messages (a first-person perception).

One explanation for third-person perceptions, derived from attribution theory, is that people's judgments about their own and others' behavior is based on different sources of information (the fundamental attribution error), leading to biased perceptions. In an effort to explain the different patterns for negative and positive media content, scholars have suggested that self-enhancement may explain motivation. Third-person perceptions may be grounded in people's motivation to feel in control and maintain a positive self-image. Individuals can enhance their self-esteem by judging themselves as smarter, more knowledgeable, and more resistant to persuasion than others.

This tendency to see oneself as relatively unaffected by the media extends to one's close associates. Third-person perceptions are greater when the others being compared are described as more socially distant (students at the same school versus people in the same state). For example, children's third-person perceptions for cigarette ads were larger when the comparison others were children their age rather than their best friends. One explanation is that, when considering distant and unfamiliar others, people tend to generate a stereotyped image of someone likely to be more influenced by the media. Another explanation suggests that this pattern may reflect assumptions about media exposure. People may assume that more distant others are more likely to be exposed to harmful media content—for example, people in general watch more violent TV than the people in one's own neighborhood.

Group processes, such as those described by social identity theory, have also been proposed as an underlying mechanism. More distant others are likely to be seen as less similar and as more likely to belong to an out-group, that is, a social group different from one's own. People judged to be members of an out-group are evaluated less favorably—and as more influenced by the media—than members of one's in-group.

With regard to the behavioral component, studies have shown that the third-person perception is associated with a greater willingness to support restrictions on various forms of negative media, such as television violence and violent rap lyrics. A few studies have documented other behavioral consequences. For example, third-person perceptions of the effects of television are related to parental mediation of children's television viewing. Studies have also examined how third-person perceptions relate to young people's intentions to engage in behaviors such as smoking and safer-sex practices. In one study, the more likely youth were to smoke, based on stated intentions and exposure to a pro-smoking environment, the smaller their third-person perceptions for cigarette advertisements (self relative to other youth their age). This relationship may simply reflect accurate perceptions of media influence. Yet, youth who were more likely to smoke also thought their best friends were more affected by cigarette ads, raising the possibility that the perceived effects of media messages on peers may motivate young people to engage in popular behaviors to "fit in."

This interpretation is derived from a recent theoretical extension of the third-person effect, labeled "the influence of presumed influence." This model suggests that perceptions of media effects on others (rather than, or in addition to, the self–other difference) may offer a broader understanding of how beliefs about media effects may influence attitudes and behaviors. Young people may act in part on the basis of how they think their peers, parents, or others are influenced by media messages such as advertisements, blogs, or media sexual portrayals.

—*Cynthia A. Hoffner*

See also Advertising, Persuasive Intent of; Cigarette Advertising, Effects of; Peer Groups, Joint Use of Media in

FURTHER READINGS

Borzekowski, D. L. G., Flora, J. A., Feighery, E., & Schooler, C. (1999). The perceived influence of cigarette advertisements and smoking susceptibility among seventh graders. *Journal of Health Communication, 4,* 105–118.

Chapin, J. R. (1999). Third-person perception and sexual risk taking among minority "at-risk" youth. *Mass Communication & Society, 2,* 163–173.

Davison, W. P. (1983). The third-person effect in communication. *Public Opinion Quarterly, 47,* 1–15.

Duck, J. M., Hogg, M. A., & Terry, D. J. (2000). The perceived impact of persuasive messages on "us" and "them." In D. J. Terry & M. A. Hogg (Eds.), *Attitudes, behavior, and social context: The role of norms and group membership* (pp. 265–291). Mahwah, NJ: Erlbaum.

Gunther, A. C., & Storey, J. D. (2003). The influence of presumed influence. *Journal of Communication, 53,* 199–215.

Henriksen, L., & Flora, J. A. (2000). Third-person perception and children: Perceived impact of pro- and anti-smoking ads. *Communication Research, 26,* 643–665.

Hoffner, C., & Buchanan, M. (2002). Parents' responses to television violence: The third-person perception, parental mediation, and support for censorship. *Media Psychology, 4,* 231–252.

Perloff, R. M. (1999). The third-person effect: A critical review and synthesis. *Media Psychology, 1,* 353–378.

Tsfati, Y., Ribak, R., & Cohen, J. (2005). Rebelde Way in Israel: Parental perceptions of television influence and monitoring of children's social and media activities. *Mass Communication & Society, 8,* 3–22.

TOBACCO ADVERTISING, INTERNATIONAL

As with other types of consumer goods, tobacco companies use advertising and marketing strategies to promote their products. The first tobacco advertisements, dating from the 19th century, mainly describe pipe and chewing tobacco. In 1910, the manufacturing of cigarettes changed, and tobacco companies started intensive nationwide advertising campaigns for their new cigarette brands. In the early years (1880–1920), advertisements were mainly targeted toward men. During the 1920s, cigarette advertising began to be directed toward women as well. In the latter half of the 20th century, young people across the globe were targeted by tobacco ads. Today, the United States and Western Europe have banned many forms of media advertising for tobacco, but many young people are still exposed to a variety of tobacco advertising, especially in countries with few or no restrictions on such activity.

Advertising messages can be communicated through different forms of media broadcasting. Tobacco products have been advertised on television and radio, in the movies, in the printed media, and outdoors—for example, at sports and entertainment events, on billboards, and at places where tobacco can be bought. After publication of a national report on detrimental consequences of smoking by the U.S. Surgeon General in 1964, the negative health effects of tobacco smoking became widely known. The increased health risks related to smoking are considered a major threat to public health. Therefore, health policymakers aim to reduce smoking rates among the general population by smoking prevention policies and programs. Because tobacco advertising is assumed to encourage smokers to continue smoking and may possibly motivate nonsmokers to try smoking, health officials have advised bans on this type of commercial advertising.

Today, the United States and many countries in Western Europe place legal restrictions on commercial advertising of tobacco products. In the United Kingdom, the prohibition on tobacco advertising on television dates back to 1965. In the United States, tobacco advertising was banned from American broadcasting in 1971. Recent legislative restrictions ban tobacco advertising through other types of media, such as newspapers, magazines, and billboards. In past decades, legislative measures against tobacco advertising and promotion generally differed between Western European countries. However, in 2003, the member states of the European Union adopted a treaty prohibiting tobacco advertising in print media, radio broadcasting, and information society services. Furthermore, in its May 23, 2003, directive on the laws, regulations, and administrative provisions relating to the advertising and

香港政府忠告市民:吸煙危害健康

同興五金建築材料

英妮紅磚

This 1990 photograph shows a cigarette advertisement featuring Joe Camel that covers one wall of an apartment building in Hong Kong. During that time, international tobacco companies invested considerably in tobacco campaigns targeting new customers, including young smokers. In 1997, tobacco advertising was banned in Hong Kong. In the United States, the Joe Camel campaign was critized for deliberately targeting adolescents and children and was, therefore, ended by the tobacco company R. J. Reynolds in 1997.

SOURCE: © Richard T. Nowitz/CORBIS; used with permission.

free distribution of tobacco products. The implementation of the described restrictions in all member states was to have become effective in all member states before the end of 2005. According to a short communication by the European Commission in February 2006, most member states have transposed the directive into national law. The noncomplying countries and those where the directive has not been made national law may risk a fine. In sum, the directive on prohibition of advertising and tobacco sponsorship has generated a more harmonized European policy toward tobacco marketing.

Despite earlier restrictions on television and radio broadcasting of tobacco advertisements, tobacco companies have promoted the purchase of their products wherever and whenever they can legally do so. Tobacco products, particularly cigarettes, have been advertised widely during the past century. For example, in 2003, the Federal Trade Commission reported that cigarette companies in the United States spent more than $15 billion on tobacco advertising and promotional activities. The possible impact of the industry's advertising and promotion practices on young people's susceptibility to smoking initiation has been an important concern for health practitioners and health policymakers. Still, tobacco companies officially claim that their marketing practices are not aimed at the recruitment of new adolescent smokers but, instead, are intended to maintain or enhance the market share of a particular brand among adult smokers. In their review of internal documents from the United Kingdom's

sponsorship of tobacco products, the European Parliament and the European Council prohibited tobacco-related sponsorship of events as well as the tobacco industry, Gerard Hastings and Lynn MacFadyen contradict the tobacco companies' claims by showing that marketing strategies are indeed aimed at young people. Furthermore, a study by Joe DiFranza and colleagues shows that the "Old Joe Camel" cartoon advertisements for marketing Camel cigarettes had a much greater impact on children than on adults. It is obvious that the tobacco industry has an important financial interest in increasing the number of new (young) smokers. The relatively high risk of becoming dependent on the main addictive substance of tobacco smoke, nicotine, may be a substantial risk for young people experimenting with tobacco products. This assumption is confirmed by research indicating that nicotine dependence can be developed during the adolescent years. In her review of empirical research on adolescent nicotine dependence, Suzanne Colby and her colleagues found consistent evidence that a large majority of adolescent smokers show symptoms of such dependence. Thus, although the tobacco industry may not intend to increase the number of young smokers, it remains logical that future profits would benefit from increased smoking rates among adolescents.

Because most forms of tobacco advertising are prohibited in the United States and Western European countries, the effects of tobacco advertising may diminish considerably. However, globally, many countries still permit advertising or only partly restrict it. Furthermore, the possibilities for tobacco companies to circumvent advertising bans vary across countries. Therefore, tobacco companies have expanded their horizons, exporting their products to other countries, buying shares in foreign tobacco companies, starting new tobacco companies, and obtaining market shares by important joint ventures. To advertise their Western brands, tobacco companies have associated their cigarettes with glamorous aspects of Western lifestyle and attributes that the local population regards as desirable.

International trade in tobacco products has been present for several centuries. Nonetheless, since the 1980s, the U.S. Trade Representative (USTR) used the threat of trade sanctions to open Asian markets to U.S. cigarettes. The opening of the markets in Taiwan, Japan, and South Korea resulted in an increased offer of foreign tobacco products by large Western tobacco companies, such as Philip Morris and British American Tobacco (BAT). For example, research shows that between 1995 and 2000, advertising expenditures by foreign firms in Taiwan increased fourfold. In addition, based on findings from industry documents, researchers claim that tobacco companies targeted youth with their advertising campaigns. According to research findings, young smokers were recruited to provide information

about what attracted them to start smoking and about how they would describe the ideal cigarette. Furthermore, cigarette companies gathered data about whether brand appeals were product- or image-related, whether mild cigarettes would attract young smokers in Taiwan, and how young smokers would react to cigarette prices. Finally, the cartoon figure, Joe Camel, was introduced in several advertising campaigns in Taiwan. As mentioned earlier, this particular character was shown to appeal to adolescents and children in the United States.

Similar marketing activities by Western tobacco companies are present in other countries, as well. For example, a 2-week field study in Mumbai, India, in 2003 demonstrated that cigarettes of the Indian Tobacco Company (a subsidiary of BAT) were advertised in newspapers and film magazines and on billboards all over the city. In China, a large tobacco-producing country, the market opened to foreign companies in 1979. Although foreign companies are hindered by bureaucratic formalities, restrictions on joint ventures, and advertising bans, the sales of Western cigarettes in China has increased. Brands such as Marlboro, which were highly advertised before the advertising ban in 1995, achieved wide recognition and consumer preference. In African countries, Western tobacco companies hold important market shares. In most of the African countries, tobacco advertising is unrestricted, and smoking rates are increasing. In the late 1980s, Eastern Europe became an interesting market for Western tobacco companies; local production was increased via joint ventures. BAT, like other tobacco companies, heavily advertised its brands by glamorizing the Western lifestyle. As in Asia, these advertising campaigns were aimed at new smokers, youngsters, and women.

In response to the shift of tobacco marketing to non-Western, developing countries, 192 member states of the World Health Organization adopted the Framework Convention on Tobacco Control. Although the signatories agreed to impose restrictions on tobacco advertising, sponsorship, and promotion, many participating countries lack the means to impose the treaty's regulations effectively. Hence, global bans and restrictions on tobacco advertising may take time to be fully implemented. For many non-Western countries, this may mean that tobacco advertising can still play a role in adolescents' smoking initiation.

—Renske Spijkerman, Rutger C. M. E. Engels,
and Regina J. J. M. van den Eijnden

See also Cigarette Advertising, Effects of; Cigarette Advertising, History of; Cigarette Use, Music Videos and; Cigarette Use in Television and Movies

FURTHER READINGS

Bansal, R., John, S., & Ling, P. M. (2005). Cigarette advertising in Mumbai, India: Targeting different socioeconomic groups, women, and youth. *Tobacco Control, 14*(3), 201–206.

Chen, T., Hsu, C. C., Zhu, S. H., Li, D., Feng, B., Zhu, T., & Anderson, C. M. (1998). Perception of foreign cigarettes and their advertising in China: A study of college students from 12 universities. *Tobacco Control, 7,* 134– 140.

Colby, S. M., Tiffany, S. T., Shiffman, S., & Niaura, R. S. (2000). Are adolescent smokers dependent on nicotine? A review of the evidence. *Drug and Alcohol Dependence, 59*(Suppl. 1), S83–S95.

DiFranza, J. R., Richards, J. W., Paulman, P. M., Wolf-Gillespie, N., Fletcher, C., Jaffe, R. D., & Murray, D. (1991). RJR Nabisco's cartoon camel promotes camel cigarettes to children. *Journal of the American Medical Association, 266*(22), 3149–3153.

Directive 2003/33/EC of the European Parliament and of the Council on 26 May 2003 (2003). Retrieved June 6, 2006, from http://europa.eu.int/eur-lex/pri/en/oj/dat/2003/l_152/l_15220030620en00160019.pdf

Gilmore, A. B., & McKee, M. (2004). Moving East: How the transnational tobacco industry gained entry to the emerging markets of the former Soviet Union—Part I: Establishing cigarette imports. *Tobacco Control, 13*(2), 143–150.

Hastings, G., & MacFadyen, L. (2000). A day in the life of an advertising man: Review of internal documents from the UK tobacco industry's principal advertising agencies. *British Medical Journal, 321*(7257), 366–371.

Taha, A., & Ball, K. (1982). Smoking in Africa: The coming epidemic. *World Smoking Health, 7*(2), 25–30.

Wen, C. P., Chen, T., Tsai, Y. Y., Tsai, S. P., Chung, W. S., Cheng, T. Y., Levy, D. T., Hsu, C. C., Peterson, R., & Liu, W. Y. (2005). Are marketing campaigns in Taiwan by foreign tobacco companies targeting young smokers? *Tobacco Control, 14*(Suppl.1), i38–i44.

TV-TURNOFF WEEK

TV-Turnoff Week is the flagship program of TV-Turnoff Network, formerly known as TV-Free America. Held annually during the last week of April, TV-Turnoff Week calls for participants to voluntarily turn off their television sets and leave them off for a week. The slogan of this event is "Turn off TV, turn on life."

The TV-Turnoff Network was founded in 1994 by Henry Labalme and Matt Pawa on the basis of their belief that people should control the role that television plays in their lives. Aside from the amount of time children spend in front of a television set, the TV-Turnoff Network argues that television brings many negative effects to children. Obesity and aggression are two negative effects that are highlighted to support their initiatives. The TV-Turnoff Network believes that people should spend their time more meaningfully with their families, friends, and themselves. Based on their observation of benefits that some schools had from turning off television, TV-Turnoff Week asks people to turn off their television sets for a week and reassess the role TV plays in their lives.

The first TV-Turnoff Week was held in 1994, and 4,000 schools signed up that year, while 11 organizations supported the activity. Over the years, the event has gained more and more support from both local governments and private organizations. A majority of U.S. governors endorse the program. In 2004, more than 19,000 organizations participated in the event, and an estimated 7.6 million people participated. In 2005, nearly 70 national organizations lent their support. The 2005 TV-Turnoff Week also involved 10 other countries, such as Australia, Brazil, Great Britain, Canada, Japan, Taiwan, Italy, and Mexico.

The TV-Turnoff Network offers a number of activities that parents and teachers can use to help children fill up the time vacated by television viewing. It also provides parents with tips on how to reduce children's daily television viewing.

TV-Turnoff Week has been a success. Based on the feedback of the participants, 90% reported that they actually reduced their television viewing after their participation in this event. Encouraged by the success of TV-Turnoff Week, the first PC-Turnoff Week also took place in 2005.

—*Xiaomei Cai*

See also Family Environment, Media Effects on; Motherhood Project; Regulation, Television

WEBSITES

PC-Turnoff Week: http://www.pcturnoff.org
TV-Turnoff Network: http://www.tvturnoff.org/index.html

TWEENS, ADVERTISING TARGETING OF

The Media Awareness Network (2005b) describes the identification and labeling of the tween market as "one of the most important recent developments in advertising to kids." The exact origin of the word *tween* is disputed, but it generally refers to youth between the ages of 8 and 12 (although some marketers identify the demographic as extending to age 14). According to the 2000 U.S. Census, there are roughly 20.9 million tweens between the ages of 8 and 12, a figure that increases to 29 million if one includes those up to 14 years old. Studies show that tweens spend $40 billion on their own and influence billions more in parental purchases. Worldwide, tweens spend more than $300 billion a year and influence an additional $1.88 trillion in parental or family spending. To put it simply: "They have more personal power, more money, influence and attention than any other generation before them" (Lindstrom & Seybold, 2003, p. 1).

The tween phenomenon is not limited to the United States. *BRANDchild: Remarkable Insights Into the Minds of Today's Global Kids and Their Relationship With Brands* (Lindstrom & Seybold, 2003) provides what it claims is the most extensive study of tweens—a study of thousands of young people representing more than 70 cities and eight countries in Europe, Asia, South America, and the United States. This extensive research is used to provide marketers around the world with step-by-step advice for reaching tweens, in chapters titled "Tween Dreams for Sale," "Bonded to Brands: The Transition Years," and "The Peer Factor," to name just a few.

Being "in between" childhood and the teen years, tweens are particularly attractive to marketers because they are at an age when they are starting to develop and focus on their identity development—a fact that also makes them extremely susceptible to advertising messages focusing on self-esteem, popularity, and general identity issues. These are the years when the importance of brands and brand preference, especially as linked with identity, really take hold. Marketers feel they have to get tweens at this age to have their brand loyalty for life.

The publication of books such as *kidfluence: The Marketer's Guide to Understanding and Reaching Generation Y—Kids, Tweens, and Teens* (Sutherland & Thompson, 2003) and *The Great Tween Buying Machine: Capturing Your Share of the Multibillion Dollar Tween Market* (Siegel, Coffey, & Livingston, 2004) as well as a growing cadre of youth marketing agencies and self-proclaimed experts promise to help corporate America get it right in reaching this demographic. Some expert advice can be had for the price of a hardcover book, and other advice comes free on the Internet in the form of articles published in various industry publications such as *Selling to Kids*, *American Demographics*, and *Ad Age*.

Still other advice, however, comes at a steep price, evidencing the high stakes of marketing to tweens. For example, the marketing agency Buzzback provides pricey demographic reports and counseling for marketers wanting to understand and reach these young people. Their July 2003 "BuzzBack Tweens Exploratory" report can be had for $750. Online advertising for the report promises it will explain the behaviors, lifestyle, and thoughts of tweens, not to mention their social relationships and shopping habits. The BuzzBack report is a bargain when compared with the 230-page May 2005 Packaged Facts report, *The U.S. Market for Tweens and Young Teens: Attitudes, Aspirations, and Consumer Behavior of 8- to 14-Year-Olds*, 3rd edition, which sells for $3,500. Again, the online advertising for the report points out the "lucrative" nature of the tween demographic and the "invaluable" and "comprehensive" nature of the report. For marketers who want a more interactive experience, there are the KidPowerX conferences held all over the world and on specific topics related to reaching various segments of the youth market including tweens, again at a cost of attendance in the thousands of dollars.

To reach this lucrative demo, marketers are pulling out all the stops; their efforts include applying well-respected academic theories and research methods to studies of how to target tweens and children—what has been called "the marriage of psychology and marketing" (Media Awareness Network, 2005a). It's not unusual, for example, for marketing advice manuals to talk extensively about the work of Jean Piaget, Abraham Maslow, and other respected psychologists and sociologists in terms of how their theories can be applied to successfully target products to tween consumers. Similarly, as Juliet Schor (2004) points out, "the research has gone anthropological, with ethnographic methods that scrutinize the most intimate details" of youths' lives.

So what does all of this research and expense reveal about tweens? Branding is key, as brands are a high priority for tweens; they associate brands with their identities. Indeed, studies have shown that tweens are more concerned with brand name when making purchases than are older teens. Peers are also extremely important to tweens, and marketers take advantage of this fact by targeting tweens with such strategies as viral marketing, in which youth are encouraged to pass along marketing messages to friends, siblings, classmates, and so on. In addition, experts report on the nature of tweens as multitaskers who do not necessarily attend to any one medium alone at any point in time. This has led marketers to attempt to target tweens through a range of media, in particular through the Internet. Such intense marketing to tweens has not gone uncriticized, as advocacy groups including the Media Awareness Network urge parents to "fight back," in particular by educating tweens about the nature and intent of advertising messages.

—*Sharon R. Mazzarella*

See also Advertising, Market Size and; Advertising, Viewer Age and; Branding; Tweens, Media Preferences of; Viral Marketing

FURTHER READINGS

Lindstrom, M., & Seybold, P. B. (2003). *BRANDchild: Remarkable insights into the minds of today's global kids and their relationship with brands.* London: Kogan Page.

Media Awareness Network. (2005a). *How marketers target kids.* Retrieved May 8, 2006, from http://www.media-awareness.ca/english/parents/marketing/marketers_target_kids.cfm

Media Awareness Network. (2005b). *Marketing and consumerism: Special issues for tweens and teen.* Retrieved May 8, 2006, from http://www.media-awareness.ca/english/parents/marketing/issues_teens_marketing.cfm

Schor, J. (2004, Fall). America's most wanted: Inside the world of young consumers [Electronic version]. *Boston College Magazine.* Retrieved May 8, 2006, from http://www.bc.edu/publicatons/bcm/fall_2004/ft_schor.html

Siegel, D. L., Coffey, T. J., & Livingston, G. (2004). *The great tween buying machine: Capturing your share of the multibillion dollar tween market.* Chicago: Dearborn.

Sutherland A., & Thompson, B. (2003). *kidfluence: The marketer's guide to understanding and reaching Generation Y—Kids, tweens, and teens.* New York: McGraw-Hill.

TWEENS, MEDIA PREFERENCES OF

If there is one word that describes tweens' relationship with media, it is *multitasking.* Unlike any generation before them, today's tweens are surrounded by a dizzying array of media choices, a phenomenon they have learned to negotiate by consuming multiple media at the same time—talking to a friend on a cell phone and instant messaging another friend on the computer while the television plays in the background.

The exact origin of the word *tween* is disputed, but it generally refers to youth between the ages of 8 and 12 (although some marketers identify the demographic as extending to age 14). According to the 2000 U.S. Census, there are roughly 20.9 million tweens between the ages of 8 and 12, a figure that increases to 29 million if one includes those up to 14 years old. Studies show tweens spend $40 billion on their own each year and influence billions more in parental purchases. Worldwide, tweens spend more than $300 billion a year and influence an additional $1.88 trillion in parental or family spending. Network executives, advertisers, software designers, and technology manufacturers have all taken note of tweens' importance as media consumers and marketing targets.

For example, after years of being ignored by television programmers, tweens have become the darlings of the television industry worldwide, with Nickelodeon, the Disney Channel, and the Cartoon Network engaged in a fierce battle to be the network-of-choice for these young viewers. Media industry executives acknowledge the lucrative nature of this audience, but they also point out the difficulty of reaching them, in part because of their penchant for multitasking. A recent study reported that more than 50% of tweens do something else while watching television, including listening to music, reading, or using a computer. Another study reported that 21% of tweens (ages 8 to 12) report radio listening while watching television; other activities reported while watching television were 22%, instant messaging; 50%, computer use; and 54%, magazine reading. Moreover, studies show younger tweens report a stronger affinity for television than do older tweens. In fact, when it comes to media choices, another study found that if they had to choose, tweens would give up television before they would give up the Internet. These findings are supported by a March 2005 study by the Kaiser Family Foundation that found that tweens (ages 8 to 14) spend roughly 3¼ hours with television daily, while older teens watch only about 2½ hours a day.

Indeed, the above-mentioned Kaiser Family Foundation study is one of the best sources for information on tweens' media preferences. A study of some 2,000 youth ages 8-to-18, the findings reveal that youth ages 8 to 14 spend about 1 hour a day playing videogames as opposed to the half hour spent by older teens. When it comes to music listening, those in the 8-to-10 range spend 59 minutes per day listening versus the hour and 42 minutes per day spent by 11-to-14 year-olds and 2 hours and 25 minutes per day spent by 15-to-18-year-olds. Similarly, younger tweens spend less time using the computer each day, with 8-to-10-year-olds reporting 37 minutes a day, 11-to-14-year-olds reporting 1 hour and 2 minutes a day, and older teens reporting an hour and 22 minutes a day. While not statistically different, tweens (ages 8 to 14) do report watching more television than do older teens (3 hours and 16 minutes versus 2 hours and 36 minutes).

Although tweens are prone to multitasking, it is clear from these numbers that television still takes up a significant amount of time in the typical tween's life. According to one study, tweens' favorite shows are *SpongeBob SquarePants, The Fairly Odd Parents,* and *The Simpsons.* Interestingly, all three are animated, evidencing tweens' lingering connection to childhood preferences. Moreover, the first two programs are staples on the Nickelodeon cable network, aiding in their three-way ratings war for control of the lucrative tween market and solidifying Nickelodeon as tween's favorite TV destination. Anchored by their Sunday (and now also Saturday) night line-up of youth-oriented, scripted, live-action programs dubbed TEENick (targeted primarily to the 11-to-12-year-old segment of the tween market) and hyped by the network as "a Sunday-night destination" for tweens, Nickelodeon leads the ratings race. The appeal of these TEENick programs, as opposed to the type of teen dramas on other youth-oriented networks such as the WB, is that Nickelodeon uses actors who are

themselves tween- (or maybe teen-) aged instead of casting young-looking 20-somethings to play tweens.

Interestingly, while programmers are trying to encourage tweens to watch their programs, others are trying to get kids away from the tube. Spurred on by record levels of obesity in U.S. children, not to mention the fact that typical tweens spend more than 4 hours each day in front of some type of screen (television, computer, video games, etc.), the U.S. Department of Health and Human Services in 2002 launched an initiative called "VERB: It's What You Do!" intended to increase physical activity in kids of this age. The concept of the program is to encourage kids to incorporate more "verbs"—running, gardening, skateboarding, dancing, singing, hiking, and so on—into their lives so as to have fun while increasing their physical activity.

—Sharon R. Mazzarella

See also Computer Use, Age Differences in; Food Advertising, Obesity and; Instant Messaging; Internet Use, Age and; Kaiser Family Foundation; Mobile Telephones; Multitasking; Music Listening, Age Effects on; Television, Viewer Age and; Television, International Viewing Patterns and; Tweens, Advertising Targeting of

FURTHER READINGS

Lindstrom, M., & Seybold, P. B. (2003). *BRANDchild: Remarkable insights into the minds of today's global kids and their relationship with brands.* London: Kogan Page.

McConochie, R. M., & Solomon, D. (2003). *Children's media odysseys: The evolving media mix of kids ages 6 to 17 through the lenses of Arbitron's PPM cross media information and Mindshare's online research panel.* Retrieved from http://www.arbitron.com/downloads/arf_kids.doc

Rideout, V., Roberts, D. F., & Foehr, U. G. (2005). *Generation M: Media in the lives of 8-18 year-olds.* Washington, DC: Kaiser Family Foundation.

Siegel, D. L., Coffey, T. J., & Livingston, G. (2004). *The great tween buying machine: Capturing your share of the multibillion dollar tween market.* Chicago: Dearborn.

U

UNESCO VIOLENCE STUDY

The connection between actual violent threat, media violence, family environment, and aggressive behavior has been investigated in numerous empirical studies. However, the impact of cultural differences and different regional and media environments on the relationship between aggressive content and aggressive attitudes and actions has rarely been studied. To gain insight in this area, UNESCO commissioned a global study in the late 1990s covering representative samples of children from 23 different countries. The results of the study demonstrated the direct interplay between cultural influences, the characteristics of media content and infrastructure, actual violence experience, and dispositions such as gender and thrill-seeking tendencies in creating and increasing aggressive attitudes and behavior. Cultural values and their broad acceptance, therefore, can be regarded as a major moderator for the impact of media violence.

Developed and supervised by Grocbel (1999), the study used a standardized questionnaire with identical items on violent experience, media use, family and peer environment, worldviews, fear, and aggressive tendencies. The questions were distributed by the study's logistical partner, the World Scout Movement, among groups of average children; 5,500 12-year-olds from six geocultural regions around the globe—Africa, Arab States, Latin America, Asia, Europe, and Canada—replicd. The study included children from rural and metropolitan areas, high and low aggression neighborhoods, and high and low media infrastructure. The countries included were Angola, Argentina, Armenia, Brazil, Canada, Costa Rica, Croatia, Egypt, Fiji, Germany, India, Japan, Mauritius, the Netherlands, Peru, Philippines, Qatar, South Africa, Spain, Tadjikistan, Togo, Trinidad and Tobago, and Ukraine.

The results demonstrate that the combination of factors—real violence in the child's neighborhood (e.g., as a result of war, experiences in refugee camps, and gang fights, such as those in the Rio de Janeiro *favelas*), a high level of media violence (on TV, Internet, in electronic games), difficult family conditions (lack of affection, aggressive experience, physical punishment), and low levels of overall social norms—is much more likely to create aggression among children than any individual factor or partial combination of these factors. Media violence, in particular, has a strong impact only when there is a lack of immediately felt social control. This may explain why a country like Japan, where there is a high level of extremely violent media content in cartoons, animated films, movies, Internet sites, and games, has a comparatively low level of active child aggression against others. Despite the media violence in Japan, strong internalized values of a collective society apply. Where the influence of such values is much lower, violence levels go up when media violence and real aggressive experience come together, as has occurred in Brazil and South Africa. Further findings show that boys, in particular, are fascinated by aggressive heroes across cultures. Some of these, for example, Arnold Schwarzenegger as the *Terminator*, have become global icons. Studies at the end of the 20th century showed that 88% of the world's children knew this character. Children from environments with a high level of aggression were twice as likely to admire

Schwarzenegger as children from less violent environments. Overall, one third of the boys name an action hero as their primary role model whereas girls more often choose pop stars and musicians. Favorite heroes also vary by region: Action heroes are most popular in Asia (one third of participants) and least popular in Africa (one sixth of participants), where pop stars and musicians are the favorites.

Having violent role models appears to serve as a way to cope with an actual perceived threat. A remarkably large number of children seem to experience significant physical or social threats, and nearly half of the age group reported that they are anxious most of the time or extremely often. They have reason for their anxiety. About 10% of the global sample had to flee their homes at least once in their lives; nearly half report they would prefer to live in another country; in the high-aggression regions, one sixth of the children answer that most people in their neighborhood die because they are killed by others. Among children in high-aggression areas, about 10% of 12-year-olds have already used a weapon against someone. In such situations, media heroes are used for escapism and as models for ways to deal with real-life problems.

The children's worldviews are obviously influenced by actual experiences as well as media exposure. Nearly one third of children living in high-aggression environments believe that most people in the world are evil as compared to one fifth in the low-aggression areas. Slightly less than half of both groups, remarkably, report a strong overlap in what they perceive as reality and what they see on the TV screen. The importance of TV is underlined by the fact that watching television consumes about 50% more of the children's leisure time than any other activity. Three hours is the global daily average, but of course, the amount ranges from less than an hour up to more than 8 hours, depending on the availability of TV in that nation. In any case, TV was the major socialization factor around the world until the early 21st century.

The impact of media violence can be explained primarily through the fact that aggressive behavior is rewarded. Nearly 50% of those who prefer aggressive media content said they would also like to be actively involved in a risky situation (as compared to 20% with another media preference). This holds especially for boys. In addition, the risk-seeking tendency is reinforced in countries with a high level of technological development. When youngsters have access to a broad spectrum of audiovisual media, their desire to respond actively to the stimulus of aggressive media content appears to increase.

—Jo Groebel

See also Aggression, Television and; Manga (Japanese Comic Books); Television, International Viewing Patterns and; Violence, Effects of

FURTHER READINGS

Groebel, J. (1999). *The UNESCO global study on media violence* (Report to the director-general). Retrieved May 22, 2006, from htttp://www.znak.com.pl/eurodialog/ed/przemoc/raport.html.en

Groebel, J. (2002). Media violence in cross-cultural perspective. In D. G.Singer & J. L. Singer (Eds.), *Handbook of children and the media* (pp. 255–268). Thousand Oaks, CA: Sage.

UNITED NATIONS CONVENTION ON THE RIGHTS OF THE CHILD

Created over a 10-year period by a global group of experts in fields ranging from government, child development, human rights, and education, the United Nations Convention on the Rights of the Child is an international treaty designed to guarantee and safeguard the rights of those under the age of 18. The treaty focuses on the realms of personal identity, health, nationality, care, educational access, justice, and freedom from all forms of exploitation and harsh punishment. Two optional protocols aim to keep children safe during warfare and to bar their involvement in prostitution, pornography, and slavery. The convention was adopted by the United Nations General Assembly in November 1989 and went into effect in September 1990.

The primary treaty includes a preamble and 54 articles, the latter divided into three parts, and is supported by two optional protocols, one on the sale of children, child prostitution, and child pornography, and one on the involvement of children in armed conflict. The treaty and both protocols have been adopted and are in effect worldwide.

Implementation of the convention and its two optional protocols are monitored by the Committee on the Rights of the Child (CRC), under the auspices of the Office of the United Nations Commissioner for

Human Rights. No other treaty in history has gained more international support; it has been ratified by 191 of 193 UN members, excluding Somalia and the United States. Somalia has signed but is barred from ratification until it has a recognized government, and the United States has signed the treaty but is still examining every facet of compliance. As both have signed, they have thus signified that ratification at a later date is still possible.

MEDIA-RELATED ARTICLES

Two articles of the main treaty and the optional protocol on the sale of children, child prostitution, and child pornography describe in detail issues related to the media and their attendant relationships with adolescents and children.

Article 13 involves a child's right to freedom of expression and to receive and disseminate ideas through all forms of media, barring necessary legal restrictions in the interest of individual rights and reputations, the protection of national security and public order, health, and morals.

Article 17 requires ratifying nations to acknowledge the function of the mass media and to assure access for children to a diverse range of international media sources. This is to be accomplished (1) by encouraging media owners to release material relating to and intended for children; (2) by promoting international cooperation in the creation and release of child-focused audio, video, and print materials dealing with a wide range of cultures, nationalities, and internationalities, with a distinct focus on materials created in the mother-tongue of indigenous and minority populations; and (3) by endorsing the creation of guiding principles to protect children from harmful media, insofar as this will not negate other aspects of the convention.

Article 34 deals with the protection of children from sexual exploitation and specifically bars the use of children in "pornographic performances and materials." This directly relates to the optional protocol dealing with the same issue.

The optional protocol defines *child pornography* as "any representation, by whatever means, of a child engaged in real or simulated explicit sexual activities or any representation of the sexual parts of a child for primarily sexual purposes," and it explicitly prohibits the sale of such materials. This aspect of the protocol is similar in effect to Article 34; however, the protocol merely prohibits the sale of these materials, whereas Article 34 restricts their creation.

A case can be made that Article 31 has a relationship to media, as it notes the rights of children to rest and leisure time and activities, and requires ratifying nations to respect and promote the equal opportunity to freely join in artistic, cultural leisure, and recreational activities when appropriate.

—*Solomon Davidoff*

See also Child Pornography; Globalization, Media and; Internet Use, International; Knowledge Gap; Obscenity; Parental Regulation of Children's Media; Pornography (various entries); Rating Systems, Parental Use of; Sex, Internet Solicitation of; Sex in Television, Content Analysis of; Television Violence, Susceptibility to; UNESCO Violence Study; Violence, Effects of; Violence, Morality and; World Summits on Children and Television

FURTHER READINGS

Committee on the Rights of the Child. (2003). *Convention on the Rights of the Child* [Electronic version]. Retrieved from http://www.unhchr.ch/html/menu3/b/k2crc.htm

Corcos. C. A. (1991). The child in international law: A pathfinder and selected bibliography. *Case Western Reserve Journal of International Law*, 23(2), 171–197.

Detrick, S. (1999). *A commentary on the United Nations Convention on the Rights of the Child.* Boston: Martinus Nijhoff.

Detrick, S. (2001). A commentary on the United Nations Convention on the Rights of the Child. *The International Journal of Children's Rights*, 9(1), 63–67.

WEBSITE

Committee on the Rights of the Child: http://www.ohchr.org/english/bodies/crc/index.htm

USES AND GRATIFICATIONS THEORY

Uses and gratifications theory is based on these basic ideas: that media audiences are active rather than passive; that their media choices depend on perceived needs, satisfactions, wishes, or motives; and that audiences are formed on the basis of similarities of need, interest, and taste. The primary questions to be answered with uses and gratifications research are why do people choose certain media and not other media, and what are the rewards derived from attending to these media? *Media* may be a medium such as television or a subset such as a program type or a specific television program.

Communication scholars studied the uses and gratifications of various aspects of mass media before it became known as the uses and gratifications approach. Researchers in the 1940s looked at what people missed about reading the newspaper when the newspaper staff was on strike, the gratifications derived from listening to soap operas, reasons for becoming interested in serious music on radio, and how children develop an interest in the comics. In the 1960s and 1970s, a more systematic approach to studying how and why people use media led to the emergence of the uses and gratifications model. Blumler and Katz (1974) discuss the major elements in the model: The audience is considered to be active rather than passive in media consumption; initiative in linking need gratification and media choice lies with the audience member; the media compete with other sources of need satisfaction; many of the goals of mass media use can be derived from data supplied by audience members themselves; and value judgments about the cultural significance of mass communication should be suspended while audience orientations are explored. McQuail (2000) lists additional elements: Audiences are conscious of media-related needs and can voice them in terms of motivations; personal utility is a more significant determinant of audience formation than aesthetic or cultural factors; and all of the relevant factors for audience formation can be measured. With these elements in mind, researchers set out to find the attributes of different media that satisfy needs of media consumers.

They found, among other things, that television and print media were interchangeable for learning purposes; that books share an information function with newspapers and an aesthetic function with movies; and that in times of crisis, radio is the best medium for news, television is the best way to understand the significance of news, and television is best for releasing tension.

CLASSIFYING NEEDS

Based on their research in the area, McQuail, Blumler, and Brown listed four broad categories as reasons

people use the media: diversion or escapism; companionship and development of personal relationships; value reinforcement and exploring personal identity; and surveillance or getting information about the world. Katz, Gurevich, and Haas came up with a slightly different list: cognitive needs—acquiring information, knowledge, or understanding; affective needs—emotional or aesthetic experience; personal integrative needs—strengthening credibility, confidence, stability, and status; and social integrative needs—strengthening contact with family and friends.

The uses and gratifications approach has been criticized for not providing predictive ability, for being nontheoretical and vague in defining key concepts, for using self-reports to determine motives, and for relying on psychological concepts such as need.

Despite criticism dating back to the 1970s, communication researchers continue to study the uses and gratifications approach. Kaye and Johnson (2004) looked at Internet users during the 2000 presidential election to see if political attitudes, Internet experience, and personal characteristics predicted motivations for Internet use. The researchers looked at respondents' motives for using the Web, bulletin boards, chat rooms, and mailing lists and found that each of these satisfied slightly different needs. These needs could be predicted by some political attitudes, demographics, and Internet use. This study is one of many examining uses of the Internet. A study by Haridakis and Rubin (2003) examined the uses and gratifications of watching television violence and found that audience characteristics, such as loneliness, isolation, and lifestyle, often are the most important predictors of aggression and also affect media use. Other studies have integrated uses and gratifications with other theories. Hofstetter (2001) combined uses and gratifications and self-efficacy: the belief that a person can perform a task successfully and that doing so produces positive consequences. He looked at self-efficacy in connection with skill in using media and found that self-efficacy measures were correlated with media use, intellectual stimulation credibility, political efficacy, and political participation. LaRose and Eastin (2004) integrated uses and gratifications and social cognitive theory into a theory of media attendance. They write that their research both supports the uses and gratifications approach and extends it by making it more theoretical; by adding new operational measures for expected gratifications, they believe media consumption can be predicted to an unprecedented degree. Thus, some of the prior criticisms of the approach are rendered invalid.

Although children's and adolescents' use of media has not been studied as thoroughly as that of adults, one area of interest in recent years is use of violent media. Slater (2003) studied the role of alienation from school, family, and peers in predicting use of violent media content, believing that examining psychosocial disorders as predictors of the use of violent media might bridge the gap between uses and gratifications research and media effects research. He found that use of media with violent content was predicted by aggression, after controlling for sensation seeking; both having a sensation-seeking personality and being male were also predictors. Slater also found that alienation predicted use of websites with violent content.

— *Kate Peirce*

See also Cultural Identity; Media Genre Preferences; Television, Motivations for Viewing of; Violence, Experimental Studies of

FURTHER READINGS

Blumler, J. G., & Katz, E. (Eds.). (1974). *The uses of mass communications.* Beverly Hills, CA: Sage.

Haridakis, P. M., & Rubin, A. M. (2003, February). Motivation for watching television violence and viewer aggression. *Mass Communication and Society, 6,* 29–56.

Hofstetter, C. R., Zuniga, S., & Dozier, D. M. (2001). Media self-efficacy: Validation of a new concept. *Mass Communication and Society, 4,* 61–76.

Kaye, B. K., & Johnson, T. J. (2004, August). A Web for all reasons: Uses and gratifications of Internet components for political information. *Telematics & Informatics, 21,* 197–223.

LaRose, R., & Eastin, M. S. (2004). A social cognitive theory of Internet uses and gratifications: Toward a new model of media attendance. *Journal of Broadcasting and Electronic Media, 48,* 358–377.

McQuail, D. (2000). *McQuail's mass communication theory.* Thousand Oaks, CA: Sage.

Severin, W. J., & Tankard, J. W. (2001). *Communication theories.* New York: Longman.

Slater, M. D. (2003, March). Alienation, aggression, and sensation seeking as predictors of adolescent use of violent film, computer, and website content. *Journal of Communication, 53,* 105–121.

V

V-CHIP (VIOLENCE CHIP)

Since 2000, all new television sets with screens 13 inches or larger have been required to come equipped with a V-chip (violence chip). The V-chip works in conjunction with a content-rating system, allowing television sets to decode the content rating of each television program. Parents can then block programming with objectionable ratings from their television set. The V-chip requirement was passed by Congress as part of the 1996 Telecommunications Act.

The V-chip is designed to empower parents to control their children's exposure to violence (and sex, adult language, etc.). In the official findings supporting the passage of the bill, Congress cited broad parental support for a technological solution allowing parents to mitigate the negative impact of televised sex and violence on children. Congress declared a compelling government interest in giving parents a tool to limit such effects, saying the V-chip is a narrowly tailored means of achieving that interest. This language specifically addresses the criteria used by courts to review content-related legislation impinging on First Amendment freedoms.

The text of the findings, then, reflects awareness of the potential First Amendment implications of the V-chip and the ratings system necessary for it to work. Critics argue that because the technology requires the rating of programs in order to function, the law violates the principles of free expression. Supporters of the V-chip counter that it is not a content regulation because the government is not limiting television programming in any way. Rather, the V-chip provides a tool for parents to monitor their child's television use.

In reality, however, very few parents are using the V-chip. Many people are unaware of its existence. Of those who do know about the V-chip, the majority do not know how to program it. Even in a study where a group of parents received special training on the operation of the V-chip, only a small portion were actually using it a year later; those who used it were parents who already were very active in monitoring their children's media use. A public information campaign was launched in 2001 to increase public knowledge about the V-chip.

Additional criticism of the V-chip focuses on the efficacy of the technology. Children are generally more technologically savvy than their parents, raising the question of whether kids can simply reprogram the television. A password system is in place to try to avoid this pitfall. Another issue is that sports and news programming are not rated and therefore cannot be blocked by the V-chip. Content analyses have shown sports and news shows to be high in violent content. A final challenge to the V-chip's effectiveness is that broadcasters and cable stations rate their own programming. Although this alleviates some of the First Amendment concerns, it raises questions about the validity of the rating system on which the V-chip depends.

—*Jennifer L. Lambe*

See also Family Environment, Media Effects on; First Amendment; Parental Regulation of Children's Media; Rating Systems, Parental Use of; Regulation, Television; Television Rating Systems, Parental Uses of; Violence, Effects of

FURTHER READINGS

Federal Communications Commission. (2003). *V-chip: Viewing television responsibly.* Retrieved from http://www.fcc.gov/vchip/

Parental Choice in Television Programming. U.S. Code 47, Chapter 5, Subchapter 3, Section 303 (1996).

VIDEO GAMES

See ENTRIES ON ELECTRONIC GAMES

VIOLENCE, DESENSITIZATION TOWARD

Most people naturally have aversive reactions to the sight of blood and gore. Some people (e.g., soldiers, surgeons) must overcome these reactions to perform their duties effectively. Their ability to do so illustrates the process of desensitization, defined as diminished psychological responsiveness to a stimulus after repeated exposure to it. Desensitization can be adaptive because it enables people to ignore irrelevant information and focus instead on relevant information. For most people, however, becoming desensitized to blood and gore can have maladaptive social consequences, such as reducing inhibitions against behaving aggressively and limiting responsiveness to victims of violence.

Hundreds of studies have shown that exposure to media violence contributes to increased societal violence. Media violence is believed to increase aggression, at least in part, by desensitizing viewers to the effects of real violence. Media violence initially produces fear, disgust, anxiety, and other avoidance-related motivational states. Repeated exposure to media violence, however, reduces its psychological impact and eventually produces aggressive approach-related motivational states, leading to increased aggression.

EFFECTS OF VIOLENT MEDIA EXPOSURE ON DESENSITIZATION

Surprisingly few media violence studies have examined physiological-emotional indicators of desensitization. Despite the small number of studies, there does appear to be a consensus in the literature that exposure to violent television can cause short-term desensitization in viewers.

Thomas, Horton, Lippincott, and Drabman conducted two studies in the 1970s examining the desensitizing effects of violent television exposure. Children were brought into a lab and hooked up to a device that measures the amount of voltage in their skin. When people get anxious, they sweat, and voltage levels increase because the sweat conducts electricity. After a baseline measure of skin conductance levels, participants viewed either a violent or nonviolent film. Next, participants viewed a film that they believed to be a real-life live event in which two children start attacking one another. Those who had viewed the violent film earlier were significantly less aroused by the "real-life" violence film than were those who had viewed the nonviolent film. Apparently those who had watched the violent film became desensitized to real-world violence.

About the same time, Cline, Croft, and Courier examined the long-term effects of violent television exposure on children and adolescents. Participants (whose ages ranged from 7 to 14 years old) reported their weekly television exposure and were divided into high-exposure and low-exposure groups. After a baseline measure of skin conductance was taken, participants viewed nonviolent and violent film sequences. Although there were no differences in arousal while viewing the nonviolent scenes, those who watched a lot of television showed less arousal while watching the violent scenes than did those who watched relatively little. Although the researchers did not measure violent television exposure, it seems very likely that those who watched a lot of television were also exposed to more violent television.

Desensitization effects have also been shown in older age groups, suggesting that these effects are not limited to children. One such study was conducted by Thomas and his colleagues. College-age participants viewed either a violent or nonviolent film clip, then watched footage from a real-life riot. Males who were previously exposed to the violent film clip were less aroused than males who had viewed a nonviolent film (these results were not found for females).

A study conducted by Linz, Donnerstein, and Adams found similar results with a college student sample. Participants who viewed 2 hours of filmed violence toward women had significantly lower heart rates while viewing later scenes of a man abusing a woman than participants who had previously viewed 2 hours of auto racing.

A recent study by Bartholow, Bushman, and Sestir examined the relationship between violent video game exposure, desensitization to violence, and aggressive behavior. Participants first completed scales that measure trait aggression and exposure to violent video games. Next, participants viewed a series of photos while their brain waves were measured. Finally, participants completed a task in which they believed they could show aggression toward another person by blasting the person with loud noise. Results showed that violent video-game players had less physiological response to violent images, which suggests desensitization. Also, physiological response to violent images was negatively correlated with aggression levels. These findings suggest a relationship between media violence exposure, desensitization, and aggressive behavior.

In summary, despite the small amount of research, there is evidence that exposure to media violence can cause physiological desensitization to other violence, even when the viewers believe the latter is real-life violence. There is also some evidence that this physiological desensitization could be linked to later aggressive behavior.

—Nicholas L. Carnagey and
Brad J. Bushman

See also Aggression (various entries); Desensitization Effects; Fear Reactions; Television, Prosocial Behavior and; Television Violence; Television Violence, Susceptibility to

FURTHER READINGS

Bartholow, B. D., Bushman, B. J., & Sestir, M. A. (2006). Chronic violent video game exposure and desensitization to violence: Behavioral and event-related brain potential data. *Journal of Experimental Social Psychology, 42,* 532–539.

Cline, V. B., Croft, R. G., & Courier, S. (1973). Desensitization of children to television violence. *Journal of Personality and Social Psychology, 27,* 360–365.

Lazarus, R. S., Speisman, M., Mordkoff, A. M., & Davison, L. A. (1962). A laboratory study of psychological stress produced by a motion picture film. *Psychological Monographs: General and Applied, 34*(553).

Linz, D., Donnerstein, E., & Adams, S. M. (1989). Physiological desensitization and judgments about female victims of violence. *Human Communication Research, 15,* 509–522.

Thomas, M. H. (1982). Physiological arousal, exposure to a relatively lengthy aggressive film, and aggressive behavior. *Journal of Research in Personality, 16,* 72–81.

Thomas, M. H., Horton, R. W., Lippincott, E. C., & Drabman, R. S. (1977). Desensitization to portrayals of real life aggression as a function of television violence. *Journal of Personality and Social Psychology, 35,* 450–458.

VIOLENCE, EFFECTS OF

For more than 50 years, social scientists have conducted research on the effects of violent media, including TV programs, films, and video games. Researchers have found evidence of three different effects of media violence:

1. *Bystander effect:* The more violent media you consume, the more desensitized you become to violence in the real world.

2. *Aggressor effect:* The more violent media you consume, the more aggressive you become.

3. *Victim effect:* The more violent media you consume, the more afraid you are of becoming a victim of violence.

The research evidence for each type of effect is described below.

Bystander effect. People who consume a lot of violent media become less sympathetic to victims of violence. People who are exposed to violent media assign less harsh penalties to criminals than those who are not; they also perceive victims as less seriously injured and display less empathy toward them. The bystander effect appears to be an enduring one. Even several days after watching violent sex scenes, men still display an increased tolerance of aggression directed toward women.

The reduced empathy for victims of violence causes people to become less willing to help a victim of violence in the real world. Immediately after exposure to violent media, children are less willing to intervene when they see two younger children fighting. One reason why people may become more tolerant of violence and less sympathetic toward victims is because they become desensitized to violence over time. Research has shown that after exposure to violent media, people are less physiologically aroused by real depictions of violence.

The effects of violent video games on children's attitudes toward violence are of particular concern. Feeling empathy requires taking the perspective of the victim, whereas violent video games encourage players to take the perspective of the perpetrator. Exposure to violent television increases people's pro-violence attitudes, but exposure to violent video games has the additional consequence of decreasing empathy for the victim.

Aggressor effect. More than five decades of scientific data lead to the irrefutable conclusion that exposure to violent media increases aggression. About 300 studies involving more than 50,000 subjects have been conducted on this topic (Anderson & Bushman, 2002). Experimental studies have shown that exposure to media violence *causes* people to behave more aggressively immediately afterward, whereas longitudinal studies have shown that the long-term effects of exposure to violent media have a significant impact on real-world aggression and violence. In part, this is because exposure to violent media desensitizes people to violence, but it is also because violent media teach children that violent behavior is an appropriate means of resolving problems.

Experimental studies typically expose participants to violent media for relatively short amounts of time (usually 20 minutes) before measuring aggressive thoughts, feelings, and, most important, behaviors (for reviews, see Anderson et al., 2003). For example, research has shown that exposure to violent media makes people more willing to subject others to electric shocks or noise blasts.

Experimental studies have been criticized for their somewhat artificial nature (for reviews and rebuttals of these criticisms, see Anderson, Lindsay, & Bushman, 1999), but field experiments have produced similar results. For example, delinquent boys who were shown violent films every night for 5 nights were more likely than those shown nonviolent films to get into fights with other children or display verbal aggression. Similar effects have been observed with nondelinquent children who saw a single episode of a violent children's television program. It is important to note that aggression may be qualitatively different from criminal violence (Savage, 2004) and that, for the most part, laboratory and field experiments have not addressed the relationship between violent media and violent behavior. A few studies have attempted to address this relationship in a naturalistic setting by tracking changes in the occurrence of violent crime after prize fights are shown on TV or after television is introduced to a

community, but these studies are few in number and have methodological flaws.

However, it is not so much the immediate effect of media violence on violent crime rates that is of concern, but rather the aggregated long-term effects (Anderson et al., 2003). Children are exposed to about 10,000 violent crimes in the media per year, and each of these has a cumulative effect on their thoughts, feelings, and actions. Violent media exposure increases children's aggressive disposition, which in turn increases the likelihood that they will commit a violent act.

Longitudinal studies offer evidence of a relationship between long-term exposure to violent television and aggressive and violent behavior in the real world. Children who watch a lot of violent television are more likely to behave aggressively later in life. For example, in one longitudinal study, children exposed to violent media were significantly more aggressive 15 years later (Huesmann, Moise-Titus, Podolski, & Eron, 2003). It is significant that this study also found that being an aggressive child was unrelated to exposure to violent media as a young adult, effectively ruling out the possibility that this relationship is merely a result of more aggressive children consuming more violent media.

Longitudinal studies have also demonstrated that exposure to violent media is related to serious, violent antisocial behavior. For example, the amount of violent media consumed is related to aggressive behavior (e.g., fighting) in high school students. Similarly, men who had watched violent media during childhood were nearly twice as likely to have assaulted their spouses 15 years later (Huesmann et al., 2003). In another longitudinal study, consumption of violent media at age 14 predicted violent crimes committed at age 22.

Although these studies demonstrate that media violence increases aggression and is related to violent crime, a number of important moderators of this effect are of theoretical and practical importance. For example, *how* violence is depicted is important. Attractive people who commit realistic violence that goes unpunished and has no apparent consequences for the victim are particularly appealing to children. Also, *who* watches violent media is important. A number of personality traits seem to place some viewers at greater risk than others. One key personality trait is aggressiveness. People who score high in trait aggressiveness behave more aggressively after being exposed to violent media, whereas there are comparatively fewer differences before and after media exposure among those who are not aggressive. However, these findings represent trait differences at a single point in time in an experimental setting. Exposure to media violence causes trait aggressiveness, which in turn increases the likelihood of aggressive behavior. This suggests that the short-term effects of violent media observed in experimental research may become increasingly pronounced within individuals as they are repeatedly exposed to violence, leading to a downward spiral into greater levels of aggression.

Younger children appear to be particularly vulnerable to the effects of media exposure as compared to teenagers and adults. Some studies have found that boys are more influenced by media violence than girls, but these effects are inconsistent; other research has found little difference between boys and girls. This inconsistency may be a result of different measures of aggression or different gender norms in the sample populations. Longitudinal studies have shown that gender differences in aggression have decreased over time, probably because more aggressive female models have appeared on TV and because it has become more socially acceptable for females to behave aggressively. One clear difference is that the combination of exposure to sex *plus* violence appears to be particularly potent in males. In one study, college students watched a movie portraying violence, one depicting sex and violence, or a nonviolent control film. Men exposed to both sex and violence were more aggressive toward a female who provoked them than were men exposed to only violence or men exposed to no sex or violence.

The effect of violent media on aggression is not trivial, either. Although the typical effect size for exposure to violent media is small by conventional standards and is thus dismissed by some critics, this small effect translates into significant consequences for society as a whole, which may be a better standard to use in measuring the magnitude of the effect. A recent meta-analysis has suggested that the effect of exposure to violent media is stronger than other small effects, such as the effect of secondhand smoke on lung cancer, the effect of asbestos on cancer, and the effect of lead poisoning on mental functioning (Bushman & Anderson, 2001).

Although the majority of studies to date have focused on violent television and movies, the same general pattern of effects appears to be present after exposure to different forms of media, including violent music and violent video games.

Victim effect. Heavy TV viewers (defined as 4 hours per day or more) are more fearful about becoming victims of violence, are more distrustful of others, and are more likely to perceive the world as a dangerous, mean, and hostile place. In another study, television exposure was predictive of fear of crime, whereas actual exposure to crime was not. A similar but stronger relationship has been reported between watching television news and fear of crime. Like the aggressor effect, this process seems to begin early in childhood, with even 7-to-11-year-olds displaying this pattern.

In general, the victim effect seems to apply only to people's appraisals of environments with which they have relatively little experience. Although violent media make people more afraid of crime in their city, exposure to violent media has relatively little impact on people's feelings of safety in their own neighborhood. This suggests that the victim effect may be related to the *availability heuristic.* People make evaluations based on salient information, and when people have relatively little firsthand experience with an environment, they may draw on television as an additional source of information. However, the victim effect may be more complicated than a simple distortion of base rates. Some researchers have recently found that violent media do not influence people's beliefs about the prevalence of crime, but people do become more fearful of crime. This suggests that there is an emotional component to the victim effect as well.

It is clear that violent media are related to violence in the society, and they make people more likely to act aggressively, more tolerant of violence, and more fearful of crime; however, not all forms of violence are alike. Media that glamorize violence may have a particularly strong influence on the bystander and aggressor effects. In contrast, the victim effect may be constrained to media that children believe to serve an informative role about the world around them, such as television news. Whether someone is more likely to become an aggressor or a victim may also depend on who they identify with, the perpetrators of violence or their victims. However, for practical purposes, the sheer amount and variety of violence children are exposed to makes it likely that all children are vulnerable to these effects in varying degrees.

—*Brad J. Bushman and Jesse J. Chandler*

See also Aggression, Movies and; Aggression, Television and; Electronic Games, Violence in; Media Effects;

Music, Impact of Violence in; Schemas/Scripts, Aggressive; Television Violence; Violence, Experimental Studies of; Violence, Natural Experiments and

FURTHER READINGS

Anderson, C. A., Berkowitz, L., Donnerstein, E., Huesmann, R. L., Johnson, J. D., Linz, D., Malamuth, N. M., & Wartella, E. (2003). The influence of media violence on youth. *Psychological Science in the Public Interest, 4,* 81–110.

Anderson, C. A., & Bushman, B. J. (2002). Media violence and societal violence. *Science, 295,* 2377–2378.

Anderson, C. A., Lindsay, J. J., & Bushman, B. J. (1999). Research in the psychological laboratory: Truth or triviality? *Current Directions in Psychological Science, 8,* 3–9.

Bushman, B. J., & Anderson, C. A. (2001). Media violence and the American public: Scientific facts versus media misinformation. *American Psychologist, 56,* 477–489.

Huesmann, L. R., Moise-Titus, J., Podolski, C. L., & Eron, L. D. (2003). Longitudinal relations between children's exposure to TV violence and their aggressive and violent behavior in young adulthood: 1977–1992. *Developmental Psychology, 39,* 201–221.

Savage, J. (2004). Does viewing violent media really cause criminal violence? A methodological review. *Aggression & Violent Behavior, 10,* 99–128.

VIOLENCE, EXPERIMENTAL STUDIES OF

The two hallmarks of an experimental study are control and random assignment. The researcher chooses the variable of interest (e.g., violent versus nonviolent video game) and then randomly assigns participants to levels of the variable (e.g., by flipping a coin). In an experimental study on video game violence, for example, participants do not get to choose whether they want to play a violent or nonviolent game. If participants chose the game they wanted to play, differences in behavior after viewing the game might be a result of preexisting individual differences between those who preferred to play a violent game and those who selected a nonviolent game. If violent game players were more aggressive afterward, it would be impossible to tell if the increase in aggression was due to the game or to individual differences in aggressiveness.

Numerous experimental studies have shown that exposure to violent media increases aggression (e.g., Anderson & Bushman, 2002). Experimental studies have played two crucial roles in documenting and understanding the effects of violent media. First, experimental studies increase confidence that there is a causal relationship between exposure to violent media and aggressive behavior. Second, experimental studies allow researchers to examine the specific mechanisms by which violent media influence aggressive behavior.

Although other research methods, such as field studies, case studies, and correlational studies, provide compelling evidence of a correlation between violent media and aggression, correlation does not imply causation. Longitudinal studies are better at establishing causality. Such research indicates that watching violent media as a child correlates with aggression later in life, although childhood aggression does not predict adult television viewing habits (Huesmann, Moise-Titus, Podolski, & Eron, 2003). However, longitudinal studies cannot rule out the possibility that both watching violent media and aggressive behavior are caused by an unknown third variable. Longitudinal researchers try to measure as many third variables as they can think of (e.g., poverty, IQ, social skills, parenting), but it is always possible that they forgot to measure an important third variable.

Experiments help researchers determine the precise cause of aggressive behavior. For example, violent media are arousing, and arousal increases aggression. Thus, it may be that violent content does not make people any more aggressive than other arousing media. Researchers have been able to rule out this possibility by presenting movies that are equally arousing but contain differing levels of violence.

The degree of control within experimental settings allows researchers to determine not only what causes aggressive behavior but also the process by which different variables influence each other. Violent media may increase aggressive behavior because they increase the accessibility of violent thoughts. Violent media also make people more likely to attend to hostile information and to expect others to behave in a hostile manner. Studies have also shown that violent media make people experience more angry feelings.

Researchers also perform quasi-experiments, which can provide important insights into how different types of people respond to violent media. Quasi-experiments are similar to experiments in that they ensure that all participants are exposed to the same treatment. However, they are not true experiments because they do not randomly assign participants to different conditions. Instead, they look at how different populations respond to an identical situation. For example, one cannot randomly assign people to be males or females or to be aggressive or nonaggressive. Quasi-experiments have found that men respond more aggressively after exposure to violent media than women do and that people who score high in trait aggressiveness are particularly susceptible to the influence of violent media.

Individual experimental findings can be aggregated into larger models, and these can make specific predictions about the development of aggressive behavior. One such model is the general aggression model (Bushman & Anderson, 2002). This model combines experimental findings into a framework that explains how the relationship between the person, the situation, affect, arousal, and cognition can lead to violent aggressive behavior. Developing a model such as this through purely correlational research would be difficult because the only way the relationship between different variables can be determined is through systematically changing them and observing the consequences.

Although experiments allow researchers to reduce the number of alternative explanations, experimental studies have often been criticized because they lack *external validity*. That is, critics claim that people's behavior in a lab may not generalize to the real world for a number of reasons. Experiments often use convenience samples (such as college students) that may differ from the rest of the population, and they take place in a strange setting (a lab room). Experimenters may also unknowingly influence participants' responses (Rosenthal & Fode, 1963). Although these are all problems that need to be carefully addressed and can easily wreck an individual experiment, they are not fatal to the experimental method as a whole (Anderson & Bushman, 1997). Another weakness of experimental studies is that they can determine only the short-term effects of violent media. Longitudinal studies are needed to determine the long-term effects.

A more difficult problem for aggression research is the gap between the kinds of behavior that can be measured in the lab and the kinds of behavior that can be measured in the field. Some critics (e.g., Kaplan, 1984) have questioned whether shocking someone or delivering loud blasts of noise is equivalent to real-world aggression. Similarly, although field research can track the relationship between violent media and violent crime (Huesmann et al., 2003), it would be unethical to create laboratory situations where participants can commit violent acts on one another. It is a mistake to confuse aggression and violence or to assume that findings about one behavior necessarily generalize to the other (Savage, 2004).

Although these limitations prevent experimental research from conclusively establishing the connection between media violence and antisocial behavior, the burden of proof does not rely on experimental studies alone. Instead, researchers draw on converging evidence from many different research methods including case studies, correlational studies, field studies, longitudinal studies, and experiments. Although each of these techniques has its own faults, combined they provide a compelling case for the relationship between violent media and aggressive behavior.

—*Jesse J. Chandler and*
Brad J. Bushman

See also General Aggression Model (GAM); Research Methods, Experimental Studies; Research Methods, Longitudinal Studies; Research Methods, Natural Experiments; Violence, Effects of; Violence, Longitudinal Studies of; Violence, Natural Experiments and

FURTHER READINGS

Anderson, C. A., & Bushman, B. J. (1997). External validity of "trivial" experiments: The case of laboratory aggression. *Review of General Psychology, 1,* 19–41.

Anderson, C. A., & Bushman, B. J. (2002). Media violence and societal violence. *Science, 295,* 2377–2378.

Bushman, B. J., & Anderson, C. A. (2002). Violent video games and hostile expectations: A test of the general aggression model. *Personality and Social Psychology Bulletin, 28,* 1679–1686.

Bushman, B. J., & Geen, R. G. (1990). Role of cognitive-emotional mediators and individual differences in the effects of media violence on aggression. *Journal of Personality and Social Psychology, 58,* 156–163.

Huesmann, L. R., Moise-Titus, J., Podolski, C. L., & Eron, L. D. (2003). Longitudinal relations between children's exposure to TV violence and their aggressive and violent behavior in young adulthood: 1977–1992. *Developmental Psychology, 39,* 201–221.

Kaplan, R. M. (1984). The measurement of human aggression. In R. M. Kaplan, V. J. Koneni, & R. W. Novaco (Eds.), *Aggression in children and youth* (pp. 44–72). Boston: Martinus Nijhoff.

Rosenthal, R., & Fode, K. L. (1963). The effect of experimenter bias on the performance of the albino rat. *Behavioral Science, 8,* 183–189.

Savage, J. (2004). Does viewing violent media really cause criminal violence? A methodological review. *Aggression & Violent Behavior, 10,* 99–128.

VIOLENCE, EXTENT OF AND RESPONSES TO

Most children and adolescents now enjoy ubiquitous access to media. A growing body of research concludes that American media are exceedingly violent. Drawing on five decades of research on media violence, this entry provides an introduction to the extent of violence in the media, examines the impact of excessive media violence on children and adolescents, and lists some efforts to help families make wise media choices.

EXTENT OF MEDIA VIOLENCE

By age 18, an American child will have seen 16,000 simulated murders and 200,000 acts of violence, according to 1998 figures of the American Psychiatric Association. Media scholar L. Rowell Huesmann told a Senate committee in 1999 that the average seventh grader plays electronic games at least 4 hours per week, and 50% of those games are violent.

A 2006 study by the Parents Television Council, a media watchdog group in the United States, concluded that there is more violence on children's entertainment programming than on adult-oriented television. The council's study reviewed programming shown during 3 weeks from the summer of 2005. Based on a content analysis of 440 hours of entertainment programming for children ages 5 to 10 on eight networks: ABC, Fox, NBC, WB, ABC Family, Cartoon Network, Disney Channel, and Nickelodeon, the study found 3,488 instances of violence, an average of 7.9 each hour. The extent of violence was higher than in 2002, when a similar study found 4.7 violent incidents per hour in prime-time shows on six broadcast networks.

The National Television Violence Study, in a 1996 report, identified violence in 66% of children's programming. Nearly 75% of the shows with violent content demonstrated unpunished violence, and victims were not shown experiencing pain in 58% of the violent acts. The study found that 46% of all television violence took place in cartoons for children. Children's programs portrayed violence as funny 67% of the time, and only 5% depicted the long-term consequences of violence. Parental warnings and violence advisories made the programs more of a magnet than they might otherwise have been. Parental Discretion Advised and PG-13 and R ratings

significantly increased boys' interest in the shows, although they made girls less interested in watching.

The digital media—games on video, computer, and the Web—today represent the single biggest influence on children and adolescents. Interactive video games, which are based on intense violence, are emerging as the entertainment of choice for America's young people. American children with home video games play with them for an average of 90 minutes a day.

A 1993 study asked 357 seventh and eighth graders to select their preferences among five categories of video games. About 2% of the children chose educational games, whereas 32% selected fantasy violence, and 17% opted for human violence. Similar trends are found in the increasing usage of games played on the personal computer. Nearly 68.2% of the homes with children in 1999 had a personal computer, and 41% of them accessed the Internet. By the early nineties, video game revenues in the United States exceeded $10 billion, nearly double the amount Americans spend on movies.

Children and adolescents have a special liking for music. Academic studies have identified how modern music glorifies acts of violence. Modern music lyrics have become increasingly explicit, particularly concerning sex, drugs, and violence against women. Hatred and violence against women have almost become characteristic in mainstream hip hop and alternative music. Although many child advocates, parents, and policymakers have attacked such messages in music lyrics, the music industry itself has honored the musicians with annual awards.

IMPACT OF EXCESSIVE MEDIA VIOLENCE

Expressing concern over the effect of media violence on the health of children, Donald Cook, president of the American Academy of Pediatrics, told a Senate subcommittee in 2000 that more than 3,500 research studies conducted since the 1950s, using many investigative methods, have examined the association between exposure to media violence and subsequent violent behavior. All but 18 studies have shown a positive correlation between media exposure and violent behavior.

Adverse Effects of Media Violence

Numerous studies have shown that viewing media violence encourages in young people six adverse effects. They are aggression (propensity for violent behavior), desensitization (less responsive to violence in real life), pessimism (cynical beliefs and attitudes), fear and insecurity (strange fears and a perpetual feeling of being unsafe), anxiety (intense apprehension of imagined danger), and unrealistic views about violence (children either think violence is all-pervasive in society or develop notions about the body's superhuman ability to survive violent acts).

A 1995 analysis conducted by the Congressional Research Service concluded that most of the existing social and behavioral science studies indicate broad unanimity on these points: (1) Human character and attitudes are negatively affected by constant viewing of televised violence; (2) television violence encourages violent behavior and affects moral and social values about violence in daily life; (3) children who watch significant amounts of television violence may exhibit aggressive behavior; (4) television violence affects viewers of all ages, intellect, and socioeconomic levels and both genders; and (5) viewers who watch substantial levels of television violence perceive a meaner world and overestimate the possibility of being a victim of violence.

In April 2006, the American Medical Association journal, *Archives of Pediatrics & Adolescent Medicine,* published a special issue on "Media and Children." The research presented in this issue clearly illustrates that the media have disturbing potential to negatively affect many aspects of children's healthy development, including social isolation, aggressive feelings and beliefs, consumerism, body weight, and sexuality.

One of the studies in the special issue concluded that watching too much violent television and playing too many violent video games adversely affect children's social and physical development. The researchers reported that the more violent television children watch, the less time they spend with their friends. Another study in the issue found that violent video games appear to instill poor attitudes in children when it comes to their own health, while promoting risky behaviors. Video games can influence not only aggression but also attitudes toward risk-taking behavior. Men who played the more violent video game, *Grand Theft Auto,* versus the less violent video game, *The Simpsons: Hit and Run,* had greater increases in blood pressure, more negative emotions and hostile feelings, and more permissive attitudes about alcohol and marijuana use.

A third study concluded that 81% of mature-rated video games often include explicit sexual imagery and language content not described on warning labels. The games contained depictions of substances or sexual themes or profanity that was not noted on the labels. Other studies in the special issue found problems with what children and teens are watching on television. One study said that children exposed to violent media had a significant long-term increase in aggressive behaviors, aggressive thoughts, angry feelings, and arousal levels. A fifth study found that children who watch more television eat more and gain more weight than children who watch less. Another study revealed that among teens whose parents expressed disapproval of teen sex, those who watch more than 2 hours of television a day may begin having sex at a younger age than those who do not.

Researchers feel that such studies offer increasing support for the American Academy of Pediatrics' recommendation that children older than 2 years spend no more than 2 hours per day with screen media; they suggest that the 2 hours should be educational. Dr. Dimitri A. Christakis, director of the Child Health Institute at the University of Washington and the coauthor of an *Archives of Pediatrics and Adolescent Medicine* editorial commenting on the studies, feels the challenge ahead is for parents and policymakers to find ways in which media can serve the best interests of children.

HELPING FAMILIES MAKE WISE MEDIA CHOICES

Society is at risk today not only for higher levels of violence but also for a greater tolerance and acceptance of this violence. Due to their age, children and adolescents remain susceptible to adverse effects, which may lead to more complex issues as they grow up. If these effects are neither expressed nor treated, they may manifest themselves in complex mental problems, especially among those lacking strong adult and peer support.

Several organizations are now working to create awareness about these issues by urging parents, teachers, and mentors not to underestimate the impact of media violence and other objectionable content that affect young people. The American Academy of Pediatrics Violence Intervention and Prevention Program has collected and catalogued resources related to youth violence prevention. The contents of this database can be searched by age group, intended audience, item category, or key topics. The Minneapolis-based National Institute on Media and the Family, a nonprofit organization, hosts the

"MediaWise" movement, which provides information about the impact of media on children and gives people who care about children the resources they need to make informed choices.

These and other awareness efforts seek to unite communities and families and help them to make wise media choices by encouraging parents to watch what their kids watch. They also promote increased physical activity, sound nutritional choices, and moderated media time in an effort to enhance the overall health of children and adolescents.

—*Debashis "Deb" Aikat*

See also Television Violence; Television Violence, Susceptibility to; Violence, Effects of; Violence, Historical Trends and; Violence, Industry Stance on; Violence, Meta-Analyses of

FURTHER READINGS

American Academy of Pediatrics Committee on Communications. (1996). Impact of music lyrics and music videos on children and youth. *Pediatrics, 98*(6), 1219–1221.

American Psychological Association. (1993). *Violence and youth: Psychology's response.* Washington, DC: Author.

Baker, R. K., & Ball, S. J. (1969). *Violence and the media: A report of the violence and media task force to the national commission on the causes and prevention of violence.* Washington, DC: U.S. Government Printing Office.

Bandura, A., Ross, D., & Ross, S. A. (1963). Imitation of film-mediated aggressive models. *Journal of Abnormal and Social Psychology, 66,* 3–11.

Cantor, J., & Reilly, S. (1982). Adolescents' fright reactions to television and films. *Journal of Communication, 31*(1), 87–99.

Caplan, R. E. (1985). Violent program content in music video. *Journalism Quarterly, 62*(1), 144–147.

Centerwall, B. S. (1992). Television and violence: The scale of the problem and where to go from here. *Journal of the American Medical Association, 267*(22), 17–21.

Drabman, R. S., & Thomas, M. H. (1974). Does media violence increase children's toleration of real-life aggression? *Developmental Psychology, 10*(3), 418–421.

Fyfe, K. (2006). *Wolves in sheep's clothing: A content analysis of children's television.* Retrieved March 16, 2006, from http://www.parentstelevision.org/PTC/publications/reports/childrensstudy/childrensstudy.pdf

Gerbner, G., & Gross, L. (1976). Living with television: The violence profile. *Journal of Communication, 26*(2), 173–199.

Gerbner, G., Gross, L., Morgan, M., & Signorielli, N. (1994). Growing up with television: The cultivation perspective.

In J. Bryant & D. Zillmann (Eds.), *Media effects: Advances in theory and research* (pp. 17–41). Hillsdale, NJ: Erlbaum.

Kunkel, D., Wilson, B., Donnerstein, E., Blumenthal, E., Linz, D., Smith, S., Gray, T., & Potter, W. J. (1995). Measuring television violence: The importance of context. *Journal of Broadcasting and Electronic Media, 39*(2), 284–291.

Levine, M. (1996). *Viewing violence: How media violence affects your child's and adolescent's development.* New York: Doubleday.

Strasburger, V. C., & Wilson, B. J. (2002). *Children, adolescents, and the media.* Thousand Oaks, CA: Sage.

Villani, S. (2001). Impact of media on children and adolescents. *Journal of the American Academy of Child and Adolescent Psychiatry, 40*(4), 392–401.

Willis, E., & Strasburger, V. C. (1998). Media violence. *Pediatric Clinics of North America, 45,* 319–331.

WEBSITES

American Academy of Pediatrics Violence Intervention and Prevention Program (VIPP) database: http://www.aap.org/vipp

National Institute on Media and the Family's MediaWise: http://www.mediafamily.org

VIOLENCE, HISTORICAL TRENDS AND

Since 1952, there have been more than 30 separate hearings about television violence, roughly one hearing every $1\frac{1}{2}$ years. These hearings often were held in response to real-life violence, including the assassinations of Martin Luther King, Jr. and Robert F. Kennedy. However, concerns about the impact of television violence on children and adolescents have also played a part in attempts to determine the extent of television violence, to analyze effects of media violence, to educate parents, and to develop public policy in this area. In 1990s, television content rating systems and the V-chip were among the responses to television violence mandated by Congress.

Aside from network executives, witnesses at congressional hearings on television violence have included people from all walks of life and with numerous concerns—academics, industry officials, members of Congress, teachers, and children's activists. Unfortunately, the hearings rarely tried to reconcile divergent testimony. Typically, contradictory points of view were expressed with no attempt to ascertain validity. Keisha Hoerrner noted in 1999 that even though Congress had spent more than 50 years examining this issue, it had passed only two pieces of legislation.

EARLY CONGRESSIONAL HEARINGS

The first congressional hearing about television violence was held in 1952 before the Commerce Committee of the House of Representatives (chair, Oren Harris, D-Arkansas) and focused on whether radio and television programs contained offensive or immoral content or emphasized violence, crime, or corruption. The Senate Subcommittee to Investigate Juvenile Delinquency (Chair, Robert Hendrickson, R-New Jersey) held hearings in 1954 to determine if the rise in juvenile delinquency was related to television's crime and horror programs. In April 1955, the Senate Subcommittee to Investigate Juvenile Delinquency (Chair, Senator Estes Kefauver, D-Tennessee) examined the question of television violence. In 1961, at hearings held by the Senate Subcommittee on Juvenile Delinquency (Chair, Senator Thomas Dodd, D-Connecticut), social scientists testified that television influenced viewers, particular teenagers and children.

Senator Dodd held another round of hearings in 1964. Although he started out with praise for the industry, Dodd's positive statements were quickly replaced with talk of the network's broken promises about lessening the amount of violence on television. Dodd and his committee cited evidence that network violence had not decreased since the last set of hearings and also presented evidence showing a causal link between aggressive behavior and watching violent television.

PRESIDENTIAL COMMISSION ON VIOLENCE

The mid to late 1960s saw considerable turmoil, civil disobedience, and urban unrest in the country. After the assassinations of Senator Robert F. Kennedy and the Reverend Dr. Martin Luther King, Jr., President Lyndon Johnson established the Presidential Commission on the Causes and Prevention of Violence to examine and hold hearings on issues relating to violence, including the impact of the mass media. Scholars were asked to review the existing research, and one new project—a content analysis to isolate the amount of violence in prime-time and weekend-daytime network dramatic programming—was funded.

Cynthia Cooper (1996) notes that the commission's final report suggested that the constant diet of violent behavior on television had an adverse effect, especially on children, encouraged violent behavior, and fostered unacceptable values about violence. Although the report did not say that violence on television was a principal cause of violence in society, it suggested that television violence was an important contributing factor.

THE SURGEON GENERAL'S TELEVISION AND SOCIAL BEHAVIOR PROGRAM

Before this report was issued, Senator John Pastore (D-Rhode Island), chair of the Senate Subcommittee on Communications, had secured $1 million to fund research under the auspices of the U.S. Surgeon General's Television and Social Behavior Program. This program framed television violence as a public health issue. It was supervised by the National Institute of Mental Health (NIMH) Scientific Advisory Committee on Television Behavior and charged with an almost impossible task: to determine scientifically the effects of violent television programs on children.

The program had an advisory committee of 12 distinguished social scientists, whose credibility and impartiality came under scrutiny when it was revealed that five members had direct ties to the television industry and that seven distinguished social scientists had been blackballed by broadcasters when the committee was selected.

The final report summarized the results by incorporating and distilling the 23 individual studies and satisfying the differing views of committee members. It stated, in several places and in several ways, that there was some evidence of a causal relation between aggressive behavior and watching violence on television. Specifically, it asserted that although viewing violence does not affect all children in the same way, viewing violence does increase the likelihood that children will become more aggressive. It concluded that there was sufficient evidence to say that watching violent programs on television could be harmful to children.

In March 1972, congressional hearings were held, and the U.S. Surgeon General reiterated that the committee, including network executives, had come to a unanimous conclusion: There was too much violence on television, and specific remedial actions were needed. Senator Pastore called for the establishment of an annual Violence Index to map the degree of violence on television and to provide a mechanism by which to keep the issue of television violence on the public agenda.

CONGRESS AND THE FEDERAL COMMUNICATIONS COMMISSION

At the 1974 congressional hearings, Professor George Gerbner reported the ongoing results of annual analyses of television programming (Violence Index), and Dr. Eli Rubinstein reported that little had been done to reduce violence on television in the years following the release of the Surgeon General's report. Network representatives presented conflicting testimony; according to their measures, there was less violence on television. Senator Pastore concluded this hearing with a challenge to the broadcasters to show a real decrease in television violence at next year's Federal Communications Commission (FCC) oversight hearings.

Congress pressured the FCC in 1974 to make recommendations to protect children from television's plethora of violent programming. The networks agreed to schedule programs that were unsuitable for children after 9 p.m. This proposal, called the *family viewing hour*, was formally included in the National Association of Broadcasters (NAB) Television Code. This was, however, a short-lived victory because the courts ruled that the family viewing hour violated the industry's right to free speech, and it was removed from the code.

CONGRESS AND THE AMERICAN MEDICAL ASSOCIATION

In 1976 and 1977, more congressional hearings were held. The American Medical Association (AMA) testified that television violence was an environmental health risk. Yet, some witnesses said that the research on the effects of television violence was inconclusive, and many spoke out against government intervention. In September 1977, the Senate Subcommittee on Communications issued its final report, approved by a vote of 8 to 7; it noted that television violence was a cause for concern and that viewers, particularly children, might be harmed by viewing violent content. The report, however, put the blame for television's excessive violence on the American public and concluded that parents should carefully monitor what and how much television their children watched.

In the 1970s, there were several public campaigns against television violence. In 1976, the AMA issued

a policy statement (1) stating that TV violence was a risk factor threatening the health and welfare of American children, (2) committing the AMA to finding ways to make television better, and (3) encouraging people to oppose TV violence and boycott companies that sponsored violent programs. Other campaigns were undertaken by the National PTA, the American Psychological Association (APA), and the National Coalition on Television Violence (NCTV).

POLICY ISSUES IN THE 1980s

In 1982, the report of the Surgeon General's Advisory Committee on Television and Social Behavior was updated and published by NIMH. The report stated that children's aggressive behavior was related to watching violent television and that these programs often taught children that violent or aggressive behavior was an appropriate way to resolve conflict. The report also took the broadcast industry to task for maintaining high levels of violent content, despite the concerns of both Congress and citizens.

The television industry immediately claimed that the report was inaccurate, and, in 1983, ABC issued a booklet that tried to refute the major conclusions about the relationship between television violence and aggressive behavior. The NIMH seven-member advisory committee, however, responded to the ABC booklet point-by-point.

The television industry changed dramatically during the 1980s. Multinational media giants took over most of the major media companies. The broadcasting and programming code of the NAB was eliminated because it violated antitrust laws. The 1980s era of deregulation furthered the perception that television was a business whose major concern was the marketplace: attracting the most viewers for the least amount of money. This environment was perhaps best summed up by FCC Chair Mark Fowler in 1984, when he described television as a "toaster with pictures." Nevertheless, concern about television violence continued.

In June 1986, Senator Paul Simon (D-Illinois) sponsored a bill designed to extend limited antitrust immunity to the networks and cable companies so they could work together to find ways to reduce television violence. The bill was met with considerable opposition, and it took numerous attempts to get it signed into law. Despite a lack of support by the television networks and the American Civil Liberties Union, the Television Improvement Act of 1990 was passed on October 28, 1989, to be in effect for 3 years. It was signed into law by President George Bush in December of that year.

CONGRESS AND THE MEDIA IN THE 1990s

Two congressional hearings in 1992 examined youth violence. The Senate Committee on Governmental Affairs discussed television violence as one of the factors that contributed to violence by juveniles, and the House Judiciary Committee's Subcommittee on Crime and Criminal Justice discussed the relationship between watching television violence and juvenile acts of violence. Testimony indicated that while the amount of violence during the prime-time hours in 1990 and 1991 had decreased slightly, violence in children's weekend-daytime programming was at an all-time high.

Hearings continued through the spring and summer of 1993 as the Television Improvement Act of 1990 approach its expiration date. These hearings, chaired by Rep. Edward Markey (D-Massachusetts), continued to pressure broadcasters to do more to control television violence. The tone of these hearings was decidedly in favor of enacting tougher government regulation of programming on the grounds that the self-regulatory measures of the broadcast industry were not working. Once again, expert witnesses testified that violence on television was plentiful and that there was a link between viewing televised violence and aggressive behavior. Testimony was also heard about the V-chip, which parents could use to block programs on the family TV.

Six weeks into the hearings, the television industry announced that parental warnings would be displayed before programs deemed particularly violent. In addition, warnings would be shown during commercial breaks and included in all promotional materials. Reaction was mixed. Some, like Congressman Markey, thought this was an important step and that the ratings would be a real help for parents. Others felt that labeling was undertaken to prevent further government intervention and that it did not go far enough.

During 1993, congressional hearings continued, and Representative Markey proposed the implementation of a rating system similar to that used by the motion picture industry, as well as a bill that would require all new television sets be equipped with V-chips to give parents an electronic tool to block specific types of programs. Although none of the bills was passed, the Television

Improvement Act of 1990 was extended at the end of 1993. Senator Simon also called on the industry to begin to monitor its programming. Consequently, the industry undertook two projects during 1994. UCLA's Center for Communication Research was appointed by the networks to monitor their programming, while the cable industry contracted with a consortium of researchers from four universities to monitor cable and broadcast programming and to conduct the National Television Violence Study (1998).

In 1996, the Communications Act of 1934 was overhauled and replaced by the Telecommunications Act of 1996. In an unprecedented move, the act included two provisions to deal with television violence. First, the act mandated that a program rating system be implemented by the industry, and second, the act called for the installation of the V-chip in all television sets with a 13-inch screen or larger manufactured after July 1, 1999. The rating system was designed by broadcasters under the leadership of Jack Valenti, president of the Motion Picture Association of America, and put into effect in January 1997.

—*Nancy Signorielli*

See also Violence, Experimental Studies of; Violence, Extent of and Responses to; Violence, Industry Stance on; Violence, Marketing and

FURTHER READINGS

Cooper, C. A. (1996). *Violence on television: Congressional inquiry, public criticism, and industry response: A policy analysis.* Lanham, MD: University Press of America.

Hoerrner, K. L. (1999). Symbolic politics: Congressional interest in television violence. *Journalism and Mass Communication Quarterly, 76*(4), 684–698.

Murray, J. P. (1995). Children and television violence. *Kansas Journal of Law and Public Policy, 4*(3), 7–14.

National Television Violence Study (Vol. 3). (1998). Thousand Oaks, CA: Sage.

National Institute of Mental Health. (1972). *Television and behavior* (Vol. 1). Washington, DC: U.S. Government Printing Office.

Rubinstein, E. A. (1980). Television violence: An historical perspective. In E. L. Palmer & A. Dorr (Eds.). *Children and the faces of television: Teaching, violence, selling* (pp. 113–127). New York: Academic Press.

Rubinstein, E. A., & Brown, J. D. (1985). Television and children: A public policy dilemma. In E. A. Rubinstein & J. D. Brown (Eds.), *The media, social science, and social policy for children* (pp. 93–117). Norwood, NJ: Ablex.

VIOLENCE, INDUSTRY STANCE ON

Concerns about violence on television are as old as television itself. The television industry, mindful of the need for advertising revenue driven by high ratings, has typically downplayed the effects of violent programming.

The industry's response to early congressional hearings on the topic in the 1950s was to point out the lack of research conclusively establishing a causal relationship between such programming and harm in viewers and to add that any studies conducted under industry auspices would be assumed to be biased, thereby placing the burden of proof elsewhere.

When the U.S. Surgeon General's Scientific Advisory Committee on Television and Social Behavior was formed in the mid-1960s, with the goal of funding research projects on the effects of television violence, the networks and National Association of Broadcasters (NAB) vetoed the inclusion of many of the researchers considered best qualified to serve. They also challenged the validity of the committee's finding that it had evidence of a causal relation between viewing violence on television and aggressive and antisocial behavior.

When legislators attempted a solution in the 1970s by pressing broadcasters to adopt into their industry code a nightly *family viewing hour,* a period during which sexual and violent programming would not air, the concept was hotly contested by some broadcasters and was not always honored. In the mid-1980s, Senator Paul Simon proposed legislation that would grant broadcasters an antitrust exemption to meet to discuss joint solutions to the issue. However, the only industry action in which the 3-year antitrust exemption resulted was an agreement to fund a study conducted by independent researchers that would monitor the levels of violence in programming; the study, the National Television Violence Study, found no significant reduction in the amount of violence on television.

In 1982, the National Institute of Mental Health (NIMH) issued a report that concluded that children learn violent behaviors from television, that heavy television viewers were more fearful and less trusting than light viewers, and that the amount of violence on television had remained consistently high through the years. The broadcast industry tried to challenge the NIMH report, with ABC publishing its own report attacking the findings point by point.

The Telecommunications Act of 1996 made it a law that all TVs with a 13-inch or larger screen sold after a certain date be equipped with a V-chip device, and it gave the industry a year to voluntarily create a rating system to work with the V-chip. Industry leaders appointed Jack Valenti, who had helped establish ratings for the Motion Picture Association of America (MPAA), to head its implementation group, which was composed largely of executives from the major broadcast and cable networks. The group ignored parents' well-documented pleas for a content-based system, in which specific information is given about what type of content (e.g., sex, violence) a program contains, and instead implemented an age-based system, where parents are given a general guideline about how old a child should be to watch a certain program. Numerous citizens groups filed critical comments with the Federal Communications Commission, and the vocal opposition caused the industry to reconsider its stance, agreeing in 1997 to modify the system by, in some instances, accompanying the six age-based categories with content descriptors. The industry used the revision as a bargaining chip to procure a moratorium on further changes to the system to give it a chance to work, and NBC refused to go along with the use of the supplementary content ratings.

While some would claim the industry has cooperated with respect to this issue, there are many who feel that media leaders have continually dragged their heels and that their failure to create a better rating system has resulted in the V-chip being a less effective tool for parents than it could be.

—*Lara Zwarun*

See also National Television Violence Study; Telecommunications Act of 1996; Television Rating Systems, Parental Uses of; Television Violence; V-Chip (Violence Chip); Violence (various entries)

FURTHER READINGS

Cater, D., & Strickland, S. (1975). *TV violence and the child: The evolution and fate of the Surgeon General's Report.* New York: Russell Sage Foundation.

Cooper, C. A. (1996). *Violence on television: Congressional inquiry, public criticism, and industry response: A policy analysis.* Lanham, MD: University Press of America.

Hamilton, J. T. (1998). *Television violence and public policy.* Ann Arbor: University of Michigan Press.

VIOLENCE, LONGITUDINAL STUDIES OF

The newspapers of today too often scream headlines of violence, murder, and mayhem. It is hard to imagine how such violent behavior is developed, and psychologists have turned to events in childhood for explanations. Among the many factors that influence violent behavior, few have received as much attention and promoted as much controversy as violence in the media.

The vast majority of research concerning the effects of viewing violence in the media has focused on short-term effects. These studies conclude that viewing violence on television *does* have a negative effect on subsequent aggressive behavior and thoughts. However, these findings are limited to the short term, and it may well be that any effects dissipate as soon as the viewer leaves the laboratory. To overcome this shortfall, several longitudinal studies have been conducted to discover whether there are any longer-lasting implications of viewing violence in the media. Although this research lacks some of the controls that experimental studies offer, longitudinal studies can suggest whether such an effect is plausible over the long term.

The first longitudinal study to assess the long-term effects of viewing violence on television was started in the 1960s by Leonard Eron and colleagues. However, the initial aim was to examine the stability of aggressive behavior as a whole, and only fortuitously was television violence included as one predictive factor. The resulting data set revealed that preference for violent television programs at age 8 predicted being named by peers as someone who is unusually aggressive at age 18. This effect was found only for boys, not for girls. When compared to other predictors, including child IQ, parental aggressiveness, parental nurturance, and punishment of child, analyses revealed that preference for violent television at age 8 was the *major* contributor to aggression at age 18. Clearly, many factors contribute to the development of aggressive behavior; however, Eron et al.'s study showed that preference for violent television is a key factor and should be not ignored.

A follow-up study of the participants in Eron et al's study revealed similar findings, although 22 years had passed since the initial measurements were taken. Preference for violent television at age 8 still predicted aggression and criminal behavior—now at

age 30—but again only for males. This effect remained stable even after controlling for other predictive factors, such as socioeconomic status, intellectual achievement, and parental responsiveness. Interestingly, there was no relationship between current preference for violent television and aggression in adulthood. The roots of aggressive behavior appear to be developed early in childhood, and later choices concerning television viewing seem to have much less influence than early exposure.

The above studies all took place in the United States, where levels of television violence have been criticized for being exceptionally high. However, research suggests that violent television has an influence on children worldwide, although the relationship is not always as straightforward. In a cross-national study, Rowell Huesmann and colleagues collected longitudinal data from five countries: the United States, Australia, Finland, Israel, and Poland. The purpose of this study was to examine whether the relationship between TV violence viewing and aggressive behavior in children from the ages of 6 to 11 was the same regardless of different cultures. Although the countries varied widely in violence rates, language, sex-role expectations, and TV broadcasts, aggressive children viewed more television, preferred more violent programs, identified more with television characters, and perceived violence as more "real life," regardless of the country of origin. A long-term relationship between early exposure to TV violence and later aggression was also revealed for boys in Finland and for both boys and girls in the United States, Poland, and Israel, even when initial aggressiveness was controlled. Separate studies in the Netherlands and in South Africa also revealed a similar relationship. Combined, these studies have two important conclusions: They show that the long-term relationship between early TV habits and later aggression is not limited to the United States and that violence in *girls* as well as in boys is linked to early exposure to violence on television.

In a more recent longitudinal study by Huesmann and colleagues, several factors known to contribute to aggressive behavior, such as TV violence viewing, socioeconomic status, intellectual ability, and a variety of parental factors, were measured in children ages 6 to 10 and then 15 years later. As in previous studies, results revealed that childhood exposure to television violence predicted adult aggression even after controlling for other factors, including childhood aggressiveness. Males who viewed high levels of violence as children were more likely to have "pushed, grabbed, or shoved their spouse," to have been convicted of a crime, and to have a traffic violation. Females who viewed high levels of violence as children were more likely to have "punched, beaten, or choked" another adult, had more traffic violations, and were more likely to be involved in criminal behavior.

Overall, these studies show that viewing TV violence in childhood contributes to the development of aggression throughout a person's lifetime. A heavy diet of TV violence in childhood is likely to shape a child's state of mind concerning real-life violence. Although the violent cartoons preschoolers are watching today may seem relatively innocuous at first glance, it is clear that they may be having a large influence on later aggression and criminal behavior.

—*Sarah M. Coyne*

See also Aggression, Television and; Cognitive Script Theory; Research Methods, Longitudinal Studies; Schemas/Scripts, Aggressive; Television Violence; Television Violence, Susceptibility to

FURTHER READINGS

Eron, L. D., Huesmann, L. R., Lefkowitz, M. M., & Walder, L. O. (1972). Does television violence cause aggression? *American Psychologist, 27,* 253–263.

Huesmann, L. R., & Eron, L. D. (1986). *Television and the aggressive child: A cross-national comparison.* Hillsdale, NJ: Erlbaum.

Huesmann, L. R., Eron, L. D., Lefkowitz, M. M., & Walder, L. O. (1984). Stability of aggression over time and generations. *Developmental Psychology, 20,* 1120–1134.

Huesmann, L. R., Moise-Titus, J., Podolski, C., & Eron, L. D. (2003). Longitudinal relations between children's exposure to TV violence and their aggressive and violent behavior in young adulthood: 1977–1992. *Developmental Psychology, 39,* 201–221.

VIOLENCE, MARKETING AND

The abundance of marketing and advertising to children in the United States is often criticized, independently of the product being sold. However, when the marketed products are violent or aggressive in nature, the concern among parents, researchers, politicians, and health professionals intensifies. Today, not only are intensely violent media portrayals readily available to children, but the companies that make these very products target young people under 17 with movies, music, and video games created for mature audiences. For example, one might call into question the appropriateness of a movie studio running an ad for a violent R-rated movie during television programs frequently viewed by young people. Likewise, video game manufacturers frequently run print ads for violent M-rated video games (for mature audiences) in magazine publications often read by young people. At the core of this issue is the idea that the marketing of violent entertainment to young people is thought to increase their demand for, and thus consumption of, violent media, which further heightens concerns over the potential negative effects of exposure to media violence.

TO WHAT EXTENT DO ENTERTAINMENT INDUSTRIES TARGET YOUNG PEOPLE?

The issue of media violence and its effect on children has been a recurring concern to policymakers for the past several decades. However, in recent years, parents, researchers, politicians, and health professionals collectively have voiced their concern over the marketing of violent media products to young audiences. In the wake of a wave of shootings in schools, particularly the violence at Columbine High School in Littleton, Colorado, President Bill Clinton requested in 1999 that the Federal Trade Commission (FTC) conduct a study of the marketing of violent entertainment products to youths. In response to Clinton's request, the FTC prepared a report on the marketing of violent entertainment to children, which the commission presented to Congress in September 2000. This report found that the marketing plans for movies, music, and video games expressly targeted children and that media plans for these products called for advertising them in media most likely to reach children and adolescents. For instance, of the 44 R-rated movies selected for the FTC study, 80% of the marketing plans targeted children under 17. Likewise, of the 55 music recordings with explicit content, 27% of the marketing plans behind these music products explicitly identified teenagers as part of their target audience. Furthermore, of the 118 M-rated violent video games sampled in this study, 70% targeted children under 17, with 60% of the marketing plans specifically aiming to target youth under 17. In light of these findings, the FTC stated that the practice of marketing violent movies, music, and electronic games to children undermined the integrity of the industries' ratings and frustrated parents' attempts to make informed decisions about their children's exposure to media violence.

Since the release of the initial report in 2000, the FTC has conducted four follow-up reports issued in April 2001, December 2001, June 2002, and July 2004. The reports issued in 2001 and 2002 found that the entertainment industry had made some progress in providing rating information in advertising and in limiting advertising for violent media products in media popular with minors. For instance, the reports indicated some progress by the film and video game industries in terms of limiting advertising in popular teen-targeted media; however, the reports also noted little to no progress in the advertising practices of the music industry.

Unfortunately, the most recent report of 2004 indicates a resurgence of some problematic practices. For instance, the report found that while rating practices have improved, the movie studios continue to market violent R-rated films and DVDs during television programs with significant adolescent audiences; furthermore, some film studios place movie promotions in other nontraditional venues (e.g., malls, fast-food product tie-ins, etc.) likely to be seen by younger audiences. Meanwhile, despite the music industry's successful reduction of advertising in print media popular among teens, they continue to place ads during television programming with significant teen audiences. Finally, with respect to video games, the FTC found progress with the marketing of M-rated video games; however, advertisements for teen-rated video games frequently appear in media popular with preteen audiences. In short, although some progress is being made in certain areas and by certain industries, the marketing of violent entertainment content to youth is still very much a part of the current media landscape.

REACTIONS TO THE FTC REPORTS

Not surprisingly, the FTC reports have raised a great deal of concern in Congress, leading to congressional hearings and pressure on the entertainment industries to self-regulate. No specific legislative proposals to restrict the marketing of violent entertainment are likely to become law anytime soon; however, bills attempting to address the problem have been proposed. One such bill, introduced by Senator Joseph Lieberman, sought to prohibit marketing of adult-rated movies, music, or video games to minors. Certainly, efforts to regulate violent media raise First Amendment concerns, and for this reason, the FTC has largely recommended that Congress continue to encourage self-regulation.

Other activist and advocacy groups, tired of calls for industry self-regulation, have taken a more proactive stance, calling for specific actions against the entertainment industries. One such group, Lion & Lamb, a national grassroots parents' organization seeking to stop the marketing of violence to children, has put forth a set of actions for all industry groups, including (1) the creation of an independently funded ratings board, appointed by Congress, which would a create user-friendly, research-informed, uniform rating system for all entertainment products; (2) the end of deceptive advertising practices documented in the FTC report, such as advertising adult materials in media popular among youth; (3) enforcement of age-appropriate previews before feature presentations at movie theaters and on videocassette releases; and (4) the end of cross-marketing adult brands such as violent adult-rated movie characters in the guise of children's products (such as toys and Halloween costumes). Although these suggestions arc admirable and well-founded (especially in light of the body of research on media violence and young people), their implementation will probably face opposition by the entertainment industry. Yet, as the number of entertainment products continues to explode, careful consideration must be given to the innovative and deceptive techniques used by the entertainment industry to market violent entertainment products to young people.

—Angela Paradise

See also Advertising, Effects on Children of; Advertising, Exposure to; Advertising on Children's Programs; Aggression (various entries); Federal Trade Commission; Violence, Effects of

FURTHER READINGS

Federal Trade Commission. (2000). *Marketing violent entertainment to children: A review of self-regulation and industry practices in the motion picture, music recording, and electronic game industries.* Retrieved from http://www.ftc.gov/reports/violence/vioreport.pdf
Federal Trade Commission. (2004). *Marketing violent entertainment to children: A fourth follow-up review of industry practices in the motion picture, music recording,*

and electronic game industries. Retrieved from http://www.ftc.gov/os/2004/07/040708kidsviolencerpt.pdf

Roberts, D. F., Foehr, U. G., & Rideout, V. (2005). *Generation M: Media in the lives of 8-18 year-olds* (Kaiser Family Foundation Report). Retrieved from http://kff.org/entmedia/upload/Generation-M-Media-in-the-Lives-of-8-18-Year-olds-Report.pdf

Timmer, J. (2002). When a commercial is not a commercial: Advertising of violent entertainment and the First Amendment. *Communication Law & Policy, 7*(2), 157–186.

VIOLENCE, META-ANALYSES OF

Generations of communication researchers have investigated the impact of violence portrayed by the mass media on media users' aggression, especially with regard to entertainment products. A vast number of empirical studies have been reported in communication, social and developmental psychology, and medical research. For decades, this research addressed the effects of television violence. As video games became extremely popular among children and adolescents, the focus shifted to include interactive entertainment. Because video games present graphic violence with high frequency, realism, and, most important, the opportunity for the users to participate in violent scenes, they have been examined as a potentially powerful facilitator of aggressive behavior in young people.

Overall, thousands of individual experiments, surveys, longitudinal studies, and other investigations address issues of media violence and its impact on aggression. It is virtually impossible to draw integrative conclusions from this overwhelming mass of findings. Therefore, experts in the field have presented meta-research that attempts to summarize the results of many single studies to draw the big picture. One approach is a literature review that discusses findings of different studies to draw conclusions about what the findings show. However, in the domain of video game violence, the available reviews disagree on the general impact of violent games. An alternative approach is meta-analysis, which is a computation procedure that calculates comparable statistical parameters reported from individual studies into average indicators of connections between variables. Meta-analysis is a powerful and extremely important tool to assess the impact of media violence on aggression.

THE TECHNIQUE OF META-ANALYSIS

In meta-analysis of media violence effects, information is collected from as many individual studies as possible; the analysis pays special attention to effect sizes, that is, statistical values that indicate the influence of media violence on aggression as found in a given study. Effect sizes can be computed in standardized ways and allow (within certain limitations) for comparability across different studies on the same topic. Technically, the statistical fusion of effect size data from different studies creates one huge data set in which all participants from the individual studies are combined. The meta-analytic procedure then reinvestigates the effect of media violence on aggression based on a virtual sample, typically comprising several thousand participants. Consequently, the results of the meta-analysis are much more substantial and valid than any individual study because the latter is limited to one specific (usually small) group of participants and one specific operationalization of *media violence* and of *aggression*.

META-ANALYTIC FINDINGS ON THE EFFECTS OF TELEVISION VIOLENCE

One of the most widely cited meta-analyses on the impact of television violence has been published by Paik and Comstock (1994). They included data from 217 relevant studies, both experimental and nonexperimental, conducted between 1957 and 1990. This analysis found a clear and robust effect of the consumption of violent TV programs on antisocial and aggressive behavior, with the effect magnitude depending on methodological aspects but not reaching zero in any subanalysis. Anderson and Bushman (2002) summarized their meta-analytic findings from 284 studies with more than 51,000 participants similarly: Regardless of the method applied and the empirical procedures of individual studies, correlations between TV violence consumption and aggression ranged between .10 and .30, with extremely low statistical probabilities of zero-correlations. These findings clearly indicate the causal connection between TV violence and aggression, and they suggest a considerable magnitude of effect, which definitely deserves a debate on political and educational countermeasures.

META-ANALYSES OF THE IMPACT OF VIDEO GAME VIOLENCE

To keep track of the quickly growing number of studies on video game violence, two meta-analyses have already been conducted in this comparatively young branch of research. Essentially, these studies led to conclusions similar to those in the meta-analyses on TV violence. Sherry (2001) combined data from 25 thematic studies and concluded from his meta-analysis that an effect of video game violence on aggression exists; however, he interpreted the average effect size to be lower compared to effect sizes computed in TV violence research. In contrast, Anderson (2004) found an "alarming" substantial effect of video game violence. He argued that many mixed findings from various studies were due to methodological shortcomings, which contributed to hide the true, strong effect size.

CONCLUSIONS

The available meta-analyses leave very little if any doubt that there is a causal connection between frequent consumption of media violence, both on television and in video games, and the tendency to display aggressive cognitions, emotions, and behavior. The relative strength of this effect remains to be discussed in light of different theories, in comparison to alternative risk factors, and taking into account inherent problems of meta-analytical procedures (primarily the so-called publication bias: Studies that find a media effect are more likely to be published and thus included in meta-analysis than are studies that do not find a media effect). For instance, Anderson and his colleagues argue that the effect of media violence is profound and that drastic regulatory and educational countermeasures are indicated. Sherry (2001), in contrast, acknowledges the existence of media violence effects but is reluctant to consider the average effect size extremely high. Therefore, to guide political and educational response to media violence, findings from meta-analyses not only demand theoretical elaboration but need to be specified for individuals with different risk backgrounds. One very promising departure in this direction is the work by Slater and his colleagues, which demonstrates the importance of synergistic interactions between media violence consumption and other risk factors of aggression, such as rejection by peers or parental

conflicts (Slater, 2003; Slater, Henry, Swaim, & Anderson, 2003; Slater, Henry, Swaim, & Cardador, 2004). Future research on media violence, including new meta-analytic approaches, should focus on the specification of such interaction effects, rather than debating the general impact of media violence, which is too abstract to allow for direct countermeasures taken by politicians, parents, and teachers. Nevertheless, it should be clear—especially from the meta-analytic studies—that there is substantial reason to be concerned about media violence and that it is necessary to implement effective intervention strategies (see Cantor & Wilson, 2003, for a comprehensive overview).

—*Christoph Klimmt*

See also Aggression, Movies and; Aggression, Television and; Aggression, Electronic Games and; Cartoons, Violence in; Electronic Games, Violence in; Interactivity; Movies, Violence in; Music, Impact of Violence in; National Television Violence Study; Research Methods, Meta-Analyses; Television Violence; UNESCO Violence Study; Violence (various entries)

FURTHER READINGS

Anderson, C. A. (2004). An update on the effects of playing violent video games. *Journal of Adolescence, 27*(1), 113–122.

Anderson, C. A., & Bushman, B. J. (2001). Effects of violent video games on aggressive behavior, aggressive cognition, aggressive affect, physiological arousal, and prosocial behavior: A meta-analytic review of the scientific literature. *Psychological Science, 12*(5), 353–359.

Anderson, C. A., & Bushman, B. J. (2002). The effects of media violence on society. *Science, 295,* 2377–2378.

Bensley, L., & van Eenwyk, J. (2001). Video games and real-life aggression: Review of the literature. *Journal of Adolescent Health, 29*(4), 244–257.

Cantor, J., & Wilson, B. J. (2003). Media and violence: Intervention strategies for reducing aggression. *Media Psychology, 5*(4), 363–403.

Dill, K. E., & Dill, J. C. (1998). Video game violence: A review of the empirical literature. *Aggression and Violent Behavior, 3,* 407–428.

Griffiths, M. (1999). Violent video games and aggression: A review of the literature. *Aggression and Violent Behavior, 4,* 203–212.

Paik, H., & Comstock, G. (1994). The effects of television violence on antisocial behavior: A meta-analysis. *Communication Research, 21*(4), 516–546.

Potter, W. J., & Tomasello, T. K. (2003). Building upon the experimental design in media violence research: The importance of including receiver interpretations. *Journal of Communication, 53,* 315–329.

Sherry, J. L. (2001). The effects of violent video games on aggression: A meta-analysis. *Human Communication Research, 27*(3), 409–431.

Slater, M. D. (2003). Alienation, aggression, and sensation seeking as predictors of adolescent use of violent film, computer, and website content. *Journal of Communication, 53*(1), 105–121.

Slater, M., Henry, K. L., Swaim, R. C. & Anderson, L. L. (2003). Violent media content and aggressiveness in adolescents: A downward spiral model. *Communication Research, 30*(6), 713–736.

Slater, M. D., Henry, K. L., Swaim, R. & Cardador, J. (2004). Vulnerable teens, vulnerable times: How sensation seeking, alienation, and victimization moderate the violent media content–aggressiveness relation. *Communication Research, 31*(6), 642–668.

Vorderer, P. (2000). Interactive entertainment and beyond. In D. Zillmann & P. Vorderer (Eds.), *Media entertainment: The psychology of its appeal* (pp. 21–36). Mahwah, NJ: Erlbaum.

VIOLENCE, NATURAL EXPERIMENTS AND

What are the effects of media violence on the aggressive attitudes and behavior of those exposed to it? This question has for several decades been the focus of a large body of research, but its importance was not anticipated until television had become ubiquitous. As a result, there have been few opportunities to address this question through before-and-after studies of natural experiments. This entry describes three natural experiments addressing the issue of the effects of media portrayals of violence and aggression. In each study, the researchers took advantage of a natural experiment to study the impact of exposure to media violence on aggressive attitudes or behavior. They chose to study different aspects of the issue: children's aggressive behavior, homicide rates, and children's conception of crime. They obtained their data in Australia, Canada, South Africa, and the United States. In each case, the data revealed evidence that exposure to violence on television has effects.

Several different methodologies have been used to study whether violence in the media can affect aggressive attitudes and behavior, and if so, whether

effects occur not only in laboratory settings but also under real-life circumstances, where many other influences, including social controls regarding aggression, also operate. These questions have been extensively studied. They are cause for concern in part because aggressive behavior tends to be stable from childhood through adolescence into adulthood, so to the extent that portrayals of aggression and violence in the media do have an effect in childhood, this effect is likely to be maintained into adulthood. Natural experiments (and field experiments with random assignment of individuals to conditions) have the advantage that causal inferences can be made in real-life, ecologically valid settings.

CHILDREN'S AGGRESSIVE BEHAVIOR

One of the studies in the Notel, Unitel, and Multitel research project, a before-and-after natural experiment in three Canadian towns, focused on children's naturally occurring aggressive behavior. In this study, conducted by Joy, Kimball, and Zabrack, children were observed during free play on the school playgrounds before school, at recess, at lunchtime, and after school. In Phase 1 of the natural experiment, before Notel had television reception, children in Grades 1, 2, 4, and 5 were observed in all three towns. In Phase 1, Unitel had one TV channel, and Multitel had four. Two years after Notel had obtained TV reception (one channel, the same as in Unitel), children in Grades 1, 2, 3, and 4 were observed in all three towns. Reception did not change in Unitel and Multitel between Phases 1 and 2. This provided before-and-after cross-sectional comparisons (same-age but different children) between the phases for children in Grades 1 and 2. It also provided longitudinal comparisons of the children who were in Grades 1 or 2 in Phase 1 with themselves 2 years later, when they were in Grades 3 or 4 in Phase 2. Another set of cross-sectional comparisons was made for Phase 1 children in Grades 4 and 5 with Phase 2 children in Grades 3 and 4. This was possible because in all three towns and in both Phase 1 and 2, there were no grade differences (i.e., the mean aggression scores did not differ for Grades 1, 2, 3, 4, 5).

In each grade, each town, and each phase, five boys and five girls were observed, for a total of 120 in all three towns in each phase, with each child observed for 21 one-minute intervals. The children were randomly selected, but no more than one child per family was included in the entire sample. The observations were time-sampled across different days of the week and periods during the day, over the course of 2 weeks, so each child was observed on many different occasions, with the order randomly determined and not dictated by the action of the moment. Neither the children, nor their parents, nor the teachers were told that the observers were interested in either aggressive behavior or television. The two female observers used checklists of 14 physically aggressive behaviors (including hits, slaps, punches, kicks, bites, pushes, holds, grabs) and 9 verbally aggressive behaviors (including disparaging, mocking, curses, commands in a loud angry tone of voice, and threats). For each one-minute interval, each observer made a check by each behavior each time it occurred. Accidental aggression and rough-and-tumble play were not included. Interobserver reliability was established initially during training in each phase, checked periodically during the observations, and was found to be high in both phases. The Phase 2 observers were different from those in Phase 1, and they did not know the data (e.g., mean levels of each behavior or overall patterns) from Phase 1. The observers were as unobtrusive as possible. The children were aware that two women were on the playground but were not aware of which particular child was being observed. They were accustomed to adults (teachers) wandering around the playground. The observers never interfered with the children's play, so the children mostly ignored them.

In addition to the behavioral observations on the school grounds, peer ratings and teacher ratings of aggression were obtained for each child. In individual interviews, each child indicated the three students in his or her class who were the bossiest, fought the most, talked back to the teacher the most, argued and disagreed the most, and pushed, shoved, and poked the most. Each teacher rated each child in her or his class on several 7-point scales ranging from *not at all characteristic* to *very characteristic* (of the child being rated). Both positive and negative behaviors were rated and grouped into four composite teaching ratings: (1) aggressive, argumentative, bossy, and hostile; (2) active and loud; (3) competitive and dominant; and (4) friendly and honest.

In general, the peer and teacher ratings of aggression were consistent with the researchers' observations of aggressive behavior on the school playground. This indicates that the observed behaviors had external validity; that is, the children observed during this study to be relatively aggressive also were considered by the

other children and their teachers to be aggressive relative to their peers.

There were no differences in the observations of aggressive behavior related to grade level. The most important question was whether there would be an increase in the aggressive behavior of Notel children following the arrival of TV reception in their community, and there was. Notel children in the longitudinal sample increased from Phase 1 to 2 in both physical and verbal aggression. This could not be attributed to maturation (being 2 years older) because there was no evidence of differences in aggressive behavior among the grades in either phase and because there was no change for Unitel or Multitel children, who also were 2 years older. Twelve cross-sectional comparisons from Phase 1 to Phase 2 were made in each town (physical aggression: Grades 1 and 2 girls in Phase 1 versus Grades 1 and 2 girls in Phase 2; the same comparison for boys; the same comparison for the girls and boys combined; a similar set of three comparisons for Grades 3 and 4 versus 4 and 5; and a similar set of six comparisons for verbal aggression). In Notel, 10 of the 12 comparisons revealed a statistically significant increase in aggression; the other two increases were not statistically significant.

None of the 12 Unitel comparisons and only 2 of the Multitel comparisons (for girls, Grades 1 and 2, verbal aggression decreased; for boys and girls combined, Grades 3 and 4, physical aggression increased) were statistically significant. The increases in Notel occurred not only for both physically and verbally aggressive behavior and for both girls and boys, but also for children who were initially low in aggressive behavior as well as those who were initially high. This latter finding is noteworthy because some people have contended that only children initially high in aggression are affected by media violence.

The catharsis hypothesis would predict a decrease in aggression in Notel following the introduction of TV due to vicarious release of aggressive impulses while viewing. All other theories about the effects of media violence on aggression (such as modeling/imitation, disinhibition, desensitization, and arousal) would predict an increase in Notel. Predictions about comparisons among the towns within each phase are less clear. Most groups have dominance hierarchies and methods of controlling aggression among members, but tolerance of aggression varies considerably from group to group. It would not necessarily be expected, therefore, that the mean levels of aggression for the three towns would form a sensible pattern in relation to the availability of TV. In Phase 1, the mean levels of verbal aggression in Notel and Unitel were lower than that in Multitel, and there were no Phase 1 differences in physical aggression. Two years after the arrival of TV in Notel, the level of verbal aggression was significantly higher there than in either Unitel or Multitel, which did not differ. In Phase 2, Notel children were highest in physical aggression, exhibiting more than Unitel children, who were lowest; Multitel children were in between and not significantly different from Notel or Unitel.

The researchers (Joy, Kimball, & Zabrack, 1986) also compared individuals with differing amounts of reported exposure to TV. The results supported the findings described above. For example, 67% of the variance in the observed physical aggression of Unitel and Multitel children in Phase 2 was predicted by other measures. In particular, hours of TV viewing in Phase 2 added significantly to this prediction, over and above observations of physical aggression and the aggression ratings of children's peers from Phase 1. This is an important finding because aggression tends to be very stable across time, so the fact that concurrent TV viewing added significantly to such prediction underscores its effect.

The pattern of findings obtained in this study suggests that the social milieu is important. When social controls are adequate, either for individuals or groups, aggressive behaviors acquired from various models, including TV, may not be performed because of the individual's inhibitions against behaving aggressively. When the social controls are disrupted, however (which may have been what happened with the advent of TV in Notel), behaviors acquired from all sources may be more likely to be performed.

When considering these and other results regarding the influence of TV on aggression, it is important to remember that aggression is a socially disapproved behavior, albeit sometimes associated with mixed messages. Parents, teachers, and others generally try to teach children not to be physically and verbally aggressive. An effect, therefore, must be strong enough to overcome or go beyond the individual's inhibitions against behaving aggressively in order to be measurable by the researchers.

HOMICIDE RATES

In a second example of a natural experiment focused on aggressive behavior in relation to exposure to television, Centerwall (1989) used epidemiological data to compare homicide rates in the United States, Canada, and South Africa. He chose homicide as his measure of violence because homicide victim statistics are very accurate. He limited his comparisons to white homicide victims in the United States and South Africa because of the different living conditions for nonwhites in the two countries. For Canada, he used the total homicide rate because Canada's population in 1951, during the period of interest, was 97% white. The focus of his comparisons among the three countries was 1945 to 1974. Television reception became available in the United States in the late 1940s and in Canada in the early to mid 1950s, but not until 1975 in South Africa. Between 1945 and 1974, the homicide rate for white victims in the United States increased 93%. Over the same period in Canada, it increased 92%. In South Africa, where TV was banned, the homicide rate declined by 7%. Centerwall also found that within the United States, the regions that acquired television first were the first to have higher homicide rates.

Centerwall's study found a lag of 10 to 15 years between the introduction of television to a country and its increase in the homicide rate, which he attributed to childhood exposure to violent media content. Homicide is primarily a late-adolescent and adult act, so the "television generation" must come of age before a media effect is seen. Centerwall considered several alternative possible ("third variable") explanations for the pattern of homicide rates in the three countries, including differences or changes in age distribution, urbanization, alcohol consumption, capital punishment, economic growth, civil unrest, and availability of firearms. He concluded that none of these alternatives provides a viable explanation for the observed homicide trends following the introduction of television in Canada and the United States, and, by comparison, South Africa, where television reception was not available over the same period (1945–1974). He speculated that white homicide rates in South Africa would show a similar increase, beginning in the early 1990s, following a similar lag of 10 to 15 years after television became available there.

CHILDREN'S CONCEPTIONS OF CRIME

A third example of researchers who took advantage of a natural experiment to study the relationship between exposure to television and some aspect of aggression is research conducted by Murray and Kippax during 1977 and 1978. They studied three Australian towns of similar size and social structure that differed in the duration, content, and magnitude of their experiences with TV. The "high-TV" town had had 5 years of exposure to a commercial channel and 2 years of exposure to the national public channel (Australian Broadcasting Corporation). The weekly broadcast time was greater for the public (98.8 hours) than the commercial (59.5 hours) channel, and the public channel had considerably more educational/instructional programming for children and adults, as well as more news and documentaries. The second town, called "low-TV," had had 1 year's exposure to the public ABC Channel, and the "no-TV" town had no TV exposure. Murray and Kippax sampled families with children under 12 in each town and estimated that this included 40% of such families in the high-TV town, 40% in the low-TV town, and 52% in the no-TV town. They reasoned that children in the high-TV town should show a more differentiated conception of crime because it was the only town with extensive exposure to police crime dramas. To test this hypothesis, they presented children with paired comparisons from a list of illegal activities (spying, murder, drunkenness, assault, kidnapping, bank robbery, and shoplifting). The items were presented in pairs and repeated until each item had been presented with all the others. The children rated the similarity of each pair on a 5-point scale from *not at all alike* to *very much alike*. The children in the new-TV and low-TV towns had a conception of crime reflecting two dimensions: seriousness of the crime and whether it was directed toward property or people. The conception of the high-TV town children included those two dimensions and added a third dimension, possibly reflecting the frequency of the crimes of drunkenness, spying, and shoplifting in the real versus televised world.

—*Tannis M. MacBeth*

See also Aggression, Television and; Media Effects, History of Research on; Notel, Unitel, Multitel Study; Research Methods, Natural Experiments; Violence, Experimental Studies of

FURTHER READINGS

Centerwall, B. S. (1989). Exposure to television as a cause of violence. In G. Comstock (Ed.), *Public communication and behavior* (Vol. 2, pp. 1–58) New York: Academic Press.

Joy, L. A., Kimball, M. M., & Zabrack, M. L. (1986). Television and children's aggressive behavior. In T. M. Williams (Ed.), *The impact of television: A natural experiment in three communities* (pp. 303–360). Orlando, FL: Academic Press.

Murray, J. P., & Kippax, S. (1977). Television diffusion and social behavior in three communities: A field experiment. *Australian Journal of Psychology, 29*(1), 31–43.

Murray, J. P., & Kippax, S. (1978). Children's social behavior in three towns with differing television experience. *Journal of Communication, 28,* 19–29.

VIRAL MARKETING

Viral marketing (also referred to as *buzz* or *grassroots* marketing) takes advantage of preexisting social networks and new media technologies to increase brand awareness and drive product trials and sales. Viral campaigns work by *seeding* or *infecting* a select group of socially active recipients with a marketing message, which they then spread through their social networks much like a viral epidemic. Within media theory, viral marketing is consistent with the two-step flow model developed by Katz and Lazarsfeld in the 1940s, which asserts that the media influence a minority of individuals, called opinion leaders, who, in turn, influence their peers through interpersonal communication.

The founders of Hotmail, a free email service, are credited with coining the term *viral marketing* in 1996. Originally, it described the practice of appending advertising about the email service to users' outgoing messages, thus turning each user into a viral agent who infected others with every message sent. Hotmail gained 12 million subscribers in 18 months at a total cost of $500,000, compared to $20 million spent by its nearest competitor, Juno, thus demonstrating the effectiveness of viral marketing.

Viral campaigns have become increasingly sophisticated in nature and use both online channels, such as email, websites, and instant messaging, and offline channels, such as text messaging, paging, and word-of-mouth. Commonly recognized types of viral marketing include pass-along viral, which involves the forwarding of content that users find interesting or entertaining; incentive viral, which offers various rewards to users for disseminating information or providing referrals; and undercover viral, which poses as nonmarketing content in the form of websites, videos, or games. Successful viral campaigns can produce significant increases in sales or awareness but may backfire if consumers question their authenticity.

Adolescents are particularly susceptible to viral marketing for two reasons. First, having grown up with new media technologies such as email and instant messaging, they are almost constantly connected to a wide network of peers. Second, adolescents are greatly influenced by their peers and aspire to fit in within social groups. Viral marketing exploits the combination of these factors by infiltrating young people's social networks and channels of communication. Tweens (children ages 9 to 13) are a particularly attractive marketing target, as they are in the process of forming identities and lifelong consumer preferences. Viral marketing is also seen as effective in reaching media-savvy teens who have become immune to advertisements in mainstream media, such as television and radio.

Viral marketing has been used successfully to promote a wide range of product categories to children and adolescents, including carbonated drinks, cosmetics, movies, music, and even motor oil. Noncommercial actors also recognize the effectiveness of viral marketing. For example, the U.S. Department of Health and Human Services' Centers for Disease Control and Prevention incorporated viral components in a social marketing campaign aimed at increasing levels of physical exercise among tweens.

One viral technique that is gaining popularity among youth marketers involves the recruitment of highly social teens, who are seeded with marketing messages and samples of new products. Viral teens then share their opinions about these products with peers, in effect acting as brand advocates. This technique, however, has come under attack by consumer advocacy groups, which argue that viral teens often neglect to disclose that they have been solicited by marketers to endorse their brands. The stealth nature of viral marketing among youth raises a number of ethical concerns and is, perhaps, its most alarming feature, one that has yet to be adequately addressed by media researchers and policymakers.

—Nadia Kaneva

See also Branding; Peer Groups, Impact of Media on; Tweens, Advertising Targeting of

FURTHER READINGS

Rosen, E. (2000). *The anatomy of buzz: How to create word-of-mouth marketing.* New York: Doubleday.

VIRTUAL REALITY

Virtual reality (called VR for short) is a computer-generated artificial image or environment that is presented to the user in such a way that it appears and feels like a real space or situation. With a VR device, young people may "experience" flying a spaceship right at home by wearing VR goggles and headsets. A user is "virtually there," hence the term. The VR experience effectively immerses the user to interact and control the virtual world in a dynamic way.

This entry provides a basic introduction to VR, explains its application and relevance to children and adolescents, and examines its conceptual features and adaptations such as *telepresence* (remotely accessing distant but real environments). Using telepresence techniques, engineers and doctors have the potential of serving a global audience without the time and trouble of traveling across nations.

APPLICATION AND RELEVANCE OF VR FOR YOUNG PEOPLE

VR is a relatively new medium of human-computer interaction. Interlinked computers use visual and auditory stimuli to create a three-dimensional environment in which the user is immersed. Instead of seeing the real world, the user interacts with this surrogate environment. As the user's level of immersion increases, the user feels more like a part of that environment.

Widespread applications of VR for children and adolescents include entertainment (VR games that simulate space-flight adventures and dragon fights), education (a VR movie on the "Seven Wonders of the Ancient World"), medical treatment (therapeutic VR games designed to distract young people from pain), and other uses (such as VR aerospace simulators that impart the virtual experience of driving or flying). VR denotes a simulated environment in which the user interacts with a series of sensors and sophisticated output devices. Modern VR technology has widespread use in games, amusement parks, performing arts, show business, and other forms of entertainment; it requires application of the British poet Samuel Taylor Coleridge's concept of "willing suspension of disbelief."

In medical settings, VR provides children and adolescents with beneficial effects such as VR distraction, which relieves anxiety associated with chemotherapy among young people; VR diversion, which reduces distress about invasive medical procedures; and immersive VR, which can improve the attention span of children and adolescents with behavioral problems and help them learn to focus on tasks. The theoretical principle underlying such VR applications is related to diverting attention away from a noxious stimulus and focusing instead on a more pleasant environment. VR has myriad applications in different fields, notably edu-tainment, engineering, design, marketing, communication, biotechnology, and even military training.

CONCEPTUAL DIMENSIONS OF MODERN VR

The conceptual origins of the modern VR can be attributed to the vision outlined in computer scientist Ivan Sutherland's 1965 paper, *The Ultimate Display*. VR researcher Frederick P. Brooks, Jr. (1999) paraphrased Sutherland's vision in these words:

> Don't think of that thing as a *screen,* think of it as a *window,* a window through which one looks into a *virtual world.* The challenge to computer graphics is to make that virtual world look real, sound real, move and respond to interaction in real time, and even feel real. (p. 16)

Sutherland proposed an immersive, three-dimensional (3-D) display for computer graphics. To this end, the first 3-D head-mounted display helmet was designed to link more closely the user's mind and computer. Sutherland attempted to place the user "inside" the computer graphics. The head-mounted display used binocular computer screens, each displaying the same image, and a gaze-tracking device, which helped mimic 3-D.

Sutherland's head-mounted display was so heavy that it had to be suspended from the ceiling. In sharp contrast to such cumbersome creations, modern VR input devices include data gloves, which track hand positions and configurations to body suits, which sense the head-to-toe orientation of the VR participant. Output devices include complex head-mounted displays and surround-sound audio systems. Early adoption of VR, even with less-than-satisfactory technologies, enabled the U.S. military and the National Aeronautics and Space Administration to create interactive computer-generated imagery; that imagery helped them to design and refine effective applications that would otherwise have taken years of trial and error.

VR AND TELEPRESENCE

The concept of telepresence is closely associated to VR. Telepresence is the use of VR technology, especially a sophisticated robotic remote control system, to participate in events at a distant location. Applications of telepresence include working in extreme temperatures or atmospheric pressure and in perilous conditions hazardous to human life. Through telepresence, the users of a networked device can be part of the network as if they are located within the physical area of the network. Telepresence involves everything from conferencing to the use of video links.

Most telepresence functions are conducted with a complex robot (or *telechir*) operated and controlled from a distant location. Telemetry over wires, optical fibers, wireless links, or the Internet executes control and feedback. Robotic telepresence brings real-time human effectiveness, obviating the need for physical presence of a human being in that location. Telepresence has been used to defuse explosives, neutralize toxic substances, and monitor unsafe situations.

—*Debashis "Deb" Aikat*

See also Computer-Mediated Communication (CMC); Computer Use, Socialization and; Interactive Media; Interactivity

FURTHER READINGS

Biocca, F., & Levy, M. R. (Eds.). (1995). *Communication in the age of virtual reality.* Mahwah, NJ: Erlbaum.
Brooks, F. P., Jr. (1999). What's real about virtual reality? *IEEE Computer Graphics and Applications, 19*(6), 16–27.
Calvert, S. L., & Tan, S. (1994). Impact of virtual reality on young adults' physiological arousal and aggressive thoughts: Interaction versus observation. *Journal of Applied Developmental Psychology, 15*(1), 125–139.
Gershon J., Zimand E., Lemos R., Rothbaum B. O., & Hodges L. (2003). Use of virtual reality as a distractor for painful procedures in a patient with pediatric cancer: A case study. *Cyberpsychology and Behavior, 6,* 657–662.

Regenbrecht, H. T., Schubert T. W., & Friedmann, F. (1998). Measuring the sense of presence and its relations to fear of heights in virtual environments. *International Journal of Human-Computer Interaction, 10*(3), 233–249.

Sutherland, I. (1965). *The ultimate display*. Washington, DC: Advanced Research Products Agency.

Vincelli, F. (1999). From imagination to virtual reality: The future of clinical psychology. *Cyberpsychology and Behavior, 2,* 241–248.

Zimand E., Anderson P., Gershon J., Graap K., Hodges L., & Rothbaum B. O. (2002). Virtual reality therapy: Innovative treatment for anxiety disorders. *Primary Psychiatry, 9,* 51–54.

W

WEBCAMS

A *webcam* (web camera or PC camera) is a low-priced digital video camera that is connected to an Internet computer and that, combined with software, enables online video communication. There are two ways in which webcams are most commonly used:

Videoconferencing (two-way webcams). People communicating in groups of two or more on the Internet via means such as instant messaging services, Internet telephony, and online chat rooms may enhance the process by adding live video imagery of themselves. This creates a two-way video-based process of communication that often also uses an audio channel and is similar to a face-to-face conversation.

One-way webcams. The typical way of using a webcam is for uploading images onto a Web server, continuously or at regular intervals. In this context, not only the actual video cameras but also the websites that feature the one-way imagery are referred to as webcams (or *live-cams*). By analogy to broadcasting, this process is called *webcasting* to emphasize the fact that image content is publicly distributed on the Web via webcams. The live webcam videos may be watched using Web browsers. This way of using webcams represents a one-way process of communication. Webcam operators, both individuals and organizations, provide live public video imagery for a large audience. The spectrum of topics and motifs is wide. One-way webcams usually do not transmit any sound.

The quality of the images transmitted by webcams is limited and depends on the recording conditions (e.g., lighting), the camera, the software, and the bandwidth of the Internet connection. In recent years, both the efficiency of PC cameras and the bandwidth of Internet connections have increased noticeably.

PREVALENCE OF WEBCAM USE

The U.S. marketing company, IDC, estimated that 18 million webcams were sold in the year 2004; the market leader for webcams is Logitech.

In a representative telephone inquiry among adult Internet users in the United States in 2003, 7% of those surveyed were operating a one-way webcam of their own. There are more than twice as many webcam viewers as active webcam operators. According to a Pew Internet and American Life Project survey conducted in 2005, one out of six adult Internet users in the United States (16%) had viewed webcam content. The male rate (19%) is slightly larger than the female rate (13%). Webcam viewing was equally popular in all parts of the population, independent of age, income, education, and number of offspring. Statistical data concerning webcam usage by children and adolescents is yet to be published.

WEBCAM CONTENT

In 1991, computer science students from Cambridge University launched the first webcam mentioned in the literature. It displayed images of a coffee pot shared by several academics in a laboratory, thus enabling them to see on their computer desktops in their respective offices when the coffee had run through (as the laboratory was called the Trojan Room, this became known as the Trojan Room coffee pot).

The best-known webcam was the so-called JenniCam, begun in 1996 by 20-year-old college student Jennifer Ringley and operated until 2003. Jennifer equipped her apartment with several webcams and filmed her own private everyday life uncensored around the clock. The live imagery was initially available online without charge and was viewed and discussed in Internet forums by a large fan audience. The video imagery consisted of captured still images, updated once per minute. A membership fee was charged for more frequent updating of the images. Webcam operators' use of the domestic video monitoring model (home cam) may have several motives. Some are driven by the desire for attention and fame, by the urge to experiment with new technology, and by the prospect of financial benefits. The homecam concept has also been adopted as a TV format (e.g., in the reality show *Big Brother*).

Popularization of the Web in the mid-1990s brought along with it the adult entertainment industry's commercialization of webcam content. Fee-based live sex shows are transmitted via webcams, enabling viewers to communicate with the people in front of the cameras via live chatting facilities. Because webcams may be operated from private homes, a grey area of semi-professional sex providers has evolved in the field of sexcams. On the other hand, professional prostitutes welcome the fact that webcams allow them to work in a safer and more self-determined environment than the streets provide.

The spectrum of webcam content is even wider. One may label topic groups of webcams, such as trafficcams, weathercams, citycams, spacecams, petcams, peoplecams, and so on. Here, webcam operators may be commercial businesses (e.g., restaurants) and public institutions (e.g., research departments) as well as private individuals. Several online webcam directories display the variety of webcams available.

POSITIVE USES OF WEBCAMS

Webcams represent windows to the world, and, unlike TV imagery, webcam videos are uncut recordings of "real life." The webcam directory, earthcam.com, features a special section for children, enabling the observation of animals, landscapes, and urban and wildlife scenery. Other webcam directories also offer a variety of content that may be used in an educationally sensible way with parental guidance. What other chances might you have of spontaneously observing the moon or the South Pole or taking a close look at a stork's nest, a horse's stable, or a volcano? Webcams may be used in school education. Children and adolescents may acquire media competence by designing and implementing webcam projects themselves. Webcams can be integrated into the websites of schools as well as used for children's personal web pages.

DANGERS OF WEBCAMS

Webcams may result in children and adolescents being confronted with pornographic content inappropriate and unsuitable for their age. Even keywords like *webcam classroom* produce several sexcams in Google search results. Although sexcams are usually fee based and require a valid credit card number, there are usually extensive previews and trial versions available for underage Internet users.

A further risk is the possibility that children and adolescents may imprudently compromise their own privacy by identifying themselves while actively using one-way or two-way webcams. Even the privacy of relatives or friends passing by in front of the camera is endangered, as images from live webcams may be downloaded and distributed on the Web by other users. Webcams offer adolescents of both sexes the opportunity to gain attention, recruit fans, receive compliments and presents, and so on, but this opportunity may blur the boundaries between innocent use and virtual prostitution. Moreover, cases of college students installing webcams in dorms and publishing intimate images of fellow pupils on the Web have been reported. In addition to intentional misuse, lapses such as young users forgetting to turn off the webcam or third parties taking over control of the camera may cause serious problems. Teaching young users ethical standards and the appropriate technical information for safeguarding their own webcam is essential here.

The increasing surveillance of citizens by means of webcams in public spaces is a further serious sociopolitical issue. Passers-by are often identifiable on images of trafficcams. Webcams in public institutions such as prisons (jailcams) are controversial. Some political activists use webcam imagery (e.g., from abortion clinics or brothels) to pillory certain groups of people in public. On the other hand, webcams are also used in child-care institutions to enable parents to observe their children at all times from their workplaces. Equipping schools with webcams is meant to document and prevent deviant behavior, although at the same time, it has an impact on privacy.

CONCLUSION

PC cameras are becoming more effective and more affordable, mobile phone cameras are more and more common, and the bandwidth of Internet connections is growing. The trend of visualization and *videographization* continues in online communication. It is all the more important to close the existing gaps in the research into webcam use by children and adolescents and to provide them with pedagogical help for a constructive active and passive use of webcams.

—Nicola Döring

See also Chat Rooms; Chat Rooms, Social and Linguistic Processes in; Computer Use in Schools; Instant Messaging; Internet Use, Age and; Internet Use, Positive Effects of; Personal Web Pages; Websites, Children's

FURTHER READINGS

Breeden, J., & Byrne, J. (2000). *Guide to webcams.* Indianapolis, IN: Prompt.

Dyrli, O. E. (2003, October 1). Big brother 24/7: School webcams may help reduce violence but also raise privacy issues. *District Administration.* Retrieved from http://www.districtadministration.com/page.cfm?p=524

Firth, S. (1998, January 8). Live! from my bedroom. *Salon.com.* Retrieved from http://archive.salon.com/21st/feature/1998/01/cov_08feature.html

Haldane, N. (2005, March 8). Webcam lets parents peek into day care [Electronic version]. *The Detroit News.* Retrieved from http://www.detnews.com/2005/business/0503/08/C02-110370.htm

Harris, J. (2001). Virtual vantage points using webcams for teleresearch. *Learning & Leading with Technology, 28*(6). Retrieved from http://www.iste.org/inhouse/publications/ll/28/6/14h/index.cfm?Section=LL_28_6

Lenhart, A., Horrigan, J., & Fallows, D. (2004). *Content creation online* (Pew Internet & American Life Project). Retrieved from http://www.pewinternet.org/pdfs/PIP_Content_Creation_Report.pdf

Lipowicz, A. (2000, August 4). Jenni's in love. *Salon.com.* Retrieved from http://www.salon.com/tech/log/2000/08/04/jennicam/

Logitech. (2005, March 2). *Logitech reaches webcam milestone: 25 million sold* (Press release). Retrieved from http://www.logitech.com/index.cfm/about/pressroom/information/US/EN,contentid=10169

Mieszkowski, K. (2001, August 13). Candy from strangers: Teen girls flash some skin on their "cam sites," and fans shower them with gifts. Who's exploiting whom? *Salon.com.* Retrieved from http://archive.salon.com/tech/feature/2001/08/13/cam_girls/

Podlas, K. (2000). Mistresses of their domain: How female entrepreneurs in cyberporn are initiating a gender power shift. *CyperPsychology & Behavior, 3*(5), 847–854.

Rainie, L. (2005). *Use of webcams* (Pew Internet & American Life Project). Retrieved from http://www.pewinternet.org/ pdfs/PIP_webcam_use.pdf

WEBSITES

Earthcam.com section for children: www.earthcamforkids.com

Online webcam directories: www.earthcam.com, www.camcentral.com, www.webcamsearch.com, www.worldlive.cz

WEBSITES, CHILDREN'S

Children become familiar and comfortable with technology, including Web pages, at very early ages. About 6% of children ages 5 to 7, 28% of children ages 8 to 10, and almost 50% of 11-to-14-year-olds are online, mostly to get help with homework and to enjoy chat rooms, entertainment, and playing games. They are online more then 45 minutes a day, with boys spending more time online than girls in each age group. In 2000, Internet access was available in 99% of American public schools. More than 50% of children have Internet access at home, and 60% of those are regular Internet users. This entry considers children as both consumers and producers of Web pages.

CHILDREN AS CONSUMERS

The World Wide Web is shrinking the world, connecting small groups with shared interests; this may be especially important for children who cannot easily meet new people on their own. Children can talk with others without sharing their name or where they live.

The Internet also provides access to consumer-oriented information for children who visit the websites of brands that interest them. According to Nielsen NetRatings, children prefer commercial sites such as

Diva Starz, Toon Town Online, Cartoon Network, Barbie, and Disney Channel. Boys tend to like search engines and sites about sports more than girls do, and girls prefer entertainment sites. Girls see the Web more as a communication medium than a place to get information, visiting sites such as AOL Instant Messenger, and websites for magazines, *YM* and *CosmoGirl.*

Such sites have advertising content tightly woven into the content; one example is the Disney website, which features famous characters, an online store, information about theme parks, and so on. Children younger than 5 years have trouble telling advertising apart from content. Children with less experience using the Web also may not be aware of the fact that their favorite sites are commercial sites; one study found that they thought the companies just wanted to provide entertainment on commercial sites. Children click on banner ads that seem to be part of the website content, especially if there are familiar characters in the advertisement.

Children have specific design preferences. They like to move the mouse around and explore the site, looking for things that are clickable. They want age-appropriate graphics, not pictures that look like they are for babies. They like sound effects and animations. Website usability expert Jakob Nielsen found that children were best able to use straightforward sites like amazon.com and yahoo.com, even though they are primarily designed for adults. However, many of the websites he studied that had been designed specifically for children were too complex and hard to navigate, with nonstandard interface design that made too few elements look clickable. Children's sites often mix content for adults and kids on the same page or require visitors to complete complex forms before they can see information, which makes them difficult for children to use.

CHILDREN AS PRODUCERS

Children like to see content created by other children, so including children in the design of websites may help increase their usage. The Web is an ideal publishing environment; children can freely publish photographs, text, and multimedia files. Many children create their own websites; one study found that 24% of children 12 to 17 years old have personal websites. In 2000, the Pew Research Center found that while 45% of teens are using the Internet, few had made any web pages, although girls were more likely to do this because they prefer to use the Internet for communication. The more experience children have online, the more

complex sites they create; children without much previous Internet experience substitute what they have learned from their experience with other media and create linear sites similar to print magazines.

Homepages created by children can be seen as places for children to experiment with aspects of their identity. They can change the site to suit their mood or as they gain skill to create new content. However, children like to play with content created by others as a way of expressing their creativity rather than putting new original content on the Web. Girls especially like sites where they can personalize the information presented or where they can enter some information about themselves and get back customized reports.

CONCERNS

The online world for children is very commercialized. For example, toymaker Mattel established barbie.com and bratz.com to promote dolls. Each is designed to build brand loyalty through games and community features such as mailing pictures made on the site to friends, registering to see high scores on games, and using message boards. Children are attractive as consumers because they have large amounts of money to spend and are more easily swayed by advertising. Advertisements on web pages, a large part of the commercialization of the Web, are often appealing to children because of their entertainment value. Unlike advertisements on television, Web ads do not interrupt the flow of activities the child is engaged with on the website, and they can be easily accessed when the child clicks on them.

Many sites provide online forums where visitors can talk with each other; companies that provide such sites not only benefit from the increased traffic but also gain insight into children's interests, new slang, and trends. This raises concerns that such forums compromise children's privacy. In 1997, the Center for Media Education, a nonprofit advocacy group, found that 90% of child-oriented websites collected personal information, and none of the sites in the study had any mechanism in place for obtaining parental permission to collect that information. In the same year, the Federal Trade Commission (FTC) began studying the issue and found that industry self-regulation was not working; neither for-profit companies nor nonprofit organizations were following the guidelines. They issued the *Report to Congress on Privacy Online* in June 1998, which recommended that Congress force companies to get parental permission before collecting any identifying information from children. The Better Business Bureau established the Children's Advertising Review Unit (CARU) to study websites targeting children. If CARU becomes aware of sites that are not complying with FTC guidelines, it reports those companies to the FTC (Bryant, 2004). The federal Children's Online Privacy Protection Act of 2000 requires that websites for children have an understandable privacy policy available online. It also requires companies with such websites to get verifiable parental consent before any information is collected from children under 13 years old and to protect the confidentiality of the information that is collected. However, an FTC study in 2002 found that about half of the sites studied were still collecting information from children without parental consent.

—*Kimberly S. Gregson*

See also Advertising, Effects on Children of; Center for Media Education (CME); Children's Advertising Review Unit (CARU); Children's Internet Protection Act of 2000 (CIPA); Children's Online Privacy Protection Act of 1998 (COPPA); Federal Trade Commission; Internet Use, Rates and Purposes of

FURTHER READINGS

Abbott, C. (1999). Web publishing by young people. In J. Seton-Green (Ed.), *Young people, creativity, and new technologies: The challenge of digital arts* (pp. 111–121). New York: Routledge.

Agosto, D. (2004). Design vs. content: A study of adolescent girls' website designs. *International Journal of Technology and Design Education, 14,* 245–260.

Bryant, K. (2004, July 1). Not child's play: Compliance with the children's online privacy rules. *Shidler Journal of Law, Commerce and Technology, 4.* Retrieved September 25, 2005, from http://www.ictjournal.washington.edu/vol01/a004bryant.html

Chandler, D., & Roberts-Young, D. (2000). *The construction of identity in the personal homepages of adolescents.* Retrieved October 15, 2005, from http://www.aber.ac.uk/media/Documents/short/Strasbourg.html

Givens, B. (1999, Winter). *Children in cyberspace: A resource guide.* Washington, DC: American Bar Association. Retrieved October 30, 2005, from http://www.abanet.org/irr/hr/winter99_givens.html

Johnson, E. (2001, Winter). Joining the children's cyber-marketplace: A challenge for publishers. *Publishing Research Quarterly,* pp. 21–28.

Lenhart, A., Rainie, L., & Lewis, O. (2001). *Teenage life online: The rise of the instant-message generation and the Internet's impact on friendships and family relationships.* Washington, DC: Pew Internet & American Life Project. Retrieved September 30, 2005, from http://www.pewinternet.org/reports/toc?aspReport=36

Livingstone, S. (2002, March). *Children's use of the Internet: A review of the research literature.* London: London School of Economics and Political Science. Retrieved October 1, 2005, from http://www.ncb.org.uk/resources/lit_review.pdf

Nielsen, J. (2002, April). *Kids corner: Website usability for children.* Retrieved September 25, 2005, from http://www.useit.com/alertbox/20020414.html

WEBSITES

American Library Association list of "great websites for children," organized by school subjects such as literature and mathematics: http://www.ala.org/greatsites

Yahooligans!, a kid-friendly website maintained by Yahoo!, with news, games, a directory of websites, and resources for parents and teachers: http://yahooligans.yahoo.com/

WHITE HOUSE OFFICE OF NATIONAL DRUG CONTROL POLICY

The White House Office of National Drug Control Policy (ONDCP) was established by the Anti-Drug Abuse Act of 1988. The principal purpose of the ONDCP is to establish policies and objectives for the U.S. drug control program. The director of ONDCP, who is commonly referred to as the "drug czar," is in charge of the National Drug Control Strategy, which is used to direct the country's anti-drug efforts. In 1998, in the midst of an increase in crack cocaine use, the ONDCP launched the National Youth Anti-Drug Media Campaign with the goal of preventing and reducing youth drug use as one component of its strategy.

Unprecedented in size and scope (by 2005, more than $1 billion had been allocated for the media campaign), the campaign produced and distributed anti-drug advertising and related information targeted to U.S. adolescents and their parents. The campaign developed the advertising in conjunction with the Partnership for a Drug-Free America, and public relations materials in conjunction with large advertising and public relations firms such as BBDO Worldwide and Porter Novelli.

The campaign saw parents as an important target for anti-drug messages because research showed that many of the parents of teens in the early part of the 21st century had used marijuana when they were adolescents and did not think it was very dangerous. One part of the campaign was designed to educate those parents that the marijuana their children were using was more potent than what they remembered, that marijuana use affects attention spans and impedes good decision making, and that it can lead to symptoms of depression and thoughts of suicide. In 2005, the seventh year of the campaign, ads running on television and in major print publications such as the *New York Times* and *Newsweek* also encouraged parents to "be the parent and set some rules . . . because dealing with an addicted child later is a whole lot scarier than hearing a few I-hate-you's now." The tag line was: ACTION: The Anti-drug. Parents were encouraged to learn more by calling an 800 number or visiting a comprehensive website called theantidrug .com, where they could access a number of publications designed to assist them in talking about and intervening in their child's drug use.

Critics contended from its outset that the campaign's anti-drug media campaign was misdirected at marijuana. They argued that other drugs, including some legal drugs such as cigarettes and alcohol, were used by more adolescents and resulted in more significant health problems than marijuana. Later in the campaign, an increase in use of methamphetamines among adolescents engendered another round of criticism that the focus on marijuana was ill advised. The campaign maintained that marijuana is a gateway drug that leads to use of other dangerous illegal drugs.

Although the campaign claimed that it had been successful in decreasing marijuana use and increasing anti-drug attitudes among adolescents, others claimed that marijuana use had remained remarkably steady over the course of the campaign.

—*Jane D. Brown*

See also Anti-Drug Media Campaigns

FURTHER READINGS

Dreyfuss, R. (2005, July). Bush's war on pot [Electronic version]. *Rolling Stone.* Retrieved from http://www .rollingstone.com/politics/story

Satel, S. (2005, August 16). A whiff of "reefer madness" in U.S. drug policy. *New York Times,* p. D6.

WEBSITE

The Antidrug Campaign: http://www.theantidrug.com

WORLD SUMMITS ON CHILDREN AND TELEVISION

The World Summit Movement on Media for Children was conceived by Patricia Edgar, who recognized that television programming for children was changing and under threat in a variety of ways and that international efforts were needed if it was to survive with the values and objectives to which professionals in the industry aspire. In 1993, she began a process of discussions that led to the first World Summit on Television and Children, which was held in Melbourne, Australia, in March 1995 and hosted by the Australian Children's Television Foundation, where Edgar was the founding director.

The objectives of the World Summit on Media for Children were

- To achieve a greater understanding of developments in children's media around the world
- To raise the status of children's programming
- To draw to the attention of key players in broadcasting the importance of issues relating to children
- To agree on a charter of guiding principles in children's media
- To ensure the provision of programs for children will be guaranteed as the communications revolution proceeds
- To assist in the developing world to provide opportunities for quality children's programming in the future

The first summit was attended by 700 people from 72 countries. Both officially and informally, the summit provided an intense, exciting, and fertile environment for the exchange of ideas and information, and it acted as a catalyst for meetings and actions around the world.

The 2nd World Summit on Television for Children was held in London, England, in 1998, and the 3rd World Summit on Media for Children was held in Thessaloniki, Greece, in 2001. A variety of other regional summits and forums, inspired by the World Summits, have also been held since 1995 in the Philippines, Africa, and North America; they all belong to the World Summit movement. At the 3rd World Summit in Thessaloniki in March 2001, the Foundation Board conferred on Brazil the right to hold the 4th World Summit on Media for Children in Rio de Janeiro during 2004. That summit, attended by 3,000 people, was a seminal event for Brazil and Latin America. The 5th World Summit is to be held in South Africa in 2007.

In 1999, a company was established to foster the World Summit movement. The World Summit on Media for Children Foundation is a not-for-profit public company incorporated in Victoria, Australia. Its board of directors includes representatives of the principal host organizations of previous and future World Summits and regional summits. The board is responsible for overseeing the process by which specific countries and organizations are given the right to hold successive World Summits on Media for Children.

The foundation's objectives are to encourage and promote the World Summit, select host organizations for future World Summits, and assist those organizations to raise funds for and prepare for the World Summit. The foundation owns the intellectual property of the World Summit on Media for Children concept.

—Patricia Edgar

See also Computer Use, International; Entertainment-Education, International; International Clearinghouse on Children, Youth, and Media; Internet Use, International; Media Education, International

FURTHER READINGS

The Communication Initiative. Retrieved May 2, 2006, from http://www.comminit.com/experiences/pds32004/experiences-1902.html

WORLD WRESTLING ENTERTAINMENT (WWE)

Scholars, parents, and social critics are becoming increasingly worried about children's exposure to professional wrestling programs, fearful that impressionable audiences will be adversely affected by violence, profanity, and sexual content that appears both in and out of the ring. World Wrestling Entertainment (WWE), formerly known as the World Wrestling Federation (WWF) and currently the largest wrestling promoter in North America, has been the focus of this controversy.

BACKGROUND

WWE grappled its way into the American mainstream in the mid-1980s, when Chairman Vince McMahon reinvented pro wrestling as sports entertainment and garnered national attention for his company by emphasizing colorful superstars such as Hulk Hogan and star-studded super events such as *Wrestlemania.* WWE programming has maintained a national following ever since, despite a period of competition from Ted Turner's rival promotion, World Championship Wrestling (WCW). Although WCW became the most popular wrestling company for part of the 1990s, the WWE reclaimed its industry dominance by introducing edgier and more risqué content at the end of the decade, known as the "attitude" era among fans. During this time, controversial superstars such as the foul-mouthed, beer-swilling "Stone Cold" Steve Austin won the affection of WWE viewers and contributed to the eventual collapse of WCW. The WWE media reach now extends to monthly pay-per-view specials and two popular weekly television programs, WWE *Raw* and WWE *Smackdown.* These shows feature scripted wrestling matches set amid interviews, talk segments, and soap opera-esque plots involving both wrestling superstars and provocatively dressed women referred to as *divas.*

CONCERNS ABOUT YOUTHFUL VIEWERS

In 2001, WWE events drew an audience of more than 50 million Americans every week, while another 6.8 million purchased pay-per-view wrestling specials. Both weekly hours of WWE *Raw* rank in the top 10 across cable programming, drawing about 3 million viewers. Audience data from Nielsen in 2003 indicate that about 627,000 children a week watch *Raw,* and about 847,000 watch the WWE network show, *Smackdown.*

The large, young audience drawn in by WWE programming has led to substantial discourse over the potential negative consequences to them. Despite a lack of empirical research in the area, some social critics have argued that professional wrestling rewards and encourages violence that would otherwise be considered inappropriate or unjust in routine social interactions. Brendan Maguire suggests that acts considered deviant in other social settings are looked at as normative in wrestling and that the notion of behavior that deviates from an acceptable social norm is barely existent in professional wrestling. John Campbell has further posited that professional wrestling characters frequently vacillate between "face" and "heel" (good guys and bad guys), creating a scenario in which identifying particular behaviors as deviant or nonnormative is almost impossible.

In addition to the unusual construction of aggression as normative, critics have expressed alarm at the simple frequency of violence in the wrestling genre. WWE programming has consistently ranked among the least-desirable shows for family viewing according to The Parents Television Council, which has labeled it too violent for family audiences. Wrestling has been further condemned for encouraging physical violence among young, impressionable viewers and for portraying violence with no regard for human dignity.

CONTENT RESEARCH

Although there is a paucity of scientific research specifically examining the content and effects of wrestling programming, a few important studies are worthy of mention. As concern over wrestling content grew during the "attitude" era of the late 1990s, a study conducted at Indiana University received mainstream media coverage on the news program, *Inside Edition.* This content analysis of 50 episodes of WWE *Raw* reported nearly 1,500 uses of the word *hell* or *ass,* more than 1,600 instances of lewd gesturing, and more than 600 incidents in which potentially deadly weapons such as tables and chairs were used in interpersonal violence. Content analyses of British television by Barrie Gunter and colleagues revealed that 6 of the 10 most violent programs were WWE shows, and a later report suggested that the two most violent individual programs on British television were WWE productions.

A content analysis by Ron Tamborini and colleagues further suggested that WWE programming contains far more violence than conventional programming. These researchers examined 36 hours of *Raw* and *Smackdown* episodes from 2002 and found that they present violence as morally just, likely to go unpunished, and devoid of realistic consequences such as extreme harm to the victim. Additional analyses of the Tamborini data set reveal further attributes that may be problematic. Other researchers have found that violence in professional wrestling tends to be out of proportion to the events provoking it, leading to an escalating spiral of violence in which routine social interactions become bloodbaths in a very short amount of time. Studies also show that wrestling programs contain an extraordinary amount of verbal aggression (typically character and competence attacks) enacted primarily for the sake of amusement.

BEHAVIORAL RESEARCH

Concerns about the programs have been heightened by research in this area indicating that young children are more likely than adults or adolescents to perceive wrestling as realistic. Because realism strengthens the potential of television violence to increase viewer aggression, initial indications that young children are watching and likely to perceive the violence as real make it important to learn more not only about the manner in which wrestling violence is portrayed but also about its impact on impressionable young audiences in terms of attitudes toward aggression and aggressive behavior.

Scattered empirical research on televised wrestling has examined gender differences in motivations for viewing, self-reports of behavioral imitation, and perceptions of wrestling realism among young children, adolescents, and adults. In two separate studies, Dafna Lemish reported that male children and adolescents frequently imitate fighting techniques used in professional wrestling and that more than half of a sample of elementary schools principals report dealing at least once a week with schoolyard fights involving children imitating wrestling. A report by the British Broadcasting Standards Commission also indicates that many younger children are unaware of the scripted nature of professional wrestling and believe the action to be real. Despite the alarming results of these studies, little if any additional empirical research has examined the impact of wrestling entertainment on children and adolescents. Although a sizable amount of social criticism has been levied against the genre, more scientific research is needed to substantiate these concerns.

—Kenneth A. Lachlan and Paul D. Skalski

See also Aggression, Television and; Sports Television; Violence, Experimental Studies of

FURTHER READINGS

Bandura, A., Ross, D., & Ross, S. A. (1963). Imitation of film-mediated aggressive models. *Journal of Abnormal and Social Psychology, 66,* 3–11.

Broadcasting Standards Commission. (2001). *How do audiences perceive TV and video wrestling?* Retrieved January 27, 2004 from http://www.ofcom.org.uk/research/consumer_audience_research/tv_audience_reports/wrestling_how_do_viewers_perceiv

Campbell, J. (1996). Professional wrestling: Why the bad guys win. *Journal of American Culture, 19,* 127–140.

Gunter, B., Harrison, J., & Wykes, M. (2003). *Violence on television: Distribution, form, context, and themes.* Mahwah, NJ: Erlbaum.

Gunter, B., & Wykes, J. (1998). *Violence on television: An analysis of amount, nature, location, and origin of violence in British programmes.* New York: Routledge.

Lemish, D. (1997). The school as a wrestling arena: The modeling of a television series. *The European Journal of Communication Research, 22,* 395–418.

Lemish, D. (1998). "Girls can wrestle too": Gender differences in the consumption of a television wrestling series. *Sex Roles, 38,* 833–849.

Maguire, B. (2000). Defining deviancy down: A research note regarding professional wrestling. *Deviant Behavior, 21,* 551–565.

Raney, A. A. (2003). Professional wrestling and human dignity: Questioning the boundaries of entertainment. In H. Good (Ed.), *Desperately seeking ethics* (pp. 61–84). New York: Scarecrow.

Tamborini, R., Skalski, P., Lachlan, K. A., Westerman, D., Davis, J., & Smith, S. L. (2005). The raw nature of televised professional wrestling: Is the violence a cause for concern? *Journal of Broadcasting and Electronic Media, 49*(2), 202–220.

Y

YOUTH CULTURE

Popular culture includes aspects of daily life that are not considered academic or fine arts. It may be bold and colorful, or raunchy, or comforting and familiar like Mickey Mouse. Popular culture often overlaps with youth culture; one of the best examples is the *Harry Potter* series, which is read by adults, teens, and children. Typical features of youth culture include being edgy, having profane content (such as the humor of the children in *South Park*), and being off-beat and "weird."

One way to understand youth culture is through media. Buckingham (2002) refers to the "electronic generation" when discussing the use of the Internet by children and teens, but that term seems to be equally applicable to both traditional and new media use because of the vast amounts of media consumed daily by modern youth. Media are used more than 6.5 hours a day, and exposure is even higher because children and teens tend to use more than one medium at the same time (i.e., they may listen to CDs while playing video games). A 2003–2004 study of children's and teens' media habits conducted for the Kaiser Family Foundation found that more than 95% have televisions, VCRs, and CD players, 80% have cable television and video games, and more than 70% have access to the Internet at home. That media world is expanding with the introduction of devices such as personal video recorders (TiVo) and portable DVD players, Internet access through video game consoles, down-loadable ring tones for cell phones, and video content on cell phones and iPODs.

Network television, especially the WB, UPN, and Fox, target their programming to reach adolescents. Networks promote young teenage stars such as Lindsay Lohan, to appeal to teenagers. In 2004, the most popular show among both boys and girls was *American Idol* on Fox, and girls liked *The OC*. On UPN, girls liked *America's Next Top Model,* while boys liked the afternoon anime programs *Pokémon* and *Yu-Gi-Oh* on the WB. Some programs, including *The Simpsons* and *Malcolm in the Middle,* were enjoyed by all teenagers, regardless of race or gender. However, different racial groups identified different favorite programs. Black teens preferred programs with African Americans in major roles, such as *The Parkers, The Hughleys*, and *Moesha*. White teens liked 7th *Heaven* and *Survivor.*

The Internet is a big part of youth culture. Teens, tweens, and children have grown up with the Internet and are accustomed to using it for information and entertainment as well as communicating with friends. They create content on the Internet as well as con-sume content created by others. Personal homepages can reflect the owner's personality and interests, with images of movie stars and favorite bands, along with stories and poems and diary entries written by the owners. The webpage can be changed as often as own-ers like to reflect changing interests or as they want to change the aspects of their identity that they share with others. Sites like MySpace.com, recently pur-chased by News Corp., cultivate community and sense of belonging with photos, homepages, and friends lists. A long list of friends has become a status symbol among the 26 million registered MySpace users. Facebook.com has similar communication features specifically for high school and college students. Users create the content on these sites and so control the culture, rather than being limited by cultural options offered by large media companies.

Children and teens both use instant messaging (IM) to quickly communicate with friends. According to the Pew Research Center, in 2005, 48% of teens surveyed use IM daily, and 30% use it several times a day. Teens use IM to keep in touch with their friends in other cities and to coordinate their schedules, talk over homework, and chat with many people at once. They can communicate privately without parental supervision, trying out various aspects of identity and talking with members of the opposite sex in a more normal setting. To speed up the conversation, users create abbreviations and slang, so that even if parents were to see messages, the messages would be almost impossible to understand. This writing style helps users feel part of a culture separate from their parents.

One aspect of media-focused youth culture that has spread from young children to older teens is animation. Cartoons let the viewers escape the rules of the everyday (adult) world. The cartoon world is creative and childlike, with talking animals and over-the-top violence. Cartoons are no longer just Saturday morning programs for children. *The Simpsons* has been on the air since the early 1990s on the Fox network. *South Park,* on the cable network Comedy Central and syndicated on network television, has been on the air since 1997. These cartoons tell stories about family life from the perspective of the children. What makes cartoons like *South Park* and *The Simpsons* popular is the power the children have; they are able to solve problems caused by their parents. Animation is popular on the Internet, as well; youth send the online addresses of interesting new animations to their friends. One site in particular draws a large weekly audience: HomestarRunner.com features animated shorts, including the most popular feature, the fan mail answered by a character named StrongBad.

Another interesting part of youth culture is video games; in fact, the Entertainment Software Association estimates that 50% of all Americans play some form of video game, and 35% of game players are under the age of 18. Like cartoons, these games let players inhabit a fantasy world where they have the power to save the planet or to fly into outer space and battle aliens. Players get to break everyday rules with no real-world consequences. Boys and young males watch less television to make time to play PC and console-based video games. Girls and young women play casual games on the Internet. Not everyone is happy about the popularity of video games, believing that virtual activity has replaced real-world outdoor play. However, a new area of video games has gained popularity— exertainment, games that combine entertainment and exercise. Popular examples are *Dance Dance Revolution* and *Mojo!;* the latter uses a small camera and a PlayStation console.

Not all media are electronic and interactive. Comic books appeared during the Depression and were one of the first attempts to market directly to children and teens instead of to parents. The stories were violent, and authority figures, such as the police, were portrayed as corrupt and ineffective, just as they are in many video games and television programs popular with youth today. During World War II, superheroes such as Captain America were popular, not just with children but also with soldiers who needed lightweight portable entertainment. Comics were blamed for the increase in juvenile delinquency and violent youth crime. Adults reacted with alarm to a youth culture they did not understand. There were calls from parent groups for censorship and state regulation of the industry, again a direct parallel to calls for censorship of video game content.

The interest in comics continues today. One category of comics seeing high sales is manga, serialized graphic novels from Japan. This is a rapidly growing area of the publishing industry, which now has series available for all ages. Sales of manga titles have been doubling for several years, and in 2006, most of the best-selling titles in the publishing industry's graphic novel category were manga titles. Manga have been available in the United States for 20 years; however, they have exploded in popularity in the last few years with the increase in interest in series such as *Full Metal Alchemist* and *Naruto*, two examples of *shonen* or manga for boys. Both are in the top 20 positions of the graphic novel BookScan list, the publishing industry's best-selling titles list. A large part of the audience for manga is young girls buying *shoujo,* or manga for girls; typical examples include *Fruits Basket* and *Fushigi Yugi.* Even American publishers are getting into the manga business; Archie Comics will release *Sabrina the Teenage Witch* with manga-style drawings.

Mainstream youth culture in music, fashion, and even sports is driven by the preferences of African American youth, who are a key part of the urban market. Hip hop music is popular with teens of all races, as are urban street slang and fashions by designers such as music industry leaders Jay-Z and P. Diddy. Part of the popularity of urban culture involves signaling membership in a culture that seems more real than the one created by big media companies. Once a slang term gets used (and overused) by mainstream media, it loses popularity among youth, who do not want to be part of the mainstream culture.

Teenage Research Unlimited estimates that teens have almost $170 billion available in disposable income. Youth are sought after as consumers because they are open to trying new products and brands; they want to be trendsetters, and once they find something they like, they can be very loyal consumers. Teens get clues about popular brands and styles from the media and celebrities. Sports stars are effective role models in advertising; girls are more likely than boys to say positive things about a product or a brand because their favorite athletic star is featured in an advertisement. Marketers prefer age-segmented media, such as animation blocks and age-targeted programming blocks, because such programming helps them pitch their products to the right audience. Marketers also engage teens and tweens in word-of-mouth programs in which they promote products to their friends. Marketers even talk of the "nag factor" in which they see children persistently encouraging their parents to buy something, pestering until they get what they want. Companies hold focus groups and conduct surveys to determine trends and shopping habits. Some companies lose credibility with youth when they use outdated terms and images that are no longer a part of youth culture. Companies may need to advertise outside traditional media to seem credible to youth. The Toyota Scion is not advertised in any mainstream magazines; research on the media use habits of the targeted audience for this car found that they do not read traditional magazines, not even traditional car buff magazines. Toyota spent $12.2 in magazine advertisements in 2004, but mainly in nontraditional magazines.

Many adults believe that compared with children in the past, today's youth have little respect for their elders and no strong sense of right or wrong; young people are seen as materialistic and selfish. Adults form many of their impressions on the basis of images in the media rather than contact with actual teenagers. Media coverage stresses problems faced or caused by youth, trivializes academic accomplishments, and overemphasizes sporting achievements. It also may show youth as having fun and getting out of control. However, the real-world facts do not support the media's negative view; youth crime is down, as is drug and alcohol use. Youth may need to take more control of creating representations of their culture online and in traditional media. That culture may be raunchy and edgy, but it can also be very honest and hopeful.

—*Kimberly S. Gregson*

See also Advertising, Exposure to; Advertising, Market Size and; Electronic Games, Types of; Hip Hop, Youth Culture and; Instant Messaging; Internet Use, Social; Manga (Japanese Comic Books); Media Exposure; Television, Motivations for Viewing of

FURTHER READINGS

Arnold, A. (2004, February 16). Drawing in the gals: Move over, guys. *Time*, p. 97.
Entertainment Software Association. (n.d.) *Game player data.* Retrieved October 30, 2005, from http://www.theesa.com/facts/gamer_data.php
Kaiser Family Foundation. (2005, March). *Executive summary: Generation M: Media in the lives of 8- to 18-year olds.* Retrieved September 28, 2005, from http://www.kff.org/entmedia/7250.cfm
Lenhart, A., & Madden, M. (2005). *Teen content creators and consumers.* Retrieved November 3, 2005, from http://www.pewinternet.org/PPF/r/166/report_display.asp
Lenhart, A., Rainie, L., & Lewis, O. (2001). *Teenage life online: The rise of the instant-message generation and the Internet's impact on friendships and family relationships.* Washington, DC: Pew Internet & American Life Project. Retrieved September 30, 2005, from http://www.pewinternet.org/reports/toc?aspReport=36
Males, M. (1998). *Framing youth: Ten myths about the next generation.* Monroe, ME: Common Courage Press.
Nichols, S., & Good, T. (2004). *America's teenagers— Myths and realities.* Mahwah, NJ: Erlbaum.
Sternberg, J. (2004, Summer). Young, dumb, and full of lies: The news media's construction of youth culture. *Screen Education, 37,* 34–39.
Thiel, S. (2005). IM me: Identity construction and gender negotiation in the world of adolescent girls and instant messaging. In S. Mazzarella (Ed.), *Girl wide web: Girls, the Internet, and the negotiation of identity* (pp. 179–202). New York: Lang.
Wright, B. (2001). *Comic book nation: The transformation of youth culture in America.* Baltimore: Johns Hopkins University Press.

Z

ZINES

Although they are extremely diverse in form and content and thus quite resistant to generalization, *zines* are typically defined as magazines handmade by an individual or small group of people as a hobby or avocation. Unlike the "slick" (i.e., professional, technically enhanced, big budget) magazines produced by the commercial publishing industry, zines typically are created at home and thus are independent from professional presses and commercial publishers. The roots of contemporary zines often are traced back only as far as the punk fanzines of the late 1970s; yet, similar self-publications have a longer and more complex history in a variety of subcultural groups, including science fiction fans of the late 1930s, the Beat poets of the 1950s, and the underground press of the 1960s and 1970s.

Most contemporary zine makers, popularly known as *zinesters,* are teenagers and young adults who feel alienated from dominant society and commercial culture. The earliest zine producers were typically white, middle-class males; however, an increasing number of girls and people of color have become involved in zine making since the late 1980s. Because paper and writing implements are inexpensive as well as easy to access, manipulate, and transport, zines remain the media texts most easily and cheaply produced by young people. In turn, because zine production requires minimal literacy and zine makers champion amateur aesthetics, zines are an attractive alternative medium for those with minimal education and publishing skills.

The disparate communities in which zines are made and consumed today have led to a wide variety of zine genres, including: *fanzines* (created by fans of a particular cultural medium or genre, such as music or sports); *community/"scene" zines* (e.g., punks, feminists); *topic/issue zines* (e.g., work, conspiracy theories); *literary zines* (poetry, short fiction, science fiction); and *comix* (underground comic books). *Personal zines* (or *perzines*) are created by one individual and composed primarily of written text and illustrations reflecting personal experiences and opinions.

In keeping with the anti-industrial, anti-commercial ethos of countercultural production, which privileges authentic expression, zines are typically created via relatively inexpensive and unsophisticated means: handwritten or typewritten text, hand-drawn illustrations, and photocopied text and images appropriated from commercial media texts. With the increased availability of personal computers, as well as word processing and desktop publishing software, an increasing number of zine producers are using digital technologies to typeset and lay out their material. Nevertheless, these electronically technologized practices are often frowned on by zinesters interested in steering clear of the corporate, industrial sector of culture and expressing themselves as authentically as possible. Zines typically carry no paid advertisements, although they often promote other zines and handmade products.

The independent "Do It Yourself" (DIY) ethos privileged by zinesters has important connections to the anti-industrial, anti-capitalist practice known in France as *la perruque,* wherein cultural producers use office time, equipment, and supplies to create, reproduce, and distribute their texts. In addition to "scamming" the means of zine production from their places of work and photocopy businesses, zinesters freely appropriate text and images mass-produced by the commercial media industries, refusing to adhere to laws protecting intellectual and artistic property. Such text and images are rarely reproduced in their original forms, however, as zine makers deconstruct and reassemble such materials to produce new meanings. To avoid criminal prosecution and censorship for such practices, many zinesters do not reveal their real identities and use nicknames by which they are known in the zine community, thus attesting to the performance nature of this culture. Zine makers also protect their identity and limit outside interference by using post office boxes instead of home addresses, by changing the titles of their zines, and by accepting only untraceable capital as payment, such as cash and stamps. As these alternative and often illegal practices suggest, zine making affords young people an opportunity to rebel against dominant social institutions and to explore counterhegemonic identities and alternative cultural economies.

In contrast with mass-produced periodicals, zines appear irregularly, their creators waiting either for good copy and artwork to publish or, more typically, for enough capital and time to compile and print the next issue. Often, zines are produced as "one-offs," singular creations by an individual who, for whatever reason, does not or cannot produce other issues. Most one-off and first-issue zines are printed in small quantities due to their producers' lack of capital or uncertainty about readers' interest in their work. Those zinesters who are committed to the zine community and to creating alternative forms of culture usually produce multiple issues of a zine and develop a subscription list that requires a larger number of reproductions. Nonetheless, even zines created by more committed individuals are rarely the same in form and content from issue to issue; therefore, a single issue of

a zine cannot be considered representative of a zinester's *oeuvre*. Unlike most commercial magazines, which rely on formulaic rhetoric and layout practices, zines typically have no table of contents, departments or sections, or page numbers structuring their material.

Zines are typically sold or traded at cultural events, such as musical shows; however, an increasing number of zines can be purchased at independent book and music stores, as well as through online distribution companies known as *distros*. Because many zinesters often produce only one issue of their zine, reproduce their zine in small quantities, fail to keep master copies of their work, or move after their zine's initial distribution, it is quite difficult to locate back issues of most zines. Thus, although new zines continually enter the alternate media economy, just as many other zines cease being reproduced, making a zine collector's or critic's job all the more difficult and frustrating. Fortunately, several zine directories exist today in both paper and electronic form (e.g., *Factsheet Five*), which makes locating such texts and their producers easier than in the past.

—*Mary Kearney*

See also Magazines, Adolescent Boys'; Magazines, Adolescent Girls'; Personal Web Pages

FURTHER READINGS

Duncombe, S. (1997). *Notes from the underground: Zines and the politics of alternative culture.* New York: Verso.

Green, K., & Taormino, T. (Eds.). (1997). *A girl's guide to taking over the world: Writings from the girl zine revolution.* New York: St. Martin's Press.

Vale, V. (Ed.). (1996). *Zines!* (Vol. 1). San Francisco: V/Search Publication.

Vale, V. (Ed.). (1997). *Zines!* (Vol. 2). San Francisco: V/Search Publication.

Wertham, F. (1973). *The world of fanzines: A special form of communication.* Carbondale: Southern Illinois University Press.

Index

British Broadcasting Standards Commission, **2:**878
British East India Company, **1:**399
British Film Institute, **2:**497
British Legends, **1:**276
British Library Association, **1:**130
British Telecom, **1:**276, 427
Brokeback Mountain, **2:**766
Brooks, Frederick P., Jr., **2:**869
Brooks, Garth, **2:**583
Brother Iz, **1:**404
Brown, Bobby, **1:**131
Brown, J., **2:**754
Brown, James, **2:**577
Brown, Jane, **1:**71, **2:**729, 730–731
Brown, J. D., **2:**760, 761
Brown, R., **2:**591
Brown, W. J., **2:**494
Brown and Williamson, **1:**180, **2:**675
Browne, Beverly A., **1:**345
Brubeck, Dave, **2:**580
Bruckman, Amy, **1:**391, 443, **2:**563
Bruner, Jerome, **1:**183, **2:**568
Bruntz, George, **2:**510
Bryant, J., **1:**233, 324
Bryant, J. A., **1:**324
Bryce, Jennifer, **2:**722
Bucher, H.-J., **2:**719
Buckingham, David, **1:**420
Bucy, Erik P., **1:**421
Budweiser, **1:**24, 31, 132
Buena Vista Group, **1:**244, 245
Buffy the Vampire Slayer, **2:**756
Bufkin, J., **2:**551
Bugs Bunny, **1:**144, 145, 146, **2:**545
Bulgaria, **1:**442
Bulimia. *See* **Eating disorders**
Bulletin boards. *See* **Internet bulletin boards**
Bulletin of the Center for Children's Books, **1:**130
Bullies
    electronic games, **1:**274
    mobile telephones, **2:**538
Bully, **1:**13
Bumpers, **1:**21, 26, 46, 59, 60, **2:**715
Bundy, Ted, **2:**770
Burdeau, George, **1:**403
Bureau of Alcohol, Tobacco and Firearms (BATF), **1:**49
Burger King, **2:**678, 679
Burgoon, Judee K., **1:**201
Burleson, Brant, **1:**320
Burnett, Leo, **1:**178
Burstyn, Joseph, **2:**710
Burstyn v. Wilson (1952), **2:**710
Bush, George H. W., **1:**317, **2:**857
Bush, George W., **2:**569
Bush, Patricia J., **1:**35–36
Bushido, **2:**577
Bushman, B. J., **1:**90, 359, **2:**723, 847, 862
Bushman, Brad, **2:**828
Bushnell, Nolan, **1:**275

Busselle, R., **2:**777
Buster Brown, **1:**192, 193, 194
But I'm a Cheerleader, **1:**13
Butler, M., **1:**364
Butsch, Richard, **1:**331
Buzzback, **2:**835
Buzz marketing. *See* **Viral marketing**
Bybee, C., **1:**14, **2:**642
Byrds, **2:**581
Bystander effect, **2:**847

The Cabinet of Dr. Caligari, **1:**388
Cable television
    Europe, **1:**306
    Latin America, **2:**465–466
    24-hour channel for preschoolers, **1:**40
Cabot, Meg, **1:**127
Cage, John, **2:**579, 583
Cagney & Lacey, **1:**222
Caillou, **2:**465
Caldecott Medal, **1:**130
Caldwell and Bradley Home Observation Measure of the
        Environment (H.O.M.E.), **1:**257
California Beef Council, **2:**785
Calvert, Sandra, **1:**204, 206, 257, 445, **2:**606
Calvert, S. L., **1:**440
Calvin Klein, **1:**52
Cambodia, **1:**93
Camel (cigarette company), **1:**25, 31, 176
    See also Joe Camel
Cameron, L., **2:**612
Campaign for Our Children, **1:**222
Campbell, D. T., **2:**726
Campbell, John, **2:**877
Canada
    indigenous peoples, **1:**402
    school Internet use, **1:**442
    television viewing and homicide rates, **2:**866
    TV-Turnoff Week, **2:**834
    UNESCO violence study, **2:**839
Canadian Broadcasting Corporation (CBC), **2:**616, 628
Candy cigarettes, **1:**177
Caniff, Milton, **1:**193
Cannibal Corpse, **2:**575
Cannon, Walter B., **1:**102, **2:**654
Cantor, J., **1:**359, **2:**488, 761
Cantor, Joanne, **1:**183, 329, 332, 335, 344, 388, **2:**539
Cantor, Muriel, **1:**330
Cantor, P. A., **1:**157
Capital Cities/ABC Group, **1:**243
Capital Group, **1:**242
Capricho, **2:**468
Captain Kangaroo, **1:**1, 261, **2:**688
Captain Marvel, **1:**189
Captain Midnight, **2:**685
Captain Morgan, **1:**93
Cardiac reaction, **2:**654
Care Bears, **1:**129
Carey, Mariah, **1:**195

Madell, D., **1:**439
Mademoiselle, **1:**32
Madonna (singer), **1:**129, 366, **2:**575
Magazine Publishers of America (MPA), **2:**481
Magazines
    crossover readership, **1:**63–64
    eating disorders, **1:**252, 344
    gender roles, **1:**364–365
    Latin America, **2:**468
    mother portrayals, **2:**541
    pornography, **2:**658–660
    sex, **2:**754
    sexual information, **2:**765
    sexualized advertising, **1:**52
    tobacco ads in, **1:**25
    See also **Zines**
Magazines, adolescent boys', 2:481–482
    adolescent portrayals in, **1:**10
    advertising effects, **2:**482
    content analysis, **2:**481
    gender portrayals in, **1:**3
    readership, **2:**481
    sexual information, **2:**764–765
Magazines, adolescent girls', 2:482–485
    adolescent portrayals in, **1:**10
    advertising, **1:**31, 62–64
    alternatives to mainstream, **2:**485
    beliefs/behaviors and, **2:**484
    body image, **2:**483, 484
    circulation, **1:**62
    content, **2:**482–483
    gender portrayals, **1:**3, **2:**482–483
    intimacy of, **2:**482
    Latin America, **2:**468
    readership, **2:**481, 482
    reception of, **2:**484
    sexual information, **2:**764–765
    sexuality, **2:**483–484
Magazines, children's, 2:485–486
    history of, **2:**485–486
    Latin America, **2:**468
    market for, **2:**485
    readership, **2:**485
    research on, **2:**486
Magic bullet theory of media effects, **1:**76, **2:**509–510, 513
The Magic Schoolbus, **1:**262
Magnavox, **1:**275
Maguire, Brendan, **1:**77, **2:**877
Mahabharatha (television series), **1:**400
Maher, Jill K., **1:**33, 345
Maher, J. K., **1:**370
Mahiri, Jabari, **1:**382
Mahler, Gustav, **2:**579
Mahood, C., **1:**427
Mainstreaming, **1:**227
Make a Wish, **2:**807
Making the Band, **1:**131
Makkar, Jalmeen, **1:**72
Malaysia, **1:**106–107

Malcolm, John G., **2:**712
Malcolm in the Middle, **1:**9, **2:**772, 881
Males, Mike, **2:**626
Maltreated children. *See* **Media effects, maltreated children and**
Mander, Jerry, **1:**294
Mandrell, Barbara, **2:**583
Manga (Japanese comic books), 2:486–488
    Astro Boy, **1:**96, **2:**486
    humor, **2:**487
    international following, **2:**487
    origins, **2:**486
    sexuality, **2:**487
    types, **2:**487–488
    youth culture, **2:**882
The Manhattan Project, **1:**12
Manhunt, **1:**81, 281
Manson, Marilyn, **2:**594
Mantle, Mickey, **1:**177
The Many Loves of Dobie Gillis, **1:**177
Mao Ze-Dong, **1:**166
Marble Madness, **1:**188, 266
Mares, Louise, **2:**539
Mares, Marie-Louise, **1:**232, **2:**817–819
Mares, M.-L., **2:**761, 793
Margie, **1:**6
Marijuana, **2:**875–876
Marinho, Roberto, **2:**464
Mario, **1:**282
Maris, Roger, **1:**177
Marketing
    alcohol advertising, **1:**91
    children's websites, **2:**873–874
    cigarettes, **1:**175–178
    contemporary animation shows, **1:**148
    market research in schools, **1:**357–358, **2:**744
    online, **1:**27–28, 94
    relational, **1:**28
    relationship, **2:**716–717
    schools, marketing in, **2:**742–744
    sexualized advertising, **1:**53
    stealth, **1:**358, **2:**868
    sticky, **2:**788–789
    tobacco, international, **2:**833
    tweens, **2:**835–836
    violence and, **2:**860–861
    viral, **1:**358, **2:**836, 867–868
    youth culture, **2:**883
    See also **Licensing, merchandising and; Promotional tie-ins;** Target audience
Markey, Edward, **2:**857
Marlboro, **1:**177, **2:**675, 833
Marlboro Man, **1:**133, 177
Marley, Bob, **2:**582
Marnie, **2:**542
Mars, **2:**785
Marske, Amy L., **1:**253
Martin, Mary, **1:**20
Martin, Ricky, **2:**468, 472

Roach, Harold (Hal), **2:**544
Roach, Max, **2:**580
Roadrunner, **1:**149
Roberts, D., **2:**787
Roberts, D. F., **1:**8, 203, 449, **2:**551
Roberts, Don, **2:**554
Roberts, Donald, **1:**70, 71, 205, **2:**576
Roberts, Robin, **1:**378
Robertson, Eck, **2:**582
Robertson, Judy, **1:**391
Robinson, D., **1:**14, **2:**642
Robinson, J., **2:**787
Robots, **2:**560–561, 869
    See also Bots
Rock and roll. *See* **Music genres, pop/rock**
Rock en español, **2:**468
Rockstar Games, **1:**277
Rocky IV, **2:**675
Rocky movies, **1:**453
Rodgers, Jimmie, **2:**582
Roe, K., **2:**521
Roe, Keith, **1:**249, **2:**649, 696
Rogers, Everett, **1:**208
Rogers, Fred, **1:**261
Rogers, Martha, **2:**716
Rogers, Roy, **2:**545
Rokeach, Milton, **2:**511
Role experimentation, adolescent, **1:**23
Role models. *See* Identification with media portrayals
Rolling Stones, **2:**572, 578, 581, 796
Rollins, Sonny, **2:**580
Romano, Ray, **1:**330
Romantic relationships
    mobile telephones, **2:**538
    movies, **2:**550–551
    music, **2:**565, 569, 599
    online, **2:**637, 752
    sexual minorities, **2:**766
Ronald McDonald, **1:**133, 342, 348, 355
Room culture research. *See* **Bedrooms, media use in**
Rooney, Mickey, **1:**11
Roosevelt, Franklin Delano, **1:**145, 194
Rosaen, Sarah F., **2:**512
Rose, Tricia, **1:**382
Roseanne, **1:**331, **2:**761
Rosenblatt, Louise M., **2:**700
Rosengren, K. E., **2:**696, 779, 821
Rosenkoetter, Lawrence, **2:**502
Rosenkoetter, Sharon, **2:**502
Rossellini, Roberto, **2:**710
Roth v. United States (1957), **2:**663
Rotten, Johnny, **2:**572
Rottweiler, **2:**575
Rough play, aggression versus, **1:**83
Rouner, D., **1:**32, 370
Rowling, J. K., **1:**127, 130, 325, **2:**693
Roy, Rammohun, **1:**399
Rubin, Alan, **2:**688
Rubin, A. M., **1:**86, **2:**520, 521, 566, 814, 842

Rubinstein, Eli, **2:**856
Ruckmick, C. A., **1:**237
Ruditis, Paul, **1:**127
Rudman, L. A., **2:**590
Rudy Vallee, **2:**685
The Ruff and Reddy Show, **1:**146
Ruggiero, J. A., **1:**364
Rugrats, **1:**149, **2:**465, 737
The Rugrats Movie, **2:**546, 678
Rule-making behavior, for mediation,
    1:14–15, 16, 18, **2:**641–642
Run-DMC, **2:**577, 582
Rushkoff, Douglas, **1:**420
Rushton, Neil, **2:**574
Russell, Steve, **1:**275
Russia
    alcohol advertising, **1:**93
    email pen pals, **1:**293
    media education, **2:**498
    public health campaigns, **1:**457
Rutland, A., **2:**612
Ryan, R. M., **2:**636
Rydin, Ingegerd, **1:**396, 397

Saari, Timo, **1:**390
Saban, Chaim, **1:**243
Saban Entertaiment, **2:**466
Sabido, Miguel, **2:**467
Sabrina The Teen-age Witch, **2:**882
Sad entertainment, **2:**539–540
Safe Surf, **1:**429
Safety
    Internet, **1:**152, 291, 420, 430, 433, 452–453, **2:**637
    mobile telephones, **2:**537
    sponsored educational material on, **2:**785
Sailor Moon, **1:**97
Salomon, Gavriel, **1:**394, **2:**476, 619
Salt-N-Pepa, **1:**378, **2:**577
Sankey, Ira, **2:**579
Sapolsky, Barry, **1:**388, **2:**556
Sapolsky, B. S., **2:**677
Satan, **2:**572
Satellite television
    Europe, **1:**306
    India, **1:**400
    Latin America, **2:**465–466
Saturday Evening Post, **1:**196
Saturday Night Fever, **1:**12, **2:**556
Saunders, Jesse, **2:**574
Saunderson, Kevin, **2:**574
Saved!, **1:**13
Saw, **1:**388
Schachter, Stanley, **1:**102
Schaeffer, Pierre, **2:**583
Scharrer, Erica, **1:**330, 331, **2:**502, 626, 772
Schell, R., **1:**32, 370
Schemas/scripts, aggressive, 2:734–736
    cognitive script theory, **1:**185–186
Schemas/scripts, gender, 2:736–738

World Summits on Media for Children and Adolescents, **1:**422
World War I, **2:**509
World War II, **1:**194, **2:**514, 568, 687
World Wide Web, **1:**418, **2:**652, 788
    See also Internet; **Personal web pages**; **Webcams**; **Websites, children's**
World Wildlife Fund (WWF), **1:**132
World Wrestling Entertainment (WWE), 1:132, **2:877–878**
World Wrestling Federation (WWF), **1:**132, **2:**877
Wornian, K., **1:**365
Wright, Bradford, **1:**190
Wright, H. R., **2:**615
Wright, John, **1:**138, 256, 257
WWE Magazine, **2:**481

Xbox, **1:**276, 278, 282, 285
Xiaohai yuebao (The Child's Paper), **1:**165
Xiao pengyou (Little Friends), **1:**165
Xin shaonian (New Youth), **1:**165
X-Men, **1:**190
X-Men, **1:**10
X-rated movies, **2:**666–668

Yahoo!, **1:**416, 429, **2:**601, 652, 764
Yang, M., **1:**359
Yarrow, L. J., **2:**718
Yates, Andrea, **2:**541
Yellow Kid, **1:**193, 194
Yizo Yizo, **2:**776
YM, **2:**481, 483, 765
Yokota, F., **2:**554
Yokota, Fumie, **2:**555
Yokota, Junko, **1:**128
Yomiuri Shimbun, **1:**455
You Are There, **1:**262
Young, Kimberly, **1:**431
Young adult (YA) literature. *See* **Books for adolescents**
Young America Magazine, **2:**742
The Young and the Restless, **2:**777
Young People New Media, **2:**496
Your Hit Parade, **1:**176, 177
Youth as E-Citizens (Youth, Media and Democracy Project), **1:**152
Youth culture, 2:881–883
    advertising, **1:**228
    African Americans, **2:**882–883
    animation, **2:**882
    business news portrayals of, **1:**6–7
    comics, **2:**882
    consumerism, **2:**883
    electronic games, **2:**882
    fan cultures and, **1:**326
    hip hop, **1:**383–384, **2:**578

history of teenager, **2:**795–797
identity formation and, **1:**4
identity in, **1:**227–228
India, **1:**400–401
instant messaging, **2:**882
Internet, **2:**881–882
language, **1:**228
music, **1:**228
television, **2:**881
visual media, **1:**228
    See also entries on **Peer groups**
Youth Internet Radio Network, **1:**403
Youth Marketing Co., **2:**796
Youth media, **2:**525, 531
Youth, Media and Democracy Project, American University, **1:**152
Youth News Network (YNN), **1:**199
Youth Radio, **2:**686
Youth Risk Behavior Survey, **1:**248
Youth Self Report, **1:**314
Yo-Yo, **1:**378, **2:**570
Y Tú Máma También, **2:**467
Yu-Gi-Oh, **2:**881
YWCA, **2:**607

Zabrack, M. L., **2:**864
Zamora, Pedro, **2:**767
Zappa, Frank, **2:**645
Zerbinos, Eugenia, **1:**141, 142
Zeta-Jones, Catherine, **2:**541
Zhang, Ping, **1:**390
Ziegesar, Cecily von, **1:**127
Zill, N., **2:**488
Zillions, **2:**485
Zillmann, D., **2:**522, 570, 587, 589
Zillmann, Dolf, **1:**102, 104, 233, 388, **2:**540, 655, 745
Zimmerman, F. J., **1:**110
Zindel, Paul, **1:**126
Zines, 2:885–886
    adolescent girls, **2:**485
    characteristics, **2:**885–886
    definition of, **2:**885
    distribution, **2:**886
    fan cultures, **1:**325
    genres, **2:**885
Zlatar, Andrea, **1:**228
Zoboomafoo, **2:**465
Zohoori, A. R., **2:**814
Zoom, **1:**137, 262
Zuckerman, Marvin, **1:**103, **2:**748
Zuckerman's Sensation Seeking Scale, **2:**748
Zusne, Leonard, **1:**149
ZZ Top, **2:**581